Keto Diet Cookbook for Women over 50

Over **750** Easy, Effective **Low-Carb Recipes** To Balance

Hormones And Effortlessly Reach Your Weight Loss Goal. I

4-Week Meal Plan Included

Raven Foster

RAVEN FOSTER

Well-known nutritionist and best-selling author based in New York City; Raven Foster is an advocate of healthy eating. As a dietitian, her books predominantly focus on the effectiveness of dietary trends and how people can monitor their nutritional intake while still eating delicious foods.

Through her research and professional experience, she has discovered that many people are discouraged from pursuing healthy eating habits because they do not know how to make foods that are both delicious and healthy.

Thus, her patients' negative experiences with cooking inspired her to instruct people on how to follow diets, which also includes several healthy and beloved recipes that cater to different palettes.In addition to her work as a dietitian, she is an avid cook and attends many culinary events in relation to American cuisine. As such, she has advised many chefs and other cooks and her dishes are known for their rich flavors and widespread appeal. She also loves to run in her free time and often spends her days off researching eating habits in the library or partaking in cook-offs with her close friends.

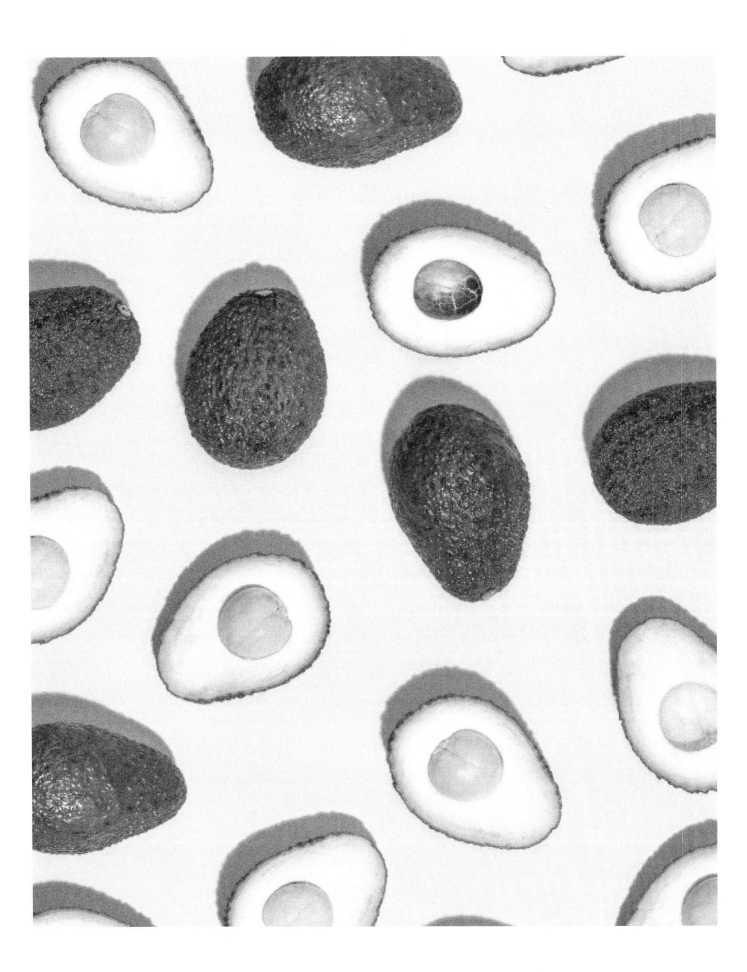

Chapter 1 — Introduction to Ketogenic Diet

A Keto diet is a source for low carbs and is used to produce ketones for energy sources in the liver. It is known with many names such as Low carb diet, ketogenic diet, low carb high fat (LCHF), etc.

The body produces Insulin and Glucose after the digestion of food with high carb content.

- The easiest molecule to produce in your body is GlucoseGlucose, and it is used as a source of energy other than any source.

- And to process GlucoseGlucose all around the body, the main chemical responsible for it is Insulin.

Since GlucoseGlucose is being used by the body as its primary energy source, the fats are stored for other activities. Glucose usually is the main energy source of the body on a high carb diet. Thus, when you reduce the amount of carbohydrate intake, the body begins a system known as Ketosis.

1.1 Types of Ketogenic Diets

A lot of times, people acquire the requirement of carbs for muscle mass.

When on a ketogenic diet, the glycogen reserves would still be refilled. An effective way to construct muscle is a keto diet, but protein intake is essential here. It is suggested that you can take in around 1.0-1.2g protein per lean pound of bodyweight if you are trying to gain mass. On a ketogenic diet, putting on muscle can be slower, but it's because your overall body fat doesn't quite increase.

The various types of Ketogenic diet when you want some fat on your body are:

- Targeted (TKD)

- Cyclical (CKD)

- Standard (SKD)

Only the standard and high proteins ketogenic diets have been widely studied. If you work out intensively, there might be a CKD or TKD for you. More complex approaches are targeted or cyclical ketogenic diets, mainly used by bodybuilders or athletes.

The Standard Ketogenic Diet (SKD) is explained in this book, and the information mentioned here can also be used with other versions of ketogenic diets.

1.2 Ketosis

Ketosis is a standard mechanism that the body initiates when food intake is poor to help us survive. We produce ketones during this state, created by the processing of fats in the liver.

A well-managed keto diet's ultimate purpose is to push the body into a metabolic state. We don't do this by calorie deprivation, but by carbohydrate starvation.

When you flood the body with fats and eliminate carbohydrates, it will start to burn ketones as the source of energy. Our bodies are extremely responsive to what you put into them. Optimal levels of ketone provide many benefits in terms of nutrition, losing weight, memory, and cognitive function.

How to Reach Ketosis

It's pretty easy to achieve Ketosis, but with all the details out there, it can be complicated and confusing. Here's the simple truth on what you need to do, organized in stages of importance:

- Limit the carbohydrates you have. The majority of individuals prefer to rely only on net carbs. Limit both if you want excellent outcomes. Try to keep net carbs below 20g and total carbohydrates under 35g per day.

- Restrict the intake of proteins. A lot of people come from an Atkins diet to keto and do not reduce their protein. Too much protein can result in lower ketosis levels. Ideally, you would like to eat 0.6g to 0.8g of protein per pound of lean body mass.

- Avoid getting concerned about fat. Fat is the main keto energy source, so make sure you give your body plenty of it. By hunger, you do not lose weight on keto.

- Drink more water. Try drinking a gallon per day of water. Not only does it help to regulate many important bodily functions, but it also helps in controlling levels of hunger.

- Avoid snacking. If you have less insulin spikes during the day, weight loss tends to be better. Unneeded snacks can result from installs or slow progression.

- Start fasting. Fasting can be a fantastic method for reliably raising ketone levels during the day.

- Add workout in. Consider adding 20-30 minutes of physical activity a day if you intend to get more out of your ketogenic diet. Even a short walk will help monitor weight loss and levels of blood sugar.

- Begin supplementation. While not normally required, a ketogenic diet can help with supplementation.

Ketosis is not like ketoacidosis

People frequently confuse these terms.

Although Ketosis is part of natural metabolism, if left unchecked, ketoacidosis is a harmful metabolic disorder that can be lethal. The bloodstream is saturated with exceptionally high levels of GlucoseGlucose (sugar) and ketones during ketoacidosis. The blood becomes acidic as this occurs, which is severely dangerous. Ketoacidosis is most associated with type 1 diabetes, which is not regulated. In individuals with type 2 diabetes, it can also occur, although this is not common. Furthermore, severe abuse of alcohol may contribute to ketoacidosis.

To achieve optimum Ketosis, there are too many tricks, hacks, and stunts out there. I would recommend you don't deal with any of that. Optimum Ketosis can be reached by dietary nutrition only (aka just eating food). To do it, you shouldn't need a magic pill. Just keep strict, remain careful, and concentrate on tracking what you eat (to make sure your protein & carb intake are correct).

How to Know if You're in Ketosis

Even though it's not worth it, you can test whether you're in Ketosis via blood or urine strips. The urine strips are known to be somewhat misleading (they address the question "Am I in ketosis?" often, and the blood strips are costly (up to $5 per strip).

You can use this brief list of physical "symptoms" instead, which will typically let you know whether you are on the right path:

- Increased Urination
- Dry Mouth
- Bad Breath
- Reduced Hunger & Increased Energy

Many individuals become crazy, testing, and measuring themselves. Focusing on the dietary element is even easier, ensuring that you take the right foods and remain within the macro limits. Your macros are the "big 3" nutrients in your daily intake: protein, fats, and carbohydrates.

1.3 What to Eat on a Keto Diet

You may want to prepare ahead in order to begin a keto diet. That implies having planned and waiting for a viable diet plan. What you eat relies on how easily you want to reach a ketogenic state. (Ketosis). (Ketosis). The stricter you are on carbs, the quicker you get into Ketosis (just under 25g of net carbs a day).

You want your carbohydrates, mostly from fruits, nuts, and dairy, to be restricted. Do not eat any processed carbohydrates, such as fruit, starch (potatoes, legumes, beans), or wheat (bread, cereals, pasta). Avocado, star fruit, and berries are the small exceptions to this that can be eaten in moderation.

Do Not Eat

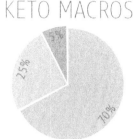

KETO MACROS

- Grains or Starches – pasta, wheat, cereal, rice, corn, etc.
- Sugar –agave, honey, maple syrup, etc.
- Sugary Foods: smoothies, soda, ice cream, fruit juice, cake, cream, candy, etc.
- Fruit – oranges, apples, bananas, etc.
- Root vegetables– potato, parsnips, carrots, yams, etc.
- Some condiments: honey mustard, barbecue sauce, teriyaki sauce, ketchup, etc.
- Unhealthy fats: mayonnaise, vegetable oils, processed, etc.
- Alcohol: liquor, wine, beer, mixed drinks
- Diet foods (Sugar-free): syrups, candies (sugar-free), sweeteners, puddings, desserts, etc.

FATS   PROTEIN   CARBS

Do Eat

- Meats – ham, steak, red meat, bacon, sausage, bacon, turkey, chicken, lamb, etc.
- Fatty Fish - trout, salmon, mackerel, and tuna.
- Eggs: pastured or whole eggs (omega-3)
- Leafy Greens – kale, spinach, etc.
- Above ground vegetables – cauliflower, broccoli, etc.
- High Fat Dairy – hard cheeses like goat, cheddar, blue, cream, or mozzarella), butter, high fat cream, etc. cheeses (unprocessed
- Seeds & Nuts– walnuts, almonds, pumpkin seeds, flaxseeds, sunflower seeds, chia seeds, etc.
- Avocado and berries – blackberries, raspberries, and other low sugar content berries
- Sweeteners – erythritol, stevia, monk fruit, and other low-carb sweeteners, etc.
- Healthy oils – coconut oil, extra virgin olive oil, and avocado oil
- Other fats – saturated fats, high-fat salad dressing, etc.
- Low Carb Veggies - tomatoes, veggies, peppers, onions, etc.
- Condiments - pepper, herbs, spices, and salt.

Try to remember that keto is very low in carbs, moderate in protein, and high in fat. Your nutrient consumption should be around **5% carbohydrate, 25% protein, and 70% fats.**

Usually, for regular dieting, somewhere between 20-30g of net carbs is suggested. However, the lower the intake of carbohydrates and glucose levels you maintain, the better the overall results. It's a good reason to take track of both your total carbs and net carbs if you're doing keto for weight loss.

With fat filling in the remaining calories in your day, protein must always be utilized as needed.

Perhaps you are wondering, "What is a net carb?" "Actually, it's easy! Your total dietary carbohydrates, excluding the total fiber, are the net carbs. I suggest that total carbs under 35g and net carbs under 25g be held (ideally, below 20g).

You can snack on cheese, seeds, nuts, or almond butter to suppress your appetite if you find yourself hungry during the day (though snacking can slow progress in the long term). We may confuse the need to have a snack with the need for a meal sometimes.

Ketogenic Diet Vegetables

Vegetable	Amount	Net Carbs
Spinach (Raw)	1/2 Cup	0.1
Bok Choi (Raw)	1/2 Cup	0.2
Lettuce (Romaine)	1/2 Cup	0.2
Cauliflower (Steamed)	1/2 Cup	0.9
Cabbage (Green Raw)	1/2 Cup	1.1
Cauliflower (Raw)	1/2 Cup	1.4
Broccoli (Florets)	1/2 Cup	2
Collard Greens	1/2 Cup	2
Kale (Steamed)	1/2 Cup	2.1
Green Beans (Steamed)	1/2 Cup	2.9

The best option for vegetables is always dark green and leafy. Much of the meals are expected to be a vegetable protein with an extra layer of fat. Olive oil-based chicken thighs with cheese and broccoli. A piece of butter and spinach side, sautéed in olive oil, topped the steak.

- There's also **2g of fiber** in 1 cup.
- There are a total of **6g carbs** in 1 cup.
- This will give us our **net carbs of 4g**.
- We take the total carbs (6g) and the dietary fiber (2g).

Here's a list of the most common low carb vegetables.

Chapter 2 – Benefits of Keto for Women over 50

If you're a woman above 50 years of age, you may be keener on weight loss than you were at 30. Many women face a decreasing metabolism at this age at a rate of around 50 calories per day. It can be exceedingly difficult to regulate weight gain by slowing the metabolism combined with less exercise, muscle deterioration, and increased cravings.

To help lose some weight, there are several diet alternatives available, but the ketogenic diet has been one of the most common lately.

We have scientific advice here to give you the answers you are searching for if you would like to lose weight.

The advantages of Keto are numerous: from weight loss and improved energy levels to clinical uses. Keto is thought of more as a diet for weight loss. Low-carb keto diets, however, give women in their 50s some substantial additional benefits. A number of the advantages you may gain from a ketogenic diet are given below.

Reduced body fat

A lot of diets guarantee weight loss, but the weight seems to be mostly water in many cases. Keto improves the burning of fat and yields greater success than most other diets. Abdominal fat, properly called visceral fat, is also preferentially targeted by Keto.

In women over 50, abdominal fat appears to increase. This increases the risk of cardiac arrest and stroke. Abdominal fat development is primarily because of the hormonal shifts associated with menopause.

Increased insulin sensitivity

the carbohydrates get digested and convert into glucose. Your body releases the hormone insulin to ferry glucose into your liver and muscles when you eat carbohydrates. With age, though, the sensitivity of your body to insulin reduces, and that means that the glucose is more likely to be converted into and processed as fat, resulting in weight. With age, though, the sensitivity of your body to insulin reduces, and that means that the glucose is more likely to be converted into and processed as fat, resulting in weight loss.

Low carb diets improve insulin sensitivity. This means that it's not going to turn the few carbohydrates you consume into fat. Increased insulin sensitivity also helps to monitor blood glucose levels. Low blood glucose levels are inseparably related to better general health and a lower risk of type 2 diabetes.

Enhanced brain function

Things like mood swings, memory loss, and difficulty focusing are also encountered by menopausal women. Anxiety and Depression can also cause them to suffer at times. This is because, during menopause, estrogen levels, the main female sex hormone, decrease, and that affects the glucose amount that enters your brain.

The keto diet gives an alternate source of fuel for your brain; ketones. Your brain works best on ketones, and on a low-carb diet, problems like mood swings and memory loss are far less likely.

The keto diet is also associated with a decreased risk of many neurological disorders, including Parkinson's disease and Alzheimer's disease, both of which are prominent in individuals over 50 years of age.

Reduced inflammation

The phase of aging can be rough on your body. In their 50s, menopausal women experience knee and hip pain and headaches, and other non-specific pain types.

Keto is a high-fat diet. Healthy anti-inflammatory fats that are expected to form part of the keto diet include:

- Avocados and avocado oil
- Olive oil
- Walnuts
- Oily fish, such as salmon, sardines, and tuna.

Whereas foods like sugar, refined carbs, and processed foods are all linked to increased inflammation. So, these are not included in the keto diet.

Improved blood lipid profile

Many women face higher triglyceride levels and "bad" LDL cholesterol in their 50s. This may lead to a Heart Attack.

Low carb diets have been shown to reduce triglycerides and LDL cholesterol while being high in fat while increasing 'healthy' HDL cholesterol.

These improvements are associated with better cardiovascular health and a lower risk of cardiovascular disease.

Reduced blood pressure

The blood pressure of women appears to be lower than that of men. However, as you reach your 50s, that can change, and menopause begins to take hold.

A number of serious health conditions, including heart failure, kidney disease, and stroke, are related to high blood pressure. It has been shown that the keto diet improves reduce blood pressure levels.

Increased bone mass

Older women are vulnerable to bone loss, which can develop into osteoporosis if left untreated. This is a medical condition marked by thin, fracture-prone bones.

The nutrients that can interact with calcium absorption are replaced by Keto. Keto can help boost bone health and density, along with plenty of leafy green vegetables that are normally rich in calcium.

Less muscle loss

Females appear to lose muscle more rapidly in their 50s than women in their 20s, 30s, and 40s. The lack of muscle decreases your metabolic rate, leading to weight gain and making weight loss more difficult. Your strength would also be impaired by muscle loss, making daily tasks harder and more exhausting.

The ketogenic diet includes eating moderate quantities of protein, and for muscle perseverance, protein is essential. The protein comprises amino acids, and the basic components of muscle tissue are amino acids. It is easy to see that Keto can be very effective for weight loss and better health for women in their 50s. Going Keto means cutting out and substituting all of the things we know are unhealthy for foods that are rich in beneficial nutrients.

Keto, in short, is not just a diet for people who are overweight; it is a diet for anybody who wants a healthier and longer life!

Basic Benefits

Weight Loss

A successful way to lose weight is by using a ketogenic diet. In reality, research indicates that a ketogenic diet can be as effective as a low-fat diet for weight loss. In essence, the ketogenic diet uses body fat as an energy source, so there are noticeable advantages to weight loss. The insulin levels drop significantly on Keto, which transforms the body into a machine for fat burning. It also resulted in declines in the amount of diastolic blood pressure and triglycerides.

A study of 34 older adults found that those who followed eight weeks of a ketogenic diet lost about five times as much overall body fat as those who adopted a low-fat diet.

Control Blood Sugar

You should consider a ketogenic diet if you are pre-diabetic or have Type 2 diabetes. A study of 349 individuals with type 2 diabetes showed that over two years, those who adopted a ketogenic diet lost an average of 11.9 kg. When considering the relation between weight and type 2 diabetes, this is a significant advantage. They also experienced better blood sugar control, and during the study, the use of some blood sugar medicines among participants decreased.

Mental Focus

For improved mental performance, many individuals use the ketogenic diet specifically.

The keto diet can help reduce and delay the progression of Alzheimer's disease symptoms. Although further research is needed, one study showed that the diet improved Parkinson's disease symptoms. Some research indicates that traumatic brain injuries may boost the effects of the diet.

Increased Energy & Normalized Hunger

You can feel more motivated throughout the day by offering your body a healthier and more stable energy form. It is proven that fats are the most efficient molecule to be burned as fuel.

Epilepsy

The ketogenic diet has been used to effectively treat epilepsy since the 1900s. Research has shown that in epileptic children, a ketogenic diet can cause a substantial reduction in seizures. For children who have untreated epilepsy today, it is also one of the most widely utilized treatments. One of the key advantages of the ketogenic diet for epilepsy is that it enables fewer medicines while also having excellent control.

Studies have also demonstrated substantial results in adults treated with Keto in the last couple of years.

Cholesterol & Blood Pressure

The reduction of triglyceride levels and cholesterol levels connected with arterial accumulation has been improved through a keto diet. More precisely, low-carb high-fat diets display a dramatic rise in HDL and a drop in LDL particle concentration. The research on ketogenic diets also shows greater improvement over other diets in blood pressure.

Insulin Resistance

When left uncontrolled, insulin resistance can escalate to type II diabetes. A significant amount of research indicates that a ketogenic diet helps individuals reduce their insulin levels to safe ranges.

Even if you're athletic, by eating foods rich in omega-3 fatty acids, you will gain from insulin regulation on Keto.

Acne

When you turn to a keto diet, it's normal to report changes in your skin.

Here's one study showing reductions in lesions and inflammation of the skin while transitioning to a low-carb diet. Another study shows that high carb eating and intensified acne are likely related, so Keto may likely help.

Polycystic ovary syndrome

A ketogenic diet helps reduce the level of insulin, which is mostly responsible for this disease.

2.1 Women's Hormones And The Keto Diet

Dr. Natasha Turner, ND, states that several of her female patients would initially lose weight. They then plateau and start gaining back all the weight and extra too. Obviously, this is not the perfect case. Cutting carbs suddenly can bring stress to the bodies of women.

At first, an increase in the stress hormone (cortisol) may be caused. Belly fat, Insulin resistance, and diabetes are associated with cortisol. The reduction of protein consumption in favor of more fats on the keto diet is one reason for this rise. Dr. Turner says that about 46 g of carbs a day are required for women (more for active women).

But that does not always qualify for the keto diet. This means the body will start eating for stores in muscles for food. Muscle wasting induces stress and cortisol spikes. Uh, not good.

Increased cortisol can alter the ratio of sex hormones in females over time. More testosterone, estrogen, and less progesterone start to be formed by the body. This could lead to disorders that are reproductive and hormonal. The exact reversal of the principle behind the diet.

The third hormonal problem has to do with the production of estrogen as well. Increased dietary fat is associated with increased development of estrogen in women. The higher the amount of estrogen, the more the thyroid is inhibited, according to Dr. Turner.

Since a healthy metabolism (weight management, sex drive cognition, and mood) is important to the thyroid, suppressing it is not pleasant. It can potentially lead to weight gain.

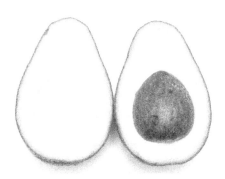

Chapter 3 – Side Effects of Keto Diet

our body gets used to the basic routine of breaking down and using carbohydrates as energy. The body has developed an army of enzymes trained for this process over time and has just a few enzymes to interact with fats, mainly to store them. Your body now needs to contend with the lack of glucose and the rise in fat, which means producing a new inventory of enzymes.

Your body will eventually use what's left of your glucose as your body becomes forced into a ketogenic state. This implies that glycogen in the muscles can be lost, triggering a lack of energy and lethargy.

3.1 Common Side Effects on a Keto Diet

In the starting week, many people report dizziness, mental fogginess, headaches, and aggravation. It is basically due to the electrolytes being released out of the body because of the diuretic effect of ketosis. The only way to deal with it is to drink enough water, maintain the sodium intake, and eat food filled with micronutrients.

Cramps

Cramps (leg cramps) are a common occurrence when a ketogenic diet is initiated. It typically occurs in the morning or at night, but overall, it's a minor problem. It's a warning that the body has a shortage of minerals, especially magnesium.

Make sure you drink lots of liquid and eat food with salt. Doing so will help minimize magnesium loss and get rid of the problem. Try supplementing it with a magnesium substitute if the problem continues.

Constipation

Dehydration is by far the most prevalent cause of constipation. An easy alternative is to raise the intake of water and aim to get as near as possible to a gallon a day.

Typically, ensuring the vegetables have some fiber in them would also help. This issue can be resolved by having some fiber from non-starchy vegetables. And if that's not enough, psyllium husk powder typically works, or a probiotic is taken.

Heart Palpitations

You will note that your heart is pounding both harder and faster when switching to keto. It's a normal one, so don't worry about that. Make sure that you drink plenty of fluid and eat enough salt if the condition continues. This is usually adequate to get rid of the issue right away.

Reduced Physical Performance

When you first start a keto diet, you will see some restrictions on your results, but it's typically only from your body adjusting to the use of fat. When your body switches to energy using fat, all of your strength and stamina will return to normal.

If you still experience performance issues, you can see benefits from eating carbs before your workout (or cycling carbs).

3.2 Less Common Side Effects on a Keto Diet

Some of the less common side effects are mentioned here.

Breastfeeding

To help the body produce milk, it is proposed to add 30-50g of extra carbs from the fruit during breastfeeding. You will have to add more calories, too. Specifically, extra fat is worth 300-500 calories to help with the production of milk. For guidance, you can always consult medical professionals.

Hair Loss

If during five months of beginning a ketogenic diet, you experience hair loss, it is most likely temporary. A multivitamin can be taken, and you can do as you usually do. Although hair loss on keto is rare, you can mitigate it by ensuring that you do not limit calories too much and make sure you get eight hours of sleep per night.

Increased Cholesterol

Generally, higher cholesterol is linked to a rise in HDL (good), decreasing the risk of heart disease. You can see elevated triglyceride levels, but in individuals that lose weight, that's very normal. When the weight is normal, these changes will dissipate.

Gallstones

The gallstones problems have been cured while on the keto diet. But the people have reported a slight discomfort when they start the keto diet. But if you stay on the keto diet for a longer period, you will see a considerable improvement.

Indigestion

Typically, the keto diet helps to remove indigestion, but if you still face problems, it is better for you to lower the daily fat intake.

Keto Flu

For individuals new to a keto diet, keto flu is a common occurrence, but it mostly goes away after only a few days, and there are ways to reduce or even eradicate it. You may experience mild discomfort when switching to keto, including nausea, exhaustion, cramps, headache, etc.

The two main reasons for this are:

1. **The keto diet is a diuretic.**
2. **You're transitioning.** Your body is prepared to process a high amount of carbs and a lower amount of fat.

Chapter 4 – How To Start Keto For Women Over 50

It may seem difficult to shift over to a ketogenic diet, but it does not have to be difficult. Although increasing the fat and protein content of meals and snacks, the focus should be on reducing carbs. Carbohydrates have to be reduced to enter and stay in a state of ketosis. Although some individuals can only achieve ketosis by consuming 20 g of carbs a day, others may need a higher intake.

Generally speaking, the lower your consumption of carbohydrates, the better it is to achieve ketosis. This is why the safest way to effectively lose weight on a ketogenic diet is to stick to keto-friendly foods and avoid products high in carbohydrates.
While keto is a simple diet, making the transition from a high carb diet to eating 50 g of carbs a day is often not easy. These instructions facilitate the shift into low carb keto dieting in a simpler way.

4.1 Guidelines

Have a planned start date
Keto is so different from other diets that, without doing any homework, you can't just jump in. Choose a start date and give yourself time to read up on low-carb dieting ins and outs. Learn more about what you can eat and what you can't. Spend this time collecting any low-carb tools, such as meal plans and recipes, that might be useful.

Clear your cupboards of unwanted carbs
Clean out any non-keto foods from your kitchen shortly before you begin your keto diet. You may think you can avoid temptation and not eat them, but the fact is that if you have easier access to high-carb foods, you are likely to exploit your diet.
However, don't make the mistake of eating any of these foods. The more carbohydrates you take, the slower and harder the transition to ketosis will be.

Use a food tracking app.
Successful dieting with keto means restricting the consumption of carb to 50 grams a day or less. Using a food monitoring app is the best way to do this effectively. Effective choices include,

- My Macros+
- My Plate
- My Fitness Pal

Understand that the first two weeks are the hardest

It's not always easy to start a keto, particularly for the first two weeks. Your body takes time to use all of its internal carb stores and instead make the transition to using ketones for energy. During this time, certain users face adverse side effects, which are typically called keto flu.

Although the keto flu is not serious and certainly not catching, once the body completely reaches ketosis, you can feel unwell. The good news is that these signs indicate that your body is beginning to switch from using energy-based carbs to using ketones. You are on the way to being a machine for fat-burning. Your symptoms will fade soon, and they will fully pass within 1-2 weeks. Often, after they leave, and unless you cheat your diet, only once can you ever suffer keto flu.

To get you started, this book will provide you with what to eat and resist when on a keto diet and include a two-week keto meal plan.

Don't cheat

By consuming unhealthy foods from time to time, many diets encourage you to take days off and even cheat. Don't be compelled to slip on keto, it's not worth it, long story short. Alternatively, reward your good eating habits.   The ketogenic diet does not contain high carb food treats.

Consider using some well-chosen supplements.

Although you don't have to use medications on the keto diet, for women over 50, they can make matters simpler. Great choices include:

1.   Exogenous ketones

Ketones from an outside source are exogenous ketones. Using exogenous ketone supplements can accelerate the burning of fat, give you energy, clear your head, and help relieve several of the keto flu symptoms. In capsules and as drink mixes, exogenous ketones are accessible.

2.   Medium-chain triglycerides

These special fats are rapidly and easily transformed into ketones by MCTs. More ketones mean better weight loss and fat burning, more control, and fewer keto flu symptoms.

Palm or coconut oil is made from MCT supplements. Coconut oil, however, is the best and environment-friendly alternative.

3.   Electrolytes

Electrolytes are elements in urine that are excreted and even lost with sweat. The keto diet increases the urine, which may mean that these essential chemicals start to run low in your body. Muscle cramps and Headaches include symptoms of low electrolyte levels. Electrolyte supplements substitute nutrients that are missing and can help avoid a variety of keto flu symptoms.

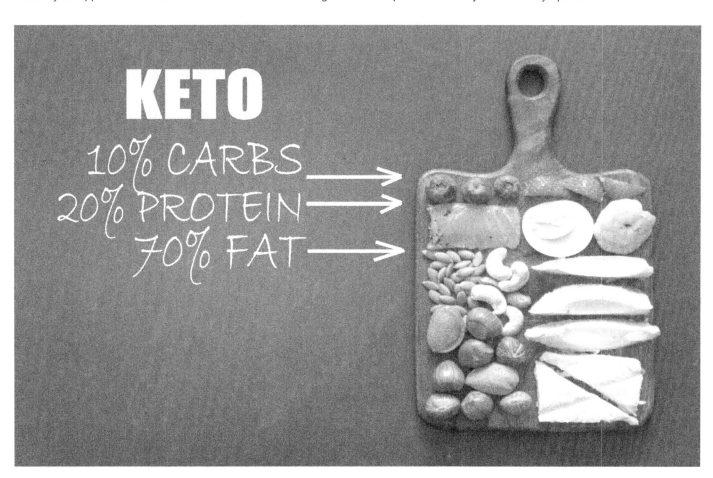

4.2 Keto Meal Plan for four Weeks

The menu below contains less than 50 g of total carbohydrates per day.
This is a general ketogenic menu for two weeks that can be changed based on individual dietary requirements.

1st Week

Keto Meal Plan		
Day	**Meal**	
Monday	Breakfast	Two eggs fried in pastured butter served with sauteed greens.
	Lunch	A bun less grass-fed burger topped with cheese, mushrooms and avocado atop a bed of greens.
	Dinner	Pork chops with green beans sauteed in coconut oil.
Tuesday	Breakfast	Mushroom omelet.
	Lunch	Tuna salad with celery and tomato atop a bed of greens.
	Dinner	Roast chicken with cream sauce and sauteed broccoli.
Wednesday	Breakfast	Bell pepper stuffed with cheese and eggs.
	Lunch	Arugula salad with hard-boiled eggs, turkey, avocado and blue cheese.
	Dinner	Grilled salmon with spinach sauteed in coconut oil.
Thursday	Breakfast	Full-fat yogurt topped with keto granola.
	Lunch	Steak bowl with cauliflower rice, cheese, herbs, avocado and salsa.
	Dinner	Bison steak with cheesy broccoli.
Friday	Breakfast	Baked avocado egg boats.
	Lunch	Caesar salad with chicken.
	Dinner	Pork chops with vegetables.
Saturday	Breakfast	Cauliflower toast topped with cheese and avocado.
	Lunch	Salmon burgers topped with pesto.
	Dinner	Meatballs served with zucchini noodles and parmesan cheese.
Sunday	Breakfast	Coconut milk chia pudding topped with coconut and walnuts.
	Lunch	Cobb salad made with greens, hard-boiled eggs, avocado, cheese and
	Dinner	Coconut chicken curry.

2nd Week

Keto Meal Plan		
Day	**Meal**	
Monday	Breakfast	Veggie and egg muffins with tomatoes
	Lunch	Chicken salad with olive oil, feta cheese, olives, and a side salad
	Dinner	Salmon with asparagus cooked in butter
Tuesday	Breakfast	Egg, tomato, basil, and spinach omelet
	Lunch	Almond milk, peanut butter, spinach, cocoa powder, and stevia milkshake (more keto smoothies here) with a side of sliced strawberries
	Dinner	Cheese-shell tacos with salsa
Wednesday	Breakfast	Nut milk chia pudding topped with coconut and blackberries
	Lunch	Avocado shrimp salad
	Dinner	Pork chops with parmesan cheese, broccoli, and salad
Thursday	Breakfast	Omelet with avocado, salsa, peppers, onion, and spices
	Lunch	A handful of nuts and celery sticks with guacamole and salsa
	Dinner	Chicken stuffed with pesto and cream cheese, and a side of grilled zucchini
Friday	Breakfast	Sugar-free greek, whole milk yogurt with peanut butter, cocoa powder, and berries
	Lunch	Ground beef lettuce wrap tacos with sliced bell peppers
	Dinner	Loaded cauliflower and mixed veggies
Saturday	Breakfast	Cream cheese pancakes with blueberries and a side of grilled mushrooms
	Lunch	Zucchini and beet "noodle" salad
	Dinner	White fish cooked in coconut oil with kale and toasted pine nuts
Sunday	Breakfast	Fried eggs with and mushrooms
	Lunch	Low carb sesame chicken and broccoli
	Dinner	Spaghetti squash bolognese

3rd Week

Details	Breakfast	Lunch	Dinner
Monday	Egg muffins with Cheddar cheese, spinach, and sun-dried tomatoes	Spiced cauliflower soup with bacon pieces or tofu cubes	Garlic and herb buttered shrimp with zucchini noodles
Tuesday	Scrambled eggs on a bed of sautéed greens with pumpkin seeds	Chicken mayonnaise salad with cucumber, avocado, tomato, almonds, and onion	Beef stew made with mushrooms, onions, celery, herbs, and beef broth
Wednesday	Omelet with mushrooms, broccoli, and peppers	Avocado and egg salad with onion and spices, served in lettuce cups	Cajun spiced chicken breast with cauliflower rice and Brussels sprout salad
Thursday	Smoothie containing almond milk, nut butter, spinach, chia seeds, and protein powder	Shrimp and avocado salad with tomatoes, feta cheese, herbs, lemon juice, and olive oil	Garlic butter steak with mushrooms and asparagus
Friday	2 eggs, fried in butter, with avocado and blackberries	Grilled salmon with a salad of mixed leafy greens and tomato	Chicken breast with cauliflower mash and green beans
Saturday	Scrambled eggs with jalapeños, green onions, and tomatoes sprinkled with sunflower seeds	Tuna salad with tomatoes and avocado plus macadamia nuts	Pork chops with non-starchy vegetables of choice
Sunday	Yogurt with keto-friendly granola	Grass-fed beef burger (no bun) with guacamole, tomato, and kale salad	Stir-fried chicken, broccoli, mushrooms, and peppers, with homemade satay sauce

4th Week

Details	Breakfast	Lunch	Dinner
Monday	Scrambled eggs in butter on a bed of lettuce topped with avocado	Spinach salad with grilled salmon	Pork chop with cauliflower mash and red cabbage slaw
Tuesday	Bulletproof coffee (made with butter and coconut oil), hard-boiled eggs	Tuna salad stuffed in tomatoes	Meatballs on zucchini noodles, topped with cream sauce
Wednesday	Cheese and veggie omelet topped with salsa	Sashimi takeout with miso soup	Roasted chicken with asparagus and sautéed mushrooms
Thursday	Smoothie made with almond milk, greens, almond butter, and protein powder	Chicken tenders made with almond flour on a bed of greens with cucumbers and goat cheese	Grilled shrimp topped with a lemon butter sauce with a side of asparagus
Friday	Fried eggs with bacon and a side of greens	Grass-fed burger in a lettuce "bun" topped with avocado and a side salad	Baked tofu with cauliflower rice, broccoli, and peppers, topped with a homemade peanut sauce
Saturday	Baked eggs in avocado cups	Poached salmon avocado rolls wrapped in seaweed (rice-free)	Grilled beef kebobs with peppers and sautéed broccolini
Sunday	Eggs scrambled with veggies, topped with salsa	Sardine salad made with mayo in half an avocado	Broiled trout with butter, sautéed bok choy

4.3 Combining Intermittent Fasting and Keto

Currently, intermittent fasting and the keto diet are the two main trends of health. These strategies are used by many health-conscious individuals to lose weight and monitor some health conditions. Although both have solid research supporting their supposed advantages, we will clarify whether combining the two is safe and efficient.

As a weight-loss method, intermittent fasting is commonly used. It is an eating strategy that cycles around calorie restriction or fasting and normal food intake during a fixed time period. There are several different kinds of fasting routines that are periodic. The popular methods are:

- **The 16/8 method**: in this one, you skip breakfast and stop eating for 8 hours, and then fast rest of the day for 16 hours. It is also known as Leans Gain.
- **Eat-Stop-Eat**: this is 24 hours of fasting once or two times a week.
- **The 5:2 diet**: 5 days of normal eating and 2 non-consecutive days of fasting in which you should limit your calorie intake to 500-600.

Potential benefits of practicing both

This will offer the following advantages if you stick to the ketogenic diet with intermittent fasting as well.

1. May smooth your path to ketosis.
2. May lead to more fat loss.

Should you combine them?

For most people, it is likely possible to combine a ketogenic diet with intermittent fasting. However, intermittent fasting should be avoided by pregnant or breastfeeding females and those with a history of disordered eating. Before attempting intermittent fasting on a keto diet, people with certain health problems, such as heart disease or diabetes, should consult a doctor.

Bear in mind that to achieve ketosis, intermittent fasting is not mandatory, although it can be used as a method to do so quickly. For those trying to boost health by cutting back on carbohydrates, simply adopting a balanced, well-balanced keto diet would be enough.

A Comprehensive Keto Diet Food List

The following are some of the best foods to eat on the keto diet, along with their serving sizes and an explanation of why they are good for people who follow this eating approach.

Avocado Oil

Per 1 tablespoon (tbsp) serving 124 calories, 0g net carbs, 0g protein, 14g fat

Benefits This is a good source of heart-healthy monounsaturated fatty acids.

Canola Oil

Per 1 tbsp serving 124 calories, 0g net carbs, 0g protein, 14g fat

Benefits Research has shown that consumption of canola oil can reduce total and bad cholesterol.

Coconut Oil

Per 1 tbsp serving 116 calories, 0g net carbs, 0g protein, 14g fat

Benefits While high in saturated fat, coconut oil may increase "good" HDL cholesterol levels.

MCT Oil

Per 1 tbsp serving 115 calories, 0g net carbs, 0g protein, 14g fat

Benefits Derived from coconut, MCT stands for medium chain triglycerides. Limited research suggests MCT oil may aid in weight loss and help promote ketosis.

Butter

Per 1 tbsp serving 100 calories, 0g net carbs, 0g protein, 11g fat

Benefits Though the serving provides 11 g of saturated fat, research has found that butter isn't a major factor in increasing risk of chronic conditions like heart disease or diabetes.

Cheddar Cheese

Per 1 slice serving 113 calories, 0g net carbs, 7g protein, 9g fat

Benefits Cheese is allowed as you please, but cheddar is a good example of its nutrition stats. One study found that cheese eaters had a 12 percent lower risk of type 2 diabetes.

Heavy Cream

Per 1 tbsp serving 52 calories, 0g net carbs, 0g protein, 5g fat

Benefits This is an easy way to add calories and fat into a ketogenic diet.

Bacon

Per 1 slice serving 43 calories, 0g net carbs, 3g protein, 3g fat

Benefits The green light on bacon may be one reason you're up for sticking to the diet, as it can make eating occasions more enticing. Just watch the sodium content, as it can add up quickly.

Chicken Thigh

Per 1 thigh serving 318 calories, 0g net carbs, 32g protein, 20g fat

Benefits Leave the skin on here for extra fat. One thigh is a good source of selenium, zinc, and B vitamins.

Eggs

Per 1 egg serving 77 calories, 1g net carbs, 6g protein, 5g fat

Benefits Eggs contain the perfect duo of satiating protein and fat; they're also high in the antioxidant mineral selenium.

Ground Beef

Per 3-ounce (oz) serving (measured raw) 279 calories, 0g net carbs, 12g protein, 24g fat

Benefits Ground beef (made with 70 percent lean meat and 30 percent fat) is a higher-fat choice — but that's the point here. You'll also get an excellent source of vitamin B12, which is necessary to keep up your energy levels.

New York Strip Steak

Per 3 oz serving 224 calories, 0g net carbs, 22g protein, 14g fat

Benefits You'll get an impressive amount of muscle-building protein plus satiating fat in this option. It's also rich in zinc, a mineral that promotes proper thyroid function.

Asparagus

Per 1 cup (raw) serving 27 calories, 2g net carbs, 3g protein, 0g fat

Benefits Asparagus contains bone-building calcium, plus other minerals, such as potassium and magnesium, which has been linked with blood sugar regulation.

Avocado

Per ½ avocado serving 160 calories, 2g net carbs, 2g protein, 15g fat

Benefits The creamy fruits are packed with fiber, something that you may lack on the keto diet. They also are an excellent source of immune-revving vitamin C.

Bok Choy

Per 1 cup (shredded) serving 9 calories, 1g net carbs, 1g protein, 0g fat

Benefits Chinese cabbage is a rich source of vitamins A and C, and offers some calcium and energy-boosting iron.

Cauliflower

Per 1 cup (raw) serving 25 calories, 2g net carbs, 2g protein, 0g fat

Benefits Provides more than three-quarters of your vitamin C quota in a day; with 3 g of fiber, it's also a good source of the heart-healthy nutrient.

Celery

Per 1 cup (raw) serving 16 calories, 1g net carbs, 1g protein, 0g fat

Benefits Celery is one of the most hydrating veggies out there. These crunchy spears also contain vitamins A and K, and folate.

Cucumber

Per ½ cup (slices) serving 8 calories, 2g net carbs, 0g protein, 0g fat

Benefits Cukes are high in water, making them a hydrating choice. They're also a surprisingly good source of vitamin K, a vitamin important for proper blood clotting and bone formation.

Green Peppers

Per 1 cup (sliced) serving 18 calories, 2g net carbs, 1g protein, 0g fat

Benefits Along with more than a day's requirements for vitamin C, they're also a good source of vitamin B6, which plays a role in more than 100 enzyme reactions in the body.

Lettuce

Per 1 cup (shredded) serving 5 calories, 1g net carbs, 0g protein, 0g fat

Benefits Leafy greens can add bulk to your meals for very few calories, as well as skin-strengthening vitamin A and vitamin C.

Mushrooms

Per 1 cup (raw) serving 15 calories, 1g net carbs, 2g protein, 0g fat

Benefits Mushrooms are known for their potential immune-boosting properties, as one study suggested.

They're also an excellent source of B vitamins.

Zucchini

Per 1 cup (sliced, raw) serving 18 calories, 3g net carbs, 1g protein, 0g fat

Benefits This is a great way to sneak in additional fiber, and the veggie also offers a good source of manganese, a mineral that helps form bone and aids in blood sugar control.

Chapter 5 – Most Common Mistakes and their Solution

You are not alone if it's happening to you. It is estimated that over 40 million women in the United States, 13 million in the United Kingdom, and many millions worldwide are going through menopause, which typically happens between the ages of 49 and 52. During this change, excess weight is very normal, no matter which diet you're on.

5.1 Problems

1. Release before you have completed the ketosis

A mandatory phase is nutritional ketosis, bringing more or less apparent and more or less lengthy aftereffects with it.

These differ depending on the amount of carbohydrates previously exploited and how stressed our liver is. We have the feeling of "poisoned" and "weighed down" as the body goes from consuming sugar to fat burning.

These above effects are due to the effect on our minds of removing sugars and carbohydrates that make us feel happy and fulfilled by activating the same opiate receptors. Now, if we stop them and this stimulation disappears, we may feel a little bit sad and anxious, on the contrary.

Many are afraid of these signs and conclude that the keto diet is not really for them, that they are much worse than when they began and left before moving to ketosis, not being well trained.

2. Incurring lack of salts and minerals

A potential lack of minerals will exasperate the desire for sugars that are sensed at first. It is also important to incorporate magnesium, potassium, and sodium into the correct doses. Eating salty snacks, eating magnesium in the evening, and using Himalayan salt may be ways of overcoming this error.

3. Consume too many proteins

Higher protein doses help solve hunger crises at the start, but then it's nice to go back to eating the right quantity. Only multiply the body weight by 0.8 (if you make a regular physical effort) or by 1.2 to know how much protein to eat (for an athlete). Another common error is the consumption of proteins of low quality, such as pork and cured meat.

4. Insufficient consumption of fats

We tend to fear using fat and not using all-natural sources: MCT oil, coconut oil, egg yolk, avocado, ghee, butter, fatty fish. The opposite fault is overdoing it with oilseeds: flax seeds, walnuts, almonds, pumpkin seeds.

5. Consume poor quality food

Another common error is, we concentrate on weight loss. Still, we tend to eat canned, frozen, fast-eating, highly processed foods, but low-quality protein, as described.

6. Do not introduce the right amount of fibers.

Vegetables should be fresh, consumed twice the number of protein, and cooked carefully, i.e., never overheated or overcooked. However, we sometimes switch to ready-made vegetables, frozen in bags. There are many berries with a low glycemic index: maqui, goji berries, berries, Inca berries, mulberries. Even about the fruit, we always resort to the very sugary one, we forget.

7. Consume raw vegetables

The consumption of vast amounts of raw vegetables, juices, cold smoothies slows down digestion over time, cools it, undermines our ability to absorb nutrients. It causes us inevitable shortcomings over time: poor teeth, nails, and hair, tiredness, joint pain, anemia, abnormal weight loss.

8. Do not drink to sufficiency.

And don't drink hot water, just that which is at room temperature. There are several advantages: higher digestibility and absorption, brighter skin and hair, deep hydration of cells, cellulite improves, retention disappears, improved kidneys, heartburn lessens, metabolism improves.

9. Eat the highest load of protein at dinner

This is an error that we all involuntarily make. The work, the many obligations, lead us to remain outside all day, to have a thrifty lunch meal or not to eat it at all. We have more time, we are more comfortable and we actually allow us a real meal complete with vegetables, proteins, sometimes even carbs and then fruit or dessert to finish. Dinner here develops into the only moment of the day when we see our family members. It eludes us that the liver is burdened by even the healthiest protein, the freshest or most organic food. He can not perform the other precious task during the night, being busy supporting digestion: that of hormones preparation, blood purification, the energy for the next day.

5.2 Solutions

For women who would like to shed fat quickly, the **keto diet** has been developed as the plan. But many women face barriers that sabotage the slimming process. Here's how to avoid them and accomplish your objectives:

Are you not losing fast enough? Eat more fat.

Annoyed because the pounds are not coming off as quickly as you would like? Odds are, you don't eat enough fat. Research indicates that women appear to neglect how much fat they can consume to meet their keto target, frequently obtaining just 30 to 40 % fat calories.

- Take 70%

Eating loads of dietary fats paves the way for the loss of weight. When the body is provided with enough fat to effectively create ketones, metabolism kicks into high gear. In just five days, cells begin to use stored fat for fuel.

Hit a plateau? Enjoy alkaline foods.

Pile your plate with alkalizing foods such as green vegetables (especially beet greens, chard, kale, dandelion greens, and collard greens), non-starchy vegetables, and lemons if your weight loss has stalled. The high amount of acid generated from having meat and dairy foods is countered by these foods, which can hinder your growth.

Craving carbs? Try keto cycling.

Try to add in "carb breaks" after a one-month keto adjustment period, two successive days a week in which you can have up to 70 total g of carbohydrate (such as oatmeal, fruit, and sweet potatoes) a day. These breaks not only make dieting feel slightly restrictive, but they can also drive you towards your goal of slimming down.

Hungry all the time? Add more oil.

All fats are pleasant, but the development of hormones that make us overeat is reduced by medium-chain triglycerides (MCTs). MCTs easily break down and go directly to the liver. Then, they are either burned for energy instantly or converted into ketones.

GI problems can be initiated by taking too much MCT oil too soon, so experts suggest taking 1 tsp. Add one more tsp. A day, every three days, until you hit a tablespoon.

5.3 Unit Conversion Table

Volume and weight conversions are an important resource to have in the kitchen. When halving or doubling a recipe, making the correct conversions can make or break your final results.

COOKING CONVERSION CHART

Measurement

CUP	ONCES	MILLILITERS	TABLESPOONS
8 cup	64 oz	1895 ml	128
6 cup	48 oz	1420 ml	96
5 cup	40 oz	1180 ml	80
4 cup	32 oz	960 ml	64
2 cup	16 oz	480 ml	32
1 cup	8 oz	240 ml	16
3/4 cup	6 oz	177 ml	12
2/3 cup	5 oz	158 ml	11
1/2 cup	4 oz	118 ml	8
3/8 cup	3 oz	90 ml	6
1/3 cup	2.5 oz	79 ml	5.5
1/4 cup	2 oz	59 ml	4
1/8 cup	1 oz	30 ml	3
1/16 cup	1/2 oz	15 ml	1

Temperature

FAHRENHEIT	CELSIUS
100 °F	37 °C
150 °F	65 °C
200 °F	93 °C
250 °F	121 °C
300 °F	150 °C
325 °F	160 °C
350 °F	180 °C
375 °F	190 °C
400 °F	200 °C
425 °F	220 °C
450 °F	230 °C
500 °F	260 °C
525 °F	274 °C
550 °F	288 °C

Weight

IMPERIAL	METRIC
1/2 oz	15 g
1 oz	29 g
2 oz	57 g
3 oz	85 g
4 oz	113 g
5 oz	141 g
6 oz	170 g
8 oz	227 g
10 oz	283 g
12 oz	340 g
13 oz	369 g
14 oz	397 g
15 oz	425 g
1 lb	453 g

Chapter 6 – Keto-Friendly Breakfast Recipes

Get ready to be amazed if you are a breakfast person who is on a keto diet. The list of keto breakfast recipes is long and scrumptious, full of delicious fat-rich foods such as eggs, bacon, sausage, cheese, butter, and avocado.

6.1 Egg Foo Young

Servings: 10 patties I Time: 45 mins I Difficulty: Easy
Nutrients per serving: Calories: 124 kcal I Fat: 9g I Carbohydrates: 3g I Protein: 7g I Fiber: 2g

Ingredients
- 6 Large Eggs
- 1/4 Cup Coconut Flour
- Kosher Salt, To Taste
- 1/2 Tsp. Apple Cider Vinegar
- 1 Cup Ham, Cooked & Diced
- 1 & 1/4 Cups Spinach, Frozen
- 2 Scallions, Sliced
- 1 Tbsp. Cilantro Fresh & Minced
- 1/2 Tsp. Baking Soda
- Black Pepper, Freshly Ground
- Avocado Oil

Method
1. Take a bowl and combine the coconut flour, eggs, apple cider vinegar, and salt together with a whisk to make a smooth mixture.
2. Add in the thawed spinach, cilantro, scallions, ham, black pepper, and baking soda. Mix them well.
3. Heat avocado oil in a non-stick frying pan and spread a spoonful of batter in it with the back of the spoon.
4. Do not turn the side for 2 minutes at medium heat and cook both sides well.
5. Once done, take out in a dish and repeat the process until the batter is finished.

6.2 Taco Bowls

Servings: 6 I Time: 35 mins I Difficulty: Easy
Nutrients per serving: Calories: 413 kcal I Fat: 33g I Carbohydrates: 8g I Protein: 22g I Fiber: 4g

Ingredients
Cauli Rice:
- 1 & 1/2 Cups Cauliflower Rice
- 6 Large Eggs, Beaten
- 3 Tbsps. Avocado Oil
- 2 Cups Ground Beef
- 1 Jalapeno Pepper, Minced
- 2 Tbsps. Lime Juice
- 2 Tbsps. Broth Or Water
- 1 Tsp. Onion Powder
- 2 Tsps. Taco Seasoning
- 2 Tsps. Milk, Dairy-Free
- Sea Salt, To Taste
- Black Pepper, To Taste

Additional Toppings:
- Fresh Salsa
- 1 Cup Cherry Tomatoes, Halved
- 1 Avocado, Sliced
- Cilantro, Minced
- Lime Juice, To Taste

Method
1. Heat one tbsp. avocado oil in a skillet and stir fry the cauliflower rice in it over medium flame. Let it cook for about 2-3 minutes, covered.
2. Then stir again and add in the lime juice, minced jalapeno, salt, and pepper. Mix until the required texture is attained. Remove from the heat and dish out. Set aside.
3. Put one tbsp. avocado oil in the same skillet and brown the ground beef in it over medium-high flame. Add the onion powder, salt, and taco seasoning in it. Stir well to combine.
4. Reduce the flame to medium-low and add the broth or water to it. Stir for a few minutes until cooked thoroughly and remove from the heat.
5. Take a bowl and whisk the eggs in it with milk and some salt and pepper.
6. Heat one tbsp. of avocado oil in a pan over medium flame and pour the whisked eggs in it. Cook and stir the eggs to scramble them. Once cooked, remove from the heat.
7. Take serving bowls and put layers of cauliflower rice, seasoned beef, scrambled eggs, and additional toppings.

6.3 Chaffles

Servings: 4 Chaffles I Time: 10 mins I Difficulty: Easy
Nutrients per serving: Calories: 115 kcal I Fat: 8g I Carbohydrates: 1g I Protein: 9g I Sugar: 2g

Ingredients
- 2 Eggs

- 1 Cup Mozzarella Cheese, Finely Shredded
- Cooking Spray

Method
1. Preheat waffle iron and spray it with cooking spray.
2. Take a bowl and put egg and cheese in it. Whisk it well.
3. Pour one-quarter of the mixture on the preheated waffle iron and let it cook until golden brown, for about 2 to 3 minutes.
4. Repeat the same for the remaining batter.
5. You can use chaffles as sandwich bread or eat with maple syrup as it is.

6.4 Pulled Pork Breakfast Hash

Servings: 4 I Time: 20 mins I Difficulty: Easy
Nutrients per serving: Calories: 153 kcal I Fat: 10g I Carbohydrates: 8g I Protein: 6g I Fiber: 1g

Ingredients
- 2 Eggs
- 2 Tbsps. Olive Oil
- 1/4 Tsp. Garlic Powder
- 1/3 Cup Pulled Pork
- 3 Brussels Sprouts, Halved
- 1/4 Tsp. Black Pepper
- 1 Cup Spinach, Chopped
- 1 Turnip, Diced
- 1/2 Tsp. Paprika
- 2 Tbsps. Red Onion, Diced
- 1/4 Tsp. Salt
- 1 Tbsp. Parsley, Finely Chopped

Method
1. Take a skillet and heat olive oil in it. Sauté the diced onion with all the spices in it for about 5 minutes, over medium-high flame.
2. Next, add in the other vegetables and cook for a few more minutes until they become soft.
3. Put the pulled pork in it as well and stir fry it.
4. Crack two eggs on it and cover it.
5. Let it cook until the egg whites are not runny anymore, for about 4-5 minutes.
6. Top with chopped parsley.

6.5 Ham and Spinach Omelet

Servings: 2 I Time: 25 mins I Difficulty: Easy
Nutrients per serving: Calories: 362 kcal I Fat: 32g I Carbohydrates: 1g I Protein: 16g I Cholesterol: 307g

Ingredients
- 1/4 Cup Ham, Chopped
- 1/4 Tsp. Black Pepper
- 1 Tbsp. Olive Oil
- 3 Eggs
- 2 Tbsps. Heavy Cream
- 1/2 Tsp. Cayenne Pepper
- 1 Tbsp. Butter
- 1/4 Cup Spinach, Chopped
- 1/2 Tsp. Italian Seasoning
- 1/4 Cup Cheddar Cheese
- 1/4 Tsp. Salt

Method
1. Take a bowl and put the eggs, salt, cayenne pepper, Italian seasoning, and black pepper in it. Whisk it well and add in cheese and cream as well. Mix well.
2. Take a pan and put olive oil and half tsp butter in it. Heat it and sauté the diced ham and spinach in it. Once they become soft, reduce the heat.
3. Add the egg mixture in it cook both sides of the omelet for a few minutes.
4. Take out once done and sprinkle parsley on top.

6.6 Breakfast Hash

Servings: 4 I Time: 20 mins I Difficulty: Easy
Nutrients per serving: Calories: 126 kcal I Fat: 9g I Carbohydrates: 3g I Protein: 7g I Fiber: 2g

Ingredients
- 1 Tbsp. Olive Oil
- 1 Turnip, Peeled & Diced
- 1 Tbsp. Parsley
- 1/4 Onion, Diced
- 1 Cup Brussel Sprouts, Halved
- 1/2 Tsp. Black Pepper
- 1/2 Tsp. Salt
- 3 Slices Bacon, Chopped
- 1/4 Cup Red Bell Pepper, Diced
- 1/2 Tsp. Paprika
- 1/2 Tsp. Garlic Powder

Method
1. Take a skillet and heat the olive oil in it over medium heat. Sauté the turnip in it along with all the spices for about 6 minutes.
2. Put the brussel sprouts and onion in it and cook for another 3 minutes, until they become soft.
3. Add in the chopped bacon and bell pepper. Sauté it until the bacon is cooked through.
4. Once done, dish out and sprinkle chopped parsley on top.

6.7 Bacon Wrapped Egg Cups

Servings: 12 I Time: 30 mins I Difficulty: Easy
Nutrients per serving: Calories: 126 kcal I Fat: 8g I Carbohydrates: 0g I Protein: 9g I Fiber: 0g

Ingredients
- 12 Eggs
- 2 Cups Bacon Strips
- Black Pepper, To Taste
- Cooking Spray

Method
1. Preheat the oven to 400 degrees F and spray on a muffin tin with cooking spray.
2. Lay the bacon strips in the muffin tin in a basket shape, covering all the sides and cut the extra bacon.
3. Put the muffin tin in the preheated oven for 5-7 minutes, do not overcook.
4. Take the tray out of the oven and crack one egg in every bacon basket.
5. Bake for another 10-15 minutes and take out of the oven.
6. Serve the bacon egg cups with a sprinkle of black pepper on top.

6.8 Granola Clusters

Servings: 8 I Time: 45 mins I Difficulty: Easy
Nutrients per serving: Calories: 327 kcal I Fat: 31.5g I Carbohydrates: 6g I Protein: 5.5g I Fiber: 3.5g

Ingredients
- 1/2 Cup Butter
- 1 Cup Pecan Halves
- 1/2 Cup Almonds
- 1/4 Cup Swerve Brown
- 1 Cup Coconut, Flaked

- 1/2 Cup Pumpkin Seeds
- 1/2 Tsp. Vanilla Extract
- 1/4 Cup Swerve Sweetener, Powdered
- 1/2 Tsp. Salt

Method
1. Preheat the oven to 300 degrees F.
2. Put the salt, pumpkin seeds, coconut, pecans, and almonds in a blender and blend for a few minutes until they are crumbled.
3. Heat the butter in a saucepan with sweeteners and stir well, until the butter melts. Take off the heat and stir in the vanilla extract.
4. Add in the nut mixture in it and mix well.
5. Put the mixture on a parchment paper-lined a baking sheet and lay down the mixture on it. Put another parchment paper on top and with a rolling pin roll it down to a uniform thickness.
6. Put the baking sheet in the preheated oven and bake until it becomes golden, for about 20-30 minutes.
7. Take out of the oven once done and cool down on a wire rack.
8. Break with hands into granola clusters and store for up to a week in an airtight container.

6.9 Deviled Eggs With Bacon

Servings: 4 I Time: 15 mins I Difficulty: Easy
Nutrients per serving: Calories: 70 kcal I Fat: 41g I Carbohydrates: 1g I Protein: 25g

Ingredients
- 12 Eggs
- 1/2 Tsp. Paprika Powder
- 1 Cup Bacon Slices
- 1/2 Cup Mayonnaise
- Parsley, Fresh & Chopped
- 1 Tbsp. Dijon Mustard
- Sea Salt, To Taste
- 1/2 Tsp. Olive Oil
- Black Pepper, To Taste

Method
1. Boil the eggs as you like them and put them under cold water to peel them easily.
2. Heat olive oil in a pan and stir fry the bacon slices in it over medium-high flame for about 5 minutes, until they are cooked through and become crispy.
3. Chop the cooked bacon into small pieces.
4. Cut the peeled eggs into halves lengthwise and take out the yolks.
5. Put the egg yolks in a bowl and add in the mayonnaise, bacon pieces, Dijon mustard, paprika powder, salt, and black pepper. Mix them well to combine.
6. Fill the egg whites hollows with a spoonful of this mixture and sprinkle chopped parsley on top.

6.10 Crustless Quiche Recipe

Servings: 6 I Time: 35 mins I Difficulty: Easy
Nutrients per serving: Calories: 216 kcal I Fat: 17g I Carbohydrates: 4g I Protein: 11g I Fiber: 1g

Ingredients
- 5 Eggs
- 1/2 Cup Cherry Tomatoes, Chopped
- 1/2 Cup Milk
- 1/2 Cup Broccoli, Chopped
- 1/2 Cup Half And Half

- 1/2 Cup Bacon, Chopped
- 2/3 Cup Mozzarella Cheese, Shredded
- 1/4 Tsp Black Pepper, Ground
- 1/2 Tsp Salt
- Cooking Spray

Method
1. Preheat the oven to 325 degrees F.
2. Take a baking dish (9-inches) and spray it with cooking spray.
3. Scatter the chopped bacon, broccoli, and tomatoes on it, evenly.
4. Take a bowl and crack the eggs in it. Add in the half-and-half, milk, salt, and pepper, and whisk them well to combine.
5. Pour this egg mixture over the scattered veggies and bacon in the baking dish.
6. Top it with shredded mozzarella cheese and put it in the preheated oven.
7. Bake it until the cheese is golden from the top and everything is cooked through, for about 25 minutes.
8. Once done, take out and let cool for a few minutes, then serve.

6.11 Keto Almond Flour Crepes

Servings: 8 to 10 crepes I Time: 35 mins I Difficulty: Easy
Nutrients per serving: Calories: 158 kcal I Fat: 13g I Carbohydrates: 3.04g I Protein: 6.28g I Fiber: 1.16g

Ingredients
- 4 Eggs
- 1 Tsp. Olive Oil
- 1/2 Cup Cream Cheese, Softened
- 1/4 Cup Almond Milk, Unsweetened
- 2 Tbsps. Swerve Sweetener, Granulated
- 3/4 Cup Almond Flour
- 1/8 Tsp. Salt

Method
1. Combine all the ingredients in a blender, except oil. Blend until a smooth consistency is attained.
2. Heat olive oil in a pan over medium-low flame and put this egg mixture in it. Swirl the pan to spread the batter evenly.
3. Cook both sides to golden brown and dish out.
4. Serve with any low carb spread of your choice.

6.12 Joe's Special Scramble

Servings: 4 I Time: 30 mins I Difficulty: Easy
Nutrients per serving: Calories: 403 kcal I Fat: 30g I Carbohydrates: 8g I Protein: 27g I Fiber: 2g

Ingredients
- 2 Tbsps. Avocado Oil
- 3 Garlic Cloves, Minced
- 1 Cup Beef, Ground
- 2/3 Cup Baby Spinach
- 10 Eggs
- 1/2 Cup Onion, Finely Chopped
- 1 Tsp. Red Boat Fish Sauce
- 1 Cup Cremini Mushrooms, Trimmed & Sliced Thinly
- 2 Tbsps. Water
- 2 Tbsps. Chives, Chopped
- Black Pepper, Freshly Ground, To Taste
- Kosher Salt, To Taste
- Cayenne Pepper Sauce (Optional)

Method
1. Combine eggs, fish sauce, salt, and pepper in a bowl and whisk well. Set aside.
2. Heat avocado oil in a skillet over a medium-high flame and sauté onions and mushrooms with a sprinkle of salt. Cook it until the mushrooms become soft and golden brown.
3. Add in the garlic and stir fry it as well until it is fragrant. Then put the ground beef in it and brown it.
4. Add more salt if you want and once the beef is browned, add the spinach, and cook it until it wilts.
5. Pour the egg mixture in it and let it sit for a few minutes and then stir it.
6. Once cooked through, dish it out and serve with hot sauce if you want.

6.13 Keto Pancakes

Servings: 4 | Time: 10 mins | Difficulty: Easy
Nutrients per serving: Calories: 395 kcal | Fat: 34g | Carbohydrates: 12g | Protein: 14g | Fiber: 6g

Ingredients
- 1/4 Cup Coconut Flour
- Mixed Berries (Raspberries Strawberries, Blueberries)
- 1/4 Cup Coconut Oil
- 1 Cup Almond Flour
- 1 Tsp. Baking Powder (Gluten-Free)
- 1/3 Cup Almond Milk, Unsweetened
- 5 Eggs
- 1 & 1/2 Tsps. Vanilla Extract
- 2-3 Tbsps. Erythritol
- 1/4 Tsp. Salt

Method
1. Preheat a griddle to 300 degrees.
2. Take a bowl and combine all the ingredients in it. Whisk them well until a smooth mixture is formed.
3. Pour a quarter cup of the batter onto the griddle and cook the pancake from both sides until it becomes golden brown.
4. Repeat the process with the remaining batter.
5. Dish out and serve with a low carb syrup or topping.

6.14 Keto Biscuit Breakfast Sandwiches

Servings: 8 | Time: 40 mins | Difficulty: Easy
Nutrients per serving (one biscuit without filling): Calories: 216 kcal | Fat: 6g | Carbohydrates: 6g | Protein: 6g | Fiber: 2g

Ingredients
- 8 Breakfast Sausage Patties, Cooked
- 1 & 1/2 Cups Almond Flour
- 1 Tbsp. Baking Powder (Aluminum Free)
- 4 Tbsps. Butter, Unsalted & Melted
- 8 Slices Cheddar Cheese
- 6 Eggs
- 1/2 Tbsp. Oil
- 3/4 Tsp. Garlic Powder
- 1/2 Cup Sour Cream, Full Fat
- 3/4 Tsp. Onion Powder
- 4 Tbsps. Milk
- Salt, To Taste
- Pepper, To Taste
- Cooking Spray

Method
1. Preheat the oven to 450 degrees F.
2. Combine the almond flour, baking powder, 1/4 tsp salt, onion, and garlic powder in a bowl and whisk well.
3. Combine two eggs, melted butter, and sour cream in another bowl and whisk them together as well.
4. Put the egg mixture in the dry mixture and whisk again until smooth.
5. Take a 12-cup muffin tin and spray it with a cooking spray.
6. Pour 1/4 cup of batter in each cup of the muffin tin and put in the oven.
7. Bake the biscuits until they become golden, for about 10-11 minutes.
8. Take out of the oven once done and allow them to cool down for about 15-20 minutes. Then take them out of the muffin tin and set them aside.
9. Combine four eggs, milk, salt, and butter as per your taste, in a bowl and whisk them well.
10. Heat oil in a pan over medium flame and pour the egg mixture in it. Swirl the pan to evenly spread it.
11. Flip the egg mixture, once cooked from one side, and cook from the other.
12. Once cooked from both sides, remove from the heat ad cut into small squares to fit the biscuits.
13. Cut the biscuits into halves like a sandwich and put the egg squares, cheese sausage patties in between.

6.15 Cheesy Ham Hash Egg Cups

Servings: 9 | Time: 35 mins | Difficulty: Easy
Nutrients per serving: Calories: 220 kcal | Fat: 18g | Carbohydrates: 1g | Protein: 15g

Ingredients
- 9 Eggs
- 1/4 Cup Almond Flour
- 2 Cups Ham, Chopped
- 1/3 Cup Mayonnaise, Sugar-Free
- 1/4 Tsp. Garlic Powder
- 1/4 Cup Onion, Chopped
- 1/3 Cup. Parmesan Cheese, Grated
- 1 Tbsp. Parsley, Fresh & Chopped
- 1/4 Tsp. Kosher Salt
- 1/8 Tsp. Black Pepper, Ground

Method
1. Preheat the oven to 375 degrees F.
2. Combine the onion, ham, garlic powder, parsley, salt, and pepper in a food processor and grind them coarsely.
3. Put this mixture in a bowl and add the almond flour, mayonnaise, and parmesan cheese in it. Stir it well to combine.
4. Spray a muffin tray with cooking spray and put the spoonful of this mixture in each muffin cup, leaving a space empty for the egg.
5. Put the tray in the preheated oven and bake for about 5 minutes.
6. Take out of the oven and crack one egg in each cup.
7. Put back in the oven for 15-20 minutes or until the eggs are cooked.
8. Once done, take out and let cool for five minutes, then take out and garnish with parsley before serving.

6.16 Easy Keto Chocolate Crepes

Servings: 4 | Time: 35 mins | Difficulty: Easy
Nutrients per serving: Calories: 186 kcal | Fat: 14.1g | Carbohydrates: 2.2g | Protein: 10.9g

Ingredients
- 4 Eggs
- 3 Tbsps. Coconut Flour
- 2 Tbsps. Cocoa Powder, Dark & Unsweetened
- 1/2 Cup Cream Cheese, Full-Fat

- 1/4 Cup Erythritol, Powdered
- 1 Tsp. Vanilla Extract (Optional)

Method

1. Take a bowl and put all the ingredients in it. Whisk the mixture well until combined.
2. Heat a non-stick pan over medium-low flame and pour a quarter of the mixture in it with a spoon, and spread it evenly with the back of the spoon.
3. Cook on both sides until golden.
4. Repeat the process with the remaining batter.
5. Dish out and serve with whipped cream and berries if you want.

6.17 Prosciutto-Wrapped Mini Frittata Muffins

Servings: 12 Muffins I Time: 30 mins I Difficulty: Easy
Nutrients per serving: Calories: 164 kcal I Fat: 14g I Carbohydrates: 4g I Protein: 7g I Fiber: 1g

Ingredients

- 4 Tbsps. Avocado Oil
- 8 Eggs
- 1/4 Cup Coconut Milk, Full-Fat
- 1 Cup Cremini Mushrooms, Sliced Thinly
- 1 Cup Cherry Tomatoes, Halved
- 1 Cup Spinach, Frozen
- 3 Garlic Cloves, Minced
- 2/3 Cup Prosciutto Di Parma
- 1 Cup Onion, Chopped
- Kosher Salt, To Taste
- Black Pepper, Freshly Ground, To Taste
- 2 Tbsps. Coconut Flour

Method

1. Preheat the oven to 375 degrees F.
2. Heat half the avocado oil in a skillet over medium flame and sauté the onions in it until they become translucent. Next, add the garlic and sauté it as well.
3. Add in the mushrooms, spinach, salt, and pepper. Stir fry until the mushroom becomes golden and spinach is wilted.
4. Once done, take out and set aside to let cool.
5. In the meantime, combine the coconut flour, eggs, coconut milk, salt, and pepper in a bowl and whisk them well until the mixture become smooth.
6. Add in the fried veggies mixture and stir well.
7. Take a muffin tin and brush it with the remaining avocado oil. Then line each cup with prosciutto, covering the bottom and sides entirely.
8. Pour a spoonful of frittata batter in each cup and put a tomato half on top.
9. Take out once done and let cool before serving

6.18 Pumpkin Chaffles

Servings: 2 Chaffles I Time: 13 mins I Difficulty: Easy
Nutrients per serving: Calories: 116.26 kcal I Fat: 9.54g I Carbohydrates: 2.61g I Protein: 4.52g I Fiber: 0.62g

Ingredients

- 1 Tbsp. Almond Flour
- 1/2 Tsp. Pumpkin Spice
- 1 Large Egg
- 1 Tbsp. Pumpkin Puree
- 2 Tbsps. Cream Cheese, Softened
- 1/4 Tsp. Baking Powder (Optional)
- Cooking Oil Spray

- 1/2 Tsp Erythritol, Granular (Optional)

Method

1. Preheat the waffle iron.
2. Combine all the ingredients in a bowl and whisk well to make a smooth batter.
3. Spray the preheated waffle iron with a cooking oil spray and then pour the batter into it. Close it and let it cook for about 4-5 minutes or until the chaffles are golden brown. Repeat this with the remaining batter and dish out once done.
4. Serve with low carb toppings and enjoy.

6.19 Keto Leek And Bacon Omelet

Servings: 4 I Time: 32 mins I Difficulty: Easy
Nutrients per serving: Calories: 124 kcal I Fat: 20g I Carbohydrates: 3g I Protein: 17g

Ingredients

- 2 Tbsps. Avocado Oil
- Sea Salt, To Taste
- 2/3 Cup Bacon, Cooked & Chopped
- Parsley, Fresh and Chopped
- 8 Eggs
- 1 Leek, Sliced
- Black Pepper, Freshly Ground, To Taste
- Chives, Fresh & Minced

Method

1. Combine the eggs with salt and pepper and whisk them.
2. Heat oil in a pan and sauté the leek in it for 5 minutes or until it becomes soft.
3. Add in the beaten egg mixture and chopped bacon.
4. Swirl the pan to evenly spread the eggs. Flip once done from one side and cook both sides for a few minutes.
5. Once cooked, dish out and sprinkle chives and parsley on top.

6.20 Keto Sheet Pan Pancakes

Servings: 15 I Time: 30 mins I Difficulty: Easy
Nutrients per serving: Calories: 221 kcal I Fat: 18.7g I Carbohydrates: 7.5g I Protein: 7.5g I Fiber: 4.2g

Ingredients

- 2 Tbsps. Coconut Flour
- 5 Eggs
- 1 Tbsp. Baking Powder
- 1 Cup Coconut Or Almond Milk
- 2 Tsps. Vanilla Extract
- 6 Tbsps. Butter, Melted
- 3 Cups Almond Flour
- 1/2 Tsp. Salt
- 6 Tbsps. Swerve Sweetener
- Cooking Spray
- 1/3 Cup Chocolate Chips, Sugar-Free

Method

1. Preheat the oven to 400 degrees F.
2. Combine all the ingredients in a large bowl except the chocolate chips. Whisk or beat it well until a smooth batter is formed.
3. Line a baking pan (11x17 inches) with parchment paper and spray it with cooking spray. Pour the batter in it and sprinkle the chocolate chips on top.
4. Put the pan in the preheated oven and bake for about 12 to 15 minutes or until the edges become golden and the center firm.
5. Take out of the oven once done and let cool for a few minutes.

6. Cut into 15 large squares and serve.

6.21 Microwave English Muffin

Servings: 1 I Time: 5 mins I Difficulty: Easy
Nutrients per serving: Calories: 141 kcal I Fat: 6g I Carbohydrates: 10g I Protein: 9g I Fiber: 4g

Ingredients

- 1 Egg
- 2 Tbsps. Milk, Nonfat
- 2 Tbsps. Coconut Flour
- 1/8 Tsp. Salt

Method

1. Combine all the ingredients in a bowl and whisk well until a smooth batter is formed.
2. Brush a ramekin (3.5 inches) inside with oil or butter and pour in the batter.
3. Put the ramekin in the microwave for about one and a half minutes or until the muffin is completely cooked.

6.22 Keto Belgian Waffles

Servings: 4 I Time: 15 mins I Difficulty: Easy
Nutrients per serving: Calories: 293 kcal I Fat: 27g I Carbohydrates: 5g I Protein: 10g I Fiber: 1g

Ingredients

- 2 Tbsps. Butter, Melted
- 4 Eggs
- 1 Tsp. Baking Powder
- 1/2 Cup Almond Flour
- 1/2 Cup Cream Cheese
- 1 Tsp. Vanilla Extract
- Cooking Spray
- Keto Maple Syrup (Optional)
- 1 Tbsp. Erythritol (Optional)

Method

1. Preheat waffle iron.
2. Combine all the ingredients in a bowl and whisk or beat them well until a smooth batter is formed.
3. Spray the waffle iron with a cooking oil spray and pour the batter into it.
4. Cook until they become crispy and golden.
5. Repeat the process with the remaining batter.

6.23 Keto Bacon And Brie Frittata

Servings: 6 I Time: 25 mins I Difficulty: Easy
Nutrients per serving: Calories: 338 kcal I Fat: 27g I Carbohydrates: 1.8g I Protein: 18g I Fiber: 0.1g

Ingredients

- 8 Eggs
- 2 Garlic Cloves, Minced
- 1 & 1/3 Cups Bacon, Chopped
- 1/2 Tsp. Salt
- 1/2 Cup Brie, Sliced Thinly
- 1/2 Cup Heavy Whipping Cream
- 1/2 Tsp. Pepper

Method

1. Take an oven-proof and non-stick skillet and stir fry the bacon in it over medium heat.
2. Once crispy, remove from the heat and set aside to let cool.
3. Combine 2/3 of the cooked bacon, eggs, garlic, cream, salt, and pepper in a bowl and mix well.

4. Take the same skillet with bacon fat in it and pour the egg mixture in it. Cook it over medium-low heat.
5. Once the eggs are half cooked, remove them from the heat and make a layer of brie slices on it and sprinkle the remaining bacon on top.
6. Put the skillet on the oven rack in the oven with a preheated broiler.
7. Broil it for about 2 to 5 minutes or until the frittata is golden brown and puffed.
8. Take out and let cool a few minutes before serving.

6.24 Omelet Muffins

Servings: 12 I Time: 30 mins I Difficulty: Easy
Nutrients per serving: Calories: 93 kcal I Fat: 6g I Carbohydrates: 1g I Protein: 7g I Cholesterol: 134mg

Ingredients

- 1 Cup Bell Peppers, Diced
- 8 Eggs
- 1/2 Cup Baby Spinach, Chopped
- 1/2 Cup Milk
- 1/4 Tsp. Salt
- 2 Scallions, Sliced Thinly
- 1 Cup Cheddar Cheese, Shredded
- Cooking Spray

Method

1. Preheat the oven to 350 degrees F.
2. Whisk the eggs with milk and add in all the other ingredients as well. Stir it until combined.
3. Spray a nonstick 12 cup muffin pan with a cooking spray and pour a spoonful mixture in every cup.
4. Put in the preheated oven and bake for about 20-25 minutes, or until the eggs are cooked through.
5. Take out of the oven, let cool for a few minutes, then dish out and eat warm.

6.25 Smoked Salmon Breakfast Frittata

Servings: 12 I Time: 22 mins I Difficulty: Easy
Nutrients per serving: Calories: 97 kcal I Fat: 6g I Carbohydrates: 1g I Protein: 8g I Fiber: 0g

Ingredients

- 2 Cups Spinach, Destemmed
- 2 Tbsps. Dill, Fresh & Minced
- 1/4 Cup Cream Cheese
- 1/2 Cup Almond Milk, Unsweetened
- 2 Tbsps. Shallot, Minced
- 2/3 Cup Salmon Filet, Smoked & Chopped
- 8 Eggs
- Coconut Oil Cooking Spray

Method

1. Preheat the oven to 350 degrees F.
2. Whisk the eggs with milk first, and then add in all the other ingredients except cream cheese. Stir well until combined.
3. Spray a muffin tin with coconut oil cooking spray and pour a spoonful of the mixture into the cups of the muffin tin.
4. Put a dollop of cream cheese evenly on each muffin.
5. Put the muffin tin in the preheated oven and bake for about 16-18 minutes.
6. Take out of the oven and let cool for a few minutes before taking the frittata out of the cups.

6.26 Egg Porridge

Servings: 1 I Time: 20 mins I Difficulty: Easy
Nutrients per serving: Calories: 661 kcal I Fat: 64.5 g I Carbohydrates: 2.9 g I Protein: 17.3g

Ingredients

- 2 Tbsps. Butter, Softened
- 1/3 Cup Heavy Cream
- 2 Eggs
- Cinnamon Powder, To Taste
- Stevia, To Taste

Method

1. Combine all the ingredients in a bowl except cinnamon and butter. Whisk them well until smooth.
2. Take a pan and heat the butter in it over medium-high heat. Once the butter is melted, add the egg and cream mixture, and cook until it thickens.
3. Once it reaches your desired consistency, take the pan off the heat and pour it into a serving bowl.
4. Sprinkle cinnamon on top and serve.

6.27 Keto Sausage Crusted Quiche

Servings: 6 I Time: 50 mins I Difficulty: Easy
Nutrients per serving: Calories: 340 kcal I Fat: 28g I Carbohydrates: 3g I Protein: 17g

Ingredients

- 6 Eggs
- 2 Tbsps. Parsley, Fresh & Chopped
- 10 Cherry Tomatoes, Halved
- 2 Tbsps. Heavy Whipping Cream
- 1 & 1/2 Cups Pork Sausage Roll (Raw)
- 2 Tbsps. Parmesan Cheese, Grated
- 1/8 Tsp. Black Pepper, Ground
- 5 Slices Eggplant, Peeled
- 1/4 Tsp. Kosher Salt

Method

- Preheat the oven to 375 degrees F.
- Whisk the eggs with cream, cheese, salt, and pepper in a bowl and set aside.
- Take a casserole dish (8-inch) and line the sausage at its bottom and sides.
- Spread the eggplant slices on it and top it with cherry tomato halves.
- Sprinkle the parsley on it.
- Pour the egg mixture over it and put it in the oven.
- Bake it for about 40 minutes or until everything is cooked thoroughly, especially sausage.
- Take out, let cool for a while, and serve.

6.28 Sheet Pan Steak And Eggs

Servings: 6 I Time: 15 mins I Difficulty: Easy
Nutrients per serving: Calories: 440 kcal I Fat: 21g I Carbohydrates: 1g I Protein: 57g I Cholesterol: 365mg

Ingredients

- 1/4 Cup Butter, Softened
- 1 Tsp. Thyme, Chopped Finely
- 6 Cups or 3 Pound Top Sirloin Steak (1-Inch Thick)
- 1 Tsp. Rosemary, Chopped Finely
- 3 Garlic Cloves, Minced
- 1 Tsp. Oregano, Chopped Finely
- 6 Eggs
- 2 Tsp. Parsley, Chopped Finely
- Black Pepper, To Taste
- Salt, To Taste

- Cooking Oil Spray

Method

- Combine butter, minced garlic, chopped thyme, parsley, oregano, and rosemary in a bowl and mix well. Set this garlic butter aside.
- Preheat the oven to high broil.
- Spray a baking pan with cooking oil spray. Divide the steaks into six pieces and season them with salt and pepper.
- Put the steaks on the baking pan and put them in the oven. Bake for 5 minutes and take out, flip the side, and put again for 5 minutes.
- Baking time can increase based on how much cooked you want it.
- Take out of the oven before they are completely cooked. Turn them in the form of a closed circle and crack an egg in each steak.
- Put in the oven again and bake until the eggs are set.
- Take out and put garlic butter on top of each egg and put in the oven again until both steak and eggs are cooked through, and butter is melted.
- Take the pan out of the oven. Brush the garlic butter again across the steaks and serve.

6.29 Chorizo And Spinach Omelet

Servings: 2 I Time: 25 mins I Difficulty: Easy
Nutrients per serving: Calories: 224 kcal I Fat: 46g I Carbohydrates: 7g I Protein: 21g I Fiber: 2g

Ingredients

- 5 Eggs
- 1/4 Cup Tomatoes, Diced
- Sea Salt, To Taste
- 2 Tbsps. Coconut Milk
- 1/4 Cup Spinach, Chopped
- 2 Chorizo Sausages
- Black Pepper, Freshly Ground, To Taste
- 1/2 Onion, Diced
- 1 Garlic Clove, Minced
- 4 Tbsps. Avocado Oil
- 1 Green Onion, Sliced

Method

- Heat half of the avocado oil in a skillet over medium-high flame. Sauté the onion and garlic in it for a minute or two, until soft and fragrant.
- Add in the chorizo sausages and cook them well for about 5-6 minutes.
- Put the spinach in it too, stir fry for a while and remove the skillet from heat.
- Combine the eggs, milk, salt, and pepper in a bowl and whisk well.
- Heat the other half of the oil in a pan and pour the beaten eggs in it. Cook one side of the omelet, flip it, and put the chorizo mixture on it. Roll the omelet and dish out.
- Top with tomatoes and green onions while serving.

6.30 Keto Sheet Pan Breakfast

Servings: 6 I Time: 45 mins I Difficulty: Easy
Nutrients per serving: Calories: 341 kcal I Fat: 24.7g I Carbohydrates: 6.9g I Protein: 16g I Fiber: 2.5g

Ingredients

- 6 Eggs
- 1/4 Cup Onion, Chopped

- 1/2 Tsp. Garlic Powder
- 1 & 1/2 Cups Radishes, Quartered
- Salt, To Taste
- 1 Cup Brussels Sprouts, Quartered
- 2 Tbsps. Butter, Melted
- 3/4 Cup Bacon, Chopped
- Pepper, To Taste
- 3/4 Cup Breakfast Sausage Links, Sliced
- Cooking Oil Spray

Method
1. Preheat the oven to 400 degrees F.
2. Take a sheet pan and spray it with cooking oil spray.
3. Spread all the vegetables and bacon on the pan and sprinkle the salt, pepper, and garlic powder on them. Drizzle the avocado oil and toss to coat them well with oil and seasoning.
4. Put in the preheated oven and bake for 15 to 20 minutes or until the sprouts and radishes become softer.
5. Take out of the oven and make six holes in between the veggies to crack the eggs in.
6. Crack the eggs in the holes and bake until the eggs are cooked, for about 5-10 minutes.

6.31 Jill's Cheese Crusted Keto Omelet

Servings: 1 | Time: 15 mins | Difficulty: Easy
Nutrients per serving: Calories: 660 kcal | Fat: 54g | Carbohydrates: 5g | Protein: 39g

Ingredients
Omelet
- 2 Eggs
- 2 Tbsps. Heavy Whipping Cream
- Salt, To Taste
- Black Pepper, Ground, To Taste
- 1/2 Tbsp. Butter
- 3/4 Cup Cheese, Shredded

Filling
- 2 Mushrooms, Sliced
- 2 Cherry Tomatoes, Sliced
- 1/2 Cup Baby Spinach
- 2 Tbsps. Cream Cheese (Optional)
- 2 Tbsps. Deli Turkey
- 1 Tsp. Oregano, Dried

Method
1. Combine the cream, eggs, pepper, and salt in a bowl and whisk them well.
2. Melt the butter in a frying pan over medium flame and scatter the cheese in it. Stir fry it until it starts to bubble.
3. Put the egg mixture on the cheese and reduce the flame to low. Cook for a minute or two without stirring.
4. Once the egg is set, put the cream cheese, tomatoes, baby spinach, turkey, mushrooms, and oregano on its one half and roll the other half over it.
5. Cook for a few minutes if needed, then dish out to serve.

6.32 Low-Carb Baked Eggs

Servings: 1 | Time: 15 mins | Difficulty: Easy
Nutrients per serving: Calories: 509 kcal | Fat: 37g | Carbohydrates: 1g | Protein: 41g

Ingredients
- 1/3 Cup Beef, Ground & Cooked
- 2 Eggs
- 1/3 Cup Cheese, Shredded
- Cooking Spray

Method
1. Preheat the oven to 400 degrees F.
2. Spray a baking dish with cooking spray and spread the cooked beef in it.
3. Make two wells or holes in between and crack the eggs in them.
4. Top it with shredded cheese and put the baking dish in the preheated oven.
5. Bake it for about 10-15 minutes or until the eggs are cooked.

6.33 Keto Biscuits And Gravy

Servings: 8 | Time: 35 mins | Difficulty: Medium
Nutrients per serving: Calories: 280 kcal | Fat: 24g | Carbohydrates: 3g | Protein: 11g

Ingredients
- 1 & 1/4 Cups Sausage, Crumbled
- 4 Egg Whites, Beaten
- 2 Tbsps. Coconut Oil
- 1 Cup Beef Broth
- Coconut Oil Spray
- Black Pepper, To Taste
- 1/2 Cup Cream Cheese
- 1/4 Tsp. Sea Salt
- 1 Tsp. Baking Powder
- Salt, To Taste
- 3/4 Cup Almond Flour
- 1 Tsp. Garlic Powder (Optional)

Method
1. Preheat the oven to 400 degrees F.
2. Combine the beaten and fluffy egg whites with the baking powder, almond flour, cold coconut oil, and sea salt. Mix them well until smooth.
3. Take a muffin tin and spray it with the coconut oil spray. Put a spoonful of batter in the cups of muffin sheet and put in the preheated oven.
4. Bake it for 10-15 minutes or until cooked well.
5. Take a skillet and sauté the sausage in it for 5-6 minutes over medium flame.
6. Add in the cream cheese and beef broth in it and mix well. Let it simmer with intermittent stirring, until the mixture becomes thick and smooth.
7. Add the salt and pepper in it as well, according to your taste. Stir well and remove off the heat, once done.
8. Finally, cut the biscuits in half with a sharp knife and put 2 biscuit halves on one serving plate with 1/3 cup gravy.

6.34 Keto French Pancakes

Servings: 4 | Time: 15 mins | Difficulty: Easy
Nutrients per serving (3 pancakes): Calories: 688 kcal | Fat: 68g | Carbohydrates: 4g | Protein: 15g

Ingredients
- 2 Tbsps. Psyllium Husk Powder
- 1/2 Cup Water
- 8 Eggs
- 6 Tbsps. Butter
- 1/4 Tsp. Salt
- 2 Cups Heavy Whipping Cream

Method
1. Combine all the ingredients, except butter, in a bowl and beat well until a smooth batter is formed.
2. Heat the butter in a frying pan and pour the batter with a spoon and spread it evenly with the back of spoon. Cook on both sides until golden.

3. Dish out and serve with a low carb topping.

6.35 Keto Caprese Omelet

Servings: 2 I Time: 20 mins I Difficulty: Easy
Nutrients per serving: Calories: 533 kcal I Fat: 42g I Carbohydrates: 4g I Protein: 33g I Fiber: 1g

Ingredients

- 2 Tbsps. Olive Oil
- 1/3 Cup Cherry Tomatoes, Halved
- Salt, To Taste
- 6 Eggs
- 1 Tbsp. Basil, Fresh & Chopped
- Black Pepper, To Taste
- 1 & 1/4 Cups Mozzarella Cheese, Sliced

Method

1. Combine the eggs, basil, salt, and pepper in a bowl, and whisk well until smooth.
2. Take a frying pan and heat olive oil in it. Sauté the halved tomatoes in the oil for a few minutes. Then pour the egg mixture in it.
3. Once the eggs are set, add in the mozzarella cheese, and reduce the heat.
4. Dish out when the omelet is cooked through.

6.36 Vegetarian Keto Breakfast Casserole

Servings: 4 I Time: 50 mins I Difficulty: Easy
Nutrients per serving: Calories: 587 kcal I Fat: 48g I Carbohydrates: 5g I Protein: 32g I Fiber: 1g

Ingredients

- 1 Cup Heavy Whipping Cream
- 1 Tsp. Onion Powder
- 12 Eggs
- 1 & 3/4 Cups Mozzarella Cheese, Shredded
- Salt, To Taste
- 1/4 Cup Leek, Trimmed & Sliced Thinly
- 1/4 Cup Parmesan Cheese, Shredded
- 1/3 Cherry Tomatoes
- Black Pepper, To Taste
- 1/4 Cup Green Olives, Pitted
- Cooking Spray

Method

1. Preheat the oven to 400 degrees F.
2. Spray a baking sheet with cooking spray and spread the leek and olives on it.
3. Whisk the eggs, onion powder, cream, salt, mozzarella cheese, and pepper together in a bowl. Pour this mixture on the baking sheet.
4. Put the baking sheet in the preheated oven and bake for 30–40 minutes, until eggs are cooked, and the top becomes golden brown.

6.37 Keto Breakfast With Fried Eggs, Tomato And Cheese

Servings: 1 I Time: 15 mins I Difficulty: Easy
Nutrients per serving: Calories: 416 kcal I Fat: 33g I Carbohydrates: 4g I Protein: 25g I Fiber: 1g

Ingredients

- 2 Eggs
- Salt, To Taste
- 1/2 Tomato
- 1/2 Tbsp. Butter
- Black Pepper, Ground, To Taste
- 1/2 Cup Cheddar Cheese, Cubed
- 1/2 Tsp. Oregano, Dried (Optional)

Method

1. Sprinkle salt and pepper on the cut side of tomato.
2. Take a frying pan and heat butter in it over medium flame.
3. Once butter is melted, put the tomato in it with the cut side down.
4. Crack the eggs in it with yolks intact. Let them cook on one side until the yolks are cooked the way you like them. Flip them once done on one side. Cook the other side for a minute or two as well.
5. Sprinkle salt and pepper on them according to your taste.
6. Dish out the tomato, eggs, and cheese on a plate and sprinkle dried oregano on them.

6.38 Keto Mushroom And Cheese Frittata

Servings: 4 I Time: 60 mins I Difficulty: Medium
Nutrients per serving: Calories: 1102 kcal I Fat: 105g I Carbohydrates: 7g I Protein: 32g I Fiber: 3g

Ingredients

Frittata

- 1/2 Cup Butter
- 2 Cups Mushrooms, Sliced
- 10 Eggs
- 1 Tsp. Salt
- 1 Cup Scallions
- 1 Tbsp. Fresh Parsley
- 2 Cups Cheddar Cheese, Shredded
- 2 Cups Leafy Greens
- 1/2 Tsp. Black Pepper, Ground
- 1 Cup Mayonnaise

Vinaigrette

- 1 Tbsp. White Wine Vinegar
- 1/4 Tsp. Black Pepper, Ground
- 1/4 Cup Olive Oil
- 1/2 Tsp. Salt

Method

1. Preheat the oven to 350 degrees F.
2. Take a pan and melt butter in it over medium-high flame. Cook mushrooms in it until become golden, for about 15 minutes.
3. Lower the flame to medium-low and add in the scallions, parsley, salt, and pepper. Stir for a few minutes and then take off the heat once done.
4. Combine the eggs, cheese, mayonnaise, salt, and pepper in a bowl and whisk well.
5. Brush a baking dish with butter and put the mushroom mixture on it. Top them with the egg mixture.
6. Put in the preheated oven and bake until the frittata is golden and eggs are cooked through, for about 40 minutes.
7. Take out of the oven and let cool for few minutes.
8. Combine the vinaigrette ingredients in a bowl and serve with the frittata and leafy greens.

6.39 Veggie Keto Scramble

Servings: 1 I Time: 20 mins I Difficulty: Easy
Nutrients per serving: Calories: 455 kcal I Fat: 34g I Carbohydrates: 4g I Protein: 32g I Fiber: 1g

Ingredients

- 3 Eggs
- 1 Tbsp. Butter
- 1/2 Tbsp. Scallion, Chopped
- 1/4 Cup Parmesan Cheese, Shredded
- 2 Tbsps. Mushrooms, Sliced

- Black Pepper, Ground, To Taste
- 2 Tbsps. Red Bell Peppers, Diced
- Salt, To Taste

Method

1. Take a frying pan and melt the butter in it over medium heat. Sauté the red peppers, mushrooms with salt and pepper in it, until tender.
2. Crack the eggs in it and stir to combine. Cook them well but do not let them become dry.
3. Dish it out and put the shredded parmesan and scallions on top.

6.40 Scrambled Eggs With Basil And Butter

Servings: 1 I Time: 10 mins I Difficulty: Easy
Nutrients per serving: Calories: 657 kcal I Fat: 61g I Carbohydrates: 3g I Protein: 25g I Fiber: 0g

Ingredients

- 2 Tbsps. Butter
- Black Pepper, Ground, To Taste
- 2 Eggs
- 1/2 Cup Cheddar Cheese, Shredded
- 2 Tbsps. Basil, Fresh
- 2 Tbsps. Heavy Whipping Cream
- Salt, To Taste

Method

1. Combine the eggs, cream, cheese, salt, and pepper in a bowl and whisk well.
2. Take a pan and heat butter in it over low heat. Once it melts, pour the egg mixture in it, and stir slightly to scramble the egg.
3. Cook on low heat if you want the eggs to be creamy and soft.
4. Once done, dish out and sprinkle fresh basil on top.

6.41 Keto Taco Omelet

Servings: 2 I Time: 25 mins I Difficulty: Easy
Nutrients per serving: Calories: 790 kcal I Fat: 63g I Carbohydrates: 8g I Protein: 44g I Fiber: 8g

Ingredients

Taco Seasoning

- 1/4 Tsp. Chili Flakes
- 1/4 Tsp. Black Pepper, Ground
- 1/4 Tsp. Onion Powder
- 1/2 Tsp. Oregano, Dried
- 1/2 Tsp. Salt
- 1/2 Tsp. Cumin, Ground
- 1/2 Tsp. Garlic Powder
- 1/2 Tsp. Paprika Powder

Omelet

- 1 Tbsp. Olive Oil
- 1 Tomato, Diced
- 3/4 Cup Beef, Ground
- 1 & 1/4 Cups Cheddar Cheese, Shredded
- 1 Avocado, Diced
- 4 Eggs
- 1/4 Tsp. Black Pepper, Ground
- 1/2 Tsp. Sea Salt
- 1 Tsp. Cilantro, Fresh
- 2 Tbsps. Lime Juice (Optional)

Method

1. Put all the taco seasoning ingredients in a bowl and mix well.
2. Take a non-stick skillet and combine the ground beef and taco seasoning in it. Cook it well and take off the heat once done.
3. Transfer to a bowl and the lime juice in it. Set aside.
4. Whisk the eggs in a bowl until they become creamy and fluffy.
5. Heat the olive oil in the same skillet over low heat and add the egg in it. Cook the eggs for a few minutes.
6. When the eggs are half done, put the ground beef, tomatoes and two third of the cheese in it. Stir slightly.
7. Dish out the omelet once done and put the remaining cheese, avocado and cilantro on it. Sprinkle the salt and pepper on top and serve.

6.42 Keto Baked Eggs With Tarragon Chive Cream Sauce

Servings: 2 I Time: 25 mins I Difficulty: Easy
Nutrients per serving: Calories: 429 kcal I Fat: 36g I Carbohydrates: 4g I Protein: 22g I Fiber: 0g

Ingredients

- 4 Eggs
- 1 Garlic Clove, Minced
- 1 Tsp. Chives, Fresh & Chopped
- 1/2 Cup Heavy Whipping Cream
- 1/4 Tsp. Sea Salt
- 1 Tsp. Tarragon, Fresh & Chopped
- 1/4 Tsp. Black Pepper, Ground
- 1/2 Cup Parmesan Cheese, Shredded
- 1/2 Tsp. Red Chili Flakes (Optional)
- 1 /8 Tsp. Nutmeg, Ground (Optional)

Method

1. Preheat the oven to 425 degrees F.
2. Brush two ramekins with oil and put them on a sheet pan.
3. Combine all the ingredients except eggs, in a bowl and mix well. Divide the mixture in two parts and pour in the ramekins.
4. Break two eggs in each ramekin and put the sheet pan in the preheated oven.
5. Bake for 15 minutes or until the eggs are cooked. Take out once done and sprinkle some chives, tarragon, and shredded parmesan cheese on top.

6.43 Keto Coconut Porridge

Servings: 2 I Time: 10 mins I Difficulty: Easy
Nutrients per serving: Calories: 481 kcal I Fat: 48g I Carbohydrates: 4g I Protein: 9g I Fiber: 5g

Ingredients

- 4 Tbsps. Coconut Cream
- 1 Tbsp. Coconut Flour
- 1/4 Tsp. Psyllium Husk Powder, Ground
- 2 Tbsps. Coconut Oil
- 1/4 Tsp. Salt
- 1 Egg, Beaten

Method

1. Take a bowl and whisk the egg with psyllium husk powder, salt, and coconut flour.
2. Put Coconut oil and cream in a pan and melt them over low heat. Add in the egg mixture and combine well until it becomes thick and creamy.
3. Pour in the serving bowls and top with a few berries if you want.

6.44 Keto Browned Butter Asparagus With Creamy Eggs

Servings: 4 I Time: 25 mins I Difficulty: Easy
Nutrients per serving: Calories: 497 kcal I Fat: 46g I Carbohydrates: 6g I Protein: 16g I Fiber: 4g

Ingredients

- 4 Eggs
- 1/2 Cup Sour Cream
- Salt, To Taste
- 6 Tbsps. Butter
- Cayenne Pepper, To Taste
- 3/4 Cup Parmesan Cheese, Shredded
- 1 & 1/2 Tbsps. Lemon Juice
- 1 Tbsp. Olive Oil
- 3 Cups Green Asparagus

Method

1. Heat 4 tbsps. butter in a pan over medium heat and crack the eggs in it. Cook them with constant stirring to scramble them. Take out once done.
2. Combine the scrambled eggs with the sour cream and cheese in a blender and blend until they become smooth. Transfer to a bowl and season with salt and cayenne pepper as per your taste. Stir well.
3. Heat olive oil in a frying pan over medium heat and sauté the asparagus in it. Season with salt and pepper and stir well. Take out after a minute or two and set aside.
4. Heat the remaining 2 tbsps. butter in the same frying pan and sauté it until becomes golden brown with a nutty smell. Take off the heat, let cool, and add in the lemon juice.
5. Put the asparagus into the frying pan again and stir with the butter over low heat until hot.
6. Serve the browned butter asparagus with the creamy eggs.

6.45 Keto BLT Baked Avocado Eggs

Servings: 2 I Time: 45 mins I Difficulty: Easy
Nutrients per serving: Calories: 790 kcal I Fat: 69g I Carbohydrates: 5g I Protein: 27g I Fiber: 14g

Ingredients

- 3/4 Cup Lettuce, Shredded
- 3/4 Cup Bacon
- 4 Cherry Tomatoes, Quartered
- Salt, To Taste
- 4 Eggs
- Black Pepper, To Taste
- 2 Avocados, Halved

Method

1. Take a skillet and cook the bacon in it over high heat. Break into pieces with the spoon, once become crispy. Take off the heat and set aside.
2. Preheat the oven to 375 degrees F.
3. Take the halved avocados and remove their pit. Enlarge their pit hole to fill an egg in it. Put them on a lined baking sheet
4. Crack an egg into every avocado hole and sprinkle with salt and pepper.
5. Put the tomatoes on the eggs and sprinkle the bacon pieces on top.
6. Put the baking sheet in the preheated oven and bake for 15 to 20 minutes, until the eggs are cooked as you like them.
7. Take the baked avocado eggs out of the oven and transfer on a serving dish with shredded lettuce on top.

6.46 Keto Dosa

Servings: 2 I Time: 25 mins I Difficulty: Medium
Nutrients per serving: Calories: 368 kcal I Fat: 33g I Carbohydrates: 4g I Protein: 13g I Fiber: 33g

Ingredients

- 1/2 Cup Coconut Milk
- 1/2 Tsp. Coriander Seed, Ground
- 1/2 Cup Mozzarella Cheese, Shredded
- 1/2 Tsp. Cumin, Ground
- 1/2 Cup Almond Flour
- Salt, To Taste
- Oil, To Taste

Method

1. Combine all the ingredients in a bowl and mix them.
2. Brush a non-stick pan with some oil and heat it over low flame.
3. Pour a spoonful batter in the pan and swirl the pan to spread it.
4. Fry the dosa from both sides until becomes golden and crispy.
5. Dish it out, once cooked and serve with coconut chutney.

6.47 Keto Oven Pancake With Bacon And Onion

Servings: 4 I Time: 40 mins I Difficulty: Easy
Nutrients per serving: Calories: 534 kcal I Fat: 49g I Carbohydrates: 5g I Protein: 16g I Fiber: 2g

Ingredients

- 1/2 Cup Bacon, Sliced
- 1 Tsp. Salt
- 3 Tsps. Psyllium Husk Powder, Ground
- 1 Cup Heavy Whipping Cream
- 2 Tbsps. Butter
- 1 Tsp. Baking Powder
- 1/2 Cup Almond Flour
- 4 Eggs
- 1/2 Yellow Onion, Sliced
- 1/2 Cup Cottage Cheese
- 1 Tbsp. Parsley, Fresh & Chopped (Optional)

Method

1. Preheat the oven to 350 degrees F.
2. Take a frying pan and melt butter in it. Sauté onion and bacon in it until the onion becomes translucent and the bacon gets crispy.
3. Combine the eggs, cream, and cottage cheese in a bowl and whisk well. Then add the almond flour, baking powder, salt, and psyllium husk in it. Whisk again to mix them thoroughly. Let the pancake batter rest for a few minutes.
4. Brush a baking pan with oil or butter and pour the batter on it. Top it with the fried onions and bacon and put in the preheated oven.
5. Bake it until the pancakes become golden brown, for about 20-25 minutes.

6.48 Keto French Toast

Servings: 2 I Time: 10 mins I Difficulty: Easy
Nutrients per serving: Calories: 408 kcal I Fat: 37g I Carbohydrates: 3g I Protein: 15g I Fiber: 3g

Ingredients

Mug Bread

- 1 Tsp. Butter

- 2 Tbsps. Almond Flour
- 2 Tbsps. Coconut Flour
- 1 & 1/2 Tsp. Baking Powder
- 1 Pinch Salt
- 2 Eggs
- 2 Tbsps. Heavy Whipping Cream

Batter

- 2 Eggs
- 2 Tbsps. Heavy Whipping Cream
- 1/2 Tsp. Cinnamon, Ground
- 1/8 Tsp. Salt
- 2 Tbsps. Butter

Method

1. Take either a big mug or a deep glass dish that has flat bottom and brush its inside with oil or butter.
2. Combine all the ingredients of mug bread in it, dry ingredients first and eggs and cream at the end. Whisk them well to make get smooth consistency, without lumps.
3. Put the mug or glass dish in the microwave for about 2 minutes, on high. You can increase the time if the bread is not cooked from the center.
4. Once done, take out and let cool for a few minutes. Take the bread out of the mug or glass dish and slice in half.
5. Whisk the eggs, salt, cinnamon, and cream in a bowl and drench the bread slices in it. Once the slices have soaked up the egg's mixture, fry them in the melted butter in a pan.
6. Dish out and serve hot.

6.49 BLTA Lettuce Wraps

Servings: 2 | Time: 20 mins | Difficulty: Easy
Nutrients per serving (2 wraps): Calories: 568 kcal | Fat: 54g | Carbohydrates: 3g | Protein: 14g | Fiber: 4g

Ingredients

- 1 Tomato, Sliced
- Salt, To Taste
- 3 Tbsps. Mayonnaise
- 2 Lettuce Leaves
- Black Pepper, To Taste
- 1/2 Avocado
- 1/4 Cup Bacon, Sliced

Method

1. Take a skillet and cook bacon slices in it over medium heat, for about 5 minutes or until they become crispy. Dish out and let cool.
2. When cool to touch, cut the bacon slices in half, lengthwise.
3. Put 1 & 1/2 tbsps. mayonnaise on each lettuce leaf and put tomato slices on top.
4. Top the tomato slices with bacon strips and avocado. Sprinkle salt and pepper on them as per your taste.

6.50 Sullivan's keDough Breakfast Pizza

Servings: 4 | Time: 40 mins | Difficulty: Medium
Nutrients per serving: Calories: 1017 kcal | Fat: 84g | Carbohydrates: 9g | Protein: 56g | Fiber: 1g

Ingredients

The Crust

- 4 Tbsps. Olive Oil
- 1 Egg
- 3/4 Cup Mozzarella Cheese, Shredded
- 1/2 Tsp. Baking Powder
- 1/2 Cup Whey Isolate Protein Powder, Unflavored
- 1/2 Tsp. Garlic, Granulated

- 3/4 Cup Parmesan Cheese, Grated
- 1/2 Tsp. Salt
- 1/4 Cup Cream Cheese
- 1/2 Tsp. Italian Seasoning

Toppings

- 2 Eggs, Scrambled
- 1/3 Cup Bacon, Chopped
- 2 Cups Cheddar Cheese, Shredded
- 1 Cup Italian Sausage, Fresh
- 1/2 Cup Cream Cheese
- 4 Tbsps. Tomato Sauce, Unsweetened

Method

1. Preheat the oven to 375 degrees F.
2. Take a large mixing bowl and mix all of the crust ingredients in it until combined. Knead the thick dough and then divide into four parts. Make four pizza crusts with them.
3. Put the pizza crusts dough on a baking sheet lined with parchment paper and put in the preheated oven. Bake until they become golden brown, for about 10–12 minutes.
4. Take out of the oven once done and top with the toppings of your choice.
5. Put back in the oven until the toppings become golden brown and cheese melts.

6.51 Keto Italian Breakfast Casserole

Servings: 4 | Time: 1 hr. | Difficulty: Easy
Nutrients per serving: Calories: 801 kcal | Fat: 71g | Carbohydrates: 7g | Protein: 16g | Fiber: 1g

Ingredients

- 8 Eggs
- 1 Cup Cheddar Cheese, Shredded
- 1/4 Cup Butter
- 1/4 Cup Basil, Fresh & Chopped
- Salt, To Taste
- 3/4 Cup Cauliflower, Chopped
- 1 Cup Heavy Whipping Cream
- Black Pepper, To Taste
- 1 & 1/2 Cups Italian Sausage, Fresh

Method

1. Preheat the oven to 375 degrees F.
2. Heat the butter in a pan over medium-high heat until it melts and sauté the cauliflower in it. When it get softer, take out and set aside.
3. Then sauté the sausage in the same pan by breaking it into crumbs with the spoon and add the salt and pepper in it. Cook it thoroughly.
4. Whisk the eggs, cheese, cream, salt and pepper together in a bowl until smooth. Set aside.
5. Brush a baking dish (8x8 inches) with oil or butter and put the sautéed cauliflower and sausage in it. Pour the egg mixture on it and top with basil.
6. Put the baking dish in the preheated oven and bake the casserole until becomes golden brown, for about 30–40 minutes.
7. Take out once all set and cooked and serve.

6.52 Keto Salmon-Filled Avocados

Servings: 2 | Time: 10 mins | Difficulty: Beginner
Nutrients per serving: Calories: 715 kcal | Fat: 64g | Carbohydrates: 6g | Protein: 22g | Fiber: 13g

Ingredients

- 3/4 Cup Sour Cream
- Black Pepper, To Taste

- 3/4 Cup Salmon, Smoked
- Salt, To Taste
- 2 Avocados, Halved & Pitted
- 2 Tbsps. Lemon Juice (Optional)

Method

1. Take the halved and pitted avocados and fill their hole with a dollop of sour cream and top with smoked salmon.
2. Sprinkle the salt and pepper on top and drizzle the lemon juice if desired.
3. Serve and enjoy.

6.53 Keto Croque Madame

Servings: 2 | Time: 25 mins | Difficulty: Medium
Nutrients per serving: Calories: 1218 kcal | Fat: 105g | Carbohydrates: 10g | Protein: 58g | Fiber: 5g

Ingredients

- 1 Cup Cottage Cheese
- 4 Eggs
- 3 Tsps. Psyllium Husk Powder, Ground
- 4 Tbsps. Butter
- 2/3 Cup Smoked Deli Ham
- 1/4 Cup Cheddar Cheese, Sliced
- 2 Tbsps. Red Onion, Chopped Finely

Serving

- 2 Eggs
- 2 Tbsps. Butter
- 1 1/2 Cups Baby Spinach
- 4 Tbsps. Olive Oil
- 1/2 Tbsp. Red Wine Vinegar
- Salt, To Taste
- Black Pepper, To Taste

Method

1. Combine the eggs, cottage cheese, psyllium husk powder in a bowl and whisk them well, until a smooth batter is formed. Set aside for five minutes to let it thicken.
2. Melt the butter in a frying pan over medium flame and put the spoonful batter in it to make pancakes. Cook the pancakes on both sides until become golden brown.
3. Put the sliced ham, onion, and cheddar cheese on one pancake and put the other on top, to make a sandwich.
4. Combine the vinegar, spinach, oil, salt, and pepper in a bowl to make the vinaigrette.
5. Make fried eggs with the remaining butter and put them on top of the sandwiches.
6. Serve the warm Croque Madame with spinach vinaigrette.

6.54 Keto Salami And Brie Cheese Plate

Servings: 2 | Time: 5 mins | Difficulty: Beginner
Nutrients per serving: Calories: 1218 kcal | Fat: 115g | Carbohydrates: 5g | Protein: 39g | Fiber: 10g

Ingredients

- 3/4 Cup Brie Cheese
- 1/2 Cup Salami
- 1 & 1/2 Cups Lettuce
- 1 Avocado
- 5 Tbsps. Macadamia Nuts
- 1/4 Cup Olive Oil

Method

1. Combine all the ingredients in a salad bowl and toss well.
2. Serve and enjoy.

6.55 Keto Mackerel And Egg Plate

Servings: 2 | Time: 15 mins | Difficulty: Beginner
Nutrients per serving: Calories: 689 kcal | Fat: 59g | Carbohydrates: 4g | Protein: 35g | Fiber: 1g

Ingredients

- 1/4 Cup Olive Oil
- Black Pepper, To Taste
- 1/4 Cup Red Onion, Sliced
- 1 Cup Mackerel In Tomato Sauce, Canned
- 1 & 1/2 Cups Lettuce
- Salt, To Taste
- 4 Eggs
- 2 Tbsps. Butter

Method

1. Melt the butter in a frying pan and fry the eggs according to your preference. Dish it out on a serving plate.
2. Put the onion slices, lettuce, and mackerel on the plate beside eggs. Sprinkle salt and pepper on it and drizzle the olive oil on the salad. Serve and enjoy.

6.56 Keto Turkey Plate

Servings: 2 | Time: 8 mins | Difficulty: Easy
Nutrients per serving: Calories: 660 kcal | Fat: 60g | Carbohydrates: 7g | Protein: 13g | Fiber: 7g

Ingredients

- 1/4 Cup Olive Oil
- 1/3 Cup Cream Cheese
- Salt, To Taste
- 1 & 1/2 Cups Lettuce
- Black Pepper, To Taste
- 3/4 Cup Deli Turkey
- 1 Avocado, Sliced

Method

1. Combine all the ingredients in a bowl and toss well.
2. Divide it into two servings.

6.57 Keto Cauliflower Hash With Eggs And Poblano Peppers

Servings: 2 | Time: 25 mins | Difficulty: Easy
Nutrients per serving: Calories: 897 kcal | Fat: 87g | Carbohydrates: 9g | Protein: 17g | Fiber: 6g

Ingredients

- 4 Eggs
- Black Pepper, To Taste
- 1 Tsp. Olive Oil
- 2 Cups Cauliflower, Grated
- Salt, To Taste
- 1/2 Cup Mayonnaise
- 6 Tbsps. Butter
- 1/3 Cup Poblano Peppers
- 1 Tsp. Garlic Powder

Method

1. Melt the butter in a pan and sauté the grated cauliflower in it. Sprinkle with salt and pepper and stir to combine. Take out once fried and set aside.
2. Stir fry the poblano peppers in the same pan in melted butter. Once their skin starts to bubble, take off the heat and set aside.
3. Whisk mayonnaise and garlic powder in a bowl and set aside.

4. Fry the eggs in the butter according to your preference and sprinkle the salt and pepper on them.
5. Serve the fried eggs with the sautéed poblanos and cauliflower hash. Put a dollop of the seasoned mayo on top.

6.58 Keto Seafood Omelet

Servings: 2 I Time: 20 mins I Difficulty: Easy
Nutrients per serving: Calories: 870 kcal I Fat: 82g I Carbohydrates: 4g I Protein: 27g I Fiber: 1g

Ingredients

- 6 Eggs
- 4 Tbsps. Olive Oil
- Salt, To Taste
- 2/3 Cup Shrimp, Cooked
- 1 Red Chili Pepper
- Black Pepper, To Taste
- 1/2 Tsp. Cumin, Ground
- 1 Tbsp. Chives, Fresh
- 1/2 Cup Mayonnaise
- 2 Garlic Cloves, Minced (Optional)

Method

1. Preheat a broiler.
2. Combine the shrimps with 2 tbsps. olive oil, garlic, red chili, ground cumin, salt, and pepper in a bowl. Mix them well and put the marinated shrimps in the broiler.
3. Once the shrimps cooked through, take out of the broiler, and let cool.
4. When cooled, add in the chives and mayo to the shrimps.
5. Whisk the eggs with salt and pepper in a bowl and fry the omelet in the remaining olive oil in a non-stick pan.
6. When the omelet is half cooked, add in the shrimp mixture and fold. Cooke at low heat and once the eggs are set dish out and serve hot.

6.59 Keto Rutabaga Patties With Smoked Salmon

Servings: 2 I Time: 30 mins I Difficulty: Medium
Nutrients per serving: Calories: 660 kcal I Fat: 60g I Carbohydrates: 7g I Protein: 13g I Fiber: 7g

Ingredients

Rutabaga patties

- 1/2 Cup Butter
- 1/2 Tsp. Onion Powder
- 1/4 Tsp. Pepper
- 3 Tbsps. Coconut Flour
- 1 Tsp. Salt
- 1 & 1/2 Cups Rutabaga, Peeled & Grated
- 4 Eggs
- 1 Cup. Halloumi Cheese, Shredded
- 1/8 Cup Turmeric (Optional)

For Serving

- 2 & 1/2 Cups Leafy Greens
- 1 & 1/4 Cups Salmon, Smoked
- 2 Tbsps. Lemon Juice
- 1 Cup Mayonnaise

Method

1. Combine all the patties ingredients in a bowl except butter and mix well. Let it rest for a few minutes.
2. Melt the butter in a skillet and put the spoonful of rutabaga mixture in it to make 12 patties out of it. Fry the patties over medium heat.
3. Cook on both sides for a few minutes and dish out once golden brown.
4. Serve with the smoked salmon, a dollop of mayonnaise, green salad with a little lemon juice squeezed on it.

6.60 Keto Rutabaga Fritters With Bacon

Servings: 4 I Time: 30 mins I Difficulty: Medium
Nutrients per serving: Calories: 955 kcal I Fat: 89g I Carbohydrates: 10g I Protein: 24g I Fiber: 6g

Ingredients

Rutabaga Fritters

- 3 Tbsps. Coconut Flour
- 2 Cups Rutabaga, Peeled & Grated
- 1/2 Tsp. Onion Powder
- 1/3 Cup Butter
- 3/4 Cup Halloumi Cheese, Shredded
- 1/4 Tsp. Pepper
- 4 Eggs
- 1 Tsp. Salt
- 1/8 Tsp. Turmeric

For Serving

- 2 & 1/2 Cups Leafy Greens
- 1 Cup Mayonnaise
- 3/4 Cup Bacon

Method

1. Combine all the fritters ingredients in a bowl except butter and mix well. Let it rest for a few minutes.
2. Melt the butter in a skillet and put the spoonful of rutabaga mixture in it to make 12 fritters out of it. Fry them over medium heat.
3. Cook on both sides for a few minutes and dish out once golden brown.
4. Serve with mayonnaise, crispy bacon, and green salad.

6.61 Keto Coconut Pancakes

Servings: 4 I Time: 40 mins I Difficulty: Medium
Nutrients per serving: Calories: 279 kcal I Fat: 24g I Carbohydrates: 3g I Protein: 11g I Fiber: 6g

Ingredients

- 3/4 Cup Coconut Milk
- 6 Eggs
- 2 Tbsps. Coconut Oil, Melted
- 1/8 Tsp. Salt
- 1 Tsp. Baking Powder
- Butter, For Frying
- 1/2 Cup Coconut Flour

Method

1. Combine all the ingredients, except butter, in a bowl and whisk or beat them well, until a smooth batter is formed, without lumps.
2. Heat the butter in a pan, until it melts and put a spoonful of batter on it and spread it with the back of spoon evenly. Flip once done from one side and cook both sides until become golden. Similarly fry the pancakes for the remaining batter at low or medium heat.

6.62 Keto Porridge

Servings: 1 I Time: 10 mins I Difficulty: Easy
Nutrients per serving: Calories: 644 kcal I Fat: 64g I Carbohydrates: 5g I Protein: 12g I Fiber: 5g

Ingredients

- 1 Tbsp. Chia Seeds
- 1 Tbsp. Sesame Seeds
- 1 Egg
- 1/3 Cup Heavy Whipping Cream
- 1/8 Tsp. Salt
- 2 Tbsps. Coconut Oil

Method

1. Combine all the ingredients, except butter, in a bowl and mix well until a smooth mixture is formed. Let it rest for 2–3 minutes.
2. Meanwhile, heat the coconut oil in a pan on medium.
3. Pour in the egg and creamy mixture in the oil and stir well. Let it simmer until your desired consistency and thickness is attained but do not boil it.
4. Transfer to a serving bowl, once done and serve hot.

6.63 Keto Western Omelet

Servings: 2 I Time: 30 mins I Difficulty: Easy
Nutrients per serving: Calories: 708 kcal I Fat: 58g I Carbohydrates: 6g I Protein: 40g I Fiber: 1g

Ingredients

- 2/3 Cup Deli Ham, Smoked & Diced
- 6 Eggs
- Salt, To Taste
- 3/4 Cup Cheddar Cheese, Shredded
- 1/2 Onion, Chopped Finely
- Black Pepper, To Taste
- 2 Tbsps. Heavy Whipping Cream
- 1/2 Green Bell Pepper, Chopped Finely
- 4 Tbsps. Butter

Method

1. Combine the eggs with whipping cream, half of the cheddar cheese, salt and pepper and whisk until the mixture becomes creamy and fluffy.
2. Heat the butter in a frying pan over medium flame until it melts and sauté the onion, peppers, and diced ham in it for a few minutes until they become soft.
3. Add in the egg mixture and cook the omelet over reduced heat to avoid the burning of egg. Once the eggs are set, sprinkle the remaining cheddar cheese on it.
4. Once the cheese melts, transfer the omelet to a serving dish and enjoy.

6.64 Keto Breakfast Tapas

Servings: 4 I Time: 15 mins I Difficulty: Easy
Nutrients per serving: Calories: 573 kcal I Fat: 50g I Carbohydrates: 6g I Protein: 24g I Fiber: 1g

Ingredients

- 1 Cup Chorizo, Diced
- 1/2 Cup Cucumber, Diced
- 1 Cup Cheddar Cheese, Shredded
- 1/2 Cup Mayonnaise
- 1/4 Cup Red Bell Peppers, Diced
- 1 Cup Prosciutto, Sliced

Method

1. Combine all the ingredients in a bowl and toss well to mix.
2. Divide into four servings and enjoy.

6.65 Keto Scrambled Eggs With Halloumi Cheese

Servings: 2 I Time: 20 mins I Difficulty: Easy
Nutrients per serving: Calories: 647 kcal I Fat: 57g I Carbohydrates: 4g I Protein: 28g I Fiber: 1g

Ingredients

- 2 Tbsps. Olive Oil
- Salt, To Taste
- 4 Eggs
- 4 Tbsps. Parsley, Fresh & Chopped
- Black Pepper, To Taste
- 1/3 Cup Halloumi Cheese, Diced
- 7 Tbsps. Olives, Pitted
- 1/3 Cup Bacon, Diced
- 2 Scallions, Chopped

Method

1. Combine the eggs, parsley, salt, and pepper in a bowl and whisk well to form a smooth mixture. Set aside.
2. Take a frying pan and heat the olive oil in it over medium-high flame.
3. Sauté the scallions, bacon, and halloumi cheese in it until they become golden brown. Then add in the egg mixture and lower the flame.
4. Cook the eggs for a while and add in the olives.
5. Stir for a few of minutes, transfer to a serving plate once done.

6.66 Prawn And Herb Omelet

Servings: 4 I Time: 25 mins I Difficulty: Easy
Nutrients per serving: Calories: 599 kcal I Fat: 15g I Carbohydrates: 11g I Protein: 45g

Ingredients

- 1 & 1/2 Cups Prawns, Cooked & Chopped
- 14 Eggs
- Nori Sheets, Toasted & Cut Into Squares
- 1 Cup Milk
- Sesame Seeds, Toasted
- 1/2 Cup Dill, Chopped
- 2 Spring Onions, Sliced
- 1/2 Cup Parsley, Chopped
- 1/4 Cup Butter, Diced
- 1/2 Cup Chives, Chopped
- 1 Cucumber, Sliced
- 1 Fennel, Sliced
- Salt, To Taste
- Black Pepper, To Taste

Lemon-Tahini Dressing

- 2 Tbsps. Chives, Chopped
- 1 Tbsp. Tahini
- 2 Tbsps. Extra Virgin Olive Oil
- 2 Tsps. Honey
- 2 Tbsps. Lemon
- 1 Tbsp. Water

Method

1. Combine all the ingredients of lemon tahini dressing in a bowl and mix well.
2. Put the eggs, milk, parsley, chives, and dill in a bowl and whisk them.
3. Put half the butter in a frying pan and heat it over medium-high heat.
4. Once melted, pour half the egg mixture in it, and swirl the pan to spread in the pan. After a minute when the eggs are half cooked, add half the cooked shrimps in it and fold gently.
5. Season with salt and pepper and cook for a minute or two until eggs are set and the prawns are warm. Transfer to a serving dish.
6. Repeat this with other half of butter, egg mixture and prawns.
7. Put the sliced spring onions, cucumber nori and sesame seeds on top of the omelet and serve with the tahini dressing.

6.67 Pumpkin Spice Overnight Oats

Servings: 2 I Time: 8 hrs. I Difficulty: Easy
Nutrients per serving: Calories: 444 kcal I Fat: 41.3g I Carbohydrates: 5.1g I Protein: 15.4g

Ingredients

- 2 Tbsps. Coconut Milk, Unsweetened

- 1/2 Cup Hemp Hearts
- 1 Tbsp. MCT Oil
- 1/3 Cup Coconut Milk, From Carton
- 3/4 Tsp. Pumpkin Pie Spice
- 1/3 Cup Coffee, Brewed
- 2 Tbsps. Pecans, Chopped
- 2 Tbsps. Pumpkin Puree
- 1 Tbsp. Chia Seeds
- 1/4 Tsp. Cinnamon, Ground
- 2 Tsps. Erythritol, Powdered
- Sea Salt, To Taste
- 1/2 Tsp. Vanilla Extract

Method
1. Combine all the ingredients except carton coconut milk, cinnamon, and pecans in a bowl and mix well.
2. Transfer to a mason jar with a lid and refrigerate overnight.
3. Add in the carton coconut milk and mix well.
4. Sprinkle the chopped pecans and cinnamon powder on top.

6.68 Keto Breakfast Grits

Servings: 2 I Time: 15 mins I Difficulty: Easy
Nutrients per serving: Calories: 484 kcal I Fat: 43.1g I Carbohydrates: 8.1g I Protein: 17.8g

Ingredients
- 1/4 Cup Cheddar Cheese
- 1/4 Tsp. Garlic Powder
- 2 Tbsps. Butter
- 1/4 Cup Hemp Hearts
- 2 Cups Cauliflower Rice
- 1/4 Cup Heavy Cream
- 1/2 Cup Cremini Mushrooms
- 1 Cup Almond Milk
- Salt, To Taste
- Black Pepper, To Taste

Method
1. Heat half the butter in a pan and sauté the mushrooms in it for 2-3 minutes over medium heat. Sprinkle some salt and pepper in it and take off the heat once become softer. Set aside.
2. Heat other half of the butter in the same pan and sauté cauliflower rice and hemp hearts in it for 2-3 minutes, over medium heat.
3. Add in the remaining ingredients and stir well. Reduce the heat to medium-low and cook for a few minutes until the mixture is thick.
4. Take off the heat and transfer to serving plates. Put the sautéed mushrooms on top and a little cheddar cheese if you want.

6.69 Keto Mushroom Sausage Skillet

Servings: 6 I Time: 30 mins I Difficulty: Easy
Nutrients per serving: Calories: 364 kcal I Fat: 29.3g I Carbohydrates: 4.3g I Protein: 20.1g

Ingredients
- 2 Tbsps. Olive Oil
- 2 Cups Pork Sausage
- 2 Cups Cremini Mushroom, Sliced
- 1 Cup Mozzarella Cheese, Grated
- 2 Green Onions, For Garnish

Method
1. Preheat the broiler in the oven.
2. Heat 1 tbsp. olive oil in a skillet over medium heat and brown the sausages in it. Take out once done and let cool. Chop them into small pieces.
3. Heat 1 tbsp. olive oil in the same skillet and sauté the sliced mushrooms in it until become golden brown.
4. Add in the chopped pork sausage and mozzarella cheese.
5. Put the skillet in the preheated broiler and cook until the cheese melts.
6. Take out of the oven and top with green onions.

6.70 Keto Lemon Donut Holes

Servings: 10 I Time: 15 mins I Difficulty: Easy
Nutrients per serving: Calories: 91 kcal I Fat: 8.3g I Carbohydrates: 1.4g I Protein: 2.4g

Ingredients
For Donut Holes:
- 1/2 Tsp. Vanilla Extract
- Wedges of 1/2 Lemon, Seeded
- 3 Tbsps. Stevia/Erythritol Blend
- 2 Tbsps. Avocado Oil
- 1/8 Tsp. Salt
- 1 Tbsp. Water
- 1 Cup Almond Flour

For Lemon Glaze:
- 2 Tsps. Lemon Juice
- 4 Tbsps. Stevia/Erythritol Blend, Powdered

Method
1. Preheat the oven to 350 degrees F.
2. Combine all the donut hole ingredients in a blender and blend well until a thick dough is formed.
3. Put spoonful of this dough on a lined baking sheet and smooth out in a ball shape using hands.
4. Put in the preheated oven and bake for 10-12 minutes.
5. Combine all the glaze ingredients in a bowl and mix well.
6. Once the donuts are done, take out of the oven and let cool.
7. Top the donut holes with lemon glaze and serve.

6.71 Keto Eggs Benedict

Servings: 2 I Time: 25 mins I Difficulty: Easy
Nutrients per serving: Calories: 781 kcal I Fat: 60.9g I Carbohydrates: 5.9g I Protein: 50g

Ingredients
Hollandaise Sauce
- 1 Tsp. Lemon Juice
- Salt, To Taste
- 2 Egg Yolks
- Paprika, To Taste
- 2 Tbsps. Butter, Melted

Eggs Benedict
- 2 Tsps. Butter
- 90 Second Keto Mug Bread For 20 Servings
- 1 Tbsp. White Vinegar
- 4 Eggs
- 1 Tbsp. Chives, Chopped
- 4 Canadian Bacon Slices
- Salt, To Taste

Method
1. Cook the keto mug bread according to package instructions, slice it and set aside.
2. Take a metal bowl and whisk the egg yolks and lemon juice in it, until combined.
3. Fill half a pot with water and boil over medium heat. Once boiled, lower the heat, and put the metal bowl in it as a double boiler.
4. Once the yolk mixture heats up, pour the melted butter in it slowly and keep stirring to mix it well with the yolks over low heat.

5. Do not let the yolks scramble and take the pot out once a thick mixture is formed. Add in the salt and pepper in it and mix well. Set the hollandaise aside.
6. To prepare the poached eggs, fill a pot with 3-4 inches of water and boil it over medium-high heat. Once it starts boiling, lower the heat and put salt and vinegar in the simmering water.
7. Crack an egg in a bowl, keeping its yolk intact. Stir the simmering water with a spoon in circular manner to create a whirlpool and slowly pour the egg into the water.
8. Allow the egg to cook for 2 to 3 minutes, then take it out with a slotted spoon and gently put on a plate with paper towels.
9. Repeat the process with the rest of the eggs.
10. Sauté the Canadian bacon slices in a pan until become crispy.
11. Take a slice of mug bread, put the bacon on it and top bacon with poached egg. Sprinkle some salt and pepper on it if you want. Assemble the egg benedicts like this with other slices too.
12. Top the benedict eggs with a spoonful of hollandaise mixture and chopped chives.

6.72 Huevos Rancheros

Servings: 4 I Time: 25 mins I Difficulty: Easy
Nutrients per serving (1 tostada): Calories: 457 kcal I Fat: 37.33g I Carbohydrates: 6.88g I Protein: 20.7g

Ingredients
Chipotle Salsa
- 1 Tbsp. Chipotle Peppers In Adobo Sauce
- Salt, To Taste
- 1/2 Cup Tomato Sauce (Low-Carb)
- 2 Tbsps. Coconut Oil
- 2 Tsps. Oregano, Dried
- Black Pepper, To Taste
- 2 Tsps. Red Pepper Flakes, Crushed
- 2 Tsps. Garlic, Fresh & Minced
- 1/2 Shallot, Diced Finely

Egg Tortilla
- 4 Lime Wedges
- 4 Eggs
- 1 Avocado, Sliced
- 1/4 Cup Cilantro, Fresh & Chopped
- 2 Cups Cheese Blend, Shredded (Mexican-Style)

Method
1. Heat coconut oil in a skillet over medium heat and sauté crushed red pepper flakes in it for aa minute and take off the heat. Let it rest for some time, strain the oil and get rid of the flakes.
2. Heat 3/4 of the drained chili oil in the skillet again and sauté the shallots and onion in it until they become fragrant. Add in the tomato sauce, chipotle chili, and oregano and cook them until the sauce thickens. Remove off the heat and set the chili salsa aside.
3. Add the 1/4 drained chili oil on a non-stick pan and spread the cheese all over the pan, making a layer at the bottom. Cook it over medium-low heat and once it starts to melt, crack the eggs on the top and cover the pan.
4. Cook at the low heat until the egg whites are cooked through. Increase the heat and let the cheese get crispy and golden. Take the egg tortilla out of the pan on a plate.
5. Repeat this process to make similar egg tortillas.
6. Put a spoonful of chili salsa on top of egg tortillas and sprinkle with cilantro. Put lime wedges and avocado slices on the plate too while serving.

6.73 Keto Breakfast Enchiladas

Servings: 4 I Time: 55 mins I Difficulty: Easy

Nutrients per serving: Calories: 524.4 kcal I Fat: 42.55g I Carbohydrates: 6.08g I Protein: 27.3g

Ingredients
Tortillas
1. 1/2 Tsp. Chili Powder
2. 6 Eggs
3. 1/4 Tsp. Black Pepper
4. 1/4 Cup Heavy Whipping Cream
5. 1/2 Tsp. Garlic Powder
6. 1/2 Tsp. Salt
7. 1/2 Tsp. Coconut Oil

Enchiladas
- 1 & 1/2 Cups Cheddar Cheese, Shredded
- 3/4 Cup Enchilada Sauce
- 1 Cup Sausage, Ground and Cooked

Method
1. Preheat the oven to 400 degrees F.
2. Combine all the tortilla ingredients in a bowl and whisk well until become smooth.
3. Heat coconut oil in a skillet, pour 1/4 cup of the batter in it and cover it.
4. Cook for 3 to 5 minutes until the eggs are cooked completely.
5. Repeat this process to make more tortillas with the remaining batter.
6. Take a tortilla and put a spoonful cooked sausage and cheese on it. Roll the tortilla and set in a casserole dish. Repeat this with all other tortillas.
7. Top them with enchilada sauce and extra cheese.
8. Put the casserole dish in the preheated oven and bake for 15 minutes or until the cheese has melted and become golden.

6.74 Keto Southern Shakshuka

Servings: 6 eggs and sauce I Time: 30 mins I Difficulty: Easy
Nutrients per serving (1 egg and sauce): Calories: 291.45 kcal I Fat: 19.14g I Carbohydrates: 11.94g I Protein: 15.17g

Ingredients
1. 1/4 Cup Olive Oil
2. 14 Garlic Cloves, Minced
3. 1/2 Cup Goat Cheese, Crumbled
4. 1 Onion, Diced
5. 6 Eggs
6. 3 Cups Collard Greens, Chopped
7. 1 Jalapeño, Chopped
8. 1/2 Green Bell Pepper, Diced
9. 3 & 1/2 Cup Tomatoes, Crushed
10. 1 Tbsp. Paprika Powder
11. Salt, To Taste
12. 1/2 Tsp. Red Pepper Flakes
13. Black Pepper, To Taste

Method
1. Preheat the oven to 425 degrees F.
2. Heat the olive oil in an oven-safe skillet over medium-high heat and put all the ingredients in it except eggs.
3. Sauté it well until everything is cooked through. Take off the heat.
4. Make wells or holes in the sauce with a spoon and put an egg into each well or hole.
5. Put the skillet in the preheated oven and bake for 5 minutes or until the egg whites are cooked.
6. Take out and serve with the crumbled goat cheese on top.

6.75 Keto Chicken and Waffle Sandwiches

Servings: 4 I Time: 25 mins I Difficulty: Easy
Nutrients per serving: Calories: 452.9 kcal I Fat: 31.68g I Carbohydrates: 5.1g I Protein: 33.73g

Ingredients
Chicken
1. Olive Oil, For Frying
2. 1 Cup Buttermilk

3. Black Pepper, To Taste
4. 1/3 Cup Almond Flour
5. Salt, To Taste
6. 1 Tsp. Paprika
7. 2 Chicken Breasts, Halved Lengthwise
8. 1/4 Tsp. Cayenne Powder
9. 1 Egg
10. Sugar-Free Syrup (Optional)
11. Bacon (Optional)
12. Pickles (Optional)
13. Mustard (Optional)

Waffles
1. 1/4 Cup Milk
2. 2 Tbsps. Butter, Melted
3. 1 Tbsp. Erythritol
4. 1/2 Tsp. Salt
5. 3 Eggs (Whites & Yolks Separated)
6. 1 Tsp. Vanilla
7. 1 Cup Almond Flour

Method
1. Preheat the oven at 350 degrees F.
2. Cut each chicken breasts halve into four strips and soak the strips in buttermilk overnight. Take the chicken strips out of the buttermilk the next day and season with cayenne powder, salt, paprika powder, and black pepper.
3. Beat the egg in a bowl and set aside.
4. Whisk the almond flour, some salt and pepper in another bowl and set aside.
5. Coat the chicken strips first in the egg, then the flour, again in the egg, and lastly the almond flour to make two layers of each.
6. Heat some olive oil in a skillet and fry the chicken strips in it on both sides until golden brown. Take out and put on a lined baking sheet.
7. Cover the baking sheet with aluminum foil and put in the preheated oven. Bake for 15 minutes or until cooked through.
8. Preheat the waffle iron.
9. Combine the melted butter, egg yolks, vanilla, milk, erythritol, almond flour and salt in a bowl and whisk well until smooth batter is formed.
10. Take the egg whites in a bowl and whisk them well until they become creamy and fluffy. Add it in the batter.
11. Spray the waffle iron with a cooking oil spray and pour the batter in it. Cook the waffles for good 5 minutes or until become golden brown.
12. Sandwich the chicken between the waffles. You can add the bacon and mustard in it if you want and top with maple syrup, if desired.

6.76 Keto Pepperoni Pizza Quiche

Servings: 8 | Time: 55 mins | Difficulty: Easy
Nutrients per serving: Calories: 416.66kcal | Fat: 38.43g | Carbohydrates: 4.41g | Protein: 14.29g

Ingredients
The Pie Crust:
- 6 Tbsps. Butter, Diced (Cold)
- 1 & 1/2 Cups Almond Flour
- 1 Egg, Beaten
- 1 Tsp. Xanthan Gum
- 1/4 Cup Coconut Flour
- 1 Tsp. Vinegar
- 1 Tsp. Salt

Quiche Filling:
- 6 Eggs
- 1/4 Tsp. Red Pepper Flakes
- 1 Cup Mozzarella Cheese, Shredded
- 1/2 Tsp. Italian Seasoning
- Salt, To Taste
- 15 Pepperoni Slices
- Black Pepper, To Taste
- 1 Cup Heavy Cream

Method
1. Preheat the oven to 350F.
2. Combine the coconut flour, xanthan gum, almond flour, vinegar, salt, egg, and butter in a blender and blend until a smooth dough is formed. Take out the dough and cover the dough with plastic wrap. Chill it for 45-60 minutes.
3. Roll the dough into a 10-inch pie crust. Put in a lined pie plate.
4. Put half of the mozzarella cheese and pepperoni inside the pie crust.
5. Combine the eggs, Italian seasoning, heavy cream, salt, red pepper flakes, and black pepper in a bowl and whisk well.
6. Pour the eggs into the pie crust and sprinkle the remaining cheese and pepperoni on top.
7. Cover the pie plate with aluminum foil and put in the preheated oven. Bake for about 35-45 minutes.
8. Take off the foil and bake again until the eggs are fully set, for about 15 minutes.

6.77 Keto Blueberry Pancake Bites

Servings: 6 | Time: 35 mins | Difficulty: Easy
Nutrients per serving: Calories: 174.77 kcal | Fat: 13.27g| Carbohydrates: 7.07g | Protein: 6.52g

Ingredients
- 1/4 Cup Butter, Melted
- 1/2 Cup Blueberries, Frozen
- 4 Eggs
- 1/3 Cup Water
- 1/2 Cup Coconut Flour
- 1/4 Tsp. Cinnamon
- 1/4 Cup Erythritol
- 1 Tsp. Baking Powder
- 1/2 Tsp. Vanilla Extract
- 1/2 Tsp. Salt

Method
1. Preheat the oven to 325 degrees F.
2. Combine the eggs, erythritol, coconut flour, baking powder, butter, vanilla extract, salt, and cinnamon in a blender and blend well until smooth. Let it sit for a few minutes. If the batter is very thick, add in the water and blend again.
3. Pour the batter into a greased muffin tin and put the blueberries on top and press some inside the batter.
4. Put the muffin tin in the preheated oven and bake for 25 minutes or until the cake bites cooked thoroughly.

6.78 Gooey Keto Cinnamon Rolls

Servings: 9 | Time: 55 mins | Difficulty: Easy
Nutrients per serving: Calories: 386.73 kcal | Fat: 31.55g | Carbohydrates: 6.82g | Protein: 16.62g

Ingredients
Cinnamon Rolls
- 3 Eggs
- 6 Tbsps. Golden Flaxseed, Ground
- 1/4 Cup Sour Cream
- 5 Tbsps. Erythritol
- 2 & 1/4 Tsps. Baking Powder
- 3 Tbsps. Water (Lukewarm)
- 1 & 1/2 Tbsps. Butter, Unsalted & Melted
- 5 Tbsps. Whey Protein Isolate
- 1/8 Tsp. Ginger, Ground
- 2 & 1/4 Cups Almond Flour

- 1 Tbsp. Yeast (Active Dry)
- 1 Tbsp. Maple Syrup
- 1 Tbsp. Apple Cider Vinegar
- 2 & 1/4 Tsps. Xanthan Gum
- 1 & 1/2 Tsp. Kosher Salt

Cinnamon Filling
- 2 Tbsps. Cinnamon, Ground
- 6 Tbsps. Erythritol
- 3 Tbsps. Butter, Softened

Glaze
- Heavy Cream, To Taste
- 3 Tbsps. Butter, Unsalted
- 1 Tsp. Vanilla Extract
- 1/3 Cup Cream Cheese
- Salt, To Taste
- 3-6 Tbsps. Erythritol, Powdered

Method
1. Line a baking sheet with parchment paper.
2. Combine the sour cream, maple syrup, active dry yeast, and warm water in a bowl and mix them well. Cover the bowl, set it aside for 10 minutes to activate the yeast.
3. Meanwhile, combine the almond flour, whey protein powder, flaxseed meal, baking powder, erythritol, xanthan gum, and salt in another bowl and mix them well.
4. Once the yeast has been activated – the foam of bubbles is formed at the surface, add in the melted butter eggs, and apple cider vinegar. Whisk them well and put the flour mixture in it too.
5. Mix the batter well to make it smooth, without any lumps, and slowly a thick dough is formed. Put the dough on a large piece of cling film laid out, knead it into a ball and divide the dough ball into 3 parts. Wet your hands with a mixture of oil and water while handling the dough.
6. Take one part of the dough and roll/spread it into a rectangle, brush it with melted butter and scatter the erythritol and cinnamon powder on it. Make a roll out of the rectangle and seal it with the help of cling film.
7. Cut the roll into three mini rolls, take them off the cling film, flatten them with your hands and put on a lined baking pan. Repeat this process with the other two parts of the dough.
8. With a kitchen towel, cover the pan and set the pan aside in a warm place for an hour, to let the dough rise.
9. Meanwhile, preheat the oven to 400 degrees F and whisk the glaze ingredients well to make a thick cream.
10. Once the dough is double in size, put the pan in the preheated oven for about 20-25 minutes, until they become golden brown. Check in between and do not let them brown too much.
11. Once done, take out of the oven and glaze them before serving. Serve warm.

6.79 Berry Coconut Oatmeal

Servings: 1 l Time: 8 mins l Difficulty: Easy
Nutrients per serving: Calories: 445 kcal l Fat: 38.16g l Carbohydrates: 6.34g l Protein: 10.45g

Ingredients
- 1/4 Cup Mixed Berries
- 1/2 Cup Almond Milk
- 1 Tbsp. Almond Meal
- 2 Tbsps. Flaxseed, Ground
- 1 Tsp. Pumpkin Seeds, Dried
- 1 Tbsp. Coconut, Dried
- 1/2 Tsp. Cinnamon
- 1/3 Cup Coconut Milk
- 1/2 Tsp. Vanilla Powder

Method

1. Combine all the ingredients in a saucepan, except berries and pumpkin seeds. Heat them over medium flame, with continuous stirring until it thickens and looks like an oatmeal.
2. Transfer into a bowl and put pumpkin seeds and mixed berries on top.

6.80 Keto Breakfast Bowl

Servings: 4 l Time: 25 mins l Difficulty: Easy
Nutrients per serving: Calories: 887.68 kcal l Fat: 75.4g l Carbohydrates: 8.2g l Protein: 40.95g

Ingredients
- 4 Eggs
- 1 Cup Coconut Oil
- 2 Cups Beef Sirloin
- 6 Garlic Cloves, Minced
- 2 Cups Cauliflower Rice
- 1 Tbsp. Erythritol, Granulated
- 1/8 Cup Calamansi Juice
- 3 Tsps. Garlic Powder
- 1/4 Cup Soy Sauce
- Salt, To Taste
- Black Pepper, To Taste

Method
1. Take a bowl and put the erythritol, calamansi juice, soy sauce, salt, half the garlic powder and black pepper in it. Mix well until dissolved.
2. Pour it over the beef in a Ziploc bag and put in the refrigerator overnight.
3. In the morning, heat one tsp. of coconut oil in a frying pan and sauté the marinated beef in it until cooked through.
4. Take out and let cool. Then cut into thin strips.
5. Heat the rest of the coconut oil in the same pan and sauté the garlic in it until fragrant.
6. Stir in the cauliflower rice and stir well until become soft and dry, sprinkle the other half of the garlic powder, salt, and pepper on it. Stir for a while and take out.
7. Fry the eggs in the pan, as you like them and serve with cauliflower rice and beef strips.

6.81 Asparagus and Gruyere Keto Quiche

Servings: 6 l Time: 1 hr. 30 mins l Difficulty: Easy
Nutrients per serving: Calories: 520 kcal l Fat: 46.39g l Carbohydrates: 4.82g l Protein: 21.17g

Ingredients
Crust
- 1/4 Cup Butter, Melted
- 1 Cup Almond Flour
- 1/2 Tsp. Xanthan Gum
- 1 Egg White
- 1/2 Cup Gruyere, Grated
- 2 Tbsps. Coconut Flour

Filling
- 2/3 Cup Gruyere, Cubed
- 1 Egg Yolk
- 1 Shallot, Sliced
- 1 Tsp. Salt
- 4 Eggs
- 1 Cup Heavy Cream
- Oil, To Taste

Method
1. Preheat the oven to 350 degrees F.
2. Combine all the crust ingredients in a bowl and whisk or beat well to make a smooth dough.
3. Knead the dough into a ball and refrigerate it for 30 minutes.

4. Take out the dough and press in a lined pie pan to spread till the edges.
5. Put in the preheated oven to bake for 10 minutes, then take out and let cool.
6. Whisk the egg yolk with heavy cream, eggs, and salt to form a creamy mixture.
7. Heat oil in a pan and sauté the shallot and asparagus in it until they become tender. Set aside.
8. For the assembly, first put the gruyere in the base of the quiche crust, then put the cheese, onion and asparagus on its top, then our in the eggs mixture.
9. Bake for 45-60 minutes or until the surface is golden brown and the eggs are completely cooked.

6.82 Keto Lemon Sugar Poppy Seed Scones

Servings: 8 I Time: 45 mins I Difficulty: Easy
Nutrients per serving: Calories: 206.81 kcal I Fat: 18.5g I Carbohydrates: 3.53g I Protein: 6.6g

Ingredients

- 4 Tbsps. Butter
- 1 & 1/2 Cups Almond Flour
- 1/2 Tsp. Baking Powder
- 1 Tbsp. Lemon Juice
- 2 Tbsps. Coconut Flour
- 1/4 Tsp. Baking Soda
- 1/4 Cup + 2 Tbsps. Erythritol
- 1 Tbsp. Poppy Seeds
- 1 Tbsp. Lemon Zest
- 2 Eggs
- 1 Tbsp. Psyllium Husk Fiber

Method

1. Preheat the oven to 350 degrees F.
2. Combine all the ingredients in a bowl, except the lemon zest and 2 tbsps. erythritol. Whisk them well to make a smooth dough, without lumps.
3. Combine the lemon zest and 2 tbsps. of erythritol in a bowl and mix well. Set aside to let dry.
4. Knead the dough into a ball, then roll I on a clean surface to form a thick dough sheet and cut eight triangles out of it.
5. Put the dough triangles on a lined baking sheet and bake in the preheated oven for 20 minutes.
6. Take out of the oven, sprinkle with lemon sugar, and bake for another 10 minutes.

6.83 Eggs Benedict Casserole

Servings: 8 I Time: 45 mins I Difficulty: Medium
Nutrients per serving: Calories: 483 kcal I Fat: 33.41g I Carbohydrates: 2.78g I Protein: 18.54g

Ingredients

- 2 Tbsps. White Vinegar
- 1/4 Cup Heavy Whipping Cream
- Lemon Juice, To Taste
- 1 Cup Butter, Unsalted & Melted
- 6 Egg Yolks
- 1/4 Tsp. Peppercorns, Crushed
- Salt, To Taste
- 1 Tbsp. Water
- 2 & 1/2 Cups Eggplant, Peeled & Diced
- 2 Cups Ham, Cooked & Diced
- 12 Eggs
- Black Pepper, To Taste

Method

1. Preheat the oven to 375 degrees F.
2. Take a greased casserole dish and spread the diced eggplant in the bottom and make a layer of ham on top of it.
3. Whisk the eggs, cream, salt, and pepper in a bowl and pour over the ham layer and stir to let it reach to the bottom.
4. Cover the casserole dish with a foil and put in the preheated oven for 30 minutes.
5. Take out of the oven and remove the foil. Bake it again for 20-30 minutes or until the egg is completely cooked.
6. Add vinegar and crushed peppercorns in a preheated skillet and stir until the vinegar evaporates, add the water and transfer this to a metal bowl.
7. Boil water in a pan, lower the heat to let it simmer and put the metal bowl in it. Add the egg yolks into the metal bowl and whisk well. Do not let the yolk scramble and whisk at low heat until the yolks thicken.
8. Take the bowl out of the water pot and slowly add the clear melted butter in it while whisking the yolks continuously.
9. Add lemon and salt to taste and 2-3 Tbsps. of water if the consistency of the sauce is very thick. Do not dilute it out too much though.
10. Once the casserole is cooked, pour the sauce over it and serve hot.

6.84 Bacon Kale and Tomato Frittata

Servings: 6 I Time: 35 mins I Difficulty: Easy
Nutrients per serving: Calories: 292.5 kcal I Fat: 24.88g I Carbohydrates: 1.61g I Protein: 13.77g

Ingredients

- 7 Eggs
- 1 Tbsp. Mayonnaise
- 7 Bacon Strips
- 1/2 Cup Parmesan Cheese, Shredded
- 2 Parsley Sprigs, Chopped
- 1/4 Cup Heavy Whipping Cream
- 1 Cup Kale, Destemmed & Chopped
- 5 Cherry Tomatoes, Sliced

Method

1. Preheat the oven to 400 degrees F.
2. Combine the eggs with whipping cream, mayonnaise, and cheese in a bowl and whisk well until combined. Set aside.
3. Sauté the bacon strips in a non-stick pan over medium-low flame until they become crispy. Take out once done and put on a paper towel. Let cool and then crumble the strips.
4. Sauté the kale in the same pan until it becomes tender and put the 3/4 of the crumbled bacon back in the pan. Stir well.
5. Pour in the egg mixture and stir to combine, once the eggs are about to set, add in the 3/4 of the tomato slices and cook for another minute.
6. Then remove the skillet off the heat and put the frittata in preheated oven for 5-10 minutes or until cooked thoroughly.
7. Sprinkle with crumbled bacon and tomato slices and parsley on top.

6.85 Caprese Egg Casserole

Servings: 2 I Time: 45 mins I Difficulty: Easy
Nutrients per serving: Calories: 151 kcal I Fat: 11.38g I Carbohydrates: 1.68g I Protein: 9.8g

Ingredients

- 8 Eggs
- 1/2 Cup Mozzarella Balls, Fresh
- Black Pepper, To Taste
- 2 Tbsps. Olive Oil
- Salt, To Taste
- 1 Tbsp. Basil, Fresh & Chopped
- 2 Cups Cherry Tomatoes, Halved

Method

1. Preheat the oven to 350 degrees F.

2. Heat the olive oil in a skillet and sauté the halved tomatoes in it util they have softened, and do not dry them out. Set aside to let cool.
3. Whisk the eggs with chopped basil, salt, and pepper in a bowl until smooth.
4. Brush a casserole dish with some oil or butter and pour the eggs mixture in it. Add the cooked tomatoes and mozzarella balls on top.
5. Bake for 25-30 minutes in the preheated oven, or until the eggs are cooked through.

6.86 Keto Sausage Gravy and Biscuit Bake

Servings: 6 I Time: 35 mins I Difficulty: Easy
Nutrients per serving: Calories: 374.67 kcal I Fat: 33.21g I Carbohydrates: 4.75g I Protein: 14.48g

Ingredients

Biscuits:

- 1/2 Tsp. Xanthan Gum
- 1 Cup Almond Flour
- 2 Egg Whites
- 2 Tbsps. Butter, Cold & Grated
- 1 Tsp. Baking Powder

Sausage Gravy:

- 3/4 Cup Pork Sausage, Ground
- 1/2 Tsp. Onion Powder
- 1/2 Cup Half And Half
- 1 Tsp. Black Pepper
- 1 Tsp. Xanthan Gum
- 1/4 Tsp. Salt
- 1 & 1/2 Cups Chicken Broth

Method

1. Preheat the oven to 375 degrees F.
2. Put all the biscuit ingredients in a bowl and mix well until combined and refrigerate it for some time.
3. Meanwhile, brown the ground pork in a skillet over medium heat until cooked through. Take out and set aside.
4. Sauté the xanthan gum in the same skillet in the pork fat for 1 minute or until become light brown, over medium-low heat.
5. Stir in the chicken stock, black pepper, onion powder, and salt. Let the gravy simmer for about 5 minutes then add half and half and mix well.
6. Let it simmer for another 3 minutes or until the gravy becomes thick and creamy.
7. Add the pork in it as well and stir to heat up. Take off the heat.
8. Grease a casserole dish with oil or butter and pour the sausage gravy in it.
9. Spread the biscuit mixture on the top, making an even layer.
10. Put the casserole dish in the preheated oven and bake for 18-20 minutes, until the biscuit mixture is cooked through.

6.87 Mini Pizza Egg Bakes

Servings: 1 I Time: 15 mins I Difficulty: Easy
Nutrients per serving (2 Mini Pizza): Calories: 333 kcal I Fat: 22.66g I Carbohydrates: 4.28g I Protein: 25.59g

Ingredients

- 1 Tbsp. Red Bell Pepper, Diced
- 3 Eggs, Egg & Yolks Separated
- 2 Black Olives, Sliced
- 4 Tbsps. Mozzarella Cheese, Shredded
- 4 Large Mild Pepper Rings
- 1 Tbsp. Tomato Sauce
- 1 Tsps. Italian Herb Blend

Method

1. Whisk the egg whites slightly in an oven safe dish and put the 1 tbsp. of mozzarella cheese and beaten yolks in it and stir slightly.
2. Microwave it for one and a half minute and let cool for some time.
3. Put the mild pepper rings on it and spread tomato sauce on the top.
4. Top it with the diced bell pepper, and olives.
5. Sprinkle the shredded cheese on it and microwave for a minute or until the cheese melts and become golden.
6. Serve hot!

6.88 Inst. Pot Crustless Quiche Lorraine

Servings: 4 I Time: 45 mins I Difficulty: Easy
Nutrients per serving: Calories: 572.5 kcal I Fat: 52.54g I Carbohydrates: 3.46g I Protein: 22.03g I Fiber: 0.03g

Ingredients

- 1 & 1/3 Cups Swiss Cheese, Shredded
- 1/4 Tsp. Nutmeg
- 4 Eggs
- 1 & 1/2 Cups Heavy Whipping Cream
- Pepper, To Taste
- 8 Bacon Slices, Chopped
- 1/4 Tsp. Salt

Method

1. Sauté the bacon slices in a pan until become crispy. Put on the paper towel and set aside.
2. Combine the eggs, nutmeg, heavy whipping cream, salt, and pepper in a bowl and whisk well until smooth.
3. Brush a cake pan with butter or oil and spread 1 cup cheese at the bottom of pan. Pour in the creamy egg mixture on top. Cover the pan with foil.
4. Pour the water in an Inst. Pot and put the steam rack inside it. Put the cake pan on the rack carefully and close the Inst. Pot lid.
5. Set high pressure setting, and 25 minutes timer.
6. Once done, take the cake pan out carefully and top with remaining 1/3 cup shredded cheese.
7. Broil it for 5-10 minutes or until the cheese becomes golden and let cool.
8. Serve by flipping out on a serving plate.

6.89 Vegetarian Three Cheese Quiche Stuffed Peppers

Servings: 4 I Time: 55 mins I Difficulty: Easy
Nutrients per serving: Calories: 245.5 kcal I Fat: 16.28g I Carbohydrates: 5.97g I Protein: 17.84g I Fiber: 1.13g

Ingredients

- 1/2 Cup Parmesan Cheese, Grated
- 4 Eggs
- 1/4 Cup Baby Spinach Leaves
- 1/2 Cup Mozzarella Cheese, Shredded
- 1 Tsp. Garlic Powder
- 2 Bell Peppers, Deseeded and Halved Lengthwise
- 1/2 Cup Ricotta Cheese
- 2 Tbsps. Parmesan Cheese, For Garnishing
- 1/4 Tsp. Parsley, Dried

Method

1. Preheat the oven to 375 degrees F.
2. Put the eggs, cheeses, garlic powder, and parsley in a food processor and blend until combined. Take out and stir in the spinach leaves.
3. Put the Bell pepper halves on a lined baking sheet and pour the egg and cream mixture in each and cover with foil.
4. Put in the preheated oven and bake for 35-45 minutes or until the egg is set.

5. Take out, remove the foil, and sprinkle the 2 Tbsps. Parmesan cheese on top.
6. Broil for 3-5 minutes or until the cheese melts and becomes golden.

6.90 No-tatoes Bubble 'n' Squeak

Servings: 3 I Time: 35 mins I Difficulty: Easy
Nutrients per serving: Calories: 332.67 kcal I Fat: 28.11g I Carbohydrates: 8.6g I Protein: 10.65g I Fiber: 3.23g

Ingredients

- 2 Tbsps. Butter
- Black Pepper, To Taste
- Florets Of 1/2 Cauliflower
- Salt, To Taste
- 2 Tbsps. Heavy Whipping Cream
- 1/4 Cup Leek, Sliced
- 2 Tbsps. Duck Fat
- 1/4 Cup Parmesan Cheese, Grated
- 1/4 Cup Brussels Sprouts, Chopped
- 3 Bacon Slices, Diced
- 1/4 Cup Mozzarella Cheese, Grated
- 1/4 Onion, Diced
- 1 Green Onion Stalk, Sliced
- 1 Tsp. Garlic, Minced

Method

1. Combine 1 tbsp. butter, cauliflower florets, cream, salt and pepper in a bowl, microwave for 4 minutes on high, and stir well.
2. Microwave for another 4 minutes, take out and blend with an immersion blender until it becomes smooth.
3. Add in the mozzarella cheese and stir to melt in the hot mixture. Set aside.
4. Sauté the chopped bacon in a pan until becomes crispy and put on a paper towel.
5. Put the remaining butter in the same pan and sauté the garlic in it over medium heat until fragrant.
6. Add in the onion and sauté it until becomes translucent and then put brussels sprouts and leeks in it. Cook them for about 5-10 minutes or until become soft.
7. Add in the green onions and cook for another minute. Then take the pan off the heat and let cool.
8. Combine the veggies with the bacon and mashed cauliflower.
9. Heat the duck fat in a pan over medium heat and add the mixture in it once the duck fat is melted, top with Parmesan cheese and stir for a while until the cheese melts. Remove from heat.
10. Transfer on the serving plates and enjoy.

6.91 Bacon Breakfast Bagels

Servings: 3 I Time: 25 mins I Difficulty: Easy
Nutrients per serving: Calories: 605.67 kcal I Fat: 50.29g I Carbohydrates: 5.76g I Protein: 30.13g I Fiber: 3.87g

Ingredients

Bagels
- 1 Egg
- 2 Tbsps. Cream Cheese
- 1 Tsp. Xanthan Gum
- 1 & 1/2 Cups Mozzarella Cheese, Grated
- 3/4 Cup Almond Flour

Fillings
- 6 Bacon Slices, Grilled & Chopped
- 2 Tbsps. Cream Cheese
- 2 Tbsps. Pesto
- 1 Cup Arugula Leaves

Toppings

- Sesame Seeds, To Taste
- 1 Tbsp. Butter, Melted

Method

1. Preheat the oven to 390 degrees F.
2. Combine the mozzarella cream cheese and melt in the oven, add in the almond flour and xanthan gum, and mix well to form a smooth dough.
3. Knead the dough into a ball, microwave it for 10 seconds if becomes hard.
4. Divide the dough into 3 parts and roll each part to form three circles.
5. Line a baking dish with parchment paper and put the three dough circles on it, cut a hollow circle within each using a cookie cutter or jar cap.
6. Brush the bagels top with melted butter and sprinkle sesame seeds on it.
7. Put the baking sheet in the preheated oven for about 18 minutes or until bagels become golden brown. Take out once done and let cool.
8. Cut the bagels in half, spread cream cheese on them, pour the pesto over it, sprinkle with arugula leaves and chopped bacon.

6.92 Spinach, Herb & Feta Wrap

Servings: 2 I Time: 20 mins I Difficulty: Easy
Nutrients per serving: Calories: 361.5 kcal I Fat: 25.27g I Carbohydrates: 4.06g I Protein: 27.55g I Fiber: 0.9g

Ingredients

- 3 Tomatoes, Sundried & Chopped
- 1/2 Cup Feta Cheese, Crumbled
- 2 Cups Spinach Leaves
- 1/2 Tsp. Salt
- 5 Eggs
- 1 Tsp. Sesame Oil
- 4 Basil Leaves, Chopped
- 3 Egg Whites
- 1 Tsp. Olive Oil (Optional)

Method

1. Combine the eggs, egg whites, sesame oil, and salt in a bowl and whisk well to form a foamy mixture.
2. Heat a non-stick pan over medium heat, lower the heat, and pour half the mixture in it and spread with back of the spoon.
3. Cook on both sides and put on a plate once done. Make another wrap similarly.
4. Sauté the spinach in a pan until it wilts and becomes soft.
5. On each wrap first put the cooked spinach leaves, then feta cheese and basil leaves. Drizzle some oil too if you want and roll the wrap in parchment paper.

6.93 Salmon Benny Breakfast Bombs

Servings: 2 I Time: 55 mins I Difficulty: Easy
Nutrients per serving: Calories: 295 kcal I Fat: 23.53g I Carbohydrates: 0.96g I Protein: 18.25g I Fiber: 0.05g

Ingredients

Breakfast Bombs
- 1/2 Tbsp. Butter, Salted
- 2 Tbsps. Chives, Fresh & Chopped
- Salt, To Taste
- 1/2 Cup Salmon, Smoked & Diced
- 2 Eggs, Hard Boiled
- Black Pepper, To Taste

Hollandaise Sauce
- Salt, To Taste
- 1/4 Tsp. Dijon Mustard
- 2 Tsps. Lemon Juice
- 1 Egg Yolk

- 2 Tbsps. Butter, Melted
- 1/2 Tbsp. Water

Method

1. Boil half the pot full of water over medium heat and then lower the heat to let it simmer.
2. Take metal bowl and combine the lemon juice, egg yolk, salt, and Dijon mustard in it. Put the bowl in the simmering water and whisk the mixture until smooth.
3. Once the mixture starts to thicken, add in the melted butter slowly and keep whisking to emulsify the mixture. Once thicken, take the bowl out of the pot. Add a little water if hollandaise sauce seems too thick. Let it cool down.
4. Mash the boiled eggs in a large bowl really well and add in the smoked salmon, hollandaise sauce, and half the chives in it. Mix well until combined. Do not make it too wet. Limit the sauce.
5. Divide the mixture into four parts and make four balls out of it.
6. Coat balls with remaining chives by rolling in them and serve.

6.94 Ham, Ricotta, and Spinach Casserole

Servings: 2 I Time: 40 mins I Difficulty: Easy
Nutrients per serving: Calories: 151.8 kcal I Fat: 9.09g I Carbohydrates: 1.35g I Protein: 15.1g I Fiber: 0.41g

Ingredients

- 1 Cup Spinach, Frozen
- 1/2 Yellow Onion, Chopped Finely
- 12 Eggs
- 1 Cup Ricotta Cheese
- 1/2 Tbsp. Garlic And Herb Seasoning
- 2 Cups Ham, Diced
- 1/4 Tsp. Salt
- 1/4 Cup Heavy Whipping Cream
- Cooking Spray

Method

1. Preheat the oven to 350 degrees F.
2. Combine all the ingredients in a bowl and mix well.
3. Spray a casserole dish with cooking spray and pour in the batter.
4. Bake in the preheated oven for 30-35 minutes or until cooked thoroughly.

6.95 Keto Zucchini Bread with Walnuts

Servings: 16 I Time: 1 hr. 30 mins I Difficulty: Easy
Nutrients per serving: Calories: 200.13 kcal I Fat: 18.83g I Carbohydrates: 2.6g I Protein: 5.59g I Fiber: 2.3g

Ingredients

- 1/2 Cup Olive Oil
- 1/4 Tsp. Ginger, Ground
- 3 Eggs
- 1/2 Cup Walnuts, Chopped
- 1 Tsp. Vanilla Extract
- 1 Cup Zucchini, Grated & Dried
- 1 Tsp. Cinnamon, Ground
- 2 & 1/2 Cups Almond Flour
- 1/2 Tsp. Salt
- 1 & 1/2 Cups Erythritol
- 1/2 Tsp. Nutmeg
- 1 & 1/2 Tsps. Baking Powder
- Cooking Spray

Method

1. Preheat oven to 350 degrees F.
2. Combine all the ingredients in a bowl and whisk well.
3. Spray a loaf pan with cooking spray and put the batter in it.

4. Put in the preheated oven and bake for 60-70 minutes.

6.96 Lemon Raspberry Sweet Rolls

Servings: 8 I Time: 45 mins I Difficulty: Easy
Nutrients per serving: Calories: 272.25 kcal I Fat: 23.18g I Carbohydrates: 5.24g I Protein: 10.04g I Fiber: 2.28g

Ingredients

Lemon Cream Cheese Filling & Raspberry Sauce

- 1/2 Cup Cream Cheese
- 1/2 Cup Raspberries, Frozen
- 2 Tbsps. Butter, Melted
- 1 Tsp. Lemon Extract
- 4 Tbsps. Stevia/Erythritol Blend
- 1/4 Tsp. Xanthan Gum
- 1/2 Tsp. Vanilla Extract
- 1 Tbsp. Water
- 2 Tsps. Lemon Zest
- 3 Tsp. Lemon Juice

Dough

- 1 Egg
- 1 Tsp. Vanilla Extract
- 1 Cup Almond Flour
- 2 Cups Mozzarella Cheese
- 1/4 Tsp. Xanthan Gum
- 1/4 Cup Stevia Erythritol Blend
- 1 & 1/4 Tsps. Baking Powder

Method

1. Combine the softened cream cheese, 2 tbsps. sweetener melted butter, vanilla extract, lemon zest, lemon extract and 1 tsp. of lemon juice in a bowl and whisk well to make a smooth and creamy mixture. Set this lemon cream cheese filling aside.
2. Heat 2 tbsps. of sweetener, xanthan gum and 2 Tsps. of lemon juice in a saucepan over medium-low heat with constant stirring.
3. Add in the frozen raspberries and mix well. Once the raspberries become warm, turn off the heat and set this raspberry sauce aside.
4. Preheat the oven to 350 degrees F.
5. Combine all the dough ingredients in a metal bowl and mix.
6. Fill one quarter of a pot with water and boil it over medium heat. Once boiled, lower the heat to let the water simmer, and put the metal bowl on it. Melting the cheese will make the mixing of the dough easier. Whisk the batter well until smooth, then take out of the pot.
7. Knead the dough well and roll to form a 12x15 inches rectangle.
8. Spread the lemon cream cheese filling on the dough evenly, and then make layer of raspberry sauce on top, leaving 1-inch dough from a side.
9. Roll the dough into a log starting at the long side and press to seal at the other side.
10. With a sharp knife cut the log into 8 pieces, gently and put these pieces on a lined baking sheet.
11. Put in the oven and bake for 24-26 minutes, or until the rolls become golden brown.

6.97 Keto Faux Sous Vide Egg Bites

Servings: 16 (8 per flavor) I Time: 30 mins I Difficulty: Easy

Bacon & Gruyere Egg Bite

Nutrients per serving: Calories: 140.63 kcal I Fat: 11.05g I Carbohydrates: 0.65g I Protein: 9.19g I Fiber: 0.01g

Ingredients

- 1 Tsp. Hot Sauce
- Salt, To Taste
- 2 Tbsps. Monterey Jack Cheese, Grated

- 6 Bacon Strips, Cooked
- Black Pepper, To Taste
- 2 Tbsps. Chives, Chopped
- 6 Eggs
- Additional Seasonings, To Taste
- 1/4 Cup Gruyere Cheese, Grated
- 2 Tbsps. Butter
- 1/4 Cup Cottage Cheese

Method
Bacon & Gruyere

1. Combine all the ingredients in a bowl except bacon and whisk well until a smooth mixture is formed.
2. Take poaching pan and pour water in the bottom. Set the heat to medium-high and in each well of the pan put a slice of bacon at the bottom and spoonful whisked mixture on top.
3. Once the water of the pan begins to simmer, lower the heat to medium and cover the pan. Cook for 5-7 minutes or until the egg bites are firm from center. Take out.

6.98 Savory Sage and Cheddar Waffles

Servings: 12 | Time: 25 mins | Difficulty: Easy
Nutrients per serving: Calories: 195.5 kcal | Fat: 17.47g | Carbohydrates: 3.49g | Protein: 5.49g | Fiber: 5.35g

Ingredients

- 1 & 1/3 Cup Coconut Flour
- 1/4 Tsp. Garlic Powder
- 2 Cups Coconut Milk
- 1/2 Cup Water
- 3 Tbsps. Coconut Oil, Melted
- 3 Tsps. Baking Powder
- 1 Cup Cheddar Cheese, Shredded
- 2 Eggs
- 1 Tsp. Sage, Dried & Ground
- 1/2 Tsp. Salt

Method

1. Preheat the waffle iron.
2. Combine all the ingredients in a bowl and whisk well to form a smooth batter.
3. Put the batter in the waffle iron in the quantity that fits in it and close it.
4. Cook until they become golden brown.
5. Take out and serve with a low carb topping.

6.99 Keto Lemon Poppyseed Muffins

Servings: 12 | Time: 45 mins | Difficulty: Easy
Nutrients per serving: Calories: 99.89 kcal | Fat: 11.69g | Carbohydrates: 1.73g | Protein: 4.04g | Fiber: 1.65g

Ingredients

- 1 Tsp. Vanilla Extract
- 3/4 Cup Almond Flour
- 3 Eggs
- 4 Tsps. Lemon Zest
- 1/4 Cup Heavy Cream
- 2 Tbsps. Poppy Seeds
- 1/4 Cup Golden Flaxseed Meal
- 1/3 Cup Erythritol
- 1/4 Cup Butter, Melted
- 3 Tbsps. Lemon Juice
- 1 Tsp. Baking Powder
- 25 Drops Liquid Stevia

Method

1. Preheat the oven to 350 degrees F.

2. Combine all the ingredients in a bowl and whisk well to form a smooth batter.
3. Grease a 12-cup muffin tin and put the batter in them equally.
4. Bake in the preheated oven for 18-20 minutes or until cooked through.
5. Take out and let cool, then serve.

6.100 Low Carb Mock McGriddle Casserole

Servings: 8 | Time: 1 hr. 15 mins | Difficulty: Easy
Nutrients per serving: Calories: 447.63 kcal | Fat: 36.04g | Carbohydrates: 2.87g | Protein: 26.16g | Fiber: 2.3g

Ingredients

- 6 Tbsps. Maple Syrup
- 1/2 Tsp. Garlic Powder
- 1 Cup Almond Flour
- Salt, To Taste
- 1/4 Cup Flaxseed Meal
- 2 Cups Breakfast Sausage
- 1/2 Tsp. Onion Powder
- 10 Eggs
- Black Pepper, To Taste
- 1/2 Cup Cheddar Cheese
- 4 Tbsps. Butter, Melted
- 1/4 Tsp. Sage

Method

1. Pre-heat the oven to 350 degrees F.
2. Cook the breakfast sausage in a pan over medium heat and break it while cooking.
3. Combine all the ingredients in a bowl, including the sausage and mix well.
4. Put the mixture in a lined casserole dish and put in the preheated oven.
5. Bake for 45-55 minutes until cooked through and golden brown from top.

6.101 Keto Breakfast Brownie Muffins

Servings: 6 | Time: 20 mins | Difficulty: Easy
Nutrients per serving: Calories: 193 kcal | Fat: 14.09g | Carbohydrates: 4.37g | Protein: 6.98g | Fiber: 7.18g

Ingredients

- 1/4 Cup Caramel Syrup (Sugar-Free)
- 1 Cup Golden Flaxseed Meal
- 1/4 Cup Cocoa Powder
- 1/2 Tbsp. Baking Powder
- 1/4 Cup Almonds, Slivered
- 1 Tsp. Vanilla Extract
- 1/2 Cup Pumpkin Puree
- 1/2 Tsp. Salt
- 1 Tsp. Apple Cider Vinegar
- 1 Egg
- 1 Tbsp. Cinnamon
- 2 Tbsps. Coconut Oil

Method

1. Preheat the oven to 350 degrees F.
2. Combine all ingredients in a bowl except slivered almonds and whisk well to make a smooth batter.
3. Put 1/4 cup of the batter in a lined muffin tin and sprinkle the slivered almonds on top.
4. Put in the preheated oven and bake for about 15 minutes or until cooked through.

6.102 Keto Breakfast Tacos

Servings: 3 | Time: 15 mins | Difficulty: Easy

Nutrients per serving: Calories: 443.67 kcal | Fat: 35.68g | Carbohydrates: 2.38g | Protein: 26.41g | Fiber: 1.53g

Ingredients

- 1/2 Small Avocado
- Salt, To Taste
- 6 Eggs
- 2 Tbsps. Cheddar Cheese, Shredded
- Black Pepper, To Taste
- 1 Cup Mozzarella Cheese, Shredded
- 3 Bacon Strips, Cooked
- 2 Tbsps. Butter

Method

1. Take a non-stick pan and heat 1/3 cup of mozzarella cheese on it for 2-3 minutes, over medium flame.
2. Once the cheese becomes golden brown at the edges, lift it with tongs and put on the back of a wooden spoon.
3. Repeat these steps to make 2 other taco shells like this.
4. Heat butter in a pan and make scrambled eggs with salt and pepper seasoning, as you like it.
5. Divide the scrambled eggs, bacon, and avocado into three parts and put on each hardened taco shell.
6. Sprinkle the shredded cheddar cheese on their top before serving.

6.103 Breakfast Keto Pizza Waffles

Servings: 2 | Time: 15 mins | Difficulty: Easy
Nutrients per serving: Calories: 604 kcal | Fat: 48.14g | Carbohydrates: 7.59g | Protein: 30.65g | Fiber: 5.5g

Ingredients

- 1 Tbsp. Bacon Fat
- 1/2 Cup Tomato Sauce
- 4 Eggs
- 4 Tbsps. Parmesan Cheese, Grated
- 1 Tsp. Italian Seasoning
- 3 Tbsps. Almond Flour
- 1/3 Cup Cheddar Cheese
- 14 Slices Pepperoni (Optional)
- 1 Tbsp. Psyllium Husk Powder
- 1 Tsp. Baking Powder
- Salt, To Taste
- Black Pepper, To Taste

Method

1. Preheat the waffle iron.
2. Combine all the ingredients (except cheese and tomato sauce) in a bowl and blend using an immersion blender until the mixture thickens.
3. Pour half of the mixture in the waffle iron and close it. Cook until the waffles become golden brown in color. Repeat it for the other half.
4. Top the waffles with tomato sauce and shredded cheese and broil them for 3-5 minutes or until the cheese melts. Add pepperoni to the top if you want.

6.104 Keto Breakfast Burger

Servings: 2 | Time: 30 mins | Difficulty: Easy
Nutrients per serving: Calories: 481 kcal | Fat: 37.97g | Carbohydrates: 1.28g | Protein: 31.76g | Fiber: 0.5g

Ingredients

- 1 Tbsp. Butter, Melted
- 1 Tbsp. Peanut Butter Powder
- Salt, To Taste
- 4 Bacon Slices, Cooked
- 1/4 Cup Pepper jack Cheese, Shredded
- Black Pepper, To Taste
- 2 Eggs
- 1/2 Cup Sausage

Method

1. Combine the melted butter with peanut butter powder in a bowl and mix well. Set it aside.
2. Chop the cooked bacon and shape into sausage patties. Fry the patties in a pan until become golden brown on both sides.
3. Put the cheese on the patties and cover the pan at low heat until the cheese melts.
4. Take out of the pan and put in a serving plate.
5. Whisk the egg in a bowl with seasonings and fry it in a non-stick pan.
6. Put the egg over the patties' cheese and top with peanut butter mixture.

6.105 Jalapeno Cheddar Waffles

Servings: 2 | Time: 10 mins | Difficulty: Easy
Nutrients per serving: Calories: 334 kcal | Fat: 27.28g | Carbohydrates: 4.88g | Protein: 15.84g | Fiber: 2.87g

Ingredients

- 3 Eggs
- Salt, To Taste
- 2 Tbsps. Cheddar Cheese, Shredded
- 1 Jalapeno
- 1 Tsp. Baking Powder
- 1 Tbsp. Coconut Flour
- 1/3 Cup Cream Cheese
- Black Pepper, To Taste
- 1 Tsp. Psyllium Husk Powder

Method

1. Preheat the waffle iron.
2. Combine all the ingredients in a bowl and blend using an immersion blender until the batter becomes smooth.
3. Pour the batter in the waffle iron and close it.
4. Cook until the waffles become golden brown in color, about 5-6 minutes.
5. Put a low carb topping and serve.

6.106 Mini Keto Pancake Donuts

Servings: 22 | Time: 8 mins | Difficulty: Easy
Nutrients per serving: Calories: 32.32 kcal | Fat: 2.68g | Carbohydrates: 0.53g | Protein: 1.41g | Fiber: 0.27g

Ingredients

- 1/3 Cup Cream Cheese
- 4 Tbsps. Erythritol
- 3 Eggs
- 1 Tsp. Baking Powder
- 4 Tbsps. Almond Flour
- 10 Drops Liquid Stevia
- 1 Tsp. Vanilla Extract
- 1 Tbsp. Coconut Flour

Method

1. Preheat a donut maker and spray it with coconut oil spray.
2. Combine all the ingredients in a bowl and blend using an immersion blender until the mixture becomes smooth.
3. Pour the batter in each well and cook until become golden brown in color, for about 3 minutes on each side.
4. Take out and make donuts similarly with the remaining batter.

6.107 Bacon Cheddar Chive Omelet

Servings: 1 | Time: 10 mins | Difficulty: Easy
Nutrients per serving: Calories: 386 kcal | Fat: 30.25g | Carbohydrates: 1.86g | Protein: 24.86g | Fiber: 0g

Ingredients

- 2 Eggs

- 2 Tbsps. Cheddar Cheese, Shredded
- Black Pepper, To Taste
- 2 Bacon Slices, Cooked
- Salt, To Taste
- 1 Tsp. Chives, Chopped
- 1 Tsp. Bacon Fat

Method

1. Crack the eggs in a bowl and season with salt, pepper and chopped chives, whisk well.
2. Take a pan and heat the bacon fat in it over medium-low heat. Pour the egg mixture in it.
3. When the egg sets, add the bacon in its middle. Cook the omelet until done and take the pan off the heat.
4. Sprinkle the shredded cheese on top of the bacon and fold the omelet around it.

6.108 Keto Peanut Pancakes

Servings: 2 I Time: 35 mins I Difficulty: Easy
Nutrients per serving: Calories: 744 kcal I Fat: 72.79g I Carbohydrates: 6.61g I Protein: 16.83g I Fiber: 5.15g

Ingredients

- 1 Egg
- 1/2 Tsp. Baking Powder
- 1/4 Tsp. Coconut Oil
- 1/4 Cup Almond Milk
- 3 & 1/2 Tbsps. Shelled Peanuts
- 1/2 Cup Almond Flour
- 1/2 Tsp. Vanilla Extract
- 1/4 Cup Heavy Whipping Cream
- 1/2 Tsp. Stevia
- Salt, To Taste
- 7 Drops Liquid Sucralose
- 1 Tbsp. Butter, Unsalted & Softened
- 1/2 Tsp. Baking Soda

Method

1. Pour heavy cream in a small saucepan and add 2 drops of liquid sucralose, heat them, and stir until combined and thickened. Set this condensed milk aside.
2. Roast the peanuts in a pan until they become brown. Then grind them with some salt and stevia. Set aside.
3. Combine the egg, liquid sucralose, almond milk, and vanilla extract in a bowl and whisk well, slowly add the almond flour, baking powder, baking soda, and 1/8 tsp salt in it. Whisk until combined.
4. Heat some coconut oil in a pan and once it melts pour spoonful of the pancake mixture in it and spread evenly with the back of the spoon. Cook the pancake on both sides until become golden.
5. Repeat this to make other pancakes.
6. Transfer the pancakes on plates, spread the condensed milk and softened butter on top of each pancake.
7. Sprinkle the ground peanuts on top and serve.

6.109 Bacon Avocado Muffins

Servings: 16 I Time: 55 mins I Difficulty: Easy
Nutrients per serving: Calories: 144.19 kcal I Fat: 11.81g I Carbohydrates: 1.71g I Protein: 6.22g I Fiber: 2.66g

Ingredients

- 2 Tbsps. Butter
- 2 Avocados, Diced
- 5 Eggs
- 3 Spring Onions, Chopped
- 1 Tsp. Garlic, Minced
- 5 Bacon Slices
- 1/2 Cup Almond Flour

- 1 Tsp. Chives, Dried
- 1/4 Cup Flaxseed Meal
- Salt, To Taste
- 1 & 1/2 Tbsps. Psyllium Husk Powder
- 1 Tsp. Cilantro, Dried
- 2/3 Cup Colby Jack Cheese, Grated
- 1 Tsp. Baking Powder
- 1 & 1/2 Tbsps. Lemon Juice
- 1 & 1/2 Cup Coconut Milk
- 1/4 Tsp. Red Chili Flakes
- Black Pepper, To Taste

Method

1. Preheat the oven to 350 degrees F.
2. Combine the eggs, lemon juice, almond flour, coconut milk, flaxseed meal, psyllium husk powder, and spices in a bowl and whisk well to make smooth batter. Cover it and set aside.
3. Fry the bacon slices in a non-stick pan over medium-low heat, until become crispy.
4. Add in the butter, spring onions, cheese, and baking powder when the slices are almost done.
5. Stir fry them while crumbling the bacon with the spoon. Add this mixture to the batter with diced avocados and mix well.
6. Brush a muffin tin with oil and put the batter in each cup.
7. Put it in the preheated oven and bake for 24-26 minutes.

6.110 Raspberry Brie Grilled Waffles

Servings: 2 I Time: 15 mins I Difficulty: Easy
Nutrients per serving: Calories: 551.5 kcal I Fat: 45.46g I Carbohydrates: 8.71g I Protein: 22.29g I Fiber: 6.8g

Ingredients

The Waffles
- 1/2 Cup Almond Flour
- 2 Tbsps. Flaxseed Meal
- 1/3 Cup Coconut Milk
- 1 Tsp. Vanilla Extract
- 1 Tsp. Baking Powder
- 2 Eggs
- 2 Tbsps. Swerve
- 7 Drops Liquid Stevia

The Filling
- 1/2 Cup Raspberries
- 1 Tsp. Lemon Zest
- 1 Tbsp. Lemon Juice
- 2 Tbsps. Butter
- 1 Tbsp. Swerve
- 1/3 Cup Brie, Double Cream

Method

1. Take a pan and brown the butter and swerve in it, then add the raspberries, lemon juice and zest in it. Cook them until everything is heated through. Set this raspberry compote aside.
2. Preheat the waffle iron.
3. Combine all the waffle ingredients in a bowl and blend it until a smooth batter is formed.
4. Pour it on the waffle iron. Cook until both sides become golden brown. Transfer to a dish having brie slices.
5. Broil them for a few minutes and then serve with raspberry compote on top.

6.111 Pumpkin Spiced French Toast

Servings: 2 I Time: 15 mins I Difficulty: Easy
Nutrients per serving: Calories: 429.73 kcal I Fat: 36.7g I Carbohydrates: 7.33g I Protein: 13.36g I Fiber: 9.02g

Ingredients

- 2 Tbsps. Butter
- 2 Tbsps. Cream
- 1/8 Tsp. Orange Extract
- 1/4 Tsp. Pumpkin Pie Spice
- 1/2 Tsp. Vanilla Extract
- 1 Egg
- 4 Pumpkin Bread Slices

Method

1. Combine all the ingredients in a bowl except the bread and butter and mix them well.
2. Put the bread slices in this mixture and let it soak the mixture.
3. Melt the butter in pan and fry the soaked bread slices in it. Cook both sides until become golden brown.
4. Transfer to plate and serve with keto toppings.

6.112 Keto Pumpkin Bread Loaf

Servings: 10 slices I Time: 1 hr. 45 mins I Difficulty: Easy
Nutrients per serving: Calories: 117.96 kcal I Fat: 8.69g I Carbohydrates: 3.23g I Protein: 4.83g I Fiber: 4.45g

Ingredients

- 1 & 1/2 Tsps. Pumpkin Pie Spice
- 3 Egg Whites
- 1/2 Cup Coconut Milk
- 1/2 Cup Pumpkin Puree
- 1 & 1/2 Cup Almond Flour
- 1/4 Cup Swerve
- 1/4 Cup Psyllium Husk Powder
- 1/2 Tsp. Kosher Salt
- 2 Tsps. Baking Powder

Method

1. Preheat the oven to 350 degrees F.
2. Combine all the ingredients in a bowl and whisk/beat well to make a smooth dough, without lumps.
3. Brush a loaf pan with butter or oil and put the dough in it.
4. Put in the preheated oven and bake for 1 hour and 15 minutes.
5. Once done, let cool, slice it and serve.

6.113 Breakfast Cauliflower Waffles

Servings: 4 I Time: 35 mins I Difficulty: Easy
Nutrients per serving (half waffle): Calories: 181.5 kcal I Fat: 12.59g I Carbohydrates: 2.86g I Protein: 13.43g I Fiber: 0.98g

Ingredients

- 1/2 Cup Cheddar Cheese, Grated
- 3 Eggs
- Black Pepper, To Taste
- 1 & 1/2 Cups Cauliflower, Grated
- 3 Tbsps. Chives, Chopped
- 1/2 Tsp. Garlic Powder
- 1/4 Cup Parmesan Cheese, Grated
- 1/4 Tsp. Red Pepper Flakes
- 1/2 Cup Mozzarella Cheese, Grated
- Salt, To Taste
- 1/2 Tsp. Onion Powder

Method

1. Preheat the waffle iron.
2. Combine all the waffle ingredients in a bowl and blend it until a smooth batter is formed.
3. Pour it on the waffle iron. Cook until both sides become golden brown.
4. Transfer to a plate and top with keto toppings of your choice.

6.114 BBQ Pulled Pork and "Cornbread" Waffles

Servings: 4 I Time: 55 mins I Difficulty: Easy
Nutrients per serving (1 waffle and 4oz. of pulled pork): Calories: 556 kcal I Fat: 45.3g I Carbohydrates: 5.7g I Protein: 26.4g I Fiber: 6.1g

Ingredients

- 2 Tbsp. Butter
- 1/4 Cup Sour Cream
- 2 Cups Pork, Pulled
- 1 Tbsp. Psyllium Husk
- 2 Tbsps. Golden Flaxseed Meal
- 2 Tbsps. Red Pepper, Chopped
- 1 Cup Almond Flour
- 1/4 Cup Coconut Milk
- 1 Tsp. Baking Powder
- 1/2 Tsp. Salt
- 3 Eggs
- 1/4 Cup BBQ Sauce

Method

1. Sift all the dry ingredients (except pork), combine them in one bowl and mix them.
2. Combine all the wet ingredients (except BBQ sauce) in another bowl, whisk them well and pour in the dry ingredients. Blend them well to make a smooth batter.
3. Put the batter on to the preheated waffle maker and cook both sides of the waffle until become golden brown.
4. Mix the pork with 3/4 of the BBQ sauce in a pan and stir fry over medium-low heat for a few minutes.
5. Transfer the waffles to the serving plate and put a spoonful pork on it. Top with extra BBQ sauce and serve.

6.115 Cinnamon Roll "Oatmeal"

Servings: 6 I Time: 35 mins I Difficulty: Easy
Nutrients per serving: Calories: 368.83 kcal I Fat: 34.43g I Carbohydrates: 4.08g I Protein: 5.85g I Fiber: 7.44g

Ingredients

- 1 Cup Pecans, Crushed
- 1/4 Tsp. Allspice
- 1/8 Tsp. Xanthan Gum (Optional)
- 1/4 Tsp. Nutmeg
- 1/3 Cup Flax Seed Meal
- 1/2 Tsp. Vanilla
- 3 Tbsps. Erythritol, Powdered
- 1/3 Cup Chia Seeds
- 1 & 1/2 Tsps. Cinnamon
- 1/2 Cup Cauliflower Rice
- 3 & 1/2 Cups Coconut Milk
- 10-15 Drops Liquid Stevia
- 1/4 Cup Heavy Cream
- 1/3 Cup Cream Cheese
- 3 Tbsps. Butter
- 1 Tsp. Maple Flavor

Method

1. Chopped the cauliflower rice in a food processor. Toast the crushed pecans on a pan for a minute.
2. Heat the coconut milk in a saucepan over medium heat and add the cauliflower in it, boil the milk once and let it simmer at low heat. Season with all the spices, add roasted pecans and mix well.
3. Add the erythritol, stevia and chia seeds, crushed pecans, cream, butter, and cream cheese as well. Mix well and heat until the desired thickness is attained.
4. Add xanthan gum if you want to make thicker.

6.116 Maple Pecan Fat Bomb Bars

Servings: 12 | Time: 1 hr. 25 mins | Difficulty: Easy
Nutrients per serving: Calories: 298.58 kcal | Fat: 29.71g | Carbohydrates: 2.51g | Protein: 4.74g | Fiber: 4.04g

Ingredients

- 2 Cups Pecan, Toasted & Crushed
- 1/4 Tsp. Liquid Stevia
- 1/2 Cup Coconut Oil
- 1/4 Cup Maple Syrup
- 1/2 Cup Coconut, Unsweetened & Shredded
- 1 Cup Almond Flour
- 1/2 Cup Golden Flaxseed Meal

Method

1. Preheat the oven at 350 degrees F.
2. Combine all the ingredients in a bowl and mix well to make a smooth batter.
3. Put in a casserole dish, press to even it out and bake for 20-25 minutes.
4. Take out and let cool down to room temperature.
5. Put in the refrigerator for 1 hour at least, then cut and serve.

6.117 Ham Cheddar Chive Souffle

Servings: 5 | Time: 45 mins | Difficulty: Easy
Nutrients per serving: Calories: 406.4 kcal | Fat: 35.85g | Carbohydrates: 3.58g | Protein: 19.63g | Fiber: 0.24g

Ingredients

- 1 Tbsp. Butter
- 1/4 Cup Ham Steak, Cooked & Cubed
- 1 & 1/2 Tsps. Garlic, Minced
- 1/4 Tsp. Black Pepper
- 1/2 Tsp. Salt
- 1/2 Onion, Diced
- 1 Cup Cheddar Cheese, Shredded
- 3 Tbsps. Olive Oil
- 1/2 Cup Heavy Cream
- 2 Tbsps. Chives, Fresh & Chopped
- 6 Eggs

Method

1. Preheat the oven to 400 degrees F.
2. Heat olive oil in a pan and sauté the onions in it until become soft, then add in the garlic and sauté it too.
3. Add all the other ingredients except butter in a bowl and mix well until combined.
4. Brush the butter in ramekins and pour the mixture in them.
5. Put the ramekins in oven and bake for 20 minutes until golden on top.

6.118 Maple Sausage Pancake Muffins

Servings: 12 | Time: 45 mins | Difficulty: Easy
Nutrients per serving: Calories: 160.5 kcal | Fat: 12.88g | Carbohydrates: 2.16g | Protein: 7.6g | Fiber: 2.7g

Ingredients

- 20 Drops Liquid Stevia
- 4 Tbsps. Coconut Milk
- 3/4 Cup Sausage, Ground
- 1 Tsp. Vanilla Extract
- 4 Tbsps. Maple Syrup
- 1 Tsp. Baking Powder
- 1/4 Tsp. Salt
- 1/4 Cup Erythritol
- 2 Tbsps. Psyllium Husk Powder
- 1 & 1/2 Cups Almond Flour
- 4 Eggs

Method

1. Preheat the oven to 350 degrees F.
2. Crumble the sausage and fry it in a pan until cooked.
3. Combine all the ingredients, including sausage in a big mixing bowl, first add all the wet ingredients, then wet ingredients with intermittent mixing. Make a smooth batter.
4. Take a 12-cup muffin tin and divide the mixture among them.
5. Put in the preheated oven and bake for 20-25 minutes.
6. Let cool and serve warm.

6.119 Sausage And Spinach Crustless Quiche

Servings: 10 | Time:1 hr. 5 mins | Difficulty: Easy
Nutrients per serving: Calories: 429 kcal | Fat: 38g | Carbohydrates: 2g | Protein: 18g

Ingredients

- 2/3 Cup Baby Spinach, Fresh
- 1 Cup Heavy Cream
- 2 Cups Breakfast Sausage Ground
- 1 Cup Cheddar Cheese, Shredded
- 1 Cup Cream Cheese, Cubed
- 6 Eggs
- 2 Tbsps. Water

Method

1. Preheat oven to 375 degrees F.
2. Cook the ground breakfast sausage in a skillet over medium high heat. Drain out the excess fat and add cream cheese in it.
3. Stir well until cream cheese melts completely, then remove from the heat.
4. Pour the water in an oven-safe bowl and put the baby spinach in it. Microwave it for 2-3 minutes until spinach wilts and become soft.
5. Whisk the eggs and cream together in a bowl. Set aside.
6. Take casserole dish, brush it with oil or butter and put the sausage cream cheese mixture at its base.
7. Next, spread the spinach on it and sprinkle the shredded cheddar cheese over it.
8. At last, pour the egg mixture in it and stir slightly so the egg can reach to the bottom.
9. Bake for 35-40 minutes or until the eggs are cooked through.
10. Once done, let cool for about 5 minutes, then cut and serve.

6.120 Bacon, Red Pepper, and Mozzarella Frittata

Servings: 6 | Time: 25 mins | Difficulty: Easy
Nutrients per serving: Calories: 424 kcal | Fat: 34.82g | Carbohydrates: 3.63g | Protein: 22.9g | Fiber: 0.67g

Ingredients

- 7 Bacon Slices, Chopped
- 8-9 Eggs
- 1/4 Cup Parmesan Cheese, Grated
- 1 Red Bell Pepper, Chopped
- Salt, To Taste
- 1/2 Cup Mozzarella, Fresh & Cubed
- 1 Tbsp. Olive Oil
- 1/4 Cup Heavy Cream
- Black Pepper, To Taste
- 1/4 Cup Goat Cheese, Grated
- 4 Mushroom Caps, Chopped
- 2 Tbsps. Parsley, Fresh
- 1/2 Cup Basil, Fresh & Chopped

Method

62

1. Preheat the oven to 350F.
2. Heat the olive oil in a pan and brown the bacon in it. Then add the chopped red pepper and cook it until becomes soft. Add in the chopped mushrooms and sauté it too.
3. Sprinkle the basil and cubed mozzarella cheese in it, stir well.
4. Combine the eggs, 1/4 cup parmesan cheese, 1/4 cup heavy cream in a bowl and season with freshly ground black pepper. Whisk them well.
5. Pour the eggs mixture in the pan as well and stir well to combine everything.
6. Sprinkle the goat cheese on top and put it in the preheated oven for 6-8 minutes.
7. Put in the broiler and broil it for 4-6 minutes more.
8. Let cool for some time and then take the frittata out of the pan. Cut and serve it.

6.121 Low Carb Cinnamon Orange Scones

Servings: 8 scones with icing I Time: 35 mins I Difficulty: Easy
Nutrients per serving (scone with extra icing): Calories: 660 kcal I Fat: 60g I Carbohydrates: 7g I Protein: 13g I Fiber: 4.5g

Ingredients

Scones
- 1/4 Cup Butter, Cubed (Unsalted)
- 2 Eggs
- 1/4 Tsp. Xanthan Gum
- 2 Tbsps. Coconut Oil
- 2 Tbsps. Maple Syrup
- 1/4 Tsp. Salt
- 1 Tbsp. Golden Flaxseed
- 1/4 Cup Erythritol
- 7 Tbsps. + 1 Tbsp. Coconut Flour
- 1 & 1/2 Tsps. Baking Powder
- 2 Tsps. Cinnamon Ground
- 1/3 Cup Heavy Whipping Cream
- 1 Tbsp. Orange Zest
- 1 Tsp. Vanilla Extract
- 1/4 Tsp. Stevia

Icing
- 20 Drops Liquid Stevia
- 1 Tbsp. Orange Juice
- 1/4 Cup Coconut Butter

Method

1. Preheat the oven to 400 degrees F.
2. Combine the golden flaxseeds, 7 tbsps. coconut flour, baking powder, cinnamon and orange zest in a bowl and mix well. Add in coconut oil and butter and whisk well.
3. Whisk the eggs well with sweetener in another bowl until becomes creamy and fluffy. Put the heavy cream, maple syrup, vanilla extract, xanthan gum and remaining coconut flour in it too. Keep mixing until a thick mixture is formed.
4. Pour this mixture in the flaxseed mixture and mix until a firm dough is formed. Knead the dough into ball and roll it into a circle.
5. Cut the flattened dough circle into 8 pieces or triangles and put them on a lined baking sheet.
6. Sprinkle some cinnamon on it if you want and bake for 15-17 minutes in the preheated oven.
7. Meanwhile combine the icing ingredients in a bowl and mix well.
8. Once done, take the scones out of the oven and let cool. Top with icing and serve.

6.122 Maple Pecan Keto Muffins

Servings: 11 I Time: 45 mins I Difficulty: Easy
Nutrients per serving: Calories: 231.36 kcal I Fat: 21.9g I Carbohydrates: 1.96g I Protein: 5.03g I Fiber: 3.19 g

Ingredients
- 1 Cup Almond Flour
- 1/4 Tsp. Liquid Stevia
- 1/2 Cup Golden Flaxseed
- 1/2 Tsp. Baking Soda
- 1 Tsp. Vanilla Extract
- 1/2 Tsp. Apple Cider Vinegar
- 3/4 Cup Pecan, Chopped
- 2 Tsps. Maple Extract
- 1/2 Cup Coconut Oil
- 2 Eggs
- 1/4 Cup Erythritol

Method
1. Preheat the oven to 325 degrees F.
2. Combine all the ingredients in a bowl except 1/3 chopped pecans. Mix them well into a smooth batter.
3. Put the batter in the cups of muffin tin, line with muffin liners.
4. Sprinkle the reserved pecans on the top and put in the oven.
5. Bake for 25-30 minutes until completely cooked and let cool before taking out of the muffin tin.

6.123 Sausage and Cheese Breakfast Pie

Servings: 2 I Time: 45 mins I Difficulty: Easy
Nutrients per serving: Calories: 900 kcal I Fat: 77.6g I Carbohydrates: 6.86g I Protein: 41.93g I Fiber: 5.45g

Ingredients
- 2 Tsps. Lemon Juice
- 5 Egg Yolks
- 1 & 1/2 Cheddar Chicken Sausages, Cubed
- 1/8 Tsp. Kosher Salt
- 3/4 Cup Cheddar Cheese Grated
- 1/4 Tsp. Baking Soda
- 1/4 Cup Coconut Oil
- 1/4 Tsp. Cayenne Pepper
- 1/4 Cup Coconut Flour
- 1/2 Tsp. Rosemary
- 2 Tbsps. Coconut Milk

Method
1. Preheat the oven to 350 degrees F.
2. Sauté the cubed sausages in a pan over medium heat, until cooked through.
3. Combine all the ingredients in a bowl and mix well to make a smooth and lump free batter.
4. Brush 2 ramekins with oil or butter and divide the prepared batter in them, filling them about 3/4. Press the sausages into the batter.
5. Put the ramekins in the oven and bake for 20-25 minutes, or until they become golden brown on top.

6.124 Pumpkin Cardamom Donut Holes

Servings: 18 I Time: 45 mins I Difficulty: Easy
Nutrients per serving: Calories: 87.68 kcal I Fat: 6.98g I Carbohydrates: 1.78g I Protein: 3.1g I Fiber: 3.15g

Ingredients
- 2 Tsps. Psyllium Husk Powder
- 1/2 Cup Pumpkin Puree
- 1/2 Tsp. Cardamom
- 1/4 Cup Erythritol/Stevia Blend
- 1/2 Cup Ricotta Cheese
- 1/2 Cup Coconut Flour
- 2 Eggs
- 1/2 Tsp. Pumpkin Pie Spice
- 1/4 Cup Butter, Salted

Method

1. Preheat the oven at 325 degrees F.
2. Combine all the ingredients in a bowl and mix well to make a smooth and lump free dough.
3. Knead the dough and make balls with about handful dough, total 18 balls can be made out of it.
4. Put in the oven and bake for 20-25 minutes or until become light golden brown in color.
5. Once done, take out and sprinkle some erythritol over them if you want.

6.125 Pork Rind Caramel Cereal

Servings: 1 I Time: 1 hr. 5 mins I Difficulty: Easy
Nutrients per serving: Calories: 514 kcal I Fat: 48.38g I Carbohydrates: 2.05g I Protein: 17.12g I Fiber: 1.3g
Ingredients
- 1/4 Tsp. Cinnamon
- 2 Tbsps. Butter
- 2 Tbsps. Heavy Whipping Cream
- 1 Cup Vanilla Coconut Milk
- 2 Tbsps. Pork Rinds
- 1 Tbsp. Erythritol
Method
1. Take a pan and caramelize the butter in it over medium heat. Once the butter's color changes to brown, take it off the heat and add the erythritol and cream in it.
2. Mix them well and heat to caramelize the whole mixture.
3. Once the desired color is attained, take it off the heat and add the pork rinds in it. Break the pork into small pieces to coat them well.
4. Cover the coated pork rinds in a foil and refrigerate for 20-45 minutes.
5. Once chilled, if you want to, you can garnish them with nuts serve with milk.

6.126 Almond Crusted Keto Quiche

Servings: 8 slices I Time: 35 mins I Difficulty: Easy
Nutrients per serving: Calories: 356.5 kcal I Fat: 30.54g I Carbohydrates: 3.91g I Protein: 16.41g I Fiber: 2.65g
Ingredients
Quiche Crust
- 1/4 Cup Olive Oil
- 1 & 1/2 Cups Almond Flour
- 1/4 Tsp. Salt
- 1 Tsp. Oregano, Dried
Quiche Filling
- 1/2 Tsp. Pepper
- 1 Tsp. Mrs. Dash Table Blend
- 6 Bacon Slices, Diced
- 1/4 Tsp. Salt
- 6 Eggs
- 1 Green Bell Pepper
- 1 Tsp. Garlic
- 1 & 1/2 Cups Cheddar Cheese
Method
1. Preheat the oven to 350 degrees F.
2. Sauté the bacon pieces in a pan until cooked and put on the paper towels, set aside. Sauté the garlic and green peppers in the same pan. Take out once done.
3. Combine the eggs, bacon, garlic, green peppers, cheese, Mrs. Dash, salt, and pepper in a container. Mix everything well and set aside.
4. Combine all the crust ingredients in a bowl and mix well to form a smooth, lump free dough.
5. Knead the dough and press it in a casserole dish.
6. Put in the oven and bake for 20 minutes. Take out even when not fully cooked, it can later be cooked with filling. Fill it with the eggs mixture and bake for another 15-18 minutes.

7. Take out and let cool.

6.127 Pistachio and Pumpkin Chocolate Muffins

Servings: 8 I Time: 55 mins I Difficulty: Easy
Nutrients per serving: Calories: 269 kcal I Fat: 23.54g I Carbohydrates: 5.45g I Protein: 7.99g I Fiber: 4.89g
Ingredients
- 2 Eggs
- 1/2 Cup Pistachios, Salted
- 1/2 Tsp. Nutmeg
- 1 & 1/2 Cups Almond Flour
- 1/2 Tsp. Apple Cider Vinegar
- 1/4 Cup Coconut Oil
- 1/2 Cup Pumpkin Puree
- 1 & 1/2 Tsp. Cinnamon
- 1/2 Tsp. Ginger
- 1/2 Tsp. Cloves
- 1/2 Cup Erythritol
- 3 Bars Dark Chocolate, Sugar-Free
- 2 Tsps. Vanilla
- 1/2 Tsp. Baking Soda
Method
1. Preheat the oven to 325 degrees F.
2. Combine all the ingredients in a bowl, first dry, then wet, and mix them well until a smooth batter is formed, without lumps.
3. Pour the batter into eight lined cups of a muffin tin and put in the oven.
4. Bake for 25-30 minutes, or until their tops become golden brown.

6.128 Low Carb Breakfast Stax

Servings: 1 I Time: 45 mins I Difficulty: Easy
Nutrients per serving: Calories: 330 kcal I Fat: 27.47g I Carbohydrates: 1.78g I Protein: 17.83g I Fiber: 0.68g
Ingredients
- 1/4 Tsp. Black Pepper, Ground
- 4 Eggs
- 2 Tbsps. Heavy Cream
- 1/4 Tsp. Kosher Salt
- 10 Bacon Slices
- 1/4 Tsp. Mrs. Dash Table Blend
- 1/2 Cups Cheddar Cheese
- 2 Tbsps. Bacon Grease
- 4 Cups Spinach
Method
1. Preheat the oven to 400 degrees F.
2. Weave the bacon slices together into a 5x5 bacon weave. Put it on a baking tray.
3. Bake the bacon weave for 25 minutes in the oven.
4. In the meantime, whisk the eggs with the cream and set aside.
5. Once the bacon weave is cooked put it on a paper towel to absorb the grease.
6. But take the bacon grease from the baking tray and put in a pan. Sauté the spinach in it. Add in the eggs and cream mixture and sprinkle the salt and pepper according to your taste.
7. Scramble the eggs, and once cooked through, put them on bacon weave. Top with cheese and broil for about 3-4 minutes in the oven.
8. Let cool for a few minutes and then serve.

6.129 Almond Flour & Flax Seed Pancakes

Servings: 8 | Time: 15 mins | Difficulty: Easy
Nutrients per serving: Calories: 225.5 kcal | Fat: 20.42g | Carbohydrates: 2.05g | Protein: 6.43g | Fiber: 5.24g

Ingredients

- 2 Tbsps. Butter
- 1/2 Cup Coconut Milk
- 1/2 Tsp. Nutmeg
- 2 Tbsps. Erythritol
- 1/2 Cup Almond Flour
- 1/2 Cup Flax Seed Meal
- 1/2 Tsp. Cinnamon
- 1 Tbsp. Coconut Flour
- 4 Eggs
- 5 Tbsps. Coconut Oil
- 1 Tsp. Baking Powder
- 1/8 Tsp. Salt

Method

1. Combine all the ingredients in a bowl (except butter and coconut oil), dry ingredients first, then wet ones. Blend them well to form a smooth batter.
2. Heat the coconut oil and butter in a pan over medium-high heat. Pour 1/4 Cup batter in it and lower the heat to medium-low.
3. Cook on both sides for some minutes, until become golden brown and serve with butter and low carb toppings if you want.

6.130 Low Carb Cinnamon Roll Waffle

Servings: 1 | Time: 25 mins | Difficulty: Easy
Nutrients per serving: Calories: 536 kcal | Fat: 44.52g | Carbohydrates: 7.65g | Protein: 24.2g | Fiber: 5.5g

Ingredients

- 2 Eggs
- 1/2 Tsp. Vanilla Extract
- 1/2 Tsp. Cinnamon
- 6 Tbsps. Almond Flour
- 1/4 Tsp. Baking Soda
- 1 Tbsp. Erythritol

Frosting

- 2 Tsps. Leftover Batter
- 1 Tbsp. Heavy Cream
- 1/4 Tsp. Vanilla Extract
- 2 Tbsps. Cream Cheese
- 1/4 Tsp. Cinnamon
- 1 Tbsp. Erythritol

Method

1. Combine all the ingredients in a bowl and mix well to make a smooth batter.
2. Pour the batter in the waffle maker.
3. In the meantime, whisk together the cream cheese ingredients in a bowl.
4. Slice the waffle into quarters. Pour the cream cheese filling over the half waffle and spread it evenly.

6.131 Crispy Stuffed Bacon Baskets

Servings: 4 | Time: 1 hr. 15 mins | Difficulty: Easy
Nutrients per serving: Calories: 325 kcal | Fat: 26g | Carbohydrates: 1.5g | Protein: 19.8g | Fiber: 0.2g

Ingredients

- 1 Tbsp. Olive Oil
- 4 Eggs
- 2 Tbsps. Heavy Cream
- 4 Cups Spinach
- 2/3 Cup Cheddar Cheese
- 1 Tsp. Pepper
- 12 Bacon Slices

Method

1. Preheat the oven to 350 degrees F.
2. Weave the bacon slices together into a 6x6 bacon weave and cut into quarters.
3. Put these slices on back of a muffin tray cups at the four corners, that are covered with foil and put it in the oven for 50 minutes.
4. Once cooked through, take out of the oven and let cool for 10 minutes.
5. Whisk the eggs and cream in a bowl and set aside.
6. Sauté the spinach in heated olive oil in a pan and season with black pepper. Once it is cooked, pour in the egg mixture, and cook over low heat.
7. Put the egg and spinach mixture in the bacon baskets and sprinkle the cheese on top.
8. Put in the oven and broil until the cheese becomes golden brown. Take out and serve hot.

6.132 Bacon Wrapped Low Carb Scotch Eggs

Servings: 2 | Time: 15 mins | Difficulty: Easy
Nutrients per serving: Calories: 477.5 kcal | Fat: 42.36g | Carbohydrates: 2.95g | Protein: 18.91g | Fiber: 3g

Ingredients

- 1/2 Tbsp. Olive Oil
- 1 Egg
- 1 Tbsp. Coconut Oil
- 2 Tbsps. Coconut Flour
- 4 Bacon Slices
- 2 Eggs, Hard Boiled
- 2 Tbsps. Parmesan Cheese

Method

1. Combine the coconut flour and parmesan cheese in a bowl and mix them. Set aside.
2. Whisk 1 egg in another bowl. Set aside.
3. Wrap each hard-boiled egg in two slices of bacon – one vertical, one horizontal.
4. Put the bacon-wrapped egg first in the egg mixture and then in the parmesan and coconut flour mixture, again in egg and once again the flour mixture.
5. Heat the olive oil and coconut oil in a pan over medium-high heat and put the scotch eggs in it. Keep turning it sides to brown from all the sides.
6. Once browned, lower the heat and fry over it for a while to cook the bacon thoroughly.
7. When cooked satisfactorily, transfer to paper towel to absorb excess oil.

6.133 Bacon Crusted Frittata Muffins

Servings: 7 | Time: 45 mins | Difficulty: Easy
Nutrients per serving: Calories: 467.57 kcal | Fat: 41.83g | Carbohydrates: 2.23g | Protein: 19.35g | Fiber: 0.1g

Ingredients

- 1/2 Tsp. Cayenne Pepper
- 18 Bacon Slices
- 1/2 Tsp. Onion Powder
- 1/2 Tsp. Celery Salt
- 7 Eggs
- 1/2 Tsp. Black Pepper, Ground
- 1 Cup Cheddar Cheese
- 4 Tbsps. Heavy Whipping Cream

Method

1. Preheat the oven to 375 degrees F.
2. Cut the bacon slices in half and put two to three slices per cup in a muffin tray to cover the cup. Put in the oven and cook for 15 minutes.
3. Whisk the eggs, cream, and spices in a bowl and set aside.
4. Put the cheddar cheese in each bacon frittata and pour the egg mixture on top, making sure the egg does not come out.
5. Bake them for 12-15 minutes more, until their tops begin to brown.
6. Take out, let cool and serve.

6.134 Low Carb Mushroom Crustless Quiche

Servings: 6 I Time: 40 mins I Difficulty: Easy
Nutrients per serving: Calories: 373 kcal I Fat: 34.4g I Carbohydrates: 5g I Protein: 13.32g I Fiber: 0.5g

Ingredients

- 5 Eggs
- 1 Cup Mushrooms, Sliced
- 1 Tbsp. Chives, Snipped
- 1 & 1/4 Cups Heavy Cream
- 1/4 Tsp. Black Pepper
- 3 Tbsps. Butter, Divided
- 1/2 Cup Gouda Cheese, Smoked & Grated
- 1/2 Tsp. Salt
- 1/4 Cup Onion, Minced
- 1/4 Cup Water

Method

1. Preheat the oven to 375 degrees F.
2. Heat 2 tbsps. butter in a pan over medium heat, and sauté mushrooms in it for a few minutes until they become dry. Take out and let cool.
3. Add the remaining butter in the same pan and once it melts, sauté the onions in it until become soft. Take off the heat.
4. Beat the eggs with water, cream, salt, and pepper in a bowl until mix well and become frothy.
5. Spray a pie dish with cooking oil spray and spread 1/3 of the cheese at the base to form a layer. Make a second even layer of the onions, mushrooms, and chives. Spread the egg cream on top and sprinkle the reserved cheese on it.
6. Put in the oven on a rack placed in the center and bake for 25 minutes or until it is set in the center and golden brown on top.

6.135 Hunger Buster Low Carb Bacon Frittata

Servings: 8 frittatas I Time: 30 mins I Difficulty: Easy
Nutrients per serving: Calories: 248.63 kcal I Fat: 19.33g I Carbohydrates: 1.66g I Protein: 16.03g I Fiber: 0.08g

Ingredients

- 1/2 Cup Half And Half
- 2 Tsps. Parsley, Dried
- 1/2 Tsp. Pepper
- 8 Eggs
- 1/2 Cup Cheddar Cheese
- 1/4 Tsp. Salt
- 1 Tbsp. Butter
- 1/4 Cup Bacon, Cooked & Chopped
- Cooking Spray
- Spinach, Sauteed (Optional)
- Broccoli, Minced (Optional)
- Spring Onion (Optional)

Method

1. Preheat the oven to 375 degrees F.

2. Combine all the ingredients in a bowl and mix well.
3. Spray an 8-cup muffin tin with cooking spray and fill 3/4 of cups with batter.
4. Put them in the oven and bake for about 15-18 minutes or until become golden.
5. Take out of the oven and let cool for a while.

6.136 Low Carb Pumpkin Pancakes

Servings: 8 I Time: 35 mins I Difficulty: Easy
Nutrients per serving: Calories: 141.18 kcal I Fat: 12.59g I Carbohydrates: 3.53g I Protein: 5g I Fiber: 3g

Ingredients

- 1 Tsp. Pumpkin Pie Spice
- 2 Tbsps. Butter
- 1 Cup Almond Meal
- 1/4 Cup Sour Cream
- 1 Tsp. Baking Powder
- 1/4 Cup Pumpkin Puree
- 2 Eggs
- 1/4 Tsp. Salt

Method

1. Combine all the ingredients in a bowl, first dry, then wet and blend until a smooth batter is formed.
2. Grease a skillet with butter and heat it over medium flame.
3. Pour 1/3 cup of the batter in it, for one pancake, and spread with the back of a spoon.
4. Cook both sides of the pancake until they become golden brown. Transfer to a plate once done.
5. Repeat this with rest of the batter and serve the pancakes warm.

6.137 Fluffy Buttermilk Pancakes

Servings: 1 I Time: 25 mins I Difficulty: Easy
Nutrients per serving: Calories: 422 kcal I Fat: 19.28g I Carbohydrates: 13.01g I Protein: 32.75g I Fiber: 9.8g

Ingredients

- 1/4 Cup Coconut Flour
- 1/8 Tsp. Cinnamon
- Oil Or Butter, As Needed
- 2 Eggs, Divided
- 1 Tsp. Vanilla Extract
- 1/2 Cup Egg Whites
- 1 Tbsp. Protein Powder
- Salt, To Taste
- 1 Tsp. Baking Powder
- 2 Tbsps. Stevia
- 1/2 Cup Buttermilk

Method

1. Take the separated egg whites and beat well until become fluffy.
2. Combine all the other ingredients in a bowl, first dry, then wet and blend until a smooth batter is formed. Add in the egg whites' cream and fold in the batter.
3. Grease a skillet with butter and heat it over medium flame.
4. Pour 1/4 cup of the batter in it, for one pancake, and spread with the back of a spoon.
5. Cook both sides of the pancake until they become golden brown. Transfer to a plate once done.
6. Repeat this with rest of the batter and serve the pancakes warm.

6.138 Fast and Easy Coffee Cubes

Servings: 1 I Time: 5 mins I Difficulty: Easy
Nutrients per serving: Calories: 403 kcal I Fat: 36.86g I Carbohydrates: 6.21g I Protein: 7.7g I Fiber: 5.6g

Ingredients

- 3 Drops Liquid Stevia
- 1 Tbsp. Coconut Oil
- 1 Baking Chocolate Square, Unsweetened
- 1 Tbsp. Peanut Butter

Method
1. Put all the ingredient in a ramekin or any other oven safe container and microwave for a minute and stir well until combined and smooth.
2. Pour the mixture in an ice cubes tray or small cups and freeze.
3. Whenever you want to use them, just put a cube in your cup and pour the coffee on top. Stir it and serve.

6.139 Keto Lemon Chia Pudding

Servings: 4 I Time: 5 hrs. I Difficulty: Easy
Nutrients per serving: Calories: 343 kcal I Fat: 30.8g I Carbohydrates: 5.9g I Protein: 6.4g I Fiber: 8.75g

Ingredients
- 2 Tsps. Lemon Zest
- 1 Cup Coconut Milk
- 1/2 Cup Heavy Cream
- 1/2 Cup Chia Seeds
- 1 Cup Almond Milk, Unsweetened
- 1/2 Cup Lemon Juice
- 3 Tbsps. Stevia/Erythritol Blend

Method
1. Combine all the ingredients in a blender and blend until a smooth mixture is formed.
2. Put this lemon chia pudding in the serving cups and cover them with cling film.
3. Put the cups in refrigerator for 5 hours at least and serve later.

6.140 Two ingredient Pasta

Servings: 1 I Time: 5 mins I Difficulty: Easy
Nutrients per serving: Calories: 520 kcal I Fat: 34g I Carbohydrates: 11g I Protein: 41g I Fiber: 34g

Ingredients
- 1 Egg Yolk
- 1 Cup Mozzarella Cheese, Shredded

Method
1. Line a baking sheet with parchment paper. Set aside.
2. Melt the mozzarella cheese in microwave for a minute or two.
3. Let it cool for a minute and then add the egg yolk in it gradually and mix well.
4. Once smooth, pour the mixture onto the lined baking sheet, cover it with another piece of parchment paper. Press it with the hand or rolling pin to spread it evenly until a thin dough sheet is formed.
5. Take off the upper parchment sheet and slice the dough sheet into thin pasta like strips.
6. Put these pasta strips on a tray and put in the refrigerator overnight.
7. The next day, boil water in a pan and put the pasta in it for a minute. Drain it and run cold water over it.
8. Serve with low carb toppings.

6.141 Low Carb Keto Bagels

Servings: 6 I Time: 22 mins I Difficulty: Easy
Nutrients per serving: Calories: 245 kcal I Fat: 21g I Carbohydrates: 6g I Protein: 12g I Fiber: 3g

Ingredients
- 1 & 1/2 Cups Almond Flour
- 1 Egg
- 1/4 Cup Cream Cheese

- 1 & 1/2 Cups Mozzarella Cheese, Shredded
- 1 Tbsp. Baking Powder

Method
1. Preheat the oven to 400 degrees F.
2. Mix the cream cheese and mozzarella cheese in a bowl and microwave it for 30 seconds.
3. Put all the other ingredients in it and whisk well to form a smooth dough. Cover the bowl with cling film and put in the freezer for 10 minutes.
4. Once the dough is set, knead it and divide it into six pieces. Roll the pieces with hands to form long rods and join their ends to make bagels.
5. Put the bagels on a lined baking sheet.
6. Put a rack in the middle of the oven and put the baking sheet on it.
7. Bake for 12 minutes or until the bagels become golden brown in color.
8. Take out and let cool and then serve.

6.142 Steak and Avocado Salad

Servings: 4 I Time: 30 mins I Difficulty: Easy
Nutrients per serving: Calories: 577 kcal I Fat: 44g I Carbohydrates: 15g I Protein: 32g I Fiber: 8g

Ingredients
- 2 Cups Cherry Tomatoes, Halved
- 3 Eggs, Hard-Boiled & Diced
- Salt, To Taste
- 1 Sirloin Steak, 1/2 Inch Thick
- 2 Tbsps. Oil
- 2 Hearts Romaine Lettuce, Chopped
- Pepper, To Taste
- 3 Tbsps. Caesar Dressing
- 2 Avocados, Diced

Method
1. Take a pan and heat the oil in it over high heat.
2. Rub the salt and pepper on both sides of the steak and cook it in the pan until it is seared on both sides.
3. Once done, let cool for 10 minutes, then slice it into strips.
4. Combine all the ingredients in a bowl, including steak strips and toss well.
5. Serve and enjoy.

6.143 Paleo Beef and Veggie Stir-fry

Servings: 6 I Time: 35 mins I Difficulty: Easy
Nutrients per serving: Calories: 213 kcal I Fat: 11g I Carbohydrates: 4g I Protein: 22g I Fiber: 1g

Ingredients
- 2 Tbsps. Avocado Oil
- 1 Tbsp. Ginger, Grated
- 1 Flank Steak, Sliced
- 4 Garlic Cloves, Minced
- 3 & 1/2 Cups Cabbage, Sliced Thinly
- 2 Tsps. Lime Juice
- 3 Carrots, Peeled & Sliced
- 2 Tsps. Coconut Aminos
- 3 Scallions, Fresh & Minced

Sauce
- 1 & 1/2 Tsps. Tapioca Flour
- 2 Tbsps. Lime Juice
- 3/4 Cup Coconut Amino

Method
1. Mix the coconut aminos and lime juice in a bowl and marinate the steak slices with it. Set aside for 10 minutes.
2. Heat 1 tbsp. avocado oil in a nonstick skillet over medium-high flame and cook the steak slices in it. Once done, take out the steak slices in a bowl.

3. Add the remaining avocado oil in it and sauté the carrot slices in it until softened, then add the sliced cabbage and stir fry it.
4. Add in the ginger, garlic, and scallions and fry for half a minute or until fragrant. Mix everything well and add the steak slices as well.
5. Add in the sauce ingredients as well, mix well and cook for about 1-2 minutes or until a thick sauce is formed. Take off the heat and serve with some chopped scallions on top.

6.144 Keto Oatmeal

Servings: 1 I Time: 5 mins I Difficulty: Easy
Nutrients per serving: Calories: 327 kcal I Fat: 27.3g I Carbohydrates: 15.6g I Protein: 11g I Fiber: 11.5g

Ingredients
- 1/2 Cup Vanilla Almond Milk, Unsweetened
- 2 Tbsps. Coconut Flakes, Unsweetened
- 1/2 Tsp. Cinnamon
- 1 Tbsp. Flax Meal
- 1/2 Tsp. Vanilla
- 1/4 Cup Almond Flour
- 1/8 Tsp. Salt
- 1/2 Tbsp. Monkfruit
- 1 Tbsp. Chia Seeds

Method
1. Combine all the ingredients in a pan except the vanilla and milk, heat them and mix well.
2. Then pour in the vanilla and milk and boil the mixture over high heat.
3. After boiling, lower the heat to medium and let it simmer until the mixture thickens to the desired consistency.
4. Take off the heat and let cool. Add the low carb toppings and enjoy.

6.145 Low Carb Meatloaf

Servings: 6 I Time: 1 hr. 10 mins I Difficulty: Easy
Nutrients per serving: Calories: 208 kcal I Fat: 12.4g I Carbohydrates: 8.4g I Protein: 17g I Fiber: 1.8g

Ingredients
Sauce
- 3 Deglet Noor Dates, Halved
- 2 Tbsps. Water
- 1/4 Cup Tomato Paste
- 1/2 Cup Tomato Sauce
- 1 Tsp. Onion Powder
- 1 Tbsp. White Vinegar
- 1/2 Tsp. Sea Salt
- 1/2 Tsp. Garlic Powder

For The Meatloaf:
- 1/4 Cup Green Onion, Sliced
- 1/2 Tsp. Sea Salt
- 2 Cups Beef, Ground
- 1/8 Tsp. Black Pepper
- 4 Tsps. Coconut Flour
- 3/4 Cup Green Bell Pepper, Diced
- 1 Egg

Method
1. Preheat the oven to 350 degrees.
2. Make the sauce my heating all its ingredients in a saucepan over high heat. Boil them with constant stirring until combined and thickened to desired consistency.
3. To further chop the dates, take it off the heat and blend in a food processor or a blender until smooth.
4. In a bowl combine all the meatloaf ingredients, dry first and wet ones later. Mix them well to make a smooth batter.

5. Put the batter into a lined loaf pan even it out by pressing it. Pour the sauce over it and spread on top.
6. Bake for 45-55 minutes or until cooked through.

6.146 Inst. Pot Green Beans

Servings: 4 I Time: 16 mins I Difficulty: Easy
Nutrients per serving: Calories: 19 kcal I Fat: 0.1g I Carbohydrates: 4.4g I Protein: 1.1g I Fiber: 1.9g

Ingredients
- 2 Tsps. Garlic, Minced
- 1 Cup Water
- 2 Cups Green Beans, Trimmed
- 1/2 Tsp. Salt

Method
1. Put all the ingredients into an Inst. Pot and stir well. Cover it and seal.
2. Cook on pressure for 10 minutes.
3. Drain the beans, sprinkle more salt if needed and serve.

6.147 Keto Baked Cauliflower Au Gratin

Servings: 6 I Time: 45 mins I Difficulty: Easy
Nutrients per serving: Calories: 174 kcal I Fat: 12.2g I Carbohydrates: 8.6g I Protein: 9.1g I Fiber: 2.5g

Ingredients
- 1 Tbsp. + 1 Tsp. Almond Flour
- 1 & 1/2 Cups Milk
- 1/4 Tsp. Onion Powder
- 4 & 1/2 Cups Cauliflower Florets
- 1/4 Tsp. Garlic Powder
- 2 Tbsps. Butter
- 1 Cup Cheddar Cheese, Grated
- 1 Tbsp. + 1 Tsp. Coconut Flour
- 1/8 Tsp. Black Pepper
- 3/4 Tsp. Salt

Method
1. Put water in a pot and add the salt in it. Boil the water and add cauliflower florets in it. Cook them for about 5-7 minutes or until they become softer. Drain them and soak dry with paper towels.
2. Heat the butter in a pan over medium high heat until it melts. Brown the almond and coconut flour in it for about 1 minute and then stir in the milk.
3. Add in the garlic powder, onion powder, salt, and pepper in it too. Bring it to boil and lower the heat to medium.
4. Then keep stirring for about 7-8 minutes until the sauce thickens. Take off the heat and add in the 1/2 cup of the grated cheese. Whisk it well to make the sauce smooth.
5. Preheat the oven to 375 degrees F.
6. Take an 8×8-inch casserole dish and spread the 1/3 of the sauce at the bottom, Make a layer of cooked cauliflower florets on top, and top it with the remaining sauce.
7. Sprinkle the remaining cheese on top and put it in the oven.
8. Bake it for 25-30 minutes or until the cheese becomes golden brown.

6.148 Low Carb Mock Cauliflower Potato Salad

Servings: 8 I Time: 30 mins I Difficulty: Easy
Nutrients per serving: Calories: 165 kcal I Fat: 16g I Carbohydrates: 3.8g I Protein: 4.4g I Fiber: 1.7g

Ingredients
- 4 Eggs, Boiled & Diced
- 1/4 Cup Red Onion, Diced
- Black Pepper, To Taste
- Sea Salt, To Taste

- 5 Cups Cauliflower Florets
- 1/2 Cup Celery, Sliced Thinly

Dressing:

- 5 Tsps. Dijon Mustard
- 2 Tsps. Sea Salt
- 2 Tsps. Dill Paste
- 1/2 Tsp. Paprika
- 1/8 Tsp. Black Pepper
- 1/2 Cup Mayonnaise
- 1 Tbsp. Apple Cider Vinegar

Method

1. Put water in a pot and add the salt in it. Boil the water and add cauliflower florets in it. Cook them for about 8 minutes or until they become softer. Drain them and soak dry with paper towels.
2. In the meantime, combine all the dressing ingredients in a bowl and whisk them well.
3. Combine the cauliflower, diced eggs, celery and red onion in a bowl and mix. Add in the dressing and toss the salad well.
4. Cover the bowl and put in the refrigerator for 2 hours at least.
5. Sprinkle the salt and pepper according to your taste and serve.

6.149 Cauliflower Tabbouleh

Servings: 2 I Time: 22 mins I Difficulty: Easy
Nutrients per serving: Calories: 660 kcal I Fat: 60g I Carbohydrates: 7g I Protein: 13g I Fiber: 7g

Ingredients

- 2 Tbsps. Olive Oil
- 1 Tbsp. Garlic, Fresh & Minced
- 3 Cups Cauliflower Rice
- 1 Green Onion
- 1 Tomato, Diced
- 2 Tsps. Lemon Juice, Fresh
- 1/2 Cucumber, Diced
- 1/2 Tsp. Salt
- 1/4 Cup Mint Leaves
- 1/2 Cup Parsley Leaves

Method

1. Put the cauliflower rice in a bowl and microwave for 3 minutes, covered. Take out, stir once, put back for 3 minutes more. Transfer to a kitchen towel and let cool.
2. Soak them well with kitchen towel to dry them as much as you can and put in a bowl.
3. Combine all the other ingredients in the bowl as well and toss well to combine.
4. Put in the refrigerator for an hour, covered. Serve cold.

6.150 Keto Banana Bread

Servings: 2 I Time: 1 hr. 10 mins I Difficulty: Easy
Nutrients per serving: Calories: 241 kcal I Fat: 22.4g I Carbohydrates: 7.4g I Protein: 7.9g I Fiber: 4.4g

Ingredients

- 4 Eggs
- 1/3 Cup Almond Milk, Unsweetened
- 1 Tsp. Baking Soda
- 3 Cups Almond Flour
- 1 Tsp. Salt
- 1/2 Cup Coconut Oil, Melted
- 1 & 1/2 Tsps. Cinnamon Powder
- 1/4 Cup Coconut Flour
- 1 & 1/2 Tbsps. Banana Extract

- 2/3 Cup Monkfruit
- 1 Tbsp. Baking Powder

Method

1. Preheat the oven to 350 degrees F.
2. Combine all the ingredients in a bowl, first dry, then wet and blend until a smooth batter is formed.
3. Line a loaf pan's bottom with parchment paper and brush coconut oil on the sides.
4. Pour the batter into it and bake for 50 to 60 minutes or until cooked through.
5. Take out of the oven once done and let cool for an hour. Then, remove gently out of the loaf pan and slice it.

6.151 Cod Scrambled Eggs

Servings: 2 I Time: 30 mins I Difficulty: Easy
Nutrients per serving: Calories: 286 kcal I Fat: 17g I Carbohydrates: 3.9g I Protein: 28.1g I Fiber: 0.4g

Ingredients

- 1 Tbsp. Olive Oil
- 4 Eggs
- 1/4 Tsp. Sea Salt
- 1/2 Tbsp. Water
- 1/2 Cup Leeks, Sliced Thinly
- Salt, To Taste
- 1 Cod Fillet, Fresh

Method

1. Take cold water in a bowl and put the sliced leeks in it. Cover it and set aside.
2. Season the cod fillet with salt after drying. Heat 1 tsp oil in a skillet over medium-high flame and fry the fish in it for 2-3 minutes on each side until become golden. Reduce the flame to medium-low and break the fish with the spoon into pieces.
3. Drain the leeks, pat dry them. Add 1/2 tsp more oil in the pan, heat it and cook the leeks in it with fish for about 2-3 minutes until become soft.
4. Take the pan off the stove and let cool for a few minutes.
5. Combine eggs and water in a bowl and whisk until become frothy.
6. Place the pan back on the stove, add the remaining oil in it and heat it over low flame.
7. Pour the eggs in the pan, let them set for a while, then scramble them. Sprinkle salt over the cod scramble eggs, mix to combine, and take off the stove once done.

6.152 Inst. Pot Breakfast Casserole With Sausage

Servings: 6 I Time: 40 mins I Difficulty: Easy
Nutrients per serving: Calories: 327 kcal I Fat: 22.8g I Carbohydrates: 0.4g I Protein: 26.7g

Ingredients

- 4 Eggs
- 2/3 Cup Cheddar Cheese, Grated
- 2/3 Cup Chicken Broth
- 2 Cups Italian Sausage, Ground
- Cooking Spray

Method

1. Set sauté mode on Inst. Pot and sauté the ground sausage in it until cooked thoroughly.
2. Combine all the ingredients in a bowl and whisk well. Add in the sausage as well, once cooked.
3. Spray a cake pan with cooking oil spray and pour the mixture in it.
4. Pour one cup water in a trivet and put it in the Inst. Pot. Put the cake pan in the Inst. Pot and seal it.
5. Cook for about 28 minutes or until the eggs are cooked.
6. Wait for 10 minutes before opening the Inst. Pot.

6.153 Low Carb Quiche With Almond Flour Crust

Servings: 8 I Time: 1 hr. 10 mins I Difficulty: Easy
Nutrients per serving: Calories: 311 kcal I Fat: 24.8g I Carbohydrates: 11.8g I Protein: 12.5g I Fiber: 2.5g

Ingredients

- 1 Cup Pork, Ground
- 1/2 Tsp. Sea Salt
- 1/8 Tsp. Paprika Powder
- 1 Pie Crust, Low Carb
- 1/8 Tsp. Fennel Seed
- 1/4 Tsp. Salt
- 1/2 Tsp. Parsley, Dried
- 1/4 Tsp. Red Pepper Flakes
- 1/2 Cup Coconut Milk
- 1/2 Tsp. Italian Seasoning
- 1/4 Tsp. Onion Powder
- 1/4 + 1/8 Tsp. Black Pepper, Ground
- 5 Eggs
- 1 Cup Spinach, Chopped

Method

1. Preheat the oven to 375 degrees F.
2. Brown the ground pork in a skillet over medium heat with all the spices. Remove from heat once done.
3. Combine the eggs with coconut milk spinach, cooked pork, and salt in a bowl and whisk well.
4. Pour the mixture in the pie crust and put in the preheated oven.
5. Bake for 20 minutes, take out and cover with foil, put back and bake for another 18-20 minutes or until the quiche is cooked.

6.154 Keto Low Carb Egg Wraps

Servings: 2 I Time: 15 mins I Difficulty: Easy
Nutrients per serving: Calories: 240 kcal I Fat: 18g I Carbohydrates: 6g I Protein: 14g I Fiber: 3g

Ingredients

- 1/2 Tomato, Sliced
- 2 Bacon Strips, Cooked
- Salt, To Taste
- 2 Eggs
- 1/2 Avocado, Sliced
- Black Pepper, To Taste
- 1 Tbsp. Almond Milk
- Cooking Spray
- 1/4 Cup Cheddar Cheese, Grated (Optional)

Method

1. Spray a pan with cooking spray and heat it over low flame.
2. Whisk the eggs with salt and pepper in a bowl and pour 1/4 cup of this mixture into the pan. Swirl the pan to spread he mixture in the pan evenly.
3. Cover the pan and let it cook for a few minutes, then flip and cook on the other side, until becomes golden.
4. Similarly make another egg tortilla with the remaining egg mixture.
5. Place the egg tortillas on serving plates, put one bacon strip on each and top with sliced tomatoes and avocados.
6. Sprinkle with grated cheese on top.

6.155 Savory Egg Custard

Servings: 4 I Time: 50 mins I Difficulty: Easy
Nutrients per serving: Calories: 240 kcal I Fat: 18g I Carbohydrates: 6g I Protein: 14g I Fiber: 3g

Ingredients

- 1/4 Cup Greek Yogurt, Plain
- 3 Eggs
- 1 Tbsp. Water
- 1/4 Tsp. Salt
- 1 Cup Almond Milk, Unsweetened
- 1/2 Tsp. Garlic Powder
- 1 Red Pepper, Roasted
- Cooking Spray
- Goat Cheese, To Taste

Method

1. Preheat the oven to 325 degrees F.
2. Take 4 ramekins and grease them with cooking spray.
3. Put the roasted red pepper with almond milk in a blender and blend until become smooth. Strain it for any chunks and put in the blender again.
4. Add all the other ingredients in it too except for goat cheese.
5. Blend until a smooth mixture is formed.
6. Divide this mixture into 4 ramekins and put them in the preheated oven.
7. Bake for 35-40 minutes or until cooked through.
8. Let cool for an hour and then garnish with goat cheese.

Chapter 7 – Keto-Friendly Lunch Recipes

Look at our selection of lunch recipes that will not only align with your keto diet but offer your taste buds a treat. And with a small number of ingredients, what's better than a tasty meal? A simple salad, a balanced soup, or a Bar BQ meal and casseroles can be made.

7.1 Mediterranean Tuna Salad with Olives

Servings: 1 I Time: 10 mins I Difficulty: Easy
Nutrients per serving: Calories: 351 kcal I Fat: 20g I Carbohydrates: 13.2g I Protein: 35.2g I Fiber: 2.9g
Ingredients
- 1 & 1/2 tsp Lemon juice, or to taste
- 1 Can Tuna, packed in water (5 oz. Drained)
- 1 Tbsp Paleo Mayo
- 1 Tbsp Sun-Dried Tomatoes Packed in Olive Oil, drained and diced
- 1 tsp Lemon zest
- 1 tsp Pine nuts
- 1/2 tsp Dried parsley
- 1/4 tsp Dried Basil
- 1/4 tsp dried oregano
- 2 Tbsp Roasted red peppers, sliced
- 4 Cherry Tomatoes, diced
- 4 Kalamata olives, sliced
- Salt, to taste

Method
1. Take oven to 350 °F.
2. On a small baking sheet, cook around 5-7 minutes until the pine nuts turn to a light brown color. Don't burn them.
3. Put all ingredients in the mug and stir. Use salt as seasoning and taste with lemon juice.
4. Chop and mix the pine nuts into the tuna.
5. Serve in wraps of lettuce or on toast.

7.2 Keto Green Bean Casserole

Servings: 6 I Time: 50 mins I Difficulty: Easy
Nutrients per serving: Calories: 159 kcal I Fat: 11g I Carbohydrates: 10.3g I Protein: 6.2g I Fiber: 3.3g
Ingredients
- 1 1/4 tsp. Sea salt
- 1 cup Onion, diced
- 2 cups Green beans, trimmed
- 1/3 cup 2% milk (or 1/2 cup almond milk)
- 1/4 Cup Full fat cream cheese (dairy-free works too)
- 1/4 tsp. Pepper
- 2 Cups Mushrooms, sliced
- 2/3 cup Half and half cream (or 1/2 cup full-fat coconut milk)
- 6 Slices Bacon

Method
1. Heat the oven to 350°F.
2. Take a frying pan over medium heat.
3. Cook until the bacon turns to golden brown color and crispy on sides.
4. Then remove excess fat after transferring it to a paper towel. Reserve only 1 Tbsp. of fat.
5. Add onions & mushrooms in a medium to high heated pan.
6. Cook until golden brown by stirring sporadically for about 3 minutes.
7. Boil all ingredients except beans.
8. Boil for 4 minutes until the mixture thickens by stirring continuously.
9. Cook by stirring continuously on reduced heat, and cook until mixture is very thick, for 7-8 minutes.
10. Boil salted water in a large pot. Cook green beans until they become fork tender. It should take 7-8 minutes. Dry them by draining excess water and patting them with a paper towel.
11. Then, add cooked beans into the sauce and stir to coat beans with sauce.
12. Put into a pan of size 8x8 inch and cook for 15-20 minutes.
13. While you are cooking beans, make crumbs of bacon in a food processor. Use casserole to sprinkle and bake for 5 minutes.

7.3 Keto Chicken Taco Soup

Servings: 4 I Time: 25 mins I Difficulty: Easy
Nutrients per serving: Calories: 215 kcal I Fat: 10.62g I Carbohydrates: 10.75g I Protein: 16.2g I Fiber: 2.1g
Ingredients
- shredded cheddar cheese optional
- fresh sliced jalapeno optional
- 8 oz full-fat cream cheese room temperature
- 4 tbsp fresh chopped cilantro optional
- 3 tbsp Low Carb Taco Seasoning
- 3 cups chicken broth
- 1 lime, cut into wedges optional

- 2 cups chicken breast tenders
- 1 cup of salsa

Method

1. Take an Inst. Pot and put the chicken broth, taco seasoning, and chicken in it.
2. Make sure that the release valve is sealed. Choose a cycle time of about 15 minutes in manual mode. The cycle will start automatically.
3. Once the cycle is completed, let it for 10 minutes. Then release the valve.
4. Take chicken out of the pot and use a fork to shred it.
5. Choose sauté setting on the Inst. Pot.
6. Whisk the cream with chicken broth mixture.
7. Simmer the shredded chicken in the pot for about 3-4 minutes.
8. If desired, top with cilantro, cheddar cheese shredded, lime wedge, and jalapeno.

7.4 Crunchy Asian Cabbage Salad

Servings: 4 | Time: 50 mins | Difficulty: Easy
Nutrients per serving: Calories: 519 kcal | Fat: 52g | Carbohydrates: 10g | Protein: 2.2g | Fiber: 2.9g

Ingredients

For Salad Dressing
- 1 tsp Bragg's Amino Acids
- 1 tsp Dijon Mustard
- 2 tbsp Rice Wine Vinegar
- 1/4 cup Coconut Oil Liquid

Cabbage
- 1/4 tsp Freshly Cracked Pepper
- 3 tbsp Rice Wine Vinegar
- 1/2 head Green Cabbage Cored and finely shredded
- 1/2 tsp Kosher Salt
- 1/2 cup Coconut Oil Liquid

Cucumbers
- 1/4 cup Cilantro Chopped with no stems
- 1/2 Hothouse Cucumber Seeded
- 1 tbsp Sesame Seeds (Optional)
- 1/4 Fresh Red Chili Pepper (Optional) Sliced thin
- 1/4 tsp Kosher Salt
- 1 tbsp Olive Oil

Red peppers (Asian)
- 2 tsp Sesame Oil
- 1 Red Pepper cored, seeded, and sliced very thin
- 1/2 tsp Ginger Fresh, from a jar or 1/4 tsp dried ginger
- 1/4 cup Scallion Greens Sliced or
- 1/4 tsp Ground Cumin
- 2 tbsp finely diced shallots.

Remaining Ingredients
- 1 Avocado Peeled, sliced and seeded
- 1 cup Snow Pea Pods

Optional Quick Pickled Onions
- 2 tbsp Red Wine Vinegar
- 1/4 cup Red Onion Finely diced

Method

Asian cabbage
1. Take a large bowl and shred the cabbage in it. Mix well after adding the remaining ingredients.
2. Don't let it sit at the bottom.

Asian cucumbers
1. Take a medium bowl and slice cucumbers in it.
2. Put rest of the ingredients and rest it for 30 minutes.

Asian red peppers
1. Take a medium bowl and slice red peppers in it.
2. Put rest of the ingredients and rest it for 30 minutes.

Quick Pickled Onions
1. Take a medium bowl and diced onions in it.
2. Take red wine vinegar and cover the onions with it.
3. Rest it for 20 minutes.

Salad Dressing
1. Take a bowl and add all the ingredients.
2. Set it aside at room temperature after mixing.

Cabbage Salad
1. After marinating all the ingredients of the salad, put the cabbage in a bowl.
2. Top it with equal portions of marinated red peppers, marinated cucumber, and sliced avocado. (In the case of snow peas, put peas into the salad.)
3. Whereas, in the case of pickled onions, top them with a pinch of cilantro.
4. And to garnish, use sesame seeds.

7.5 Keto Dutch Baby with Chocolate and Macadamia

Servings: 4 | Time: 20 mins | Difficulty: Easy
Nutrients per serving: Calories: 272 kcal | Fat: 23.62g | Carbohydrates: 8.74g | Protein: 8.52g | Fiber: 5.7g

Ingredients

- 4 large eggs
- 2 tbsp coconut flour
- 2 tbsp butter
- 1/8 tsp salt
- 1/4 cup monk fruit sweetener
- 1/4 cup heavy whipping cream
- 1/4 cup almond flour
- 1/2 cup sugar-free whipped cream optional
- 1/2 cup strawberries optional
- 1 tsp vanilla extract
- 1 tbsp sugar-free chocolate syrup

Method

1. Preheat the oven to 400°F.
2. Put butter (2 tbsps.) in a preheated oven.
3. In a large bowl, whisk together 1/4 cup Sweetener (Monk fruit), 2 tbsp coconut flour, 1/8 tsp salt, and 1/4 cup almond flour.
4. In a second bowl, add 1 tsp vanilla extract, 4 large eggs, and 1/4 cup heavy whipped cream.
5. Stir until well combined.
6. Combine mixtures of egg and almond flour.
7. Remove skillet from the oven and pour batter (Dutch Baby) in skillet.
8. Bake skillet in the oven for 15 minutes to brown the Dutch Baby top.
9. Take 1 tbsp. ChocZero syrup and drizzle the pancake.
10. Take 1 tbsp. nuts (macadamia) and sprinkle the pancake.
11. Serve with fresh strawberries and sugar-free whipped cream.

7.6 Parmesan Roasted Ranch Cauliflower with Avocado

Servings: 4 | Time: 35 mins | Difficulty: Easy
Nutrients per serving: Calories: 179 kcal | Fat: 14.5g | Carbohydrates: 11g | Protein: 5g | Fiber: 6.5g

Ingredients

- 2 Tbsp. Olive oil
- 2 cups Cauliflower, cut into large florets
- 1 large avocado, cubed
- 2 Tbsp. Finely grated Parmesan cheese
- 2 Tbsp. Ranch mix (recipe below)
- Pinch of sea salt

Ranch Seasoning:

- 3/4 tsp Salt
- 1 Tbsp Dried Parsley
- 1 tsp Garlic powder
- 1/3 tsp Pepper
- 1 tsp Onion powder
- 1 tsp Dried Dill

Method

1. Preheat the oven to 400°F.
2. Take a bowl, mix the oil and cauliflower in it.
3. Add 2 Tbsp. of mixed ranch mix to cauliflower. Coat by tossing.
4. Spread a single layer of cauliflower on a baking sheet. Leave space between the flowers.
5. First, cook for 15 minutes and then cook again for 12 minutes after stirring until the color changes to Golden Brown.
6. Toss with avocado, cheese, and some salt in a bowl.

7.7 Spinach Salad with Warm Bacon Dressing

Servings: 4 | Time: 30 mins | Difficulty: Easy
Nutrients per serving: Calories: 445 kcal | Fat: 32g | Carbohydrates: 5.14g | Protein: 28g | Fiber: 1.8g

Ingredients

- 2 oz Mushrooms, sliced very thinly (about 4 large)
- 10.5 oz Baby Spinach
- 4 large boiled eggs, chopped
- 8 oz Bacon, diced

Warm Bacon Dressing

- 1/4 cup bacon grease
- 2 tbsp Red wine vinegar
- 1 tbsp Low carb brown sugar
- 2 tbsp Shallot, finely chopped
- Salt and pepper to taste
- 1/2 tsp Dried tarragon
- 1 tbsp Whole Grain Mustard

Customize

- Mandarin oranges, apple, walnuts, strawberries, shrimp, blue cheese

Method

1. Put diced bacon in a pan on medium heat.
2. Cook for 5-6 minutes by stirring sporadically.
3. Pour bacon oil into a small bowl after removing it from the pan.
4. Chop or slice the eggs, mushrooms, and shallot.
5. Heat mushrooms in a pan over medium heat to lightly cook them.
6. Take shallots and sauté them.
7. Turn the heat to medium-low and add the Sukrin Gold, bacon oil, tarragon, vinegar, and whole grain mustard. Combine all of these by stirring continuously.
8. Add pepper and salt to taste.
9. Toss the hot dressing with the spinach and divide between 4 serving bowls. Taste to adjust seasoning. Top with bacon, eggs, and mushrooms.

7.8 Chicken Cobb Salad with Cobb Salad Dressing

Servings: 2 | Time: 20 mins | Difficulty: Easy
Nutrients per serving: Calories: 632 kcal | Fat: 54g | Carbohydrates: 9.5g | Protein: 29g | Fiber: 5g

Ingredients

- 4 oz cooked chicken breast, diced (about 1 medium breast)
- 180 grams romaine lettuce, chopped (2 hearts of romaine)
- 2 large boiled eggs, quartered, sliced, or chopped
- 6 tbsp Cobb Salad Dressing (or blue cheese dressing)
- 2 oz cheddar cheese, cubed
- 4 slices cooked bacon, crumbled
- 2-3 green onions, sliced
- 1/2 Hass avocado, cubed or sliced

Method

1. Take lettuce and toss it with cobb salad dressing.
2. Divide it into 2 bowls.
3. Serve

7.9 Broccoli Cheddar Quiche with Bacon

Servings: 6 | Time: 50 mins | Difficulty: Easy
Nutrients per serving: Calories: 457 kcal | Fat: 40g | Carbohydrates: 3.8g | Protein: 20g | Fiber: 0.5g

Ingredients

- 1/4 cup almond milk (or water)
- 6 large eggs
- 1/4 cup raw onions, finely chopped (1 ounce)
- 1 1/4 cup heavy cream
- 2 cups shredded cheddar cheese (8 ounces)
- 1/4 tsp salt
- 6 oz bite-sized broccoli florets (steamed until crisp-tender)
- 1/4 tsp white pepper
- 4 slices cooked bacon, crumbled

Method

1. Preheat oven to 350°F.
2. Spray a baking spry on a 10" plate.
3. Cook the bacon and crumble it.
4. Now, steam broccoli. And dice onions.
5. Layer the ingredients on a quiche plate: 1/3 each of the broccoli, onion, 1/4 of the cheese, and bacon.
6. Add the almond milk, heavy cream, salt, eggs, and pepper to a medium bowl and use a hand mixer to beat it.
7. Then, take custard and pour over the quiche ingredients.
8. Bake it for 40 minutes to brown the top.
9. Serve.

7.10 Avocado Chicken Salad

Servings: 3 | Time: 15 mins | Difficulty: Easy
Nutrients per serving: Calories: 267 kcal | Fat: 20g | Carbohydrates: 4g | Protein: 19g | Fiber: 1g

Ingredients

- 1 medium Hass Avocado, mashed
- 2 cups poached chicken diced (10 oz)
- 1/3 cup celery, finely diced (1 large rib)
- 2 tbsp cilantro, finely chopped
- salt and pepper to taste
- 2 tbsp red onion or scallion, minced
- 1 tbsp fresh lemon juice (or lime juice)
- 2 tbsp avocado oil (or your favorite)

Method

1. Prepare the onion, celery, and cilantro in a bowl.
2. Take diced chicken and vegetables in the bowl.
3. Cut avocado in half.
4. Then scoop the flesh from the avocado.
5. Use a fork to mash it and turn it to smoot and creamy texture.
6. Take oil and lemon juice and stir the ingredients.
7. Add all ingredients together in a bowl and mix by stirring.
8. Serve with lettuce.

7.11 Low Carb Chicken Soup

Servings: 6 | Time: 30 mins | Difficulty: Easy

Nutrients per serving: Calories: 274 kcal I Fat: 15g I Carbohydrates: 8g I Protein: 26g I Fiber: 2g

Ingredients

- 6 cups bone broth
- 2 cups cooked chicken, diced

Vegetable Base

- 1 cup celery, sliced
- 4 tbsp butter, avocado oil, or olive oil
- 1/2 cup onion, diced
- 1 large garlic clove, sliced
- 8 ounces celery root, cubed
- 1 whole bay leaf
- 1/3 cup carrot
- 2 tsp chicken base
- 1 tsp lemon zest
- 2 tsp lemon juice mixed with water
- salt and pepper to taste
- 1 tbsp garlic herb seasoning blend
- 1/4 cup dry white wine

Method

1. Take diced chicken.
2. Take vegetables. Peel and cut them.
3. Add butter, lemon zest, bay leaf, and vegetables in a quart pot on medium heat.
4. Stir continuously to coat everything.
5. Add chicken base, wine, and garlic herb blend after reducing the heat to medium.
6. Cook vegetables for about 3-4 minutes until they turn brown.
7. Boil the chicken broth, then simmer the vegetables over reduced heat until they become tender. Add the chicken broth and bring it to just under a boil.
8. Add pepper and salt to taste.

7.12 Sweet and Sour German Green Beans with Bacon and Onions

Servings: 4 I Time: 18 mins I Difficulty: Easy
Nutrients per serving: Calories: 166 kcal I Fat: 11g I Carbohydrates: 8g I Protein: 9g I Fiber: 4g

Ingredients

- 4 slices bacon, diced
- 2 cups green beans
- 2 tbsp apple cider vinegar
- 1/4 cup onion, finely chopped
- 1 tbsp Low carb brown sugar
- 2 tbsp water
- 1 tsp wholegrain mustard
- 1/4 tsp salt

Method

1. Take trimmed beans, chopped onions, and diced bacon.
2. Turn beans tender by cooking.
3. Cook bacon in a pan over medium heat for 4 minutes.
4. Sauté the onions.
5. Add the Sukrin Gold, water, onions, and cider vinegar to the bacon.
6. Take a pan and put grain mustard in it.
7. At last, take green beans and coat by stirring at heat thoroughly.
8. Use pepper and salt to taste.

7.13 Thai Chicken Satay with Peanut Sauce

Servings: 4 I Time: 35 mins I Difficulty: Easy
Nutrients per serving: Calories: 279 kcal I Fat: 15g I Carbohydrates: 4g I Protein: 30g I Fiber: 1g

Ingredients

- 2 cups chicken tenders

Chicken Satay Marinade

- 1 tbsp Hot Madras Curry Powder
- 1/3 cup full fat coconut milk from a can
- 1/4 cup chopped fresh cilantro (optional)
- 1/2 tsp ground coriander
- 2 tbsp Red Boat Fish Sauce (optional)
- 2 tbsp Low carb brown sugar

Peanut Sauce

- 1/3 cup full fat coconut milk from a can
- 1 tsp soy sauce
- 1/4 cup smooth peanut/almond butter
- 1-2 tsp chile-garlic sauce
- 1 tbsp Low carb brown sugar
- 1/2 tsp Thai Red Curry Paste

Extras

- soaked bamboo skewers
- lime wedges
- chopped fresh cilantro

Method

1. take warm water and soak the skewers in it.
2. Cut the chicken in half and place it in zip-lock bags.
3. Take the satay marinade in a bowl and put a chicken in it to coat all sides of the chicken.
4. Marinate overnight or for 30 minutes.
5. Warm peanut butter in a small bowl.
6. Whisk in the chile-garlic sauce, Sukrin Gold, Thai curry paste, and soy sauce.
7. Then, add coconut milk slowly.
8. Season it to taste.
9. Refrigerate it.
10. Thread the chicken tenders onto the bamboo skewers.
11. Cook the chicken on the grill, either indoor or outdoor.
12. Garnish it with fresh cilantro (chopped).
13. Serve with the peanut sauce and a lime wedge.

7.14 Fajita Hasselback Chicken

Servings: 4 I Time: 5 mins I Difficulty: Easy
Nutrients per serving: Calories: 368 kcal I Fat: 11g I Carbohydrates: 9g I Protein: 53g I Fiber: 1g

Ingredients

- ½ red bell pepper, diced
- 4 chicken breasts
- ½ yellow bell pepper, diced
- ½ onion, diced
- 2 Tbsps. fajita spice mix
- ½ cup cheddar cheese (50 g), grated
- 3 Tbsps. salsa
- ½ green pepper, diced

Method

1. Take the oven to 350°F.
2. Cut and slice the chicken but not deep enough to keep the bottom intact.
3. Take fajita mix, and mix the cooked onions and pepper on medium heat.
4. Take salsa and stir in the mixture. Use cheese to sprinkle over it.
5. Melt the cheese and mix all ingredients.
6. Fill chicken slices with 1 tbsp of mixture.
7. Bake the chicken in the oven for 20 minutes, and juice run through it.

7.15 Chicken Spinach Blueberry Salad with Parmesan Cheese

Servings: 2 I Time: 20 mins I Difficulty: Easy

Nutrients per serving: Calories: 519 kcal I Fat: 38g I Carbohydrates: 10g I Protein: 35g I Fiber: 4g

Ingredients

Chicken Spinach Blueberry Salad

- 6 cups baby spinach (170 g)
- 8 ounces chicken tenders or chicken breast
- 4 cups fresh blueberries
- Two slices of red onion (paper-thin)
- 2 cups shaved Parmesan cheese
- 1 cup sliced almonds (toasted or raw)

Balsamic Dressing

- 1 tbsp red wine vinegar
- 1/4 cup extra light olive oil
- 1 tbsp balsamic vinegar
- 2 tsp minced red onion
- 1/2 tsp dijon mustard
- 1 tbsp water
- 1 pinch each salt and pepper
- 1/8 tsp dried thyme
- 1/2 tsp low carb sugar

Method

1. Grill the chicken thoroughly. And cut it into small pieces.
2. Take almonds, and minced the onions, and make the dressing (balsamic).
3. Brown the almonds slightly in a frying pan. Cool it after removing it from the pan.
4. Add all ingredients of the dressing and blend them well with a stick blender.
5. Take spinach and arrange it evenly on two plates.

7.16 Keto Tuna Melt

Servings: 4 I Time: 15 mins I Difficulty: Easy
Nutrients per serving: Calories: 227 kcal I Fat: 14g I Carbohydrates: 3g I Protein: 21g I Fiber: 1g

Ingredients

- 3 Tbsps. Mayonnaise
- 1.5 cups Canned Tuna
- ¼ cup Sliced celery
- 1 Tbsp. Finely diced red onion
- 4 slices Cheddar Cheese
- 2 Tbsps. Dill pickle relish
- ¼ Tsp. Salt
- 4 Tomato slices from a large tomato

Method

1. Take a bowl. Add and stir mayonnaise, tuna, celery, red onion, and dill relish.
2. Sprinkle some salt on the tomato slices placed on a baking sheet.
3. Then, on each slice, add 1/4 of the tuna mixture.
4. Take slices of cheese to top each tomato slice.
5. Cook until cheese melts. It should take about 3-5 minutes.
6. Serve

7.17 Cheesy Baked Zucchini Casserole

Servings: 6 I Time: 45 mins I Difficulty: Easy
Nutrients per serving: Calories: 275 kcal I Fat: 21g I Carbohydrates: 7g I Protein: 13g I Fiber: 1g

Ingredients

- 2 Tbsps. Butter
- 4.5 cups (approximately) zucchini, large, sliced 1/4 inch thick
- 1/2 cups Onion, diced
- 1 Tsp. Salt
- 1/2 cups Parmesan Cheese, grated and divided

- ½ cup Heavy Cream
- 2 cloves garlic, minced
- 1/2 cups Gruyere Cheese, grated and divided

Method

1. Heat the oven to 450°F.
2. Prepare and pace the salted zucchini slices on a paper towel.
3. Let sit each side for 15 minutes each.
4. Put zucchini slices on a dish.
5. Take a skillet and heat the butter to melt it.
6. Then add onion and garlic to cook them for 3 minutes and 2 minutes, respectively.
7. Add the heavy cream while stirring in a pan.
8. Add Gruyere cheese and Parmesan cheese and melt the cheese while stirring.
9. Add the sauce (cheese) to the zucchini.
10. Bake zucchini with parmesan and Gruyere for 5 minutes by covering the casserole dish with a foil. Remove it when tender.
11. Serve.

7.18 Mexican Keto Meatballs

Servings: 15 meatballs I Time: 50 mins I Difficulty: Easy
Nutrients per serving (2 meatballs): Calories: 220 kcal I Fat: 18g I Carbohydrates: 2g I Protein: 14g I Fiber: 2g

Ingredients

- 2 Tbsps. Chili Powder
- 2 Tsps. Salt
- 2 Tbsps. Cumin
- 2 cups Ground Beef
- 1/4 cup Jalapenos, finely diced
- 1 Egg
- 85 g Cheddar Cheese, shredded

Method

1. Take oven to 400°F.
2. Take a large bowl and mix every ingredient in it.
3. Bake balls of 2-inch size after rolling meat in balls like shape.
4. For 25-30 minutes, bake them on a sheet (baking).

7.19 Meat Lovers' Keto Stuffed Peppers

Servings: 6 I Time: 1 hr 10 mins I Difficulty: Easy
Nutrients per serving: Calories: 284 kcal I Fat: 22g I Carbohydrates: 6g I Protein: 16g I Fiber: 2g

Ingredients

- 225 g Mozzarella cheese
- 50 g Pepperoni small pieces
- 3 Bell peppers, any color
- ¾ cup Pasta sauce
- Cooked 175 g Italian sausage

Method

1. Heat oven to 400°F.
2. Cut pepper and place them on the dish after removing seeds in them.
3. On the bottom side of each pepper, put 1 tbsp. Sauce.
4. Use pepperoni pieces and 30 g of Italian sausage as a topping.
5. Put some mozzarella.
6. Put sauce, pepperoni, and mozzarella again as the topping. Make sure to fill pepper with enough mozzarella.
7. Bake peppers in the oven for 40 minutes until cheese is · melted.

7.20 Inst. Pot Short Ribs

Servings: 4 I Time: 2 hrs 30 mins I Difficulty: Easy

Nutrients per serving: Calories: 363 kcal I Fat: 21g I Carbohydrates: 4g I Protein: 33g I Fiber: 1g

Ingredients

- Kosher salt
- 4 cups Short Ribs
- 1 Tbsp. Olive Oil
- Pepper
- 2 sprigs Rosemary
- 2 Bay Leaves
- 1 Onion, cut into quarters
- 4 sprigs thyme
- 3 large Carrots, cut into quarters
- 2-4 cups Beef Broth
- ½ cup Red Wine

Method

1. Put pepper and salt on all sides of the ribs.
2. Add olive oil 1 tbsp. in the pot on sauté setting.
3. Brown sides of ribs, it takes 2 minutes for each side.
4. Set aside beef ribs.
5. Cook onions and carrots in the pot for 5 minutes.
6. Cook with red wine.
7. Put herbs wrapped in cheesecloth with onions and carrots in a pressure cooker.
8. Now, Put beef ribs in the pot.
9. Take out the broth in another pot.
10. For 1.5 hours, cook everything in a pressure cooker on high pressure.
11. When done, release the pressure.
12. Strain vegetables and beef in a bowl and put away herbs and vegetables.
13. Serve.

7.21 Cheesy Artichoke Chicken Bake

Servings: 8 I Time: 1 hr. I Difficulty: Easy
Nutrients per serving: Calories: 399 kcal I Fat: 27g I Carbohydrates: 3g I Protein: 34g I Fiber: 1g

Ingredients

- 6 slices bacon, chopped and cooked
- 200 g Quartered artichoke hearts,
- 4 cups chicken breasts
- 1/4 c Mayonnaise
- 150 g Smoked Gouda
- 30 g Fresh baby spinach, chopped
- 1/2 Tsp. Onion powder
- 60 g Cream cheese, softened
- 85 g Havarti or Gruyere
- 1 Tsp. Garlic powder

Method

1. Heat the oven to 400°F.
2. Cut each chicken breast horizontally into two slices.
3. Stir all ingredients together except chicken.
4. Put the chicken in an oiled dish and use salt to sprinkle over it.
5. Then, spread cheese on chicken.
6. Put 4 breasts on cheese mixture.
7. Bake in the oven for 30 minutes by covering with foil.
8. Keep cooking until the chicken is cooked thoroughly.

7.22 Keto Club Sandwich

Servings: 2 I Time: 10 mins I Difficulty: Easy
Nutrients per serving: Calories: 413 kcal I Fat: 28g I Carbohydrates: 5g I Protein: 35g I Fiber: 1g

Ingredients

- 1 Tbsp. Mayonnaise
- 60 g Cheddar Cheese sliced
- 6 Iceberg lettuce leaves
- 180 g Deli Turkey sliced
- 2 slices Cooked Bacon
- 150 g Tomato slice
- 120 g Deli Ham sliced

Method

1. Take out the core of iceberg lettuce.
2. Peel off lettuce leaves.
3. Spread mayonnaise on top of the two lettuce leaves.
4. Put 30 g of cheese on the lettuce slice and use the deli ham slice as topping on leaves.
5. Similarly, use two lettuce leaves to spread over the ham with mayonnaise. Top with sliced tomato, the cooked bacon, sliced deli turkey, and cheese.
6. Again, use mayonnaise on turkey and put lettuce leaves on it.
7. Cut in 4 pieces and put a toothpick in each piece.

7.23 Keto Antipasto Salad

Servings: 8 I Time: 1 day 25 mins I Difficulty: Easy
Nutrients per serving: Calories: 444 kcal I Fat: 36g I Carbohydrates: 10g I Protein: 19g I Fiber: 4g

Ingredients

- 250 g Prosciutto
- 1 head Cauliflower
- 250 g Genoa Salami
- 150 g Roasted red peppers
- 5-6 leaves Fresh Basil
- 90 g Pepperoncini
- 90 g Black olives
- 240 g Fresh mozzarella
- 410 g Artichoke Heart quatres, drained

DRESSING:

- 2 Tsp. Garlic powder
- 1 cup Olive oil
- 2 Tsp. Dried oregano
- 1/2 cup Red wine vinegar
- 3/4 Tsp. Salt
- 1 Tsp. Onion powder
- 2 Tsp. Lemon juice
- 1/2 Tsp. Pepper

Method

1. Whisk together all the dressing ingredients in a small cup.
2. Cut cauliflower into bite-sized florets and position them with about 1 inch of water in a pot. Place the lid on the pot and bring the cauliflower to a boil for 3-5 minutes, steaming until slightly tender.
3. Drain and pat the cauliflower and rinse. Place in a gallon-size resealable bag, and pour half of the dressing over it. Place it in the refrigerator for at least 1 hour or overnight to marinate.
4. Toss all the ingredients together the next day and pour the rest of the dressing over the antipasto salad.
5. Chill until it's ready for serving.

7.24 Zucchini Soup

Servings: 8 I Time: 30 mins I Difficulty: Easy
Nutrients per serving: Calories: 64 kcal I Fat: 3g I Carbohydrates: 6g I Protein: 2g I Fiber: 1g

Ingredients

- 800 g Zucchini
- ¼ Tsp. Pepper
- 2 cloves Garlic
- ¼ cup Heavy cream
- 210 g sliced onion

- ½ Tsps. Kosher salt
- 400 g Chicken Broth

Method
1. Place a lid on it and add the onion, garlic cloves, chicken broth, and zucchini to a large pot. Bring to a boil, then reduce heat to medium and let it simmer, occasionally stirring, for 20 minutes.
2. Remove the pot from the heat until the zucchini is incredibly soft and use an immersion blender to combine it into a smooth puree.
3. Using the puree to add salt and pepper and then mix in the heavy cream.
4. Serving and loving!

7.25 Grilled Shrimp Citrus Marinated

Servings: 8 shrimp I Time: 30 mins I Difficulty: Easy
Nutrients per serving: Calories: 244 kcal I Fat: 3g I Carbohydrates: 4g I Protein: 46g

Ingredients
- 2 Tbsp. Orange zest
- 1 cup Olive oil
- 900 g Medium - Large shrimp
- 2 Tbsp. Lime zest
- 1/2 cup Orange Juice
- 2 Tbsp. Lemon zest
- 1/2 cup Lime juice
- 1/2 cup Lemon juice
- 1/2 Tsp. Ginger, grated
- 1/2 Tsp. Pepper
- 1/4 cup Cilantro
- 3 Tbsps. Garlic, minced
- 1/4 cup Parsley
- 1 Tsp. Salt

Method
1. Combine the olive oil, zest, orange juice, lemon and lime juice, minced garlic, parsley, ginger, salt, cilantro, and pepper in a large cup. Together, whisk.
2. Set to the side of 1/2 cup of the marinade.
3. In a large freezer bag or airtight tub, put the shrimp and pour the leftover marinade on them. To coat, toss the shrimp and seal them in a jar or bag and put them in the refrigerator for 30 minutes - 1 hour to marinate.
4. Take it out of the jar once the shrimp is marinated, avoiding any excess marinade when you put the shrimp on skewers. Dispose of the remaining marinade after skewering all the shrimp.
5. Grill each side for 2-3 minutes or until the shrimp is pink and cooked.
6. Until serving, drizzle the unused marinade over the cooked shrimp (no raw shrimp should have touched the marinade).

7.26 Taco Zucchini Boats

Servings: 8 I Time: 40 mins I Difficulty: Easy
Nutrients per serving: Calories: 242 kcal I Fat: 16g I Carbohydrates: 6g I Protein: 19g I Fiber: 1g

Ingredients
- 2 cups Ground beef
- 4 Zucchini
- 1 Tbsp. Chili Powder
- 1/4 cup Water
- 1/2 cup Bell Peppers, mixed Red & Yellow
- 1/2 Tsp. Salt
- 2 Tsps. Cumin
- 1/2 cup Salsa
- 240 g Cheddar cheese, shredded

Method
1. Preheat the oven to 400°F.
2. Have your zucchini ready by cutting off the end of the stem.
3. Place the zucchini boats and sprinkle a small amount of salt over them in a greased baking dish.
4. Brown the ground beef in a skillet over medium heat.
5. Connect the ground beef to the chili powder, bell peppers, salt, cumin, and 1/4 cup of water. Keep cooking until the vegetables are softened and water is absorbed.
6. Fill each zucchini vessel with the beef and vegetable mixture until the beef mixture is ready.
7. Top the vessels with zucchini and cheddar cheese.
8. Bake for 20 minutes or until you have softened the zucchini and melted the cheese.
9. Before serving, pour salsa over the boats.

7.27 Keto Buffalo Chicken Cauliflower Casserole

Servings: 8 I Time: 45 mins I Difficulty: Easy
Nutrients per serving: Calories: 372 kcal I Fat: 30g I Carbohydrates: 5g I Protein: 19g I Fiber: 1g

Ingredients
- ⅓ cup Frank's Red-Hot Sauce
- 520 g Cauliflower
- ¼ cup Ranch dressing
- 1 cup Celery, chopped
- 2 Eggs
- 250 g Cream Cheese, softened
- 240 g Cheddar cheese
- 350 g Chicken

Method
1. Preheat the oven to 350°F.
2. Remove the core from the head of your cauliflower and cut into bite-sized pieces.
3. By sticking it in boiling water for 3 minutes or steaming in the microwave until it is fork-tender, blanch the cauliflower. Dry and set aside.
4. Stir the hot sauce, ranch dressing, cream cheese, and eggs together in a big bowl.
5. To the cream cheese mixture, add the cauliflower, 4 ounces of cheddar cheese, chicken, and celery and toss until well coated.
6. Pour the remaining cheddar cheese into an 11x7 inch casserole dish and sprinkle with it.
7. Bake for 30 minutes or until the cheese is melted and bubbly and the cauliflower is cooked.

7.28 Creamy Asparagus Soup

Servings: 8 I Time: 30 mins I Difficulty: Easy
Nutrients per serving: Calories: 110 kcal I Fat: 8g I Carbohydrates: 6g I Protein: 3g I Fiber: 2g

Ingredients
- 2 Tbsps. Butter
- 900 g Asparagus, trimmed
- 5 cups Chicken broth
- 1 Onion, thinly sliced
- 1-2 Tbsps. Lemon juice
- Salt and pepper to taste
- 1/2 cup Heavy Cream

Method
1. Break the asparagus and roughly chop the onion into 1-inch pieces.
2. Heat a medium pot over medium-high heat with butter on the burner.
3. Add the onion and asparagus and cook for 2 minutes.
4. Add the broth and cover it with a lid, then boil.

5. Reduce it to a simmer once it reaches a boil and cook for 20 minutes or until the vegetables are extremely tender.
6. Remove the pot from the heat and puree the contents using a stick blender until it's smooth.
7. Stir the cream in. Note: At this stage, you should add more broth until it has the perfect consistency, if the soup is thicker than you prefer.
8. Connect the lemon juice and, to taste, salt and pepper.

7.29 Low Carb Sausage And Kale Soup

Servings: 6 I Time: 25 mins I Difficulty: Easy
Nutrients per serving: Calories: 164 kcal I Fat: 3g I Carbohydrates: 9g I Protein: 20g I Fiber: 3g

Ingredients
- 450 g Italian turkey sausage, sliced
- 960 g Chicken broth
- 1/2 cup Onion, diced
- 240 g Kale, stem removed
- 450 g Diced tomatoes

Method
1. Set the Inst. Pot to sauté the sausage.
2. Turn off the Inst. Pot and add to the pot the onions, diced tomatoes, and chicken broth.
3. Fasten the cap and shut the steam valve on your Inst. Pot or pressure cooker. Set to manual, high energy, 15 minutes.
4. While the soup heats, put the chopped kale in a microwave dish with about 1/2 a cup of water.
5. After the time is up, let the pressure cooker sit for about 10 minutes and then carefully open the valve to release the rest of the steam.
6. Open the lid and add kale to your pressure cooker before serving.

7.30 One Pot Low Carb Sausage And Riced Veggies

Servings: 4 I Time: 20 mins I Difficulty: Easy
Nutrients per serving: Calories: 660 kcal I Fat: 60g I Carbohydrates: 7g I Protein: 13g I Fiber: 7g

Ingredients
- 120 g Onion
- 2 tbsp Olive oil
- 1.5 c Kale
- Salt and pepper to taste
- 1 bag Green Giant Riced Cauliflower & Sweet Potato
- 1/4 c Goat cheese
- 4 cups Italian sausage

Method
1. Apply the olive oil and the Italian sausage to a skillet over medium-high heat. For 5 minutes, cook.
2. Add the diced onions to the pan and sauté them for another 5 minutes with the Italian sausage or until the sausage is cooked.
3. Add the rice and vegetables and kale to cook for 5 minutes or until the kale and the riced veggies are tender and warmed up.
4. To taste, apply salt and pepper.
5. Serve and sprinkle with some goat's crumbled cheese.

7.31 Sriracha Grilled Leg Of Lamb

Servings: 10 I Time: 1 hr 10 mins I Difficulty: Easy
Nutrients per serving: Calories: 337 kcal I Fat: 23g I Carbohydrates: 2g I Protein: 32g

Ingredients
- 2 cloves Garlic
- 5 cups Leg of Lamb
- 1 tsp Paprika
- 2 Tbsp Sriracha
- 1/2 c Mayonnaise
- 1 tsp Salt

Method
1. In a cup, combine salt, paprika, mayonnaise, garlic, and Sriracha, then dump into a freezer bag for a gallon.
2. In the freezer bag, add a leg of lamb and rub it with the marinade. Seal the bag and put it in the refrigerator for at least 30 minutes, up to 4 hours, to marinate.
3. Remove the lamb from the bag and put it on a grill that is 400 °F F. Sear for 5 minutes on either side.
4. Close the grill lid and cook for 30-40 minutes or until the inside temperature of the lamb reaches 130 °F F.
5. Take it off the grill and let it rest for 10 minutes. Slice and serve.

7.32 Tandoori Grilled Lamb Chops

Servings: 2 I Time: 51 mins I Difficulty: Easy
Nutrients per serving: Calories: 475 kcal I Fat: 24g I Carbohydrates: 15g I Protein: 59g I Fiber: 2g

Ingredients
- 1 1/2 tbsp Garam masala
- 6 Lamb chops
- 3/4 c Greek yogurt
- 3 Garlic cloves, minced
- 2 tbsp Lemon juice
- 1 tbsp Turmeric
- 1 tsp Ginger, minced
- 1 tsp Salt
- ¼ tsp Cayenne Pepper
- 2 tsp Paprika

Method
1. Combine the garlic, mayonnaise, paprika, salt, and Sriracha in a cup, then pour a gallon in a freezer bag.
2. Rub a lamb leg with the marinade. Put it in the bag and refrigerate for 0.5-4 hours.
3. Remove the lamb from the bag and place it on a 400°F grill.
4. Sear on either side for 5 minutes.
5. Close and cook the grill lid for 30-40 minutes or until the lamb's inside temperature reaches 130°F.
6. Take it off the grill and leave for 10 minutes to rest. Slicing and serving.

7.33 Low Carb Meatball And Vegetable Casserole

Servings: 4 I Time: 30 mins I Difficulty: Easy
Nutrients per serving: Calories: 474 kcal I Fat: 39g I Carbohydrates: 10g I Protein: 25g I Fiber: 2g

Ingredients
- 1 c Eggplant
- 16 Cooked Perfect Fresh Meatballs
- 2 c Bell peppers
- 1 c Zucchini
- 1 c Squash
- 2 tbsp Olive oil
- ½ c Red onion, (diced)
- 240 g Fresh mozzarella
- 1 c Low carb pasta sauce
- Salt and pepper to taste

Method
1. In a wide bowl, put the diced vegetables and toss them in olive oil.
2. To taste, apply salt and pepper.

3. Spread low carb pasta sauce in a casserole dish and then add vegetables to spread them out evenly.
4. Nestle meatballs with vegetables and top with fresh mozzarella bites.
5. Cover the dish with foil and cook for 20 minutes in the oven at 350 ° F or until the vegetables are tender.

7.34 Jalapeno Chicken And Broccoli Casserole

Servings: 6 I Time: 45 mins I Difficulty: Easy
Nutrients per serving: Calories: 387 kcal I Fat: 27g I Carbohydrates: 7g I Protein: 31g I Fiber: 1g

Ingredients
- 240 g Cream cheese, softened
- 4-5 cups Chicken breast, cubed
- ½ c Heavy cream
- ½ c Parmesan, shredded
- 1 tsp Garlic powder
- 2 c fresh broccoli florets
- 1 tsp Onion powder
- 1 c Mozzarella, shredded
- ½ tsp Pepper
- ½ tsp Salt
- 1 Jalapeno, seeded & diced

Method
1. In a big bowl, add the heavy cream, garlic powder, onion powder, cream cheese, salt and pepper.
2. Add the jalapenos diced and stir until mixed.
3. To the cheese mixture, add the cubed chicken and fold them together until the chicken is covered in the cheese.
4. Spoon into a 13x9-inch baking dish that is greased.
5. Florets of Nestle broccoli into the chicken.
6. Mozzarella and Parmesan cheese topping.
7. Cover and bake for 25 mins at 400°F. Uncover and bake for an extra 5 minutes.

7.35 Bacon Cheddar Egg Salad

Servings: 6 I Time: 15 mins I Difficulty: Easy
Nutrients per serving: Calories: 458 kcal I Fat: 42g I Carbohydrates: 1g I Protein: 15g

Ingredients
- Salt to taste
- 12 Hard-boiled eggs
- 1/2 cup Bacon, diced
- 1/2 cup Cheddar cheese, shredded and diced
- 1 Tbsp. Mustard
- 1 cup Mayonnaise

Method
1. Take a large bowl and add chopped boiled eggs.
2. Add mustard and mayonnaise, stir it.
3. Add cheddar and bacon, fold mixture together.
4. Salt to taste.

7.36 Sheet Pan Lemon Chicken And Asparagus

Servings: 4 I Time: 25 mins I Difficulty: Easy
Nutrients per serving: Calories: 272 kcal I Fat: 4g I Carbohydrates: 5g I Protein: 41g I Fiber: 2g

Ingredients
- 2 fresh lemons, sliced
- 5 ½ cups Chicken tenders
- 1 tsp Kosher salt
- 1 bunch Asparagus
- Olive oil
- 60 g Parmesan, shaved
- 2-3 Tbsp Lemon Pepper

Method
1. Place the slices on a oiled baking sheet and slice the lemons into circles.
2. Place the tender asparagus and chicken over the lemon slices.
3. Drizzle it all with olive oil and sprinkle it with salt.
4. Using lemon pepper to sprinkle the chicken tenders.
5. Bake for 15-20 minutes at 425 °F or until the chicken is fully cooked.
6. Shaved Parmesan garnish.

7.37 Curried Chicken Salad

Servings: 6 I Time: 20 mins I Difficulty: Easy
Nutrients per serving: Calories: 422 kcal I Fat: 33g I Carbohydrates: 6g I Protein: 29g I Fiber: 3g

Ingredients
- 1-2 tsp Curry Powder
- 5 ½ cups Chicken Breast
- 1/2 c Red Bell Pepper
- Salt to taste
- 1 c Almonds
- 3/4 c Mayonnaise

CURRY POWDER
- 2 Tbsp Ground Cumin
- 2 Tbsp Ground Cardamom
- 1/4 tsp Cayenne
- 1 Tbsp Ground Turmeric
- 1 Tbsp Dry Mustard
- 2 Tbsp Ground Coriander

Method
1. Mix all the curry powder spices and store them in an airtight jar.
2. Place in a wide bowl the sliced, cooked chicken breast and add the mayonnaise and the 1 Tsp. Curry powder, with a pinch of salt.
3. Thoroughly mix and taste. Until you are pleased with the taste, continue adding curry powder and salt.
4. Gently fold in and add the sliced almonds and diced red bell pepper.
5. Store until ready to eat in the refrigerator.

7.38 Memphis BBQ Sausage And Cheese Platter

Servings: 8 I Time: 35 mins I Difficulty: Easy
Nutrients per serving: Calories: 660 kcal I Fat: 60g I Carbohydrates: 7g I Protein: 13g I Fiber: 7g

Ingredients
- 4 Tbsps. Stubb's Original BBQ Sauce
- 240 g Cheddar Cheese
- 10 Dill Pickles
- 1 Jar Pepperoncinis
- 2 cups Smoked Sausage
- 240 g Pepper Jack Cheese

Method
1. Put the sausage on the heated grill and baste it with the Original BBQ Sauce.
2. Put sausage on both sides and let it cook for about 10 minutes.
3. Flip the sausage over when it is ready and proceed to cook.
4. From the grill, detach the sausage and cut it into slices.
5. Put the pepperoncini, pickles, cheese, and some more Stubb's sauce on a plate for dipping.

7.39 Keto Fideo

Servings: 4 | Time: 20 mins | Difficulty: Easy
Nutrients per serving: Calories: 409 kcal | Fat: 29g | Carbohydrates: 7g | Protein: 29g | Fiber: 4g

Ingredients

- 2 cups ground beef (or venison)
- 1/2 cup diced onion
- 1 tsp. salt
- 2 Tbsp. chili powder
- 3/4 cup chicken stock or bone broth
- 1 package of Palmini linguini, drained and rinsed
- 2 Tbsp. grated parmesan
- 1/3 cup grated mild cheddar
- 1 tsp. garlic powder

Method

1. Start to brown the ground meat in a skillet over medium-high heat and use salt to season it.
2. Cook until meat is browned and onions become translucent.
3. First put palming drain and cook for 2 minutes then add chili and garlic and again cook for 1 minute.
4. Cook for another 3 minutes and add cheese while stirring.
5. Serve.

7.40 Loaded Baked "Potato" Soup

Servings: 5 | Time: 17 mins | Difficulty: Easy
Nutrients per serving: Calories: 204.97 kcal | Fat: 17.1g | Carbohydrates: 10.62g | Protein: 3.45g | Fiber: 3.26g

Ingredients

- 1/4 cup chopped onion
- 3 Tbsp. Butter
- 340 g bag frozen cauliflower
- 2 cups medium turnips
- 1 tsp. Salt
- 1 rib celery cut into 1" pieces
- 2 1/3 cups chicken broth
- 1/2 tsp. Garlic powder
- Crispy bacon, crumbled
- 1/2 cup heavy cream
- Sliced scallions or green onion
- Cheddar cheese
- 2 Tbsp. Sour cream

Method

1. Cook according to package instructions or steam the cauliflower until tender.
2. In a medium saucepan over medium heat, melt the butter. Add the onions, diced celery and turnips. Season with garlic powder and salt and sauté until onions are translucent and turnips start to gather a little golden brown color and start to soften, around 7-10 minutes, over medium heat. Connect the cauliflower and continue cooking for 2-3 more minutes.
3. Add the chicken stock to the vegetables and bring to a boil and reduce the heat for 5-7 minutes or until the turnips are fork-tender.
4. Pour the vegetable and stock mixture into the mixer carefully. Apply the milk and sour cream and mix until creamy and smooth. This is best achieved in a high-powered blender, but it can also work well in a conventional blender or immersion blender, although the texture might not be as smooth. When mixing hot liquids, use care and cover the top of the mixer with a towel. If you want a thinner soup, use some extra broth!
5. If needed, taste and re-season with salt and pepper. Top and enjoy with bacon, cheese and green onion!

7.41 Texas Style Keto Venison Chili

Servings: 6 | Time: 1 hr | Difficulty: Easy
Nutrients per serving: Calories: 360 kcal | Fat: 19g | Carbohydrates: 10g | Protein: 36g | Fiber: 4g

Ingredients

- 3 1/3 cups ground venison or beef
- 3 Tbsps. Lard or bacon fat
- 1 bell pepper chopped
- 1/2 medium onion chopped
- 4 cloves garlic minced
- 3 Tsps. Garlic powder
- 1 poblano pepper seeded and chopped
- 1 Tbsp. Pepper
- 1 Tsp. paprika
- 2 Tbsps. Kosher salt
- 400 g cans diced tomato
- 2 Tbsps. chili powder
- 250 ml bottle low carb beer
- Cups of water
- 3 Tbsps. tomato paste
- 1/2 Tbsp. cumin

Method

In a large pot add lard, fat or oil and ground meat. Season meat with 1 Tbsp kosher salt, 1/2Tbsp pepper and 2 tsp garlic powder. Cook ground meat on medium high to high heat until brown and caramelized. This will give amazing depth of flawor to the chili do don't rush this step!

Turn heat down to medium high and add onion, peppers and garlic and cookj for 5-7 minutes or until veggies start to soften. The veggies will help pick up all browned meat bits and help deglaze the pan.

Add tomatoes, tomato paste, beer, water, and remaining seasonings.

Cover and simmer on low for about 30 minutes, stirring occasionally. Remove lid and simmer for another hour more, until meat is tender and the chili is your uncovered. If you like a thinner chili, just leave the cover on. The longer the chili simmers the more tender and decadent it gets...I have let is sit on the stove on a low simmer all afternoon!

Serve uo loaded with topping and alongside your favorite low carb corn bread !

7.42 Keto Mexican Street Cauliflower Salad

Servings: 12 | Time: 40 mins | Difficulty: Easy
Nutrients per serving: Calories: 152 kcal | Fat: 13g | Carbohydrates: 7g | Protein: 4g | Fiber: 2g

Ingredients

- 1 ½ tsp. salt
- 2 large heads fresh cauliflower cut into small florets
- 1/4 cup diced purple onion
- 1 tsp. garlic powder
- 4 Tbsp. avocado oil
- 2 Tbsp. chopped cilantro
- 1 cup cherry or grape tomatoes, halved
- 1 jalapeno
- ½ tsp. pepper
- 1/2 cup diced bell pepper

For the Dressing:

- 1/2 cup sour cream

- 1 Tbsp. fresh lime juice
- ¼ cup mayonnaise your favorite
- 1/4 tsp. paprika
- 1/3 cup + 2 Tbsp. crumbled Cotija cheese
- 1/2 tsp. cumin
- ¼ tsp. salt
- 2-3 cloves garlic finely minced
- 1/2 tsp. chili powder

Method

1. Preheat to 425°F the oven. Using the salt, avocado oil, pepper and garlic powder to toss the florets and put the cauliflower florets on a lined sheet tray. For 20-25 minutes or until tender, roast at 425°F.
2. Combine the cooled cauliflower, jalapeno, bell pepper, cabbage, tomatoes and coriander in a broad bowl and shake.
3. Stir the mayo, sour cream, and the next 7 ingredients together. Combine the vegetables with the dressing and gently toss to cover them. You cannot need any of the dressing, depending on the size of the cauliflower heads. As needed, wear. In a serving dish, spoon the salad and finish with more cheese and minced cilantro. Immediately serve. Cover and chill before served, to serve afterwards.

7.43 Keto Mexican Spaghetti Casserole

Servings: 8 I Time: 1 hr I Difficulty: Easy
Nutrients per serving: Calories: 365 kcal I Fat: 27 I Carbohydrates: 9g I Protein: 22g I Fiber: 2g

Ingredients

- 2 Tbsp. tomato paste
- 2 Tbsp. chili powder
- 2 oz. cream cheese softened
- 1/3 cup diced bell pepper
- 1/2 tsp. cumin
- 1/2 cup diced onion
- 1 spaghetti squash about 10.8 cups or 4 cups cooked
- 1 cup water
- 1 1/2 cups shredded medium cheddar divided
- 1 ½ tsp. salt divided
- 1 ½ tsp. garlic powder
- 5.4 cups ground beef or venison
- ¼ cup sliced green onion

Method

1. Preheat the oven to 400°F. Using a fork or knife to pierce the squash numerous times and microwave it for 3-4 minutes. Remove it gently from the oven, cut off the sides. Drizzle with avocado oil on the cut side, sprinkle with salt and put on a sheet pan lined with parchment, cut side down. For 30-45 minutes or until soft, roast. Roast time can depend on your squash's size.
2. Meanwhile, roast the beef or venison over medium heat in a large skillet with bell pepper, onion, garlic powder and half a teaspoon of salt. Continue cooking until the caramelization of the meat occurs and the vegetables are tender. Add the cumin and chili powder and simmer for an additional minute. Add the tomato paste, water, the rest of the salt and cook for 1-2 minutes or until the paste is thickened. Taste the mixture of chili and change the salt as needed. Stir in the cream cheese and 1 cup of the shredded cheese and remove from the sun. Stir until it is melted and thoroughly mixed in with the cheese.
3. Attach the spaghetti squash that has been prepared and toss to blend. Pour the mixture of chili and squash into a lightly greased saucepan, cover with the remaining cheese and bake for 15 minutes at 400 °F or until the cheese is melted and bubbly.
4. Top and eat soft with sliced green onions.

7.44 Keto Zucchini Gratin with Poblanos

Servings: 8 I Time: 25 mins I Difficulty: Easy
Nutrients per serving: Calories: 230 kcal I Fat: 20g I Carbohydrates: 6g I Protein: 7g I Fiber: 2g

Ingredients

- ½ tsp. garlic powder
- ¾ cup heavy cream
- 1 ¼ tsp. cumin
- 1 ¼ tsp. salt divided
- 1 ½ cup shredded Monterey Jack cheese or Pepper Jack divided
- 1 clove garlic
- 1 small onion diced
- 2 poblano peppers seeded and diced
- 2 Tbsp. sour cream
- 3 Tbsp. butter
- 4 zucchinis cut in half lengthwise and sliced

Method

1. Preheat the oven to 400°F.
2. Melt the butter, put the onion, poblano, ½ tsp. in a large oven-safe skillet over medium heat. Add salt and simmer for 5-7 minutes until tender. Connect the cumin and garlic and simmer for an additional minute. Stir in the sliced zucchini and season with ½ tsp. Continue to cook for another 5 minutes or until the zucchini is tender.
3. Stir in the milk and simmer for an additional minute. Stir in 1 cup of cheese, sour cream, and the remaining ¼ tsp. salt.
4. Add the remaining cheese to the top and bake for 10-12 minutes or until bubbly. Switch the broiler on high and cook for 2-3 more minutes or until browned on top. Remove from the oven and let sit before serving for 5 minutes.

7.45 Keto Shrimp Etouffee with Crawfish

Servings: 4 I Time: 30 mins I Difficulty: Easy
Nutrients per serving: Calories: 427 kcal I Fat: 32g I Carbohydrates: 8g I Protein: 24g I Fiber: 3g

Ingredients

- ¼ cup sliced green onions
- ¼ tsp. cayenne pepper
- ½ cup heavy cream
- ½ tsp. pepper
- ½ tsp. salt
- ¾ cup diced onion
- 1 cup diced bell pepper
- 1 cup diced celery
- 1 cup shrimp or chicken stock
- 1 pound crawfish tails thawed
- 1 pound raw large shrimp peeled & deveined,
- 1 tsp. dried oregano
- 1 tsp. dried thyme
- 1 tsp. paprika
- 3 oz. cream cheese softened
- 4 cloves garlic finely chopped
- 4 Tbsp. butter

Method

1. Over medium heat in a large pan, add butter. Melt the butter and proceed to cook for 3-5 minutes or until the butter is finely browned, stirring regularly. For around 5-7 minutes, add the diced celery, onion, and pepper to the butter and proceed to cook until the onion is translucent and the vegetables begin to brown.

2. Mix the paprika, the oregano, the thyme, the peppers and the salt in a small bowl and put aside. Attach the vegetables to the minced garlic and simmer for another minute.

3. Apply the spice mixture to the vegetables and simmer, stirring continuously, for another minute. To blend, apply the stock to the veggie and spice mixture and whisk well. Simmer showed himself for 6-8 minutes. Apply the cream to the skillet and proceed to cook for a further 5-7 minutes or until the mixture is thickened and the back of the spoon is coated.

4. Add the crawfish and shrimp to the pan after the sauce has thickened. Cook for 2-3 minutes until the shrimp is thoroughly cooked. Remove the pan from the heat and swirl until it is thoroughly melted and mixed into the cream cheese.

5. Sprinkle over the top of the shrimp and crawfish with the green onions and garnish with chopped parsley if desired. Over steamed cauliflower rice, serve.

7.46 Keto Lemon & Garlic Grilled Chicken Quarters

Servings: 8 I Time: 7 hrs I Difficulty: Easy
Nutrients per serving: Calories: 438 kcal I Fat: 34g I Carbohydrates: 1g I Protein: 31g

Ingredients

- Garnish: Chopped Parsley & Lemon Wedges
- Fiesta Brand Lemon Pepper & Salt
- 14.4 cups chicken leg quarters about 4 quarters
- 10 cloves garlic smashed and roughly chopped
- 1/2 tsp. dried thyme crushed
- 1 cup fresh lemon juice
- 1 cup avocado oil
- 1 ½ Tbsp. salt
- ½ tsp. pepper
- ½ tsp. paprika
- ¼ tsp. onion powder

Method

1. In a tub, combine the first 8 ingredients and whisk them together to combine. For basting, scrape 1/2 cup of the marinade and set aside for later. Divide the chicken into 2 ziptop bags and dump into each bag ½ of the remaining marinade. Let the air out of the bags and combine with the marinade to coat the chicken. Refrigerate for 6-8 hours while marinating, spinning the bags 2-3 times.

2. Preheat the grill to 325°F or so. Remove and put the chicken from the bag on a sheet pan; discard the marinade. Lightly season the chicken with salt and lemon pepper. Grill covered for 20-25 minutes on the skin side up. Switch the chicken and grill for an extra 20-25 minutes or until finished, always basting the chicken with the marinade reserved. Sprinkle with minced parsley and serve with lemon wedges. Put the chicken on the serving platter.

7.47 Grilled Salmon with Cilantro Lime Crema

Servings: 4 I Time: 30 mins I Difficulty: Easy
Nutrients per serving: Calories: 380 kcal I Fat: 25.6g I Carbohydrates: 5.5g I Protein: 33.9g I Fiber: 0.5g

Ingredients

- Olive oil
- 1 ½ pound salmon fillet cut into four pieces

For the Spice Rub:
- 1/8 tsp. Cayenne pepper
- 1 tsp. salt
- 1 ¼ tsp. dried oregano crushed
- ¾ tsp. garlic powder
- ½ tsp. paprika
- ½ tsp. chili powder

For the Cilantro Lime Crema
- 1/8 tsp. cumin
- 1 Tbsp. fresh lime juice
- 1 Tbsp. chopped cilantro
- 1 clove garlic finely minced
- ¼ tsp. salt
- ¼ tsp. lime zest
- ¼ cup sour cream
- ¼ cup mayonnaise your favorite

Method

1. For the Crema: Add all the ingredients for the cream in a small mixing bowl and stir to combine. Before serving, cover and refrigerate.

2. Preheat to 350-400°F on your barbecue.

3. Mix all the ingredients for the spice rub in a small bowl and mix well to combine. Drizzle the bits of salmon with olive oil and season the spice mixture liberally on both sides. Set the side of the salmon skin down on the hot barbecue. Cook on each side for about 8 minutes, turning once.

4. To serve: drizzle the cream and sprinkle with minced cilantro over the grilled salmon. With new lime, serve.

7.48 Mexican Shredded Beef

Servings: 6 I Time: 1 hr 5 mins I Difficulty: Easy
Nutrients per serving: Calories: 421 kcal I Fat: 27g I Carbohydrates: 3g I Protein: 38g I Fiber: 1g

Ingredients

- Salt Pepper & Garlic Powder
- 3 cloves garlic finely chopped
- 2.5 pound chuck roast
- 2 Tbsp. avocado oil
- 2 Tbsp. adobo sauce from the can of chipotles
- 2 chipotle peppers seeded and diced
- 1/2 onion diced
- 1 tsp. salt
- 1 tsp. garlic powder
- 1 tsp. chili powder
- 1 cup beef broth or stock
- 1 1/2 tsp. cumin
- ½ cup chopped bell pepper

Method

1. By choosing the sauté setting and turning it up to heavy, preheat the Inst. Pot. With salt, pepper and garlic powder, season the chuck roast on both sides. Once it's warmed, stir in the oil and add the roast. Sear for 4-5 minutes or until golden brown on either foot.

2. Turn the heat off until the beef is seared and add the next 10 ingredients. Place the cap on the Inst. Pot and put the valve in the position of the seal. Cook on high pressure for 55 minutes and normal release for 20 minutes.

3. Turn the valve gently so that any residual strain is removed and close the lid. Remove the beef from the liquid and put and shred it on a plate or tray. On the sauté setting, turn the Inst. Pot back on high and bring the remaining liquid to a boil to minimize the pot. Simmer for about 10 minutes… there should be about 1-½ cups of liquid left. Carry the shredded beef back to the pot. Serve with diced coriander, new lime, pico de gallo and sliced avocado served with cauliflower rice!

7.49 Chipotle Lime Grilled Pork Chops

Servings: 6 I Time: 4 hrs 30 mins I Difficulty: Easy

Nutrients per serving: Calories: 317 kcal I Fat: 19g I Carbohydrates: 5g I Protein: 29g I Fiber: 1g

Ingredients

For the marinade:

- Salt Pepper & Garlic Powder
- 6 pork ribeyes ¾" to 1" thick
- 6 cloves garlic finely minced
- 4 Tbsp. oil
- 2 tsp. Lakanto Monkfruit Sweetener golden or classic
- 2 chipotle peppers seeded
- 1 tsp. salt
- 1 tsp. onion powder
- 1 tsp. cumin
- 1 tsp lime zest
- ½ cup fresh lime juice

Method

1. Mix all the marinade ingredients into a glass jar and shake well to combine. Combine in a mixer for a creamier marinade and a basting sauce. With ½ of the marinade, placed the pork chops in a ziptop bag. Remove from the air and cool for 4-6 hours.
2. Preheat the grill to 450°F until preparing for grilling. From the marinade, cut the pork chops and season with salt, pepper and garlic powder on both sides. Place chops on a preheated grill and cook 5-7 minutes on each side, basting chops sometimes during cooking with the reserved marinade. Depending on the chops' thickness, the grilling time can vary, and the internal temperature should be 160°F. Remove from the grill and serve as needed, with any leftover marinade.

7.50 Asian Inspired Ground Venison Lettuce Wraps

Servings: 8 I Time: 25 mins I Difficulty: Easy
Nutrients per serving: Calories: 158 kcal I Fat: 9g I Carbohydrates: 3g I Protein: 14g I Fiber: 0g

Ingredients

- Garnish: sliced green onions and chopped dry roasted salted peanuts
- 6 oz. cremini or white button mushrooms cleaned and diced in ¼" pieces
- 4 cloves garlic finely minced or grated
- 3 Tbsp. rice wine vinegar
- 3 Tbsp. gluten-free soy sauce or Tamari
- 2 tsp. sriracha hot sauce optional
- 2 Tbsp. natural smooth peanut butter
- 1/3 cup water
- 1/2 tsp. granulated garlic
- 1 tsp. salt
- 1 Tbsp. sesame oil
- 1 Tbsp. olive oil
- 1 Tbsp. Lakanto Monkfruit sweetener
- 1 Tbsp. fresh grated ginger
- 1 pound ground venison
- 1 head iceberg lettuce washed and separated into individual leaves
- 1 8 oz. can water chestnuts drained and diced
- ¼ cup sliced green onions

Method

1. Combine the vinegar, soy sauce, sesame oil, peanut butter, sugar or a substitute, and the sriracha in a little dish. To mix and set aside, stir.
2. Apply the olive oil and venison to the pan in a large skillet over medium-high heat and start browning. Season with 1

teaspoon. 1/2 tsp and salt. Powder and garlic. Add the sliced mushrooms, garlic, chestnuts, ginger, and green onions after 2-3 minutes, and begin to cook until the meat is brown and begins to caramelize. You should have several bits stuck to the bottom of the pan at this stage. Apply the water to the pan and stir, wiping off the bottom of the pan with all the caramelized pieces.

3. Pour in the sauce that has been cooked and apply to the meat mixture. Continue to cook, stirring continuously, for another 2-3 minutes, until no liquid is left in the pan.
4. Place about half a cup of the meat mixture in the middle of the lettuce leaf to serve. Cover with green onion diced and peanuts diced, roll up and enjoy!

7.51 Chili Lime Steak Fajitas with Squash & Peppers

Servings: 4 I Time: 30 mins I Difficulty: Easy
Nutrients per serving: Calories: 482 kcal I Fat: 32g I Carbohydrates: 11g I Protein: 39g I Fiber: 3g

Ingredients

For the Fajitas:

- ½ tsp. chili powder
- ½ tsp. cumin
- ½ tsp. paprika
- 1 ½ pound skirt steak membrane removed
- 1 ½ Tbsp. fresh lime juice
- 1 ½ tsp. pink Himalayan salt
- 2 Tbsp. olive oil
- 2-3 garlic cloves finely minced or For the Veggies:
- 2 zucchinis sliced in ½" rounds
- 1 yellow squash sliced in ½" rounds
- ½ purple onion sliced
- 1 poblano pepper seeded and sliced into strips
- 1 colored bell pepper seeded and sliced into strips
- 3 Tbsp. olive oil
- ½ tsp granulated garlic
- 1 ½ tsp. pink Himalayan salt
- ½ tsp. pepper
- ¼ tsp. cumin

Method

1. Combine the chili powder, cinnamon, cumin, paprika, and granulated garlic in a small cup, if necessary. To mix, stir well. In both ends, brush the seasoning generously over the skirt steak, rubbing it in. Place the steak in a ziptop bag and, if used, apply the fresh garlic, olive oil, and the juice. Cover the bag and shake it to guarantee it is covered with the whole steak. For 30 minutes to 3 hours, refrigerate.
2. Grill meat until meat is to the perfect doneness, around 3 minutes per hand, over a hot, intense heat. To broil, put the rack near the broiler in the oven and broil until it is charred, between 2-4 minutes on either side. Tent the foil with the grilled beef and let the steak sit for 5-10 minutes. Slice the grain in half and eat with the vegetables.
3. Preheat the oven to 425°F and set aside and line a large sheet pan with parchment. Combine all vegetables and the next 5 ingredients in a large bowl and toss to cover the veggies. Spread them on the lined sheet pan and bake for 15-20 minutes at 425°F or until needed.

7.52 Keto Jambalaya with Shrimp & Andouille Sausage

Servings: 6 I Time: 30 mins I Difficulty: Easy
Nutrients per serving: Calories: 431 kcal I Fat: 28g I Carbohydrates: 11g I Protein: 32g I Fiber: 3g

Ingredients

- 1 Tbsp. bacon fat
- 1 cup diced celery
- 1 cup diced onion
- 1 cup diced green bell pepper
- 4 cloves garlic finely chopped
- ½ tsp. salt
- ½ tsp. dried thyme
- 2 tsp. Fiesta Brand Cajun-All Seasoning
- ½ tsp. paprika
- 1 pound medium shrimp 41/50, peeled and deveined
- 3 Tbsp. heavy cream optional
- Chopped Green Onions
- Chopped Parsley
- 1 15 oz can diced tomatoes
- 1 pound andouille sausage cut into ¼-1/2 inch slices then cut in half
- 1 12 oz package of frozen cauliflower rice

Method

1. In compliance with the box directions, cook the cauliflower rice. Push between paper towels to dry while cooling and remove excess vapor. You want the cauliflower rice to be dry, so there is no water in your final bowl. Place aside the cauliflower rice.
2. Over medium prepare, heat a large skillet and add the sausage. Cook the sausage until golden brown; take it out of the grill. In the pan, add celery, onion, bell pepper, and 1/2 tsp of salt and cook for 5-7 minutes or until the onion is translucent and the vegetables are tender. Add garlic and cook, stirring continuously, for another 1-2 minutes.
3. Lower the heat to medium and put the sausage back in the pan. To mix, add onions, thyme, Cajun-All, paprika and dry cauliflower rice and stir. Apply the vegetables and sausage to the shrimp and cook until the shrimp is finished, stirring regularly, for about 5 minutes. Apply the milk and mix softly to blend. Top up and eat with sliced green onions and chopped parsley!

7.53 Blackened Venison Tenderloin with Spicy Brussels Sprouts & Cajun Cream Sauce

Servings: 8 I Time: 45 mins I Difficulty: Easy
Nutrients per serving: Calories: 319 kcal I Fat: 24g I Carbohydrates: 10g I Protein: 17g I Fiber: 3g

Ingredients

For the Crispy Brussels Sprouts:
- ¾ tsp. salt
- 1 tsp. Fiesta Brand Cajun Redfish & Meat Seasoning
- 1 tsp. Fiesta Brand Cajun-All Seasoning
- 1 tsp. garlic powder
- 3 cups Brussels Sprouts washed, trimmed and halved
- 3 Tbsp. bacon drippings or olive oil

For the Venison:
- 1 tsp. pink Himalayan salt
- 2 Tbsp. Fiesta Brand Cajun Redfish & Meat Seasoning
- 2 Tbsp. salted butter
- 2 venison tenderloins cleaned & trimmed
- 3 tsp. garlic powder

For the Cajun Cream Sauce
- ¼ cup sliced green onion
- ½ tsp. Blackened Redfish Seasoning
- 1 cup heavy cream
- 1 medium tomato seeded & diced
- 1/3 cup chicken broth or stock

- 2 cloves garlic finely minced
- 2 Tbsp. butter

Method

To Prepare the Brussels Sprouts:
1. 1. Preheat the oven to 400°F. Place halved Brussel sprouts on a sheet pan lined with parchment. Drizzle with olive oil or bacon drippings and scatter with seasonings. Toss sprouts with seasoning and oil to coat. 35-45 minutes or until crispy and browned, put in a 400°F oven.

For the Venison
1. Prepare the venison when the sprouts are frying. Sprinkle the blackening sauce, garlic and salt generously with the tenderloins and transform them to ensure that they are uniformly covered. Preheat the skillet.
2. Apply the butter until the pan is healthy and hot and the tenderloins go in as soon as it melts. Cook on each side for around 3-4 minutes and put the skillet in the oven with the tenderloins and cook to the appropriate thickness. The amount of time depends on the size and how you want your tenderloin to be prepared. I like my medium and it took about 7-8 minutes in the oven.
3. Take the tenderloins out of the pan and let them rest while preparing the cream sauce, loosely coated with foil. Move the skillet cautiously back to medium heat.

To Prepare the Cajun Cream Sauce
1. Add onion, garlic, tomato, and butter to the pan. Sauté for 2 minutes.
2. cook until broth is reduced by half.
3. Simmer by stirring continuously for 4 minutes after adding cream.

To Plate:
1. Take venison and slice it in sizes between ¼ and ½ inch.
2. Top with cream, sprouts roasted.
3. Serve!

7.54 Mexican Tomato Soup

Servings: 4 I Time: 25 mins I Difficulty: Easy
Nutrients per serving: Calories: 69 kcal I Fat: 4g I Carbohydrates: 7g I Protein: 1g I Fiber: 2g

Ingredients

- ¼ medium red onion
- ¼ red, yellow or orange bell pepper
- ¼ tsp. chili powder
- ¼ tsp. cumin
- ¼ tsp. paprika
- ½ tsp. granulated garlic
- 1 ½ tsp. salt
- 1 cup chicken broth (for vegan or vegetarian use Vegetable broth or stock)
- 1 fresh jalapeno, halved, deveined and seeded
- 1 stalk celery peeled or strings removed
- 1 Tbsp. olive oil (additional for drizzling veggies)
- 2 tsp fresh lime juice
- 4 medium vine-ripened tomatoes

Topping Ideas
- Chopped Cilantro
- Diced Avocado
- Queso Fresco
- Shredded Cabbage
- Shredded Chicken
- Sliced Green Onion
- Sour Cream
- Thinly sliced radishes

Method

1. Preheat the oven to 400 ° F and put a sheet of parchment in the pan. Place the tomatoes, celery, onion, bell pepper,

and jalapeno on a baking sheet, drizzle with the olive oil and roast for 20-25 minutes in the oven until the skin starts to char and break.

2. In a blender, put all of the vegetables. Just a note... add just 1/4 to 1/2 of the jalapeno to start if you're worried about the soup being too spicy. To raise the sun, you can always add more! Connect the garlic pellets and the next 7 ingredients. Blend on high for 5-10 seconds for a smooth soup. You may also puree the soup using an immersion blender. In a large bowl or saucepan, place all the ingredients and blend until the perfect consistency is reached, creating a soup with a little more texture. Top with the toppings needed and enjoy!

7.55 Keto Mexican Shredded Chicken

Servings: 8 I Time: 20 mins I Difficulty: Easy
Nutrients per serving: Calories: 126 kcal I Fat: 9g I Carbohydrates: 5g I Protein: 6g I Fiber: 2g

Ingredients

- 3 Tbsp. butter
- 1 Tbsp. chili powder
- 2 tsp. cumin
- 2 tsp. granulated garlic
- 1 Tbsp. paprika
- 1 tsp. salt
- 4 cups cooked chicken (dark & white) shredded or pulled
- 8 oz. tomato sauce
- 1/2 cup diced onion
- 1/3 cup chicken stock or water

Method

1. Melt the butter in a broad skillet over a moderate heat heat and add the chopped onions. Sauté the onions for around 5-7 minutes until they are translucent.
2. Add the butter, onions, and spices. Cook for the next 30 seconds. Then add the cooked chicken, water and tomato sauce and stir to mix. Switch the heat to low and leave for 5-10 minutes to simmer. When needed, taste and change the seasoning. If you've used water rather than stock, you can need more salt.
3. Serve hot.

7.56 Chicken Verde Enchilada Soup

Servings: 6 I Time: 1 hr I Difficulty: Easy
Nutrients per serving: Calories: 252 kcal I Fat: 17g I Carbohydrates: 7g I Protein: 18g I Fiber: 0g

Ingredients

Verde Sauce
- 1 poblano
- 1/2 tsp. salt
- 1/2 white onion, cut in half
- 1/4 cup fresh cilantro
- 1-2 jalapeno peppers, fresh
- 2 tbsp. lime juice (about two lime)
- 4 large garlic cloves
- 5 tomatillos

For the Soup
- 1 cup chopped celery
- 1 cup chopped onion
- 1 tbsp. butter
- 1 tsp. cumin
- 1/2 cup heavy cream
- 1/3 cup sour cream
- 2 quarts chicken broth
- 2 tsp salt
- 2 tsp. minced garlic
- 2/3 cup diced yellow bell pepper
- 3 cups shredded chicken**

Toppings
- Avocado Slices
- Chopped Cilantro
- Monterrey Jack Cheese

Method

To make the Verde Sauce:
1. Preheat the furnace to 350 °F. Place the poblano, tomatillos, onion, and jalapeno on a sheet pan lined with parchment. In a small piece of foil, wrap your garlic cloves and drizzle the cloves with oil.
2. Wrap them up and position them with the veggies on the sheet pan. Drizzle with olive oil on the remaining vegetables and roast in the oven for 35-30 minutes or until the peppers are blistered and slightly charred. Set to cool aside.
3. Seed the peppers and put them in a blender with the onion, tomatillos, garlic cilantro, cloves, lime juice and salt when the vegetables are cool.
4. Taste the peppers first to test the heat or start with 1/2 a jalapeno at a time and increase to the desired heat level to ensure that your sauce is not too spicy. Mix well until the sauce is smooth. Set aside.

To prepare the soup:
1. Melt the butter over medium heat in a big stockpot. Add the celery, onion, pepper, and salt to the pot and sauté for 5-7 minutes over medium heat or until the veggies begin to soften. Put the garlic and cumin and cook for a further 2 minutes.
2. Add the vegetables to the chicken stock and simmer for 20 minutes. To the stock and vegetable mixture, add 1 cup of the prepared Verde sauce, cream and the chicken and whisk to combine. Simmer for 10 more minutes. Remove and stir in the sour cream from the sun. Taste the salt and change it if necessary. Serve immediately with slices of avocado, Monterrey Jack Cheese, sliced cilantro and wedges of lime.
3. It makes perfect leftovers with this soup! Reheat it gently.

7.57 Bayou Shrimp Salad with Avocado

Servings: 4 I Time: 15 mins I Difficulty: Easy
Nutrients per serving: Calories: 493 kcal I Fat: 38g I Carbohydrates: 13g I Protein: 26g I Fiber: 8g

Ingredients

- 2 cups shrimp
- 1 lemon
- 1/2 cup celery, finely diced
- 2 avocados halved
- 2 scallions, thinly sliced
- 3 Tbsp. Fiesta Cajun All Seasoning
- 8 cups water

For the Sauce
- 1 tbsp. fresh lemon juice
- 1 tsp. hot sauce, Louisiana or Tabasco
- 1/2 cup mayonnaise your favorite
- 1/2 tsp. Fiesta Cajun All Seasoning
- 1/2 tsp. Worcestershire sauce, gluten-free
- 1/8 tsp. granulated garlic
- 2 1/2 tsp. brown mustard

Method

1. Combine the mayonnaise in a small bowl and the next 6 ingredients for the sauce and whisk to combine. Cover and put the mixture in the refrigerator until you are ready for use.
2. Combine 8 cups of water and 3 Tbsp of seasoning with the saucepan. In the water, juice the whole lemon and add the lemons as well. Bring this mixture to a boil and let it boil for

5 minutes over medium heat. Add the shrimp and boil for 2-3 minutes or until pink and done with the shrimp... don't overcook. Drain and move the shrimp into a bowl of ice to cool them down and avoid the cooking process. Peel the shrimp until cold. You can keep the shrimp whole or cut in half... I left the small ones whole and cut the others in half.

3. Combine the boiled, cooled shrimp, celery, scallion, and sauce in a medium dish. Add diced avocado here, if you are not serving on avocado vessels. Gently throw to mix and serve on lettuce leaves or simply eat up straight! Do not add avocado until ready to eat, if prepared in advance.

7.58 Loaded Chorizo Burgers with Cilantro Lime Crema

Servings: 6 I Time: 35 mins I Difficulty: Easy
Nutrients per serving: Calories: 473 kcal I Fat: 40g I Carbohydrates: 0g I Protein: 26g

Ingredients

Chorizo Burger Mix
- 1 pound ground beef (80/20 or 73/27)
- 1 pound ground pork
- 1 Tbsp. kosher salt
- 2 tsp. apple cider vinegar
- 2 tsp. garlic powder (granulated)
- 3 Tbsp. water
- 6 Tbsp. Bolner's Fiesta Brand Chorizo Mix

Cilantro Lime Crema
- 1 Tbsp. fresh lime juice,
- 1 Tbsp. chopped cilantro
- salt & pepper to taste
- 1/2 tsp. garlic powder (granulated)
- 1/4 cup sour cream, full fat
- 1/4 cup mayonnaise (your favorite)

Optional Burger Toppings
- iceberg or butter lettuce
- low carb / keto / gluten-free burger buns
- Monterrey Jack Cheese
- pickled jalapenos
- sliced avocado or guacamole
- sliced red onion
- sliced tomato

Method

1. In a big bowl, combine all the burger ingredients together and mix well to mix all the seasonings with the ground meat. Place the mixture in a large zip-top bag and cool for at least 4 hours, but it is best for 12-24 hours!
2. Remove the mixture of the burger from the fridge and break into 6 portions and shape a patty for each piece. Season with salt and pepper on both sides and leave to sit for 10 minutes.
3. Over medium heat, preheat a large skillet. Cook 3 patties for around 4-5 minutes per side at a time. Top with cheese if desired and cover for 1 minute with a lid to allow the cheese to melt.
4. Combine all 6 of the crema ingredients and blend to combine. Season with salt and pepper to taste.
5. On a bed of lettuce or on your favorite toasted bun, serve up these beautiful burgers. Top with sliced avocado or guacamole, sliced onion, new tomato, and cream and enjoy!

7.59 Tangy Cucumber Salad With Feta & Dill

Servings: 3-4 I Time: 15 mins I Difficulty: Easy

Nutrients per serving: Calories: 660 kcal I Fat: 60g I Carbohydrates: 7g I Protein: 13g I Fiber: 7g

Ingredients

- 1 large English cucumber, sliced or diced
- 1 ripe avocados, peeled & diced
- 1 Tbsp Rodelle's Sesame Dill Seafood Seasoning
- Fresh Dill (optional)
- 1/2 cup grape or cherry tomatoes, halved
- 1 1/2 T fresh lemon juice or white wine vinegar
- 1/2 tsp salt
- 1/3 cup Feta cheese
- 1/4 medium purple onion, thinly sliced
- 1/4 cup olive oil
- 1/4 tsp Dijon mustard
- 1/4 tsp black pepper
- 1/4 tsp garlic powder

Method

1. In a wide bowl, mix the first 5 ingredients and toss to blend. Whisk together the oil, lime juice / vinegar, the mustard, and the next four seasonings in a small bowl. Pour the dressing over the vegetables, toss and coat gently. Before serving, refrigerate for at least 2 hours. Garnish with fresh chopped dill for extra dill flavor before serving.
2. Prepare without the avocado if you are cooking and serving the next day, and substitute the avocado around 2 hours before serving.

7.60 Roasted Vegetable Salad

Servings: 6 I Time: 1 hr I Difficulty: Easy
Nutrients per serving: Calories: 210 kcal I Fat: 17.3g I Carbohydrates: 9g I Fiber: 5g

Ingredients

- ½ medium onion, cut into 1" wedges
- ½ tsp. granulated garlic
- 1 bell pepper, cut in ½" dice
- 1 head cauliflower, cleaned and cut into florets
- 1 small eggplant or about 1 1/2 cups, peeled and diced in 1" cubes
- 1/2 cup olive oil
- 10 asparagus spears, cut into 2" pieces
- 2 small turnips, wedged or diced
- 2 squash (zucchini or summer), sliced in ½" slices
- 20 radishes, cut in half if large
- 3 cups fresh broccoli florets
- 4 T. of basil pesto, heaping (homemade or your favorite brand)
- Salt & Pepper
- Shredded or shaved Parmesan cheese

Method

1. Line the two large parchment sheet pans. On one saucepan and radishes, turnips and cauliflower on the other, put squash, bell pepper, broccoli, onion, eggplant, and asparagus.
2. Drizzle ¼ cup of olive oil into each pan of vegetables. Sprinkle with ¼ tsp of garlic in each pan and usually season vegetables with salt and pepper and toss to cover.
3. In the oven, put the pans and roast for 30-45 minutes at 425°F or until the veggies begin to brown and caramelize. The broccoli and squash pan will finish first and it will take a little more time to pan with the cauliflower. Do not hurry this segment... this makes the veggies so incredibly delicious! Place them all in a wide bowl, add the basil pesto and toss to coat until all the veggies are done.
4. Sprinkle with Parmesan cheese and serve at room temperature or high!

7.61 Chicken Poblano Chowder

Servings: 4 | Time: 45 mins | Difficulty: Easy
Nutrients per serving: Calories: 660 kcal | Fat: 60g | Carbohydrates: 7g | Protein: 13g | Fiber: 7g

Ingredients
- ¼ Tsp. chili powder
- ¼ Tsp. pepper
- ½ Tsp. cumin
- ¾ Tsp. salt
- 1 ½ Tbsp. cornstarch (optional)
- 1 large carrot, diced
- 1 medium onion, chopped
- 1 quart chicken stock
- 1/8 Tsp. poultry seasoning
- 2 cups shredded or diced chicken
- 2 poblano peppers, seeded, deveined & diced
- 2 Tbsps. butter
- 3 cloves garlic, chopped
- 3 oz. cream cheese, softened
- 3 stalks celery, chopped (about 1 cup)
- 3 Tbsps. heavy cream

Method
1. Melt the butter over medium heat in a saucepan.
2. Add the celery, garlic, carrot, onion, and peppers and sauté for 7-10 minutes or until the onion is translucent. For 2-3 more minutes, add salt, pepper, cumin, poultry seasoning, and chili powder and continue cooking.
3. Stir in the cream cheese and continue stirring until it is fully melted. To mix, add the chicken stock and stir well. Bring the mixture to a boil, add the chicken and continue to cook for 15-20 minutes until the vegetables are tender.
4. Whisk the cornstarch and cream together if you are using cornstarch for a slightly thickened soup. When the soup is up to a boil and the vegetables are soft, whisk the cornstarch/cream slurry continuously into the simmering soup. Carry the soup back to a boil to thicken completely. To taste and serve, add salt and pepper!
5. If you do not use cornstarch, apply the cream to the soup when the vegetables are tender and stir to mix. Salt to taste and eat with mustard! Add avocado, sour cream or chopped cilantro to garnish.

7.62 Tomato and Basil Salad

Servings: 4 | Time: 20 mins | Difficulty: Easy
Nutrients per serving: Calories: 127 kcal | Fat: 11g | Carbohydrates: 7g | Protein: 1g | Fiber: 2g

Ingredients
- ¼ Tsp. freshly ground pepper
- ½ Tsp. fleur de sel
- 1 small shallot thinly sliced
- 2 Tbsps. aged balsamic vinegar
- 2 Tbsps. fresh basil leaves finely sliced
- 3 Tbsps. extra virgin olive oil
- 4 medium heirloom tomatoes cut into wedges

Method
1. Place the sliced shallots in a shallow bowl and cover to mellow their bite for at least 15 minutes with your favorite aged balsamic.
2. Place the marinated shallots and vinegar on the sliced tomatoes, a splash of olive oil, a sprinkle of fleur de sel, a few slices of freshly ground black pepper and a chiffonade of basil.

7.63 Watercress & Chicken Soup

Servings: 4 | Time: 40 mins | Difficulty: Easy
Nutrients per serving: Calories: 295 kcal | Fat: 15g | Carbohydrates: 8g | Protein: 33g | Fiber: 2g

Ingredients
- ½ pound fresh watercress or two containers of Go Green hydroponic/living watercress, washed and drained
- ½ Tsp. Red Boat fish sauce
- ½ Tsp. toasted sesame oil
- 1 large shallot thinly sliced
- 1 pound boneless skinless chicken thighs, thinly sliced
- 1 Tsp. avocado oil ghee, or fat of choice
- 2 large carrots peeled and sliced into ¼" coins
- 2 Tsps. coconut aminos
- 4 large shiitake mushrooms thinly sliced
- 6 cups bone broth or chicken broth
- kosher salt to taste

Method
1. If you're using live stuff, grab your watercress and cut off the root end. In cold water, rinse the leaves well and dry them in a salad spinner.
2. Slice the chicken's boneless, skinless thighs into strips and drop them in a bowl. Add the aminos, sesame oil, and fish sauce to the coconut and mix to ensure that the marinade is well distributed.
3. Heat the avocado oil over medium heat in a large saucepan and cut up the remainder of the vegetables.
4. Toss in the shallots, carrots, and shiitake mushrooms and a pinch of salt when the pan is warmed. Sauté until softened by the shallots and mushrooms
5. Pour in the broth and carry over high heat to a boil.
6. Attach the chicken and bring it all to a boil again. Reduce the heat to low and cook for 5-10 more minutes, or until the chicken is cooked through and the carrots are softened. Boneless, skinless chicken breast can cook quicker than the thighs, so if the carrots are not yet as tender as you want them, you may need to fish out the chicken first. Thighs, on the other hand, are more forgiving if you overcook them, so once the carrots are cooked through, you should leave them in the pot.
7. Remove the heat from the pot and stir the watercress into it. Season to taste with more salt and/or fish sauce as soon as the watercress has wilted.

7.64 Inst. Pot Cowboy Chili

Servings: 8 | Time: 1 hr 30 mins | Difficulty: Easy
Nutrients per serving: Calories: 520 kcal | Fat: 34g | Carbohydrates: 10g | Protein: 47g | Fiber: 3g

Ingredients
For the chili:
- 1 cup bone broth or chicken broth
- 1 medium yellow onion cut into ½-inch dice
- 1 ounce unsweetened chocolate shaved
- 1 Tbsp. dried oregano
- 1 Tbsp. smoked paprika
- 2 Tbsps. ground cumin
- 2 Tbsps. tomato paste
- 2 Tsps. Diamond Crystal kosher salt use 1 Tsp. if Morton's brand
- 3 Tbsps. ancho chili powder
- 4 garlic cloves peeled and minced
- 14.4 cups beef chuck roast cut into 2-inch cubes
- 4 slices bacon cut into ¼-inch pieces
- Freshly ground black pepper

- Juice from ½ small lime

For the garnish:

- ½ cup julienned radish
- ½ cup minced fresh cilantro
- ½ medium white onion cut into ¼-inch dice
- 2 limes cut into wedges
- plain full-fat coconut yogurt optional

Method

1. Toss the beef with the salt in a large bowl and set it aside.
2. Switch on your Inst. Pot's sauté feature and throw in the sliced bacon. To ensure browning, stir the bacon regularly.
3. Move them to a paper-towel once the bacon bits are crunchy.
4. Throw in the tomato paste and onion and sauté until the onions are tender, around 2-3 minutes.
5. Meanwhile, in a small bowl or measuring cup, mix the oregano, ancho chili powder, paprika, cumin, and the broth. Mix until the chocolate shavings are smooth and then stir them in
6. Stir in the garlic and chili-chocolate mixture when the onions have softened. Cook until fragrant or for 1 minute.
7. Add the lime juice, salted beef, and fried bacon. Stir well.
8. Cook for 35 minutes under high pressure.
9. Release the pressure when the chili is done cooking.
10. Taste the stew with salt and pepper and season accordingly. With your favorite garnishes, top up the chili.

7.65 Inst. Pot Oxtail Stew

Servings: 8 I Time: 1 hr 35 mins I Difficulty: Easy
Nutrients per serving: Calories: 767 kcal I Fat: 40g I Carbohydrates: 11g I Protein: 89g I Fiber: 2g

Ingredients

- ¼ cup minced Italian parsley
- 1 pound yellow onions finely sliced
- 1 Tbsp. ghee olive oil, avocado oil, or fat of choice
- 1 Tbsp. aged balsamic vinegar
- 1 Tbsp. Red Boat fish sauce
- 1½ cups marinara sauce I like Rao's brand
- 3 medium carrots roughly chopped
- 18 cups oxtails cut crosswise into 3-inch segments
- 8 garlic cloves peeled and smashed
- Freshly ground black pepper
- Magic Mushroom Powder or Diamond Crystal kosher salt

Method

1. In a wide bowl, put the oxtails and add 1 Tbsp. Magic Mushroom Powder.
2. Toss well and place on a rimmed baking sheet in a single layer.
3. Under the broiler, pop the oxtails. On each hand, broil for around 5 minutes or until well browned. Alternatively, in the Inst. Pot on the "Sauté" feature, you can brown the meat in batches, but it will be tedious and messy.
4. While under the broiler the oxtails are browning, grab your Inst. Pot and turn the "Sauté" feature on. Add the ghee or fat of choice when the metal insert is heavy. Toss in the carrots and sliced onions and cook until the onions are softened.
5. Sprinkle with any extra kosher salt or Magic Mushroom Powder. Attach the crushed garlic and stir for approximately 30 seconds or until the garlic is fragrant.
6. Grab the pan with the browned oxtails and nestle them into the vegetables. Pour in some of the pan's stored juices. Mind not to fill more than 2/3rds of your pressure cooker absolutely
7. Pour on the meat with the marinara sauce, fish sauce, and aged balsamic vinegar. Stir well, making sure the bottom of the pot is reached by the liquid.

8. Lock the lid on and program the Inst. Pot to cook for 45 minutes under high pressure.
9. Enable the pressure to release naturally when the oxtails are finished cooking. If you are impatient, after 30 minutes have passed, you can release the pressure manually.
10. The meat should fall off the bone and be tender. If required, taste the stew and change the pepper, Magic Mushroom Powder, salt, and/or balsamic vinegar seasoning.

7.66 Ginger-Scallion Chicken

Servings: 4 I Time: 1 hr I Difficulty: Easy
Nutrients per serving: Calories: 409 kcal I Fat: 22g I Carbohydrates: 1g I Protein: 48g I Fiber: 1g

Ingredients

- ¼ cup avocado oil, softened duck fat ghee, or fat of choice
- ½ cup thinly sliced scallions about 3 scallions
- 1 Tbsp. grated fresh ginger
- 1 Tbsp. melted duck fat ghee, or fat of choice
- 4 chicken breasts bone-in, skin-on (10-12 ounces each)
- Diamond Crystal kosher salt

Method

1. Preheat the oven to 450°F. Add the ginger, scallions, fat, and 2 teaspoons to a small cup of Kosher salt. Mix thoroughly.
2. Carefully split the skin of each chicken breast away from the meat using your fingers to create a pocket. Now, add 1 Tbsp. the "pesto" under each breast's surface.
3. Press and rub the skin gently to spread the pesto uniformly. You can continue cooking the chicken at this stage, or refrigerate it for up to a day and roast it later.
4. Atop a foil-lined baking sheet, place the chicken skin-side up on a wire rack.
5. Brush the chicken breasts with the melted fat and season with more salt.
6. Oven-roast for 30 to 35 minutes or until 150°F is inserted into the thickest portion of the chicken registers by an instant-read thermometer.
7. Give the chicken 5 to 10 minutes to rest. Just serve!

7.67 Umami Chicken

Servings: 6 I Time: 55 mins I Difficulty: Easy
Nutrients per serving: Calories: 488 kcal I Fat: 38g I Carbohydrates: 3g I Protein: 32g I Fiber: 1g

Ingredients

- ⅔ cup plain coconut yogurt or use ½ cup full fat coconut milk
- 1 Tsp. Red Boat fish sauce
- 2 Tbsps. lemon juice
- 2½ Tsps. Magic Mushroom Powder
- 10.8 cups bone-in skin-on chicken thighs
- 6 cloves of garlic minced

Method

1. Mix the Magic Mushroom Powder, coconut yogurt, the garlic, and the fish sauce in a big cup.
2. Toss in the thighs of the chicken and blend until well coated. Marinate for at least 30 minutes and for up to a day in the fridge.
3. When you are ready to cook the chicken, heat the oven to 400 ° F convection or 425 ° F traditional. Shake off the excess marinade and place the chicken on a rimmed baking sheet, skin-side down, on a stainless-steel wire rack.
4. Roast the chicken for 45 minutes, turn the tray and, at the halfway stage, flip the thighs skin-side up.
5. When the skin is browned and the chicken's temperature in the thickest part is 165 °F, the thighs are done.

7.68 Meatza

Servings: 4 I Time: 30 mins I Difficulty: Easy

Nutrients per serving: Calories: 510 kcal I Fat: 43g I Carbohydrates: 7g I Protein: 23g I Fiber: 2g

Ingredients

- ¼ cup Castelvetrano olives pitted
- ¼ cup marinara sauce
- ¼ pound cremini mushrooms
- ½ cup goat cheese or almond ricotta
- 1 pound bulk mild Italian sausage
- 1 small red bell pepper
- 1 small red onion

Method

1. On the parchment, layer the bulk sausage, and use your hands to turn the meat into a rectangle.
2. Press sausage on parchment paper. Then, using a rolling pin, flatten the sausage evenly until it is around 1⁄4-inch thick.
3. Put the baking sheet in the hot oven and bake at 425 °F and at the halfway point for about 10 minutes.
4. Blot the crust well with towels. Remove the meat crust.
5. Put a layer of marinara sauce on the crust of the steak, and add your favorite toppings.
6. Put the meat in the oven and cook for another 5-10 minutes or until the toppings are browned.
7. Remove from the oven and allow it to rest for 5 minutes.
8. Serve.

7.69 Dan Dan Noodles

Servings: 6 I Time: 45 mins I Difficulty: Easy
Nutrients per serving: Calories: 580 kcal I Fat: 50g I Carbohydrates: 12g I Protein: 23g I Fiber: 4g

Ingredients

For the noodles:
- 2 Tsps. salt
- 7.2 cups zucchini

For the chili oil:
- ½ cup light-tasting olive or avocado oil
- ½- inch piece of cinnamon stick
- 1 Tbsp. whole black peppercorns
- 2 Tbsps. crushed red pepper flakes

For the pork:
- ½ Tsp. ground black pepper
- 1 jalapeño
- 1 Tbsp. extra-virgin olive oil
- 1 Tsp. salt
- 4.4 cups ground pork
- 2- inch piece fresh ginger
- 3 cloves garlic

For the sauce:
- ¼ cup coconut aminos
- ¼ Tsp. ground black pepper
- ⅓ cup cornichons
- ½ Tsp. Chinese five-spice powder
- 2 Tbsps. tahini or almond butter
- 2 Tbsps. unseasoned rice vinegar
- 2 Tsps. toasted sesame oil
- garnish: a handful cashews 2–3 scallions
- pinch coconut sugar

Method

1. Take noodles and toss with salt in a colander.
2. Make the oil with chili. Combine the peppercorns, oil, red pepper, and cinnamon. Heat the oil as you cook, over medium-low heat.
3. Only cook the pork. Heat the oil for 2 minutes in a large skillet over medium-high heat. Peel and grind the ginger as the oil heats, mince the jalapeño, and peel and smash the

garlic. Apply the aromatics to the oil and cook for about 1 minute, until fragrant. Season with the pepper and salt, and cook, breaking up the meat with a wooden spoon, until it is browned, 7-10 minutes. Crumble the pork into the pan.
4. Make the gravy. Place the sesame oil, tahini, black pepper, and Chinese five-spice in a small bowl while the pork is cooking.
5. Add the vinegar, aminos, and sugar from the coconut; whisk until mixed. Set aside.
6. In the pan, coat the meat with sauce.
7. To the skillet, add the cornichons, toss to combine, and move the meat mixture to a big cup. Over medium-high heat, reheat the skillet. Rinse the zucchini noodles in a clean dish towel under running water, drain well, and dry them.
8. In the heated pan, add the noodles and stir-fry until hot for 2–3 minutes. Return the meat to the pan and mix with two wooden spoons; allow it to heat.
9. Remove the cinnamon stick from the chili oil using a slotted spoon and discard it. To cool, set the oil aside. Chop the cashews and scallions.
10. Break the noodles into separate bowls to serve and cover with a drizzle of chili oil, then sprinkle with scallions and cashews.

7.70 Big-O Bacon Burgers

Servings: 4 I Time: 30 mins I Difficulty: Easy
Nutrients per serving: Calories: 484 kcal I Fat: 41g I Carbohydrates: 3g I Protein: 24g I Fiber: 1g

Ingredients

- ½ pound cremini mushrooms finely chopped
- 1 pound ground beef
- 1½ Tsps. kosher salt
- 2 Tbsps. ghee lard, or fat of choice, divided
- 4 ounces bacon frozen and cross-cut into small pieces
- Freshly ground black pepper

Method

1. Take 1 Tbsp Ghee and heat it in a skillet over medium heat.
2. Sauté the mushrooms. Set the cooked mushrooms aside in order to cool to room temperature.
3. Combine the bacon, ground beef, and mushrooms in a large bowl and season with salt and pepper. Gently mix the ingredients.
4. Divide the mixture into four parts and flatten each into 3⁄4-inch-thick patties using the hands.
5. Melt the leftover Ghee in a skillet over medium heat, and fry the patties for 3 minutes in the warm fat, turning once.
6. To allow any excess fat to drain off, move the patties to a wire rack. Pile them with your favorite burger toppings, wrap them in roasted Portobello mushrooms or lettuce leaves, and serve.

7.71 Cantonese Egg Custard with Minced Pork

Servings: 4 I Time: 45 mins I Difficulty: Easy
Nutrients per serving: Calories: 228 kcal I Fat: 17g I Carbohydrates: 4g I Protein: 15g I Fiber: 1g

Ingredients

For the filling:
- ½ pound ground pork or your favorite protein
- 1 small shallot minced
- 1 Tsp. ghee
- 1 Tsp. Red Boat fish sauce
- 2 Tsps. coconut aminos
- 3 fresh shiitake mushrooms thinly sliced
- 3-4 asparagus stalks thinly sliced
- freshly ground black pepper

For the custard:
- ¾ cup water
- 1 Tsp. Red Boat fish sauce
- 3 large eggs

For the garnish:
- ½ Tsp. toasted sesame oil
- 2 green onion stalks thinly sliced
- 2 Tbsps. chopped cilantro

Method
1. Heat the ghee over a medium-high heat in a large skillet. Break up the pork using a spatula and add shallots to it.
2. When the shallots are softened, sauté the filling.
3. Toss in the chopped mushrooms of asparagus and shiitake and stir-fry for about a minute or until the asparagus turns pink.
4. Season the meat and vegetables with the coconut, fish, and freshly ground pepper sauce.
5. Next, put cooked meat and vegetables in a shallow bowl.
6. With approximately two inches of water, fill a large stockpot. In the coated kettle, boil water.
7. Making the egg custard by mixing the eggs and water as the water in the steamer comes to a boil.
8. Add 1 Tsp. Sauce with fish and whisk to mix.
9. Over the meat and vegetables filling, pour the egg mixture.
10. Place the egg custard carefully in the pot.
11. For 15-20 minutes or until the custard is fully set, replace the lid on the pot and steam.
12. Sprinkle with sesame oil and garnish with chopped fresh cilantro and green onions over the savory egg custard.

7.72 Lamb with Spinach Sauce

Servings: 2 I Time: 4 hrs I Difficulty: Easy
Nutrients per serving: Calories: 511 kcal I Fat: 37g I Carbohydrates: 14g I Protein: 32g I Fiber: 7g

Ingredients
- ¼ Cup full-fat coconut milk
- ½ cup diced tomatoes
- 1 tbsp. Diamond Crystal kosher salt
- 1 tbsp. ground cumin
- 1 tbsp. Lemon juice or more to taste
- 1 tsp. Ground turmeric
- 1½ tbsps. Garam masala
- 2 medium onions thinly sliced
- 2 tbsps. Ghee
- 2 tbsps. Ground coriander
- 3 tbsps. Minced ginger
- 30 ounces frozen spinach defrosted and squeezed dry
- 4 garlic cloves minced
- 14.4 cups lamb necks, cut into 1½ inch cubes, cut crosswise into 2-inch pieces or 7.2 cups of boneless lamb shoulder
- Freshly ground black pepper

Method
1. Preheat the oven to 300°F. Meanwhile, heat the ghee over medium-high heat in a Dutch oven.
2. With paper towels, dry the lamb necks well and sprinkle with 1 Tsp. Kosher salt.
3. Sear the lamb in batches in fat until browned on all sides.
4. Take the browned lamb to a dish and reduce the heat to low. To the empty pan, add the onions and sauté until translucent and smooth (about 10 minutes).
5. Add the ginger, garlic, coriander, cumin, and turmeric when the onions are soft and whisk until fragrant.
6. Add the coconut milk and tomatoes and cook until the sauce has thickened. Using the stick blender to mix the sauce until smooth.

7. Nestle the sauce with the browned lamb parts and add boiling water about 2 cups. Stir in 2 teaspoons. of kosher salt and bring to a boil the contents.
8. Place the pot in the oven for 2½ hours or until the meat is tender.
9. Mix the defrosted spinach and garam masala and stir. Cook until the spinach is soft, over medium heat.
10. Change the salt and pepper and apply the lemon juice to the seasoning.

7.73 Spicy Ethiopian Chicken Stew

Servings: 6 I Time: 2 hrs I Difficulty: Easy
Nutrients per serving: Calories: 660 kcal I Fat: 25g I Carbohydrates: 6g I Protein: 32g I Fiber: 1g

Ingredients
- ¼ cup ghee
- ¼ Tsp. Freshly ground black pepper
- ¼ Tsp. ground cardamom
- 1 Tbsp. berbere seasoning
- 1 Tbsp. minced ginger
- 2 cups chicken broth
- 2 medium red onions thinly sliced
- 2 Tbsps. freshly squeezed lime juice optional
- 3 garlic cloves minced
- 10.8 cups chicken drumsticks skin on or off
- 4 hardboiled eggs
- Diamond Crystal kosher salt

Method
1. Apply slat to the drumsticks thoroughly and set aside.
2. Heat the ghee over medium heat in a big Dutch oven. Put the sliced onions and let them cook for 1 to 2 minutes, uninterrupted. To ensure even cooking, season liberally with salt, and gently turn over the pile of onions every 3 to 4 minutes.
3. Until the onions are softened and greatly reduced in volume, switch the heat to medium-low for approximately 15 minutes.
4. Cook for another 40 minutes to turn the onions golden brown.
5. Stir in the caramelized onions with the garlic and ginger, and cook until fragrant, about 30 seconds.
6. Garnish with cardamom, Berber, and black pepper. Cook the spices until they are fragrant, then add the chicken stock in and stir well to blend.
7. Nestle the drumsticks into the liquid and carry to a low simmer the contents of the jar. Cover and cook, sometimes rotating the drumsticks, for 45 minutes or until the meat is tender and fried.
8. Take off the lid of the Dutch oven once the chicken is finished and turn the heat up to medium-high. Cook for 5 to 10 minutes until approximately one-third of the liquid is reduced.
9. Break the eggs that are hard-boiled into wedges. Switch the chicken drumsticks to a serving plate, garnish with wedges of eggs, and top with the spicy sauce.

7.74 Pressure Cooker Lamb Shanks

Servings: 4 I Time: 1 hr I Difficulty: Easy
Nutrients per serving: Calories: 711 kcal I Fat: 44g I Carbohydrates: 12g I Protein: 63g I Fiber: 3g

Ingredients
- 1 cup bone broth
- 1 large onion roughly chopped
- 1 pound ripe Roma tomatoes
- 1 Tbsp. aged balsamic vinegar
- 1 Tbsp. tomato paste
- 1 Tsp. Red Boat fish sauce

- 1/4 cup minced Italian parsley (optional)
- 2 celery stalks roughly chopped
- 2 medium carrots roughly chopped
- 2 Tbsp. ghee divided
- 3 garlic cloves smashed and peeled
- 10.8 cups lamb shanks
- Diamond Crystal kosher salt

Method

1. Melt 1 Tbsp. Ghee in a 6-quart pressure cooker over high heat.
2. Sear the lamb shanks until all sides have browned (8-10 minutes).
3. Chop up the onion, celery, carrots, and tomatoes while the lamb is browning.
4. Take the lamb out of the pot and put it on a plate.
5. Lower the heat.
6. Season with salt and pepper and add the celery, carrots, and onion to the pot.
7. Add the tomato paste and garlic cloves once the vegetables have turned translucent and mix for one minute.
8. Along with the tomatoes, add the shanks back into the pot and pour the fish sauce, bone broth, and balsamic vinegar in.
9. Grind on some fresh pepper before locking on to the lid.
10. Bring the contents of the pot up to high pressure.
11. Maintain low heat to achieve high pressure for 45 minutes.
12. When you finish cooking the braised shanks, let the pressure drop naturally.
13. Plate the shanks and change the seasoning sauce. Ladle shanks with the sauce.
14. Mince the Italian parsley on top of the braised meat and sprinkle with it.

7.75 Sous Vide Wild Alaskan Cod

Servings: 2 I Time: 40 mins I Difficulty: Easy
Nutrients per serving: Calories: 499 kcal I Fat: 17g I Protein: 82g

Ingredients

- 2 Tbsps. coconut oil or fat of choice
- 2 wild Alaska cod fillets
- Aleppo chile finishing salt
- Freshly ground black pepper

Method

1. Preheat SousVide Supreme to 130°F.
2. Drop the frozen cod into the bath for 30 minutes from the fridge.
3. Pull out. Dry them off and season with Aleppo chile salt-finishing and pepper.
4. Heat up the oil in a high cast-iron skillet.
5. Sear for 1 minute on either side of the fish. Serve with some baby spinach and guacamole sautéed!

7.76 Keto Crab Stuffed Mushrooms With Cream Cheese

Servings: 4 I Time: 40 mins I Difficulty: Easy
Nutrients per serving: Calories: 267 kcal I Fat: 20.44g I Carbohydrates: 4.67g I Protein: 15.31g I Fiber: 0.7g

Ingredients

- 1 can lump crabmeat, drained (6 ounce can)
- 1 pinch salt
- 1 tbsp green onion, minced
- 1 tsp fresh parsley, minced
- 1/2 cup finely grated cheddar cheese (divided use)
- 1/2 tsp garlic, minced
- 1/4 tsp red pepper flakes
- 1/4-1/2 tsp lemon zest

- 2 tbsp mayonnaise
- 2 tsp lemon juice
- 2 tsp prepared horseradish
- 4 ounces cream cheese, softened
- 8 large white button or brown mushrooms (1/2 pound)
- black pepper to taste

Method

1. Wash and then dry the mushrooms. Make a large hole in it for filling. Place them on a baking tray.
2. Preheat the oven to 375°F.
3. Put cream cheese, mayonnaise, horseradish, lemon juice, green onion, parsley, red pepper flakes, and lemon juice. And stir to melt the cream cheese.
4. Cheddar cheese folded in half and put it in crab. Add seasoning to the taste.
5. With the filling, stuff the mushrooms and top with the remaining cheddar cheese.
6. The mushrooms can be refrigerated overnight at this point, and baked the next day.
7. Carefully cover it in cling film. Continue with the directions for baking when ready.
8. Add an extra 5-10 minutes of baking time to prepare the mushrooms.
9. Put water in baking tray to cover mushrooms. Bake mushrooms for 20-25 minutes.
10. Refrigerate the remaining mushroom in a tight container. Reheat in the microwave or cover with foil and warm for 30 minutes in a 350°F oven.

7.77 Sous Vide Lamb Burgers

Servings: 4 I Time: 4 hrs 20 mins I Difficulty: Easy
Nutrients per serving: Calories: 323 kcal I Fat: 27g I Carbohydrates: 1g I Protein: 19g I Fiber: 1g

Ingredients

- 1 pound ground lamb
- 1 Tsp. Table seasoning
- Diamond Crystal kosher salt
- Freshly ground black pepper

Method

1. Preheat your SousVide Supreme to 137 ° F.
2. Apply pepper and salt the ground lamb generously. Then, apply the seasoning Table and mix the meat gently to spread the seasoning.
3. Divide the meat into four patties and then freeze for two hours.
4. Vacuum seal them after the patties are solidified, two per container.
5. Put them for about 2 hours at SousVide Supreme. Then, cut out the patties and use paper towels to rinse them.
6. Arrange the patties on top of a foil-lined tray on a baking rack. Make circular shapes with the help of a kitchen torch.

7.78 Sous Vide Black Cod Fillets

Servings: 3 I Time: 1 hr 20 mins I Difficulty: Easy
Nutrients per serving: Calories: 352 kcal I Fat: 32g I Carbohydrates: 1g I Protein: 15g I Fiber: 1g

Ingredients

- 1 cup water
- 1 pound black cod fillets skin-on and scaled
- 3 sprigs thyme
- 3 Tbsp. ghee or fat of choice
- 4 Tbsp. Diamond Crystal kosher salt
- Diamond Crystal kosher salt
- Fleur de sel
- lemon wedges

Method

1. Preheat the oven to and use the SousVide Supreme to heat it to 125°F.
2. Make kosher salt by mixing 2 tbsps. of table salt and 1 cup of water, it will create 10% brine.
3. Cut each fillet in 2 pieces.
4. Remove skin and use salt as seasoning on both sides.
5. Put them in the oven for 35 minutes at 300°F.
6. Remove the pine bones from the fillets.
7. In a bag, put the fillets and pour the brine into the mixture. Let them sit in a bowl of ice in the fridge for 10 minutes.
8. Wash with water and dry the fillets with paper towel.
9. With a pat of ghee or butter and a thyme sprig, each fillet is vacuum sealed.
10. Dunk the sealed fillets in the water furnace for 20 minutes.
11. The skins in the oven should be done. To cool when they are done, remove them from the pan to a wire rack.
12. When the fillets are finished cooking, place them on a platter and top with the reserved cooking liquid.
13. On top of the fillets, place fleur de sel, pepper, and a squeeze of fresh lemon juice.

7.79 Broiled Bacon-Wrapped Tuna Medallions

Servings: 4 I Time: 30 mins I Difficulty: Easy
Nutrients per serving: Calories: 193 kcal I Fat: 5g I Carbohydrates: 6g I Protein: 32g I Fiber: 1g

Ingredients
- ¼ cup coconut aminos
- ¼ cup freshly squeezed orange juice
- ¼ Tsp. Freshly ground black pepper
- ½ Tsp. Aleppo pepper (optional)
- ½ Tsp. Red Boat fish sauce
- 1 pound tuna albacore loin skinless
- 1 Tbsp. balsamic vinegar
- 2 slices bacon thin-cut

Method
1. Cut the tuna loin crosswise, about 1.5-inch thick, into five mini steaks.
2. Mix coconut amino acids, orange juice, fish sauce, black pepper, Aleppo pepper, and vinegar in a measuring cup. Pour over the fish with the marinade and marinate for 15 minutes.
3. Place the bacon on a plate lined with four sheets of paper towel on a microwave-safe plate and cover with two sheets.
4. For 1-2 minutes, microwave the bacon on high so that it is cooked halfway but still pliable.
5. Wrap a slice of par-cooked bacon with each marinated tuna medallion and put them on a rack on top of a foil-lined baking tray.
6. Broil the bacon-wrapped tuna on one side for about 4 minutes and turn over and cook for an extra 2 minutes.
7. Serve.

7.80 Lemongrass and Coconut Chicken Drumsticks

Servings: 6 I Time: 4 hrs 20 mins I Difficulty: Easy
Nutrients per serving: Calories: 319 kcal I Fat: 22g I Carbohydrates: 7g I Protein: 24g I Fiber: 1g

Ingredients
- ¼ cup fresh scallions chopped
- 1 large lemongrass stalk
- 1 large onion thinly sliced
- 1 thumb-size piece of ginger microplaned
- 1 Tsp. five spice powder
- 10 chicken drumsticks skin removed
- 1¼ cups full-fat coconut milk divided
- 2 Tbsps. Red Boat fish sauce
- 3 Tbsps. coconut aminos
- 4 garlic cloves minced
- Diamond Crystal kosher salt
- Freshly ground black pepper

Method
1. Rip off the drumsticks' meat. Put it in a large bowl and season with salt and pepper.
2. With a grater or beat the stalk and cut finely, trim the fresh lemongrass stalk and grate finely.
3. Place in a high-powered blender and blitz the garlic, lemongrass, coconut milk, ginger, coconut amino acids, fish sauce, and five spice powder until smooth.
4. Pour on the chicken with the marinade and blend well.
5. Dump the onion into the slow cooker's bottom and dump the chicken on top with the marinade. Set low on the slow cooker and cook for 4-5 hours.
6. Move the chicken and the sauce to a storage container to cool in the fridge for a few days if you're saving it for later. Place the drumsticks in a pot to reheat and bring them to a simmer.
7. When the stew has finished cooking, remove the chicken and place the sauce and onions in a blender for an extra creamy sauce. Puree the sauce and, at the last moment, pour ¼ cup more coconut milk into the blender. Return the sauce and chicken to the cooker and keep it warm.

7.81 Crispy Sous Vide Duck Confit Legs

Servings: 3 I Time: 1 hr I Difficulty: Easy
Nutrients per serving: Calories: 302 kcal I Fat: 60g I Carbohydrates: 7g I Protein: 13g I Fiber: 7g

Ingredients
- 2 Tbsps. duck fat
- 1 package of Grimaud Farms duck

Method
1. For about 45 minutes, put the sealed legs into the SousVide Supreme at 140°F.
2. Take out the legs and dry them with a pat.
3. In a cast iron skillet, melt the duck fat over medium-high heat and sear the skin side-down of the legs for around 2 minutes. Flip them over, and brown for about a minute on the other side.

7.82 Spaghetti and Meatballs

Servings: 4 I Time: 25 mins I Difficulty: Easy
Nutrients per serving: Calories: 398 kcal I Fat: 34g I Carbohydrates: 5g I Protein: 18g I Fiber: 1g

Ingredients
- 1 package of kelp noodles or zoodles
- 1 pound uncooked Italian sausage
- 1 Tbsp. ghee
- 12 oz marinara sauce

Method
1. Make small meatballs of sausage.
2. Melt one Tbsp. of ghee on medium heat in an iron skillet.
3. Fry and brown the meatballs in the pan.
4. Apply about half of Rao's marinara sauce jar and bring to a boil with the sauce.
5. Cover the pan and cook the sauce for 5 minutes on low heat.
6. In a colander, put noodles in meatballs and sauce.
7. Cover and cook for some time, until the noodles are tender.

7.83 Tuna and Avocado Wraps

Servings: 1 I Time: 15 mins I Difficulty: Easy
Nutrients per serving: Calories: 364 kcal I Fat: 19g I Carbohydrates: 14g I Protein: 37g I Fiber: 8g

Ingredients

- 1 scallion thinly sliced
- 1/2 jalapeño pepper diced small
- 1/2 limes
- 1/2 medium avocado
- 2 butter lettuce leaves
- 2 Pure Wraps or toasted nori optional
- 5 oz canned wild albacore tuna (in water)
- Diamond Crystal kosher salt

Method
1. Put tuna in a medium cup and break it gently with a fork.
2. Add Jalapeño and chopped scallions. Then, toss them with the tuna in the tub.
3. Mix in the pepper, the salt, and the lime spritz.
4. Mash half an avocado with salt, pepper, and the remainder of the lime juice in a separate dish.
5. Scoop the guacamole up, add seasoned tuna to the bowl and mix to blend.
6. Grab two Pure Wraps and put on each one a slice of lettuce. Break the lettuce with the tuna salad, roll it up, and serve.

7.84 Oven-Braised Mexican Beef

Servings: 6 I Time: 3 hrs 10 mins I Difficulty: Easy
Nutrients per serving: Calories: 379 kcal I Fat: 22g I Carbohydrates: 6g I Protein: 38g I Fiber: 1g

Ingredients
- ½ cup chicken stock
- ½ cup minced cilantro optional
- ½ cup roasted salsa I use Trader Joe's Double Roasted salsa
- ½ Tsp. Red Boat Fish Sauce
- 1 medium onion thinly sliced
- 1 Tbsp. chili powder I use Penzeys Arizona Dreaming
- 1 Tbsp. coconut oil or fat of choice
- 1 Tbsp. tomato paste
- 1½ Tsps. kosher salt Diamond Crystal brand
- 2 radishes thinly sliced (optional)
- 2½ pounds boneless beef short ribs beef brisket, or beef stew meat cut into 1½-inch cubes
- 6 garlic cloves peeled and smashed

Method
1. Mix the chili powder, cubed beef, and salt in a large cup.
2. Melt fat in a big dutch oven over medium heat.
3. Sauté onions until translucent.
4. Stir in the tomato paste and garlic and cook for 30 seconds.
5. Add the seasoned beef and add the stock, salsa, and sauce to the fish. Boil it.
6. Cover the pot and put it in the oven at 300 ° F until the beef is tender, or for 3 hours.
7. Spoon the beef on a serving dish and cover it with cilantro and/or radishes.

7.85 Grilled Calamari and roasted Peppers

Servings: 3 I Time: 45 mins I Difficulty: Easy
Nutrients per serving: Calories: 334 kcal I Fat: 22g I Carbohydrates: 10g I Protein: 24g I Fiber: 1g

Ingredients
- 1 medium red bell pepper
- 1 pound squid cleaned and gutted
- 1 small shallot thinly sliced
- 1 Tbsp. balsamic vinegar
- 1/4 cup Italian parsley
- 2 Tbsp. extra virgin olive oil
- 2 Tbsp. melted ghee or fat of choice
- Diamond Crystal kosher salt

- Freshly ground black pepper
- Juice from 1/2 a lemon

Method
1. Place the pepper in a bowl and cover with plastic wrap or foil tightly and steam it for at least 15 minutes.
2. Rub off the skin that has been blackened and cut the seeds, stem, and ribs.
3. Break and set aside the bell pepper into thin strips.
4. Rinse and squid dry. Cut open each one so that it'll lay flat on the grill.
5. With the cooking fat, put salt and pepper to taste, toss the squid.
6. In a small cup, mix the thinly sliced shallots with balsamic vinegar and let them mellow out.
7. Heat up your gas grill. Toss on the squid once it's super-hot and cook on each side for 20-30 seconds.
8. Cut them up and throw them in a bowl until the squid is flash-grilled.
9. Over the squid, add juice from half a lemon and pour in the olive oil.
10. Toss the sliced peppers, shallots, pepper, and salt into the balsamic-marinated ones.
11. Mix well with everything and sprinkle with the parsley. Taste and change as required for seasoning.

7.86 Chicken Spaghetti Squash Bake

Servings: 6 I Time: 1 hr 50 mins I Difficulty: Easy
Nutrients per serving: Calories: 553kcal I Fat: 42g I Carbohydrates: 12g I Protein: 30g I Fiber: 2g

Ingredients
- 1 whole spaghetti squash
- 2 ounces cream cheese
- 2 Tbsps. butter
- 6 ounces cheddar, shredded
- 3 ounces mozzarella, shredded
- 3 cups cooked, shredded chicken
- 2 cloves garlic, minced
- 1 Tsp. onion powder
- Chives, for garnish
- 1/2 Tsp. ground mustard
- 1/2 Tsp. pepper
- 1 1/4 cups heavy whipping cream
- 10.5 ounces Ro*Tel, drained

Method
To cook the spaghetti squash:
1. Preheat the oven to 400 °F.
2. Break the squash in half lengthwise and scoop out the seeds. Dispose of the seeds.
3. Drizzle with olive oil. Cook for 1 hour on a baking sheet in oven or until the squash is tender with a fork.
4. Follow these instructions to cook in the Inst. Pot.
5. When the squash is cooked, shred the squash by using a fork to scrape the squash widthwise into long spaghetti-like strands.
6. Place the squash strands in a large mixing bowl.
To make the cheese sauce:
1. In a medium saucepan, add the cream cheese, heavy cream, and butter and melt them on medium heat.
2. Whisk the mustard and pepper into the field.
3. Remove the cheddar and mozzarella from the heat and whisk until the mixture is smooth.
To assemble:
1. Heat the oven to 350 °F. With non-stick spray, spray a baking dish.
2. To the mixing bowl with the spaghetti squash, add the chicken, garlic, and onion powder.
3. To coat, pour the cheese sauce over the top and stir gently.

4. In the prepared baking dish, pour the mixture into it and bake for 20 minutes or until hot and bubbly.
5. Before serving, sprinkle it with chives.

7.87 Inst. Pot Cajun Ranch Chicken Soup

Servings: 2 | Time: 40 mins | Difficulty: Easy
Nutrients per serving: Calories: 412 kcal | Fat: 23g| Carbohydrates: 5g | Protein: 44g | Fiber: 1g

Ingredients

- ½ cup shredded white cheddar
- 1 1/2 pounds chicken breast
- 1 jalapeno, minced, see note
- 1 Tsp. dried chives
- 1 Tsp. dried dill
- 1 Tsp. dried parsley
- 1 Tsp. onion powder
- 2 cups baby spinach
- 2 cups reduced sodium chicken broth
- 2 Tsps. Cajun seasoning, more as needed
- 3 cloves garlic
- 4 slices bacon, diced
- 8 ounces cream cheese
- Cilantro, jalapeno slices, green onions, for garnish

Method

1. Add bacon to the pot and cook till it becomes crisp.
2. Pour the broth into the pot.
3. To mix, add the garlic, chicken, Cajun seasoning, jalapeno, parsley, dill, and chives to the pot and stir.
4. Cover, close the vent, and cook for 18 minutes under high pressure. Enable 10 minutes to relieve the pressure naturally.
5. Remove the chicken from the pot and use two forks to shred it.
6. In a small cup, microwave the cream cheese.
7. Add the cream cheese and set the pot to sauté. Whisk well until the soup has completely melted into the cream cheese.
8. Put the chicken along with the spinach and cheddar back in the pot.
9. Ladle it into bowls and serve, if needed, with jalapeno, cilantro, and green onions.

7.88 Keto Chicken Fajita Soup

Servings: 6 | Time: 38 mins | Difficulty: Easy
Nutrients per serving: Calories: 392 kcal | Fat: 26g | Carbohydrates: 11g | Protein: 29g | Fiber: 4g

Ingredients

- ½ Cup chopped cilantro
- ½ tsp. Chili powder
- 1 fresh lime, juiced
- 1 medium onion, chopped
- 1 pound chicken breasts
- 1 tbsp. Avocado oil
- 1 tbsp. Chipotles
- 1 tbsp. Cumin
- 1 tsp. Salt
- 2 bell peppers, chopped
- Diced avocado,
- 2 cloves garlic, minced
- Cheddar
- 2 cups chicken broth
- Diced tomatoes,
- 8 ounces cream cheese
- Sour cream,

Method

1. Add the onion and peppers and cook for about 5 minutes.
2. To coat the vegetables, add the chipotle, garlic, chili powder, cumin, and salt to the pot and mix.
3. To the pot, add the lime juice, chicken broth, and chicken.
4. Cover and turn the vent to seal, and cook for 18 minutes at high pressure.
5. Remove the chicken and use two forks to shred it.
6. To sauté, turn the Inst. Pot on and add the cream cheese.
7. Put the cilantro and stir well.
8. Using sour cream, onions, avocado, or cheese to serve.

7.89 Keto Burrito Bowl

Servings: 1 | Time: 5 mins | Difficulty: Easy
Nutrients per serving: Calories: 374 kcal | Fat: 25g | Carbohydrates: 15g | Protein: 27g | Fiber: 6g

Ingredients

- 1 cup Mexican Cauliflower Rice
- 1 Tbsp. chopped cilantro
- 1/2 cup Mexican Shredded Beef
- 1/4 cup Keto Guacamole
- 1/4 cup Pico de Gallo
- 1/4 cup shredded cheddar cheese

Method

1. Mix ingredients in a small bowl and season to taste.
2. Add pepper and salt or hot sauce (optional).
3. Serve.

7.90 Dill Pickle Egg Salad Sandwiches

Servings: 3 | Time: 30 mins | Difficulty: Easy
Nutrients per serving: Calories: 465 kcal | Fat: 35g | Carbohydrates: 7g | Protein: 30g | Fiber: 1g

Ingredients

For the egg salad:

- ½ cup chopped dill pickles
- 1 Tbsp. dill pickle juice
- 1 Tbsp. fresh dill
- 1 Tbsp. prepared yellow mustard
- 3 Tbsps. mayonnaise
- 6 hard boiled eggs
- Salt and pepper, to taste

For the chaffles:

- 1 1/2 cups finely shredded mozzarella
- 1 Tbsp. coconut flour
- 3 eggs, beaten
- 3/4 Tsp. baking powder

Method

To make the egg salad:

1. Peel and cut into small bits with the shells.
2. Including the rest of the ingredients, add the eggs to a bowl and mix.
3. serve or store in fridge.

To make the chaffles:

1. To preheat, connect the waffle iron to electricity.
2. Whisk the coconut flour, eggs, and baking powder together. Mix the mozzarella.
3. To cover the bottom of the waffle iron, spoon just enough batter and close the waffle iron.
4. For 3 minutes, cook. Remove the waffle and repeat until you have 6 chaffles fried, with the remaining batter.

To assemble:

1. Divide the egg salad evenly between three chaffles.
2. Serve.

7.91 Bruschetta Chicken

Servings: 4 | Time: 45 mins | Difficulty: Easy

Nutrients per serving: Calories: 355 kcal I Fat: 18g I Carbohydrates: 6g I Protein: 45g I Fiber: 1g

Ingredients

For the chicken:

- ½ Tsp. salt
- 1 Tsp. Italian seasoning
- 2 cloves garlic, minced
- 2 Tbsps. balsamic vinegar
- 2 Tbsps. olive oil
- 3/4 cup shredded mozzarella
- 4 chicken breasts, about 6 ounces each

For the bruschetta:

- ½ cup chopped basil
- ½ small red onion, chopped
- ½ Tsp. salt
- 1 ½ cups cherry tomatoes, halved
- 1 Tsp. balsamic vinegar
- 1 Tsp. olive oil
- 3 cloves garlic, minced

Method

1. Add the chicken breasts in baking dish.
2. In a small cup, add the balsamic vinegar, oil, Italian seasoning, garlic, and salt. Whisk them to mix. Place the chicken over it and switch to coat it.
3. While the oven heats to 425 ° F, let the chicken set for 10 minutes.
4. Put the chicken in the oven and bake until the chicken reaches 165 ° F or for 25-30 minutes.
5. Blend all ingredients for the bruschetta to a bowl.
6. Remove from the oven when the chicken is baked, and top with the mozzarella.
7. To melt the cheese and warm the tomatoes, pour the bruschetta over the chicken and return to the oven for 5 minutes.

7.92 Crispy Baked Chicken Thighs

Servings: 2 I Time: 50 mins I Difficulty: Easy
Nutrients per serving: Calories: 796 kcal I Fat: 54g I Carbohydrates: 2g I Protein: 80g I Fiber: 0g

Ingredients

- ½ Tsp. cracked pepper
- 1 Tsp. chopped parsley
- 1 Tsp. garlic powder
- 1 Tsp. onion powder
- 1 Tsp. paprika
- 1 Tsp. salt
- 2 Tbsps. avocado oil
- 3 pounds bone-in chicken thighs

Method

1. In a big zip top bag, add all the ingredients except for the parsley and seal them. Smush the chicken in bag to season it.
2. On the baking sheet, arrange the chicken and bake 400°F for 35-45 minutes.
3. sprinkle the chicken with parsley.
4. Serve.

7.93 Baked Salsa Chicken

Servings: 4 I Time: 45 mins I Difficulty: Easy
Nutrients per serving: Calories: 216 kcal I Fat: 11g I Carbohydrates: 4g I Protein: 22g I Fiber: 2g

Ingredients

- ½ Tsp. chili powder
- ½ Tsp. cumin
- 1 ½ cups salsa
- 1 cup shredded pepper jack cheese
- 1 Tbsp. chopped cilantro
- 1 Tsp. garlic salt
- 4 chicken breasts, about 6 ounces each

Method

1. Pound the breasts of the chicken to an even size.
2. Add the chili powder, garlic salt, and cumin to the chicken seasoning.
3. Add ½ cup of salsa and spread to cover the bottom of dish.
4. On top of the salsa, put the chicken. Then, pour the remaining salsa over it.
5. Bake for 30 minutes at 375 °F, or until the chicken reaches 165 °F.
6. Sprinkle the top of the chicken with the cheese and remove it from the oven.
7. For 3-4 minutes, return to the oven to melt the cheese.
8. Sprinkle with cilantro.

7.94 Chicken Alfredo Pizza

Servings: 8 I Time: 35 mins I Difficulty: Easy
Nutrients per serving: Calories: 660 kcal I Fat: 60g I Carbohydrates: 7g I Protein: 13g I Fiber: 7g

Ingredients

For the crust:

- ¾ cup almond flour
- 1 egg
- 2 cups shredded mozzarella
- 2 Tbsps. cream cheese

For the Alfredo sauce:

- 1 clove garlic, minced
- 1 ounce cream cheese
- 1/3 cup heavy whipping cream
- 1/4 cup shredded Parmesan cheese
- 2 Tbsps. butter

For assembling:

- 1 cup chicken, cooked and cubed
- 1/4 cup spinach, chopped
- 2 cups Mozzarella cheese

Method

To make the crust:

1. Preheat the furnace to.
2. Microwave the cream cheese and mozzarella for 1 minute.
3. Add egg and almonds.
4. On a large sheet of parchment paper, place the dough. Top it with a second parchment cover.
5. Roll the dough out into a circle with a diameter of 12 inches.
6. Take out the top piece of parchment and pass the bottom sheet to a pizza pan with the dough on it.
7. Bake for 10 minutes at 425 °F or until finely golden in the crust.

To make the Alfredo sauce:

1. Add the butter, cream, garlic, and cream cheese to a small saucepan over medium heat to melt cheese and butter.
2. Add parmesan cheese and stir to make it creamy and smooth.

To assemble:

1. Place the Alfredo sauce uniformly over the crust of the pizza.
2. Cover the mozzarella cheese with 3/4 of it.
3. Attach the spinach and chicken and top with the remainder of the mozzarella.
4. Return for 10 minutes to the oven.
5. Let set before slicing and serving for 2 minutes.

7.95 Pork Chops with Dijon Sauce

Servings: 4 I Time: 17 mins I Difficulty: Easy

Nutrients per serving: Calories: 201 kcal I Fat: 17g I Carbohydrates: 1g I Protein: 12g I Fiber: 0g

Ingredients

- 4 boneless pork chops, about 6 ounces each
- 1 Tbsp. avocado oil
- 2 Tbsps. dijon mustard
- 1 Tsp. minced parsley
- 1/2 Tsp. salt
- 1/2 Tsp. cracked pepper
- 1/3 cup chicken broth
- 1/3 cup heavy cream

Method

1. Sprinkle with salt and pepper on both sides of the pork chops.
2. Heat oil over medium heat in a large skillet until it shimmers.
3. Add the pork chops to the skillet and cook, about 5 minutes per side, until golden on each side and cooked through.
4. Remove the pork chops and set them aside on a tray.
5. To scrape up any browned bits from the bottom of the plate, add the chicken broth to the skillet and whisk well.
6. Apply the dijon and cream and cook until the sauce reduces and thickens to your liking, stirring frequently.
7. Put the pork chops back in the skillet and sprinkle them with parsley.
8. Serve over the pork chops with a drizzle of Dijon cream sauce.

7.96 Baked Chicken Drumsticks

Servings: 6 I Time: 50 mins I Difficulty: Easy
Nutrients per serving: Calories: 323 kcal I Fat: 18g I Carbohydrates: 1g I Protein: 37g I Fiber: g

Ingredients

- 2 pounds chicken drumsticks
- 2 Tbsps. avocado oil
- 1 Tsp. paprika
- 1 Tsp. garlic powder
- 1 Tsp. onion powder
- 1 Tsp. chopped parsley
- ½ Tsp. salt
- ½ Tsp. cracked pepper

Method

1. In a big zip top bag, add all the ingredients and seal them. Smush the chicken in bag to season it.
2. On the baking sheet, arrange the chicken and bake 400°F for 45 minutes.
3. Serve.

7.97 Pizza Stuffed Chicken

Servings: 4 I Time: 45 mins I Difficulty: Easy
Nutrients per serving: Calories: 402 kcal I Fat: 26g I Carbohydrates: 6g I Protein: 32g I Fiber: 1g

Ingredients

- ¼ cup Parmesan cheese
- ½ Tsp. Italian seasoning
- ½ Tsp. salt
- 1 cup pizza sauce
- 1 Tsp. garlic powder
- 1 Tsp. minced parsley
- 2 cups grated mozzarella, divided
- 2 Tsps. avocado oil
- 32 slices pepperoni
- 4 chicken breasts, about 6 ounces each

Method

1. Place the chicken breasts on a cutting board.
2. Drizzle oil on the chicken and season with garlic powder, salt and Italian seasoning.
3. In the chicken breast, position 1/4 cup of mozzarella. Over the cheese, add 4 slices of pepperoni.
4. In the prepared baking dish, put the chicken and drizzle it with the pizza sauce. Spread the sauce over the chicken tops to coat them.
5. Sprinkle the remaining mozzarella with it. Top with the slices of Parmesan and the remaining pepperoni.
6. Bake chicken for 30-35 minutes at 375°F.
7. Until serving, sprinkle it with fresh parsley.

7.98 Low Carb Chicken Patties

Servings: 10 I Time: 16 mins I Difficulty: Easy
Nutrients per serving: Calories: 373 kcal I Fat: 25g I Carbohydrates: 5g I Protein: 33g I Fiber: 3g

Ingredients

- 2 cups cooked, shredded chicken breasts
- 2 Tbsps. mayonnaise
- 1 egg
- 2 green onions, minced
- 1 Tsp. fresh dill
- 1 Tsp. fresh parsley
- 1 Tsp. salt
- 2 Tbsps. butter, for frying
- 1/2 cup almond flour
- 1/2 Tsp. pepper

Method

1. To a mixing bowl, add all the ingredients except for the butter and whisk well to combine.
2. In order to scoop the mixture into your hand, use a medium cookie scoop.
3. Heat a large skillet with a heavy bottom over medium heat and add butter.
4. Add the chicken patties to the skillet once the butter has melted and cook until golden brown on each side, about 3 minutes on each side.
5. Immediately serve.

7.99 Ranch Grilled Chicken

Servings: 6 I Time: 8 hrs 20 mins I Difficulty: Easy
Nutrients per serving: Calories: 494 kcal I Fat: 19g I Carbohydrates: 4g I Protein: 71g I Fiber: 1g

Ingredients

- ½ cup avocado oil
- ½ cup ranch dressing
- 1 Tbsp. apple cider vinegar
- 1 Tbsp. chopped parsley
- 1 Tsp. hot sauce
- 1 Tsp. salt
- 2 Tbsps. buttermilk
- 2 Tbsps. Worcestershire sauce
- 3 pounds boneless, skinless chicken breasts

Method

1. To a mixing bowl, add all but the chicken.
2. Add the chicken breasts and add the marinade to a baking dish or gallon zip top container. To coat the chicken, stir well.
3. For at least 30 minutes and up to 8 hours, marinate the chicken in the refrigerator. The longer you marinate the chicken, the more delicious it will be.
4. Heat the grill to a heat that is medium.
5. Remove the chicken from the marinade and let the chicken drip off a lot of it, then return it to the hot grill.
6. Grill on each side for 5-10 minutes until cooked through, depending on your chicken's thickness.

7.100 Lemon Caper Chicken

Servings: 4 I Time: 25 mins I Difficulty: Easy
Nutrients per serving: Calories: 326 kcal I Fat: 19g I Carbohydrates: 2g I Protein: 36g I Fiber: 0g

Ingredients

- ¼ cup heavy cream
- 1 cup chicken broth
- 1 pound thin sliced chicken breasts
- 1 Tbsp. avocado oil
- 1 Tbsp. lemon juice
- 1 Tsp. pepper
- 1 Tsp. salt
- 2 Tbsps. butter
- 3 Tbsps. capers

Method

1. With salt and pepper, season the chicken on both sides.
2. Heat the avocado oil over medium heat in a big, heavy-bottomed skillet.
3. Cook the chicken, flipping for about 8 minutes halfway through cooking.
4. Remove the chicken and set it aside on a tray.
5. Apply the butter and the chicken broth to the skillet and bring it to a boil.
6. Reduce the chicken broth by half, about 5 minutes or so.
7. Apply the lemon juice and cream to the skillet and boil until the sauce is thick enough to cover the back of the spoon, stirring occasionally, for around 5 minutes.
8. Add the sauce to the capers and stir to combine.
9. Put the chicken back in the skillet and coat it with sauce. To re-warm the chicken, cook for 1 more minute.
10. Immediately serve.

7.101 Creamy Tuscan Shrimp

Servings: 4 I Time: 17 mins I Difficulty: Easy
Nutrients per serving: Calories: 368 kcal I Fat: 29g I Carbohydrates: 8g I Protein: 20g I Fiber: 2g

Ingredients

- ½ cup sun-dried tomatoes
- 1 cup chopped spinach
- 1 cup heavy cream
- 1 Tsp. garlic powder
- 1 Tsp. paprika
- 1 Tsp. salt
- 16 ounces large raw shrimp, peeled, deveined, tail off
- 2 cloves garlic, minced
- 2 Tbsps. butter

Method

1. Over medium heat, heat a big, heavy-bottomed skillet. The butter is added to the skillet.
2. Attach the shrimp when the butter has melted and sprinkle with the ground garlic and paprika.
3. Cook for 5 minutes or until the shrimp is pink and opaque, stirring occasionally.
4. Remove the shrimp and set it aside on a tray.
5. To mix, add the sun-dried tomatoes, heavy cream, and garlic to the pan and stir well. Let the sauce cook over a low heat for 2 minutes to thicken.
6. Put in the spinach and stir thoroughly. Continue cooking over low heat for about 2 minutes until the spinach has wilted and the sauce has thickened.
7. Put the shrimp back in the skillet and coat it with the sauce. Sprinkle, to taste, with salt.
8. Immediately serve.

7.102 Low Carb Tamale Pie

Servings: 4 I Time: 35 mins I Difficulty: Easy

Nutrients per serving: Calories: 580 kcal I Fat: 43g I Carbohydrates: 13g I Protein: 31g I Fiber: 5g

Ingredients

- ¼ Tsp. baking soda
- ⅓ cup heavy cream
- ½ cup coconut flour
- ½ Tsp. salt
- 1 cup grated cheddar cheese
- 1 Tbsp. taco seasoning
- 1/2 cup enchilada sauce, see note
- 2 cups shredded chicken breasts
- 2 Tbsps. 1:1 sugar substitute
- 3 large eggs
- 4 ounces diced green chiles
- 6 Tbsps. butter, melted
- Cilantro, hot sauce, sour cream, lime, avocado - for serving

Method

1. Preheat the furnace to 350 °F.
2. To a mixing bowl, add the milk, melted butter, and eggs and whisk to blend.
3. To mix, add the coconut flour, green chiles, salt, sugar replacer, and baking soda to the bowl and stir well.
4. In the prepared dish, spread the mixture and bake for 15 minutes. The cornbread in the center should only be put on top, but still quite jiggly.
5. To poke holes all over the cornbread, use a fork.
6. Drizzle the enchilada sauce on top of the cornbread.
7. Top a bowl with the cooked chicken and taco seasoning and stir to coat.
8. Over the top of the cornbread, arrange the chicken and sprinkle with grated cheddar.
9. Return for 10 minutes to the oven.
10. With your favorite toppings, serve.

7.103 Skillet Cabbage Lasagna

Servings: 6 I Time: 35 mins I Difficulty: Easy
Nutrients per serving: Calories: 413 kcal I Fat: 29g I Carbohydrates: 14g I Protein: 30g I Fiber: 4g

Ingredients

For the lasagna:
- ½ onion, minced
- 1 clove garlic, minced
- 1 medium head cabbage, cored and chopped
- 1 pound ground beef
- 2 cups shredded mozzarella
- 24 ounce jar Rao's Marinara

For the ricotta topping:
- ¼ cup shredded Parmesan
- 1 clove garlic, minced
- 2 cups ricotta
- 2 Tbsps. freshly chopped parsley

Method

1. Over medium prepare, heat a large skillet and add the ground beef.
2. Brown the beef until cooked about halfway, breaking it up as it heats.
3. Apply the garlic and onion to the meat mixture and cook until the meat has cooked through, stirring regularly.
4. Apply and blend marinara to the meat.
5. Using the skillet to add the cabbage and gently stir to coat the meat sauce on cabbage.
6. Continue to cook over low heat for 15 minutes or until the cabbage is as soft as you like.
7. Remove the cover and replace the skillet with the mozzarella. To mix, stir well.

8. Add the parmesan, ricotta, parsley, and garlic to a small bowl to create the ricotta topping, and whisk to mix.
9. Spread the mixture of ricotta over the cabbage and cook for 2 minutes to warm up over low heat.
10. Immediately serve.

7.104 Cilantro Lime Shrimp

Servings: 4 I Time: 11 mins I Difficulty: Easy
Nutrients per serving: Calories: 239 kcal I Fat: 7g I Carbohydrates: 2g I Protein: 38g

Ingredients

- 1 Tbsp. avocado oil
- 1 Tsp. salt
- 1/2 Tsp. cumin
- 1/4 cup chopped cilantro
- 1/4 Tsp. cayenne more to taste
- 2 Tbsps. lime juice
- 24 ounces large shrimp peeled and deveined
- 4 cloves garlic minced

Method

1. Heat the oil over medium heat in a large skillet. Sprinkle the cumin, flour, and cayenne with the added shrimp.
2. Cook for 4-5 minutes or until the shrimp is pink, stirring frequently.
3. In the skillet, add the garlic and cook for 1 minute more.
4. Remove and add the cilantro and lime juice from the sun. To mix, stir well.
5. Immediately serve.

7.105 Crockpot Cabbage Soup with Beef

Servings: 6 I Time: 4 hrs 10 mins I Difficulty: Easy
Nutrients per serving: Calories: 205 kcal I Fat: 10g I Carbohydrates: 8g I Protein: 25g I Fiber: 3g

Ingredients

- ½ onion, chopped
- 1 carrot, chopped
- 1 medium head cabbage, chopped
- 1 pound lean ground beef
- 1 Tbsp. Italian seasoning
- 1 Tsp. salt
- 2 cloves garlic, minced
- 2 stalks celery, chopped
- 5 cups beef broth

Method

1. Brown the beef in a medium skillet over medium heat.
2. Add the onion to the beef and completely cook the meat.
3. Drain the oil and add onion and beef in a crockpot.
4. Top the crockpot and fill with the carrot, beef broth, Italian seasoning, celery, cabbage, garlic, and salt.
5. Cook for 4 hours on high heat.

7.106 Guacamole Chicken Melt

Servings: 4 I Time: 22 mins I Difficulty: Easy
Nutrients per serving: Calories: 501 kcal I Fat: 30g I Carbohydrates:11g I Protein: 47g I Fiber: 5g

Ingredients

For the chicken:
- 1 Tbsp. avocado oil
- 1 Tsp. cumin
- 1 Tsp. garlic salt
- 1 Tsp. paprika
- 4 chicken breasts

For the avocado:
- 1 Tbsp. lime juice
- 1 Tsp. cumin
- 1 Tsp. salt
- 2 avocado
- 2 Tbsps. minced cilantro
- 2 Tbsps. minced red onion

For assembling:
- ½ cup grated Pepper jack cheese
- 4 slices bacon, fried crisp

Method

1. Add the oil to a large and heat over medium heat.
2. Season the chicken on all sides with paprika, cumin, garlic, and salt.
3. Add the chicken to the pan and cook until the chicken is fully cooked.
4. In a small bowl, add the red onion, avocado, cumin, salt, coriander, and lime juice and mash together with a fork.
5. Spoon the guacamole uniformly over each piece of chicken.
6. Break the pieces of bacon in half and lay 2 halves on each breast of chicken. Sprinkle cheese with it.
7. Cover the pan with a lid and let the cheese melt for 2 minutes.
8. Serve.

7.107 Creamy Tuscan Chicken

Servings: 4 I Time: 20 mins I Difficulty: Easy
Nutrients per serving: Calories: 485 kcal I Fat: 32g I Carbohydrates: 8g I Protein: 42g I Fiber: 2g

Ingredients

- 4 thin sliced chicken breasts
- 1 Tsp. paprika
- 1 Tsp. garlic powder
- 1 Tsp. salt
- 2 Tbsps. butter
- 1 cup heavy cream
- ½ cup oil-packed sun-dried tomatoes
- 2 cloves garlic, minced
- 1 cup chopped spinach

Method

1. Combine the salt, paprika, and garlic powder and scatter evenly over the chicken.
2. Add butter to a heated skillet over medium heat.
3. Add the chicken breasts when the butter has melted and cook for 5 minutes on each side or until cooked through.
4. Remove the chicken and set it aside on a tray.
5. To mix, add the sun-dried tomatoes, heavy cream, and garlic to the pan and stir well. Let the sauce cook over a low heat for 2 minutes to thicken.
6. Attach the spinach and stir thoroughly. Continue cooking over low heat, about 3 minutes, until the spinach has wilted and the sauce has thickened.
7. Put the chicken back in the skillet and coat it with sauce.
8. Immediately serve.

7.108 Chicken Lazone

Servings: 4 I Time: 20 mins I Difficulty: Easy
Nutrients per serving: Calories: 507 kcal I Fat: 37g I Carbohydrates: 3g I Protein: 39g I Fiber: 0g

Ingredients

- ½ Tsp. garlic powder
- ½ Tsp. onion powder
- ½ Tsp. paprika
- 1 cup heavy cream
- 1 Tsp. chili powder
- 1 Tsp. salt
- 4 Tbsps. butter, divided

- 4 thin sliced chicken breasts

Method
1. In a small cup, add the garlic powder, chili powder, onion powder, salt, and paprika and whisk to mix.
2. To season, sprinkle half the spice mixture on both sides of the chicken breasts.
3. Heat butter in a heated skillet over medium heat.
4. Add the chicken breasts and cook until they are cooked through.
5. Remove the chicken and set it aside on a tray.
6. Put the heavy cream and 2 tsps. Butter, and spices in the skillet. Whisk to blend well.
7. Bring to a boil and let the sauce get thick around 2 minutes.
8. Put the chicken back in the pan to coat it with the sauce.
9. Immediately serve.

7.109 Low Carb Zuppa Toscana

Servings: 8 I Time: 40 mins I Difficulty: Easy
Nutrients per serving: Calories: 295 kcal I Fat: 18g I Carbohydrates: 10g I Protein: 20g I Fiber: 3g

Ingredients
- 1 cup heavy cream
- 1 pound spicy Italian sausage
- 1 yellow onion, diced
- 2 turnips, sliced, about 10 ounces total
- 3 cloves garlic, minced
- 4 cups chopped kale
- 4 slices bacon, diced
- 6 cups chicken broth
- Salt and pepper

Method
1. Over medium heat, heat a Dutch oven or big sauce pot. Add the Italian sausage to the pot and start browning the meat as it cooks, breaking it up.
2. Add the onion, bacon, and garlic when the meat is about half browned, and continue to cook and stir until the sausage is cooked completely.
3. Attach the turnips and broth of chicken and bring to a boil. Reduce the heat and cook for 10 minutes to simmer.
4. Add the kale and cook for 5 minutes or until both the kale and the turnips are tender.
5. Remove and stir in the cream from the sun. Taste and, as needed, add salt and pepper.
6. Immediately serve.

7.110 Low Carb Goulash

Servings: 8 I Time: 45 mins I Difficulty: Easy
Nutrients per serving: Calories: 239 kcal I Fat: 16g I Carbohydrates: 7g I Protein: 18g I Fiber: 2g

Ingredients
- 1 bay leaf
- 1 cup beef broth
- 1 pound ground beef
- 1 Tbsp. Italian seasoning
- 1 Tbsp. soy sauce
- 1 Tsp. seasoned salt
- 1 yellow onion, diced
- 2 cloves garlic, minced
- 24 ounces Rao's Marinara
- 3 medium zucchini, chopped

Method
1. In a dutch oven, add the onion, garlic, and ground beef and brown over medium heat. Drain the fat and return the meat to the pan when the beef is cooked.
2. The remaining ingredients are added to the pot and brought to a boil. Simmer for 20 minutes, cover, and cook, stirring periodically, or until the zucchini is as soft as you like.
3. Prior to serving, remove the bay leaf.

7.111 Quick prawn, coconut & tomato curry

Servings: 4 I Time: 30 mins I Difficulty: Easy
Nutrients per serving: Calories: 335 kcal I Fat: 26g I Carbohydrates: 7g I Protein: 19g I Fiber: 1g

Ingredients
- 1 green chilli, deseeded and sliced
- 1 medium onion, thinly sliced
- 1 tbsp tomato purée
- 2 garlic cloves, sliced
- 2 tbsp vegetable oil
- 200ml coconut cream
- 200ml vegetable stock
- 3 tbsp curry paste
- 350g raw prawn
- coriander sprigs and rice, to serve

Method
1. In a large frying pan, heat the oil. Fry the garlic, half the chilli and onions for at least 5 minutes.
2. Then, put curry paste and cook for additional 1 minute.
3. Add the creamy coconut, purée of tomatoes, and stock.
4. Add the prawns after 10 mins simmer on medium heat.
5. Cook for three minutes.
6. Sprinkle with the remaining sprigs of coriander and green chilies.
7. Serve with rice.

7.112 Peppered Mackerel & Pink Pickled Onion Salad

Servings: 6 I Time: 15 mins I Difficulty: Easy
Nutrients per serving: Calories: 318 kcal I Fat: 25g I Carbohydrates: 7g I Protein: 13g I Fiber: 4g

Ingredients
- 100g bag honey-roasted mixed nuts
- 100g bag watercress
- 240g pack peppered smoked mackerel, torn into pieces
- 250g pack ready-cooked beetroot

For the dressing
- 1 small red onion , very thinly sliced
- 3 tbsp sherry vinegar
- 4 tbsp extra virgin olive oil
- pinch of sugar

Method
1. Mix the vinegar, onion, sugar, and some salt. Then, chop the nuts and dice the beetroot.
2. Divide the smoked mackerel and the watercress between six plates. Sprinkle nuts and beetroot over it and top with pickled onions.
3. Drizzle the dressing with oil in pickled vinegar.

7.113 Mediterranean Sardine Salad

Servings: 4 I Time: 15 mins I Difficulty: Easy
Nutrients per serving: Calories: 140 kcal I Fat: 10g I Carbohydrates: 1g I Protein: 10g I Fiber: 1g

Ingredients
- 1 tbsp caper, drained
- 1 tbsp olive oil
- 1 tbsp red wine vinegar
- 2 x 120g cans sardines in tomato sauce, drained and sauce reserved

- 90g bag salad leaves
- handful black olives, roughly chopped

Method
1. Divide the salad leaves, then drizzle over the capers and olives.
2. Cut the sardines roughly and put it into the salad.
3. Mix the tomato sauce with the vinegar and oil and sprinkle over the salad.

7.114 Smoked Trout, Watercress & Beetroot Salad

Servings: 4 I Time: 10 mins I Difficulty: Easy
Nutrients per serving: Calories: 436 kcal I Fat: 38g I Carbohydrates: 7g I Protein: 17g I Fiber: 2g

Ingredients
- 1 tbsp creamed horseradish
- 1 tbsp French mustard
- 145g bag watercress, large stalks removed
- 150ml/¼ pint olive oil
- 250g pack cooked beetroot
- 2x 135g packs smoked trout fillets
- 50ml vinegar

Method
1. Put a bit of salt, ground pepper, olive oil, plus mustard, and vinegar in an empty bottle with a lid.
2. Refrigerate it.
3. Break the beetroot in quarters in a bowl.
4. Then, put 2 tbsps. of dressing and horseradish creamed and stir well.
5. Remove the skin and cut the tuna fish into pieces.
6. Mix the beetroot and watercress then put the smoked trout on top.

7.115 Avocado, Prawn & Fennel Cocktails

Servings: 4 I Time: 10 mins I Difficulty: Easy
Nutrients per serving: Calories: 223 kcal I Fat: 18g I Carbohydrates: 2g I Protein: 13g I Fiber: 2g

Ingredients
For the dressing
- 1 segmented orange
- 4 tbsp extra-virgin olive oil
- juice 1 lemon

For the salad
- 1 avocado, quartered, peeled and sliced
- 1 fennel bulb, trimmed, halved and finely sliced
- 200g cooked king prawn
- 3 spring onions, sliced
- 55g bag wild rocket

Method
1. Mix the citrus juices and oil in a bowl with some pepper and salt to make dressing. Then set aside.
2. In a bowl, mix all the other ingredients, except the rocket, together with the half of the dressing and orange segments.
3. Put the rocket leaves into 4 Martini glasses.
4. Pile the salad, then sprinkle with the remaining dressing.
5. Serve

7.116 Spinach Artichoke Stuffed Peppers

Servings: 8 I Time: 45 mins I Difficulty: Easy
Nutrients per serving: Calories: 178 kcal I Fat: 13g I Carbohydrates: 7g I Protein: 9g I Fiber: 2g

Ingredients
- ¼ cup grated Parmesan
- ¼ Tsp. pepper
- ¼ Tsp. red pepper flakes

- ¼ Tsp. salt
- 1 clove garlic, minced
- 1 cup chopped baby spinach
- 1 cup cooked shredded chicken
- 1/3 cup grated Mozzarella
- 2 Tbsps. mayonnaise
- 4 bell peppers, any color
- 4 ounces artichoke hearts, diced
- 6 ounces cream cheese, room temperature

Method
1. Add water about 2 tbsps. in a bakery dish.
2. Cut pepper in half and place them in baking dish.
3. To a medium mixing bowl, add the spinach, mozzarella, artichoke hearts, red pepper flakes, cream cheese, mayonnaise, garlic, parmesan, salt and pepper. To mix, stir well.
4. To the mixture, add the chicken and whisk to blend.
5. Spoon the filling into each pepper evenly and put the peppers back in the dish.
6. Tightly cover the pan with foil and bake for 35 minutes.
7. Immediately serve.

7.117 Mozzarella Stuffed Meatballs

Servings: 4 I Time: 25 mins I Difficulty: Easy
Nutrients per serving: Calories: 562 kcal I Fat: 37g I Carbohydrates: 7g I Protein: 48g I Fiber: 1g

Ingredients
- ½ Tsp. oregano
- 1 cup crushed pork rinds
- 1 cup marinara
- 1 large egg
- 1-pound ground beef, 90% lean
- 1 Tsp. garlic powder
- 1 Tsp. onion powder
- 2 Tbsps. chopped parsley
- 2 Tbsps. heavy cream
- 2 Tbsps. water
- 6 ounces mozzarella, cut into 12 small cubes

Method
1. In a medium mixing bowl, add the pork rinds, water, ground beef, onion powder, milk, egg, garlic powder, and oregano and blend well with clean hands to combine.
2. Divide 12 separate portions of the meatballs and form each piece into a tiny patty.
3. In the middle of each patty, put a slice of cheese and carefully fold the edges around the cheese to seal it in.
4. Be sure to seal the meatball completely around the cheese so that when baking it does not leak out.
5. In a 12-inch cast iron skillet that has been sprayed with non-stick spray, put the meatballs.
6. For 15 minutes, bake at 400°F.
7. Spoon marinara over each meatball.
8. Sprinkle just before serving with parsley.

7.118 Slow Cooker BBQ Chicken Wings

Servings: 8 I Time: 1 hr 40 mins I Difficulty: Easy
Nutrients per serving: Calories: 495 kcal I Fat: 32g I Carbohydrates: 4g I Protein: 43g

Ingredients
- 1 Tsp. garlic powder
- 1 Tsp. pepper
- 1 Tsp. salt
- 1/2 cup chicken broth
- 1/4 cup reduced sugar ketchup
- 3 Tbsps. Italian salad dressing

- 4 pounds chicken wing pieces, thawed

Method

1. To a cooker, add the chicken wings.
2. Sprinkle garlic powder, pepper, and salt over the chicken.
3. Cook for 1.5 hour at a high temperature.
4. Take out the chicken and place on a baking sheet.
5. For 2-3 minutes, place the chicken on the broiler to allow the skin to become crisp.
6. Stir together the Italian salad dressing and ketchup in a small bowl until smooth.
7. Brush the mixture uniformly between the pieces of chicken.
8. Place the coated chicken to caramelize the sauce under the broiler and watch closely for about 2 minutes.
9. Take out of oven and quickly serve.

7.119 Lemon Baked Cod

Servings: 4 I Time: 25 mins I Difficulty: Easy
Nutrients per serving: Calories: 136 kcal I Fat: 12g I Carbohydrates: 1g I Protein: 7g I Fiber: 0g

Ingredients

- ¼ cup butter, softened
- ½ Tsp. pepper
- ½ Tsp. salt
- 1 Tbsp. lemon juice
- 1 Tbsp. minced parsley
- 1 Tsp. minced garlic
- 4 cod fillets, 4 ounces each
- 4 slices lemon

Method

1. Spray with non-stick spray on a baking sheet.
2. In a small bowl, add the lemon juice, butter, garlic, salt, parsley, and pepper and mix with a fork until well mixed.
3. Spread the butter mixture evenly and top with a slice of lemon over each cod filet.
4. Bake at 400°F for 15-20 minutes.

7.120 Teriyaki Chicken Stir Fry

Servings: 4 I Time: 30 mins I Difficulty: Easy
Nutrients per serving: Calories: 271 kcal I Fat: 10g I Carbohydrates: 5g I Protein: 24g I Fiber: 4g

Ingredients

- 1 cup broccoli florets
- 1 cup cauliflower florets
- 1 pound boneless skinless chicken breasts
- 1 Tsp. chili paste
- 1 Tsp. minced garlic
- 1 Tsp. minced ginger
- 1/4 cup honey substitute
- 1/4 cup soy sauce
- 1/4 cup vinegar
- 2 cups chopped bell peppers
- 2 Tbsps. vegetable oil, divided

Method

1. Over medium-high heat, heat a large skillet.
2. Add vegetable oil about 1 tbsp. to a heated skillet.
3. Add diced chicken to a skillet.
4. Cook, stirring frequently, until cooked through.
5. Remove and set aside on a tray.
6. Add a different oil about 1 Tbsp. in the skillet.
7. Stir in the broccoli, cauliflower, and peppers and cook for 5 minutes or until tender-crisp with stirring frequently.
8. In a small cup, whisk together the vinegar, soy sauce, garlic, ginger, sugar, and chili paste.
9. Apply to the mixture and stir to coat. Cook for 3 minutes, stirring often.
10. Cook it while stirring for 2 minutes.

11. Immediately serve.

7.121 Broiled Lobster Tails

Servings: 2 I Time: 10 mins I Difficulty: Easy
Nutrients per serving: Calories: 208 kcal I Fat: 10g I Carbohydrates: 5g I Protein: 23g I Fiber: 1g

Ingredients

- 2 Lobster tails
- celtic sea salt
- 1 tsp garlic powder
- 1 tsp smoked paprika
- 1 1/2 tbsp butter, divided
- 1/2 tsp white pepper

Method

1. Preheat the broiler to a high degree.
2. On a baking sheet or in an oven-safe bowl, put the lobster tails.
3. Cut the top of the lobster tail shell carefully down to the tip of the tail with sharp kitchen scissors or a knife, avoiding the meat. Devein and, if necessary, remove any grit.
4. Pull the shell down carefully, so the meat looks like it's lying open on top of the shell.
5. Slide a lemon wedge or two under the lobster meat, between the meat and the tail, to make it look even better.
6. In a small tub, combine the spices.
7. Sprinkle spices on them.
8. Using the lobster tail to add tiny pats of butter.
9. Place the upper middle rack in the oven.
10. Cook for about 8-10 minutes, until the meat is opaque and white.
11. Remove and serve with the drawn butter right away.

7.122 Rotisserie Prime Rib

Servings: 2 I Time: 4 hrs 45 mins I Difficulty: Easy
Nutrients per serving: Calories: 124 kcal I Fat: 8g I Carbohydrates: 6g I Protein: 8g I Fiber: 2g

Ingredients

- 2 prime rib roast, about 5 pounds
- 2 tbsp fresh cracked pepper
- 2 Tbsp. garlic powder
- 4 tbsp Italian seasonings or Aleppo pepper
- 4 Tbsps. kosher, Celtic, or other coarse salt

Method

1. Roast well.
2. Let it sit for around 2 hours at room temperature.
3. Take grill temperature to 350°F.
4. Place rotisserie forks in the roast.
5. Cook roast for 2 – 2.5 hours over charcoal. Keep the grill temperature about 350°F while cooking.
6. Remove the prime rib from the rotisserie and cover, loosely, with foil for 30-45 minutes before the meat rests.
7. Slice them and serve.

7.123 Smoked Brisket

Servings: 12 I Time: 8 hrs 45 mins I Difficulty: Easy
Nutrients per serving: Calories: 137 kcal I Fat: 9g I Carbohydrates: 6g I Protein: 7g I Fiber: 1g

Ingredients

- 1 15 lb brisket

Brisket Baste:

- 1 cup beer
- 5 tbsp butter, melted
- 1/4 cup apple cider vinegar
- 1/4 cup beef stock

Brisket Rub:

- 1 tbsp brown sugar

- 2 tbsp chili powder
- 2 tbsp coarse ground black pepper
- 2 tbsp garlic powder
- 2 tbsp kosher salt
- 2 tbsp onion powder
- 2 tbsp paprika

Method
1. Start the Traeger grill.
2. Set the temperature to 225°F and preheat for 10 minutes with the lid closed.
3. In a small cup, blend the chili pepper, onion powder, kosher salt, garlic powder, paprika, and pepper together.
4. Season Brisket on all sides.
5. Place the brisket on the grill rack, fat side down.
6. Cook the brisket until the internal temperature exceeds 160°F.
7. Remove from the grill.
8. Double seal the aluminum foil with the meat and apply the beef broth to the foil package.
9. Grill, cook up to 204°F.
10. Remove from the grill once done.
11. Split and serve.

7.124 Smoked Turkey

Servings: 6 | Time: 2 hrs 20 mins | Difficulty: Easy
Nutrients per serving: Calories: 110 kcal | Fat: 2g | Carbohydrates: 7g | Protein: 3g | Fiber: 2g

Ingredients
Brine:
- 1 cup kosher salt
- 1 gallon vegetable stock
- 2 Tbsp. black peppercorns
- 2 Tsps. savory
- 1 gallon iced cubes
- 1/2 cup light brown sugar
- 1 1/2 Tsps. allspice berries
- 1 1/2 Tsps. rosemary

Turkey:
- 1 turkey, 12-14lb
- Bag of charcoal
- Chips or chunks for smoking (fruit wood or oak)

Method
1. Bring all the ingredients to a boil.
2. Then, let it cool.
3. Put the cooled brine with ice in a cooler.
4. Put turkey in it and seal it in cooler.
5. Remove the turkey and air dry it to reach at room temperature.
6. Use a damp cloth or towel to cover the turkey.
7. When smoker reaches around 250°F add the turkey directly to the grates.
8. Keep rotating turkey and maintain fire at constant level.
9. Smoke the turkey for 30-40 minutes per pound at 235-250 °F before it reaches an internal temperature of 160 °F.
10. Smoke, cover, and let stand for 30 minutes prior to carving.

7.125 Brown Bag Herb Roasted Turkey

Servings: 8 | Time: 3 hrs 5 mins | Difficulty: Easy
Nutrients per serving: Calories: 99 kcal | Fat: 9g | Carbohydrates: 4g | Protein: 2g | Fiber: 1g

Ingredients
- 1 carrot, chopped
- 1 celery stick, chopped
- 1 cup chicken broth
- 1 lemon, quartered
- 1 onion, peeled and cut into large pieces

- 1 turkey, 10 to 20 lbs, brought to room temperature
- 2 tbsp italian herb blend
- 6 tbsp butter, softened
- Large parchment paper bag, or brown paper shopping bag
- Salt and pepper

Method
1. To 375°F, preheat the oven.
2. Generally, rub the turkey with salt and pepper.
3. Within the turkey, place the celery, onion, lemon, and carrot as well as the collar and giblets.
4. Rub butter all over the turkey.
5. Sprinkle the herbs generously over the turkey.
6. Put the turkey in the bag and place it in a pan for roasting.
7. Within the turkey cavity, pour the chicken broth.
8. Fold the bag closed, and tuck it under the turkey so that it locks while it cooks in the steam.
9. Place the turkey in the preheated oven's center rack.
10. For the first 10 lbs, the cooking time is calculated to be around 2.5 hours, plus 12 minutes for each additional pound.
11. Remove from the oven and leave in the bag for 15 minutes until the turkey is completely cooked.
12. Then break open the bag, carve it, and serve.

7.126 Swiss Steaks

Servings: 4 | Time: 3 hrs 10 mins | Difficulty: Easy
Nutrients per serving: Calories: 333 kcal | Fat: 19g | Carbohydrates: 9g | Protein: 27g | Fiber: 3g

Ingredients
- 1 (14.5-ounce) can diced tomatoes
- 1 large onion, thinly sliced
- 1 Tbsp. Worcestershire sauce
- 1 tsp cracked pepper
- 1 tsp kosher salt
- 1 Tsp. dried oregano
- 1 Tsp. smoked paprika
- 1/2 can tomato sauce (7 oz)
- 14 oz beef stock
- 2 stalks celery, chopped
- 2 tbsp olive oil
- 4 cube steaks
- 5 cloves garlic, minced

Method
1. Preheat the furnace to 325 °F.
2. Generous steaks with salt and pepper.
3. Add olive oil to a wide pan or dutch oven and heat to a shimmery condition.
4. On both sides of the brown steaks, around 4 minutes per hand.
5. Remove from the pan when the steaks are browned, and set aside.
6. Add the onion and celery to the pan and cook until slightly browned and tender.
7. Stir in the garlic and cook until fragrant, about 45 seconds, with the onions and celery.
8. Combine onions, tomato sauce, spices, and sauce with Worcestershire.
9. Cook for about 5 minutes, before it bubbles.
10. Stir in the beef broth and placed the steaks back in the pan.
11. The cover pan has a close-fitting lid.
12. Braise for 2 1/2 hours in the oven until the steaks are tender and when pressed with a fork, the meat slightly pulls away.
13. Add up to 1 cup of water to continue cooking until the steaks are soft if the liquid cooks too much.
14. Place a little sauce in the pan and enjoy it!

7.127 One Pot Garlic Butter Chicken Thighs And Mushrooms

Servings: 6 | Time: 25 mins | Difficulty: Easy
Nutrients per serving: Calories: 335 kcal | Fat: 24g | Carbohydrates: 7g | Protein: 25g | Fiber: 1g

Ingredients

- 1 cup chicken stock
- 1 pinch to 1 tsp red pepper flakes
- 1/2 cup diced cilantro, optional
- 1/4 cup parmesan cheese
- 2 tbsp lemon juice
- 4 chicken thighs, bones removed
- 4 tbsp butter, divided
- 6-10 cloves garlic, sliced in half or finely diced
- 8 oz cremini mushrooms, stems removed and wiped clean
- PINCH of salt

Method

1. Over a heated pan, add and melt the butter.
2. Then add chicken with a minute amount of salt.
3. Cook until chicken is turned to slight brown color.
4. Remove from pan and save left over oil.
5. Then, add garlic and stir.
6. Add mushrooms and to stop them from burning stir continuously.
7. Then, add butter second time and melt it.
8. Brown the mushroom and garlic without burning them.
9. Add cilantro and red pepper flakes.
10. Add lemon juice, stock, and cheese.
11. Boil and let it rest for 2 minutes to become thicken.
12. Add chicken thighs and let cook for about 8 minutes.
13. Take out of pan and serve!

7.128 Avocado Tomatillo Salsa

Servings: 16 | Time: 15 mins | Difficulty: Easy
Nutrients per serving: Calories: 32 kcal | Fat: 2g | Carbohydrates: 3g | Protein: 1g | Fiber: 1g

Ingredients

- ½ cup of chicken broth or vegetable broth
- ½ Tsp. of salt
- 1 avocado, mashed
- 1 jalapeño, seeded
- 1 serrano, seeded
- 10 tomatillo tomatoes
- 3 garlic cloves, peeled
- 3 slices of white onion

Method

1. Begin by heating the oven to 425 °F.
2. Spray olive or avocado oil on a baking sheet lined with aluminum foil.
3. Cut tomato husks into four pieces after washing them.
4. Mix them with the whole serrano, jalapeño, and onion slices on baking sheet.
5. Sprinkle with a little salt and bake for about 10 minutes or until a nice char is created from the tomatoes.
6. To encourage them to bake evenly, flip the peppers and onion slices halfway through.
7. In a mixer, combine the tomatillos, peppers, garlic, onions, chicken broth avocado, and salt and mix until smooth.
8. Put salt to taste and immediately serve.

7.129 Oven Broiled Ribeye Steaks With Mushrooms

Servings: 4 | Time: 55 mins | Difficulty: Easy

Nutrients per serving: Calories: 660 kcal | Fat: 60g | Carbohydrates: 7g | Protein: 13g | Fiber: 7g

Ingredients

- 1 tsp peanut oil
- 1/2 tsp celtic sea salt
- 1/4 tsp freshly cracked pepper
- 2 16 oz ribeye steaks
- 2 garlic cloves, crushed
- 3 tbsp garlic herb butter
- 3-4 thyme sprigs
- 8 oz cremini mushrooms, sliced

Method

1. Preheat an iron pan in oven.
2. Season the steak with pepper and salt, and let it stay at room temperature for 30 minutes.
3. Cut and slice mushrooms.
4. Add the steaks to the pan carefully, then the mushrooms, and shut the oven.
5. Flip the steaks after 4 minutes and stir up the mushrooms.
6. In a pan, add thyme and garlic.
7. Keep tossing and stirring steaks and mushrooms, depending on the thickness of steaks, until steaks are at your desired doneness.
8. Add butter on top of the steaks with pats of garlic.
9. Stir and leave to rest for at least 10 minutes before serving.

7.130 Grilled Spot Prawns With Garlic Herb Butter

Servings: 2 | Time: 10 mins | Difficulty: Easy
Nutrients per serving: Calories: 660 kcal | Fat: 60g | Carbohydrates: 7g | Protein: 13g | Fiber: 7g

Ingredients

- 1 lb spot prawns
- 2 large cloves garlic, pressed or minced
- 2 Tbsp chopped flat leaf parsley
- 1 tsp fresh lemon juice
- Avocado oil
- 1/2 cup butter or ghee, melted
- 1/2 shallot, minced
- 1/2 tsp sea salt
- 1/4 tsp freshly ground black pepper
- 1/4 tsp red pepper flakes

Method

1. Prep butter for the spice. Melt butter over medium heat in a shallow casserole dish. Once it is warmed, add the garlic and minced shallot and cook until the butter is infused, stirring occasionally, for about 5 minutes.
2. Add the lemon juice, parsley, pepper, sea salt, and red pepper flakes and remove from the sun. Only set aside.
3. Prepare a spot of prawns.
4. Brush the flesh with some avocado oil on the foot. Set the prawn halves flesh side down on the grill when the grill is hot at 450°F.
5. For 90 seconds, barbecue.
6. Place the prawns carefully on a serving platter.
7. Serve with lemon wedges immediately and enjoy!

7.131 Spinach Strawberry Pecan Salad with Homemade Balsamic Dressing

Servings: 2 | Time: 25 mins | Difficulty: Easy
Nutrients per serving: Calories: 524 kcal | Fat: 42g | Carbohydrates: 11.5g | Protein: 27g | Fiber: 4g

Ingredients

Salad

- 1 ounce crumbled feta cheese
- 1 ounce pecans (raw or toasted)
- 2 tbsp red onion, thinly sliced
- 3 oz strawberries, sliced
- 4 oz grilled chicken, sliced
- 6 oz baby spinach or spinach mix (170 g)

Vinaigrette Dressing (makes 1/2 cup)

- 1 pinch each salt and pepper
- 1 tbsp balsamic vinegar
- 1 tbsp red wine vinegar
- 1 tbsp water
- 1/2 tsp sweetener
- 1/4 cup light olive oil (or avocado oil)
- 1/8 tsp dried thyme
- 2 tsp minced red onion

Method
1. Make the dressing.
2. Slice the strawberries, chicken, and onions.
3. Put the ingredients in different bowls and drizzle over the dressing.

7.132 Cauliflower Broccoli Rice Salad

Servings: 4 | Time: 18 mins | Difficulty: Easy
Nutrients per serving: Calories: 188 kcal | Fat: 18g | Carbohydrates: 6g | Protein: 2g | Fiber: 3g

Ingredients
- 1/2 cup walnut pieces, toasted (2 oz)
- 1/2 tsp black pepper (start with less)
- 1/3 cup avocado oil (or olive oil)
- 1/4 cup Champagne vinegar (or rice vinegar)
- 1/4 cup chopped parsley
- 1/4 tsp salt (or more to taste)
- 2 tbsp minced onion
- 8 oz broccoli florets
- 8 oz cauliflower florets

Method
1. Bake walnut pieces at 350°F for 15 minutes on a sheet or until they become fragrant.
2. Cool them with a tea towel. Rubbing the towel vigorously also removes walnuts bitter skin.
3. Take a small cup and add minced onions, vinegar and oil.
4. Pulse the cauliflower florets to rice grain shape and put in a serving bowl.
5. Similarly, pulse the broccoli florets, and mix both cauliflower and broccoli pulsed florets together.
6. Use cling film to cover the bowl for about 3 minutes and then microwave it.
7. Add ample oil in heated pan and add broccoli mixture. Cook it and stir for half a minute. Again, cook it for an additional 1 minutes. Now, let it cool under the sun.
8. Add walnuts and chopped parsley in riced broccoli mixture and blend them.
9. Add vinegar and oil according to your taste.
10. Immediately serve.

7.133 Big Mac Salad

Servings: 6 | Time: 20 mins | Difficulty: Easy
Nutrients per serving: Calories: 368 kcal | Fat: 31g | Carbohydrates: 3g | Protein: 18g | Fiber: 1g

Ingredients
Salad
- 1 cup Tomatoes (chopped)
- 1 lb Ground beef
- 1 tsp Sea salt
- 1/2 cup Pickles (diced)
- 1/4 tsp Black pepper
- 3/4 cup Cheddar cheese (shredded)
- 8 oz Romaine lettuce (or iceberg if desired)

Dressing
- 1 1/2 tbsp Besti Powdered Erythritol
- 1 tsp White vinegar
- 1/2 cup Mayonnaise
- 1/2 tsp Smoked paprika
- 2 tbsp Pickles (diced)
- 2 tsp Mustard

Method
1. Cook beef over high heat in a skillet.
2. Season with black pepper and sea salt.
3. Fry while stirring and break beef pieces using spatula for about 7-10 minutes.
4. Make dressing. To do this, puree dressing's ingredient in a blender.
5. Refrigerate until ready to serve.
6. Mix the salad with beef and dressing.

7.134 Low Carb Jicama Pizza Fries

Servings: 2 | Time: 25 mins | Difficulty: Easy
Nutrients per serving: Calories: 548 kcal | Fat: 48g | Carbohydrates: 17g | Protein: 17g | Fiber: 7g

Ingredients
- 1 package cut Jicama
- 1/2 package good-quality pepperoni
- 1/4 cup oil
- 1/4 cup shredded mozzarella cheese
- 3/4 cup Low Carb Pizza Sauce

Low Carb Pizza Sauce
- 3 medium cloves garlic minced
- 1 jar tomato sauce crushed tomatoes, no sugar added
- 1 tsp. powdered rosemary
- 1 tsp. dried thyme
- 2 tsp. dried parsley
- 1 tsp. smoked paprika
- salt to taste
- liquid stevia to taste (optional)
- 1/2 cup chopped yellow onion
- 1/3 cup + 1 tbsp. olive oil

Method
Pizza Sauce
1. Sauté the garlic and onions in 1 tbsp. of olive oil in a small skillet.
2. Mix every ingredient in a pot of medium size.
3. Cook for 3 minutes with stirring.
4. Cool and refrigerate it.

Pizza Fries
5. Toss the oil with the cut jicama.
6. Bake the jicama for 20 minutes at 400°F.
7. Remove from the oven, cover with pepperoni, cheese, sauce, and bake for another 10 minutes.

7.135 Low Carb Spinach, Strawberry, Bacon and Artichoke Heart Salad

Servings: 4 | Time: 15 mins | Difficulty: Easy
Nutrients per serving: Calories: 141 kcal | Fat: 10g | Carbohydrates: 4g | Protein: 9g | Fiber: 1g

Ingredients
- 3 oz. washed spinach leaves
- 1 tbsp. white balsamic vinegar
- 4 large fresh strawberries, sliced
- salt and pepper to taste

- 1/2 lb. bacon, cooked and broken into small pieces
- 1/4 (14.5 oz.) jar artichoke hearts + 1/2 the oil they are packed in

Method
1. Mix every ingredient in a bowl and serve.

7.136 Low Carb Chicken Tomato and Avocado Salad

Servings: 4 I Time: 15 mins I Difficulty: Easy
Nutrients per serving: Calories: 341 kcal I Fat: 29g I Carbohydrates: 10g I Protein: 12g I Fiber: 5g

Ingredients
- 2 cups cooked, chopped chicken
- 2 medium avocados
- 1 tsp. garlic powder
- salt and pepper to taste
- 1/2 medium tomato, chopped (about 1 cup)
- 1/2 small yellow onion, chopped
- 2-3 large fresh basil leaves, minced
- 1/4 cup olive oil

Method
1. Mix every ingredient in a large bowl and use pepper and salt as seasoning to your taste.
2. Serve.

7.137 Low Carb Tuna Vegetable Salad

Servings: 2 I Time: 10 mins I Difficulty: Easy
Nutrients per serving: Calories: 339 kcal I Fat: 28g I Carbohydrates: 5g I Protein: 21g I Fiber: 1g

Ingredients
- 1 stalk celery
- 1/2 lime, juiced
- 1/2 medium cucumber, peeled
- 1/3 cup mayo, no sugar added
- 1/4 small red onion
- 2 cans water packed tuna
- salt & pepper to taste

Method
1. Mix all ingredients in a medium bowl and stir.
2. Eat as a single dish, or use salad as side dish.

7.138 Low Carb Keto Spinach Cobb Salad

Servings: 2 I Time: 10 mins I Difficulty: Easy
Nutrients per serving: Calories: 355 kcal I Fat: 23g I Carbohydrates: 6g I Protein: 31g I Fiber: 4g

Ingredients
- 1/2 large avocado, cut into small chunks
- 1/3 cup chopped cucumber
- 1/3 cup chopped tomatoes
- 1/4 lb. good quality bacon, cooked and crumbled
- 2 cups raw baby spinach
- 2 large hard boiled eggs
- 4 oz. cooked chicken

Method
1. Put spinach in a bowl.
2. Add other ingredients on top of spinach and put dressing.

7.139 Avocado Tuna Salad

Servings: 4 I Time: 15 mins I Difficulty: Easy
Nutrients per serving: Calories: 295 kcal I Fat: 29g I Carbohydrates: 9g I Protein: 2g I Fiber: 7g

Ingredients
- 2 Tbsps. yellow mustard

- 2 avocados, sliced and pitted
- 1/3 cup mayonnaise
- 1/4 Tsp. onion powder
- 1/4 cup celery, diced
- 1/4 Tsp. crushed red pepper flakes
- 1/8 Tsp. garlic powder
- 1 (6.4oz) canned tuna fish, drained

Method
1. In a small bowl mix mayonnaise, tuna fish, celery, onion powder, red pepper flakes, mustard, and garlic powder.
2. Put half cup of tuna salad in each avocado.
3. Serve.

7.140 Smoked Salmon Sushi with Cauliflower Rice

Servings: 24 I Time: 25 mins I Difficulty: Easy
Nutrients per serving: Calories: 150 kcal I Fat: 10g I Carbohydrates: 7g I Protein: 8g I Fiber: 3g

Ingredients
- ½ avocado
- ½ Tbsp. "squeezable" ginger
- ½-1 Tbsp. soy sauce
- 1 small cucumber
- 1 Tbsp. rice wine vinegar
- 10 ounces frozen cauliflower
- 4 ounces smoked salmon
- 4 seaweed wrappers
- 4 Tbsps. cream cheese

Method
1. Heat the frozen cauliflower in a large skillet.
2. Add soy sauce, vinegar, and squeezable ginger. Stir well.
3. Add four chunks of the cream cheese.
4. Melt the cheese while stirring and make it is completely mixed with cauliflower.
5. Set aside the mixture and allow it to cool at room temperature. Divide in 4 equal servings.
6. Place four wrappers (seaweed) on a plastic wrap and spread cauliflower mixture on top of it.
7. Layer the cucumber strips, salmon and avocado slices with cauliflower rice.
8. Roll the wrapper to make sushi rolls.
9. Cut into half inch-thick rolls and drizzle dipping sauces and spicy mayo on them.
10. Serve.

7.141 Keto Ham And Cheese Rolls

Servings: 6 I Time: 20 mins I Difficulty: Easy
Nutrients per serving: Calories: 198 kcal I Fat: 13g I Carbohydrates: 3g I Protein: 17g I Fiber: 0g

Ingredients
- 1 cup diced ham
- 2 eggs
- 1/2 cup shredded cheddar cheese.
- 1/2 cup grated parmesan cheese
- 3/4 cup shredded mozzarella cheese.

Method
1. Take oven to 375°F.
2. In a bowl, combine the egg and shredded cheese.
3. Mix well to blend them perfectly.
4. Add diced ham and stir well to blend.
5. Take a parchment lined or an oiled baking sheet.
6. Make round rolls by dividing the mixture in 6 equal parts.
7. Bake at 375 °F for around 20 minutes or when a faint brown crust is formed.
8. Serve.

7.142 Easy Keto Naan

Servings: 6 I Time: 25 mins I Difficulty: Easy
Nutrients per serving: Calories: 411 kcal I Fat: 34g I Carbohydrates: 8g I Protein: 21g I Fiber: 4g

Ingredients

For the Naan:
- 1 1/2 cups Blanched almond flour.
- 1 tbsp Gluten-free baking powder.
- 2 large Eggs.
- 2 tbsp Full-fat Greek yogurt.
- 3 cups Mozzarella.

For The Garlic Butter Topping:
- 2 tbsp Butter.
- 1 tbsp Fresh parsley (chopped)
- 1/2 tsp Garlic powder.

Method

1. Take oven to 350°F temperature.
Prepare a baking sheet with parchment paper.
2. Microwave sour cream and mozzarella in a large bowl, stirring every 30 seconds.
3. Add and mix the flour, eggs, and baking powder to the melted dough.
4. Knead until not sticky (add some almond flour to avoid stickiness).
5. Divide into 6 balls.
6. Spread the rolls on baking sheet.
7. Bake them until they are light brown in color.
8. Melt butter in pot and mix in garlic and powder parsley.
9. Bake naan in oven for 5 minutes after brushing garlic butter on them.
10. Then, Serve.

7.143 Pan Seared Scallops With Garlic And Lemon

Servings: 4 I Time: 15 mins I Difficulty: Easy
Nutrients per serving: Calories: 190 kcal I Fat: 5g I Carbohydrates: 7g I Protein: 14g

Ingredients

- 1 lb scallops, defrosted, patted dry
- 1 tsp pepper, freshly cracked
- 1 tsp salt, celtic sea salt
- 1/2 cup white wine
- 1/2 lemon, sliced into half-wedges
- 2 tbsp garlic, diced
- 3 tbsp butter, grass-fed

Method

1. Melt the butter in pan.
2. Lightly season the dry scallops with pepper and salt.
3. Put scallops in a pan.
4. Heat until a golden crust is formed on one side of scallop.
5. Then, add garlic and let it brown but do not let it burn.
6. Add wine, lemon slices, and mix.
7. When scallops are browned and are springy, serve them topped with sauce.

7.144 Garlic Butter Broiled Lobster Tails

Servings: 2 I Time: 15 mins I Difficulty: Easy
Nutrients per serving: Calories: 416 kcal I Fat: 31g I Carbohydrates: 12g I Protein: 24g I Fiber: 1g

Ingredients

- 1 tsp smoked paprika
- 1.2 tsp white pepper
- 1/4 cup minced garlic
- 2 Lobster tails
- 2 tbsp diced parsley
- 4 tbsp butter + 2 one Tbsp. pats of butter
- celtic sea salt
- juice of 1 lemon

Method

1. Add garlic and 4 tbsp butter in a large pan and cook on medium low heat.
2. Place lobster tails in an oven safe dish or on a baking sheet.
3. Carefully cut the lobster tail dodging the meat.
4. Pull the shell down and take out the meat.
5. Season with spices.
6. Add some butter.
7. Let cook in the oven for 10 minutes.
8. Add garlic and some butter to the lobster after 6 Minutes.
9. Remove and serve.

7.145 Low Carb Corn Dog Muffins

Servings: 4 I Time: 35 mins I Difficulty: Easy
Nutrients per serving: Calories: 419 kcal I Fat: 24g I Carbohydrates: 8.5g I Protein: 42g I Fiber: 2.7g

Ingredients

- 1 pound boneless top sirloin steak, cut into 1/4-inch-thick slices
- 1 Tbsp. black and/or white sesame seeds
- 1 Tbsp. fish sauce
- 1 Tbsp. toasted sesame oil
- 1 Tbsp. unseasoned rice wine vinegar
- 1 Tsp. grated fresh ginger
- 12 cremini mushrooms, thinly sliced
- 2 cloves garlic, minced
- 4 (8-ounce) packages spaghetti-style shirataki noodles
- 4 green onions, sliced on a bias, white and green parts separated
- 4 soft-boiled eggs
- 5 cups beef stock
- 5 Tbsps. gluten-free soy sauce or coconut aminos, divided
- Pinch of red pepper flakes
- Sea salt and black pepper

Method

1. Use pepper and salt to season the steak.
2. Rinse and soak the shirataki noodles.
3. Add the noodles to the heated pan and dry fry for 4 minutes.
4. Simmer the beef in a Dutch oven at medium heat.
5. Add the sesame oil, fish sauce, garlic, red pepper flakes, vinegar, ginger, and 4 Tbsps. of the soy sauce to the noodles.
6. Brown the noodles by frying for 5 minutes.
7. Add the sauce and noodles to the pot having the stock.
8. Scorch the steak for 2 minutes in the hot pan.
9. Add the green onions, the mushrooms, and the soy sauce to the skillet on medium heat. Fry them with stirring constantly.
10. Split the noodle among 4 bowls.
11. Top each bowl with the mushroom and mixture the steak.
12. Transfer the broth on each bowl.
13. Finish each bowl with sesame seeds, an egg, some green parts of green onions.

7.146 Keto Mongolian Beef

Servings: 4 I Time: 35 mins I Difficulty: Easy
Nutrients per serving: Calories: 339 kcal I Fat: 19g I Carbohydrates: 1.9g I Protein: 37g

Ingredients

- 1/4 Tsp. crushed red pepper flakes, optional
- 1/2 cup golden monk fruit sweetener
- 1 1/2 pounds flank steak

- 1 ½ Tsps. glucomannan powder or xanthan gum
- 1 Tbsp. fish sauce
- 1 Tbsp. grated fresh ginger
- 1 Tbsps. avocado oil
- 2 Tbsps. gluten free soy sauce or coconut aminos
- 2 Tbsps. thinly sliced green onions
- 2 Tbsps. toasted sesame oil
- 3 cloves garlic, minced

Method
1. Cut the steak into thin strips, then into pieces. Set aside.
2. Mix the minced garlic, red pepper flakes, soy sauce, fish sauce, monk fruit sweetener, and sesame oil in a small bowl.
3. Add steak coated in marinade in a large bowl.
4. Refrigerate for 30 minutes to marinate properly.
5. Once the avocado oil is hot, add the marinade, steak, and grated ginger.
6. Cook the steak until color is brown.
7. Spoon out sauce and put in a bowl.
8. Use glucomannan powder to sprinkle on the sauce and mix the ingredients to thickens the sauce.
9. Serve beef with thick sauce and use green onions (sliced) to garnish.

7.147 Creamy Cajun Sausage And Potato Soup

Servings: 8 I Time: 55 mins I Difficulty: Easy
Nutrients per serving: Calories: 323 kcal I Fat: 25.6g I Carbohydrates: 15.2g I Protein: 11.3g I Fiber: 1.8g

Ingredients
- ¼ Tsp. garlic powder
- ¼ Tsp. onion powder
- ¼ Tsp. rubbed sage
- ½ Tsp. dried oregano
- ½ Tsp. smoked paprika
- 1 medium carrot, diced
- 1 pound yukon gold potatoes, peeled and diced
- 1 red bell pepper, seeded and diced
- 1 small onion, diced
- 1 Tsp. sea salt
- 12 ounces andouille sausage links, sliced into rounds
- 2 cups full fat coconut milk
- 2 ribs celery, diced
- 2 Tbsps. olive oil
- 4 cups chicken stock
- 5 cloves garlic, minced
- pinch cayenne pepper
- pinch red pepper flakes
- sliced green onions, optional for garnish

Method
1. Heat the olive oil in a Dutch oven.
2. Then, add the andouille sausage and cook until color turns to brown.
3. Add the bell pepper, onion, garlic, carrot, and other seasonings to the sausage pan.
4. Sauté to tender the veggies.
5. Add the potatoes and chicken stock to the pot and boil them. Then, simmer for 20 minutes.
6. Stir in the coconut milk with andouille.
7. Simmer for 15 minutes.
8. Use green onions as garnish.

7.148 Sesame Ginger Noodles

Servings: 6 I Time: 35 mins I Difficulty: Easy

Nutrients per serving: Calories: 281 kcal I Fat: 24.39g I Carbohydrates: 16g I Protein: 7.8g I Fiber: 6.6g

Ingredients
- (4) 8-ounce packs spaghetti style shirataki noodles
- ¼ cup gluten free soy sauce
- 1 ½ Tbsps. unseasoned rice vinegar
- 1 cup tahini, almond butter, or natural peanut butter
- 1 Tbsp. fresh lime juice
- 2 cloves garlic, minced
- 2 Tbsps. toasted sesame seeds
- 2 Tsps. ground ginger
- 3 Tbsps. golden monk fruit
- 4 green onions, sliced on a bias
- fresh lime wedges, for serving

Method
1. Mix the soy sauce, monk fruit, tahini, ginger, rice vinegar, lime juice, and garlic in a bowl to make the sauce.
2. Transfer the sauce over the prepared noodles and mix into coat the noodles.
3. Cook for 7-10 minutes on low heat.
4. Top with sesame seeds, fresh lime juice (squeeze), and green onions.

7.149 Low Carb Zuppa Toscana Soup

Servings: 10 I Time: 1 hr 15 mins I Difficulty: Easy
Nutrients per serving: Calories: 283 kcal I Fat: 22g I Carbohydrates: 4.5g I Protein: 13g I Fiber: 1.4g

Ingredients
- 1 cup heavy cream, more to taste
- 1 medium onion, chopped (about 1 cup)
- 1 pound bulk ground Italian sausage
- 1 small head cauliflower, cored and cut into small florets (about 4 cups)
- 2 packed cups fresh spinach or kale
- 2 Tbsps. butter
- 4 cloves garlic, minced
- 6 cups chicken stock
- 6 slices bacon, chopped
- Grated parmesan cheese, for serving (optional)
- Pinch of red pepper flakes
- Sea salt and ground black pepper

Method
1. Cook the bacon in a Dutch oven until it is crispy.
2. Add the garlic, butter, a pinch each of salt, onion, and pepper to the bacon drippings.
3. Sauté until the garlic is fragrant and the onion is translucent.
4. Add the red pepper flakes and the Italian sausage to the pot.
5. Cook for 10 minutes.
6. Boil the stock. Then add cauliflower. Simmer it for 5 minutes.
7. Stir in the spinach and cream and cook for 10 minutes.
8. Put the cooked bacon to the soup.
9. Serve.

7.150 Creamy Roasted Garlic And Mushroom Soup With Bacon

Servings: 4 I Time: 35 mins I Difficulty: Easy
Nutrients per serving: Calories: 250 kcal I Fat: 20g I Carbohydrates: 9.5g I Protein: 11.6g I Fiber: 2g

Ingredients
- ⅓ cup heavy cream
- ½ Tsp. ground black pepper, more to taste
- 1 bulb garlic (about 10 cloves)

- 1 small yellow onion, diced
- 1 Tbsp. butter
- 1 Tbsp. chopped fresh thyme or 1 Tsp. dried thyme leaves
- 1 Tsp. olive oil, extra to garnish
- 1 Tsp. sea salt, more to taste
- 14 ounces mixed mushrooms, cleaned and chopped
- 2 small celery stalks, sliced
- 2 Tbsps. chopped flat-leaf parsley, extra for garnish
- 4 ¼ cups chicken stock
- 8 slices bacon, cooked and chopped

Method

1. Cut the top quarter inch off the garlic bulb and place on an aluminium foil.
2. Drizzle the bulb of garlic with the olive oil, then sprinkle with salt and pepper.
3. Bake at 400°F for 30 minutes.
4. Melt the butter in a Dutch oven.
5. Add the celery and onion.
6. Sauté for 5 minutes.
7. Add the thyme, mushrooms, salt, parsley, and pepper to the pot.
8. Sauté for an additional 5 minutes.
9. Spoon out some to use as a garnish.
10. Add the cream, chicken stock, and 6 cloves of roasted garlic to the pot.
11. Simmer the soup for about 30 minutes.
12. Pulse in a blender until smooth.
13. Top with reserved vegetables, chopped bacon, parsley, roasted garlic cloves, and olive oil.
14. Serve.

7.151 Roasted Butternut Squash Soup With Sausage

Servings: 12 I Time: 1 hr 15 mins I Difficulty: Easy
Nutrients per serving: Calories: 272 kcal I Fat: 22.4g I Carbohydrates: 8.8g I Protein: 9.2g I Fiber: 1.4g

Ingredients

- ¼ Tsp. nutmeg
- ½ Tsp. ground ginger
- 1 ½ Tsps. rubbed sage
- 1 cup heavy cream
- 1 large butternut squash (about 4 pounds), peeled and cubed
- 1 medium onion, chopped
- 1 pound ground sausage
- 1 Tsp. sea salt
- 2 Tbsps. olive oil
- 3 Tbsps. butter or olive oil
- 4 cups chicken stock, divided
- 6 cloves garlic, minced
- fried sage leaves, optional garnish
- Pinch of cayenne pepper
- roasted pepitas, optional garnish
- Sea salt and ground black pepper
- sour cream, optional garnish

Method

1. Layer the squash on a baking sheet.
2. Season with pepper and salt and drizzle with olive oil.
3. Roast for 40 minutes at 375°F.
4. Melt the butter in a Dutch oven.
5. Add the ginger, garlic, onion, salt, cayenne, sage, and nutmeg.
6. Blend the onion mixture.
7. Blend the roasted squash, the onions the chicken stock.
8. Cook the sausage on medium heat.

9. Put the pureed squash with the sausage.
10. Cook on medium heat for 10 minutes, stirring frequently,
11. Then reduce heat to low and let simmer for 30 minutes.
12. Top with fried sage, pepitas, and sour cream.
13. Serve.

7.152 Reuben Stuffed Mushrooms

Servings: 5 I Time: 30 mins I Difficulty: Easy
Nutrients per serving: Calories: 190 kcal I Fat: 20g I Carbohydrates: 1.5g I Protein: 0g I Fiber: 0g

Ingredients

- ¼ cup Keto Russian Dressing, more to taste
- ½ cup sauerkraut, chopped
- ½ cup shredded Swiss cheese, or 5 slices
- 1 Tbsp. chopped fresh chives
- 5 large portobello mushrooms, cleaned, with gills and stems removed
- 8 ounces corned beef, sliced or chopped
- cracked black pepper, to taste

Russian Dressing

- ½ cup ketchup
- 1 cup mayonnaise
- 1 Tbsp. chopped fresh chives
- 1 Tbsp. chopped fresh parsley
- 1 Tbsp. Worcestershire sauce
- 1 Tsp. chopped fresh dill
- 2 Tbsps. spicy brown mustard

Method

1. In a large bowl, Mix ketchup, mayonnaise, Worcestershire sauce, mustard, chives, parsley, and dill to make Russian Dressing.
2. In a mixing bowl, combine the corned beef, sauerkraut, and Russian dressing.
3. Put mixture in each cap of mushroom and add swiss cheese on top of it.
4. Bake them at 400°F for 15 minutes.
5. Top with black pepper and chives.
6. Serve.

7.153 Reuben Stuffed Sweet Potatoes With Russian Dressing

Servings: 6 I Time: 25 mins I Difficulty: Easy
Nutrients per serving: Calories: 660 kcal I Fat: 60g I Carbohydrates: 7g I Protein: 13g I Fiber: 7g

Ingredients

FOR THE REUBEN STUFFED SWEET POTATOES

- ¼ cup butter (½ stick)
- ⅓ cup Russian Dressing
- 1 lb precooked deli style corned beef, chopped
- 1 tsp caraway seeds
- 1 tsp onion powder
- 1½ cups sauerkraut
- 2 large sweet potatoes
- 2 tbsp olive oil
- 3 cloves garlic, minced
- 4 slices Swiss cheese
- Chopped green onion, for garnish

FOR THE RUSSIAN DRESSING

- ½ cup ketchup (reduced sugar, organic preferred)
- 1 cup mayonnaise
- 1 tbsp fresh chives, chopped
- 1 tbsp fresh parsley, chopped
- 1 tbsp Worcestershire sauce

- 1 tsp fresh dill, chopped
- 2 tbsp spicy brown mustard

Method

FOR THE REUBEN STUFFED SWEET POTATOES

1. Put butter on sweet potato.
2. Sprinkle with the caraway seeds and onion powder. Bake them for 45 minutes to 1 hour.
3. Add the sauerkraut, corned beef, and garlic in heated olive oil.
4. Sauté for 10 minutes.
5. Put corned beef mixture on top of sweet potato baked.
6. Add a slice of Swiss cheese on top and drizzle with Russian dressing.

FOR THE RUSSIAN DRESSING

1. In a large mixing bowl, mix ketchup, mayonnaise, chives, parsley, mustard, Worcestershire sauce, and dill.
2. Mix well. Serve
3.

7.154 One Pot Keto Sesame Chicken And Broccoli

Servings: 4 | Time: 25 mins | Difficulty: Easy
Nutrients per serving: Calories: 204 kcal | Fat: 6.1g | Carbohydrates: 7g | Protein: 30g | Fiber: 2.1g

Ingredients

- ¼ cup coconut aminos, or soy sauce
- ½ Tsp. sesame seeds, plus extra for garnish
- 1 ½ Tsp. arrowroot powder (get it here)
- 1 clove garlic, minced
- 1 pound boneless, skinless chicken breast, cubed
- 1 Tbsp. avocado oil (I usc this brand)
- 1 Tsp. sesame oil
- 12 ounces broccoli florets
- Green onions, sliced, for garnish
- Red pepper flakes, for garnish
- Salt and pepper, to taste

Method

1. Microwave the broccoli florets with some water to tender it.
2. Mix the arrowroot powder and coconut aminos in a small bowl.
3. Add the garlic and avocado oil and sauté until fragrant in a large skillet.
4. Sauté the chicken with pepper and salt to taste in a skillet.
5. Sauté the broccoli and sesame oil in a pan then put coconut amino mixture on top of it.
6. Garnish with sesame seeds, red pepper flakes, and green onions.
7. Serve.

7.155 Cabbage Noodle Tuna Casserole

Servings: 8 | Time: 45 mins | Difficulty: Easy
Nutrients per serving: Calories: 377 kcal | Fat: 28g | Carbohydrates: 10g | Protein: 23.5g | Fiber: 3g

Ingredients

- ½ cup frozen peas
- 1 ¼ cup Parmesan cheese, grated, divided
- 1 ½ cup heavy cream
- 1 cup onion, chopped
- 2 cloves garlic, minced
- 2 tbsp grass-fed butter
- 2 tbsp lemon zest
- 2 tbsp olive oil
- 2 tsp dried dill or 2 tbsp fresh dill
- 2 tsp dry mustard powder (get it here)
- 3 - 5oz cans albacore tuna, drained (I use this brand)

- 3 ribs celery, chopped
- juice of 1 lemon
- medium head green cabbage (about 1 ½ lbs), cut into large shreds
- sea salt and black pepper, to taste

Method

1. Heat the butter and olive oil in skillet.
2. Once heated, add the onion, cabbage, garlic, celery, black pepper, and sea salt to the pan.
3. Sauté to crisp the vegetables for about 10 minutes.
4. Mix in the mustard powder, dill, lemon juice, and lemon zest.
5. Pour the 1 cup Parmesan cheese and heavy cream into the pan.
6. Melt cheese while stirring.
7. Decrease heat and let the sauce to thicken.
8. Stir in the peas and the tuna.
9. Drizzle Parmesan cheese over the dish and put it in the oven.
10. Cook until the cheese top is golden brown.

Chapter 8 – Keto-Friendly Dinner Recipes

The following easy keto-friendly dinner recipes will help you create meal plans with a focus on a low-carb and high-fat diet. You will find range of meat recipes, soups, seafood, cauliflower rice and pastas etc.

8.1 Keto Shrimp Courgette Boats On The Grill

Servings: 4 I Time: 30 mins I Difficulty: Easy
Nutrients per serving: Calories: 180 kcal I Fat: 7.5g I Carbohydrates: 13.8g I Protein: 17g I Fiber: 4.1g

Ingredients
For The Courgette:
- Two Large Courgette Squashes
- 1 Tsp Olive Oil
- 1/4 Tsp Salt
- 1/4 Tsp Ground Cayenne Pepper

For The Cauliflower Rice Salad:
- One Small Onion, Roughly Chopped, Around 2 Cups
- One Large Bunch Of Asparagus
- 1 Tbsp Olive Oil, Plus 1 Tsp, Divided
- 1 Tsp Garlic, Chopped
- Salt & Pepper
- 3 Tbsp Fresh Juice Of Lemon
- 3 Tbsp Fresh Basil, Chopped
- 2 Cups Cauliflower Florets, Cut Into Bite-Sized Pieces

For The Shrimp:
- 1 Tsp Olive Oil
- 1/2 Tsp Ground Cayenne Pepper
- Lemon Zest, For Garnish
- 1 Tsp Honey
- 1/2 Pound Fresh Shrimp, Peeled & Deveined

Method
1. Put the BBQ on a grill basket & preheat for around ten min on high heat.
2. Slice the courgette lengthwise in half & scoop out a few of the inside, creating a boat. As the courgette softens when grilled, make sure to leave several along the edges. Use the olive oil to brush the courgette and sprinkle with cayenne pepper & salt.
3. Toss the minced Onion and Asparagus only with oil & garlic in a wide bowl, then season with pepper & salt.
4. Reduce the heat to med-high on the grill & put the Onion & Asparagus in the grill basket. Also, put the courgette directly on the grill, slice-side-down. Fry the vegetables for around ten min, till gently charred & excellent grill marks are created. Turn halfway through the courgette and stir the vegetables around. Remove & cover the vegetables from the grill & put them aside till ready for usage.
5. Put the cauliflower in a big food processor as the vegetables cook & process till it falls into what appears like rice. Put in a wide bowl & microwave till soft, for 5-6 mins. If you like, you can steam the cauliflower in the oven as well.
6. Put the barbecue heat back up to full again. Toss the oil, pepper, salt &honey with the shrimp, ensuring that the spices are spread equally. Put them on the grill & cook for around five min, till they are opaque & gently charred. Flip through halfway.

To Serve:
1. Chop the onion as well as the grilled asparagus and put them into the cauliflower rice. Mix the leftover one tablespoon of olive oil, lemon juice & Basil together. Sprinkle with salt to taste.
2. Scoop the mixture of cauliflower into the courgettes, really pack it in as far as you can, & add the shrimp on top. Add fresh lemon zest to garnish it.
3. Now enjoy it.

8.2 No Bean Keto Chili In The Inst. Pot

Servings: 6 I Time: 35 mins I Difficulty: Easy
Nutrients per serving: Calories: 222 kcal I Fat: 12.7g I Carbohydrates: 11.5g I Protein: 16.8g I Fiber: 3.3g

Ingredients
- 1/2 cup Onion, diced
- 1 1/2 Tbsp Olive oil, divided
- 1/2 Cup Celery sliced
- 1 Red pepper, diced
- 1 Tbsp Garlic, minced
- 4 tsp Chile powder
- 1 Lb Grass-fed 85% lean Ground beef
- 1 Tbsp Smoked Paprika
- 1/8 tsp Ground Allspice
- 1/4 tsp Cayenne pepper
- 1 Can Crushed tomatoes (14 oz)
- 1/2 Cup Water
- 1 Can Fire-roasted minced tomatoes (14oz)
- 2 Tbsp Tomato paste
- Pinch of pepper
- 1 tsp Sea salt
- 1/4 cup Parsley chopped
- 2 Bay leaves

Method
1. In the Instant Kettle, place 1/2 Tablespoon of the oil & switch to sauté mode. When it's hot, sauté the pepper, onion, celery & garlic for around 3 mins before they start to soften.
2. Put the remaining oil and the beef & cook for around 3 to 4 mins, till it starts to turn brown. Drain out the extra fat.
3. Put the paprika, chili powder, cayenne, then allspice, & simmer for 3 to 4 mins till the beef is entirely brown & no longer pink.
4. Except for the Parsley, combine all the leftover ingredients & stir till well mixed. Cover your Inst. Pot (please ensure it is sealed) & switch it to manual mode (high pressure should be

adjusted instantly) & set it for ten min. Allow it to release steam naturally when cooked.

5. Remove the cover and switch it to sauté mode when the steam is released. Cook, constantly stirring, for 2 to 4 mins, till some of the water has evaporated.
6. Mix it in the Parsley & enjoy it.

8.3 Keto Sloppy Joes

Servings: 2 I Time: 5 mins I Difficulty: Easy
Nutrients per serving: Calories: 276 kcal I Fat: 18.8g I Carbohydrates: 4.4g I Protein: 23.2g I Fiber: 0.9g

Ingredients

- 1/2 tbsp Olive Oil
- 1 pound Ground Beef, (85%)
- 1/3 cup Green Onions, thinly sliced
- 3/4 cup Tomato Sauce (canned)
- 1 1/2 tbsp Tomato Paste
- 1/2 cup Low-Sodium Beef Broth
- 1 tbsp Monkfruit Sweetener
- 1 tbsp Worcestershire Sauce
- 1 tsp Red Wine Vinegar
- 1 tsp Chili Powder
- 1/2 tsp Sea Salt
- 1/2 tsp Prepared Yellow Mustard
- pinch of Black Pepper
- Lettuce, for serving
- pinch of Crushed Red Pepper Flakes

Method

1. Heat the olive oil in the big frying pan over med-high. Place the green onions & boil for a minute.
2. Place the ground beef & cook for around five min till the beef is no different pink.
3. In the bowl, mix all the rest of the ingredients up to Parsley. Place into the cooked beef & carry to a simmer.
4. Decrease the heat to med after boiling & simmer till the sauce is thickened, around 9 to 10 mins.
5. Spoon the combination over the lettuce & fill it with cheese & Parsley if necessary.
6. Enjoy it.

8.4 Keto Steak With Garlic Butter Mushrooms

Servings: 4 I Time: 25 mins I Difficulty: Easy
Nutrients per serving: Calories: 292 kcal I Fat: 21.7g I Carbohydrates: 1.1g I Protein: 23.5g I Fiber: 0.4g

Ingredients

- 4 tsp Ghee, softened to room temperature
- Sea salt
- 1 tsp Fresh garlic, chopped
- 1 Lb Grass-fed Top Sirloin Steak

For The Mushrooms:

- 2 Cups thinly sliced White mushrooms
- 2 tsp melted ghee
- Sea salt
- 1 tsp minced fresh garlic

Method

1. Preheat the barbecue to high heat
2. With the paper towel, pat the steak off. Mix the ghee & garlic in the small bowl & scatter half of it on one steak side. Drizzle salt on it.
3. Put the steak on it once the grill is hot, butter the side down & cook for 4 to 5 mins, till charred. Rub ghee combination on the top side, turn & cook till done-ness is desired. Take it from the heat, cover & leave to rest when cooking the mushrooms.

4. In a cup, Add the melted ghee, mushrooms, garlic, and a splash of salt. Put two layers of tin foil over the top of each other & put the mushrooms in one layer in the middle. To make a packet, cover the sides up firmly.
5. On the barbecue, put the mushrooms to fold a packet face up & grill for five min. Another 4 to 5 mins, or till the mushrooms are soft.
6. Serve your mushrooms on the steak & enjoy it.

8.5 Keto Beef And Broccoli

Servings: 2 I Time: 1 hr 25 mins I Difficulty: Easy
Nutrients per serving: Calories: 344 kcal I Fat: 20.4g I Carbohydrates: 11.9g I Protein: 26.7g I Fiber: 3.3g

Ingredients

- 1 tsp minced & divided Fresh ginger
- 1/4 Cup Coconut aminos, divided
- 1 tsp minced & divided Fresh garlic
- 1 1/2 Tbsp Avocado oil, divided
- 8 Oz Flank steak, thinly sliced against the grain
- 1/4 Cup Reduced-sodium beef broth
- 2 1/2 Cups Broccoli, cut into big florets
- Salt
- 1/2 tsp Sesame oil
- Sesame seeds for garnish
- Green onion for garnish
- Fried cauliflower rice

Method

1. In a tiny bowl, mix 1 Tablespoon of the amino coconut, 1/2 Teaspoon of Garlic & ginger. Put & mix your beef into the marinade. For at least 1hr, cover & refrigerate.
2. Heat 1 Tablespoon of oil over med heat in a big saucepan. Put the broccoli & cook for around 3 to 4 mins, constantly stirring, till it just starts to soften. Put the remaining garlic & ginger into the mixture and cook for 1 min.
3. Lower the heat, cover the pan & cook for around 4-5 mins, till the broccoli is soft and crisp. Occasionally, stir it.
4. Move the broccoli to the plate when cooked. Turn the heat to med/high & put the leftover 1/2 Tablespoon of oil to it. Put the marinated beef & cook for around 2 to 3 mins, till golden brown. Stir back the broccoli in.
5. Mix the remaining amino coconut, sesame oil & broth in a shallow bowl. Place it into the skillet & simmer till it is only starting to thicken, stirring continuously for around 1-2 min—season with salt.
6. Serve with sesame seeds & green onion on cauliflower rice.

8.6 Keto Philly Cheesesteak With Cauliflower & Stuffed Peppers

Servings: 6 I Time: 50 mins I Difficulty: Easy
Nutrients per serving: Calories: 379 kcal I Fat: 22.9g I Carbohydrates: 11g I Protein: 32.7g I Fiber: 2.3g

Ingredients

For the Onions:

- 1 Tbsp Olive oil
- Salt
- Two big onions sliced around 1/2 thick

For the Peppers:

- Six tiny Green bell peppers
- 1 Lb Beef top sirloin steak
- 1 Tbsp Olive oil
- Salt
- 2 cups Cauliflower, cut into tiny florets
- 12 Oz sliced Provolone cheese

Method

1. Heat 1 Tablespoon of olive oil in a wide pan over med heat till shiny. Put sliced onions to it. & a pinch of salt, stirring till it is

coated with oil. Cook, regularly mixing, till the onions become golden brown & caramelized, for 30 to 45 mins. You will need to switch the heat to med-low if you have a boiling burner since you don't want it to burn. Do not mix very much since you want to fully caramelize the bottom.

2. Put the ready peppers in a big pot when the onions are cooking & cover them with water. Carry to a simmer & simmer for 2 to 3 mins, till just softened. Drain & put on a sheet of paper towel, softly patting a few liquids off; in the 9x13 inch pan, place the peppers, & preheat the oven to 350 deg C.
3. Heat the leftover 1 Tablespoon of oil over med heat in a wide skillet. Cook your sliced steak till golden brown and the extra fat is drained away. Transfer to a dish.
4. 4. Put the cauliflower in a big food processor when the beef is cooking & process till "rice-like." Put it right in the skillet that your beef was in & cook over med heat, regularly mixing, till golden brown.
5. When the beef & caramelized onions are cooked, add them to the skillet & sprinkle them with sea salt. Stir till it's mixed properly.
6. Stuff each pepper with the combination & put a cheese slice to each seed. (1 oz cheese per pepper half). Bake for around 10 to 15 mins, till the cheese is melted and the peppers are soft. Switch the oven to the high grill & cook till the cheese becomes golden brown for about 2 to 4 mins.
7. Enjoy it.

8.7 Asparagus Stuffed Chicken Breast

Servings: 4 I Time: 30 mins I Difficulty: Easy
Nutrients per serving: Calories: 241.8kcal I Fat: 9.1g I Carbohydrates: 2.9g I Protein: 34.2g I Fiber: 0.7g

Ingredients

- Italian seasoning
- 1 Lb Chicken Breast
- Garlic powder
- 4 tsp Honey mustard
- Sea salt
- 3 Oz Provolone cheese
- 1 Tbsp Olive oil
- 8 Stalks of Asparagus

Method

1. Oven preheated to 425 degrees.
2. Cut the chicken breasts in half about the entire way, but leave them intact so that each chicken may fold up. Scatter on the inside of every breast the garlic powder, Italian seasoning & a bit of salt. Drizzle the Italian seasoning on chicken breast outside.
3. From around inside of every chicken breast, scatter one teaspoon of honey mustard. Lay a piece of provolone, followed by Two asparagus spears, on the top of every chicken. Fold your chicken over &, if needed, protect it with toothpicks.
4. Warm the oil up over med heat in a big, oven-safe skillet. Put the chicken in & cook for around 2 to 3 mins, till golden brown. On the other hand, flip & repeat.
5. Cover the skillet with tinfoil & bake till the thermometer inserted into your chicken breast reaches 165 degrees, around 15 mins.

8.8 Chipotle Healthy Pulled Pork In The Slow Cooker

Servings: 5 I Time: 8 hrs 15 mins I Difficulty: Easy
Nutrients per serving: Calories: 428 kcal I Fat: 33.7g I Carbohydrates: 3g I Protein: 27g I Fiber: 0.4g

Ingredients

For The Pork And Rub:
- ½ Med sliced yellow Onion
- 1/2 Cup Water
- 1 Tbsp minced fresh garlic
- ½ Tbsp of Coconut sugar
- ½ Tbsp of Salt

- ½ tsp of Chili powder
- ¼ tsp Cumin powder
- ¼ Tbsp Adobo sauce from a can of chipotle peppers in adobo sauce
- 1/6 tsp smoked paprika
- Whole wheat for serving
- 2 Lbs Pork shoulder extra fat removed.
- Paleo ranch
- Coleslaw mix
- Lime Juice
- Green tabasco

Method

1. Put the onion in the bottom of the slow cooker & cut the onion & chop the garlic. One cup of water, pour in.
2. Mix all of the spices for spice rub in a shallow bowl.
3. Slice off the pork shoulder with some big, noticeable pieces of fat & after this, rub it all over with spice rub till it is equally coated.
4. Put the pork on the highest part of the garlic, water & onions, then cook for 6 to 8hrs on high till soft and moist.
5. If the pork is baked, drain much of the liquid from the slow cooker & put the solids back into the slow cooker.
6. On a chopping board, move the pork & shred it with two forks.
7. Move the chopped pork to the slow cooker & combine it with the garlic & onions. Cover till ready to serve
8. Serve your pulled pork on the bun/lettuce, garnished with ranch coleslaw, mix & a squeeze of the juice of lime & green tabasco.

8.9 Greek Turkey Meatballs With Feta

Servings: 4 I Time: 30 mins I Difficulty: Easy
Nutrients per serving: Calories: 230.4 kcal I Fat: 12.6g I Carbohydrates: 3.2g I Protein: 26.1g I Fiber: 1.5g

Ingredients

- 2 oz full-fat feta cheese
- 1 lb lean ground turkey
- One big egg whisked
- 3 tbsp minced fresh parsley
- 1 tbsp minced fresh mint
- 2 tbsp coconut flour
- 1 1/2 tsp ground basil
- 1 1/2 tsp garlic powder
- 1 1/2 tsp ground oregano
- 3/4 tsp ground dill
- 3/4 tsp cumin
- 3/4 tsp ground thyme
- 1/4 tsp ground nutmeg
- 1/2 tsp salt
- 1/4 tsp cinnamon

Method

1. Oven preheated to 400 degrees & use bakery release paper to line a rimmed cookie sheet.
2. In a big bowl, combine all the ingredients till mixed well. To heap 1 Tablespoon sized balls, use a cookie scoop to put them on the skillet, forming them into a ball. Twenty balls you can have.
3. Bake till the thermometer reaches 165 degrees F for a moment, around 10 to 13 mins.
4. Serve & Enjoy.

8.10 Air Fryer Salmon

Servings: 2 I Time: 12 mins I Difficulty: Easy
Nutrients per serving: Calories: 183.2 kcal I Fat: 11.6g I Carbohydrates: 0g I Protein: 20g I Fiber: 0g

Ingredients

- 8 Oz Wild-caught salmon
- Sea salt

- 1 tsp Olive oil

Method

1. Rub a salmon with the oil of olive & drizzle it with sea salt.
2. Put in the air fryer's mesh basket & cook at 400 degrees till the temperature reaches 120 degrees F.
3. Cover & stop for ten min.

8.11 BBQ Chicken Low Carb Healthy Quesadillas

Servings: 2 | Time: 35 mins | Difficulty: Easy
Nutrients per serving: Calories: 459 kcal | Fat: 14.4g | Carbohydrates: 19.5g | Protein: 59.2g | Fiber: 7g

Ingredients

- 1 Cup shredded Chicken breast
- 2 Cups Liquid Egg whites
- Avocado Oil Spray
- 1/4 cup BBQ sauce of choice + extra for drizzling
- 2-4 Tbsp Coriander chopped
- 2/3 cup grated Cheddar cheese

Method

1. Carry a tiny pot of salted water to a simmer, & cook the chicken breast for around 10-15 mins till it is no longer pink inside.
2. Preheat the broiler & adjust the oven rack from the top position to the 2nd position. Use Avocado Oil to spray a cookie sheet.
3. Spray a tiny skillet with Avocado Oil & heat over high heat. Lower the heat when hot, & slowly place a half cup of the white egg in. Cover & cook till just set, around five min, on top of the white egg. Slide the "tortilla" egg on the prepared cookie sheet, & repeat till you have four "tortillas" with the leftover egg whites. Put all the tortillas on the cookie sheet & spray with Avocado Oil on top of them.
4. Cut the chicken using two forks, then put it in a bowl. Please put it in the BBQ sauce till the chicken is very well covered.
5. Split the shredded chicken into two of the "tortillas" then stretch out to surround the "tortilla." Split on top of the chicken, the cheese & Coriander, & spray with avocado oil. Cover with the extra tortillas, the un-cooked egg white side down. With Avocado Oil, brush the tops of the quesadillas.
6. Put the quesadillas underneath the broiler & broil for around fifteen min, till slightly crisp as well as the egg whites start to bubble.

8.12 Chocolate Coffee Rubbed Steak With Coconut

Servings: 2 | Time: 20 mins | Difficulty: Easy
Nutrients per serving: Calories: 286 kcal | Fat: 19g | Carbohydrates: 5g | Protein: 24g | Fiber: 1g

Ingredients

- 1/4 tsp Salt
- 1 tsp ground coffee
- 1/4 tsp Garlic powder
- 1/2 tsp Chili powder
- 1/4 tsp Onion powder
- 1/2 tsp smoked paprika
- 1 tsp cocoa powder, Unsweetened
- 1/8 tsp Cinnamon
- 1 tsp sugar of coconut
- Pepper Pinch
- 2 Tbsp coconut flakes, Unsweetened
- 1/2 Lb Strip steak, New York

Method

1. Combine the ingredients of the rub in a med bowl & set aside.
2. Cut the steak off some big, noticeable chunks of fat & cover it with the rub. Get in there for good to ensure that the steak is properly covered.
3. Cover your steak & let it stay in the fridge for at least one hour, ideally longer to incorporate the flavor.
4. Spray with cooking spray on a grill skillet (or normal pan) & preheat over high heat. Oven preheated to 400 degrees as well.
5. Cook the steak, around 1-2 mins per side, till pleasant & seared on either side.
6. Switch the heat down to med and continue cooking till the appropriate amount of done-ness is met
7. Move to a plate after the steak is cooked & cover this with tinfoil to sit for 5-7 mins.
8. Toast the coconut flakes on a tiny, bakery release paper lined cookie tray whereas the steak is resting. See carefully as it requires just 2 min for them to get soft & golden.
9. Enjoy your steak garnished with a flake of coconut.

8.13 Pistachio Crusted Chicken With Coriander Yogurt Sauce

Servings: 2 | Time: 30 mins | Difficulty: Easy
Nutrients per serving: Calories: 409 kcal | Fat: 11g | Carbohydrates: 21g | Protein: 51g | Fiber: 7g

Ingredients

For The Chicken

- Salt
- 1/2 Cup Roasted Pistachios
- 8 Oz Chicken
- One big egg white

For The Cauliflower Rice

- 4 Cups Cauliflower (cut into bite-sized slices)
- 1/2 cup Coriander, roughly minced
- Salt & pepper
- Fresh juice of a lime, to taste

For The Sauce

- 1/2 tsp Ground cilantro
- 1/2 cup non-fat Greek yogurt
- 1/8 tsp Cayenne pepper
- Juice of half a lime
- Salt Pinch

Method

1. Oven preheated to 425 degrees & put it on top of a wide cookie sheet with a little cooling rack.
2. Grind your pistachios & a salt pinch in a tiny food processor till the pistachios are processed but still a little bit chunky. This preserves the crunchy chicken. Place the pistachios into a dish with shallow sides. Put the white egg in a med dish.
3. Pat your chicken to dry & put in the white egg, shaking off all the surplus. After this, roll about softly, put in the pistachios, so the full chicken is coated, pressing firmly to stick the nuts to a chicken. Put it on the rack & bake for around 12-15 mins till the chicken is no further pink from the inside, & the outside becomes golden brown & crunchy.
4. Put the cauliflower in a big food processor, whereas the chicken cooks & processes till it appears like rice.
5. Put in a big bowl & microwave the cauliflower rice till tender, around 3-4 mins. Combine with the Coriander & sprinkle to taste with the salt & new lime juice. Place aside
6. In a tiny bowl, mix all the sauce ingredients & serve on top of the chicken & rice of cauliflower.
7. Decorate with it, Coriander.

8.14 Crock Pot Low Carb Buffalo Chicken Soup

Servings: 4 | Time: 4 hrs 10 mins | Difficulty: Easy
Nutrients per serving: Calories: 305 kcal | Fat: 26.2g | Carbohydrates: 6.9g | Protein: 11.9g | Fiber: 0.6g

Ingredients

- 3/4 cup thinly sliced Celery

- 1/2 Tbsp Ghee
- 1/4 cup diced Onion
- 2 cups chicken broth (Low-sodium)
- 1/2 cup coconut milk (Full fat)
- 1/4 Cup Hot sauce
- 1/2 Cup full 30 Ranch dressing
- 1/2 tsp Sea salt
- 1/2 Lb Chicken thighs
- 1/4 tsp Paprika
- sliced Green Onion for garnish
- 1 Tbsp Tapioca starch

Method
1. Warm the ghee on med-high heat in a wide bowl. Put in the celery & onion, then cook for around 3-4 mins before they start to soften & brown. Put into the 7-quart crockpot.
2. Cover the chicken with all the leftover ingredients & stir till mixed—Nestle your chicken into a liquid, on HIGH, cover & cook for three hrs.
3. Stir together the tapioca starch & 2 teaspoons of the liquid of cooking in a med bowl till smooth. Mix it back into the crockpot to ensure that it's smooth & blended—Cook for 1 to 2 more hours, or till the soup hardens a bit.
4. Remove & chop the chicken from your crockpot. Through the crockpot, mix it back.
5. Serve it with onion

8.15 Cauliflower Fried Rice

Servings: 2 | Time: 20 mins | Difficulty: Easy
Nutrients per serving: Calories: 236 kcal | Fat: 11.4g | Carbohydrates: 24.5g | Protein: 11.8g | Fiber: 6.1g

Ingredients
- 2 Slices smoked bacon (Thick-cut)
- 3/4 cup diced Onion
- 4 Cups Cauliflower florets
- 1 Tbsp minced Garlic
- 1/2 cup sliced Green Onion plus extra for garnish
- 2 Tbsp Water
- 1 Egg
- 2 1/2 Tbsp Coconut aminos
- Salt and pepper to taste
- 1/2 Tbsp sesame oil (Cold-pressed)
- Sesame seeds for garnish

Method
1. On med heat, heat a broad wok & cook the bacon till brown & crispy golden, turning once. Remove to a lined paper-towel plate & pat the extra fat off. Set that bacon fat in the skillet aside.
2. Put the cauliflower florets in a broad food processor as the bacon cooks, and pulsate till rice-like. Place aside
3. 3. Lower the heat to med/high when the bacon is cooked & removed from the grill, & put the onions & garlic. Cook till slightly becomes golden brown, for 1 min.
4. Put the riced cauliflower along with the green onions sliced & cook for around 5 mins, stirring regularly, till the cauliflower becomes golden brown & soft.
5. Heat a tiny non-stick skillet on med heat as the cauliflower cooks. Mix the water with the egg & put it in the skillet. Use a cap to protect & cook till the egg is ready. Don't scramble around it. Cut it onto a chopping board till cooked & break it into small slices.
6. Take it from the heat & stir in the cut egg, coconut amino & sesame oil till the cauliflower is fried. Season with salt & pepper. After this, crumble & whisk in the fried bacon till fairly combined.
7. Decorate with additional sesame & onion seeds.

8.16 Coconut Chicken Curry

Servings: 6 | Time: 40 mins | Difficulty: Easy

Nutrients per serving: Calories: 660 kcal | Fat: 60g | Carbohydrates: 7g | Protein: 13g | Fiber: 7g

Ingredients
- 2 Tbsp divided Coconut oil
- 1 1/2 lbs chicken thighs (boneless skinless)
- One thinly sliced Red pepper
- 1/2 cup diced Onion
- 1/2 Tbsp minced fresh garlic
- 1/2 Tbsp minced fresh ginger,
- 2 tsp Turmeric
- 4 tsp yellow curry powder
- 1 tsp ground cumin
- 1 tsp Salt
- 1 tsp Garam masala
- 1 1/2 Cups Chopped tomatoes
- 1 Can coconut milk Full fat (14 oz)
- 1/2 cup minced Coriander
- Rice/cauliflower rice for serving

Method
1. Heat 1 tablespoon of coconut oil on med/high heat in a big, high-sided frying skillet. Include the chicken thighs & cook till seared & golden brown for 1-two min on each side, then move to a tray.
2. The residual oil is applied as well as the heat is switched to med. Put the onion, red pepper, garlic, curry powder, ginger, garam masala & turmeric , then simmer for around five min, till the vegetables start to soften.
3. Put the Coriander to the remaining ingredients, & bring to a simmer. After this cover, boil for 3 mins, lower the heat & boil for ten min. Uncover & cook for another 5-ten min till the sauce has thickened significantly.
4. Take the chicken to a chopping board & chop2 it with two forks, then, together with the Coriander, mix it back into the curry.
5. Serve with the preferred rice.

8.17 Low Carb Keto Chicken Stir Fry

Servings: 2 | Time: 25 mins | Difficulty: Easy
Nutrients per serving: Calories: 238 kcal | Fat: 9.6g | Carbohydrates: 15g | Protein: 27g | Fiber: 4.3g

Ingredients
- 1 1/2 Tbsp divided Olive oil
- 1/2 Lb thinly sliced chicken breast (boneless skinless)
- 1/2 courgette Sliced
- One thinly sliced Red pepper
- 1/4 sliced Onion
- 1/2 tsp minced fresh ginger
- 1/2 tsp minced fresh garlic
- 2 Tbsp soy sauce (reduced sodium)
- 1/2 Tbsp Rice vinegar
- Salt
- 1/2 tsp Sesame oil
- Cauliflower rice for serving
- Green onion for garnish

Method
1. In a wide, elevated side skillet or wok, heat one tablespoon of oil over med/high heat. Cook the chicken for around 5-6 mins, till the center is golden brown & no further pink. Move to the skillet.
2. In the skillet, Put the leftover oil & switch the heat to a med amount. Put all the vegetables into the soy sauce & cook for around 5-8 mins, till the vegetables are brown & soft.
3. Return to the chicken & the sesame oil, rice vinegar & soy sauce to the skillet & cook for around 30 sec.
4. Garnish it with green onion & Serve with rice or cauliflower.

8.18 Cilantro Lime Cauliflower Rice

Servings: 4 | Time: 20 mins | Difficulty: Easy
Nutrients per serving: Calories: 113.2 kcal | Fat: 7.1g | Carbohydrates: 11.7g | Protein: 3.4g | Fiber: 4.4g

Ingredients

- 2/3 cup diced Onion
- 2 Tbsp Olive oil
- One big head of cauliflower, riced
- 1 Lime juice
- 1/2 tsp Sea salt
- 1/2 cup roughly chopped Coriander

Method

1. In a wide saucepan, heat olive oil to med-high, add onion & cook till soft & slightly browned, around 2-3 mins.
2. Put the cauliflower rice & cook for around 5-6 mins, constantly stirring, till tender & brown.
3. Remove & mix in the salt & juice of lime from the heat. Put it all back on the heat & simmer for another 1-2 mins till a little bit of rice dries out.
4. Change the salt & lime to taste.

8.19 Dairy-Free Paleo Casserole With Chicken

Servings: 4 | Time: 1 hr 15 mins | Difficulty: Easy
Nutrients per serving: Calories: 321 kcal | Fat: 19.8g | Carbohydrates: 13.9g | Protein: 25.2g | Fiber: 4g

Ingredients

The Casserole:

- 1 Tbsp plus 1 tsp divided Olive oil
- 1 Lb Lean Ground turkey
- 1/2 cup diced onion
- Pepper
- 1/4 cup plus 2 Tbsp Tomato paste
- One big sliced courgette 1/4 thick
- 1 tsp minced Garlic
- 1/2 tsp Salt
- 1/8 tsp Cardamom powder
- 1/8 tsp Oregano flakes
- 1/4 tsp Cumin powder
- 1/4 tsp Chili powder
- 1/2 tsp minced Fresh Tarragon plus extra for garnish
- 1 big thinly sliced tomato
- 1 cup diced orange bell pepper

For The Sauce:

- 1 1/2 Tbsp Olive oil
- 1 Tbsp plus 1 tsp Coconut flour
- 1 Tbsp plus 1 tsp Almond meal
- 1 cup Almond milk Unsweetened
- Salt & pepper

Method

1. oven preheated to 350 degrees & spray the olive oil with an 8x8 inch skillet. Place aside
2. Heat 1 Tablespoon of olive oil on med heat in a big saucepan.
3. 3. Put the turkey & roast till it's no further pink, & the outside is soft & brown. Put the minced tomato paste & onion, then sprinkle with salt.
4. Put the sliced courgette and toss with the leftover tsp of olive oil & garlic in a wide bowl. Stir together the cumin, salt, cardamom, chili powder & oregano in a different, shallow bowl. Put & throw in the courgette, ensuring that the spices are uniformly covered.
5. Scatter the courgette on the bottom of the prepared skillet and scatter the fresh tarragon on the rest of the skillet.

6. On top of the courgette, scoop the turkey combination & push back so the turkey is soft & wrapped. Place the sliced tomato with an even layer on the turkey top. Finish by splashing the sliced bell pepper uniformly over the surface of the tomato.
7. Cover and bake the casserole for 15 minutes.
8. Create the sauce as the casserole bakes by boiling the olive oil over medium/high heat in a wide skillet.
9. Put flour of coconut & almond meal, then simmer till the flour begins to soak into the oil & give a dark brown color for around 1 min. Think of black peanut butter.
10. Put in the milk of almond, put it to a boil & whisk continuously. Decrease the heat to mild until boiling so that the sauce remains at a steady low simmer. To make sure it does not smoke, stir regularly.
11. Cook for around 10-11 mins, till the sauce starts to thicken. With salt & pepper, season.
12. Place the sauce uniformly till the casserole is cooked & roast, exposed, for another 45 mins.
13. Let sit for 10 mins; after this slice, Put extra tarragon & enjoy it.

8.20 Chicken Pesto Spaghetti Squash

Servings: 2 | Time: 1 hr 15 mins | Difficulty: Easy
Nutrients per serving: Calories: 515 kcal | Fat: 37g | Carbohydrates: 19g | Protein: 31g | Fiber: 4.6g

Ingredients

- 1 Med spaghetti squash
- 1 Tbsp divided Oil
- 8 Oz cubed chicken breast, Boneless & skinless
- Salt
- Onion powder
- Garlic powder

The Pesto:

- 2 cups lightly packed Basil (32g)
- 6 Tbsp Pine nuts
- 1 tsp minced fresh garlic
- 1 Tbsp fresh lemon juice
- 2 Tbsp Olive oil
- 1/2 tsp Salt

Method

1. Heat the oven to 400 degrees & use aluminum foil to cover a rimmed cookie sheet.
2. Break the half-length spaghetti squash carefully & scoop out all the seeds. With 1/2 Tablespoon of oil, massage the inside & season with salt. Put on the cookie sheet, cut-side-down, & bake till the fork is soft, approximately 45 minutes to 1 hour. Additionally, on a small cookie sheet, scatter the pine nuts & bake till about golden brown, around 5-10 mins.
3. Heat another 1/2 Tablespoon of oil in a wide pan over low heat until the squash is finished. Sprinkle garlic powder, onion powder & salt on the chicken cubes & simmer for around five min, till golden brown.

Make the Pesto

1. In a Tiny food processor, place the pine nuts & pulse till broken. Put in all the leftover ingredients, excluding the oil, then scrape the sides if required when mixed.
2. With the food processor going, once well mixed, stream in the liquid.
3. Split the squash into Two bowls & combine each squash with 1/2 of the pesto. If needed, finish with chicken & extra sliced Basil. Sprinkle with salt to taste.

8.21 Keto Mexican Cauliflower Rice

Servings: 4 | Time: 15 mins | Difficulty: Easy
Nutrients per serving: Calories: 109.2 kcal | Fat: 7.2g | Carbohydrates: 10.5g | Protein: 3.5g | Fiber: 4.4g

Ingredients

- 2 Tbsp Olive oil
- 2 Lbs cauliflower cut into florets

- 2 tsp Fajita seasoning
- 1/4-1/2 tsp Salt
- 3/4 Cup Salsa of your choice
- 1/2 cup diced Coriander
- Fresh lime juice

Method
1. In a big food processor, put the cauliflower & pulse till you prefer rice.
2. Heat oil over med-high heat in a wide skillet. Put the rice & simmer till golden brown, stirring often. Usually 5-6 mins
3. Put seasoning & salt to the fajita and cook for 1 minute.
4. Put the salsa & simmer for around 3-4 mins, till the rice starts to dry up.
5. Mix in the Coriander & enjoy it.

8.22 Keto Creamed Spinach

Servings: 4 I Time: 10 mins I Difficulty: Easy
Nutrients per serving: Calories: 203.2 kcal I Fat: 18.5g I Carbohydrates: 7.4g I Protein: 0g I Fiber: 2.4g

Ingredients
- 1 Lb Baby spinach
- 2 tsp Olive oil
- 2 Tbsp Butter
- 2 tsp minced Garlic
- 2/3 cup diced Onion
- 4 Oz cream cheese Full fat
- 1/2 cup almond milk Unsweetened
- 1/2 tsp Salt
- 1/2 tsp Nutmeg

Method
1. Heat oil over med heat in a big skillet. Cook your spinach till it is nice & wilted; after this, transfer it to a colander to rinse it.
2. On a med boil, heat the butter. Put the onion & garlic, then roast for around 3 mins, till golden brown.
3. Put the almond milk, cream cheese, nutmeg & salt, then mix till the creamy cheese is melted & smooth. Cook for 2-3 mins, constantly stirring, till mildly thickened.
4. Squeeze out enough water as needed from the spinach & then mix it till well covered in the skillet.

8.23 No Bean Low Carb Keto Turkey Chili

Servings: 6 I Time: 50 mins I Difficulty: Easy
Nutrients per serving: Calories: 195.6 kcal I Fat: 10.1g I Carbohydrates: 7.1g I Protein: 20.6g I Fiber: 2g

Ingredients
- 1 1/2 Tbsp divided Olive oil
- 1/2 cup diced Onion
- One big diced red pepper
- 1/2 cup thinly sliced Celery
- 1 Tbsp minced fresh garlic
- 4 tsp Chile powder
- 1.25 Lbs Lean ground turkey
- 1 Tbsp Paprika
- 1/4 tsp Cayenne pepper
- 1 1/2 tsp ground cumin
- 1 Can Fire-roasted minced tomatoes
- 1 Can Chopped tomatoes
- 2 Tbsp Tomato paste
- 1/2 Cup Water
- 1 tsp Salt
- Pepper Pinch
- 2 Bay leaves
- 1/4 cup chopped Parsley

Method
1. Heat 1 Tablespoon of oil over med-high heat in a big saucepan. Put the pepper, onion, garlic & celery, and then simmer for around 3 mins until the onion starts to soften.
2. To the skillet, put the remainder of the oil as well as the turkey. Cook for approximately 3-4 mins, till the turkey, starts to brown. Drain some of the liquid away.
3. Put in the spices & cook for around 3-4 mins till the turkey is no further pink & the spices become fragrant.
4. Put the roasted tomatoes, water, smashed tomatoes, tomato paste, pepper & salt on the burner & mix till well mixed. Now Carry it to a simmer.
5. Mix in the bay leaves after boiling, lower the heat to med-low, & cover the skillet. Boil for thirty min, sometimes stirring.
6. Remove the bay leaves & mix in the Parsley till they have simmered.

8.24 Middle Eastern Keto Slow Cooker Chicken Thighs

Servings: 4 I Time: 4 hr 10 mins I Difficulty: Easy
Nutrients per serving: Calories: 596 kcal I Fat: 35g I Carbohydrates: 3g I Protein: 63g I Fiber: 1g

Ingredients
- 2 pounds Chicken Thighs Boneless & Skinless
- 1 tbsp Za'atar Seasoning
- 1/3 cup Chicken Broth
- 2 ounces Goat Cheese
- 3 tbsp Tahini Paste
- One tbsp Fresh Juice of Lemon
- 1/2 tsp Sea Salt
- 1/2 Lemon
- sliced Fresh Mint for garnish

Method
1. Break off some of the chicken's big noticeable pieces of fat (optional) & place the thighs in the crockpot's rim. Drizzle seasoning on the zaatar & brush all around the chicken to thoroughly cover it.
2. Put the goat cheese in a med, microwave-safe bowl & microwave for around 15-30 sec, till the goat cheese only starts to soften. Put all the remaining ingredients & mix in a bowl until the cheese is smooth & broken down.
3. Place on the chicken to make sure that everything is covered. In the crockpot, bring the two halves of Lemon.
4. Cover & simmer for 4-5 hours on low heat till the chicken is soft and fried.
5. Squeeze all the juice out from the lemons into the crockpot once it is cooked. Move the chicken to the bowls, mix the leftover sauce till it's mixed in the crockpot.
6. Spoon the sauce on the chicken & if needed, top with mint.

8.25 Dairy-Free Vegan Cauliflower Soup

Servings: 6 I Time: 1 hr 5 mins I Difficulty: Easy
Nutrients per serving: Calories: 152 kcal I Fat: 11.7g I Carbohydrates: 10.8g I Protein: 4.8g I Fiber: 4.4g

Ingredients
- 1 Garlic head
- 10 Lightly Heaping Cups Cauliflower, cut into florets (one medium head that is 2 lbs 10 oz)
- 3 Tbsp plus 1 tsp Olive oil
- 1/2 big roughly chopped Onion
- 1 1/4 tsp divided Salt
- 4 Cups Chicken
- 4 Tbsp cream cheese of Full fat

Method
1. Oven preheated to 400 degrees.
2. Break off the top of the head of garlic, reveal the cloves & strip all of the papery skin away. Put the garlic on the highest point of

a double layer of the tinfoil, cut-side-up. Put one teaspoon of olive oil on the garlic. To build a tiny package over the garlic, fold the tinfoil from the end, making sure it's securely closed. Put it on a small cookie sheet & bake for around 40-45 mins till the garlic is soft.

3. Put the cauliflower & the onion in a wide bowl, then toss with three teaspoons of olive oil & 3/4 teaspoon salt. Divide into two cookie sheets equally.
4. Bake for around 20-25 mins, often stirring, till tender & golden brown.
5. Put the onion, half Garlic head & cauliflower in a high-powdered processor till it has been roasted. Put 1/2 teaspoon of salt, broth & cream cheese to the leftover 1/2 teaspoon, and combine until smooth and fluffy. If you like, sample the broth, change some salt, and incorporate some garlic.

8.26 Low Carb Buffalo Chicken Meatballs

Servings: 4 I Time: 30 mins I Difficulty: Easy
Nutrients per serving: Calories: 378 kcal I Fat: 18g I Carbohydrates: 28.3g I Protein: 30.4g I Fiber: 8.8g
Ingredients
The Zoodles
*   Eight big courgettes
*   Salt
For The Cauliflower Alfredo
*   3 Cups Water
*   5 Cups (cut into bite-sized pieces) Cauliflower
*   3 Cups broth of Vegetable
*   1 1/2 Tbsp minced Garlic
*   1 Tbsp Olive oil
*   1/2 cup roughly chopped onion
*   Pepper
*   1/2 tsp Salt
*   2 Tbsp Milk
The Meatballs
*   1 Lb additional Lean Ground chicken
*   1/2 cup grated Mozzarella cheese
*   1/4 cup plus 2 Tbsp old fashioned oatmeal (Rolled)
*   1/4 cup diced Green Onion plus extra for garnish
*   1 1/2 tsp minced Garlic
*   1 tsp Salt
*   1 Tbsp Ranch seasoning
*   Pepper Pinch
*   Buffalo chicken sauce
*   One big egg white
Method
1. oven preheated to 400 degrees & spray the cooking spray on a baking dish.
2. On a mandolin, use a 5/7 millimeters julienne blade & slice courgette lengthwise to produce long noodles.
3. Toss the courgette noodles & let them hang in the strainer on a cup for 20 to 30 mins. A couple of times, mix them around as they strain.
4. In a big kettle, mix the water and vegetable broth and bring it to a boil. When it is cooked, add the cauliflower and cover it. Cook for around 6-7 minutes until the cauliflower is soft. Remove from the sun, and to stay safe, cover. Don't drain them!
5. Combine cheese, ground chicken, 1/4 cup of green onion, 1 tsp of salt, 1 1/2 tsp of garlic, ranch powder, oatmeal, pepper & egg whites in a big bowl. Mix, so it's blended equally.
6. Make the meat into balls & put it on the cookie sheet that has been prepared. Put them in the oven & bake for 10 to 15 mins.
7. In a med skillet, heat one tablespoon of olive oil & cook the garlic & onion until finely golden brown. In a big food processor/blender, incorporate the cooked garlic & onion.
8. Move the cauliflower into the food processor with a slotted spoon & put salt, a pepper pinch & cream. Blend & then put 3 to 4 more

cooking liquid teaspoons till the required consistency is obtained in the sauce.
9. Squeeze the courgette noodles out of the excess water and split them between bowls. If required, cover with meatballs, cauliflower sauce & sprinkle with buffalo sauce & additional green onions.

8.27 Low Carb Pizza Meal Prep Bowls

Servings: 4 I Time: 20 mins I Difficulty: Easy
Nutrients per serving: Calories: 453.5 kcal I Fat: 29.4g I Carbohydrates: 10.2g I Protein: 36.8g I Fiber: 1.9g
Ingredients
*   24 uncured Pepperonis
*   Eight slices of Ham
*   Four slices of Bacon
*   Two sliced Green Peppers
*   1 tbsp Italian Seasoning
*   1 pound Lean Grass-Fed Ground Beef
*   1/2 tsp Sea Salt
*   3/4 cup divided Tomato Sauce
*   1/4 cup sliced Black Olives
*   3 ounces grated Mozzarella Cheese
Cheese Sauce:
*   1 cup Roasted Cashews (soaked in water)
*   2 tbsp Nutritional Yeast
*   1/3 cup Water
*   1 tsp Sea Salt
*   1 tsp Garlic Powder
*   1/4 tsp Stone Ground Mustard
*   1/2 tsp Onion Powder
*   Black Pepper pinch
Method
1. Oven preheated to 185 °c & use bakery release paper to line a baking sheet. Put the pepperonis & ham out and bake for around 5-10 mins, till lightly crisp. Monitor carefully as before the pepperoni; the ham would most definitely be done.
2. Fry the bacon till golden brown & on each side in a wide frying pan on med heat, switching to a towel-lined plate & extracting the excess oil once cooked.
3. Into the skillet, Put the peppers & mushrooms with the remaining bacon fat & fry, constantly stirring, till golden brown & soft, around ten min.
4. Heat a separate big frying pan on med-high as the vegetable fry, then fry the beef, breaking it as it cooks, till it's no further pink from inside, around 10 mins. Drain the extra fat away.
5. Stir in the beef with Italian seasoning & salt till well combined. Then put 1/2 cup tomato sauce & stir.
6. Divide the pepperoni, ham, vegetables, bacon, olives & meat. Divide per bowl (1 Tablespoon each) with the remaining tomato sauce. Eventually, split the shredded cheese & cover every bowl, then refrigerate till ready to serve! The bowls could last in the refrigerator for 3 to 5 days.
7. Reveal & microwave for around one minute before ready to eat, or when the cheese melt. Mix & enjoy it.
    To make Paleo cheese sauce
1. Put all the ingredients & blend in a Tiny food processor, preventing scraping down the sides till smooth.
2. Store in a small separate meal prepared jars.

8.28 Turkey Meatballs With Basil Black Walnut Pesto Cream

Servings: 4 I Time: 30 mins I Difficulty: Easy
Nutrients per serving: Calories: 458 kcal I Fat: 34.6g I Carbohydrates: 11.1g I Protein: 26.4g I Fiber: 3.9g
Ingredients
The Meatballs:

- 1 Egg
- 1 Lb Lean ground turkey
- 1/4 cup sliced Fresh Basil plus extra for garnish
- 2 tsp minced fresh garlic
- 2 tsp Italian seasoning
- 1 tsp packed Lemon zest
- 4 tsp Coconut flour
- 1/2 tsp Sea salt
- 1/2 cup chicken broth Reduced sodium
- Four small courgettes

For The Sauce:
- 2 1/4 cups very tightly packed Fresh Basil (35g)
- 1/3 Cup Black Walnuts, Hammons
- 2 tsp Lemon zest
- 2 Tbsp Fresh juice of Lemon
- 1 tsp minced fresh garlic
- 2 tbsp additional Virgin Olive oil
- 3/4 tsp Sea salt
- 6 Tbsp coconut milk Full fat
- 6 Tbsp chicken broth Reduced sodium

Method

1. Mix all the meatball components with the coconut flour in a wide bowl till it's combined. Place the coconut flour in & mix till it's combined. Form into 20 slightly heaping balls.
2. Heat a big, non-stick skillet on med-high heat. Cook the meatballs along both sides till golden brown - around 1 min per side. Stir in the broth of the chicken, decrease the heat to med/low & cover. Cook for around 8-11 mins, stirring regularly, till the meatballs are cooked as well as the broth has been absorbed.
3. Put the black walnuts into a Tiny food processor as the meatballs cook, & pulse till broken down. Put all the leftover ingredients & pulse to the olive oil till it is broken down & mixed.
4. With the food processor going, when well combined, stream in the olive oil
5. Mix the milk of coconut & chicken broth in a big frying pan over med/high heat. Just get it to a simmer.
6. Mix in all the pesto till just mixed & cook for 1 min after boiling, mixing continuously. Then lower the heat to med/low, then boil till the sauce starts to thicken, for 2 to 3 mins.
7. On med-high heat, heat a dry frying pan & cook the courgette noodles till they are only softened around 3-4 mins. Transfer to a sheet of paper towel & the remaining moisture is gently squeezed out—split b/w four bowls.
8. Mix the meatballs into the sauce & serve with fresh Basil and a squeeze of Lemon, if needed, over the zoodles.

8.29 Chicken Zoodle Soup

Servings: 22 I Time: 8 hrs 20 mins I Difficulty: Easy
Nutrients per serving: Calories: 344 kcal I Fat: 20.4g I Carbohydrates: 11.9g I Protein: 26.7g I Fiber: 3.3g

Ingredients

For The Broth:
- 3 Med Carrots
- 1 Pasture raised stewing hen
- Four Celery Stalks
- One big onion
- Six leaves of Bay
- Two full bundles of Parsley, covered & tied with twine
- full Peppercorns
- 2 Boxes (not sodium-reduced) chicken broth
- Whole Star anise seed

For the Zoodles:
- courgettes
- Salt

Method

1. Put the chicken in the big stockpot
2. Break each carrot & celery stalk into three big pieces & put them on the chicken's highest point.
3. Break the onion into big pieces & put the carrots & celery on top.
4. On top of the herbs, place the packed Parsley & bay leaves.
5. Fill two black peppercorn steel diffusers & put them in the stockpot.
6. Repeat this, in a different diffuser, along with the star anise seed.
7. In the stockpot, place a chicken broth box over the top of it.
8. Till all the components are covered, fill the remainder of the pot with water.
9. Carry the pot to a simmer on high heat, after the switch to med & cover & cook all day long.
10. Remove the vegetables & put them aside till the supply is through simmering. Cut the chicken; it will all fall off the bone & put the fat & any little floaty parts off its top of the stock on the plate & skim.
11. Remove extra fat off the chicken, chop & set aside
12. Depending on the 'chicken flavor you want, taste the stock, and see if it needs some extra salt or any more chicken broth.
13. Using a paper towel, gently push out any extra moisture from the zoodles & then split them b/w bowls. Stock the spoon on top & incorporate shredded chicken.

8.30 Mediterranean Egg Muffins With Ham

Servings: 6 I Time: 25 mins I Difficulty: Easy
Nutrients per serving: Calories: 109 kcal I Fat: 6.7g I Carbohydrates: 1.8g I Protein: 9.3g I Fiber: 1.8g

Ingredients

- Nine slices deli ham
- 1/3 cup minced fresh spinach
- 1/4 cup crumbled Feta cheese
- Five big eggs
- Salt Pinch
- Pepper pinch
- Fresh Basil for garnish
- 1 1/2 Tbsps Pesto sauce
- 1/2 cup roasted & sliced red pepper (Canned) plus extra for garnish

Method

1. Oven preheated to 400 degrees. GENEROUSLY brush with cooking spray on a baking tray.
2. Line every muffin tin with 1 & a half pieces of ham, ensuring that you do not leave gaps to explode out.
3. On the bottom of each muffin tin, put a tiny bit of roasted red pepper.
4. On top of every red pepper, put one tablespoon of chopped spinach.
5. With a heaping 1/2 Tablespoon of crumbled feta cheese, round off the pepper & spinach.
6. Whisk the eggs along with salt & pepper in a med dish. Divide the mixture of eggs equally between the Six muffin tins.
7. Bake till the eggs become puffy & sound ready, for 15-17 mins.
8. Remove the muffin tin from each cup & garnish with 1/4 tsp of pesto sauce, extra red pepper slices & fresh basil.

8.31 Steak and Shrimp Surf

Servings: 2 I Time: 50 mins I Difficulty: Easy
Nutrients per serving: Calories: 566 kcal I Fat: 38g I Carbohydrates: 10g I Protein: 41.5g I Fiber: 3g

Ingredients

Filet Mignon
- 8 ounces filet mignon
- salt & pepper
- 1 tbsp olive oil
- 1 cup Monterey Jack cheese
- 4 ounces softened Philadelphia cream cheese

- 8 ounces thawed & squeezed dry, frozen spinach
- 1 tbsp butter
- 13.75 ounces can quarter artichoke hearts
- 1/4 cup minced onion
- 1 tsp minced garlic
- 1/4 tsp white pepper
- 1 tsp red wine vinegar

Shrimp Scampi
- Six med shrimp (remove the shell)
- salt & pepper
- 1 tsp minced garlic
- 2 tsp olive oil
- 1 tbsp white wine
- 2 tbsp butter
- 1 tsp juice of Lemon
- 1 tbsp minced parsley

Steamed asparagus (prepare in advance, steam before serving)
- 6 ounces trimmed asparagus
- salt & pepper
- 1 tbsp water

Method

1. On med heat, put a non-stick plate. When it is hot, Put the onion, garlic & butter, cook till tender. Place the leftover ingredients & mix till the cheeses have melted & cooked through the spinach artichoke sauce. Thin it with water, if you wish. Change the salt & pepper seasonings. Refrigerate until it is cold. It can be completed some days in advance. Heat & stir. Makes 3 cups per serving with 1/2 cup.
2. Trim asparagus by chopping 1 inch from the bottom and using a vegetable peeler to peel the last Three inches. Bend one spear if the asparagus is small, and it may crack if it is tender. Use it to slice the thickness of the remaining asparagus. Put the asparagus with one tablespoon water in a secure microwave dish & cover with clinging film.
3. Have the sliced and ready ingredients for its shrimp scampi. Drain a shrimp on a towel, then add salt & pepper on the plate & season.
4. In a secure microwave dish, place the Spinach artichoke dip & prepare to reheat (or in a small pot on the stove with 1 tbsp of water to reheat on medium-low). Take the asparagus from the refrigerator & prepare it for cooking.
5. At least 20 to 30 mins before serving, remove the steaks from the fridge. Rub with around one teaspoon of oil on the outer surface, then sprinkle with salt & pepper liberally.
6. Put a skillet with a hard bottom over the med fire. Place the remaining Two teaspoons of oil when heated, then swirl the skillet to cover the top. Place the steaks as the oil shimmers & do not move for 4 mins. Work a spatula under steaks softly & turn for the next 4 mins to cook. Based on the hardness of the steaks & how cold they become.
7. Remove your steaks & cover them lightly with foil to settle on a tray.
8. On med heat, put a non-stick pan. Put the olive oil & tilt when heated to cover the bottom of the plate. Once the oil shimmers, Put the shrimp. Cook the shrimp around 1/2 way up till opaque. Turn over the shrimp & cook for an extra 1 1/2-2 mins.
9. Remove the shrimp from the bowl, lower the heat, then add the butter & the garlic—1 min to cook. Put the wine and the lemon juice, then simmer till the smell of alcohol in the wine burns away. Take it from the heat & bring the shrimp into the plate, mix in the Parsley & cover loosely with foil.
10. For 1/2-2 minutes, steam the asparagus. Uh, drain.
11. Split the steak, shrimp & asparagus into two bowls. Every spinach artichoke dip measures 1/2 cup, saving the remainder for another day. Spoon garlic butter on the asparagus & steak. Now enjoy it.

8.32 Keto Chicken Marinade

Servings: 1 | Time: 5 mins | Difficulty: Easy
Nutrients per serving: Calories: 253 kcal | Fat: 27.5g | Carbohydrates: 1.5g | Protein: 1.5g| Fiber: 0.5g

Ingredients

- 1 lb Chicken breast
- 2 Tbsps Olive oil
- 6 Tbsps Chicken broth
- 1 Tbsp Yellow mustard
- 2 Tbsps of lemon juice
- 1 Tsp Dried Italian seasoning
- 1 Tbsp Minced garlic
- Sea salt

Method

1. Add mustard, garlic, chicken broth, olive oil, lemon juice, seasoning, and salt in a bowl and toss well.
2. Add the chicken to the bowl and mix everything well. Keep it aside for three hours to marinate.
3. Heat the grill over medium flame for 15 minutes.
4. Place the chicken over the grill and grill from both sides for 10 minutes.
5. Serve and enjoy it.

8.33 Keto Pork Tenderloin with Pistachio Pesto

Servings: 4 | Time: 30 mins | Difficulty: Difficult
Nutrients per serving: Calories: 486 kcal | Fat: 27.1g | Carbohydrates: 9.7g | Protein: 50.7g | Fiber: 3.5g

Ingredients

The Pesto:
- 1/3 Cup Salted Pistachios
- 1/2 Cup cilantro
- 1 1/2 Cups Basil
- ½ Tsp salt
- ½ Lemon zest
- 1 Tbsp lemon juice
- 3 Tbsps Olive oil
- 1 Tbsp Water
- ½ tsp black pepper

The Zoodles:
- Salt to taste
- Four grated Zucchinis

For The Pork:
- 2 lb Pork tenderloin
- Salt to taste
- 1 1/2 Tbsp Olive oil
- Black pepper to taste

Method

1. Place pork tenderloin in a bowl and sprinkle salt, olive oil, and pepper and mix well. Set aside for 15 minutes.
2. Heat olive oil in a skillet over medium flame and add pork pieces.
3. Cook for 5 minutes from each side.
4. Transfer the pork to a baking tray and bake in a preheated oven at 400 degrees for 15 minutes.
5. Blend the pistachios, basil, lemon zest, cilantro, and lemon juice in a blender to get a granular mixture. Slowly pour in water and oil too to get a creamy mixture.
6. Now, cook zoodles in a skillet over medium flame until they get soft.
7. Drain and dry the zoodles and set them aside.
8. Pour pesto sauce over zoodles and mix well.
9. Top the zoodles with pork cut into slices and sprinkle pistachios and squeeze lemon juice according to taste.

8.34 Inst. Pot Turmeric Chicken and Vegetables

Servings: 2 I Time: 10 mins I Difficulty: Easy
Nutrients per serving: Calories: 320 kcal I Fat: 17.3g I Carbohydrates: 10.4g I Protein: 28.4g I Fiber: 4.1g

Ingredients

- 8 oz Chicken breast
- 2 Tbsps melted Coconut oil
- 1/2 Cup coconut milk
- 1 Tsp minced ginger
- 2 Tsp Tomato paste
- 1/4 tsp Ground cinnamon
- 3/4 Tsp Ground turmeric
- Pinch of pepper
- Cilantro, for garnish
- 1/4 tsp Salt
- 1 Cup Brussels sprouts
- 1 Cup sliced Broccoli
- 1/2 sliced Red Bell Pepper

Method

1. Place the Inst. Pot on sauté mode and heat coconut oil in it.
2. Cook chicken in an Inst. Pot from both sides for five minutes.
3. Now, mix coconut milk, tomato paste, ginger, turmeric, salt, and pepper in a bowl.
4. Transfer the milk mixture to an Inst. Pot and mix well.
5. Stir in Brussels and shift the mode from sautéing to the manual, and put it on high pressure with a lid on the pot for one minute.
6. Release the pressure and add bell pepper and broccoli and mix well.
7. Cover the pot and let it cook for 25 minutes.
8. Sprinkle cilantro and serve.

8.35 Asian Miso Steak Sheet Pan Dinner

Servings: 4 I Time: 25 mins I Difficulty: Easy
Nutrients per serving: Calories: 317 kcal I Fat: 18.7g I Carbohydrates: 11.1g I Protein: 38.5g I Fiber: 4g

Ingredients

- 4 Baby Boy Choy
- 4 Cups sliced Broccoli
- 2 Tbsps White miso paste
- Sesame seeds as required to garnish
- 2 Tsps Sesame oil
- 2 Tsps Olive oil
- 1 Lb Sirloin Steak
- 2 Tsps minced ginger

The Miso Butter
- 4 Tsps White miso paste
- 4 Tsps Garlic ghee

Method

1. In a bowl, add boy choy, ginger, broccoli, Misco, and oil and mix well.
2. Transfer the broccoli over a baking tray lined with a parchment sheet.
3. Bake for eight minutes in a preheated oven at 400 degrees.
4. After eight minutes, broil the broccoli for few minutes until they are done.
5. Now, add all the ingredients of miso butter in a bowl and toss well.
6. Spread the butter mixture over the steak and set aside.
7. Sauté the steak in a pan over medium flame for two minutes from both sides.
8. Transfer the steaks to the side of broccoli and let them broil for five minutes.
9. Again spread butter mixture over the steak and add boy choy to the other side of the pan.
10. Let them broil for five more minutes.
11. Spread the butter mixture again over the steaks and drizzle sesame seeds.
12. Serve and enjoy it.

8.36 Sheet Pan Za'atar Chicken Thighs

Servings: 4 I Time: 10 mins I Difficulty: Easy
Nutrients per serving: Calories: 515 kcal I Fat: 35g I Carbohydrates: 13.4g I Protein: 35g I Fiber: 5.5g

Ingredients

- 1 ½ Lbs chicken thighs
- 6 Cups diced Cauliflower
- 1/4 Cup Pistachios
- One sliced onion
- 2 Tbsps chopped mint
- Salt to taste
- 2 1/4 Tbsps Avocado oil
- 2 Tbsps Zahtar
- 2 Tsps lemon juice
- 4 Tsps Tahini
- 1/4 Cup chopped Cilantro
- 2 Tsps Dukkah

Method

1. Lightly roast the pistachios in a preheated oven at 450 degrees for 10 minutes in a baking tray. Place them aside.
2. Add salt, olive oil, and cauliflower in a bowl and mix well.
3. Transfer the cauliflower over a baking sheet. Set aside.
4. Add zahtar and chicken pieces in a bowl.
5. Drizzle some salt and transfer it to a cauliflower pan.
6. Bake the chicken and cauliflower in a preheated oven at 450 degrees for 20 minutes.
7. Mix tahini, olive oil, and lemon juice in a bowl.
8. Pour the tahini mixture over the baked chicken pieces and bake for another eight minutes.
9. Then let them broil for five more minutes.
10. Drizzle lemon juice over the chicken pieces and sprinkle mint, pistachios, cilantro, and Dukkah, and toss well.
11. Serve and enjoy it.

8.37 Tomato Grilled Moroccan Chicken with Yogurt Mint Sauce

Servings: 2 I Time: 25 mins I Difficulty: Easy
Nutrients per serving: Calories: 205 kcal I Fat: 2.4g I Carbohydrates: 13.1g I Protein: 32.4g I Fiber: 2.8g

Ingredients

- 1/2 Lb Boneless Chicken breast
- 2 Tbsps Tomato paste
- 1/2 Tsp minced Garlic
- One chopped onion
- 1/4 Tsp Salt
- 1/2 Tsp paprika
- Pinch of pepper
- 1 Tsp Olive oil
- 1/4 Tsp Cumin powder
- 1/8 Tsp Cinnamon

Mint Yogurt Dip
- 1/2 Tsp minced Garlic
- 1/2 Cup Greek yogurt
- 1/4 Tsp Salt
- 1/4 Cup grated Cucumber

- 2 Tbsp chopped mint
- Pinch of pepper

Method

1. Whisk salt, paprika, garlic, olive oil, tomato paste, pepper, garlic, cumin, and cinnamon in a bowl.
2. Mix in chicken pieces. Place the bowl in the fridge overnight to marinate and to get better results.
3. Thread the chicken and onion over skewer with alternating fashion.
4. Place the threaded skewers over a preheated grill and from 15 minutes from all the sides.
5. Whisk the ingredients of dipping sauce and cucumber in a blender and blend to obtain a smooth mixture.
6. Sprinkle the mint over grilled skewers and serve with dipping sauce.

8.38 Oven Baked Mahi Mahi with Macadamia Crust

Servings: 2 I Time: 20 mins I Difficulty: Easy
Nutrients per serving: Calories: 369 kcal I Fat: 27.5g I Carbohydrates: 5.1g I Protein: 28.6g I Fiber: 2.4g

Ingredients

- 10 oz Mahi Mahi Fillets
- 1/2 Cup Roasted and chopped Macadamia nuts
- 1/2 Tbsp Coconut oil
- Cilantro as required for garnishing
- Salt to taste

Method

1. Blend nuts in a food processor.
2. Transfer crushed nuts into a plate.
3. Drizzle coconut oil over fillets and sprinkle crushed macadamia nuts.
4. Lightly press the nuts so that they get stick to the fillets. Sprinkle some salt.
5. Place mahi-mahi fillets in a baking tray lined with parchment paper.
6. Bake in a preheated oven at 450 degrees for 10 minutes.
7. Later broil it for five minutes.
8. Sprinkle cilantro and serve.

8.39 Spinach Artichoke Greek Yogurt Chicken

Servings: 4 I Time: 30 mins I Difficulty: Easy
Nutrients per serving: Calories: 320 kcal I Fat: 10.2g I Carbohydrates: 16.9g I Protein: 41.3g I Fiber: 7.1g

Ingredients

For The Chicken:

- 1/4 Tsp minced Garlic
- 3 Tbsps Greek yogurt
- 2 Tbsps artichoke preserving liquid
- Four artichoke hearts
- ½ Tsp salt
- 1 Lb Chicken breasts
- Italian seasoning
- ½ Tsp black pepper
- Spinach as required

The Greek Yogurt Sauce:

- 1/2 Cup Greek yogurt
- 1 Tsp chopped Garlic
- 4 Artichoke hearts
- Salt to taste
- 1/3 Cup blend of grated Parmesan and Romano Cheese
- Black pepper to taste

Method

1. Add yogurt, artichoke liquid, salt, garlic, and pepper in a large mixing well. Whisk everything well.
2. Add chicken in the bowl and toss well to evenly coat the chicken.
3. Place the bowl in the fridge for three hours to marinate.
4. Using a sharp knife, make small pockets in chicken pieces and fill them with spinach and place one artichoke heart in each pocket.
5. Use a toothpick to close the opening.
6. Drizzle seasoning over the filled chicken pieces.
7. Place the chicken pieces over a preheated grill and grill for 10 minutes from each side.
8. Whisk all the ingredients of yogurt sauce in a bowl and blend them in a food processor.
9. Serve the chicken with yogurt sauce and enjoy it.

8.40 Indian Salmon Curry Zucchini Noodles with Coconut Milk

Servings: 2 I Time: 20 mins I Difficulty: Easy
Nutrients per serving: Calories: 408 kcal I Fat: 26g I Carbohydrates: 17.8g I Protein: 27.2g I Fiber: 5g

Ingredients

- 3/4 Cup coconut milk
- Salt to taste
- 2 tsp Curry paste
- 8 oz Salmon fillets

The Zucchini Noodles:

- Three zucchinis
- Salt to taste
- Chopped Mint for garnishing

Method

1. Add salt, coconut milk, and curry paste in a bowl and whisk well. Set aside. The coconut milk sauce is ready.
2. Place salmon fillets in a baking tray.
3. Pour the coconut milk sauce over the salmon.
4. Cover the tray and place in the fridge for three hours.
5. Drain excess water for zucchini noodles and mix some salt in it.
6. Place the zucchini noodles aside for 30 minutes with occasional stirring.
7. Bake salmon fillets in a preheated oven at 450 degrees for 15 minutes.
8. Add coconut milk sauce in cooked and drained noodles and toss well.
9. Place baked salmon fillets over the zoodles and sprinkle mint and serve.

8.41 Low Carb Paleo Zucchini Lasagna

Servings: 8 I Time: 1 hr 45 mins I Difficulty: Medium
Nutrients per serving: Calories: 367 kcal I Fat: 25.1g I Carbohydrates: 16.7g I Protein: 19.4g I Fiber: 4.2g

Ingredients

The Zucchini Noodles:

- 1 Tbsp salt
- Five zucchinis

For The Meat:

- 1/2 Lb Pork
- 1 Cup chopped Onion
- 1/2 Lb Beef
- 1 Tbsp chopped Garlic
- 1 Tsp Dried oregano
- 1 Tbsp Italian seasoning
- 1/4 Tsp salt

For The Cheese

- 2 Cups Raw cashews
- 1 1/4 Tsp Salt

- 2 Tbsps lemon juice
- 1 Tsp Onion powder
- Pepper to taste
- 1/2 Tsp Garlic powder
- 6 Tbsp Water

Other:

- 3/4 Cup Tomato sauce
- 3/4 Cup Crushed tomatoes
- 1/2 Cup minced Parsley

Spice Blend

- 1/2 Tbsp minced Garlic
- 1 Tsp Italian Seasoning
- 1/2 Tsp Red pepper flakes
- 1 Tsp Dried parsley
- 1 Tsp salt
- 1/4 Tsp Fennel Seed
- 3/4 Tsp Black pepper
- 1/4 Tsp Paprika
- 1/2 Tsp Minced onion

Method

1. Make thin slices out of zucchini and arrange them on a baking sheet.
2. Sprinkle salt over the zoodles.
3. Bake the zoodles in a preheated oven at 350 degrees for 25 minutes.
4. Add all the items of spice blend in a bowl and mix them well. Divide the mixed spices into two equal portions.
5. Sprinkle one spices mix portion over the pork pieces and set aside.
6. Cook sausage, onion, garlic, and beef in a pan over medium flame for ten minutes.
7. Stir in Italian seasoning, salt, oregano, and black pepper and cook for three minutes.
8. Transfer the cooked mixture to a bowl and place them aside.
9. Blend cashews, spices, and lemon juice in a food processor to get a smooth mixture.
10. Transfer the blended cashew mixture to a bowl and place it aside.
11. In another bowl, add crushed tomatoes and tomato sauce and whisk well.

Assemble:

1. In the bowl, first pour a small portion of sauce, followed by the placement of cooked meat, zucchini noodles, cheese mixture, and parsley.
2. Repeat the same process until everything is used up.
3. Cover the bowl and bake in a preheated oven for 45 minutes.
4. Then cook for 15 more minutes while the cover is removed.
5. Sprinkle parsley over the top and serve.

8.42 Ham and Asparagus Quiche

Servings: 8 I Time: 1 hr 20 mins I Difficulty: Easy
Nutrients per serving: Calories: 493 kcal I Fat: 42g I Carbohydrates: 7.5g I Protein: 22.5g I Fiber: 3.8g

Ingredients

- One recipe packet of Flaky Pie Crust
- 1 Cup cubed Ham
- 8 oz Asparagus
- 1 Tbsp butter
- 1 oz chopped onion
- ¼ Tsp white pepper
- 2 Cups grated Gruyere cheese
- 1 Cup heavy cream
- Five eggs
- ¼ Tsp salt
- ¼ Cup water

Method

1. Prepare the pie's crust according to the directions given over the packet and chill it until further use.
2. Melt the butter in a pan over medium flame.
3. Sauté asparagus, ham, and onions in the butter with constant stirring until they are done.
4. In the end, add asparagus spears and mix well. Later, separate the spears and set them aside to use them for quiche garnishing.
5. Whisk eggs, salt, pepper, thyme, cream, and water in a mixing bowl.
6. Beat until frothy mixture is obtained.
7. Start making layers of cheese, ham mixture and repeat the process until both are used up over the pie dough in a baking tray.
8. Add custard mixture at the end and spread asparagus spears over the top.
9. Bake in a preheated oven at 375 degrees for 40 minutes.
10. Then, broil for five minutes.
11. Prepare the pie crust per instructions. While the dough chills, move on to the preparation of the quiche ingredients (below).
12. Serve and enjoy it.

8.43 Crockpot BBQ Chicken

Servings: 2 I Time: 3 hrs 35 mins I Difficulty: Easy
Nutrients per serving: Calories: 321 kcal I Fat: 16g I Carbohydrates: 5g I Protein: 37g I Fiber: 1g

Ingredients

- 3 Lbs boneless Chicken breasts
- 4 oz butter

Sauce Ingredients

- 6 oz tomato paste
- 3 Tbsps cider vinegar
- 1 Tsp dried thyme
- 1/3 cup brown sugar
- 3 Tbsps red wine vinegar
- 1 Tsp onion powder
- 1/2 Tsp celery salt
- 2 Tbsps yellow mustard
- 1 Tsp garlic powder
- 1 Tsp salt
- 1 Tsp liquid smoke
- 1 Tsp black pepper
- 1/8 Tsp ground cloves

Method

1. Whisk all the items of sauce in a bowl.
2. Place the chicken pieces in the crockpot and pour sauce mixture over it.
3. Cover the pot and cook for four hours on high mode.
4. Shred the chicken and add back to the pot.
5. Add butter and heat to melt it.
6. Adjust the taste accordingly.
7. Serve and enjoy it.

8.44 Chicken Florentine

Servings: 2 I Time: 30 mins I Difficulty: Easy
Nutrients per serving: Calories: 560 kcal I Fat: 42.72g I Carbohydrates: 6.63g I Protein: 38g I Fiber: 1.2g

Ingredients

- 6 oz boneless Chicken breasts
- 1/2 Cup Heavy cream
- 1/4 Lb sliced Mushrooms
- 1/4 Cup White Wine

- 1/4 Cup Cream cheese
- 1 Tsp minced Garlic
- 1 1/2 Tbsp Olive oil
- 1 Cup Spinach

Method
1. Rub the chicken with salt, oil, and pepper and set aside for a while.
2. Heat olive oil in a skillet over medium flame.
3. Add chicken and cook for 15 minutes from both sides.
4. Transfer the chicken to the plate and cover it to keep it warm.
5. Heat olive oil again in the same pan and sauté garlic and mushrooms in it with occasional stirring.
6. Add wine or chicken broth and mix well.
7. Stir in spinach and cook for few minutes with stirring until they wilt.
8. Now create a space in the middle of the pan and add heavy cream and cream cheese in the center and cook to melt them.
9. Sprinkle pepper and salt and serve.

8.45 Keto Chinese Pepper Steak

Servings: 3 | Time: 25 mins | Difficulty: Easy
Nutrients per serving: Calories: 267 kcal | Fat: 16g | Carbohydrates: 5.54g | Protein: 25.32g | Fiber: 1.3g

Ingredients
- 12 oz sliced Flank steak
- 3/4 Red bell pepper
- 3/4 Green bell pepper
- 1/4 sliced Onion
- 1 Tbsp Olive oil
- 1 Tbsp soy sauce
- 1 Tsp toasted sesame oil

Method
1. Heat olive oil in a pan over medium flame.
2. Add beef and cook for two minutes without touching it.
3. After two minutes, stir it and cook for two more minutes.
4. Transfer cooked beef pieces into the plate and set aside.
5. Heat olive oil again in the same pan over medium flame.
6. Sauté all the veggies in it. Stir in soy sauce and water and toss well.
7. Cover the pan and let it cook for three minutes.
8. Add beef back to the pan and cook for two minutes.
9. Sprinkle salt, sesame oil, and pepper and serve.

8.46 Keto Eggplant Lasagna Stacks

Servings: 4 | Time: 1 hr | Difficulty: Easy
Nutrients per serving: Calories: 255 kcal | Fat: 16g | Carbohydrates: 10g | Protein: 19g | Fiber: 5g

Ingredients
- 1 1/4 Lbs sliced Eggplant
- 1 Tsp Salt
- 1 Egg beaten with 3 Tsps of Water
- 4 oz sliced Mozzarella cheese
- 1 Cup Tomato Sauce
- 1/4 Cup grated Parmesan cheese
- 1 Tbsp olive oil

Low Carb Keto Breading
- 1 Cup pork rind panko
- 1/4 Tsp onion powder
- 1 Tsp dried oregano
- 1/2 Cup grated Parmesan cheese
- 1 Tsp dried basil
- 1/4 Tsp garlic powder
- 1/2 Tsp salt

- 1/4 Tsp ground pepper

Method
1. Slice eggplants and sprinkle salt over them.
2. Place them aside for a while.
3. In a large bowl, beat eggs and set aside.
4. Whisk all the ingredients of breading in a bowl and set aside.
5. Drain and dry eggplants.
6. Dip each of the eggplant slices in the egg mixture and then in breadcrumbs to thoroughly coat the eggplant slices from all the sides.
7. Place the coated eggplant slices on a baking tray.
8. Bake in a preheated oven at 400 degrees for ten minutes.
9. After ten minutes, coat eggplant with tomato sauce and place mozzarella cheese and parmesan cheese over eggplants.
10. Bake again for five minutes to melt the cheese.
11. Serve and enjoy it.
12. Preheat oven to 400 F.

8.47 Keto Chicken Broccoli Alfredo

Servings: 2 | Time: 30 mins | Difficulty: Easy
Nutrients per serving: Calories: 534 kcal | Fat: 37g | Carbohydrates: 9.6g | Protein: 42.7g | Fiber: 2.8g

Ingredients
- 6 oz boneless chicken breasts
- 1 Cup Broccoli
- 2 Tbsp Butter
- 2 Tbsp Water
- Black pepper to taste
- 1/3 Cup Heavy cream
- 1 Tsp minced Garlic
- 2 oz grated Parmesan cheese
- Salt to taste
- 1 Cup Cauliflower rice
- Chopped parsley for garnish

Method
1. Rub black pepper and salt over the chicken and set aside for a while.
2. Melt the butter in a pan over medium flame.
3. Add the chicken and cook for seven minutes from both sides.
4. Transfer the cooked chicken to a plate and cover it to keep it warm.
5. In the same pan, add broccoli and water. Mix and cover the pan and let it steam for three minutes.
6. Shift the broccoli to the plate with chicken.
7. Again melt butter in the pan.
8. Sauté garlic in butter over medium flame.
9. Stir in heavy cream and cheese and cook while stirring for seven minutes.
10. Pour in water to bring sauce to the required consistency.
11. In the end, add pepper and salt and stir well.
12. Take another pan and melt butter in it over medium flame.
13. Sauté cauliflower rice and cook for few minutes until cauliflower gets soft.
14. Sprinkle salt and pepper and toss well.
15. Serve cauliflower with sauce, chicken, and broccoli, and enjoy it.

8.48 Vegetarian Keto Lasagna with Mushroom Ragu

Servings: 8 | Time: 1 hr 30 mins | Difficulty: Easy
Nutrients per serving: Calories: 347 kcal | Fat: 24.64g | Carbohydrates: 11g | Protein: 21.55g | Fiber: 3g

Ingredients
- 1 ½ Lbs Eggplant

- 1/2 Tsp dried Basil
- 1 Lb Mushrooms
- 1/2 Cup (30 g) Parmesan cheese
- 3 Tbsps Olive oil
- Three sliced Garlic cloves
- 1 1/2 Cup Marinara Sauce
- 15 oz Ricotta cheese
- 1 Egg beaten
- 3 Cups grated Mozzarella cheese

Method
Eggplant (Preheat oven to 400F)
1. Sliced the eggplants in eight parts and cut them vertically.
2. Arrange the eggplants pieces in a baking tray sprayed with oil.
3. Bake in a preheated oven at 400 degrees for ten minutes from both sides.
4. Transfer the eggplants to a plate and place them aside.

Mushrooms Ragu
1. Roughly chop the mushrooms in a food processor using metal blades.
2. Heat olive oil in a pan over medium flame.
3. Sauté garlic in heated oil for one minute.
4. Stir in chopped mushrooms and cook for few minutes.
5. Pour in marinara sauce and basil and mix well.
6. Let the mixture simmer till the point when the desired consistency of the sauce is achieved.
7. Remove the pan from the flame and set it aside.

Ricotta Cheese
1. Whisk ricotta cheese with mozzarella and parmesan cheese, and egg. Set aside.

Layer
1. Spread sauce in a pan, add eggplant slices, spread ricotta cheese mixture, mushroom ragu, parmesan cheese, and at the end, a layer of mozzarella cheese.
2. Continue making layers in the same manner.

Bake
1. Cover the pan with foil and bake in a preheated oven at 375 degrees for 30 minutes.
2. Uncover the pan and bake for ten more minutes.
3. Cool the lasagna and slice it to the desired size.
4. Serve and enjoy it.

8.49 Low Carb BBQ Chicken Enchiladas

Servings: 8 I Time: 1 hr I Difficulty: Easy
Nutrients per serving: Calories: 306 kcal I Fat: 13.55g I Carbohydrates: 18g I Protein: 30g I Fiber: 9g

Ingredients
- 4 Cups shredded Chicken
- 1/2 Tsp granulated garlic
- 3/4 Tsp ground Cumin
- 2/3 Cup BBQ sauce
- 2 Tbsps water
- 1/4 Cup chopped onions
- 1/4 Tsp white pepper
- 2 Cups shredded cheddar cheese
- 1/2 Tsp Pink Salt
- 8 Tortillas
- 1 1/4 Cup enchilada sauce
- Cilantro for garnish

Method
1. Whisk BBQ sauce, water, and enchilada sauce in a bowl and set aside.
2. In another bowl, add chicken, onions, salt, cumin, pepper, and garlic, and toss well.
3. Add cheese and BBQ enchilada sauce mixture and toss well.
4. Spread the BBQ sauce mixture in a casserole pan.

5. Lightly toast the tortillas.
6. Spread filling over the half section of the tortilla.
7. Place the tortilla in a casserole pan facing the filling side downwards.
8. When you are done with all the tortillas, then spread the BQQ sauce and cheese mixture over the casserole.
9. Cover the pan with foil.
10. Bake in a preheated oven at 375 degrees for 30 minutes.
11. Uncover the pan and broil for five minutes.
12. Sprinkle cilantro and serve.

8.50 Keto Eggplant Lasagna with Meat Sauce

Servings: 8 I Time: 1 hr 30 mins I Difficulty: Easy
Nutrients per serving: Calories: 410 kcal I Fat: 28.33g I Carbohydrates: 8.85g I Protein: 29.55g I Fiber: 2.4g

Ingredients
- 1 1/2 Lbs Eggplant
- Two chopped Garlic cloves
- 3 Tbsps Olive oil
- 1 Lb lean ground beef
- 3 Cups Mozzarella cheese
- 1/2 Tsp dried Basil
- 1 Tsp Roasted Beef Base
- 1 1/2 Cups Keto Tomato Sauce
- 1 Egg
- 15 oz Ricotta cheese
- 1/2 Cup grated Parmesan cheese

Method
1. Cut the top and bottom sides of the eggplant. Put the eggplant vertically on the cutting board and make eight pieces out of it.
2. Arrange the eggplant slices over the cookie sheets sprayed with oil.
3. Bake in a preheated oven at 400 degrees for ten minutes from both sides.
4. Transfer the baked eggplant slices into the plate and place it aside.

Meat Sauce
1. Sauté garlic in heated olive oil in a saucepan over medium heat for a minute.
2. Add beef in garlic and cook while breaking it.
3. Add marinara sauce, basil, and beef base and mix well.
4. Let it simmer for a few minutes.
5. When the sauce becomes thick, remove the pan from the flame and set it aside.
6. The meat sauce is ready.

Ricotta Cheese
1. Add egg and ricotta cheese in a bowl and whisk well.
2. Add parmesan cheese and mozzarella cheese and mix well again. Set aside.

Layer
1. Pour half of the sauce into a lasagna pan.
2. Place eggplant slices in a pan.
3. Then pour ricotta cheese sauce followed by spreading of meat sauce.
4. Repeat the process and make layers until all the items are used up.

Bake (Preheat oven to 375 F)
1. Cover the pan with butter paper.
2. Bake in a preheated oven at 375 degrees for 30 minutes while covering the pan with foil.
3. Uncover the pan and bake for ten more minutes.
4. Let it cool, and then slice it.
5. Serve and enjoy it.

8.51 Keto Shepherd's Pie

Servings: 6 I Time: 1 hr. 30 mins I Difficulty: Difficult

Nutrients per serving: Calories: 476 kcal I Fat: 37g I Carbohydrates: 10g I Protein: 26g I Fiber: 3g

Ingredients

- 1 1/2 Lbs ground beef
- 2 Cups Water or Beef broth
- One cubed Carrot
- 1/2 Cup chopped Onion
- One cubed Turnip
- 1/2 Tsp Black pepper
- 2 Tsps Worcestershire Sauce
- 1 Tsp Beef Base
- 1 Tbsp Tomato paste
- 1 Tsp dried thyme
- 1 Tbsp Porcini powder dried
- 1/2 Tsp Salt
- 1/4 Tsp Xanthan gum
- 1/4 Cup chopped parsley

Mashed Cauliflower Topping

- 1/4 Cup Sour cream
- 1 Lb tendered cauliflower florets
- 1/2 Cup sliced Scallion tops
- 2 oz soft Cream cheese
- 1/4 Tsp Salt
- 1 Cup grated Gruyere Cheese
- ¼ Tsp white pepper

Method

1. Collect and prepare all the ingredients.
2. Mix xanthan hum and spices in a bowl. Try not to form clumps.

Cottage Pie Filling

1. Cook ground beef in a pan over medium flame and use a spoon to break it while cooking and stirring.
2. Increase the flame and stir in veggies, Worcestershire, mixed spices, water, beef base, and tomato paste.
3. Mix well to dissolve tomato paste and beef base.
4. Cover the pan and let it simmer for 22 minutes over a low flame or until veggies are done.
5. After 20 minutes, increase the flame and let the gravy to get a thicker consistency.
6. Sprinkle parsley and add salt and pepper to adjust the taste.

Mashed Cauliflower Topping

1. Place cauliflower in a bowl and add a little water.
2. Place the bowl in the microwave and let it steam for ten minutes with occasional stirring.
3. Transfer the tender cauliflower to a blender and blend it.
4. Pour in sour cream, pepper, cream cheese, and salt and blend again to get a smooth mixture.
5. Shift the cauliflower mixture in a container and mix in cheese and scallion.
6. Spread shepherd's pie filling in casserole sprayed with oil and add cauliflower mixture over it.
7. Sprinkle cheese over the tip.
8. Bake in a preheated oven at 375 degrees for 50 minutes.
9. Serve and enjoy it.

8.52 Keto Lasagna Stuffed Peppers

Servings: 6 I Time: 1 hr I Difficulty: Difficult
Nutrients per serving: Calories: 660 kcal I Fat: 20g I Carbohydrates: 9.92g I Protein: 26.63g I Fiber: 1.3g

Ingredients

- 1 Cup ricotta cheese
- 3 Bell peppers
- 1/4 Tsp Fennel seeds
- 1 Tsp Olive oil
- 1 Lb ground Beef
- 1 1/2 Cup shredded Mozzarella cheese
- 1 Cup Tomato sauce
- 1/4 Cup Parmesan cheese

Method

1. First, cut the peppers in half and deseed them.
2. Place the deseeded bell peppers in a baking tray.
3. Heat olive oil in a skillet over medium flame.
4. Sauté fennel seeds in heated oil with constant stirring.
5. Add ground beef and cook while breaking it with the spoon.
6. Add tomato sauce and cook for few minutes or when the sauce gets thickened.
7. Now, remove the skillet from the flame.
8. Add mozzarella cheese and set aside for a while. The meat sauce is ready.
9. Then, fill the center of the bell peppers with meat sauce.
10. Add ricotta cheese and again place a layer of meat sauce.
11. Place the bell pepper in a baking tray and cover them with aluminum foil.
12. Keep them aside for 25 minutes.
13. Bake in a preheated oven at 350 degrees for 30 minutes.
14. After 30 minutes, uncover the bell peppers, add mozzarella and ricotta cheese at the top and bake again for 12 minutes.
15. Sprinkle parmesan cheese.
16. Serve and enjoy it.

8.53 Herb Crusted Eye Round Roast Beef

Servings: 12 I Time: 1 hr 50 mins I Difficulty: Difficult
Nutrients per serving: Calories: 348 kcal I Fat: 15.37g I Carbohydrates: 1.91g I Protein: 47.63g I Fiber: 0.4g

Ingredients

- 1/4 Cup Dijon mustard
- 4 Lb eye round roast
- Salt to taste
- 2 Tbsps Olive oil
- Black pepper to taste

Herb Crust

- 1/2 Cup crushed pork rinds
- 1/4 Cup minced Shallots
- 2 Tbsps minced Parsley
- 1/4 Tsp Pepper
- 1/2 Cup grated Parmesan Cheese
- 1/4 Cup Butter
- 2 Tbsps minced Garlic
- 1 Tbsp chopped Thyme
- 1/4 Tsp Salt

Method

1. Combine minced shallots, herbs, parmesan cheese, pepper, garlic, and salt in a mixing bowl.
2. Add pork rinds and toss well. Keep it aside for a few minutes.
3. Rub roast with salt, olive oil, and pepper and set aside for few minutes.
4. Heat olive oil in a pan with a heavy bottom.
5. Add roast and cook from all sides until they turned brown.
6. Transfer them to a plate and set them aside.
7. Sprinkle Dijon mustard over the roast.
8. Heat butter in the same pan and add all the ingredients of herb crust, and stir well.
9. Lightly coat the roast with the herb mixture by pressing the mixture over it.
10. Bake the roast in a preheated oven at 275 degrees until the roast's internal temperature reaches 135 degrees.
11. Remove the roast pan from the oven and let it cool.
12. Slice the roast with a sharp knife and serve.

8.54 Keto Korean Beef Bowls

Servings: 2 I Time: 15 mins I Difficulty: Easy

Nutrients per serving: Calories: 462 kcal | Fat: 25.25g | Carbohydrates: 7.48g | Protein: 48.83g | Fiber: 2.5g

Ingredients

- 1 Tbsp Sesame oil
- 1 Tsp Ground Ginger
- 1 Lb Lean Ground Beef
- 1 pressed Garlic clove
- 2 Tbsps Tamari Soy Sauce
- 1/4 Tsp Chile flakes
- 1 Tbsp brown sugar
- 1 Tbsp Siracha
- 1 Tbsp White vinegar
- 1 1/2 Cups Cauliflower rice
- 1 Tbsp lime juice

Method

1. Heat sesame oil in a skillet over medium flame.
2. Add beef and stir well.
3. Cook while stirring and break it using a spoon.
4. Let it cook for five minutes until beef turned brown and no pink color is seen.
5. Stir in garlic, chili flakes, and ginger.
6. Increase the flame to high and cook for five minutes.
7. Add soy sauce, sriracha, vinegar, and sugar.
8. Cook for two minutes with constant stirring to evenly mix everything well.
9. Remove the skillet from flame and mix in lime juice.
10. Serve and enjoy it with cauliflower.

8.55 Keto Keema Curry

Servings: 2 | Time: 30 mins | Difficulty: Medium
Nutrients per serving: Calories: 268 kcal | Fat: 14.6g | Carbohydrates: 9g | Protein: 25g | Fiber: 3.3g

Ingredients

- 1 Lb ground Beef
- 3/4 Cup diced Onion
- 1 Cup sliced green Beans
- One sprig Cilantro
- 1 Tbsp minced garlic
- 1 Tbsp Ghee
- 1 Tbsp minced Ginger
- 1 Tbsp Coconut Manna
- 3/4 Cup Water

Spices
- 1 Tsp ground Coriander
- 1/4 Tsp Red pepper flakes
- 1 Tsp ground Cinnamon
- 3/4 Tsp Salt
- 1/4 Tsp Turmeric
- 1/4 Tsp Black pepper

Grind
- 1/4 Tsp Fennel seeds
- Three whole Green cardamon pods
- Four whole Cloves
- 2 Tbsp Poppy seeds

Garnish
- Thin plain yogurt
- Chopped Cilantro
- Lime wedges

Method

1. First ground fennel, poppy seeds, cloves, and cardamom in mortar and pestle and transfer them to a bowl. Set aside.
2. Heat olive oil in a skillet over medium flame.
3. Sauté onions in heated oil for six minutes.
4. Stir in ginger and garlic and cook for one minute.
5. Mix in ground beef and, using a spoon breaking it and cook until it turned brown.
6. Bow pour in coconut mana or coconut milk, whatever you are using.
7. Add spices and mix well—Cook for two minutes.
8. Add green beans, water, and cilantro.
9. Cover the pan and let simmer for 15 minutes, until beans are done.
10. Sprinkle salt and pepper to adjust the taste.
11. Sprinkle cilantro and lime.
12. Pour in the yogurt and serve; enjoy it.

8.56 Tofu Lettuce Wraps

Servings: 2 | Time: 20 mins | Difficulty: Easy
Nutrients per serving (4 wraps): Calories: 338 kcal | Fat: 28.3g | Carbohydrates: 7.8g | Protein: 17.7g | Fiber: 3g

Ingredients

- 2 Tsps Sesame Oil
- 12 oz Firm Tofu
- One thumb-sized Ginger
- 2 Green Onions
- Eight leaves of Baby Gem Lettuce

For the Peanut Sauce:
- 1 Tbsp Peanut Butter smooth
- 1 Tsp Rice Vinegar
- 1 Tbsp Sesame Oil
- 1 Tbsp Soy Sauce
- 1 Tbsp Water

Method

1. Whisk all the items of peanut sauce in a bowl and keep it aside until further use.
2. Heat sesame oil in a skillet over medium flame.
3. Sauté onions and ginger in heated oil for three minutes.
4. Now add chopped tofu and cook for six more minutes with frequent stirring.
5. Pour in peanut sauce and toss well to coat everything in.
6. Remove the pan from the flame and let it cool for a few minutes.
7. Spread tofu mixture over a lettuce leaf.
8. Sprinkle onions and sesame seeds.
9. Serve and enjoy with peanut sauce as dipping.

8.57 Cajun Shrimp and Avocado Chaffle

Servings: 4 sandwiches | Time: 25 mins | Difficulty: Medium
Nutrients per serving: Calories: 488 kcal | Fat: 32.22g | Carbohydrates: 6.01g | Protein: 47.59g | Fiber: 2.6g

Ingredients

Cajun Flavored Chaffle
- 4 Eggs
- 2 Cups shredded Mozzarella cheese
- 1 Tsp Cajun Seasoning

Chaffle Sandwich Filling
- 1 Lb Raw Shrimp
- 4 Slices cooked Bacon
- 1 Tbsp Bacon fat
- One sliced Avocado
- One recipe Bacon Scallion Cream Cheese Spread
- 1/4 Cup sliced Red onion
- 1 Tsp Cajun seasoning

Method

1. Whisk eggs in a bowl.
2. Mix in mozzarella cheese and Cajun seasoning. Toss to evenly mix everything.
3. Now transfer the batter to the waffle maker in batches and cook until they turned to brown.

4. Combine shrimp, Cajun seasoning, pepper, and salt in a bowl.
5. Heat bacon fat in skillet over medium flame.
6. Add shrimps and cook until they get opaque for five minutes from both sides.
7. Transfer the cooked shrimps to a plate and keep it aside.
8. Put some cream cheese over the chaffle, add shrimps, avocado, onion, and bacon.
9. Place another chaffle over the first one.
10. Serve and enjoy it.

8.58 Grilled Tandoori Chicken

Servings: 12 I Time: 50 mins I Difficulty: Medium
Nutrients per serving: Calories: 220 kcal I Fat: 9.7g I Carbohydrates: 0.8g I Protein: 29.4g I Fiber: 0.3g

Ingredients
For the Grilled Tandoori Chicken Marinade
- 2 Tbsp Garam Masala
- 1 Tsp Turmeric
- 1 Tbsp Paprika
- 1/4 Cup Water
- ¼ Tsp Cayenne Chili Powder
- 1 Tsp minced Garlic
- 1 Tsp minced Ginger
- 3 Tbsp Olive Oil
- 2 Tbsp Lime Juice

Method
For the Marinade
1. Whisk all the ingredients of marination in a bowl except for lime juice and water.
2. A smooth paste is formed.
3. Now mix in water and lime juice and adjust the consistency.
4. Add the chicken and toss well to thoroughly coat the chicken.
5. Cover the bowl and place it in the fridge for five hours to marinate the chicken.
Grilled Tandoori Chicken
1. Place the marinated chicken without marinade over the preheated grill.
2. Cook for five minutes while covering the grill.
3. Change the side of the chicken and cook for another three minutes.
4. Repeat the process and continue it for 15 minutes until the whole chicken is fully tenderized.
5. Serve and enjoy it.

8.59 Keto Chicken Stuffed Peppers

Servings: 4 I Time: 35 mins I Difficulty: Medium
Nutrients per serving: Calories: 468 kcal I Fat: 30g I Carbohydrates: 11g I Protein: 39g I Fiber: 2g

Ingredients
- 4 Bell peppers
- 2 Tbsps Olive oil
- 1/2 Tsp chopped Garlic
- 1 Lb ground chicken breast
- One pinch of Salt
- 1 Tsp Pepper
- 1 Tbsp Lemon juice
- 1/2 Cup Pesto
- 1/4 Cup Parmesan cheese shredded
- Four slices of Mozzarella cheese

Method
1. Remove the seeds from bell peppers.
2. Place deseeded bell peppers over a baking tray and bake in the preheated oven at 375 degrees for 15 minutes.
3. Heat olive oil in a pan over medium flame.
4. Add chopped bell peppers and cook for five minutes.

5. When bell peppers get a little soft, add chicken breast pieces, salt, garlic, lemon juice, and pepper.
6. Cook for few minutes with occasional stirring until chicken is turned golden.
7. Drain the liquid released from the chicken and mix parmesan cheese and pesto.
8. Toss everything well and remove the pan from the flame. The chicken filling is ready.
9. Now take one baked bell pepper at a time and fill it with chicken filling.
10. Drizzle mozzarella cheese and again bake for 18 minutes.
11. Serve and enjoy it.

8.60 Egg Masala

Servings: 4 I Time: 30 mins I Difficulty: Medium
Nutrients per serving: Calories: 268 kcal I Fat: 21.8g I Carbohydrates: 8.7g I Protein: 11g I Fiber: 1.8g

Ingredients
- Six hard-boiled eggs
- ¾ Cup chopped Onions
- 1 Lb chopped tomatoes
- 1/2 cup water
- 4 Tbsp Olive oil or ghee
- Eight curry leaves
- 1-inch Cinnamon piece
Masala
- One chopped Serrano pepper
- Two chopped Garlic cloves
- 1 Tbsp Tomato paste
- 1 Tsp Chicken base
- One sprig Cilantro
- 3/4 Tsp Coriander powder

Method
1. Add all the ingredients of masala to a food processor and grind them to form a paste.
2. Now add tomatoes without seeds in the processor and make a puree out of them.
3. Add cinnamon and little water and blend.
4. Transfer the puree to a bowl and set aside.
5. Heat ghee in a pan over medium flame.
6. Sauté curry leaves and cinnamon for 30 seconds.
7. Now add onions and cook until they get brown color.
8. Stir in masala mixture puree and cook until their raw smell goes off.
9. Pour in a half cup of water and mix well.
10. Cover the pan and let it simmer until everything is done.
11. Add ghee, salt, and pepper, and toss well.
12. Now mix in boil eggs and let them simmer for two minutes.
13. Sprinkle cilantro and serve.

8.61 Juicy Keto Oven-Baked Ribs

Servings: 6 I Time: 3 hrs I Difficulty: Difficult
Nutrients per serving: Calories: 445 kcal I Fat: 32.5g I Carbohydrates: 3.39g I Protein: 37g I Fiber: 0.6g

Ingredients
- 2 Baby back ribs racks
- 2 Tbsps BBQ Dry Rub
- Black pepper to taste
- 2 Tbsps Olive oil
- Salt to taste
- 1/2 Cup Keto BBQ Sauce

Method
1. First, remove the skin from the ribs using a sharp knife. Do it very carefully.
2. Drizzle olive oil over the skinless dried ribs.
3. Sprinkle salt and pepper over the ribs. Rub the seasoning to thoroughly coat the ribs.

4. Place the ribs in a baking tray lined with aluminum foil and cover them.
5. Bake in a preheated oven at 275 degrees for two hours or until ribs are fully tenderized.

For Keto Dry Ribs:
1. Take the ribs out of the oven.
2. Uncover the ribs and message them with salt and pepper again.
3. Bake again for 22 more minutes without covering them.

For Sauced Keto Ribs:
1. Take the ribs out of the oven and remove the foil from them.
2. Spread BBQ sauce over the ribs.
3. Let them boil for five minutes over medium flame or until dark spots appears over the sauce.
4. Repeat the process with the second side.
5. Serve and enjoy it.

8.62 Indian Chicken Curry

Servings: 4 I Time: 40 mins I Difficulty: Medium
Nutrients per serving: Calories: 352 kcal I Fat: 24.5g I Carbohydrates: 5.7g I Protein: 29g I Fiber: 1.2g

Ingredients

- 1 1/4 Lb boneless Chicken breast
- 1/2 Cup sliced Onion
- 2 Tbsp Ghee
- 2 Tbsps Olive oil
- 1/4 Cup chopped cilantro
- 1/2 Cup Water
- 1/4 Tsp Salt
- 1 Tsp Chicken base
- 1/4 Tsp Turmeric

Masala
- Two chopped Serrano peppers
- 3/4 inch chopped Ginger
- One chopped green bell pepper
- One chopped Garlic clove

Method

1. Add all the ingredients of masala to the blender and blend them to form a paste. You can add a few drops of water too.
2. Heat olive oil in a pan over medium heat.
3. Add onions to heated oil and sauté them for three minutes.
4. Stir in the masala paste and cook until their raw smell diminishes.
5. Then add cinnamon, chicken base, turmeric, olive oil, and half Cup of water. Mix well.
6. Now add chicken and toss well to mix everything.
7. Cover the pan and cook for 15 minutes over low flame.
8. After 15 minutes, remove the cover from the pan and increase the flame to evaporate all the water to thicken the chicken sauce.
9. The oil will be seen over the sauce's surface, which indicates that the chicken is done.
10. In the end, add ghee and sprinkle cilantro, and toss.
11. Serve and enjoy it.

8.63 Stuffed Poblano Peppers with Mexican Ground Beef

Servings: 4 I Time: 50 mins I Difficulty: Medium
Nutrients per serving: Calories: 395 kcal I Fat: 23.6g I Carbohydrates: 11.6g I Protein: 35.6g I Fiber: 3.6g

Ingredients

- 4 Poblano peppers
- 1 Tbsp Olive oil
- 2 Tbsps minced Cilantro
- 1 Lb ground Beef
- 1/2 Cup Diced onion
- 2 Tbsps Tomato paste
- Two chopped Garlic cloves
- 1 Tbsp ground Chile powder
- 1 Cup Beef broth
- Salt to taste
- 1 1/2 Tsp Ground cumin
- One pinch of Cinnamon
- 1 1/2 Cup grated Monterey Jack Cheese
- 1 Cup cooked Cauliflower rice
- Black pepper to taste

For Topping
- Salsa
- Cilantro
- Pumpkin seeds
- Cheese
- Lime wedges
- Sour cream

Method

1. Arrange poblano pepper in a baking tray.
2. Place the tray in the broiler and let them roast for minutes or until the pepper gets blacken.
3. Transfer the roasted pepper onto the plate and cover. Keep it aside until further use.
4. Heat olive oil in a skillet over medium flame.
5. Sauté garlic and onion in heated oil for three minutes.
6. Mix in ground beef and cook while breaking it using the spoon.
7. When beef is cooked for ten minutes, mix in tomato paste, cinnamon, chili powder, beef broth, and cumin with constant stirring to combine everything.
8. Let the mixture simmer until the liquid is reduced to half.
9. Sprinkle salt, cilantro, and pepper.
10. Now, peel the skin from roasted peppers and make a vertical slit at the top using a knife.
11. Remove the seeds from the center of the pepper.
12. Place the poblano peppers in a baking tray. Set aside.
13. Mix in cheese and cauliflower rice with the beef mixture and toss to combine everything well.
14. Fill the poblano pepper with the beef mixture.
15. Sprinkle some of the cheese at the top.
16. Bake the stuffed poblano peppers in a preheated oven at 350 degrees for 15 minutes.
17. Squeeze time juice over the top and serve with salsa and green salad.

8.64 Cast Iron Sloppy Joe Casserole

Servings: 8 I Time: 55 mins I Difficulty: Medium
Nutrients per serving: Calories: 371 kcal I Fat: 24g I Carbohydrates: 11g I Protein: 28g I Fiber: 3g

Ingredients

Casserole Filling
- 1 Cup Cheddar cheese
- One recipe Sloppy Joes

Cornbread Base
- 3 Eggs
- 1 Cup grated Mozzarella cheese
- 1/4 Tsp Sweet Corn Extract
- 2 oz Cream cheese
- 2 Cups Almond flour
- 1 Tbsp Baking powder

Method

1. First, prepare the joe filling following the instruction written over the packet.
2. Transfer the filling into the plate and sprinkle the cheese. Set aside until further use.

3. Add extract, almond flour, cheese, baking powder, and eggs in a blender. Blend to get a thick batter.
4. Transfer the batter into the bowl.
5. Now spread the thick batter over a skillet sprayed with oil.
6. Then, spread joe filling over the batter.
7. Bake in a preheated oven at 350 degrees for 40 minutes.
8. Again sprinkle cheese and bake to melt the cheese.
9. Serve and enjoy it.

8.65 Slow Cooker Mississippi Pot Roast

Servings: 6 | Time: 6 hrs 20 mins | Difficulty: Difficult
Nutrients per serving: Calories: 503 kcal | Fat: 37.74g | Carbohydrates: 1.22g | Protein: 37g

Ingredients

- 2 1/2 Lbs Chuck roast
- 1/2 Tsp Salt
- 2 Tbsp Butter
- 1 Tbsp Olive oil
- 8 Pepperoncini peppers
- 1/2 Tsp Black pepper
- 1 Tsp Beef base
- 1/3 Cup Water
- 1 Tbsp Ranch Seasoning

Method

1. Rub salt, oil, and pepper all over the surface of the chuck. Set aside until further use.
2. Heat olive oil in a skillet over medium flame.
3. Add chuck roast and cook well from all the sides.
4. When the roast gets brown color, remove the skillet from the heat and transfer the roast to the slow cooker.
5. Now add beef base in the same skillet and cook over low flame.
6. Pour in water and let it simmer.
7. Transfer the beef base mixture into the slow cooker.
8. Add butter and ranch seasoning in a slow cooker and toss well.
9. In the end, add pepperoncini and cook for six hours on high flame.
10. When roast is done, transfer it to the plate.
11. Mix in 1 tsp of ranch seasoning and serve.

8.66 Lamb Chops with Mint Sauce and Roasted Rutabaga

Servings: 2 | Time: 50 mins | Difficulty: Medium
Nutrients per serving: Calories: 730 kcal | Fat: 56.7g | Carbohydrates: 10.23g | Protein: 39g | Fiber: 3.2g

Ingredients

- Four sliced Lamb loin chops
- Salt to taste
- 2 Tsp Olive oil
- Black pepper to taste

Rutabagas
- 1/8 Tsp Salt
- One cubed Rutabaga
- 2 Tsp Chopped Rosemary
- 2 Tsp Olive oil
- 1/8 Tsp Pepper

Mint Sauce
- One pinch of Red chili flakes
- 1/4 Cup Champagne vinegar
- 1 Tbsp Minced Mint
- 2 Tbsp sugar
- One pinch of salt

Method

1. Rub lamb with salt, olive oil, and pepper and set aside for a while.
2. Add rutabaga, salt, olive oil, rosemary, and pepper in a bowl and toss to coat the rutabaga evenly.
3. Transfer the rutabaga to a baking pan and cook with occasional stirring for about 32 minutes.
4. Heat the olive oil in the same pan over medium flame.
5. Add lamb chops and cook for 10 minutes from both sides.
6. Shift the lamb chops into the plate and cover to keep it warm.
7. In the same pan, add sweetener and vinegar.
8. Let it simmer over low flame for seven minutes.
9. Sprinkle salt, mint, and red chilies and toss well. The sauce is ready.
10. Now cook rutabaga in the pan over medium flame for few minutes until it gets a golden color. Add salt and pepper and toss well.
11. Transfer the rutabaga into the plate with cooked lamb.
12. Pour the sauce over lamb and rutabaga and serve.

8.67 Ham Steak with Red-Eye Gravy

Servings: 4 | Time: 15 mins | Difficulty: Easy
Nutrients per serving: Calories: 417 kcal | Fat: 32g | Carbohydrates: 0.26g | Protein: 31g

Ingredients

- 1 1/4 Lbs Ham steak
- 1/4 Cup black coffee
- 2 Tsps Bacon fat
- 2 Tbsps Butter
- 1/4 Cup Water
- 1 Tbsp Ketchup

Method

1. Let ham steak come to temperature for 20 minutes. Blot it with a dry paper towel, so it browns and doesn't steam in the pan.
2. Heat the olive oil in a skillet over medium flame.
3. Add ham in heated oil and cook for seven minutes from both sides.
4. Transfer the brown color cooked ham to the plate.
5. Add water and coffee in the same skillet and cook over a low flame with constant stirring.
6. Stir in ketchup and butter and cook for one minute.
7. Pour the sauce over ham and serve.

8.68 Filet Mignon Steak Pizzaiola

Servings: 2 | Time: 40 mins | Difficulty: Medium
Nutrients per serving: Calories: 580 kcal | Fat: 42g | Carbohydrates: 8.8g | Protein: 40g | Fiber: 1.6g

Ingredients

Filet Mignon Steaks
- Salt to taste
- 2 Steaks Filet Mignon
- Black pepper to taste
- 1 Tbsp Olive oil

Peppers and Mushrooms
- 2 Tbsp Dry white wine
- 1 Tbsp Olive oil
- 1/2 sliced green bell pepper
- 4 oz Sliced mushrooms
- 1/2 sliced Red bell pepper
- 1/4 Cup sliced Onion
- 1/4 Tsp thyme leaves

Butter (Garlic Parmesan)
- 2 oz Butter
- 1/4 Tsp grated Raw garlic
- 2 oz grated Parmesan cheese

129

Red Sauce

- 1/2 Cup Rao's Arrabiatta Sauce

Method

1. Keep steaks at room temperature.
2. Rub salt, oil, and pepper over the surface of filet mignon and set aside.
3. Add butter, cheese, and garlic in a bowl and toss well.
4. Transfer the mixture to cling film. Roll the film and give a log shape to it. Place the cling film with butter mixture in the fridge until further use.
5. Heat olive oil in a pan over medium flame.
6. Add steaks in heated oil and sear for three minutes.
7. Now place the pan in the oven at 375°F and cook until steaks are done.
8. Transfer the steaks into the plate and cover to keep them warm.
9. Again heat olive oil in the same pan over medium flame.
10. Add bell peppers and onion and cook for five minutes with occasional stirring.
11. Sprinkle thyme and toss.
12. Remove the pan from the flame and transfer the veggies to the plate. Set aside.
13. Now add red sauce to a pan and lightly warm it up.
14. Pour the sauce into the serving plate and place the steak over it.
15. Pour the butter cheese mixture over the steaks, and at the end, top steaks with stirred fried veggies.
16. Serve.

8.69 Inst. Pot Vegetable Beef Soup

Servings: 6 I Time: 1 hr 20 mins I Difficulty: Easy
Nutrients per serving: Calories: 321 kcal I Fat: 14.87g I Carbohydrates: 10g I Protein: 32.83g I Fiber: 2.5g

Ingredients

- 1 1/2 Lbs cubed beef chuck
- 6 oz diced Turnip
- 1 Tbsp Olive oil
- 5 oz sliced Celery
- 4 oz cut String beans
- 4 oz sliced Carrots
- 3 oz diced Onions
- 32 oz beef broth
- Two sliced Garlic cloves
- Salt to taste
- 1/2 Cup red wine
- 2 Tsps beef base
- 2 Tbsps tomato paste
- 1 Tbsp mushroom powder
- 2 Tsps gelatin powder
- Two bay leaves
- 4 Tbsps butter
- Two whole cloves
- 1/2 Tsp rubbed dried marjoram
- 1 Tsp rubbed dried thyme
- Black pepper to taste

Method

1. Heat the pan over medium flame and add beef to it.
2. Cook beef until it gets brown.
3. Transfer the beef into the pressure cooker with 4 tbsps beef broth.
4. Now add all the remaining ingredients to the cooker and mix well.
5. Cover the pressure cooker and shift it to soup mode.
6. When beef is done, add in marjoram and thyme and mix.
7. Sprinkle salt and pepper to adjust the taste.
8. Serve and enjoy it.

8.70 Low Carb Beef Stroganoff

Servings: 4 I Time: 30 mins I Difficulty: Medium
Nutrients per serving: Calories: 466 kcal I Fat: 36.6g I Carbohydrates: 5.86g I Protein: 26.5g I Fiber: 0.4g

Ingredients

- 2 oz Philadelphia Cream Cheese
- 1 Lb ground Beef, lean
- 1/4 Cup sliced Onions
- 4 oz sliced Mushrooms
- 3 Tbsps Butter
- 1 Tbsp Worcestershire sauce
- 2 Tbsps Brandy
- Black pepper to taste
- 1 Tsp Beef base
- 1 Cup sour cream
- 1 Tbsp chopped parsley
- 1 1/2 pinches grated Nutmeg
- Salt to taste

Method

1. First, cook cauliflower rice in heated oil over medium flame for a few minutes.
2. When the cauliflower rice is done, transfer them to a bowl and cover them to keep them warm.
3. Heat olive oil in a skillet and sauté mushrooms for five minutes with occasional stirring.
4. Add some more butter and stir in onions.
5. Cook onions for few minutes and then transfer onions and mushrooms into the plate.
6. Now, add ground beef in the same pan and cook it while breaking it with a spoon for a few minutes.
7. Pour in Worcestershire sauce and toss well.
8. Stir in beef base and brandy.
9. In the end, add mushroom mixture and spread nutmegs.
10. Let it simmer for a few minutes.
11. Mix in cream cheese and cook to melt it.
12. Then add sour cream and let it simmer.
13. When the sauce gets thicken, sprinkle parsley, salt, and black pepper and toss well.
14. Serve and enjoy it.

8.71 Pulled Pork Keto Stuffed Mushrooms

Servings: 2 I Time: 50 mins I Difficulty: Medium
Nutrients per serving: Calories: 548 kcal I Fat: 41g I Carbohydrates: 6.7g I Protein: 39.3g I Fiber: 1.4g

Ingredients

- 1/2 Cup keto coleslaw
- 2 Portobello mushroom caps
- 1 Cup shredded Cheddar cheese
- 1 Cup pulled Pork
- 1/4 Cup BBQ sauce

Optional for the Mushroom Caps:

- 2 Tbsps Italian Dressing
- 1 Tbsp Olive oil

Method

1. Lightly warm the pulled pork and add it to a bowl.
2. Add cheese, salt, BQQ sauce, and black pepper.
3. Now, make a small cavity in the center of the mushroom cap and fill it with a pulled pork mixture.
4. Arrange the stuffed mushroom caps in a baking tray sprayed with oil and lined with parchment paper.
5. Bake in a preheated oven at 400 degrees for 35 minutes.
6. Spread coleslaw over baked mushroom caps.
7. Serve and enjoy it.

8.72 Homemade Sloppy Joe Hot Pockets

Servings: 6 | Time: 35 mins | Difficulty: Medium
Nutrients per serving: Calories: 379 kcal | Fat: 28.5g | Carbohydrates: 8g | Protein: 23g | Fiber: 3g

Ingredients

- 2 Cups Sloppy Joe Filling

Hot Pocket Dough

- 1 1/2 Cups shredded Mozzarella cheese
- 1 Egg, beaten
- 2 oz Cream cheese
- 1 1/3 Cups Almond flour
- 1/4 Tsp Baking soda
- 3 Tbsps Whey protein powder

Method

Hot Pocket Dough:
1. Add mozzarella cheese and cream cheese in a bowl and microwave the bowl for three minutes to melt the cheese. Whisk them well.
2. Crack an egg in the cheese mixture and mix.
3. Stir in almond flour, baking soda, and protein powder.
4. Mix to combine everything well. Keep the dough aside for 30 minutes.
5. Now roll out the dough between butter paper sprayed with oil.
6. Spread the dough with the butter paper in a baking tray.

Assembly:
1. Slice the dough in the required size and number.
2. Spread sloppy joe filling at the center of each slice of the dough.
3. Fold the dough and press the edges gently.
4. Bake in a preheated oven at 400 degrees for 20 minutes.
5. Serve and enjoy it.

8.73 Juicy Smoked Chicken Leg Quarters

Servings: 4 | Time: 2 hrs 10 mins | Difficulty: Difficult
Nutrients per serving: Calories: 261 kcal | Fat: 21g | Carbohydrates: 1.5g | Protein: 16g | Fiber: 0.1g

Ingredients

- Four sliced Chicken leg
- 1 Tbsp Olive oil
- 3 Tsp Dry Rub for Chicken
- Salt to taste

Smoker Pellets

- signature blend, pecan

Method

1. Dry chicken leg quarters with a paper towel. Remove any extra pieces of fat from the back of the chicken.
2. Mix chicken rub and oil in a small bowl.
3. Brush the chicken with oil mixture and set aside for one hour.
4. Preheated the grill on smoke mode.
5. Place the chicken over a preheated grill and let it cook on smoke mode for one hour.
6. When the internal temperature of the chicken reaches 165 degrees, remove the chicken from the grill.
7. Serve and enjoy it.

8.74 Italian Sausage, Peppers and Onions with Sauce

Servings: 4 | Time: 30 mins | Difficulty: Medium
Nutrients per serving: Calories: 420 kcal | Fat: 32.5g | Carbohydrates: 8g | Protein: 23.5g | Fiber: 1.5g

Ingredients

- 1 Lb Italian sausage
- 2 oz sliced Onion
- 9 oz sliced Bell pepper, any one color or mix
- Salt to taste
- 1 Tbsp Olive oil
- 1/2 Cup Rao's Marinara Sauce
- 1 Tsp minced garlic
- Black pepper to taste

Method

1. Add sliced onions, sausage, oil, and pepper in a bowl.
2. Transfer the mixture to a baking tray.
3. Bake in a preheated oven at 400 degrees for 40 minutes.
4. After 40 minutes, remove the pan from the oven and pour in marinara sauce.
5. Serve and enjoy it.

8.75 Smoked Beer Can Chicken with Dry Rub

Servings: 4 | Time: 1 hr 25 mins | Difficulty: Difficult
Nutrients per serving: Calories: 337 kcal | Fat: 18g | Carbohydrates: 1.3g | Protein: 36g

Ingredients

- 1 Tbsps oil
- One whole Chicken
- 3 Tbsps Chicken Rub
- 2 Cups Beer

Method

1. Remove the chicken bits from the cavity. Dry the chicken well with paper towels.
2. Mix oil and chicken rub in a small bowl.
3. Brush the oil mixture over the whole surface of the chicken.
4. Add 2 cups of beer to the chicken throne.
5. Mix in two spoons of chicken rub into the liquid.
6. Put the chicken throne in the chicken's cavity. Chicken should stand stable over the chicken throne.
7. Place the chicken with the chicken throne over the pan.
8. Cook, bake, or grill the chicken, whatever you want, for one hour till the chicken's central temperature reaches 16 degrees.
9. Remove the chicken from the chicken throne.
10. Slice the chicken and serve.

8.76 Creamy Keto Mac and Cheese with Ham

Servings: 4 | Time: 25 mins | Difficulty: Medium
Nutrients per serving: Calories: 404 kcal | Fat: 60g | Carbohydrates: 7g | Protein: 13g | Fiber: 7g

Ingredients

- 1 Lb Cauliflower
- Three slices Bacon
- 10 oz cubed Ham
- 1/4 Cup Onion
- 1 Tsp Chicken Base
- 1 Tsp Garlic
- 1/4 Cup dry White wine
- 2 oz Cream cheese
- 1/4 Tsp White pepper
- 1/4 Cup Water
- 1/2 Cup Mozzarella cheese
- 1 Tsp Worcestershire sauce
- 1 Cup Cheddar cheese

Method

1. Steam the chopped cauliflower until they get soft and wilt.
2. Transfer cauliflower in a bowl and set aside.
3. Cook bacon in a skillet over medium flame until bacon becomes crispy; it will take seven minutes.
4. Transfer the bacon to the plate and leave the bacon fat in the pan.

5. Add garlic and onion to the same pan and cook for three minutes.
6. After three minutes, pour water and wine. Mix.
7. Add cream cheese and chicken base. Stir and cook until cheese melts.
8. Now add mozzarella cheese, white pepper, cheddar cheese, and Worcestershire.
9. Let it simmer for seven minutes.
10. When the sauce gets a little thick, add ham and steamed cauliflower into the pan and toss gently.
11. Place bacon at the top and serve.

8.77 Easy Sausage and Cabbage Dinner

Servings: 4 I Time: 30 mins I Difficulty: Medium
Nutrients per serving: Calories: 306 kcal I Fat: 21g I Carbohydrates: 8.5g I Protein: 20g I Fiber: 2g

Ingredients

- 1 Lb Italian sausages
- Four strips Raw bacon
- 1 Lb sliced cabbage
- 2 oz sliced onion
- Salt to taste
- One chopped Garlic clove
- Black pepper to taste

Method

1. Now, preheat the grill.
2. Place sausage over the heated grill and cook for few minutes or until they are done.
3. Now cook bacon in heated oil in a pan until they become crispy.
4. Mix garlic and onions and cook for five minutes.
5. Add chopped cabbage and cook until it gets soft.
6. Add cabbage in batches to cook them properly.
7. In the end, add sliced grilled sausage, pepper, and salt to the pan and toss well.
8. Serve and enjoy it.

8.78 Baja Fish Tacos with Chipotle Lime Crema

Servings: 4 I Time: 20 mins I Difficulty: Easy
Nutrients per serving: Calories: 524 kcal I Fat: 42g I Carbohydrates: 11.5g I Protein: 27g I Fiber: 4g

Ingredients

BAJA FISH TACOS
- 2 Tbsp Avocado oil
- 1 Lb Halibut
- Black pepper to taste
- Tortillas
- Sea salt to taste

Simple Red Cabbage Slaw
- 1 Tsp Sea salt
- 1/2 shredded red cabbage
- One diced Jalapeño
- 1/2 Red sliced onion
- 2 Tbsps of Lime juice

CHIPOTLE LIME CREMA
- 1/2 Cup Plain yogurt
- 1/2 Tsp Sea salt
- 1/4 Tsp Chipotle powder
- 1/4 Tsp Garlic powder
- 1 Tbsp Lime juice

TOPPINGS
- 1/2 Cup chopped Cilantro
- Two sliced Jalapeños
- One diced avocado, diced
- 2 Tbsps lime wedges

Method

1. Rub fish with salt and pepper and set aside for a while.
2. Whisk all the ingredients of red cabbage slaw in a bowl.
3. Mix them using hands, do message to thoroughly mix them. Keep it aside.
4. In another bowl, mix all the items of chipotle lime crema and place the bowl in the fridge for a while. The chipotle lime crema is ready
5. Heat oil in a pan over medium flame.
6. Add fish and cook for five minutes from both sides.
7. Transfer the cooked fish strips to a plate and set them aside.
8. Lightly toast the tortillas in a pan.
9. Place fish strips over each tortilla followed by cabbage slaw, jalapeno slices, sprinkle cilantro, place avocado, and at the end spread chipotle lime crema.
10. Serve and enjoy it.

8.79 Spinach Artichoke Pizza

Servings: 4 I Time: 40 mins I Difficulty: Medium
Nutrients per serving: Calories: 366 kcal I Fat: 28g I Carbohydrates: 8g I Protein: 22g I Fiber: 3g

Ingredients

Fathead Pizza Crust
- 1/4 Cup Almond flour
- 1 1/2 Cup grated Mozzarella cheese
- 1 Egg
- 2 oz Cream cheese
- 2 Tbsps Whey protein powder

Spinach Artichoke Dip
- 1/4 Tsp White pepper
- 4 oz Cream cheese
- 8 oz Spinach
- 1 Cup Shredded Jack cheese
- 1 Tsp Red wine vinegar
- 8 Cups artichoke hearts
- 1/4 Cup chopped Onion
- 1 tbsp butter
- 1 Tsp minced Garlic

Additional Cheese
- 1 Tbsp mayonnaise
- 1/2 cup Monterey Jack Cheese

Method

1. Combine cream cheese and mozzarella cheese in a bowl and microwave them for half a minute to melt them.
2. Crack an egg in a cheese mixture and mix.
3. Stir in protein powder and almond flour and toss well to mix everything.
4. Knead the dough a little.
5. Now roll the dough between butter paper and spread it in a pan.
6. Cook the dough in a preheated oven at 400 degrees for about 15 minutes.
7. Melt the butter in a skillet over medium flame and sauté garlic and onions in heated butter for two minutes.
8. Mix in artichokes and spinach and mix.
9. Pour red wine and add pepper and salt.
10. Add mayonnaise and mix. The dipping is ready.
11. Spread jack cheese over the baked crust and then spread artichoke dipping over the curst.
12. Place the pan in the oven again for a few minutes to lightly melt and warm the toppings.
13. Serve and enjoy it.

8.80 White Chicken Enchiladas

Servings: 8 I Time: 40 mins I Difficulty: Medium

Nutrients per serving: Calories: 433 kcal I Fat: 33g I Carbohydrates: 3g I Protein: 30g I Fiber: 0.5g

Ingredients

- Eight crepes

Chicken Enchilada Filling

- Salt to taste
- 1 Lb shredded Rotisserie chicken
- Black pepper to taste

White Cheese Sauce

- 1/4 Tsp Salt
- 2 Cups grated Monterey Jack cheese
- 4 oz diced Green chills
- 4 oz Cream cheese
- 1/2 Tsp White pepper
- 1 1/2 Tsp ground Cumin
- 1/2 Tsp granulated Onion powder
- 1/2 Tsp granulated Garlic powder

Method

1. Mix salt and pepper with shredded chicken.
2. Heat the skillet over medium flame.
3. Add all the items of sauce into the pan and cook until they melt with occasional stirring.
4. Bring it to simmer for a few minutes to thicken the sauce.
5. When required, consistency of the sauce is achieved, then remove the pan from the flame.
6. Spread half of the sauce over a casserole tray sprayed with oil.
7. Now spread chicken mixture over the tortilla ad roll them up.
8. Place the rolled tortilla in a casserole with the seamed side facing downwards.
9. Spread the remaining sauce over the tortilla and bake in a preheated oven at 350 degrees for 30 minutes.
10. Serve and enjoy it.

8.81 Mexican Cornbread Casserole Taco Pie

Servings: 8 I Time: 45 mins I Difficulty: Medium
Nutrients per serving: Calories: 436 kcal I Fat: 30g I Carbohydrates: 8g I Protein: 31g I Fiber: 3g

Ingredients

Ground Beef Taco Meat

- 2 Tbsps Tomato paste
- 1 Lb Ground beef
- Salt to taste
- 2 Tbsps Taco seasoning
- Black pepper to taste
- 1 Cup Cheddar cheese
- 1/2 Cup Beef broth

"Cornbread" Base

- 1 Cup grated Mozzarella Cheese
- 2 Cups Almond flour
- 2 oz Cream cheese
- 3 Eggs
- 1 Tbsp Baking powder
- 1/4 Tsp Sweet Corn Extract

Method

1. Cook ground beef in a pan over medium flame.
2. Use a spoon to break the beef while cooking.
3. After ten minutes, add taco seasoning, beef broth, and tomato paste. Cook for few minutes until liquid is reduced to half.
4. Sprinkle salt, cheese, and pepper. Remove the pan from the flame.

5. Blend eggs, extract, cheese, baking powder, and almond flour in a processor to form a thick batter.
6. Transfer the batter to a pan sprayed with oil and spread it evenly.
7. Spread taco meat over the batter.
8. Bake in a preheated oven at 30 degrees for 40 minutes.
9. Spread cheese and bake again to melt the cheese.
10. Serve and enjoy it.

8.82 Chicken Pizza Crust

Servings: 4 I Time: 40 mins I Difficulty: Medium
Nutrients per serving: Calories: 222 kcal I Fat: 11g I Carbohydrates: 1g I Protein: 30g

Ingredients

- 1 Cup grated Mozzarella cheese
- 1 Lb shredded chicken breast
- Salt to taste
- 2 Eggs
- Black pepper to taste

Method

1. Add shredded chicken, pepper, and salt in a bowl. Toss well.
2. Add all the remaining ingredients and mix them using your hands.
3. Transfer the mixture over a baking tray lined with parchment paper.
4. Bake in a preheated oven at 400 degrees for 20 minutes.
5. Spread the desired toppings over the baked pizza and place them in the oven again.
6. Bake the pizza for 12 minutes.
7. Serve and enjoy it.

8.83 Low Carb Mexican Chicken Casserole

Servings: 8 I Time: 55 mins I Difficulty: Medium
Nutrients per serving: Calories: 184 kcal I Fat: 11g I Carbohydrates: 8g I Protein: 12g I Fiber: 2g

Ingredients

- 1 1/4 Cups Enchilada sauce
- 6 Cups cooked cauliflower rice
- 1 Egg
- 2 cups cooked and shredded Chicken
- 2 cups grated Mexican Blend Cheese
- 4 oz diced Green chilies
- 1/4 Tsp Salt
- 1 Tsp Ground cumin

Optional Toppings:

- Diced Avocado
- Extra enchilada sauce
- Diced Tomatoes
- Sour cream
- Cilantro

Method

1. Mix cauliflower, cheese, chilies, salt, egg, and cumin in a bowl. Set aside.
2. Spread cauliflower rice over the casserole tray sprayed with oil. Press the rice firmly.
3. Bake the casserole in a preheated oven for 35 minutes.
4. Mix enchilada sauce and meat in a bowl.
5. Spread the meat mixture over cauliflower rice and add cheese.
6. Bake again for ten minutes to melt the cheese.
7. Serve and enjoy it.

8.84 Low Carb Taco Salad

Servings: 4 I Time: 25 mins I Difficulty: Medium

Nutrients per serving: Calories: 530 kcal I Fat: 42g I Carbohydrates: 9g I Protein: 32g I Fiber: 5g

Ingredients

- Black pepper to taste
- 1 Lb Ground beef
- One cubed Avocado
- Two chopped Romaine hearts
- 4 oz cubed Cheddar cheese
- Salt to taste
- 2 Tbsps sliced Red onion
- 3 oz Grape tomatoes
- 1 Tsp Ground cumin

Mexican Vinaigrette

- 1 Cup Cilantro Lime Vinaigrette

Optional Ingredients

- Sour cream
- Salsa

Method

1. Cook beef in a pan over medium flame for ten minutes and use a spoon to break it while cooking.
2. Stir in salt, cumin, and pepper.
3. Add taco seasoning and cook for one minute.
4. Prepare the vinaigrette by following the instructions written in the packet.
5. Transfer all the ingredients, including the cooked beef, to a bowl.
6. Pour in the dressing over the mixture in the bowl and toss well.
7. Spread salsa and cream and serve.

8.85 Ground Beef Taco

Servings: 6 I Time: 25 mins I Difficulty: Medium
Nutrients per serving: Calories: 432 kcal I Fat: 33g I Carbohydrates: 7g I Protein: 28g I Fiber: 2g

Ingredients

Ground Beef Taco Meat

- One recipe Taco Seasoning
- 1 Lb Ground beef
- 2 Tbsps Tomato paste
- Salt to taste
- 1/2 Cup Beef broth
- Pepper to taste

Taco Shells

- 6 Cheese Taco Shells

Toppings

- 1/2 Cup Salsa
- 2 Cups chopped Lettuce
- 1/2 Cup shredded Cheese
- 1/4 Cup Mined Purple onion
- One sliced Avocado
- 1/2 Cup Sour cream
- 1/4 Cup chopped Cilantro

Method

1. Add lemon juice and avocado in a bowl and set aside until further use.
2. Cook ground beef in a pan over medium flame with constant stirring to break the beef during cooking.
3. Add taco seasoning and cook for two minutes.
4. Stir in beef broth and let it simmer for few minutes.
5. Sprinkle salt and pepper according to the taste.
6. Spread the taco meat in taco cheese shells and add toppings according to your taste.
7. Serve and enjoy it.

8.86 Herb Roasted Chicken

Servings: 6 I Time: 2 hrs 45 mins I Difficulty: Difficult
Nutrients per serving: Calories: 409 kcal I Fat: 30g I Carbohydrates: 2g I Protein: 30g

Ingredients

- 1 Tbsp Avocado oil
- Salt to taste
- One whole Chicken
- Black pepper to taste

Compound Butter

- 2 Tsps chopped Parsley
- 4 Tbsps Butter
- 1 Tsp shredded lemon zest

Ingredients for Chicken Cavity and Pan

- Two crushed Garlic cloves
- One chopped Onion
- 1/2 Cup Water
- One whole Lemon
- Parsley sprigs as required

Method

1. Combine lemon zest, butter, lemon juice, and parsley in a bowl.
2. Rub the butter mixture over the chicken pieces to coat them well.
3. Then rub lemon, salt, olive oil, and pepper over the chicken pieces
4. Preheat oven to 350 degrees F and position rack to the middle of the oven.
5. Fill the chicken cavity with lemon, garlic, and parsley.
6. Place the chicken in a pan and spread onion, parsley, garlic, and lemon around the chicken.
7. Then roast the chicken in a preheated oven at 350 degrees for 100 minutes.
8. You can add water when the pan starts getting dry during roasting.
9. Transfer the chicken onto the plate.
10. Serve and enjoy it.

8.87 Keto Beef Stew

Servings: 6 I Time: 2 hrs 30 mins I Difficulty: Difficult
Nutrients per serving: Calories: 288 kcal I Fat: 20g I Carbohydrates: 8g I Protein: 20g I Fiber: 2g

Ingredients

- 6 oz chopped Celery root
- 1 1/4 Lbs cubed Beef chuck roast
- Two sliced Celery ribs
- 8 oz chopped whole mushrooms
- 4 oz sliced Pearl onions
- Two sliced Garlic cloves
- Black pepper to taste
- 3 oz sliced Carrot
- 2 Tbsps Tomato paste
- 5 Cups Beef broth
- 2 Tbsps Olive oil
- 1 Bay leaf
- Salt to taste
- 1/2 Tsp Dried thyme

Method

1. Rub beef with the oil and set aside.
2. Heat the oil in a heavy bottom pan over medium flame.
3. Sauté mushrooms in heated oil for two minutes.
4. Transfer the cooked mushrooms to the bowl where other veggies are added.
5. Again heat the olive oil over medium flame in the same pot.

6. Cook beef in heated oil for a few minutes.
7. Add tomato paste, thyme, and bay leaf and toss well.
8. Cook for two minutes.
9. Slowly pour in broth with constant stirring.
10. Let it simmer for two minutes.
11. Cover the pot and let it cook for 90 minutes over low flame.
12. When beef is done, add veggies and mix well.
13. Simmer for five minutes over medium flame.
14. Cover the pot and cook for 40 minutes over low flame.
15. Sprinkle salt and pepper to adjust the flavor.
16. Serve and enjoy it.

8.88 Bacon Wrapped Pork Chops with Apple Cider Vinegar Glaze

Servings: 4 I Time: 25 mins I Difficulty: Medium
Nutrients per serving: Calories: 358 kcal I Fat: 24g I Carbohydrates: 1.5g I Protein: 32.5g

Ingredients

Pork Chops

- Four slices Bacon
- 1 1/4 Lbs boneless Pork chops
- 1 Tbsp Olive oil
- Black pepper to taste
- Salt to taste

Apple Cider Vinegar Glaze

- 1/2 Cup Water
- 1/4 Cup diced Onion
- 1 Tsp Chicken base
- Two minced Garlic cloves
- 1/4 Cup Apple cider vinegar
- 2 Tbsps Butter
- 3 Sprigs of thyme
- 1 Tsp sugar

Method

1. Rub pork chops with salt, oil, and pepper and set aside.
2. Heat olive oil in a skillet over medium flame.
3. Add pork chops and cook from both sides for five minutes.
4. Transfer the chops into the plate and cover to keep them warm.
5. Now sauté garlic and onions for two minutes.
6. Stir in thyme and chicken base—Cook for one minute.
7. Add vinegar and water and mix well.
8. Cook until half of the sauce is evaporated.
9. Add butter and cook to mix it with the sauce.
10. Let it simmer for a few minutes.
11. At this point, you can adjust the taste by adding salt and pepper.
12. Pour the sauce over pork and serve.

8.89 Hamburger Steak and Gravy

Servings: 4 I Time: 25 mins I Difficulty: Medium
Nutrients per serving: Calories: 612 kcal I Fat: 52g I Carbohydrates: 5g I Protein: 29g I Fiber: 1g

Ingredients

Hamburger Steaks

- 2 Tsps Montreal Steak Seasoning
- 1 1/4 Lbs Ground beef
- 2 Tsps Worcestershire sauce
- 1 Tbsp minced Parsley
- 1 Tsp Oil
- 1/4 Cup crushed Pork rinds
- Salt to taste
- 1/4 Cup Heavy cream
- Black pepper to taste

Mushroom and Onion Gravy

- 1/4 Cup Water
- 1/4 Cup diced Onions
- 1 Tsp Beef base
- 8 oz sliced Mushrooms
- 2 Tbsps Whisky
- 1/3 Cup Heavy cream
- 1 Tbsp Butter

Method

1. Soak pork rinds in cream for ten minutes. The panade is ready. Set aside.
2. Combine beef, soaked pork rinds, steak seasoning, Worcestershire, and parsley. Use your hands to mix all the ingredients evenly.
3. Make patties of the required size out of the mixture.
4. Season the patties with salt and pepper.
5. Heat olive oil in a skillet over medium flame.
6. Cook patties in heated oil for five minutes from both sides.
7. Transfer cooked patties (hamburger steak) into the plate and set aside.
8. Now melt butter in the same pan and sauté mushrooms for two minutes with constant stirring.
9. Add onion and stir. Cover the pan and cook for two minutes.
10. Stir in the beef base, whisky, and water.
11. Mix in heavy cream and stir well.
12. Let it simmer until the sauce gets thickens.
13. Add butter and salt and pepper to adjust the flavor.
14. Pour the sauce over the patties and serve.

8.90 Easy Pan-Seared Lamb Chops with Mustard Cream Sauce

Servings: 4 I Time: 30 mins I Difficulty: Medium
Nutrients per serving: Calories: 426 kcal I Fat: 30g I Carbohydrates: 4g I Protein: 31g

Ingredients

Pan-Seared Lamb Chops

- 1 Tbsp chopped Rosemary
- 1 1/2 Lbs Lamb chops
- Salt to taste
- Two crushed Garlic cloves
- 2 Tbsps Olive oil
- Black pepper to taste

Mustard Cream Pan Sauce

- 2 Tbsps Brandy
- 1 Tbsp minced Shallot
- Sprig of Rosemary
- 1 Tbsp grainy Mustard
- 1/2 Cup Beef broth
- 2/3 Cup Heavy cream
- 2 Tsps Worcestershire sauce
- Salt to taste
- 2 Tsps Lemon juice
- 1 Tsp Erythritol
- Sprig of Thyme
- 2 tbsps Butter
- Black pepper to taste

Method

1. Add garlic, rosemary, lamb chops, and olive oil in a bowl and toss well.
2. Place chops in a baking tray and sprinkle salt, pepper, and rosemary mixture.
3. Cover the tray and place in the fridge for several hours.
4. Heat olive oil in a skillet over medium flame.
5. Add chops and cook for eight minutes.
6. Change the side of the chops and cook the other side for seven minutes.

7. Transfer the cooked lamb chops to a plate and set aside.
8. Sauté shallots in a pan over a low flame.
9. Pour in brandy and beef broth.
10. Increase the flame to medium and let it simmer for one minute.
11. Now add mustard, erythritol, and Worcestershire and toss well.
12. Add rosemary, cream, and thyme and simmer for ten minutes.
13. Squeeze lime juice and add butter. Toss and simmer until desired consistency is achieved—the mustard cream sauce is ready.
14. Pour the sauce over lamb chops; serve and enjoy it.

8.91 Low Carb Pork Stir Fry

Servings: 4 I Time: 15 mins I Difficulty: Easy
Nutrients per serving: Calories: 226 kcal I Fat: 12g I Carbohydrates: 10g I Protein: 19g I Fiber: 4g

Ingredients

- 1 Tbsp minced Ginger
- 3/4 Lb stripped Pork loin
- 12 oz Broccoli florets
- 1 Tbsp Extra dry sherry
- 2 Tbsps Avocado
- 1 Tsp minced Garlic
- 1 Cup Green onions
- 1 Tsp cornstarch
- One sliced Red bell pepper
- 2 Tbsps Tamari soy sauce
- 1 1/2 Tbsps sugar
- 1 Tsp sesame oil

Optional Ingredients
- Sesame seeds
- Red pepper flakes

Method

1. Combine minced garlic, ginger, pork loin, and oil in a mixing bowl.
2. Now add chopped bell pepper, sliced onions, chopped broccoli in layer form in bowl.
3. Mix in cornstarch and sweetener. Toss well.
4. Then add sesame oil, soy sauce, and sherry and mix.
5. Heat olive oil in a wok over medium flame.
6. Add pork and cook for a few minutes without touching it.
7. Cook from both sides, and when they are completely cooked, transfer them to the plate.
8. Now shift the veggies into the wok and cover the wok.
9. Cook for one minute.
10. Add pork and mix well.
11. Mix in the sauce and let it boil with occasional stirring for one minute.
12. When the sauce gets thickens, remove the wok from the flame.
13. Serve and enjoy it.

8.92 Low Carb Malibu Chicken

Servings: 4 I Time: 50 mins I Difficulty: Medium
Nutrients per serving: Calories: 696 kcal I Fat: 55g I Carbohydrates: 4g I Protein: 46g

Ingredients

- Salt to taste
- 4 Chicken breasts
- Black pepper to taste

Malibu Dipping Sauce
- 3 Tbsps Yellow mustard
- 1/2 Cup Mayonnaise
- 1 Tbsp powdered sugar

Crumb Topping
- 2 Tsps Granulated garlic
- 3/4 Cup crushed Pork rinds
- 3/4 Cup grated Parmesan cheese
- 1/4 Tsp Salt
- 1 Tsp granulated Onion
- 1/8 Tsp Pepper

Top With
- 4 oz Swiss cheese
- Eight pieces of sliced Deli ham

Method

1. First, add pork rinds in a food processor and crush them.
2. Transfer the crushed pork rinds to a bowl and set aside.
3. Rub dry chicken with salt and pepper and set aside.
4. Whisk mustard, mayonnaise, and sweetener in a bowl.
5. Pour less than half of the mayo mixture over the chicken and reserve the remaining for further use.
6. Toss to evenly coat the chicken with the mayo mixture and place it in the fridge for two hours to marinate.
7. Now, in another bowl, combine seasoning, cheese, and pork rinds.
8. Spread half of the mixture in a baking tray.
9. Place the chicken in the tray and spread the other half of the mixture on the chicken pieces' top.
10. Bake in a preheated oven at 350 degrees for 40 minutes until the chicken is done.
11. Sprinkle ham and cheese and bake again to melt the cheese.
12. Serve and enjoy it.

8.93 Grilled Buffalo Shrimp Tacos with Blue Cheese Crema

Servings: 4 I Time: 30 mins I Difficulty: Medium
Nutrients per serving: Calories: 188 kcal I Fat: 18g I Carbohydrates: 6g I Protein: 2g I Fiber: 3g

Ingredients

GRILLED BUFFALO SHRIMP TACOS
- 2 Tbsps Lime juice
- 1 Lb Shrimp
- ½ diced Red onion
- 1 Cup Hot Sauce
- 1/4 Cup Avocado oil
- 12 Corn tortillas

SIMPLE RED CABBAGE SLAW
- One diced Jalapeño
- 1/2 chopped Red cabbage
- ½ Red sliced onion
- 1 Tsp Sea salt
- 3 Tbsps lime juice

BLUE CHEESE CREMA
- 1 Tbsp Lime juice
- 1 Cup Greek yogurt
- 1/2 Tsp Sea salt
- 2 oz crumbled Blue cheese
- Coldwater as required

TOPPINGS
- One diced Avocado
- 1 Cup chopped Cilantro
- 2 Tbsps Lime wedges
- Two sliced Jalapeños

Method

1. Whisk lime juice, onions, hot sauce, and avocado oil in a bowl.
2. Add shrimps and mix well to evenly coat the shrimps.

3. Place the bowl in the fridge for two hours to marinate the shrimps.
4. Combine jalapeno, lime juice, red cabbage, onion, and salt in a bowl and mix well.
5. Message all the ingredients using hands to soften the cabbage.
6. The red cabbage slaw is ready. Set aside.
7. Mix yogurt, lime juice, salt, and blue cheese in a mixing bowl.
8. Pour in water and transfer the mixture to a blender and blend to get a smooth mixture.
9. You can add more water to get the desired consistency.
10. Lightly toast the tortillas over a preheated grill for half a minute.
11. Now place the shrimps over the grill sprayed with oil.
12. Grill shrimps for three minutes from both sides.
13. Spread cabbage slaw over tortillas, place cilantro, jalapeno, shrimp, blue cheese crema, and avocado.
14. Serve with hot sauce and enjoy it.

8.94 Cream of Mushroom Pork Chops

Servings: 4 I Time: 30 mins I Difficulty: Easy
Nutrients per serving: Calories: 483 kcal I Fat: 40g I Carbohydrates: 6g I Protein: 21g I Fiber: 1g

Ingredients

- Four thin, bone-in pork chops
- 2 1/2 tbsp divided avocado oil
- 1 pound mushrooms, sliced
- 1 tbsp minced onion
- One clove minced garlic
- 1/3 cup chicken broth unsalted
- 1/3 cup dry white wine
- 1/8 tsp powdered dried sage
- 1/2 cup heavy cream
- salt & pepper
- 1/4 tsp chopped fresh thyme leaves

Method

1. Let the chops of pork stand for at least 20 min at room temp. This guarantees that they cook equally & don't get rough. With around 2 tsp of oil, rub all sides of the pork & sprinkle with salt. Chop the onion & garlic, then cut the thyme. In a shallow bowl, put the wine & chicken broth along.
2. On med-high heat, heat a wide skillet. Once hot, put 2 to 3 teaspoons of Oil or sufficiently for the skillet's bottom to swirl & coat. Once the surface shimmers, the oil is hot. In the pan, Put the chops of pork & lower the heat to med. Cook on each side for around 3 1/3 mins. Take it from the plate & cover with foil.
3. In the skillet, pour one tablespoon of oil & swirl to coat. Put the mushrooms as the oil shimmers, then stir to coat—Cook for two mins undisturbed. Mix the mushrooms & put the garlic & onions in the skillet. 1 min to cook & stir. Cook for the extra min. Then scrape all the brown bits from the skillet's bottom with the wine & chicken broth. Let it boil & decrease by half.
4. Cook till the sauce thickens & put the powdered sage, fresh thyme & heavy cream (this is a thinner sauce). (this is a thinner sauce). Sprinkle with salt.
5. Put the pork chops in the skillet & carry them to the plate or place the pork chops on the mushrooms & sauce and eat.

8.95 Indian Chicken Tikka Wings

Servings: 4 I Time: 40 mins I Difficulty: Easy
Nutrients per serving: Calories: 396 kcal I Fat: 33g I Carbohydrates: 2g I Protein: 23g

Ingredients

- Ten whole chicken wings
Tikka Marinade
- 1 cup coconut milk full fat

- 1 1/2 tbsp ground cilantro
- 2 tsp ground chili pepper
- 1 1/4 tsp salt
- 1/2 chopped cilantro
- Three cloves chopped garlic
- 1/4 cup fresh juice of the lemon
Citrus Cilantro Sauce
- 1/4 cup fresh juice of a lemon
- 1/4 cup coconut milk full fat
- 1/8 tsp salt
- 1/2 bunch coriander
- 1-2 tbsp erythritol

Method

1. Preparation: Split the wings into wings & drums with a fine knife. Throw away the tips or reserve them for soup. Mix the ingredients in a big plastic zip-lock bag for your Tikka Chicken marinade & put the wings. For 24 to 48 hrs, marinate.
2. Roast the Wings: Take the Tikka Chicken wings back from the marinade & blot with paper towels. Sprinkle with salt. Make the grill preheat. Oil the barbecue grill & cook the wings - around ten min each side - till cooked through.
3. Sauce: Mix the ingredients for your sauce in a processor when the wings are frying, & blend. Uh, taste.
4. Take the chicken tikka wings from the barbecue & either spill over the sauce & serve or place it on the side with the sauce.
5. Oven Method: Put & spread the chicken wings on the sheet skillet. Bake for 30-40 mins at 350 & finish for a few mins more under the broiler till the wings have a good color on them.

8.96 Low Carb City Chicken

Servings: 4 I Time: 25 mins I Difficulty: Easy
Nutrients per serving: Calories: 300 kcal I Fat: 16.93g I Carbohydrates: 2.84g I Protein: 33g I Fiber: 1.2g

Ingredients

- salt & pepper
- 1 pound boneless pork loin
- One big egg
- 2 tbsp divided olive oil
- Low Carb Coating Gluten Free
- 1/4 cup Parmesan Cheese
- 1/2 cup almond flour
- 1 tbsp minced parsley
- 1/4 tsp pepper
- 1/2 tsp salt
- 1/4 tsp garlic powder, coarse
- 1/4 tsp onion powder, granulated
- Eight wooden skewers

Method

1. Break the pork into cubes of around 1 inch. Onto Eight skewers, string the pork. With salt & pepper, season.
2. In a jar big enough to accommodate a whole skewer, combine the ingredients to coat.
3. On a broad dinner plate, put the threaded skewers. Break the egg and spill the pork over it. Switch each of the skewers that are covered in the egg.
4. Heat a med skillet on med heat to cook or saute. Apply one tablespoon of oil when hot & swirl to cover the plate.
5. Take the skewer of the pork, allowing any excess egg to drain back onto the plate, & roll it into the breading combination. Ensure that it is properly coated. Put it in the skillet. Three more skewers, repeat the same process.
6. Fry the City Chicken on either side for around 1 1/2 mins, on all four sides. Remove & cook the leftover skewers of City Chicken on a paper towel. Serve at room temp.

8.97 Peri Peri Chicken

Servings: 4 I Time: 4 hrs 45 mins I Difficulty: Easy
Nutrients per serving: Calories: 520 kcal I Fat: 44g I Carbohydrates: 8g I Protein: 27g I Fiber: 4g

Ingredients

- 2 cups divided Peri-Peri sauce
- 4 Chicken quarters

Method

1. Before putting them in the freezer bag with one cup of Peri-Peri sauce, drizzle the chicken thighs with one tsp of salt. For Four hours or overnight, seal & put in the freezer to marinate.
2. Oven preheated to210 degrees C.
3. Pull off the extra marinade & cut the marinated chicken from the frozen bag.
4. In a shallow bowl, put ½ cup of the Peri-Peri sauce.
5. In a broad casserole bowl or on a cookie sheet, put the chicken parts & bake for 20 to 30 mins. As the chicken cooks, baste this with the peri-peri sauce you put in the bowl every 10 mins.
6. Serve on the side with the leftover 1/2 cup Peri-Peri sauce.

8.98 Easy Keto Pad Thai

Servings: 2 I Time: 23 mins I Difficulty: Easy
Nutrients per serving: Calories: 300 kcal I Fat: 22g I Carbohydrates: 13g I Protein: 13g I Fiber: 4g

Ingredients

- 2 tbsp Rice wine vinegar
- 2 tbsp Fish sauce
- 1 tbsp Lime juice
- 1 tbsp Granulated artificial sweetener, we used Splenda
- Two big Eggs
- 2 tbsp Peanut oil
- 2 tsp minced garlic
- 14 ounces spiralized courgette
- Four chopped Scallions
- 5 ounces Bean sprouts
- 2 tbsp finely chopped Fresh Coriander
- 4 tsp minced peanuts

Method

1. In a tiny saucepan, mix fish sauce, rice vinegar, artificial sweetener & lime juice, then carry to a simmer on med-high heat.
2. Fry the eggs in a tiny cup. Place the egg on the boiling sauce & whisk the full time. Let the eggs boil till they are finished. Take it from the heat.
3. Sauté the peanut oil & garlic for 1 min in a pan on med-high heat. Stir in the scallions.
4. Put the scallions & courgette and finish cooking for 1 min.
5. Over the courgette, spill the sauce & put the bean sprouts. Sauté and after this take it from the heat.
6. Add the coriander & peanuts to the garnish. Immediately serve.

8.99 Air Fryer Pork Chops

Servings: 4 I Time: 14 mins I Difficulty: Easy
Nutrients per serving: Calories: 248 kcal I Fat: 13g I Carbohydrates: 2g I Protein: 29g I Fiber: 1g

Ingredients

- 4 Boneless pork chops
- 1 tbsp Olive oil
- 2 tsp Garlic powder
- 2 tsp Onion powder
- Two tsp Paprika
- 1 tsp Salt
- 1/2 tsp Pepper

Method

1. Mix the onion powder, garlic powder, paprika & salt in a shallow bowl.
2. Use a thin layer of olive oil to brush the chops of pork & then rub the spice mix onto them.
3. Put the chops of pork in the basket of the airy fryer, operating in batches. Put the pork chops side-by-side.
4. Set the temp to 185 degrees C for 9 mins. Begin cooking the chops with the pork.
5. Stop the timer halfway through & remove the basket, tossing the pork chops over. Remove the basket as well as the timer begins.

8.100 Inst. Pot Roast Beef

Servings: 6 I Time: 1 hr. 17 mins I Difficulty: Easy
Nutrients per serving: Calories: 473 kcal I Fat: 29g I Carbohydrates: 5g I Protein: 45g I Fiber: 1g

Ingredients

- 3 pounds Chuck roast
- 2 tsp Italian seasoning
- 2 tsp Garlic powder
- 2 tsp Onion powder
- 1 tsp Kosher salt
- 1 tbsp Olive oil
- One roughly chopped Carrot
- ½ roughly chopped Onion
- Two crushed cloves Garlic
- 1 tbsp Tomato paste
- 5 cup Red wine
- 1 tbsp Worcestershire
- 2 cups Beef broth

Method

1. Slice the chuck roast into pieces of 1 pound.
2. Mix the onion powder, Italian Seasoning, Kosher salt & garlic powder in a tiny bowl.
3. Rub it over the beef with the seasoning combination.
4. Set SAUTE as your Inst. Pot & add olive oil. Put in the pot brown on either side for 2 mins with the seasoned chuck roast bits. Remove & set aside the browned beef.
5. Leave the saute for the Inst. Pot. Put the red wine, then simmer for five mins.
6. Whisk together the red wine & put the tomato paste, Worcestershire & beef broth in the pot.
7. With the onion, garlic & carrots, put your browned beef in the liquid in a pot.
8. Secure the lid input and placed SEALING on the valve. For 40 mins, set to HIGH Intensity.
9. Click CANCEL whenever the timer goes off & let it release the natural pressure release for ten min. Transfer the valve to VENTING after ten min to relieve the excess pressure.
10. Set aside & extract the cooked beef from a liquid. For the veggies to be removed, strain the liquid into a fine-mesh strainer.

8.101 Keto Inst. Pot Cabbage Rolls

Servings: 12 I Time: 1 hr 20 mins I Difficulty: Easy
Nutrients per serving: Calories: 218 kcal I Fat: 14g I Carbohydrates: 6g I Protein: 14g I Fiber: 2g

Ingredients

- 1 cup of water
- One head cabbage

FILLING:

- 1 pound ground Pork
- 1 pound ground beef
- 2 tsp onion powder
- 1 tsp garlic powder
- 2 tsp finely chopped parsley
- 2 tsp salt
- ½ tsp pepper

- 1 tbsp Worcestershire
- One big egg

SAUCE:

- 2 tbsp additional-virgin olive oil
- 2 tsp dried oregano
- 1/2 chopped cup onion
- Three minced cloves garlic
- 2 tbsp tomato paste
- 28 ounces canned crushed tomatoes
- 1 tbsp Worcestershire
- 1 tsp Salt

Method

SAUCE:
1. On med boil, heat the olive oil in a frying pan.
2. Put the onions when the olive oil is hot and cook for 2 mins. Put the garlic & cook for another min to finish cooking.
3. Put the leftover sauce ingredients mix together for around 15-20 mins, cooking on med heat, stirring periodically, while the stuffed cabbage is being cooked.

FILLING:
1. In a big bowl, mix all the filling ingredients & work them together with the hands.
2. Until going on to the next move, wash your hands carefully.
3. Assemble rolls of cabbage.
4. With the lid on, fill a pot big enough to accommodate your cabbage. Get things to a boil with a kettle of water.
5. Core your cabbage & put it in the water. Cover it with a lid.
6. For 5-7 mins, cook.
7. Take the cabbage from water & peel off the cabbage's head with a pliable cabbage leaf & position it on the flat surface.
8. At the end of a leaf, put 3 ounces of the meat combination along with the stem.
9. If you roll the leaf on the meat, fold it into the side of the cabbage leaf & begin rolling till the end is reached.

COOK IN THE INST. POT/COOKER Under PRESSURE:
1. In the Slow Cooker Insert, put a trivet & place one cup of water into the rim.
2. Put on the trivet for the first cabbage rolls and cover with 1 cup of sauce.
3. Put the 2nd row of cabbage rolls in different directions on top of the 1st row. Put 1 cup of sauce.
4. Repeat & top with the leftover sauce for a third coat, allowing it to spill down the sides of cabbage rolls to cover everything.
5. Secure the cover in place & set up the SEALING valve. Set to HIGH PRESSURE for 20 mins & cook.
6. Before carefully moving the valve to vent & allowing the residual steam to escape, allow the Inst. Pot to perform a natural release for fifteen min after it has done.
7. From the jar, extract the stuffed cabbage & put it aside.
8. Set the Inst. Pot to sauté & boil the sauce in the pot, stirring continuously—Cook for ten min or till thickened to a pasta sauce's consistency.
9. Plate a stuffed cabbage in a wide bowl. Now enjoy it.

8.102 Inst. Pot Chicken Bone Broth

Servings: 12 I Time: 2 hrs 30 mins I Difficulty: Easy
Nutrients per serving: Calories: 45 kcal I Fat: 1g I Carbohydrates: 1g I Protein: 5g

Ingredients

- 4 Chicken Wings
- 2 Rotisserie Chicken carcasses
- 2 roughly chopped stalks Celery
- 1 roughly chopped Carrot
- 1 big quartered Onion
- 1 bunch fresh thyme
- 2 Bay Leaves
- 2 to 3 sprigs Fresh Rosemary

- 2 tsp Salt
- ½ tsp Pepper
- Water

Method

1. In the Slow Cooker, put all the ingredients & fill the pot with water till it reaches just below the peak fill mark.
2. Turn the valve on top to SEALING & set the Slow Cooker to HIGH pressure for 120 mins. Lock the Inst. Pot lid in position.
3. Click CANCEL when the timer goes off & then allow it to make a natural release for thirty min.
4. After thirty min, flip your valve to VENTING to clear the lid & let out some residual steam.
5. To strain the vegetables, herbs & chicken bones, spill the broth into a bowl via a fine mesh strainer. Add salt
6. Please place it in a sealed jar in the fridge. Till ready for usage, or ice for up to six months in a sealed jar.

8.103 Keto Chicken Parmesan Roll-Ups

Servings: 10 I Time: 1 hr 10 mins I Difficulty: Easy
Nutrients per serving: Calories: 155 kcal I Fat: 9g I Carbohydrates: 5g I Protein: 15g I Fiber: 2g

Ingredients

- Two full aubergine
- 16 ounces chicken breast, Cooked & shredded
- 1 tbsp Italian seasoning
- 1 tsp Salt
- 2 cups divided Rao's Marinara Sauce
- ½ cup Mozzarella Cheese
- 1 cup Parmesan cheese

Method

1. Oven preheated to 210 degrees C.
2. Carefully slice the aubergine into long vertical slices that are 1/4 inch wide by using a mandolin.
3. Layer the slices in a single layer on a cookie sheet lined with bakery release paper. Cook 12 to 15 mins. This move is to dry the aubergine such that it does not leak a lot of water when it heats, so it is finished as it seems that any have shrunk & are partially dry and not brown/burned.
4. Take it from the oven when the aubergine has completed baking & let it cool for 10 mins.
5. Lower the temperature of the oven.
6. Mix the chopped chicken, Italian Seasoning, 1/4 cup of marinara sauce, Parmesan cheese, & salt in a wide bowl while the aubergine is cooling.
7. To the bottom of even an oven-safe baking dish, apply half a cup of marinara.
8. At one end of an aubergine strip, put roughly 2.5 ounces of chopped chicken combination & roll it up gently. Put the roll with the overlapping end face down in the baking dish. For any of the aubergine slices, repeat this.
9. Top with two teaspoons of marinara sauce for each aubergine roll. Drizzle the mozzarella cheese on the rolls & put for 20 mins in the oven to roast.

8.104 Provolone And Prosciutto Stuffed Pork Loin

Servings: 10 I Time: 1 hr 15 mins I Difficulty: Easy
Nutrients per serving: Calories: 323 kcal I Fat: 18g I Carbohydrates: 1g I Protein: 37g I Fiber: 1g

Ingredients

- 3 pounds trimmed Pork loin
- 6 ounces Prosciutto
- 6 slices Provolone
- 1 tbsp Olive Oil
- 3 tsp Salt
- 2 tsp Pepper

Method

1. oven preheated to 400 degrees.
2. Trim the pork loin's excess fat & butterfly it.
3. On the open pork loin, put the provolone slices & then finish with sliced prosciutto.
4. "Safe roast tightly spaced 1 to 2 apart with butcher's twine.
5. Brush with olive oil on the top of the pork loin & drizzle with salt & ground pepper.
6. Bake & cover for 45 mins. Then cut the foil & resume cooking for ten min or till the internal temp has reached 80 degrees C.
7. Take it from the oven before cutting the twine & slicing, then allow the roast to stand for ten mins.

8.105 Low Carb Pizza Casserole

Servings: 10 | Time:1 hr 15 mins | Difficulty: Easy
Nutrients per serving: Calories: 519 kcal | Fat: 43g | Carbohydrates: 7g | Protein: 27g | Fiber: 3g

Ingredients

- ounces Pepperoni
- 14 ounces Cauliflower florets
- 2 pounds Italian Sausage
- 1 tbsp Olive Oil
- 8 ounces sliced Mushrooms
- 1 Green Pepper
- 12 ounces shredded Mozzarella cheese
- 1.5 cups Low Carb Pasta Sauce
- 1/4 cup powdered Parmesan cheese
- 1 tsp Italian Seasoning

Method

1. steam your cauliflower. In a safe microwave bowl with one cup of water, put the cut cauliflower. Cover with a wet paper towel & microwave for around 3 mins or till the cauliflower is soft.
2. Drain your cauliflower with a towel.
3. Oven preheated to 200 degrees C
4. Cook the Italian sausage in a big pan over med heat for around 15 mins. Drain the extra fat once the sausage has done cooking.
5. Put the olive oil & sauté the mushrooms for ten min on med-high heat to extract the excess water in the same saucepan.
6. Coat it with non-stick spray. Prepare a 13 to a 9-inch baking dish and then spread 1/2 cup of pasta sauce on the bottom.
7. Place the cooked Italian sausage, cauliflower, green peppers & mushrooms in a wide dish. Toss together once blended well.
8. In the baking dish, spread 1/2 of the combination. Cover with 1/2 cup of pasta sauce, accompanied by 1/2 cup of pepperoni & then 6 ounces of mozzarella cheese.
9. Then spread the leftover combination of toppings over the egg, accompanied by the pepperonis, the remaining 1/2 cup of pasta sauce, & Six ounces mozzarella cheese.
10. Mix the Italian Seasoning & parmesan cheese in a tiny bowl.
11. Drizzle over the casserole with the Parmesan combination & finish with Ten pepperoni slices.
12. Put the cheese in the oven & cook for thirty min or till the casserole is fully cooked & the cheese is melted.

8.106 Keto Big Mac Casserole

Servings: 10 | Time: 50 mins | Difficulty: Easy
Nutrients per serving: Calories: 487 kcal | Fat: 41g | Carbohydrates: 5g | Protein: 25g | Fiber: 1g

Ingredients

- 1/2 cup diced Onion
- 2 pounds Ground beef
- 1 tbsp Worcestershire
- 2 tsp Garlic powder
- 2 tsp divided Salt
- 1 tsp divided Pepper
- 2 tbsp Dill pickle relish

- 2 ounces Cream cheese
- Four big Eggs
- 8 ounces shredded Cheddar cheese
- 1/4 cup Heavy cream

BIG MAC SAUCE
- 4 tbsp Dill pickle relish
- 1/2 cup Mayonnaise
- 2 tbsp Yellow mustard
- 1 tsp Paprika
- 1 tsp White wine vinegar
- 1 tsp Garlic powder
- 1 tsp Onion powder

Method

1. Oven preheated to 175 degrees C.
2. In a pan on med-high pressure, prepare the ground beef. Put the Worcestershire sauce, diced onions, garlic powder, 1 tsp & 1/2 tsp of pepper after cooking for around 7 mins. Continue cooking the ground beef for 3 mins or till the ground beef is completely cooked.
3. Until putting the beef back in the skillet, move the ground beef to the strainer & let the excess fat drain out.
4. To the ground beef, put the cream cheese & heat over med-low heat till your cream cheese is melted & the beef is covered.
5. Mix in the dill relish & extract the combination from the heat.
6. Scoop the beef combination into an 11-7 inch baking dish.
7. Beat the heavy cream, eggs, 1 tsp of salt & 1/2 tsp of pepper together in a shallow bowl.
8. Shake the baking dish softly and place the egg combination over the ground beef such that the egg combination is equally distributed.
9. Cover with the grated cheese.
10. For thirty min or till the casserole is set, put the dish in an oven to bake.
11. The casserole dish gives the Large Mac sauce by stirring all the ingredients in the tiny bowl.
12. Sprinkle it with a Big Mac sauce before serving as the casserole falls out of the oven.

8.107 Big Mac Keto Meatloaf

Servings: 8 | Time: 1 hr 25 mins | Difficulty: Easy
Nutrients per serving: Calories: 499 kcal | Fat: 40g | Carbohydrates: 4g | Protein: 30g | Fiber: 1g

Ingredients

KETO MEATLOAF:
- 2 pounds Ground beef
- 2 cup finely crushed Pork rinds
- 1 Egg
- 2 tsp Onion powder
- 2 tbsp Worcestershire sauce
- 1 tsp Salt
- 8 ounces American Cheese
- 1/2 tsp Garlic powder

BIG MAC SAUCE:
- 2 tbsp Dill pickle relish
- 1/4 cup Mayonnaise
- 1 tbsp Yellow mustard
- 1/2 tsp Paprika
- 1/2 tsp White wine vinegar
- 1/2 tsp Garlic powder
- 1/2 tsp Onion powder

Method

1. Oven preheated to 175 degrees C.
2. Mix the pork rinds, ground beef, egg, onion powder, Worcestershire sauce, salt & garlic powder in a big bowl. Mix the components till they're fully mixed.

3. Press 1/2 of the ground beef combination onto the bottom of a loaf pan lined with bakery release paper. Leave a 1-inch lip to create a small indentation in the middle of the ground beef.
4. Put the cubed American cheese in the indentation & press it into the bottom half with the leftover ground beef combination, so the meatloaf is covered.
5. For 60 to 70 mins, bake.
6. All the Big Mac sauce components are whisked together in a bowl as the meatloaf bakes.
7. Take the meatloaf from the oven when you stop baking and let it rest for ten min.
8. Take it from the pan & then line it with Big Mac sauce.

8.108 Italian Sausage And Pepper Foil Packet Meal

Servings: 6 I Time: 30 mins I Difficulty: Easy
Nutrients per serving: Calories: 553 kcal I Fat: 48g I Carbohydrates: 8g I Protein: 23g I Fiber: 2g

Ingredients
- Two large dice Red Bell Peppers
- 2 pounds Italian Sausage
- Two large dice Yellow Bell Peppers
- One thinly sliced Red Onion
- Pepper
- Salt

Method
1. Cut the Italian sausage into strips.
2. Cut the veggies into wedges.
3. Mix the meat & veggies & put salt & pepper.
4. Cover & barbecue in a foil packet for 20 mins or till the sausage has cooked through.

8.109 Chimichurri Steak

Servings: 6 I Time: 25 mins I Difficulty: Easy
Nutrients per serving: Calories: 395 kcal I Fat: 27g I Carbohydrates: 1g I Protein: 32g

Ingredients
- 2 pound Flank Steak
- 1/2 tsp Salt
- Chimichurri Sauce
- 1/2 tsp Pepper

Method
1. Salt & pepper the flank steak gently & let it hang out & hit room temp.
2. Heat the grill at 225 C.
3. Make the chimichurri sauce, whereas the steak hits room temp & the barbecue heats up.
4. Put the flank steak on the barbecue when the barbecue is prepared, & cook on each side for around five min or till the steak reaches an internal temp of 125 F - 145 F.
5. Carry it in & let it rest for fifteen min till the steak is finished. Then break the beef into thin pieces & split through the grain.
6. Put chimichurri sauce on top & enjoy!

8.110 Inst. Pot Big Mac Soup

Servings: 8 I Time: 45 mins I Difficulty: Easy
Nutrients per serving: Calories: 492 kcal I Fat: 43g I Carbohydrates: 6g I Protein: 20g I Fiber: 1g

Ingredients
- 1 tbsp Butter
- 1 pound Ground Beef
- 1/2 cup diced Onion
- 1 cup diced Celery
- 1 finely minced clove Garlic
- 6 ounces thinly sliced Cabbage
- 1 big Dill pickle
- 1 tbsp Worcestershire sauce
- 1 cup Heavy cream
- 3 cups Beef broth
- 12 ounces American Cheese
- Sesame Seeds for garnish

SPECIAL SAUCE
- 4 tbsp Dill pickle relish
- 1/2 cup Mayonnaise
- 2 tbsp Yellow mustard
- 1 tsp Paprika
- 1 tsp White wine vinegar
- 1 tsp Garlic powder
- 1 tsp Onion powder

Method
1. Your ground beef is brown. Put ground beef & mix till browned. Set Inst. Pot to SAUTE. Press cancel to end the saute feature
2. Drain the ground beef grease & return to the Inst. Pot.
3. Put the celery, onion, cabbage, garlic, Worcestershire sauce, beef broth & dill pickle. Fasten the cover, place the pressure valve on top for SEALING & cook at HIGH PRESSURE for ten min.
4. Click cancel to finish the cooking when the timer goes off and leave for five min to release it naturally. Turning the valve to VENTING to relieve the remaining pressure.
5. Remove the cover of the Inst. Pot & switch on the SAUTE feature. Put Heavy cream & American cheese, stirring till the cheese is fully melted.
6. Mix the special sauce ingredients in the tiny bowl.
7. Serve the soup with a topping of sesame seeds & a drizzle of a special sauce till the cheese has melted.

8.111 Low Carb Moo Shu Pork

Servings: 4 I Time: 2 hrs 11 mins I Difficulty: Easy
Nutrients per serving: Calories: 660 kcal I Fat: 60g I Carbohydrates: 7g I Protein: 13g I Fiber: 7g

Ingredients
- 1 pound pork, cut into thin pieces
- 4 Carb Balance tender Taco Flour Tortillas
- 2 eggs
- 2 tbsp vegetable oil
- 5 ounces shiitake mushrooms
- 8 ounces slaw Mix
- 2 ounces bean sprouts
- 3 ounces bok choy
- 2 tbsp sliced scallions

MARINADE:
- 1 tsp fresh ginger
- 2 crushed cloves garlic
- 6 tbsp soy sauce
- 2 tbsp rice vinegar
- 1 tsp sesame oil
- 1 tsp five Spice Powder

HOISIN SAUCE
- 1/2 teaspoon fresh ginger
- 3 to 5 drops liquid sweetener
- 2 tbsp black bean paste
- 3 tbsp soy sauce
- 1/2 tsp sesame oil
- 1 tbsp rice vinegar
- 1 tsp Sriracha hot sauce
- 1/2 tsp 5 spice powder

Method

1. In a little bowl, mix all of the marinade ingredients. Divided in two.
2. In the bowl, put the thinly sliced pork and add 1⁄2 of the marinade on the pork. Stir such that the meat is completely coated, then cover & allow to marinate for at least 2hrs in the freezer. Place the excess marinade in the refrigerator in a little jar till ready for usage.
3. Mix the hoisin ingredients in a tiny bowl & put aside.
4. In a shallow bowl, put the eggs together.
5. On med-high heat, heat a wide skillet. Put 1 tbsp of marinated pork & vegetable oil. Cook for about five min, till most of the pork, is ready.
6. Put the eggs into the skillet & proceed to mix, then cook for around 1 min, till the eggs are scrambled.
7. Put the slaw mix, vegetable oil, bean sprouts, mushrooms, bok choy, & the reserved marinade to the second tbsp. Continue cooking for five min or till the
8. Serve it with the extra bean sprouts, scallions to garnish, a sprinkle of low carb hoisin sauce & Moo Shu Pork. Heat the Project Carb Balance Tortillas for the greatest taste.

8.112 Inst. Pot Butter Chicken

Servings: 8 I Time: 32 mins I Difficulty: Easy
Nutrients per serving: Calories: 394 kcal I Fat: 30g I Carbohydrates: 9g I Protein: 20g I Fiber: 2g

Ingredients

- 2 cups diced Onion
- Five cloves minced Garlic
- 4 tbsp Butter
- 15 ounces Tomato sauce
- 2 pounds chicken thighs
- 2 tbsp Red curry paste
- 3 tbsp Tomato paste
- 1 1/2 tsp ground ginger
- 2 tsp Garam masala
- 1 tsp Salt
- ½ tsp Smoked paprika
- 1/2 cup Heavy cream
- Coriander for garnish

Method

1. Put onion, garlic & butter, and prepare your Slow Cooker to SAUTE. Saute till the onions are soft, for about five min. Cancel the saute by pressing OFF.
2. To the slow cooker, put the tomato sauce, chicken, tomato paste, garam masala, red curry paste, ground ginger, salt & smoked paprika. Close it with the lid in position & switch the pressure valve for 7 mins at HIGH PRESSURE.
3. Do the natural release for five min once the timer goes off & then move the valve over the top to VENTING to get the excess steam out from the pressure cooker.
4. Take the cover off & extract the chicken from the sauce with a slotted spoon, and put it aside.
5. Put the heavy cream in a pot &, till creamy, puree the sauce using the immersion blender.
6. Set the slow cooker to SAUTE & mix the sauce for 7 to 10 mins till boiling, or till it thickens. Turn the Saute OFF.
7. Return the chicken to the sauce, mix & serve with the coriander garnish.

8.113 Roasted Cauliflower Steaks With Brown Butter

Servings: 2 I Time: 5 mins I Difficulty: Easy
Nutrients per serving: Calories: 249 kcal I Fat: 23g I Carbohydrates: 9g I Protein: 4g I Fiber: 3g

Ingredients

- ¼ cup Olive Oil
- 2 heads Cauliflower
- ½ tsp Salt
- ½ cup salted Butter
- 4 tbsp capers
- 1 Lemon
- ½ Walnuts cup

Method

1. oven preheated to10 degrees C.
2. Cut cauliflower into "steaks" 1 inch deep.
3. Brush the cauliflower steaks with oil of olive on both sides & put them on a cookie sheet. Do not use bakery release paper, or the lovely caramelization would not be obtained.
4. Season with salt & bake for around 10 mins in the oven. Before flipping, the cauliflower must have a good brown color to it. Then flip for the next ten min and begin to roast.
5. Make the brown butter as the cauliflower bakes. Put the butter on medium heat to a hot skillet.
6. It will foam when the butter cooks, & then you would see tiny brown bits start developing on the bottom. It is finished till the color of the batter hits a rich golden-brown color. In the bowl, put in the brown butter. To remove brown bits from the bottom, you should strain the butter or not. It depends on you!
7. On med heat, put the capers & walnuts in the pan & gently toast them for 2 to 3 mins. Then place the brown butter again in the skillet.
8. Take it from the oven & spoon the capers, walnuts & brown butter on the cauliflower steaks once the cauliflower has done baking.
9. Squeeze lemon on your cauliflower & enjoy.

8.114 Sheet Pan Curried Chicken And Vegetables

Servings: 6 I Time: 40 mins I Difficulty: Easy
Nutrients per serving: Calories: 397 kcal I Fat: 28g I Carbohydrates: 14g I Protein: 21g I Fiber: 5g

Ingredients

- 4 tbsp divided Olive oil
- 4 tsp divided Curry powder
- 2 tsp divided Salt
- 3 cups Carrots
- 4 cups Cauliflower florets
- 2 Red bell peppers
- 1 tbsp shredded fresh ginger
- 6 Chicken thighs
- 2 cups chopped Green onions
- 1 cup finely chopped coriander

Method

1. Oven preheated to 220 degrees C.
2. Combine 2 tsp of curry powder, two tablespoons of olive oil, & 1 tsp of salt in a wide bowl. Put the carrots, cauliflower, bell pepper, and ginger, then toss gently till fully surrounded in a bowl.
3. Arrange a greased/ lined sheet pan with the veggies.
4. Put the leftover two tbsp of olive oil, 2 tsp of curry powder & 1 tsp in another cup. To the dish, put the chicken thighs & toss till it's covered.
5. Put chicken thighs on the sheet pan above the veggies.
6. Cook your chicken in an oven for 20 mins, extract it from the oven & sprinkle the chicken & veggies with the green onions. Put it back in the oven & proceed to bake for another ten mins or till the chicken is completely cooked.
7. Sprinkle with coriander & take the tray from the oven.

8.115 Grilled Chicken Fajita Skewers

Servings: 4 I Time: 28 mins I Difficulty: Easy
Nutrients per serving: Calories: 195 kcal I Fat: 4g I Carbohydrates: 12g I Protein: 26g I Fiber: 4g

Ingredients

- 1 lb cubed Chicken Breast
- 3 Tbsp Chili powder
- 1/2 Tbsp Garlic powder
- 2 Tbsp Cumin
- 1/2 tsp salt plus extra to taste
- 1 Green Bell Pepper
- 1 Red Bell Pepper
- 1 Yellow Bell Pepper
- 1 Red Onion

Method
1. Mix the garlic powder, chili powder, salt & cumin in a wide bowl.
2. In spice mix, Put cubed chicken & toss till it's covered.
3. On a skewer, alternate b/w peppers, onions & chicken till every skewer is filled.
4. Sprinkle the skewers with a little extra salt.
5. Grill 4 to 5 mins per side or till chicken is baked through, on med-high heat.
6. Serve the fajitas with tortillas of corn/flour, salsa, sour cream, guacamole, & something else you want!

8.116 Fire Roasted Red Pepper Soup

Servings: 2 | Time: 5 mins | Difficulty: Easy
Nutrients per serving: Calories: 39 kcal | Carbohydrates: 8g | Protein: 1g | Fiber: 2g

Ingredients
- 28 oz canned Tomatoes
- 9 oz diced Onion
- 3 cloves Garlic
- 16 oz Roasted Red Peppers
- 2 Tbsp Tomato Paste
- 1/2 tsp Salt
- 2 c Broth, chicken/ vegetable

Method
1. Saute the onions in a big pot on med heat till the onions are soft. Put the garlic & finish cooking for two min.
2. Put the tomatoes, roasted red peppers, broth & tomato paste.
3. Carry to a boil & then simmer it on low pressure & cover it.
4. Cook for thirty mins.
5. Just use the immersion blender to puree the soup components till the soup becomes smooth.
6. .Sprinkle with salt to taste

8.117 Herb Crusted Grilled Leg Of Lamb

Servings: 10 | Time: 50 mins | Difficulty: Easy
Nutrients per serving: Calories: 273 kcal | Fat: 21g | Carbohydrates: 1g | Protein: 70g

Ingredients
- 2.5 lb butterflied & trimmed Aussie Boneless leg of lamb
- 4 minced Garlic cloves.
- 2 Tbsp juice of Lemon
- 1 Tbsp True Aussie Lamb Rub
- ½ c Parsley
- 6 Tbsp Unsalted softened butter
- ¼ c Coriander

Method
1. heat barbecue to 175 degrees C.
2. In the bowl, mix the rub, butter, garlic, parsley, coriander & lemon juice.
3. Cover the lamb's butterfly leg in herbal butter.
4. Put a leg of lamb on a barbecue & sear on each side for five min.
5. Cover the barbecue lid & cook for 30 to 40 mins until the lamb's inside temp exceeds 130 degrees F.
6. Take it off the barbecue & let it sit for ten mins. Slice & eat.

8.118 Keto Chicken Tenders

Servings: 2 | Time: 16 mins | Difficulty: Easy
Nutrients per serving: Calories: 474 kcal | Fat: 60g | Carbohydrates: 7g | Protein: 13g | Fiber: 7g

Ingredients
- 1 cup almond flour
- 8 ounces chicken breast tenderloins
- 1 tsp salt
- 1 tsp pepper
- 1 big egg
- 1/4 cup Heavy Whipping

Method
1. Beat the egg & put milk in the big bowl to cover them. Sprinkle With salt & pepper. Put the chicken & let it rest for ten min.
2. In a shallow dish/pan, put the almond flour & sprinkle with pepper & salt.
3. Coat the chicken with flour on all ends.
4. Fry till golden brown & the internal temperature exceeds 160o in tiny batches.
5. Dip in the favorite keto-friendly sauce of your choosing.

8.119 Keto Salisbury Steak With Mushroom Gravy

Servings: 6 | Time: 30 mins | Difficulty: Easy
Nutrients per serving: Calories: 457 kcal | Fat: 34g | Carbohydrates: 5g | Protein: 32g

Ingredients
For the Salisbury Steaks:
- 3/4 cup almond flour
- 2 lbs ground chuck
- 1 Tbsp chopped fresh parsley
- 1 Tbsp Worcestershire sauce
- 1/4 cup beef broth
- 1 Tbsp dried onion flakes
- 1/2 tsp garlic powder
- 1/2 tsp ground black pepper
- 1 1/2 tsp kosher salt
For the gravy:
- 2 Tbsp bacon grease
- 2 Tbsp butter
- 1 cup sliced yellow onions
- 2 cups sliced button mushrooms
- 1/2 cup beef broth
- 1/2 tsp Worcestershire sauce
- salt & pepper
- 1/4 cup sour cream

Method
1. In a med sized bowl, mix all the steak components & blend well.
2. Shape into six oval patties around 1 inch thick & put on a baking sheet.
3. Bake for 18 mins in the preheated 185 degrees (C) oven.
4. In a wide skillet, melt the butter & bacon fat.
5. Put the mushrooms & cook till golden brown on med heat (about 3 minutes per side.)
6. Put the onions & simmer on med heat for five min, till golden & smooth.
7. Put the Worcestershire sauce & broth, mix & simmer for 3 mins, stirring to brush off any pieces from the bottom of a pan.
8. Stir well, put the sour cream & take it from the heat.
9. Sprinkle with salt.
10. If needed, serve on the hot Salisbury Steaks with additional parsley for topping.

8.120 One Pot Cheesy Taco Skillet

Servings: 6 I Time: 20 mins I Difficulty: Easy
Nutrients per serving: Calories: 341 kcal I Fat: 20g I Carbohydrates: 9g I Protein: 30g I Fiber: 1g

Ingredients

- One large diced yellow onion
- 1 lb lean ground beef
- 2 diced bell peppers
- 1 large shredded courgette
- 1 can diced tomatoes with green chilis
- 3 cups baby kale or spinach combination taco seasoning
- green onions for garnish
- 1 1/2 cup shredded cheddar & jack cheese

Method

1. In a wide skillet, put lightly brown beef & crumble it good.
2. Drain the excess fat.
3. Put the peppers & onions, then fry till browned.
4. Put canned tomatoes, taco seasoning, as well, as any water required for taco seasoning to cover the combination evenly (up to 1 tbsp- the liquid from the tomatoes will help)
5. Put the greens & leave to wilt absolutely.
6. Mix thoroughly.
7. Cover with the grated cheese & allow the cheese to melt.
8. Serve on a plate of lettuce, rice/taco/burrito whether the cheese is melted!

8.121 Thai Red Curry Shrimp & Veggies

Servings: 4 I Time: 30 mins I Difficulty: Easy
Nutrients per serving: Calories: 368 kcal I Fat: 31g I Carbohydrates: 3g I Protein: 18g I Fiber: 1g

Ingredients

- 1.5 lb peeled raw wild-caught shrimp
- 1 large head riced cauliflower
- 2 Tbsp coconut oil (28g)
- 2 sliced shallots
- 4 big minced/pressed cloves garlic
- 2 sliced red bell peppers
- 2 peeled & thinly sliced stalks of lemongrass
- 6 sliced green onlons
- 2 Tbsp freshly grated/finely minced ginger
- 1 can coconut milk full fat
- 1/2 cup organic chicken stock low sodium
- 2 Tbsp red curry paste
- 2 cups snap peas (250g)
- 8 Thai aubergines (135g)
- 2 small zested & juiced limes
- 1 small bunch of coriander
- 1 tsp fish sauce

Method

1. Prepare the shrimp. Take the shrimp out of the fridge and pat it dry.
2. Sauté rice with cauliflower. Heat 1 Tablespoon of coconut oil over med heat in the large pan. Sauté the cauliflower rice till tender but not fluffy (around 3 mins over med-high heat) (about 3 minutes over medium-high heat).
3. Saute any veggies. In a wide pot, on med heat, heat the leftover 1 Tbsp of coconut oil. Put the garlic, shallot, red bell pepper, green onion & lemongrass (reserve some green onion for garnish). (reserve some green onion for garnish). Cook for six mins or till the veggies are tender, but they do not turn orange. Occasionally stir.
4. Put curry paste & ginger. Cook for one min, sometimes stirring.

5. Put the aubergine & liquids. Put coconut milk, chicken stock, fish sauce, & Thai aubergine. Carry & stir regularly to a boil, scraping the bottom & edges. For four mins, cook.
6. Put snap peas & shrimp. Boil for around five min or till the shrimp is pink & opaque.
7. Switch the heat off & put the lime juice & coriander to the mixture (reserve a few coriander for topping) (reserve some cilantro for garnish) (reserve some cilantro for garnish).
8. Sprinkle to taste.
9. Garnish it. Serve with the additional green onions, cilantro, & lime zest on cauliflower rice & garnish.

8.122 Low Carb Beef Stroganoff Meatball

Servings: 4 I Time: 5 mins I Difficulty: Easy
Nutrients per serving: Calories: 452 kcal I Fat: 34g I Carbohydrates: 6g I Protein: 24g

Ingredients

For the meatball mix:

- 1 egg
- 1 lb ground beef
- 1 tsp kosher salt
- 1/4 cup almond flour
- 1/2 tsp garlic powder
- 1/2 tsp onion powder
- 1/4 tsp black pepper
- 1 tsp Worcestershire sauce
- 1 tsp dried parsley
- 2 Tbsp butter to fry

For the sauce:

- 2 cups sliced mushrooms
- 1 Tbsp butter
- 1 minced clove garlic
- 1 cup sliced onions
- 3/4 cup sour cream
- 1 1/2 cups beef broth
- salt & pepper to taste
- 1/4 tsp xanthan gum
- 2 Tbsp chopped fresh parsley

Method

1. In a med bowl, mix the meatball components & combine well.
2. Form them into Twelve meatballs.
3. In a large, non-stick saute skillet, heat 2 Tablespoons of butter.
4. On med pressure, fry the meatballs in butter till browned on each side & cooked fully (2-3 minutes per side.)
5. Set aside & take the meatballs off the pan.
6. Put 1 tbsp of butter & two cups of mushroom slices in the skillet.
7. Cook till golden & fragrant mushrooms (4-5 minutes) (4-5 minutes.)
8. From the pan, remove the mushrooms.
9. Put the garlic & onions, then simmer for 3 to 4 mins, or till smooth & translucent.
10. From the pan, remove the onions.
11. To have all the yummy bits off, put the beef broth in the skillet & scrape a bottom.
12. Place the sour cream & xanthan gum & whisk till smooth.
13. Return to the skillet, put the mushrooms, meatballs, onions & garlic, then mix.
14. Boil for twenty mins at low.
15. Sprinkle with salt.
16. Right before eating, Top with the new parsley.

8.123 Low Carb Bacon Bok Choy

Servings: 2 I Time: 15 mins I Difficulty: Easy
Nutrients per serving: Calories: 154 kcal I Fat: 13g I Carbohydrates: 4g I Protein: 4g I Fiber: 1g

Ingredients

- 2 cups baby bok choy, chopped
- 2 slices pastured bacon
- 2 big cloves garlic

Method

1. Start by frying the bacon in a pan. Take it from the pan & set it aside to cool when finished, retaining the pan's bacon grease.
2. The garlic & the bok choy stems then cook for about 2-3 mins, stirring continuously to the pan.
3. Put the leaves & stir till the leaves wilt.
4. Enjoy & serve.

8.124 Korean Spicy Pork

Servings: 4 I Time: 40 mins I Difficulty: Easy
Nutrients per serving: Calories: 189 kcal I Fat: 9g I Carbohydrates: 9g I Protein: 15g I Fiber: 1g

Ingredients

For Marinating and Cooking

- 1 lb Boneless Pork Shoulder
- 1 sliced Onion
- 1 tbsp Minced Ginger
- 1 tbsp Minced Garlic
- 1 tbsp Soy Sauce
- 1 tbsp rice wine
- 1 tbsp Sesame Oil
- 2 packets Splenda
- 2 tbsp gochujang
- 1/4-1 tsp Gochugaru
- 1/4 cup Water (62.5 ml)

For Finishing

- 1 tbsp Sesame Seeds
- 1 Sliced Onion
- 1/4 cup Green Scallions, Chopped

Method

1. Combine all the marinating & boiling supplies in the/ Inst. Pot /Pressure Cooker's inner lining. If necessary, allow it to sit for at least an hour & up to 24 hrs.
2. Cook for 20 mins at high pressure, then let it slowly relieve pressure for ten min. Release the residual pressure after ten minutes have gone.
3. You can see the excellent meat & a yummy-looking sauce once you open the pot.
4. Heat the pan.
5. Put the cubes of pork & the finely diced onion in the hot skillet.
6. Let it get warm, then place 1/4-1/2 cup of the sauce. This sauce can begin to sizzle & caramelize easily. Mix with the pork well.
7. You attempt to evaporate this sauce, leave behind its delicious goodness on the meat.
8. Drizzle with sesame seeds & green onions till the sauce has evaporated & the onions had softened & serve.
9. To serve on the side, you should use the remainder of the sauce from the pressure cooker.

8.125 Prosciutto-Wrapped Cod with Lemon Caper Spinach

Servings: 2 I Time: 20 mins I Difficulty: Easy
Nutrients per serving: Calories: 660 kcal I Fat: 60g I Carbohydrates: 7g I Protein: 13g I Fiber: 7g

Ingredients

- 4 cups of baby spinach
- 2 Tbsps. of ghee, or grass-fed butter, or avocado oil
- 1 tsp. of lemon juice (fresh)
- Salt & freshly ground black pepper
- 1 lemons' zest
- 12 to 14 oz. of cod fillets
- 1 minced clove of garlic
- 1.5 oz. of prosciutto de Parma
- 2 Tbsps. of capers

Method

1. With paper towels, dry the fish fillets completely, and thaw them (if frozen) for half an hour until they reach room temperature.
2. After they have come to room temperature, dry them again if necessary. Sprinkle the fillets with salt and freshly ground black pepper. Please keep in mind; prosciutto also has salt in it.
3. Gently Wrap the prosciutto around seasoned fish fillets, so they would not tear up.
4. Lay prosciutto's strips into a sheet on a flat surface, if they are in strips, and then wrap the fish fillets.
5. In a cast-iron skillet, on medium flame, melt ghee or butter or the oil you are using.
6. Place prosciutto-wrapped fish fillets in skillet and let them cook, until fish flakes with a fork easily, for five minutes on each side.
7. It will take you about ten minutes to cook. Although this cooking time is for fillet (one-inch thickness), it may vary depending upon fish fillets' thickness and size.
8. Cook until the meat thermometer shows 140 F or 160 C.
9. Take the fillets out and let them cool on a wire rack. Keeping them on the rack will not let the bottom get soggy.
10. Add minced garlic to the used pan, and sauté for half a minute.
11. Add capers, lemon juice, and spinach.
12. Keep mixing and cook for two minutes, or until the spinach wilts.
13. Take spinach mix out on serving plates, place fish on top, and drizzle lemon juice and zest.
14. Serve right away and enjoy.

8.126 Creamy Shrimp & Bacon skillet

Servings: 4 I Time: 10 mins I Difficulty: Easy
Nutrients per serving: Calories: 340 kcal I Fat: 29g I Carbohydrates: 3.5g I Protein: 17g I Fiber: 1g

Ingredients

- 4 oz. of smoked salmon
- Half cup of coconut cream
- 1 cup of mushrooms, sliced
- 4 oz. of shelled raw shrimp
- Freshly ground black pepper, to taste
- 1 pinch of Sea Salt
- 4 slices of uncured bacon (organic)

Method

1. Slice the bacon into one-inch pieces.
2. In a cast-iron skillet, add bacon pieces to the skillet, cook on medium heat for almost five minutes.
3. Do not make the bacon crispy; slightly cook it, add mushrooms slices sauté for five more minutes.
4. Cut the smoked salmon in strips, and add in the mushrooms, cook for 2-4 minutes
5. Add raw shrimps and cook for almost two minutes on high heat.
6. Add in the salt and cream, turn the heat low, and cook for 60 seconds, or until the sauce becomes thick enough for your liking.
7. Serve right away with zucchini noodles if you like.

8.127 One-Pot Chicken Cacciatore

Servings: 6 I Time: 1 hour I Difficulty: Medium
Nutrients per serving: Calories: 451 kcal I Fat: 23g I Carbohydrates: 24g I Protein: 29g I Fiber: 4g

Ingredients

- 28 oz. of crushed tomatoes
- 1 cup of White wine

145

- 2 Chicken breasts skin on, bone-in,
- 1 bell pepper (red), cut into slices
- 4 thighs of Chicken, or skin on drumsticks & thighs both, bone-in
- Half cup of all-purpose Flour
- 1 and a half tsp. of Salt, add more to taste
- 1 bell pepper (green), cut into slices
- 2 tbsps. of Olive oil
- 1 sliced Onion, large-sized
- 1 tsp. of freshly ground black pepper
- 3/4 cup of Chicken Broth
- 2 cups of Mushrooms, cut into slices
- 2 minced cloves of garlic

Method
1. Season the chicken with salt and freshly ground black pepper.
2. Coat the seasoned chicken in all-purpose chicken.
3. In a Dutch oven, add olive oil, brown the chicken in batches on a medium flame for three minutes for each side.
4. Take the chicken out and place it on a plate, set it aside.
5. In the pot, add garlic, peppers, mushrooms, half tsp. of salt and onions, cook for 2 to 3 minutes.
6. Add the white wine and let it simmer, cook until it is reduced by half.
7. Add broth, one tsp. of salt, and tomatoes to the pot.
8. Add the chicken in sauce in the pot.
9. With the lid on, let it simmer.
10. Cook for almost half an hour until the chicken is tender and cooked through.
11. Serve with bread or over rice or pasta to your liking.

8.128 Texas Chicken Nachos

Servings: 4 | Time: 20 mins | Difficulty: Easy
Nutrients per serving: Calories: 660 kcal | Fat: 60g | Carbohydrates: 7g | Protein: 13g | Fiber: 7g

Ingredients
- 1 and a half tsp. of smoked paprika
- 1 and a half cups of cheddar cheese
- 3 tbsp. of green onion
- 1 and a half lbs. of chicken tenders
- 3/4 tsp. of chili powder
- 1 tbsp. of olive oil
- 1 and a half tsp. of kosher salt
- 6 bacon slices, cooked & crumbled
- Half tsp. of cayenne pepper
- 1 jalapeno
- 3/4 tsp. of cumin

Method
1. Let the oven preheat to 350 F.
2. In a bowl, mix paprika, cumin, salt, cayenne pepper, and chili powder.
3. Coat the chicken pieces well in the spice rub. Add olive oil on spice coated chicken and distribute the oil well over chicken.
4. Place the seasoned chicken pieces on a baking sheet and do not overcrowd the baking sheet leaving at least half an inch of space between chicken pieces.
5. Bake for 3 to 4 minutes at 350 F, flip the chicken pieces once and bake for another 3 to 4 minutes.
6. Add jalapeno and cheese to the chicken. Place back in the oven and bake at 425 F until cheese melts for almost 3 to 4 minutes.
7. Take out from the oven and garnish with bacon and green onion on top.
8. Serve right away, or serve with blue cheese dressing or ranch dressing.

8.129 Keto Cheesy Spinach Stuffed Chicken Breast

Servings: 4 | Time: 55 mins | Difficulty: Medium
Nutrients per serving: Calories: 491 kcal | Fat: 33g | Carbohydrates: 3.5g | Protein: 43g

Ingredients
- Half tsp. of minced garlic
- 2 cups of chopped spinach
- 4 skinless chicken cutlets or breasts, boneless
- 1/3 cup of parmesan cheese (grated)
- 6 oz. of softened cream cheese
- 1/4 tsp. of kosher salt
- Half cup of mozzarella cheese (grated)
- 1/8 tsp. of ground nutmeg
- 1/4 tsp. of freshly ground black pepper

For the breading
- 1/8 tsp. of garlic powder
- 1/3 cup of parmesan cheese (grated)
- 1/8 tsp. of onion powder
- Half tsp. of dried parsley
- 1/3 cup of superfine almond flour
- 2 tbsp. of olive oil
- 2 whole eggs
- Half tsp. of kosher salt

Method
1. In a bowl, mix garlic, cream cheese, freshly ground black pepper, nutmeg, salt, parmesan, spinach, and mozzarella. Mix well and set it aside.
2. Clean the chicken if any visible membrane or fat is present.
3. (If chicken breasts are large, then slice them in half lengthwise and flatten them, so use 2 of chicken breasts cut into four pieces).
4. On a clean surface, place one layer of plastic wrap and wrap one piece of chicken in plastic wrap.
5. Flatten the chicken by pounding with a mallet, from one side to the center. Do not flatten it too much so that it may become very thin.
6. Repeat the process on all chicken pieces.
7. Place ¼ of spinach mixture in the center of chicken pieces and roll them tightly.
8. Seal the edges with your clean hands. So, the filling will not get out.
9. On a baking sheet, place all pieces of chicken seam side down.
10. Keep in the fridge for 15 minutes.
11. In a bowl, whisk the eggs.
12. In another bowl, mix all the ingredients of breading and mix well (do not add olive oil).
13. In a cast-iron skillet, heat the olive oil.
14. Let the oven preheat to 375 F.
15. Coat the chicken in the whisked egg, then in breading, then fry in oil on all sides until light brown.
16. Place the chicken on a baking pan.
17. Bake for 18 to 22 minutes, at 375 F, or until internal temperature shows 165 F.
18. Serve with alfredo sauce or rice.

8.130 Low Carb Muffuletta Chicken

Servings: 4 | Time: 25 mins | Difficulty: Easy
Nutrients per serving: Calories: 846 kcal | Fat: 64g | Carbohydrates: 6g | Protein: 57g | Fiber: 1g

Ingredients
Muffuletta Chicken
- 4 oz. of mortadella, cut into slices
- 1 and a half lb. of chicken breasts

- 4 oz. of salami, cut into thin slices
- 4 oz. of capocollo, cut into thin slices
- 2 cups of Olive Salad
- 4 oz. of provolone cheese, cut into slices
- ¼ cup of butter (half of the stick)
- 4 oz. of mozzarella cheese, cut into slices

Olive Salad

- 1 cup of green olives
- Half tsp of freshly ground black pepper
- 1 and a half cups of Giardiniera vegetables (pickled)
- 1 tsp. of dried oregano
- ⅓ cup of red wine vinegar
- ¼ cup of olive oil
- 4 large garlic cloves
- Half cup of pepperoncini
- 1 cup of Kalamata olives
- ¼ cup of red peppers (roasted)
- Half cup of capers
- 1 tsp. of dried basil

Method

For Chicken

1. Sear the chicken breast: add butter in a skillet, over medium flame, and cook chicken for 8 minutes on every side until light brown.
2. Let the oven preheat to 350 F.
3. In a rimmed cookie sheet, add chicken and layer the chicken with capocollo, provolone, mozzarella, salami, and mortadella.
4. Bake for ten minutes on the middle rack.
5. Take chicken out of the oven, add the olive salad on top, and serve right away.

For Olive Salad

1. Add the garlic, Kalamata olives, olive oil, pickled vegetables, pepperoncini, roasted red peppers, red wine vinegar, and green olives in a food processor.
2. Pulse until roughly chopped.
3. Add in freshly ground black pepper, oregano, and basil. Pulse until combined.
4. Add in the capers. Keep in the fridge for at least 60 minutes before serving with chicken

8.131 Pistachio Crusted Salmon

Servings: 4 I Time: 20 mins I Difficulty: Easy
Nutrients per serving: Calories: 298 kcal I Fat: 18g I Carbohydrates: 6g I Protein: 27g I Fiber: 2g

Ingredients

- Salt and freshly ground black pepper, to taste
- 3 tbsp. of Dijon mustard
- 3/4 cup of Pistachios, finely diced
- 16 oz. of Salmon

Method

1. Let the oven preheat to 400F.
2. Season the salmon with salt and freshly ground black pepper.
3. Spread mustard on every filet, and press in finely cut pistachios.
4. Put on an oiled baking pan and bake at 400 F for 10 to 15 minutes, until fish flakes easily and tender.
5. Serve right away and enjoy.

8.132 Grouper Caprese

Servings: 4 I Time: 25 mins I Difficulty: Easy
Nutrients per serving: Calories: 442 kcal I Fat: 18g I Carbohydrates: 3g I Protein: 63g

Ingredients

- 2 Roma Tomatoes, cut into thin slices

- 8 oz. of grated Mozzarella
- Salt and freshly ground Black Pepper
- 4 Grouper fillets
- 2 tbsp. of Pesto

Method

1. Let the oven preheat to 350 F.
2. Season the Grouper with salt and freshly ground black pepper.
3. Fry in a skillet for two minutes on every side.
4. Put on a baking sheet.
5. Rub each side with pesto, add 3 to 4 thin slices of tomatoes, top with grated cheese.
6. Bake for eight minutes in the oven.
7. Serve right away.

8.133 Roasted Shrimp with Lemon & Herb Spaghetti Squash

Servings: 4 I Time: 70 mins I Difficulty: Difficult
Nutrients per serving: Calories: 235 kcal I Fat: 10.4g I Carbohydrates: 25.7g I Protein: 9.7g I Fiber: 4.3g

Ingredients

- 12 oz. of peeled large shrimp, deveined
- 2 tbsp. of grass-fed butter
- ¼ cup of plain Greek yogurt
- Juice of one lemon
- Salt & freshly ground black pepper, to taste
- Half cup of dry white wine
- 1 tbsp. of olive oil
- ¼ tsp. of red pepper flakes
- 3 minced cloves of garlic
- 1 tsp. of lemon zest
- 2 spaghetti squash, small sized
- 2 tbsp. of chopped parsley, fresh
- 1 tsp. of Dijon mustard

Method

1. Let the oven preheat to 350 F, cut the squash in half lengthwise, take all the seeds out.
2. Put the middle side squash down on an oiled baking sheet.
3. Bake for 45 minutes at 350 F, till squash is tender.
4. In a skillet, add butter and oil on medium flame. Season the shrimp with freshly ground black pepper and salt and sauté in butter oil mixture for almost two minutes.
5. Add garlic and sauté for another two minutes until the shrimp is completely cooked, but do not overcook the shrimp. Turn off the heat and set it aside.
6. Add Dijon mustard, lemon juice, red pepper flakes, white wine, and lemon zest. Let it boil. Turn the heat low and let it simmer till the squash has completely baked. Turn off the heat.
7. Take the squash out of the oven. With a fork, scrape out the spaghetti flesh.
8. Add spaghetti squash in a strainer and let the excess water drip, carefully press with a paper towel.
9. Add yogurt in sauce, till smooth and creamy. Add in chopped fresh parsley.
10. Coat the spaghetti squash in shrimp and sauce and serve.

8.134 Skillet Salmon with Avocado & Basil

Servings: 4 I Time: 15 mins I Difficulty: Easy
Nutrients per serving: Calories: 232 kcal I Fat: 9g I Carbohydrates: 7g I Protein: 32g I Fiber: 3g

Ingredients

- 1 and a half pounds of skinless salmon filet, boneless
- 2 tsp. of coconut oil
- 1 tbsp. of lime juice
- Half tsp. of crushed red pepper

- 1 tsp. of Italian seasoning
- ¼ tsp. of freshly ground black pepper
- 1 and a half tsp. of kosher salt
- One whole avocado
- For garnish, sliced scallions
- ¼ cup of chopped basil

Method
1. In a cast-iron skillet, add oil on medium flame.
2. Season the salmon with crushed red pepper, ¾ tsp. of salt, freshly ground black pepper, Italian seasonings.
3. Place the seasoned salmon filet in oil.
4. Let it cook, do not flip until crispy and browned along the edge, cook for 4-6 minutes. Cooking time depends on thickness.
5. Flip the fish over and turn off the heat.
6. Let it cook on the other side in the heated skillet, for about four minutes or until cooked to your liking.
7. Peel and pit the avocado and mix with the rest of the salt, lime juice, and basil.
8. Serve salmon with avocado mash.
9. Top with sliced scallions and serve.

8.135 Cedar Plank Grilled Fish

Servings: 2 I Time: 20 mins I Difficulty: Easy
Nutrients per serving: Calories: 147 kcal I Fat: 5g I Carbohydrates: 2g I Protein: 23g

Ingredients
- 1 pinch of paprika
- 1 Cedar plank
- 1 Lemon, thinly sliced
- 1 pinch of garlic powder
- 3 parsley sprigs
- 1 to 2 pounds of cleaned Fish
- 1 pinch of freshly ground black pepper
- 1 tbsp. of olive oil
- 1 pinch of salt

Method
1. Let the grill preheat to high.
2. Pre-soak the plank and coat with olive oil.
3. Place the fish on the plank.
4. Season the inside of the fish with paprika, salt, garlic powder, and freshly ground black pepper.
5. Stuff the fish with parsley and thin slices of lemon.
6. Grill for 10 to 14 minutes on the covered grill.
7. Serve right away.

8.136 Balsamic Glazed Rosemary Steak Skewers

Servings: 6 I Time: 36 mins I Difficulty: Easy
Nutrients per serving: Calories: 660 kcal I Fat: 60g I Carbohydrates: 7g I Protein: 13g I Fiber: 7g

Ingredients
- Fresh Rosemary, thick stalks
- 1-pound of Grape or cherry tomatoes
- 2 and a half pounds of Sirloin steak, slice into 1 and a half-inch cubes

Marinade
- 1 tsp. of Salt
- ¼ cup of Balsamic glaze
- 1 tsp. of Dijon mustard
- ¾ cup of Vegetable oil

Method
1. In a bowl, add all ingredients of the marinade and add in a zip-lock bag.

2. Add beef to the bag and coat well. Keep in the fridge for 60 minutes or more.
3. Take leaves of rosemary stalks and leave some on the top.
4. Thread the meat on rosemary skewers with tomatoes and beef.
5. Repeat the process until the meat is gone.
6. Grill the meat for three minutes on every side until tender.

8.137 Balsamic Steak Roll-Ups

Servings: 4 I Time: 1 hour 10 mins I Difficulty: Easy
Nutrients per serving: Calories: 327 kcal I Fat: 12g I Carbohydrates: 12g I Protein: 39g I Fiber: 3g

Ingredients
- Half cup of Balsamic Vinegar (Aged)
- freshly ground black pepper, to taste
- 1 and a half pounds of Sirloin or Flank Steak
- 2 to 3 Carrots
- Salt, to taste
- Olive Oil, as needed
- 1 pound of Asparagus

Method
1. Slice the steak into three-inch of strips.
2. Place every piece in plastic wrap and pound with a mallet to 1/4 inch of thickness.
3. Put the steak in a dish and pour balsamic vinegar on top, cover with plastic wrap, let it rest for 1 to 2 hours.
4. Season the steak with freshly ground black pepper and salt.
5. Wrap the trimmed asparagus bunch in a moist paper towel and microwave for two minutes.
6. Slice carrots into thin pieces.
7. Wrap the vegetables in meat and make a roll, secure with a toothpick.
8. Make all meat rolls with vegetables.
9. In a pan, add olive oil and add steak rolls and cook for 1 to 2 minutes on each side.
10. Let it rest for five minutes before serving.

8.138 Greek Chicken Roll-Ups

Servings: 4 I Time: 30 mins I Difficulty: Easy
Nutrients per serving: Calories: 660 kcal I Fat: 60g I Carbohydrates: 7g I Protein: 13g I Fiber: 7g

Ingredients
- 2 Chicken Breasts, cut in halves
- Salt, to taste
- 4 oz. of softened Cream Cheese
- Half cup of Black Ripe Olives, chopped
- 4 oz. of Feta Cheese

Method
1. Let the oven preheat to 400 F.
2. Pound the chicken breast in plastic wrap with a mallet until they all are the same thickness.
3. In a bowl, mix ripe olives, cream cheese, and feta cheese.
4. Add 2 to 3 tbsp. of olive mix into every chicken breast piece and roll it up.
5. Put all rolls in an oiled baking pan—Bake for 20 to 30 minutes.
6. Serve right away and enjoy.

8.139 Almond Parmesan Baked Salmon

Servings: 1 I Time: 20 mins I Difficulty: Easy
Nutrients per serving: Calories: 412.8 kcal I Fat: 29.19g I Carbohydrates: 3.5g I Protein: 34.34g I Fiber: 1.48g

Ingredients
- 1 bunch of cilantro
- 3/4 cup of almond flour
- 1/3 cup of melted butter
- Salt & freshly ground black pepper, to taste

- 3/4 cup of Parmesan cheese (grated)
- 1 salmon fillet

Method

1. Let the oven preheat to 400 F.
2. Trim and clean the cilantro, cut the stems. Chop the cilantro leaves.
3. In a bowl, add almond flour, chopped cilantro, melted butter, and parmesan. Mix with a fork.
4. Place a baking paper on a baking sheet, place fish skin side down, and season with freshly ground black pepper and salt.
5. Coat the fish with parmesan mix and press with your hands on the fish.
6. Bake at 400 F for 15 minutes.
7. Serve and enjoy.

8.140 Keto Creamy Cajun Chicken

Servings: 6 I Time: 35 mins I Difficulty: Easy
Nutrients per serving: Calories: 547 kcal I Fat: 39g I Carbohydrates: 5g I Protein: 42g I Fiber: 1g

Ingredients

- 1 cup of grated parmesan
- 2 tbsp. of butter
- 2 tbsp. of avocado oil
- Blackened Seasoning
- 2 lbs. of chicken breasts, cut into cutlets
- 1 onion, cut into slices
- 1 and a half cup of heavy cream
- 3 green onions, cut into slices
- 1 bell pepper, cut into slices
- 1 and a half cup of chicken broth
- 2 minced cloves of garlic

Method

1. Season the chicken with blackened seasoning generously and set it aside.
2. In a skillet, add avocado oil and butter on medium flame.
3. Sear the chicken in batches for 3 to 4 minutes on each side until the chicken's internal temperature reaches 165 F.
4. Use a smoke vent if smoke is too much.
5. Cut the chicken into slices.
6. Add pepper and onion to the pan, cook for 2 to 3 minutes.
7. Add garlic and cook for 60 seconds more.
8. Add chicken stock to the pan and let it boil. Turn the heat low, and let it simmer for 8 to ten minutes, reduce it by half.
9. Add cream and let it simmer until it also reduces by half and becomes thick.
10. Turn the heat low, add in the cheese. Mix until cheese melts.
11. Add sliced chicken back into the sauce with its juices.
12. Serve with cheese and green onion on top.

8.141 Bacon Wrapped Chicken Diablos

Servings: 6 I Time: 40 mins I Difficulty: Easy
Nutrients per serving: Calories: 660 kcal I Fat: 60g I Carbohydrates: 7g I Protein: 13g I Fiber: 7g

Ingredients

- Six slices of smoked bacon
- 3 jalapenos, cut into halves, seeds removed
- Half purple or sweet onion, slice into 4 to 5 wedges
- 6 oz. of Pepper Jack Cheese, cut into 6 slices
- 2 to 3 chicken breast, horizontally cut into thin slices
- Your preferred seasoning rub, as needed

Method

1. Season the chicken generously with seasoning. Season the onion and peppers too.
2. Place one chicken piece on a clean surface, add cheese, onion pieces on chicken with jalapeno cut side down over cheese.
3. Roll the chicken tightly with cheese, onion, and pepper inside. With bacon, wrap around the chicken roll and close with a toothpick.
4. Keep repeating for all slices of chicken breast.
5. Now, either keep these in the fridge in a closed container or cook them right away.
6. Let the grill heat up for 15 to 20 minutes to 350 to 400 F. Grill the chicken until it is completely cooked and cheese melts.
7. You can bake the chicken at 400 F for 15 to 20 minutes.
8. Cooking time depends upon the thickness of chicken pieces.

8.142 Roasted Red Pepper & Caramelized Onion Frittata

Servings: 8-10 I Time: 1 hr I Difficulty: Medium
Nutrients per serving: Calories: 660 kcal I Fat: 60g I Carbohydrates: 7g I Protein: 13g I Fiber: 7g

Ingredients

- 1 and a half cup of shredded Fontina cheese
- 1 tbsp. of butter
- Half cup of roasted bell pepper (2 peppers)
- 2 tsp. of salt
- 1 tsp. of freshly ground black pepper
- 12 whole eggs
- Half cup of sour cream
- 2 sweet onions, large-size, cut into halves and ¼" strips

Method

1. Let the oven preheat to 350 F.
2. In a cast-iron skillet, melt the butter on medium flame, and saute onions for 40 minutes or until caramelized and soft.
3. Meanwhile, whisk the eggs with sour cream, salt, freshly ground black pepper, cheese. Mix well, but do not over whisk the eggs.
4. Spread the caramelized onions in the pan in one layer. Add roasted red pepper on caramelized onions.
5. Pour the whisked eggs over onion and peppers. Cook for 3 to 5 minutes on low flame just as eggs start to set.
6. Place the pan in the oven and bake for 15 to 17 minutes. Eggs should have a custard-like consistency.
7. Make sure to use an oven-proof skillet, and I used a 12" skillet.
8. Serve and enjoy.

8.143 Poached Cod in Tomato Sauce

Servings: 4 I Time: 25 mins I Difficulty: Easy
Nutrients per serving: Calories: 169 kcal I Fat: 1g I Carbohydrates: 7g I Protein: 34g I Fiber: 2g

Ingredients

- Kosher or sea salt, to taste
- 2 cups of marinara sauce
- 4 skinless & boneless cod fillets (6-oz.)
- ¼ cup of fresh herbs (chopped) such as basil, chives, cilantro, or Italian parsley
- Freshly ground black pepper, to taste

Method

1. Thaw the cod the whole night in the fridge if the fish is frozen. Or keep in cool water for 10 to 15 minutes.
2. With paper towels, dry the fish and season with salt.
3. In a ten-inch skillet, add 2 cups of marinara sauce. Fish should fit in one single layer in the skillet.
4. Keep the skillet on medium flame and boil the sauce. As the sauce is boiling, add fish into the sauce.
5. Turn the heat low, and let it simmer.

6. Cover the skillet and let it cook for 5-8 minutes or until fish flakes easily.
7. The internal temperature of fish should be 130 to 140 F with a meat thermometer.
8. Sprinkle fresh herbs and freshly ground black pepper on fish.
9. Serve right away with rice or sautéed vegetables.

8.144 Inst. Pot Zucchini Bolognese

Servings: 4 I Time: 1 hr I Difficulty: Difficult
Nutrients per serving: Calories: 498 kcal I Fat: 43g I Carbohydrates: 9g I Protein: 19g I Fiber: 2g

Ingredients

- 3 minced cloves of garlic
- 1 yellow, large-sized onion, diced
- 2 tbsp. of avocado oil or olive oil
- 1 and a half pounds of zucchini chopped into half" pieces
- 1 pound of Italian sausage (bulk)
- Juice from half lemon
- Magic Mushroom Powder, 1 tsp.

Method

1. Turn on the function of sauteing in the Inst. Pot, then add in the olive oil.
2. Add in the chopped onion and cook for 2-3 minutes, keep stirring, until onion softens.
3. Add sausage and break it up with a spoon. Cook until it is cooked through.
4. Add in garlic, zucchini, magic mushroom powder. Mix it well.
5. Do not add any liquid; zucchini will have some liquid of its own.
6. Lock the Inst. Pot, and cook for 35 minutes under high pressure.
7. Let the pressure release on its own, or manually vent.
8. Vegetables should be soft; mash with a spoon to make the sauce chunky.
9. Taste and adjust the seasoning of the sauce with salt, black pepper, or mushroom powder.
10. Add in the lemon juice. Season it again if required.
11. Make the noodles from zucchini in a spiralizer. Add the spiralized noodles to the sauce and coat them well.
12. Sprinkle with herbs and serve.
13. You can freeze the sauce also, for later use.

8.145 Lemon Garlic Chicken Parchment Packets

Servings: 4 I Time: 30 mins I Difficulty: Medium
Nutrients per serving: Calories: 425 kcal I Fat: 27g I Carbohydrates: 11g I Protein: 36g I Fiber: 3g

Ingredients

- 2 minced garlic cloves
- ⅓ cup of olive oil
- Freshly cracked black pepper, to taste
- ¼ cup of lemon juice (freshly squeezed)
- 1 shallot large-size cut into thin slices
- Kosher salt, to taste
- 4 skinless chicken boneless breasts or thighs (almost 6 oz. each)
- 1 and a half tsp. of dried oregano
- 8 tomatoes (cherry) slice in half
- 4 summer squash medium-sized, cut into thin coin
- 8 green olives, pitted, sliced in half

Method

1. Let the oven preheat to 450 F.
2. In a bowl, mix kosher salt, olive oil, ¼ tsp. freshly ground black pepper, lemon juice, oregano, and minced garlic.

3. Add the meat and coat well, and let it rest for ten minutes or 2 hours. Do not marinate for more than that.
4. Take four sheets of parchment paper and double in half. Make one side of the heart on it. Cut it so one will get full hearts.
5. Lay these hearts on a flat surface. Add ¼ of Zucchini or summer squash on each side of the heart. Add onion rings to it and season with freshly ground black pepper and salt.
6. Put one chicken piece over the vegetables, and pour 2 tbsp. of the marinade on the chicken.
7. Add ¼ of cherry tomatoes and olives over them. Do the same for the rest of the packets.
8. Place the other half of the heart over the chicken and fold the edges tightly.
9. On a baking sheet, place the packets in one layer.
10. Bake for 15 to 20 minutes, until the internal temperature of the chicken shows 165 F.
11. Cut the packet to release the steam and serve right away and enjoy.

8.146 Rack of Lamb

Servings: 4 I Time: 1 day 55 mins I Difficulty: Difficult
Nutrients per serving: Calories: 417 kcal I Fat: 32g I Carbohydrates: 3g I Protein: 30g I Fiber: 1g

Ingredients

- 4 minced cloves of garlic
- 2 lamb racks French cut almost 1 and a half pounds of each rack
- ⅓ cup of olive oil (extra virgin)
- Half tsp. of freshly cracked black pepper
- 3 tbsp. of lemon juice
- 2 tsp. of kosher salt
- 1 tbsp. of oregano (dried)

Method

1. Clean the extra fat from the rack of lamb, only leave a thin layer.
2. Coat the rack of lamb in salt and keep it in the fridge overnight or for 3 days.
3. In a bowl, mix garlic, freshly cracked black pepper, olive oil, lemon juice, and oregano.
4. Coat the rack of lamb in marinade mix and keep in the fridge for 1 to 12 hours.
5. Let the oven preheat to 275 F, put the marinated rack of lamb on a baking sheet, and place in the middle rack in the oven.
6. Bake for 30 to 45 minutes, for medium-rare, until internal temperature shows 125°F.
7. Take the meat out and turn the broiler on to the highest temperature.
8. Broil the rack of lamb for five minutes, so the outside is browned well.
9. Slice and serve the meat after 10 minutes of resting the meat.

8.147 Crab & Avocado Temaki

Servings: 4 I Time: 20 mins I Difficulty: Easy
Nutrients per serving: Calories: 256 kcal I Fat: 15g I Carbohydrates: 7g I Protein: 23g I Fiber: 4g

Ingredients

- 1 pound of lump crab meat (cooked)
- 2 small size cucumbers slice into thin pieces
- Freshly cracked black pepper, to taste
- 8 nori sheets (toasted)
- 1 avocado large-sized, peeled & pitted, cut into thin slices
- 2 tbsp. of mayonnaise (paleo)
- Half tsp. of red pepper flakes (it is optional)
- 2 scallions cut into thin slices

- One and a half tbsp. of sesame seeds (toasted)
- 1 tbsp. of lime juice
- Diamond Crystal Kosher salt, to taste
- 1 cup of microgreens

Method

1. If you are busy and want to prepare this dish quickly, then skip this next step, but if you have time, make sure to follow it because even toasted nori sheets taste amazing when heated.
2. Heat every sheet of nori on the gas burner on medium to low flame, gradually fan it back and forth until they become bright green.
3. If one does not have a gas burner, make sure to use the oven. Switch on the broiler
   and place the rack almost six inches away from the heating source. Put 2 sheets of nori on the rimmed baking sheet and place them in the oven for about ten seconds or till they turn green and smell fragrant.
4. Slice every toasted sheet of nori in two pieces so that one will have 16 pieces of nori sheets that are toasted.
5. In a mixing bowl, add the mayonnaise, crab meat, lime juice, red pepper flakes, and scallions. Taste and adjust seasoning with salt and freshly ground black pepper to your liking. Mix well and set it aside.
6. To make nori rolls, place a piece of nori, shiny side down and place 2 tbsp. of crab mix on nori piece and, filling needs to be diagonal, from the top side of left to the center of the bottom of the sheet.
7. Add the slice of avocado on top of crab meat, sprouts, and cucumber. Roll the sheet around the vegetables and crab meat in a shape to make a cone.
8. Add sesame seeds on top; toast them if they are not toasted.
9. Serve right away so the nori will not get soft, and you will get crispy bites of nori vegetable crab meat rolls.

8.148 Pork Stew Inst. Pot

Servings: 6 I Time: 1 hr I Difficulty: Difficult
Nutrients per serving: Calories: 335 kcal I Fat: 14g I Carbohydrates: 15g I Protein: 35g I Fiber: 6g

Ingredients

- 3 and a half pounds of pork shoulder, sliced into 1 and a half-inch of cubes
- 1 onion large-sized, cut into thin slices
- 6 cloves of garlic peeled & smashed
- 1 tbsp. of olive oil (extra virgin) or ghee or avocado oil
- 1 tbsp. of balsamic vinegar (aged)
- 1 tbsp. of Mushroom Magic Powder or Crystal Diamond kosher salt
- ¼ cup of Italian parsley, finely chopped, it is optional
- 3 carrots, medium size, cut into two-inch of chunks
- 1 cup of marinara sauce
- 1 cabbage, small size, cut into eight wedges
- Diamond Crystal kosher salt, to taste
- Freshly ground black pepper, to taste
- 1 tsp. of fish sauce (Red Boat)

Method

1. In the Inst. Pot, Turn on the function of sautéing. As the inserted metal gets hot, add in the oil of your choice.
2. Add in onions, and saute till tender or fragrant.
3. Add in the smashed garlic and keep stirring until fragrant, for almost 30 seconds. Make sure not to burn it.
4. Add in the pieces of pork, and add the fish sauce and Mushroom magic powder.
5. Make sure to mix well to season the meat.
6. Add in marinara sauce over the top of the cubed pork pieces, do not mix it. Maybe a few of the recent Inst. Pots

will tell you a "Burn" message (error) if the marina sauce starts to scald.
7. Now switch off the function of sautéing. Cook for 30 to 35 minutes with the lid locked and on high pressure.
8. As the pork gets done cooking. Let the pressure release manually or let it release naturally; it is your choice.
9. Add cabbage and the carrots to the Inst. Pot and cook for three minutes on high pressure
10. Again release the pressure naturally or manually and add in the aged balsamic vinegar.
11. Taste and adjust the seasoning of the stew and adjust with freshly ground black pepper and salt if required.
12. Garnish the stew with Italian parsley freshly chopped. Serve and enjoy.

8.149 Sonoran Hot Dogs

Servings: 4 I Time: 30 mins I Difficulty: Easy
Nutrients per serving: Calories: 263 kcal I Fat: 19g I Carbohydrates: 13g I Protein: 12g I Fiber: 5g

Ingredients

- 4 sugar-free hot dogs if you are on a Whole30
- 8 lettuce butter leaves
- 1 bell pepper (red) or other colors, cut into thin slices
- 1 Hass avocado large size, peeled & cut into thin slices
- 1 onion, large size, cut into thin slices
- 4 slices of bacon sugar-free if you are on a Whole30
- Crystal Diamond kosher salt
- Half cup of pico de gallo or salsa of your choice

Method

1. Wrap every hot dog in one strip of sugar-free bacon in one later, tuck the bacon strips' ends so it would not get open every time.
2. Take a 12-inch cast-iron skillet and place it on medium flame. As it gets hot, put hot dogs wrapped in bacon strips in the center of the skillet.
3. Pan-fry the bacon-wrapped hot dogs until the bacon becomes browned. Flip to the other side and brown on the other side as well.
4. Add in the bell peppers and onions all over the hot dogs and in any space available.
5. Season with salt, vegetables, and hot dogs.
6. Keep browning the bacon-wrapped hot dogs, onions, and bell peppers, to make sure they cook evenly.
7. It will be ready when bacon is browned and slightly crispy, onion and bell peppers are caramelized and tender.
8. Serve these bacon-wrapped hot dogs, onion, and bell pepper in lettuce butter leaves.
9. Garnish with your choice of salsa or pico de gallo and thinly cut avocado slices.
10. Serve and enjoy.

8.150 Vegetable Soup in Inst. Pot

Servings: 4 I Time: 15 mins I Difficulty: Easy
Nutrients per serving: Calories: 205 kcal I Fat: 1g I Carbohydrates: 14g I Protein: 39g I Fiber: 4g

Ingredients

- 1 russet potato, medium-sized, cut into one inch of cubes
- 6 cups of Bone Broth or chicken broth (Inst. Pot)
- 1 shallot, large-sized, cut into thin slices
- 2 carrots, medium-sized, peeled & cut into ¼ inch of coins
- 3 shiitake mushrooms (dried)
- 1 tsp. of fish sauce (Red Boat)
- 2 scallions cut into thin slices
- 1 pound of baby bok choy trim the ends, & cut in half or in quartered, if too large
- 2 minced cloves of garlic
- Crystal Diamond kosher salt

Method

1. In the Inst. Pot, add in the bone broth when the metal insert turns hot.
2. Add in the shallots, carrots, and potatoes. Do not splash yourself. Add in fish sauce (red boat), shiitake mushrooms, and garlic. Add in the quartered bok choy.
3. Cook for 2 minutes, with the lid locked of Inst. Pot on high pressure.
4. As the soup gets done cooking, release the pressure naturally or manually, your choice.
5. Taste and adjust seasoning with fish sauce and salt as needed.
6. Take the soup out in the bowl, garnish with scallions.
7. Serve and enjoy this delicious soup.

8.151 Tandoori Shrimp

Servings: 4 I Time: 30 mins I Difficulty: Easy
Nutrients per serving: Calories: 247 kcal I Fat: 9g I Carbohydrates: 7g I Protein: 36g I Fiber: 3g

Ingredients

- Half cup of coconut milk (full-fat) or coconut yogurt (plain)
- 1 and a half pounds of shrimp (21 to 25 shrimps) peeled & deveined
- ¼ cup roughly chopped fresh cilantro
- 1 tbsp. of spice tandoori mix (make sure no salt is added)
- 1 tbsp. of freshly squeezed lemon juice
- 2 limes, slice into thin wedges
- Half tsp. of Crystal Diamond kosher salt

Method

1. Thaw the shrimps, if they are frozen in running water for 6 to 7 minutes, or until they thaw slightly. Clean the shrimps if they have not been cleaned before.
2. In a mixing bowl, add coconut milk, crystal Diamond kosher salt, freshly squeezed lemon juice, and spice Tandoori mix. Mix well and set it aside. If using shake up bottle, shake and take out a half cup of marinade.
3. Toss the cleaned shrimps in marinade well. Keep the marinated shrimps in the fridge for half an hour.
4. Let the oven preheat to 400 F with the middle rack.
5. Place the marinated shrimps in one even layer on the parchment-lined baking rimmed sheet.
6. Roast for 7 to 8 minutes in the oven; flip the shrimps halfway through.
7. Cooking time depends upon the size of shrimps. Even smaller shrimps will take five minutes to cook.
8. Serve the tandoori shrimps with lime wedges and top with roughly chopped fresh cilantro and few drops of lemon juice.
9. Serve and enjoy these delicious tandoori shrimps with rice.

8.152 Vietnamese Pork Stew in Inst. Pot

Servings: 8 I Time: 1 hr 25 mins I Difficulty: Easy
Nutrients per serving: Calories: 500 kcal I Fat: 34g I Carbohydrates: 6g I Protein: 41g I Fiber: 2g

Ingredients

- ¼ cup of shallots, cut into thin slices
- 3 scallions cut into thin slices
- 1 tbsp. of avocado oil, ghee, or coconut oil
- 4 cloves of garlic peeled & smashed
- 1 cup of coconut water
- ¼ pound of shiitake mushrooms cut the stems & slice in half or in quarters if they are too large
- 3 large size peeled carrots, slice into half-inch slices (diagonal)
- 3 tbsp. of fish sauce and add more if needed
- Half cup of fresh cilantro leaves
- 3 quarter size fresh slices of peeled ginger

- 3 pounds of pork shoulder slice into two" cubes

Method

1. In the Inst. Pot, turn on the function of sauteing; when the inserted metal is hot, add in the oil of your preference.
2. Add in shiitake mushrooms, shallots. Cook for about 4 to 5 minutes or until the vegetables are tender.
3. Add in garlic, ginger and cook for 4 to 5 minutes.
4. Add in the meat cubes and mix it well.
5. Add in fish sauce and coconut water.
6. Mix well, scrape the bottom of the browned bits of the Inst. Pot.
7. Turn off the function of sauteing. Lock the Inst. Pot's lids, and let it cook for 40 minutes under high pressure.
8. As it is cooked. Let the pressure release naturally or release it manually after 15 minutes.
9. The pork should be tender that it should be flake with a fork. If it does not flake easily, let it cook for 7 to 10 minutes more in high pressure.
10. Taste it and add more seasoning, salt, and fish sauce if required.
11. Keep the pork warm on a serving platter, cover it so it will remain warm.
12. Add the carrots gently to the cooking liquid so you will not splash yourself.
13. Let it cook for two minutes at high pressure.
14. Release the pressure manually or naturally, then carefully remove the lid of the Inst. Pot.
15. Take out the cooking liquid and carrots with the pork.
16. Serve with scallion slices and fresh chopped cilantro and enjoy.

8.153 Sheet Pan Meatballs & Broccolini

Servings: 6 I Time: 40 mins I Difficulty: Medium
Nutrients per serving: Calories: 531 kcal I Fat: 43g I Carbohydrates: 11g I Protein: 31g I Fiber: 3g

Ingredients

- 1 and a half cups of marinara sauce
- 2 tbsp. of avocado oil or extra virgin olive oil
- 1 and a half pounds of bulk Italian sausage, please ensure it is Whole30 suitable
- 1 pound of broccolini with trimmed ends
- 1 tsp. of Mushroom Magic Powder or Crystal Diamond kosher salt

Method

1. Let the oven preheat to 400 F or 425 F convection bake, with a middle rack.
2. Toss the broccolini with mushroom magic powder and olive oil and place on a rimmed baking sheet. Or use 1 tsp. of crystal diamond kosher salt instead of mushroom powder or half tsp. of fine grain salt.
3. Place the seasoned broccolini on a baking sheet in one even layer.
4. Make some meatballs from bulk Italian sausage. Get the meat out of links by piercing it with a fork or knife.
5. Make same size meatballs; it will make 24 meatballs that should be one and a half-inch in diameter.
6. Place the meatballs in space available around and the broccolini on a rimmed baking sheet.
7. Place the rimmed baking sheet in the oven. Roast the broccolini and meatballs until meatballs are cooked through or for 18 to 20 minutes.
8. Broccolini should be charred in some places.
9. After 7 to 10 minutes, rotate the baking tray to make sure, cooking is even.
10. Meanwhile, in a pan, heat the marinara sauce or a microwave-safe container in a microwave.
11. Take out the meatballs, and pour over the hot marinara sauce.
12. Serve right away with rice and enjoy.

8.154 Inst. Pot Orange Duck & Gravy

Servings: 4 I Time: 1 hr 30 mins I Difficulty: Easy
Nutrients per serving: Calories: 491 kcal I Fat: 27g I Carbohydrates: 11g I Protein: 49g I Fiber: 2g

Ingredients

- Kosher salt (Diamond Crystal), to taste
- Half tsp. of herbs de Provence
- ¼ tsp. of freshly cracked black pepper
- 4 legs' of duck
- 2 tbsp. of avocado oil, or ghee duck fat divided
- 1 yellow, medium-sized onion, chopped
- 1 celery rib, medium-sized, finely diced
- 1 carrot, large-sized, diced
- 8 cloves of garlic, peeled and smashed
- 1 tbsp. of tomato paste
- Half cup of chicken stock or bone broth
- 1 navel orange, medium-sized
- 2 tbsp. of Italian parsley, roughly chopped
- 1 bay leaf, dried
- 1 sprig of thyme, fresh

Method

1. In a mixing bowl, mix herbes de Provence, freshly cracked black pepper, one and a half tsp. of crystal diamond kosher salt.
2. With paper towels, dry the duck's legs, and coat with the seasoning mix you prepared earlier.
3. In the Inst. Pot, turn the sauteed function on, and add one tbsp. of oil in it.
4. Once the oil is hot, add diced carrots, onions, celery half tsp. of crystal diamond kosher salt. Keep stirring and cook until vegetables are tender for 3-5 minutes.
5. Add in tomato paste and garlic. Keep stirring and cook for 30 seconds, until garlic becomes fragrant.
6. Add in the bone broth, scrape the bottom for browned bits.
7. Peel the orange with a peeler and add in orange zest strips, but do not peel too deeply so that the bitter part would not be peeled.
8. Squeeze the orange juice in the Inst. Pot.
9. Add thyme, parsley, and bay leaf. Mix well, and turn the saute function off.
10. Add the duck legs (seasoned) in the Inst. Pot, in one even layer, on vegetables. Make sure the duck is skin side up.
11. Lock the Inst. Pot's lid, keep it in a sealed arrangement. Let it cook under high pressure for 40-45 minutes.
12. Drop the high pressure naturally of the Inst. Pot as the duck has cooked through.
13. One can release the pressure manually after 18 to 20 minutes.
14. Take the duck legs out carefully. It should be very tender that you can break apparat with a fork, so handle it gently.
15. You can serve it right away or keep it safe in a sealed container for four days and serve as you want.
16. Take out the orange zest, sprig of thyme, bay leaf. With an immersion blender, puree the rest of the sauce to turn into a thick gravy.
17. Taste and adjust seasoning with crystal diamond kosher salt and freshly ground black pepper.
18. It will make lots of gravy, so store in the freezer in ice cube trays, and use up to four months.
19. After patting them dry with paper towels, cook the meat in a cast-iron skillet on medium flame.
20. Add oil to the hot cast-iron skillet. Add legs of duck, skin side down, and pan-fry them for 2 to 3 minutes, until the skin is lightly browned and crispy.
21. Now flip the duck legs over and let them golden brown on the flip side.
22. If you do not like the frying option. One can broil the duck legs (it will not make the skin as crispy as with frying)
23. The broiling method: turn the broiler on, and place the duck legs on the middle rack in a rimmed baking sheet, place the skip side up.
24. Broil the duck legs for 5 to 10 minutes until the skin is golden brown.
25. Now serve the duck legs with thick delicious gravy. Enjoy.

8.155 Tandoori Fish

Servings: 4 I Time: 40 mins I Difficulty: Medium
Nutrients per serving: Calories: 357 kcal I Fat: 19g I Carbohydrates: 7g I Protein: 29g I Fiber: 2g

Ingredients

- 1 tsp. of kosher salt (Diamond Crystal) or half tsp. of a fine grain salt
- 4 white fish fillets (such as sea bass or cod, 6-ounce each)
- 1 lemon cut into thin wedges
- 1 tbsp. of spice tandoori mix (make sure to get no salt added)
- 1 tbsp. of lemon juice (freshly squeezed)
- Half cup of coconut yogurt or plain coconut cream, or coconut milk (full-fat)

Method

1. With a paper towel, dab the fillets dry.
2. Season with salt on every side of fish fillets.
3. In a bowl, mix freshly squeezed lemon juice, plain yogurt, spice tandoori mix.
4. Mix well, or shake in a glass bottle and take out a half cup of marinade.
5. Coat the seasoned fish fillet in marinade well. Keep in the fridge for 20 minutes to 60 minutes. (One can skip this part and cook the fish right away).
6. Let the oven preheat to 400 F with the middle rack.
7. On a rimmed baking sheet, place a sheet of parchment paper.
8. Place all four fish fillets on them.
9. Place the baking sheet in the oven on the middle rack and cook for 8 to 15 minutes or until the internal temperature of fish fillets shows 145 F. (cooking time depends on the thickness of fish fillet)
10. Fish should be flaky and opaque, and it should come apart easily with the fork.
11. As one" fish fillet takes almost ten minutes to cook and thinner fillets than that will cook faster.
12. Serve the fish right away with sautéed vegetables and thin lemon wedges.
13. I served mine over cauliflower rice and micro salad, vegetables.

Chapter 9 – Keto-Friendly Beverages

Most of the drinks contain a high amount of sugar and carbs restricted in the keto diet because they have been proven to be related to many health problems, including diabetes and obesity. But no worries, here you can find several keto-friendly and sugar-free yet flavorful options to try.

9.1 Coffee With Cream

Servings: 1 I Time: 5 mins I Difficulty: Easy
Nutrients per serving: Calories: 203 kcal I Fat: 21g I Carbohydrates: 2g I Protein: 2g I Fiber: 0g

Ingredients
- 1/4 Cup Heavy Whipping Cream
- 2 Tbsps. Nuts, Crushed (Optional)
- 3/4 Cup Brewed Coffee

Method
1. Brew your coffee according to your preference.
2. Slightly heat the cream in a pan and stir till it becomes frothy.
3. Take a cup and mix the warm cream and coffee in it.
4. Serve hot with crushed nuts on top or as it is.

9.2 Keto Coffee

Servings: 2 I Time: 5 mins I Difficulty: Easy
Nutrients per serving: Calories: 260 kcal I Fat: 27.7g I Carbohydrates: 1.05g I Protein: 1.08g I Fiber: 0g

Ingredients
- 2 Tbsps. Coconut Oil Or MCT Oil
- 2 Tbsps. Butter, Unsalted (Grass-Fed)
- 2 Cups Brewed Coffee
- 1 Tsp. Vanilla Extract (Optional)
- 1 Tbsp. Heavy Whipping Cream (Optional)

Method
1. Brew your coffee according to your preference.
2. Blend the coffee with unsalted butter, coconut or MCT oil, vanilla extract, and whipping cream if you want, in a blender for about a minute or until it becomes frothy.
3. Pour out the keto coffee in your favorite mugs and enjoy.

9.3 Vegan Keto Golden Milk

Servings: 1 I Time: 5 mins I Difficulty: Easy
Nutrients per serving: Calories: 303 kcal I Fat: 31.1g I Carbohydrates: 2.7g I Protein: 2.1g I Fiber: 2g

Ingredients
- 2 Tsps. Ginger, Fresh & Peeled
- 2 Tbsps. MCT Oil
- 1 & 1/2 Cup Almond Milk, Unsweetened
- 2 Tsps. Erythritol
- 1/4 Tsp. Cinnamon, Ground
- 2 Ice Cubes
- 3/4 Tsp. Turmeric Powder
- 1/4 Tsp. Vanilla Extract
- Sea Salt, To Taste

Method
1. Combine all the ingredients in a blender and mix for about a quarter or half a minute.
2. For the strong taste of turmeric and ginger, blend longer.
3. Decant into the glass or mug and sprinkle powdered cinnamon on top before serving.

9.4 Keto Creamy Chocolate Smoothie

Servings: 2 I Time: 10 mins I Difficulty: Easy
Nutrients per serving: Calories: 593.3 kcal I Fat: 55.7g I Carbohydrates: 7.7g I Protein: 10.6g I Fiber: 11.7g

Ingredients
- 1 Tbsp. Almond Butter
- 1 Tsp. Coconut Oil
- 1/2 Avocado
- 1 Tbsp. Flax Meal
- 1 & 1/4 Cups Almond Milk, Unsweetened
- 1 Tbsp. Cocoa Powder, Unsweetened
- 1/4 Cup Heavy Whipping Cream
- Liquid Stevia, To Taste

Method
1. Combine all the ingredients in a blender and mix until a smooth consistency is attained.
2. Decant into the serving glass and top with cocoa powdered and whipped cream if you want.

9.5 Keto Pumpkin Pie Spice Latte

Servings: 3 I Time: 10 mins I Difficulty: Easy
Nutrients per serving: Calories: 136.28 kcal I Fat: 19.83g I Carbohydrates: 2.49g I Protein: 0.68g I Fiber: 1.79g

Ingredients
- 2 Tbsps. Butter
- 1/2 Tsp. Cinnamon, Powdered
- 1 Cup Coconut Milk
- 2 Cups Brewed Coffee
- 2 Tsps. Pumpkin Pie Spice
- 1/4 Cup Pumpkin Puree
- 1 Tsp. Vanilla Extract
- 2 Tbsps. Heavy Whipping Cream
- 15 Drops Liquid Stevia

Method
1. Pour the coconut milk, butter, pumpkin puree, and spices into a small saucepan and heat over a medium-low flame.
2. Once the mixture starts to bubble, add the coffee, and mix well.

3. Remove from the heat and add the whipped cream and liquid Stevia. Mix well to blend the contents until frothy.
4. Decant in the serving mug and a dollop of whipped cream on top.

9.6 Blueberry Banana Bread Smoothie

Servings: 2 I Time: 10 mins I Difficulty: Easy
Nutrients per serving: Calories: 270 kcal I Fat: 23.31g I Carbohydrates: 4.66g I Protein: 3.13g I Fiber: 5.65g

Ingredients

- 1/4 Cup Blueberries
- 2 Tbsps. MCT Oil
- 2 1 & 1/2 Tsps. Banana Extract
- Cups Vanilla Coconut Milk, Unsweetened
- 1 Tbsp. Chia Seeds
- 3 Tbsps. Golden Flaxseed Meal
- 10 Drop Liquid Stevia
- 1/4 Tsp. Xanthan Gum

Method

1. Combine all the ingredients in a blender and let it sit for a few minutes to allow the chia and flax seeds to soak some moisture.
2. Then blend for a minute or two until a smooth consistency is attained.
3. Serve in the glasses and enjoy.

9.7 Blackberry Chocolate Shake

Servings: 2 I Time: 5 mins I Difficulty: Easy
Nutrients per serving: Calories: 346 kcal I Fat: 34.17g I Carbohydrates: 4.8g I Protein: 2.62g I Fiber: 7.4g

Ingredients

- 1/4 Cup Blackberries
- 2 Tbsps. MCT Oil
- 1 Cup Coconut Milk, Unsweetened
- 1/4 Tsp. Xanthan Gum
- 2 Tbsps. Cocoa Powder
- 12 Drops Liquid Stevia
- 7 Ice Cubes

Method

1. Combine all the ingredients in a blender and blend for a minute or two until a smooth consistency is attained.
2. Serve in the glasses and enjoy.

9.8 Dairy-Free Dark Chocolate Shake

Servings: 2 I Time: 5 mins I Difficulty: Easy
Nutrients per serving: Calories: 349.35 kcal I Fat: 33.15g I Carbohydrates: 5.73g I Protein: 7.2g I Fiber: 6.1g

Ingredients

- 1/2 Avocado
- 1/2 Cup Coconut Cream, Chilled
- 2 Tbsps. Hulled Hemp Seeds
- 2 Tbsps. Dark Chocolate (Low Carb)
- 1/2 Cup Almond Milk
- 1 Tbsp. Cocoa Powder
- 2 Tbsps. Powdered Erythritol, To Taste
- Flake Salt, To Taste
- 1 Cup Ice

Method

1. Put the cocoa powder, hemp seeds, erythritol, and dark chocolate in a blender and mix until the chocolate is chopped.
2. Add the remaining ingredients and blend for a minute or two until a smooth consistency is attained.
3. Pour in the serving glasses and enjoy.

9.9 Keto Meal Replacement Shake

Servings: 2 I Time: 5 mins I Difficulty: Easy
Nutrients per serving: Calories: 453 kcal I Fat: 42.6g I Carbohydrates: 6.9g I Protein: 8.8g I Fiber: 8.1g

Ingredients

- 1/2 Avocado
- 2 Tbsps. Almond Butter
- 1 Cup Almond Or Coconut Milk, Unsweetened
- 1/4 Tsp. Vanilla Extract
- 1/2 Tsp. Cinnamon, Powdered
- 2 Tbsps. Golden Flaxseed Meal
- 1/8 Tsp. Salt
- 2 Tbsp. Cocoa Powder
- 1/2 Cup Heavy Cream
- 15 Drops Liquid Stevia
- 8 Ice Cubes

Method

1. Combine all the ingredients in a blender and blend for a minute or two until a smooth consistency is attained.
2. Serve in the glasses and enjoy.

9.10 Keto Iced Coffee

Servings: 1 I Time: 5 mins I Difficulty: Easy
Nutrients per serving: Calories: 160 kcal I Fat: 16.1g I Carbohydrates: 1.5g I Protein: 1.6g I Fiber: 0g

Ingredients

- 3 Tbsps. Heavy Cream
- 5 Drops Liquid Stevia
- 1 Cup Brewed Coffee
- 1/2 Tsp. Vanilla Extract (Optional)
- Ice Cubes, To Taste

Method

1. Brew your coffee according to your preference and let it cool down to room temperature.
2. Combine the coffee with all the other ingredients in a blender and blend for about a minute or until it becomes frothy.
3. Pour the iced coffee in your favorite mug and enjoy.

9.11 Low-Carb Ginger Smoothie

Servings: 2 I Time: 5 mins I Difficulty: Easy
Nutrients per serving: Calories: 83 kcal I Fat: 8g I Carbohydrates: 3g I Protein: 1g I Fiber: 1g

Ingredients

- 2 Tbsps. Spinach, Frozen
- 1/3 Cup Coconut Milk Or Cream, Unsweetened
- 2 Tsps. Ginger, Fresh & Grated
- 2 Tbsps. Lime Juice, Divided
- 2/3 Cup Water

For Garnishing

- 1/2 Tsp. Fresh Ginger, Grated

Method

1. Combine all the ingredients in a blender and adjust the lime juice amount as per your taste.
2. Blend the mixture for a minute or until a smooth consistency is attained.
3. Serve with grated ginger on top.

9.12 Whipped Dairy-Free Low-Carb Dalgona Coffee

Servings: 2 I Time: 5 mins I Difficulty: Easy
Nutrients per serving: Calories: 40 kcal I Fat: 2g I Carbohydrates: 1g I Protein: 1g I Fiber: 1g

Ingredients

- 2 Tbsps. Water, Hot
- 1 & 1/2 Cups Coconut Or Almond Milk, Unsweetened
- 1 & 1/2 Tbsps. Erythritol
- 1 & 1/2 Tbsps. Espresso Instant Coffee Powder
- 1/2 Cup Ice Cubes
- 1 Tsp. Vanilla Extract (Optional)

Method

1. Take a narrow glass and combine the coffee powder, hot water, and erythritol in it and blend them well with an immersion blender for about 3 minutes or till the mixture becomes creamy and light in color.
2. Take two glasses, fill two-third of them with ice and then pour the almond or coconut milk in it along with vanilla extract if you want. Mix them well.
3. Put the spoonful of the creamy coffee mixture on the top of each glass and stir before serving.

9.13 Keto Eggnog

Servings: 4 I Time: 10 mins I Difficulty: Easy
Nutrients per serving: Calories: 249 kcal I Fat: 24g I Carbohydrates: 6g I Protein: 3g I Fiber: 1g

Ingredients

- 1/4 Cup Orange Juice
- 2 Egg Yolks
- 1/2 Tbsp. Orange Zest
- 1/4 Tbsp. Vanilla
- 1/2 Tsp. Erythritol, Powdered
- 1/8 Tsp. Nutmeg, Ground
- 1 Cup Heavy Whipping Cream
- 4 Tbsps. Bourbon Or Brandy (Optional)

Method

1. Combine egg yolks, vanilla extract, and erythritol in a deep bowl and whisk the mixture well until it becomes fluffy.
2. Add in the orange juice, orange zest, and whipping cream. Mix well until a smooth consistency is attained.
3. Pour the eggnog n the serving glasses and refrigerate for about 15 minutes.
4. Finally, serve with a sprinkle of nutmeg on top.

9.14 Iced Tea

Servings: 2 I Time: 2 hrs. & 10 mins I Difficulty: Easy
Nutrients per serving: Calories: 0 kcal I Fat: 0g I Carbohydrates: 0g I Protein: 0g I Fiber: 0g

Ingredients

- 1 Tea Bag
- 2 Cups Cold Water
- 1 Cup Ice Cubes
- 1/3 Cup Sliced Lemon or Fresh Mint Leaves

Method

1. Put the teabag and lemon slices or mint leaves in a cup of cold water in a pitcher and put in the refrigerator for an hour or two.
2. Take the tea bag, and lemon slices or mint leaves out of the water. Substitute them with new ones if you want.
3. Pour in another cup of water and ice cubes in the pitcher and serve.

9.15 Flavored Water

Servings: 4 I Time: 5 mins I Difficulty: Easy
Nutrients per serving: Calories: 0 kcal I Fat: 0g I Carbohydrates: 0g I Protein: 0g I Fiber: 0g

Ingredients

- 2 Cups Ice Cubes
- Flavoring, e.g., Fresh Mint Or Raspberries, Or Sliced Cucumber

- 4 Cups Cold Water

Method

1. Take a pitcher and add cold water along with flavorings in it.
2. Refrigerate it for about 30 minutes and then serve.

9.16 Butter Coffee

Servings: 1 I Time: 5 mins I Difficulty: Easy
Nutrients per serving: Calories: 0 kcal I Fat: 37g I Carbohydrates: 0g I Protein: 1g I Fiber: 0g

Ingredients

- 2 Tbsps. Butter, Unsalted
- 1 Tbsp. Coconut Or MCT Oil
- 1 Cup Freshly Brewed Coffee, Hot

Method

1. Brew your coffee according to your preference, and let it cool down a bit.
2. Combine the coffee with all the other ingredients in a blender and blend for about a minute or until it becomes frothy.
3. Pour the butter coffee in your favorite mug and enjoy.

9.17 Keto Hot Chocolate

Servings: 1 I Time: 5 mins I Difficulty: Easy
Nutrients per serving: Calories: 216 kcal I Fat: 23g I Carbohydrates: 1g I Protein: 1g I Fiber: 2g

Ingredients

- 1 Cup Boiling Water
- 2 & 1/2 Tsps. Powdered Erythritol
- 2 Tbsps. Butter, Unsalted
- 1/4 Tsp. Vanilla Extract
- 1 Tbsp. Cocoa Powder

Method

1. Combine all the ingredients in a full-sized mug and blend well with an immersion blender until it becomes frothy.
2. Serve hot and enjoy.

9.18 Dairy-Free Keto Latte

Servings: 2 I Time: 5 mins I Difficulty: Easy
Nutrients per serving: Calories: 191 kcal I Fat: 18g I Carbohydrates: 1g I Protein: 6g I Fiber: 0g

Ingredients

- 1 & 1/2 Cups Boiling Water
- 2 Tbsps. Coconut Oil
- 1 Tsp. Ground Ginger Or Pumpkin Pie Spice
- 2 Eggs
- 1/8 Tsp. Vanilla Extract

Method

1. Combine all the ingredients in a blender and blend for a few seconds.
2. Do not let the eggs cook in the boiling water and serve instantly.

9.19 Low-Carb Vegan Vanilla Protein Shake

Servings: 1 I Time: 10 mins I Difficulty: Easy
Nutrients per serving: Calories: 449 kcal I Fat: 34g I Carbohydrates: 8g I Protein: 28g I Fiber: 4g

Ingredients

- 4 Tbsps. Pea Protein Powder, Unflavored
- 1/2 Cup Almond Milk, Unsweetened
- 2 Tbsps. Cauliflower Rice, Frozen
- 1 Tbsp. Almond Butter
- 1/2 Cup Coconut Milk
- 1 Tsp. Vanilla Extract
- 1/2 Tsp. Cinnamon, Ground

Method
1. Combine all the ingredients in a blender and blend the mixture for a minute or until a smooth consistency is attained.
2. Decant in a serving glass and enjoy.

9.20 Electrolyte Elixir

Servings: 4 I Time: 1 min I Difficulty: Easy
Nutrients per serving: Calories: 7 kcal I Fat: 0.1g I Carbohydrates: 2g I Protein: 0.1g I Fiber: 0g

Ingredients
- 1/2 Cup Lemon Juice, Fresh
- 1/2 Tsp. Magnesium
- 1 Tsp. Salt
- 8 Cups Water

Method
1. Combine all the ingredients in a pitcher and stir well.
2. Decant in serving glasses and enjoy.

9.21 Keto Chai Latte

Servings: 2 I Time: 5 mins I Difficulty: Beginner
Nutrients per serving: Calories: 133 kcal I Fat: 14g I Carbohydrates: 1g I Protein: 1g I Fiber: 0g

Ingredients
- 2 Cups Boiling Water
- 1/3 Cup Heavy Whipping Cream
- 1 Tbsp. Chai Tea

Method
1. According to the package instructions, brew the tea in boiling water.
2. In a saucepan or microwave, heat the cream and pour it into the tea and serve.

9.22 Sugar-Free Mulled Wine

Servings: 8 I Time: 15 mins I Difficulty: Beginner
Nutrients per serving: Calories: 82 kcal I Fat: 0.1g I Carbohydrates: 3g I Protein: 0.1g I Fiber: 0g

Ingredients
- 2 Cinnamon Sticks
- 1 & 1/2 Tsps. Orange Zest, Dried
- 1 Star Anise
- 2 Tsps. Ginger, Dried
- 1 Tsp. Green Cardamom Seeds
- 3 Cups White Or Red Wine, With Or Without Alcohol
- 1 Tsp. Cloves
- 1 Tbsp. Vanilla Extract (Optional)

Method
1. Combine all the ingredients in a saucepan and simmer over medium-low flame for about 5-10 minutes. Do not bring to boil.
2. Remove from the heat and let the mixture sit overnight for a strong taste of spices.
3. Strain the wine and serve hot with snacks or nuts.

9.23 Co-Keto (Puerto Rican Coconut Eggnog)

Servings: 2 I Time: 5 mins I Difficulty: Easy
Nutrients per serving: Calories: 563kcal I Fat: 56g I Carbohydrates: 7g I Protein: 7g I Fiber: 0g

Ingredients
- 3 & 1/3 Cups Coconut Cream
- 2 Cups Heavy Whipping Cream
- 4 Egg Yolks, Beaten
- 1 & 2/3 Cups Coconut Milk, Unsweetened

- 1 Cup Rum
- 1/2 Cup Warm Water
- 2 Tbsps. Coconut Oil
- 1 Tbsp. Vanilla Extract
- Stevia, To Taste
- 2 Tsps. Cinnamon, Ground
- 1/4 Tsp. Ginger, Ground
- 1/4 Tsp. Nutmeg, Ground
- 1/4 Tsp. Cloves, Ground

Method
1. Heat the beaten egg yolks and whipping cream together in a double boiler, constantly stirring until a smooth consistency is attained and the temperature reaches 160°F.
2. Add the coconut oil and mix well until thick and smooth.
3. Pour this mixture into a blender and add all the other ingredients. Blend well and then transfer to the glass bottles and let chill.

9.24 Cinnamon Coffee

Servings: 1 I Time: 5 mins I Difficulty: Easy
Nutrients per serving: Calories: 660 kcal I Fat: 60g I Carbohydrates: 7g I Protein: 13g I Fiber: 7g

Ingredients
- 1/2 Tsp. Brown Sugar
- 1/8 Tsp. Cinnamon, Powdered
- Whipped Cream (Optional)
- 1 Cup Coffee

Method
1. According to the package instructions, brew the coffee.
2. Add the brown sugar and cinnamon powder to it and stir well.
3. Put a dollop of whipped cream on top if you want.

9.25 Sugar-Free Caramel Brulee Latte

Servings: 2 I Time: 2 mins I Difficulty: Easy
Nutrients per serving: Calories: 106 kcal I Fat: 11g I Carbohydrates: 1g I Protein: 1g I

Ingredients
- 2 Tbsps. Caramel Syrup
- 2 Cups Brewed Coffee
- 4 Tbsps. Coconut Milk Or Heavy Whipped Cream

Method
1. Brew your coffee according to your preference and add one Tbsp. of caramel syrup and 2 Tbsps. of coconut milk or heavy cream in each cup.
2. Top with a dollop of whipped cream or caramel if you want and serve.

9.26 Pumpkin Spice Latte Milkshakes

Servings: 3 I Time: 15 mins I Difficulty: Easy
Nutrients per serving (with 2 Tbsps. whipped coconut cream per shake): Calories: 364 kcal I Fat: 18.52g I Carbohydrates: 5.48g I Protein: 2.3g I Fiber: 1.83g

Ingredients
- 1 Cup Keto Vanilla Ice Cream
- 1/3 Cup Almond Milk
- 1/3 Cup Water
- 2 Tbsps. Pumpkin Puree
- 1 & 1/2 Tsp. Instant Coffee
- 1 Tsp. Pumpkin Pie Spice

Coconut Whipped Cream:
- 2 Tbsps. Sugar (Low Carb)
- 1 & 3/4 Cups Coconut Milk

Method

1. Put the coconut milk in the refrigerator overnight, take the thick cream off the milk top, and put it in a bowl. Save the milk for other recipes.
2. Whisk in the low carb sugar in the coconut cream until your desired consistency is attained.
3. Combine all the other ingredients in a blender and blend for a few minutes until it becomes smooth.
4. Decant in your preferred glasses and top with coconut whipped cream.

9.27 Keto Russian Coffee

Servings: 2 I Time: 2 mins I Difficulty: Easy
Nutrients per serving: Calories: 214 kcal I Fat: 22g I Carbohydrates: 3g I Protein: 2g I Fiber: 1g

Ingredients

- 1/3 Cup Vanilla Vodka
- 4 Tbsps. Almond Milk, Unsweetened
- 2 Tbsps. Stevia
- 2 Cups Brewed Coffee

Milk Foam (Optional)

- 1/4 Cup Heavy Cream
- 2 Tbsps. French Vanilla Whipped Foam Topping (Sugar-Free)
- 1 Stick Of Cinnamon
- 1/4 Tsp. Vanilla Extract

Method

1. Brew coffee according to your preference and divide it into two cups. Stir in half of the almond milk, Stevia, and vodka in each cup.
2. Put the milk foam on top if you want.
3. To make milk foam, combine all its ingredients in a jar and mix well until the mixture becomes frothy. Microwave for 10 sec and then put a dollop on each serving.

9.28 Creamy Matcha Latte

Servings: 1 I Time: 6 mins I Difficulty: Easy
Nutrients per serving: Calories: 255 kcal I Fat: 22.8g I Carbohydrates: 5.3g I Protein: 2.33g I Fiber: 1.3g

Ingredients

- 1/8 Tsp. Pink Sea Salt
- 1/3 Cup Almond Milk, Unsweetened
- 1 Tsp. Matcha Tea
- 2/3 Cup Coconut Milk
- Stevia, To Taste
- 4 Drops Vanilla Extract (Optional)

Method

1. Take a saucepan and add both kinds of milk to it. Heat until it starts to bubble and add the remaining ingredients to it.
2. Mix well and serve in separate cups.

9.29 Keto Avocado Smoothie

Servings: 2 I Time: 10 mins I Difficulty: Easy
Nutrients per serving: Calories: 232 kcal I Fat: 22.4g I Carbohydrates: 6.9g I Protein: 1.7g I Fiber: 2.8g

Ingredients

- 1/2 Tsp. Turmeric Powder
- 1 Tsp. Fresh Ginger, Grated
- 1/4 Cup Almond Milk
- 3/4 Cup Coconut Milk
- 1/2 Avocado
- 1 Tsp. Lime Or Lemon Juice
- 1 Cup Ice, Crushed
- Stevia, To Taste

Method

1. Combine all the ingredients in a blender and blend until a smooth consistency is attained.
2. Pour in your favorite glasses and enjoy.

9.30 Avocado Mint Green Keto Smoothie

Servings: 1 I Time: 2 mins I Difficulty: Easy
Nutrients per serving: Calories: 223 kcal I Fat: 23g I Carbohydrates: 5g I Protein: 1g I Fiber: 1g

Ingredients

- 1/2 Cup Almond Milk
- 5-6 Mint Leaves
- 1/2 Avocado
- 3/4 Cup Coconut Milk
- 1/2 Tsp. Lime Juice
- 1 & 1/2 Cups Ice, Crushed
- Stevia, To Taste
- 3 Cilantro Sprigs
- 1/4 Tsp. Vanilla Extract

Method

1. Combine all the ingredients in a blender, except ice, and blend until it becomes smooth.
2. Then, add the crushed ice and blend again till the desired consistency.
3. Pour into glasses and serve.

9.31 Keto Skinny Margaritas

Servings: 2 I Time: 10 mins I Difficulty: Easy
Nutrients per serving: Calories: 102 kcal I Fat: 1g I Carbohydrates: 1g I Protein: 1g

Ingredients

- 1/3 Cup Tequila
- 1 Tbsp. Warm Water
- 2 Tbsps. Lime Juice
- Ice Cubes, To Taste
- Stevia, To Taste
- Coarse Salt, For Glass's Rim

Method

1. Mix the warm water and Stevia in a bowl and put squeeze the lime juice in another bowl.
2. Take a jar and combine the lime juice, sweetener syrup, and the tequila in it. Close the lid of the jar and shake it well to mix the contents.
3. Slightly wet the rim of two cocktail glasses and line with salt, and pour the margarita in them.
4. Add the ice in them and garnish with a slice of fresh lime if you want.

9.32 Iced Keto Matcha Green Tea Latte

Servings: 1 I Time: 1 min I Difficulty: Easy
Nutrients per serving: Calories: 36 kcal I Fat: 2.5g I Carbohydrates: 0.8g I Protein: 1.6g I Fiber: 0.8g

Ingredients

- 5 Drops Vanilla Stevia
- 1 Tsp. Matcha Powder
- 1 Cup Coconut Or Vanilla Almond Milk, Unsweetened
- Ice, To Taste

Method

1. Combine all ingredients in a blender and blend for a few minutes until a smooth consistency is attained and match if completely dissolved.
2. Add ice in your preferred quantity and enjoy.

9.33 Spiced Gingerbread Coffee

Servings: 1 I Time: 2 mins I Difficulty: Easy

Nutrients per serving: Calories: 108 kcal I Fat: 11.2g I Carbohydrates: 1.5g I Protein: 1g

Ingredients
- 1 Cup Hot Brewed Coffee
- 1 Tbsp. Heavy Cream
- 1/2 Tsp. Sukrin Gold
- 1 & 1/2 Tsps. Sukrin Gold Fiber Syrup
- 1/4 Tsp. Ginger, Ground
- 1/8 Tsp. Cloves, Ground
- 1/8 Tsp. Cinnamon, Ground
- Whipped Cream

Method
1. Combine all the ingredients in a mug except cloves and cream. Mix well until the spices are blended thoroughly.
2. Add a dollop of whipped cream on top and sprinkle the ground cloves on it.

9.34 Coconut Milk Strawberry Smoothie

Servings: 2 I Time: 2 mins I Difficulty: Easy
Nutrients per serving: Calories: 397 kcal I Fat: 37g I Carbohydrates: 15g I Protein: 6g I Fiber: 5g

Ingredients
- 2 Tbsps. Almond Butter, Smooth
- 1 Cup Coconut Milk, Unsweetened
- 3/4 Tsp. Stevia (Optional)
- 1 Cup Strawberries, Frozen

Method
1. Combine all the ingredients in a blender and mix until a smooth consistency is attained.
2. Decant into the serving glasses and enjoy.

9.35 Peanut Butter Chocolate Keto Milkshake

Servings: 1 I Time: 1 min I Difficulty: Easy
Nutrients per serving: Calories: 79 kcal I Fat: 5.7g I Carbohydrates: 6.4g I Protein: 3.6g I Fiber: 3.3g

Ingredients
- 5 Drops Stevia
- 1/8 Tsp. Sea Salt
- 1 Tbsp. Peanut Butter Powder, Unsweetened
- 1 Cup Coconut Milk, Unsweetened
- 1 Tbsp. Cocoa Powder, Unsweetened

Method
1. Combine all the ingredients in a blender and mix until a smooth consistency is attained.
2. Decant into the serving glasses and enjoy.

9.36 Sugar-Free Fresh Squeezed Lemonade

Servings: 8 I Time: 10 mins I Difficulty: Easy
Nutrients per serving: Calories: 5 kcal I Fat: 1g I Carbohydrates: 2g I Protein: 1g I Fiber: 1g

Ingredients
- 8 Cups Water
- 1 Tsp. Lemon Monkfruit Drops
- 4 Slices Lemon (Optional)
- 3/4 Cup Lemon Juice
- Ice (Optional)

Method
1. Combine all the ingredients in a pitcher and stir well to mix.
2. Chill in the refrigerator or add ice to it before serving.
3. Put the lemon slices in it if you want.

9.37 Cucumber Mint Water

Servings: 16 I Time: 5 mins I Difficulty: Easy
Nutrients per serving: Calories: 3 kcal I Fat: 0g I Carbohydrates: 0g I Protein: 0g I Fiber: 0g

Ingredients
- 8 Cups Water
- 3/4 Cup Cucumber Slices
- 1 Tbsps. Mint Leaves

Method
1. Press the mint leaves in a pitcher with the help of a spoon and add the other ingredients to it.
2. Chill it in the refrigerator for an hour and then enjoy.

9.38 Caramel Apple Drink

Servings: 1 I Time: 10 mins I Difficulty: Easy
Nutrients per serving: Calories: 76 kcal I Fat: 3g I Carbohydrates: 16g I Protein: 1g I Fiber: 14g

Ingredients
- 2 Cups Water
- 1 Tbsp. Caramel Syrup
- 1 Tbsp. Apple Cider Vinegar (Raw)
- 1/8 Tsp. Allspice
- 1/8 Tsp. Nutmeg, Ground
- 1/8 Tsp. Orange Zest, Dried
- 1 Cinnamon Stick, Halved
- 3 Whole Cloves
- 1/4 Cup Vanilla Whipped Cream (Optional)
- 1/8 Tsp. Cinnamon, Ground (Optional)
- 5 Drops Stevia (Optional)

Method
1. Take the water in a pan and put the allspice, cinnamon stick halves, and cloves in it. Boil the water and then let it sit for 2-3 minutes off the heat, with the lid on.
2. Strain the spice water into a large mug and put the caramel syrup and apple cider vinegar in it. Stir well and add Stevia or ground cinnamon if you want.
3. Put a dollop of whipped cream on top if you ant and drizzle some caramel syrup if you want.

9.39 Keto Frosty Chocolate Shake

Servings: 1 I Time: 10 mins I Difficulty: Easy
Nutrients per serving: Calories: 346 kcal I Fat: 36g I Carbohydrates: 8.4g I Protein: 4g I Fiber: 4g

Ingredients
- 5 Tbsps. Almond Milk, Unsweetened
- 2 Tbsps. Cocoa Powder
- 1 & 1/2 Tsps. Truvia
- 1/8 Tsp. Vanilla Extract (Sugar-Free)
- 6 Tbsps. Heavy Whipping Cream

Method
1. Combine all the ingredients and whisk well to make a fluffy peak of cream.
2. Freeze the mixture for 20 minutes and then crack it open with a fork.
3. Chill it as per your preference and serve cold.

9.40 Strawberry Avocado Smoothie

Servings: 2 I Time: 2 mins I Difficulty: Easy
Nutrients per serving: Calories: 165 kcal I Fat: 14g I Carbohydrates: 11g I Protein: 2g I Fiber: 7g

Ingredients
- 1 & 1/2 Cups Coconut Milk
- 1 Tsp. Stevia
- 1 Avocado

- 1 Tbsp. Lime Juice
- 2/3 Cup Strawberries, Frozen
- 1/2 Cup Ice

Method
1. Combine all the ingredients in a blender and blend until a smooth consistency is attained.
2. Pour in your favorite glasses and enjoy.

9.41 Almond Berry Mini Cheesecake Smoothies

Servings: 2 | Time: 10 mins | Difficulty: Easy
Nutrients per serving: Calories: 165 kcal | Fat: 8.6g | Carbohydrates: 16.8g | Protein: 7g | Fiber: 4.4g

Ingredients
- 1 Cup Almond Or Coconut Milk, Chilled
- 2 Tbsps. Almond Or Coconut Flour
- 2 Cups Mixed Berries, Frozen
- 1 Tbsp. Almond Butter, Smooth
- 1/2 Cup Cottage Cheese, Organic
- 1 Tsp. Nuts Or Almonds, Toasted & Crushed
- 1 Tsp. Vanilla Extract
- 1/8 Tsp. Cinnamon
- Stevia, To Taste (Optional)

Method
1. Combine all the ingredients in a blender, except crushed nuts, and blend until a smooth consistency is attained.
2. You can add Stevia if you want and pour it into cups.
3. Top with crushed and toasted nuts and serve.

9.42 Hemp Milk And Nut Milk

Servings: 4 | Time: 12 hrs. 15 mins | Difficulty: Easy
Nutrients per serving: Calories: 44 kcal | Fat: 3.6g | Carbohydrates: 1.7g | Protein: 1.5g | Fiber: 0.9g

Ingredients
Nut milk
- 4 Cups Water
- 1/8 Tsp. Sea Salt
- 1 Cup Raw Nuts (Pecan, Almond, Walnut, Cashew, etc.)
- 1 Tsp. Vanilla Extract (Optional)
- 1/3 Cup Maple Syrup (Optional)

For Hemp Milk
- 3 Cups Water
- 1/8 Tsp. Sea Salt
- 1/2 Cup Hulled Hemp Seed
- 1/4 Cup Maple Syrup (Optional)
- 1 Tsp. Vanilla Extract (Optional)

Method
Nut Milk
1. Soak the nuts overnight and drain them the next day.
2. Blend the water and soaked nuts in a blender until a smooth consistency is attained.
3. Add in the salt, vanilla extract, and maple syrup if you want and blend again until mixed well.
4. Strain the mixture using a double layer of cheesecloth to isolate the pulp. Once done, add water to the milk to get your preferred consistency.
5. Pour the nut milk into mason jars and store them if you want for up to 5 days.
6. Cover the jars with lids and store in the refrigerator for up to 5 days.

Hemp Milk
1. Combine all the ingredients in a blender and blend for a few minutes or until a smooth consistency is attained.
2. You can strain the excess seeds using a cheesecloth and store the hemp milk in mason jars for up to 5 days.

9.43 Gut Healing Bone Broth Latte

Servings: 2 | Time: 10 mins | Difficulty: Easy
Nutrients per serving: Calories: 161 kcal | Fat: 7.2g | Carbohydrates: 5.2g | Protein: 10.8g | Fiber: 0.9g

Ingredients
- 1 Tbsp. Coconut Oil
- 1/4 Tsp. Ginger, Ground
- 2 Cups Bone Broth
- 1/8 Tsp. Cayenne Pepper
- 1/8 Tsp. Turmeric Powder
- 1/8 Tsp. Black Pepper
- 1/8 Tsp. Sea Salt
- Coconut Cream, To Taste (Optional)
- Collagen Peptides (Optional)

Savory Latte Toppings (Optional)
- Fresh Herbs
- Green Onion, Chopped
- Red Pepper Flakes

Method
1. Pour bone broth into a saucepan and add all the ingredients in it except sea salt.
2. Heat the mixture over medium flame while stirring constantly until combined.
3. You can use an immersion blender to mix coconut cream if necessary.
4. Blend well to make a frothy and creamy mixture.
5. Pour into serving mugs and sprinkle seal salt on top.
6. You can also use savory latte toppings for garnishing if you want.

9.44 Creamy Cocoa Coconut Low Carb Shake

Servings: 2 | Time: 5 mins | Difficulty: Easy
Nutrients per serving: Calories: 222 kcal | Fat: 23.1g | Carbohydrates: 5.4g | Protein: 2.5g | Fiber: 2.7g

Ingredients
- 2 Tbsps. Cocoa Powder
- 1/2 Tbsp. Almond Butter, Smooth
- 1 Cup Almond Or Coconut Milk, Unsweetened
- 2 Tbsps. Coconut MCT Oil
- 1/8 Tsp. Sea Salt
- 1/2 Cup Coconut Cream

Additional Sweeteners (Optional)
- Stevia Leaf Or Xylitol
- Banana Or Maple Syrup
- Cinnamon
- Berries

Method
1. Combine all the ingredients in a blender and mix until a smooth consistency is attained.
2. Add sweetener of your choice, if you want, and decant into the serving glasses and enjoy.

9.45 Low Carb Dark Chocolate Protein Smoothie

Servings: 1 | Time: 5 mins | Difficulty: Easy
Nutrients per serving: Calories: 220 kcal | Fat: 9g | Carbohydrates: 2.5g | Protein: 28.4g | Fiber: 19.5g

Ingredients
- 1 Cup Almond Milk, Unsweetened
- 1/4 Cup Avocado, Frozen
- 1/2 Tsp. Matcha Green Tea

- 2 Tbsps. Protein Powder, Zero Carb
- 1 Tbsp. Swerve Sweetener
- 1 Tbsp. Cocoa Powder, Dark

Method
1. Combine all the ingredients in a blender and mix until a smooth consistency is attained.
2. Decant into the serving glass and enjoy.

9.46 Mint Chocolate Green Smoothie

Servings: 2 | Time: 5 mins | Difficulty: Easy
Nutrients per serving: Calories: 359 kcal | Fat: 17.4g | Carbohydrates: 37.4g | Protein: 20.6g | Fiber: 10g

Ingredients
- 3/4 Cup Vanilla Almond Milk, Unsweetened
- 1/2 Cup Ice
- 1/2 Cup Kale, Packed Firmly
- 1/4 Cup Vanilla Protein Powder
- 1/4 Cup Vanilla Greek Yogurt (2%)
- 1/4 Cup Avocado, Mashed
- 1 Tbsp. Mini Chocolate Chips
- 1/4 Tsp. Peppermint Extract
- 1/2 Tbsp. Agave

Method
1. Combine all the ingredients in a blender and mix until a smooth consistency is attained.
2. Decant into the serving glasses and enjoy.

9.47 Low Carb Raspberry Cheesecake Shake

Servings: 1 | Time: 5 mins | Difficulty: Easy
Nutrients per serving: Calories: 560 kcal | Fat: 55g | Carbohydrates: 8g | Protein: 9g | Fiber: 3g

Ingredients
- 1/4 Cup Almond Milk, Unsweetened
- 1 Tsp. Butter, Unsalted (Cold)
- 1/4 Cup Heavy Cream
- 6-8 Raspberries, Fresh
- 1/4 Cup Cream Cheese
- 4 Tsps. Almond Flour
- Ice (Optional)
- Liquid Stevia, To Taste (Optional)

Method
1. Put the almond milk, raspberries, heavy cream, and cream cheese in a vessel and blend using an immersion blender. Add the sweetener if you want. Transfer it into a serving glass.
2. In a bowl, mix the almond flour and butter to form crumbs. Put these crumbs on top of the drink after adding ice, if you want, and serve.

9.48 Watermelon Smoothie

Servings: 1 | Time: 5 mins | Difficulty: Easy
Nutrients per serving: Calories: 39 kcal | Fat: 3g | Carbohydrates: 1g | Protein: 0g

Ingredients
- 3/4 Cup Lemon Lime Seltzer
- 1/8 Tsp. Xantham Gum
- 15 Drops Watermelon Flavoring Oil
- 8 Ice Cubes
- 1 Drop Vanilla Extract
- 2 Tbsps. Stevia
- 1 Drop Lemon Extract
- 1. Tbsp Heavy Cream

Method
1. Combine all the ingredients in a blender and mix until a smooth consistency is attained.
2. Decant into the serving glass and enjoy.

9.49 Low-Carb Blueberry Smoothie

Servings: 2 | Time: 5 mins | Difficulty: Easy
Nutrients per serving: Calories: 251 kcal | Fat: 22g | Carbohydrates: 6g | Protein: 8g | Fiber: 1g

Ingredients
- 1/4 Cup Cream Cheese
- 3/4 Cup Almond Milk, Unsweetened
- 1/2 Tsp. Vanilla Extract
- 1/2 Cup Ice
- 2 Tsps. Stevia/Erythritol Blend, Granulated
- 1/3 Cup Blueberries, Frozen
- 1-5 Drops Lemon Extract
- 1/4 Cup Heavy Whipping Cream
- 2 Tbsps. Collagen Peptides (Optional)

Method
1. Combine all the ingredients in a blender and mix until a smooth consistency is attained.
2. Decant into the serving glasses and enjoy.

9.50 Pumpkin Low Carb Smoothie With Salted Caramel

Servings: 1 | Time: 5 mins | Difficulty: Easy
Nutrients per serving: Calories: 245 kcal | Fat: 10.4g | Carbohydrates: 11.8g | Protein: 29g | Fiber: 6.4g

Ingredients
- 1 Cup Almond Milk
- 1/4 Avocado
- 2 Tbsps. Vanilla Protein Powder
- 1/4 Cup Pumpkin Puree
- 4 Ice Cubes
- 2 Tbsps. Caramel Syrup, Salted & Sugar-Free

Method
1. Combine all the ingredients in a blender and mix until a smooth consistency is attained.
2. Decant into the serving glass and enjoy.

9.51 McKeto Strawberry Milkshake

Servings: 1 | Time: 5 mins | Difficulty: Easy
Nutrients per serving: Calories: 368 kcal | Fat: 38.85g | Carbohydrates: 2.42g | Protein: 1.69g | Fiber: 1.28g

Ingredients
- 1/4 Cup Heavy Cream
- 1/4 Tsp. Xanthan Gum
- 3/4 Cup Coconut Milk
- 7 Ice Cubes
- 1 Tbsp. MCT Oil
- 2 Tbsps. Strawberry Torani, Sugar-Free

Method
1. Combine all the ingredients in a blender and mix until a smooth consistency is attained.
2. Decant into the serving glass and enjoy.

9.52 Keto Blueberry Cheesecake Smoothie

Servings: 1 | Time: 5 mins | Difficulty: Easy
Nutrients per serving: Calories: 311 kcal | Fat: 27g | Carbohydrates: 9g | Protein: 5.5g | Fiber: 2.5g

Ingredients
- 1/2 Cup Cream Cheese
- 2 Tbsps. Heavy Cream

- 1 Cup Almond Milk, Unsweetened
- 1 Tsp. Cinnamon, Ground
- 1/2 Cup Blueberries
- 6 Drops Stevia
- 1/2 Tsp. Vanilla Extract

Method
1. Combine all the ingredients in a blender and mix until a smooth consistency is attained.
2. Decant into the serving glass and enjoy.

9.53 Keto Tropical Smoothie

Servings: 2 | Time: 5 mins | Difficulty: Easy
Nutrients per serving: Calories: 355.75 kcal | Fat: 32.63g | Carbohydrates: 4.41g | Protein: 4.4g | Fiber: 3g

Ingredients
- 1 Tbsp. MCT Oil
- 1/2 Tsp. Mango Extract
- 7 Ice Cubes
- 2 Tbsps. Golden Flaxseed Meal
- 1/4 Tsp. Blueberry Extract
- 3/4 Cup Coconut Milk, Unsweetened
- 1/4 Tsp. Banana Extract
- 1/4 Cup Sour Cream
- 20 Drops Liquid Stevia

Method
1. Combine all the ingredients in a blender and mix until a smooth consistency is attained. Let it sit for a few minutes and allow the flax meal to absorb moisture.
2. Decant into the serving glasses and enjoy.

9.54 Keto Kale & Coconut Shake

Servings: 1 | Time: 5 mins | Difficulty: Easy
Nutrients per serving: Calories: 660 kcal | Fat: 60g | Carbohydrates: 7g | Protein: 13g | Fiber: 7g

Ingredients
- 4 Cups Kale, Chopped
- 1/2 Cup Coconut Milk
- 1 Cup Almond Milk, Unsweetened
- 1/4 Cup Coconut, Unsweetened & Ground
- 1 Cup Ice
- 1/4 Tsp. Kosher Salt
- 1 Tbsp. Fresh Ginger, Peeled (Optional)

Method
1. Combine all the ingredients in a blender and mix until a smooth consistency is attained.
2. Decant into the serving glass and enjoy.

9.55 Savory Cucumber Herb Sangria

Servings: 2-4 | Time: 5 mins | Difficulty: Easy
Nutrients per serving: Calories: 660 kcal | Fat: 60g | Carbohydrates: 7g | Protein: 13g | Fiber: 7g

Ingredients
- 2 Cups Sparkling Water
- 3 Cups Dry White Wine
- 2 Cups Ice
- 3 Limes, Sliced
- 1 Green Cucumber, Sliced
- 1 Cup Basil Leaves, Fresh
- 2 Lemons, Sliced
- 1 Cup Mint Leaves, Fresh

Method

1. Put all ingredients in a pitcher except wine, sparkling water, and ice. Stir well and press the lemon, lime, basil, mint, and cucumber a little to release their juices.
2. Add the wine to it and stir well.
3. Put it in the refrigerator and let it sit for about 20 minutes.
4. Take out the pitcher and pour in the sparkling water and ice.
5. Serve cold.

9.56 Sparkling Raspberry Limeade Mocktail

Servings: 2 | Time: 1 min | Difficulty: Easy
Nutrients per serving: Calories: 22 kcal | Fat: 0.2g | Carbohydrates: 5.5g | Protein: 0.5g | Fiber: 2.1g

Ingredients
- 1/2 Cup Raspberries, Unsweetened & Frozen
- 1 & 1/2 Cups Sparkling Raspberry Lemonade, Chilled
- 2 Tbsps. Lime Juice
- 1/8 Tsp. Vanilla Stevia
- 1/2 Cup Ice, Crushed

Method
1. Combine all the ingredients in a blender and mix until a smooth consistency is attained.
2. Decant into the serving glasses and enjoy.

9.57 Bailey's Irish Cream

Servings: 12 | Time: 20 mins | Difficulty: Easy
Nutrients per serving: Calories: 200 kcal | Fat: 14g | Carbohydrates: 1g | Protein: 0g | Fiber: 0g

Ingredients
- 1/2 Tsp. Vanilla Extract
- 1 & 1/4 Cups Irish Whiskey
- 2 Cups Heavy Cream
- 1 Tbsp. Cocoa Powder
- 1/2 Tsp. Instant Espresso Powder
- 2/3 Cup Swerve
- 1 Tsp. Almond Extract

Method
1. Take a saucepan and put cocoa, instant powder, sweetener, and cream in it. Heat it over medium-low flame and bring to a boil.
2. Reduce heat to low and let it simmer for about 10 minutes.
3. Take off the heat and add in the whiskey, almond, and vanilla extracts.
4. Let cool and serve.

9.58 Low Carb Coffee Milkshake

Servings: 2 | Time: 1 min | Difficulty: Easy
Nutrients per serving: Calories: 345 kcal | Fat: 31.4g | Carbohydrates: 24g | Protein: 2.5g | Fiber: 18.2g

Ingredients
- 1 Tsp. Instant Espresso Powder
- 15 Drops Stevia
- 1 & 1/2 Cups Ice, Crushed
- 1 Cup Vanilla Ice Cream (Low Carb)
- 1/2 Cup Almond Milk
- 2 Tsps. Cocoa Powder (Optional)
- 2 Tbsps. Whipped Cream (Optional)

Method
1. Combine all the ingredients in a blender and mix until a smooth consistency is attained.
2. Decant into the serving glasses and put a dollop of whipped cream on top if you want.

9.59 Sugar-Free Strawberry Limeade

Servings: 8 | Time: 5 mins | Difficulty: Easy

Nutrients per serving: Calories: 16 kcal I Fat: 0.1g I Carbohydrates: 4.3g I Protein: 0.2g I Fiber: 1.5g

Ingredients

- 5 Cups Water
- 3/4 Cup Lime Juice, Fresh
- 1 & 1/2 Tsps. Stevia
- 1 & 1/2 Cups Strawberries, Sliced
- Ice, To Taste

Method

1. Combine all the ingredients in a blender and mix until a smooth consistency is attained.
2. Decant into the serving glasses and enjoy.

9.60 Low-Carb Keto Shamrock Shake

Servings: 1 I Time: 2 mins I Difficulty: Easy
Nutrients per serving: Calories: 660 kcal I Fat: 60g I Carbohydrates: 7g I Protein: 13g I Fiber: 7g

Ingredients

- 1 Tsp. Spinach Powder
- 1 Cup Vanilla Ice Cream, Low Carb
- 1/3 Cup Coconut Or Almond Milk, Unsweetened
- 1/8 Tsp. Pure Mint Extract
- Whipped Cream (Optional)

Method

1. Combine all the ingredients in a blender and mix until a smooth consistency is attained.
2. Decant into the serving glasses and put a dollop of whipped cream on top if you want.

9.61 Keto Smoothie With Almond Milk

Servings: 1 I Time: 5 mins I Difficulty: Easy
Nutrients per serving: Calories: 332 kcal I Fat: 28.5g I Carbohydrates: 15g I Protein: 10.2g I Fiber: 8.9g

Ingredients

- 1 Tbsp. Cocoa Powder, Unsweetened
- 2 Tbsps. Almond Butter
- 1 Cup Almond Milk
- 1/4 Cup Avocado
- 3 Tbsps. Monkfruit
- 1 Cup Ice, Crushed

Method

1. Combine all the ingredients in a blender and mix until a smooth consistency is attained.
2. Decant into the serving glass and enjoy.

9.62 Sparkling Grapefruit Frosé

Servings: 6 I Time: 5 mins I Difficulty: Easy
Nutrients per serving: Calories: 244 kcal I Fat: 0.1g I Carbohydrates: 29.1g I Protein: 1g I Fiber: 0.1g

Ingredients

- 1 Cup Ice
- 1 Cup Grapefruit Juice, Fresh
- 1/4 Cup Agave Nectar
- 1 & 1/2 Cups Rosé Wine

For Garnish (Optional)

- Grapefruit Wedges
- Mint Sprigs

Method

1. Freeze rosé in a shallow dish overnight.
2. Scrape it off the dish the next day and put in a blender with all other ingredients.
3. Blend until a smooth consistency is attained.
4. Decant into the serving glasses and garnish with mint sprigs and grapefruit wedges if you want.

9.63 Banana Oat Breakfast Smoothie

Servings: 2 I Time: 5 mins I Difficulty: Easy
Nutrients per serving: Calories: 210 kcal I Fat: 7.5g I Carbohydrates: 32.5g I Protein: 5.6g I Fiber: 4.8g

Ingredients

- 1 Banana
- 1/2 Cup Almond Milk
- 1 Tbsp. Flaxseed Meal
- 1/2 Cup Yogurt
- 1/2 Tsp. Cinnamon
- 1/3 Cup Rolled Oats

Method

1. Combine all the ingredients in a blender and mix until a smooth consistency is attained.
2. Decant into the serving glasses and enjoy.

9.64 Keto Mexican Chocolate Eggnog

Servings: 6 I Time: 15 mins I Difficulty: Easy
Nutrients per serving: Calories: 242 kcal I Fat: 23g I Carbohydrates: 4g I Protein: 7g I Fiber: 1g

Ingredients

- 1/4 Cup Whiskey Or Bourbon
- 1 & 1/2 Cups Almond Milk, Unsweetened
- 6 Eggs
- 1/4 Cup Cocoa Powder
- 1/2 Cup Monkfruit/Erythritol Blend
- 1 Cup Heavy Cream
- 1/2 Cup Whipped Cream
- 1 Tsp. Vanilla
- 1/2 Tsp. Cinnamon Powder
- 1/4 Tsp. Chili Powder
- 1/8 Tsp. Cayenne Pepper
- 1/8 Tsp. Nutmeg, Grated
- 1/8 Tsp. Salt

Method

1. Combine all the ingredients in a blender except bourbon/whiskey, vanilla, and whipped cream. Blend it until a smooth consistency is attained.
2. Then pour this mixture into a saucepan and heat it over a medium-low flame with constant stirring for about 8 minutes. Do not let it boil.
3. Take off the heat, put the saucepan in a bowl full of ice, and stir the eggnog to cool it down.
4. Add the bourbon/whiskey and vanilla in it and decant into a covered container.
5. Refrigerate for about 4 hours and add in the whipped cream or top the eggnog with it.
6. Serve and enjoy.

9.65 Keto Cranberry Hibiscus Margarita

Servings: 8 I Time: 20 mins I Difficulty: Easy
Nutrients per serving: Calories: 86 kcal I Fat: 1g I Carbohydrates: 6g I Protein: 1g I Fiber: 2g

Ingredients

- 2 & 1/2 Tbsps. Naval Orange Zest
- 1 & 1/2 Cups Cranberries, Fresh
- 1 Cup Tequila
- 5 Cup Water
- 3/4 Cups + 2 Tbsps. Monkfruit/Erythritol Blend
- 3 Tbsps. Lime Juice, Fresh
- Ice
- 4 Hibiscus Tea Bags
- Coarse Salt, For Glass's Rim

Method
1. Take a saucepan and put the 1 cup water, 3/4 cup sweetener, orange zest, and cranberries in it. Heat it over medium flame and bring to boil, reduce heat, and let it simmer until it is thickened, for about 10-15 minutes.
2. Strain the cranberry gel and let cool.
3. Boil the remaining 4 cups of water in a saucepan and put the hibiscus tea bags in it for five minutes.
4. Take out the tea bags and add the 2 Tbsps. of sweetener in it. Mix well and set aside to cool down.
5. Combine the cranberry gel, hibiscus tea, and all the remaining ingredients in a blender and blend well.
6. Slightly wet the rim of cocktail glasses and line with salt, and pour the margarita in them.

9.66 Keto Frozen Blackberry Lemonade

Servings: 2 I Time: 5 mins I Difficulty: Easy
Nutrients per serving: Calories: 155 kcal I Fat: 15g I Carbohydrates: 6g I Protein: 2g I Fiber: 2g

Ingredients
- 1 Cup Ice
- 1/4 Cup Blackberries, Fresh
- 4 Tbsps. Lemon Juice
- 1/2 Cup Almond Milk
- 1/3 Cup Coconut Cream
- 1 Tbsp. Stevia/Erythritol Blend
- 1/8 Tsp. Sea Salt

Method
1. Combine all the ingredients in a blender and mix until a smooth consistency is attained.
2. Decant into the serving glasses and enjoy.

9.67 Triple Berry Cheesecake Smoothie

Servings: 1 I Time: 5 mins I Difficulty: Easy
Nutrients per serving: Calories: 158 kcal I Fat: 11g I Carbohydrates: 12g I Protein: 3g I Fiber: 6g

Ingredients
- 2 Tbsps. Avocado
- 1/2 Cup Mixed Berries, Frozen
- 1 Tsp. Vanilla
- 2 Tbsps. Cream Cheese
- 1/8 Tsp. Sea Salt
- 1/2 Cup Almond Milk, Unsweetened
- 7-10 Drops Monkfruit Extract

Method
1. Combine all the ingredients in a blender and mix until a smooth consistency is attained.
2. Decant into the serving glass and enjoy.

9.68 Maple Almond Green Smoothie

Servings: 1 I Time: 5 mins I Difficulty: Easy
Nutrients per serving: Calories: 210 kcal I Fat: 16.8g I Carbohydrates: 10.4g I Protein: 8.1g I Fiber: 6.3g

Ingredients
- 1 Cup Baby Spinach
- 1 Tbsp. Avocado
- 1 Tbsp. Golden Flax Meal
- 1 Tbsp. Almond Butter
- 1 Cup Almond Milk, Unsweetened
- 1 & 1/4 Tsps. Stevia/Erythritol Blend
- 1/4 Tsp. Vanilla Extract
- 1/8 Tsp. Cinnamon
- 1/4 Tsp. Maple Extract
- 2-3 Ice Cubes (Optional)

Method

1. Combine all the ingredients in a blender and mix until a smooth consistency is attained.
2. Decant into the serving glass and enjoy.

9.69 Dairy Free Chocolate Pecan Keto Shake

Servings: 1 I Time: 10 mins I Difficulty: Easy
Nutrients per serving: Calories: 247 kcal I Fat: 20g I Carbohydrates: 12g I Protein: 5g I Fiber: 8g

Ingredients
- 5 Raw Pecans, Halved
- 2 Tbsps. Cocoa Powder, Unsweetened
- 1/8 Tsp. Pink Himalayan Salt
- 1 & 1/3 Cups Almond Milk, Unsweetened
- 2 & 1/2 Tsps. Stevia/Erythritol Blend
- 2 Tbsps. Avocado
- 3-4 Ice Cubes

Method
1. Combine all the ingredients in a blender and mix until a smooth consistency is attained.
2. Decant into the serving glass and enjoy.

9.70 Strawberry Colada Milkshake

Servings: 1 I Time: 3 mins I Difficulty: Easy
Nutrients per serving: Calories: 660 kcal I Fat: 60g I Carbohydrates: 7g I Protein: 13g I Fiber: 7g

Ingredients
- 1/2 Tbsp. Chia Seeds
- 3-4 Strawberries, Frozen
- 1/3 Cup Coconut Milk
- 1/3 Cup Almond Milk, Unsweetened
- 1 Tsp. Stevia/Erythritol Blend
- 4-5 Ice Cubes
- 1/8 Tsp. Pink Salt
- 1/4 Tsp. Coconut Extract
- 1/4 Tsp. Vanilla Extract
- 1/2 Tbsp. Coconut Oil (Optional)
- 1 Tbsp. Strawberries, Freeze-Dried (Optional)

Method
1. Combine all the ingredients in a blender and mix until a smooth consistency is attained.
2. Decant into the serving glass and enjoy.

9.71 Keto Frozen Hot Chocolate

Servings: 1 I Time: 5 mins I Difficulty: Easy
Nutrients per serving: Calories: 660 kcal I Fat: 60g I Carbohydrates: 7g I Protein: 13g I Fiber: 7g

Ingredients
- 1 Tbsp. Avocado
- 1/4 Cup Coconut Milk
- 1 Tbsp. Cocoa
- 1/2 Cup Almond Milk, Unsweetened
- 1/2 Cup Ice Cubes
- 1 & 1/4 Tsps. Stevia/Erythritol Blend
- 1/2 Tsp. Vanilla
- 1/8 Tsp. Pink Himalayan Salt

For Garnish
- Chocolate Chips, Sugar-Free
- Whipped Coconut Cream

Method
1. Combine all the ingredients in a blender except ice cubes. Blend until a smooth consistency is attained.

2. Decant into the serving glass, add the ice, and put the whipped cream and chocolate chips on top if you want.

9.72 Dairy-Free Keto Iced Latte

Servings: 1 | Time: 5 mins | Difficulty: Easy
Nutrients per serving: Calories: 660 kcal | Fat: 60g | Carbohydrates: 7g | Protein: 13g | Fiber: 7g

Ingredients
- 1/4 Cup Brewed Coffee, Strong
- 1 & 1/2 Cups Almond Milk, Unsweetened
- 1 Tbsp. MCT Oil

Method
1. Brew your coffee according to your preference.
2. Combine all the ingredients in a blender and mix until a smooth consistency is attained.
3. Decant into the serving cup and enjoy.

9.73 Sugar-Free Hibiscus Lemonade

Servings: 4 | Time: 10 mins | Difficulty: Easy
Nutrients per serving: Calories: 660 kcal | Fat: 60g | Carbohydrates: 7g | Protein: 13g | Fiber: 7g

Ingredients
- 1 & 1/2 Cups Sparkling Mineral Water
- 2 Tbsps. Lemon Juice, Fresh
- 1 Tbsp. Stevia/Erythritol Blend
- 2 Cups Brewed Hibiscus Tea
- Ice, To Taste

Method
1. Put all the ingredients in a pitcher except water and ice. Mix everything well until dissolved.
2. Add the water and ice and stir.
3. Decant into the serving glasses and enjoy.

9.74 Low Carb 7Up

Servings: 2 | Time: 2 mins | Difficulty: Easy
Nutrients per serving: Calories: 2 kcal | Fat: 0g | Carbohydrates: 1g | Protein: 0g | Fiber: 0g

Ingredients
- 1 & 1/2 Cups Ice
- 1/4 Tsp. Liquid Stevia
- 1/2 Tbsp. Lime Juice
- 2/3 Cup Seltzer Water

Method
1. Fill serving glass with ice and put all the other ingredients in it.
2. Stir well and enjoy.

9.75 Low Carb German Chocolate Fat Bomb Hot Chocolate

Servings: 1 | Time: 12 mins | Difficulty: Easy
Nutrients per serving: Calories: 358 kcal | Fat: 39g | Carbohydrates: 2g | Protein: 2g

Ingredients
- 2 Tbsps. Cocoa Butter
- 1/4 Cup Coconut Milk
- 1 Cup Chocolate Almond Milk, Unsweetened
- Stevia, To Taste

Method
1. In a saucepan, combine all the ingredients and heat over medium-low flame until the cocoa butter melts.
2. Remove from the heat and mix with an immersion blender till t becomes frothy.
3. Decant into your favorite mug and enjoy.

9.76 Low Carb German Gingerbread Hot Chocolate

Servings: 2 | Time: 20 mins | Difficulty: Easy
Nutrients per serving: Calories: 72 kcal | Fat: 4g | Carbohydrates: 11g | Protein: 3g | Fiber: 5g

Ingredients
- 1/4 Cup Cocoa Powder, Unsweetened
- 2 Cups Chocolate Almond Milk, Unsweetened
- 1/2 Tsp. Liquid Stevia
- 1/4 Cup Stevia
- 1/4 Tsp. Cardamom, Ground
- 1 Tsp. Cinnamon, Ground
- 1/8 Tsp. Allspice, Ground
- 1/8 Tsp. Anise Seed, Ground
- 1/8 Tsp. Cloves, Ground
- 1/8 Tsp. Nutmeg, Ground
- 1/8 Tsp. Ginger, Ground

Method
1. Combine all the ingredients in a saucepan and heat it over medium heat.
2. Once it boils, reduce the heat to low, and let it simmer for about 5 minutes with intermittent stirring.
3. Decant into serving mugs and enjoy.

9.77 Coconut Pumpkin Steamer

Servings: 1 | Time: 5 mins | Difficulty: Easy
Nutrients per serving: Calories: 241 kcal | Fat: 24g | Carbohydrates: 9g | Protein: 2g | Fiber: 1g

Ingredients
- 1 Tsp. Vanilla Extract
- 1/2 Cup Coconut Milk
- Stevia, To Taste
- 1/4 Tsp. Pumpkin Pie Spice, Without Sugar

Method
1. Combine all the ingredients in a saucepan and heat it over medium heat.
2. Once the bubbles start to form, take off the heat, and serve warm.

9.78 Low Carb Margarita Mix

Servings: 2 | Time: 5 mins | Difficulty: Easy
Nutrients per serving: Calories: 35 kcal | Fat: 0g | Carbohydrates: 9g | Protein: 0g | Fiber: 0g

Ingredients
- 1/2 Cup Lemon Juice, Fresh
- 1 & 1/2 Cups Water
- 1/4 Tsp. Liquid Stevia
- 1/3 Cup Erythritol, Powdered
- 1/8 Tsp. Orange Extract
- 1 Cup Tequila
- Ice, To Taste

Method
1. Combine all the ingredients in a pitcher except tequila and ice.
2. Mix well to dissolve the sweetener.
3. Add the tequila and stir.
4. Pour in the cocktail glasses with rims covered with salt.
5. Add the ice and enjoy.

9.79 Low Carb Electrolyte Water

Servings: 4 | Time: 5 mins | Difficulty: Easy
Nutrients per serving: Calories: 2 kcal | Fat: 0g | Carbohydrates: 1g | Protein: 0g

Ingredients
- 4 Cups Water
- 2 Tbsps. Lemon Juice
- 1/8 Tsp. Baking Soda
- Stevia, To Taste
- 1/8 Tsp. Salt

Method
1. Combine all the ingredients in a bottle, cover it, and shake well.
2. Serve and enjoy.

9.80 Low Carb Pumpkin Spice Mocha

Servings: 2 | Time: 15 mins | Difficulty: Easy
Nutrients per serving: Calories: 187 kcal | Fat: 21g | Carbohydrates: 1g | Protein: 0g

Ingredients
- 1 Tsp. Pumpkin Pie Spice, Without Sugar
- Stevia, To Taste
- 3 Tbsps. Cocoa Butter
- 1/4 Cup Coffee Grounds
- 3 Cups Water

Method
1. Brew the coffee according to your preference with the pumpkin spice in it.
2. Add the cocoa butter in it and blend with an immersion blender until a smooth consistency is attained and it becomes frothy.
3. Add the desired quantity of sweetener and enjoy.

9.81 Kombucha Sangria

Servings: 7 | Time: 10 mins | Difficulty: Easy
Nutrients per serving: Calories: 101 kcal | Fat: 0g | Carbohydrates: 6.5g | Protein: 0.1g | Fiber: 0g

Ingredients
- 4 Tbsps. Monkfruit, Powdered
- 1 Cup Orange Juice
- 2 Cups Kombucha
- 3 & 1/4 Cups Spanish Wine
- 1 Lime, Sliced
- 1 Orange, Sliced
- 1 Lemon, Sliced
- 1/2 Cup Brandy (Optional)

Method
1. Combine all the ingredients in a pitcher, except orange, lemon, and lime slices.
2. Stir well to mix and add the orange, lemon, and lime slices.
3. Serve with ice and enjoy.

9.82 Pumpkin Spice Hot Buttered Rum

Servings: 4 | Time: 10 mins | Difficulty: Easy
Nutrients per serving: Calories: 73 kcal | Fat: 60g | Carbohydrates: 1.2g | Protein: 0.2g | Fiber: 0.5g

Ingredients
- 1 Cup Butter
- 1 Cup Golden Monkfruit
- 3 Tbsps. Maple Syrup, Sugar-Free
- 2 Tsps. Vanilla Extract
- 1 Cup Heavy Cream
- 1 & 1/2 Cups Monkfruit, Powdered
- 1 Tbsp. Pumpkin Pie Spice
- 2 Cups Hot Water
- 1 Cup Rum

Method
1. Take a bowl and put the golden Monkfruit, butter, vanilla, and maple syrup in it. Whisk well for few minutes until creamy and fluffy.
2. Add all the other ingredients except rum and water and mix well. Set aside.
3. Fill each serving glass with 1/4 cup Rum, 1/2 cup water, and two to three tbsps. of the batter and stir well.

9.83 Tart Cherry Lemon Drop

Servings: 1 | Time: 5 mins | Difficulty: Easy
Nutrients per serving: Calories: 660 kcal | Fat: 60g | Carbohydrates: 7g | Protein: 13g | Fiber: 7g

Ingredients
- 4 Tbsps. Tart Cherry Juice
- 4 Lemon Wedges
- 2 Tbsps. Fresh Lemon Juice
- 3 Tbsps. Vodka
- 2 Tbsps. Water
- 1 Tbsp. Monkfruit, Powdered
- 1 Tbsp. Lemon Juice, Fresh
- 1 Tsp. Monkfruit, Granular
- Ice, To Taste

Method
1. Combine powdered lemon juice, water, and lemon wedges in a blender and blend well until a smooth consistency is attained.
2. Add the vodka, tart cherry juice, and ice in it and blend again until desires consistency.
3. Dip the rim of the cocktail glass in lemon juice and then in granular Monkfruit.
4. Pour in the juice and garnish with a lemon slice if you want.

9.84 Orange Creamsicle Mimosas

Servings: 1 | Time: 10 mins | Difficulty: Easy
Nutrients per serving: Calories: 255 kcal | Fat: 11.5g | Carbohydrates: 8g | Protein: 0.9g | Fiber: 0.1g

Ingredients
- 1 Tbsp. Vanilla Vodka
- 1/4 Cup Orange Juice, Fresh
- 2 Tbsps. Heavy Cream
- 1 Tsp. Monkfruit, Powdered
- 1/2 Cup Sparkling Wine, Dry (Prosecco Or Champagne)

Method
1. Combine all the ingredients in a blender except wine. Blend it well until a smooth consistency is attained.
2. Add the wine and serve.

9.85 Low Carb Strawberry Basil Bourbon Smash

Servings: 1 | Time: 10 mins | Difficulty: Easy
Nutrients per serving: Calories: 159 kcal | Fat: 0.4g | Carbohydrates: 3.5g | Protein: 0.5g | Fiber: 0.9g

Ingredients
- 1/4 Cup Bourbon
- 3 Basil Leaves
- 1/8 Tsp. Black Pepper, Ground
- 3 Strawberries, Sliced
- 2 Tbsps. Lemon Juice, Fresh
- 1 Tsp. Erythritol, Powdered
- Ice, To Taste

Method
1. Combine all the ingredients in a blender and blend until desired consistency is attained.
2. Decant in serving glass and enjoy.

Chapter 10 – Keto-Friendly Desserts Recipes

Are you craving something sweet but worrying about your diet at the same time? You are in the right place. By using these delicious keto-friendly recipes, you can still have dessert when on a keto diet. Just do not forget to check the ingredients and nutritional information to suit your meal-planning goals outlined by your dietitian. I bet you will find a new favorite.

10.1 Sugar-Free Keto Blueberry Muffins With Almond Flour

Servings: 12 I Time: 45 mins I Difficulty: Easy
Nutrients per serving: Calories: 247 kcal I Fat: 21.8g I Carbohydrates: 9.3g I Protein: 7.3g I Fiber: 3.9g

Ingredients

- 1 Tbsp of Baking powder
- 1 tsp of Sea salt
- 1/2 Cup Unsweetened Applesauce
- 2 tsp Vanilla extract
- 2/3 Cup Fresh blueberries
- 3 Cups Almond flour
- 1 tsp Baking soda
- 3 Large Eggs, at room temperature
- 3/4 cup of Monkfruit (or granulated sweetener of choice)
- 4 Tbsp Coconut flour, packed
- 7 Tbsp Coconut oil, melted

Method

1. Preheat the oven to 350 F and use an oil spray to spray a muffin pan.
2. Mix the coconut flour, almond flour, baking powder, baking soda, and salt in a medium dish. Just put aside.
3. In a wide cup, beat together the coconut oil, eggs, monk fruit, applesauce, and vanilla until well mixed, using the electric hand mixer.
4. Stir in the mixture of almond flour until well mixed, together with the blueberries. Let a batter stand for 5 minutes so the moisture can continue to be absorbed by the coconut flour.
5. Divide into 12 muffin cavities (use a large ice cream scoop for cooking the muffins with very domed tops) and bake until clean, approximately 24-25 minutes, golden brown, and insert a toothpick in the middle comes out.
6. Leave for 15 minutes to cool. Then, to remove them, loop a knife carefully along the sides of each muffin. Then, before attempting to take them out, let them cool perfectly in the pan.

10.2 Keto Zucchini Muffins With Almond Flour

Servings: 12 I Time: 30 mins I Difficulty: Easy
Nutrients per serving: Calories: 217 kcal I Fat: 18.5g I Carbohydrates: 8.6g I Protein: 8.2g I Fiber: 4g

Ingredients

- 1 1/2 Cups Monk fruit sweetener
- 1 Tbsp Ground Cardamom
- 1 Tbsp Ground cinnamon
- 1 tsp Baking soda
- 1 tsp Salt
- 1 tsp Vanilla extract
- 1/2 cup Tahini
- 2 Cups Grated zucchini, packed (about 2 medium zucchinis)
- 2 Large Eggs
- 2 tsp Baking powder
- 3 Cups Almond meal (10.5 oz)
- 5 Tbsp Unsweetened vanilla almond milk

Method

1. Preheat the oven to 350 F and adjust to one position below the oven rack center. Use cooking spray to spray a muffin pan.
2. Stir the almond meal, cardamom, baking powder, cinnamon, salt, and soda together in a medium bowl and set aside.
3. Using the electric hand mixer, mix the monk fruit, tahini, almond milk, eggs, and vanilla extract in a large bowl until well mixed.
4. The wet mixture adds the dry mixture and stirs until well mixed, and a thick batter emerges. Finally, fold in a grated zucchini softly when mixed uniformly.
5. Divide the mixture, filling up to the tip, into 12 muffin cavities. I like to use a huge scoop of ice cream, as it gives them a very good, domed top.
6. Bake for about 20-22 minutes, until a toothpick put in the middle, comes out clean. Let it cool for 10 minutes in the bath. Next, turn to a wire rack to cool off perfectly.

10.3 Sugar-Free Low Carb Keto Pecan Pie

Servings: 12 | Time: 1 day 55 mins | Difficulty: Easy
Nutrients per serving: Calories: 328.7 kcal | Fat: 31.1g | Carbohydrates: 18.8g | Protein: 5g | Fiber: 2.7g

Ingredients

- 6 Tbsp Unsalted butter
- 3/4 tsp Salt
- 2/3 cup Powdered erythritol sweetener (I used swerve)
- 2 large eggs
- 1 tsp Vanilla
- 1 tsp Maple extract
- 1 Almond flour pie crust
- 1 1/4 Cups Heavy whipping cream
- 1 1/2 Cups Pecans

Method

1. Whisk together all the sweetener and the butter in a big, high-sided frying pan set over medium-low heat. Cook, constantly whisking, until golden brown in the mixture, around 5-7 minutes.
2. When whisking continuously, throw in the creamy until golden and carry to a soft simmer.
3. Simmer, constantly stirring, around 8 minutes, until the mixture only starts to thicken. Remove from the heat and allow 30 minutes to cool.
4. Heat your oven to 350 F as it is cooling, then spread the pecans on the large baking sheet. Bake until browned and toasted for 10-12 minutes. Then, cut them loose and set them aside.
5. Add in eggs, salt, and the extracts and stir until smooth, until the mixture is cooled somewhat. Stir the pecans in.
6. Through the cooled pie crust, pour the filling and bake until the top feels firm, about 30 minutes. Let it cool at room temperature and cover overnight, and refrigerate.
7. Slice and devour the next day.

10.4 Low Carb Keto Mug Cake

Servings: 1 | Time: 8 mins | Difficulty: Easy
Nutrients per serving: Calories: 312 kcal | Fat: 23.9g | Carbohydrates: 19.6g | Protein: 8.2g | Fiber: 11.6g

Ingredients

- 1 Egg yolk
- 1 Tbsp Coconut oil, melted
- 1 tsp Sugar-free chocolate chips
- 1/2 tsp Baking powder
- 1/2 tsp Vanilla extract
- 2 1/2 Tbsp Monkfruit sweetener
- 2 Tbsp Unsweetened cocoa powder
- 3 Tbsp Coconut flour
- 5 Tbsp Unsweetened vanilla almond milk
- Pinch of salt

Method

1. Whisk all of the dried ingredients in a small dish (everything up to the milk.)
2. Stir the remaining ingredients, minus the chocolate chips, in a separate, shallow cup. Pour in the dry ingredients and stir until the mixture is tender. Stir the chips in.
3. Transfer to a wide mug (14-16oz at least) and distributed evenly.
4. Cook it until the top is fixed and it is no bigger than a dime on some wet spots.

10.5 Keto Chocolate Peanut Butter Fat Bombs

Servings: 12 | Time: 1 hr 10 mins | Difficulty: Easy
Nutrients per serving: Calories: 127 kcal | Fat: 11.6g | Carbohydrates: 3.7g | Protein: 3.8g | Fiber: 1.4g

Ingredients

- 30-40 Drops Liquid stevia (to taste)
- 3/4 Cup Natural creamy peanut butter (may also use almond butter)
- 3 Tbsp cocoa powder (Unsweetened)
- 3 Tbsp Coconut oil

Method

1. Line a mini muffin tin with liners for mini muffins.
2. In a big, microwave-safe dish, put the coconut oil and peanut butter and heat until smooth and molten, for about 1 min.
3. Whisk in the powder with the chocolate until smooth. Then, to taste, whisk the stevia in.
4. Cover about 3/4 of the way, complete with the muffin cavities. Place the pan gently in the refrigerator and cool for around 1 hour, until solid.

10.6 Black Walnut Chocolate Chip Muffins With Almond Flour

Servings: 12 | Time: 40 mins | Difficulty: Easy
Nutrients per serving: Calories: 292 kcal | Fat: 26.1g | Carbohydrates: 10.9g | Protein: 8.3g | Fiber: 5.8g

Ingredients

- 1 Tbsp of Baking powder
- 1 Tbsp Vanilla extract
- 1 tsp of Baking soda
- 1/2 cup + 1 Tbsp Stevia-sweetened chocolate chips
- 1/4 Cup Hammons Black Walnuts, diced
- 3 cups Almond flour (300g)
- 3 large eggs, at room temperature (important)
- 3/4 cup of Monkfruit
- 1 tsp of Salt
- 4 Tbsp Coconut flour, firmly packed (32g)
- 6 Tbsp of Full-fat coconut milk (canned)
- 6 Tbsp of melted Ghee

Method

1. Preheat the oven to 350 °F and coat a muffin pan generously with cooking spray.
2. Mix the almond flour, baking powder, coconut flour, baking soda, and salt in a big dish.
3. Beat the monk fruit, coconut milk, eggs, ghee, and vanilla in a wide cup, using the electric hand mixer, until well mixed.
4. Add the mixture of flour and whisk until it is well mixed. Stir in the black walnuts and chocolate chips. It's going to be moist for your combination, much like cookie dough. Then sit for 5 mins so that the moisture can start to absorb the coconut flour.
5. Fill your muffin tin around 2/3 of the way (we like to use ice cream scoop to make the muffins look cool and domed) and bake on until tops are golden brown, about 25-27 minutes, and insert a toothpick in the middle comes out clean.
6. Let the cool pan Full. Then, loosen them with a knife along each muffin's edges and separate them from the tray.

10.7 Keto Pumpkin Cheesecake

Servings: 12 | Time: 2 hrs 20 mins | Difficulty: Easy

Nutrients per serving: Calories: 242 kcal I Fat: 23g I Carbohydrates: 5.7g I Protein: 6.5g I Fiber: 1.5g

Ingredients

- 3/4 cup Monkfruit
- 2/3 Cup Canned pumpkin
- 2 large eggs, at room temp
- 16 Oz Full fat cream cheese, at room temperature (2 blocks)
- 1 Tbsp Vanilla extract
- 1 Tbsp Pumpkin Pie Spice
- 1 Gluten-free Graham Cracker Crust, baked in a 9-inch springform pan

Method

1. Preheat up to 325 ºF in your oven.
2. Beat the cream cheese and the monk fruit together in a large bowl using the electric hand mixer until smooth and well mixed.
3. Include all the ingredients, then beat until they are mixed. Don't beat it too hard, or the entrance of too much air in the cheesecake will cause it to sink during baking.
4. With 2 or 3 layers of tinfoil, take the graham cracker crust first from the freezer and then wrap the bottom and the sides very firmly. Place the pan in a large pan for roasting.
5. Onto the crust, pour the cheesecake, and smooth out uniformly. Switch to your oven's middle rack and cover the pan with water until the springform pan comes halfway up.
6. Bake for about 55-60 minutes, until the outside is set and a little circle in the middle is jiggly. Turn the oven off and gently break the lock, allowing the cheesecake to sit for 15 minutes in the oven. Shift to the counter to cool fully, then.
7. Cover up and refrigerate for 8 hours until cool, but better if overnight.
8. Hover a knife down the sides of a cheesecake softly, cut the pan and slice it out.

10.8 Sugar-Free No-Bake Keto Cheesecake

Servings: 2 I Time: 5 mins I Difficulty: Easy
Nutrients per serving: Calories: 292 kcal I Fat: 28g I Carbohydrates: 4.9g I Protein: 8g I Fiber: 0.9g

Ingredients

For The Crust:

- 1 tsp Powdered Erythritol Sweetener (I used Swerve)
- 2 tsp Ghee or butter, melted
- 3 Tbsp Almond flour, packed

The Cheesecake:

- 0.5 Cup Cream cheese (softened to room temperature)
- 0.5 tsp Vanilla extract
- 8-12 tsp of Powdered Erythritol Sweetener (to taste)
- 4 Tbsp 2% Plain Greek yogurt

Method

1. Stir the almond flour with sweetener together in a shallow dish. In the ghee, add in and mix until crumbly. Push a tiny ramekin onto the rim.
2. Beat a cream cheese plus sweetener in a medium bowl using the electric hand mixer. Add Cream cheese and vanilla, then beat until mixed again, keeping the sides from scraping as desired.
3. To taste sugar again. Spoon over crust and smoothly spread out. To firm up cream cheese, cool for at least 2 hours.

10.9 Sugar-Free Keto Lemon Bars

Servings: 16 I Time: 1 hr 25 mins I Difficulty: Easy
Nutrients per serving: Calories: 106 kcal I Fat: 8.9g I Carbohydrates: 4.7g I Protein: 2.5g I Fiber: 2.3g

Ingredients

For The Crust:

- Pinch of salt
- 2 Tbsp Monkfruit
- 1/2 cup Coconut oil
- 1 cup of Coconut flour (95g)

For The Topping:

- 3/4 Cup Fresh lemon juice (about 6 large juicy lemons)
- 1 1/2 tsp Coconut flour, sifted
- 1/2 cup Monkfruit
- 2 tsp of Lemon zest
- 4 Eggs

Method

1. Preheat oven to 350 ºF and use coconut oil to generously oil an 8x8 inch pan. Only put aside.
2. Include the coconut flour until it forms a dough.
3. Press the dough uniformly into the pan and bake for about 10 minutes, until just slightly golden brown.
4. Carefully stir together the lemon zest and eggs in a wide bowl until the crust has cooled.

10.10 Keto Brownies

Servings: 16 I Time: 30 mins I Difficulty: Easy
Nutrients per serving: Calories: 107 kcal I Fat: 10g I Carbohydrates: 5.7g I Protein: 2.5g I Fiber: 2.9g

Ingredients

- 1 large egg
- 1/2 tsp Baking soda
- 1/2 tsp Mint extract
- 1/4 cup Plant-based chocolate protein powder
- 1/4 tsp Sea salt
- 2 Egg yolks
- 2 Tbsp vanilla almond milk (Unsweetened)
- 5 ounces Sugar-free chocolate (roughly chopped and divided)
- 6 Tbsp Erythritol Sweetener
- 7 Tbsp Coconut oil (melted and divided)

Method

1. Preheat the oven to 350 ºF and use coconut oil to generously oil an 8x8 inch pan. Put aside.
2. Beat the coconut oil and monk fruit and a pinch of salt together in a large bowl, using an electric hand mixer, until smooth and well mixed. Include coconut flour until it forms a dough.
3. Press the dough uniformly into the pan and bake for about 10 minutes, until just softly golden brown. Leave to cool for 30 minutes.
4. Lower the oven temperature to 325 ºF and make sure that the oven rack is in the center of the oven.
5. Carefully stir together the lemon zest and eggs in a wide bowl until the crust has cooled. Don't use an electric blender here, or once fried, you can top with crack.
6. Heat the lemon juice softly in a separate, medium dish. Whisk in and stir in the monk fruit until it is dissolved. At room temperature, let it cool fully.

10.11 Peanut Butter Truffles

Servings: 10 Truffles I Time: 30 mins I Difficulty: Easy
Nutrients per serving (2 Truffles): Calories: 132 kcal I Fat: 9.9g I Carbohydrates: 10.9g I Protein: 4.4g I Fiber: 5.6g

Ingredients

- 2 tbsp Choc Zero Vanilla Syrup (Sugar-Free)
- 1/4 cup peanut butter
- 1/4 cup Coconut flour
- 1/3 cup chocolate chips (sugar-free)

Method
1. Mix all the peanut butter and the sugar-free syrup in a medium-sized dish.
2. To mix, add the coconut flour and mix. You are looking for a quality that you can roll into balls quickly. You can change the consistency if it is too moist or too dry by adding more coconut flour or the sweetener if required.
3. Take heaped Tsp. fuls of the blend and roll between your hands into balls. Move them to a plate or tray lined with paper that is oil proof.
4. Place the truffles for 10-20 minutes in the freezer until they are solid.
5. Melt the chocolate chips, meanwhile.
6. Take the truffles from the fridge and use the chocolate to decorate them. You should dip them in full or drizzle on top with a little chocolate-up it's to you.
7. For up to 1 week, you can store it in the refrigerator.

10.12 Creamy Keto Chia Pudding

Servings: 2 | Time: 6 hrs 10 mins | Difficulty: Easy
Nutrients per serving: Calories: 258 kcal | Fat: 18g | Carbohydrates: 8.15g | Protein: 3.66g | Fiber: 4.3g

Ingredients
- 1 cup Coconut milk full-fat
- 1 dash Salt
- 1/4 tsp Vanilla extract
- 1/4-1/2 tsp Stevia glycerite
- 2 tbsp Sugar-free jam
- 3 tbsp Black chia seeds

Method
1. In a small mug, mix the chia seeds and 1/2 cup of coconut milk.
2. Whisk together the vanilla, salt, and the leftover coconut milk. Use your preferred liquid sweetener to sweeten the flavor.
3. After 30 minutes, refrigerate and stir well to avoid Chia seeds from clumping at the bottom of the container. Overnight, refrigerate.
4. Layer the chia pudding in a serving cup or a small compact container of 1 Tbsp. of sugar-free jelly. Store in your refrigerator for up to 5 days.

10.13 Cranberry Almond Crumb Muffins

Servings: 12 | Time: 40 mins | Difficulty: Easy
Nutrients per serving: Calories: 330 kcal | Fat: 28.73g | Carbohydrates: 9.46g | Protein: 8.12g | Fiber: 5g

Ingredients
Dry Ingredients (divided use)
- 1/2 cup coconut flour (50 g)
- 1/2 cup low carb sugar (115 g)
- 1/2 Tsp. baking soda
- 1/2 Tsp. salt
- 1 1/2 cups fresh cranberries chopped, (115 g)
- 2 cups almond flour (185 g)
- 2 Tsp. baking powder
- 2 Tbsp. psyllium husk powder (20 gm)

Wet Ingredients
- 6 large eggs
- 1 Tsp. vanilla extract
- 1 Tbsp. white vinegar
- 1/2 Tsp. stevia glycerite
- 1/2 Tsp. almond extract
- 1/2 cup full-fat coconut milk (118 ml)

Crumb Mixture
- 1/4 cup sliced almonds a small handful
- 1/3 cup reserved dry ingredients (35 g)
- 2 Tbsp. low carb sugar
- 1 Tbsp. coconut oil melted (or butter)

Method
1. Preheat the oven to 350 °F and raise the lower third of the rack.
2. With the paper liners, line a muffin pan or brush well with the baking spray. °F
3. Dry Ingredients: Weigh into a medium bowl the first 6 ingredients - NOT the psyllium husk powder.
4. To break up any lumps and to spread the ingredients equally, whisk well.
5. Drop 1/3 cup of the dry mixture and place it in a small dish.
6. To add the muffin ingredients, add the psyllium husk powder and stir again.
7. On top, pour the chopped cranberries.
8. If the tops are well browned, insert a toothpick into the center of a muffin comes out clean, and the cranberry muffins are finished.

10.14 Buttery Keto Pecan Sandies Cookies

Servings: 18 cookies | Time: 1 hr 22 mins | Difficulty: Easy
Nutrients per serving: Calories: 126 kcal | Fat: 12.16g | Carbohydrates: 3.2g | Protein: 2.33g | Fiber: 2.4g

Ingredients
- 1 1/2 tsp Xanthan gum
- 1 cup Almond flour (90 g)
- 1 cup Pecans (4 oz/ 113 g)
- 1 Egg white beaten
- 1 tsp Vanilla
- 1/2 cup Low carb sugar (90 g)
- 1/2 cup Oat fiber (34 g)
- 1/4 tsp Baking soda
- 2 tsp Gelatin (optional)
- 8 tbsp cold salted butter cut into small pieces
- Extra sweetener for dipping tops (2 tbsp)

Method
1. Preheat the oven to 350 and place the rack in the center position. Using parchment paper to cover a sheet pan.
2. Pour pecans and cut them into tiny pieces in the food processor.
3. To combine, add the next Six ingredients and mix.
4. Cut butter into the small pieces and add it until put into the food processor, grinding.
5. Beat vanilla into the white egg in a tiny cup.
6. The food processor spread the mixture equally all around ingredients and pulse until the dough is uniformly moist.

10.15 Keto Cranberry Crumb Bars

Servings: 16 | Time: 1 hr | Difficulty: Easy
Nutrients per serving: Calories: 196 kcal | Fat: 14g | Carbohydrates: 8g | Protein: 4g | Fiber: 3g

Ingredients
Cranberry Filling
- 1 cup water (236.58 g)
- 1 pinch fresh ground nutmeg
- 1 pinch salt
- 1 Tbsp. lemon juice (15 ml) or 3 Real Lemon packets
- 1/2 cup low carbohydrates powdered sugar (80 g)
- 12 ounces cranberries (340 g) fresh or frozen

Shortbread Crust
- 2 cups almond flour (180 g)

- 1 cup shredded coconut (90 g) ground in a coffee grinder
- 1/3 cup whey protein powder (20 g)
- 1/3 cup low carb powdered sugar (50 g)
- 1/2 Tsp. salt
- 8 Tbsp. salted butter melted

Crumb Topping

- 3/4 cup of a shortbread crust mixture
- 1/2 cup chopped walnuts (40 g)
- 3 Tbsp. Low carb brown sugar (35 g)
- 3 Tbsp. Sugar-Free Chocolate Chips (40 g)

Method

1. By cutting a parchment's strips large enough to fill the pan's bottom and go up to two respective ends and hangover, prepare an 8x8 or 9x9 brownie pan.
2. With baking spray, spray the pan and placed the piece of parchment in the pan, smoothing it to match. Then you have to chop the walnuts.
3. Place all of the cranberry filling ingredients in a medium pot and bring it to a boil.
4. For 10-15 minutes, simmer gently until a mixture thickens.
5. When the cranberries are frying, process the crushed coconut until it is finely ground in a coffee grinder or small food processor.
6. In a medium dish, place all the dry ingredients for a shortbread crust.
7. The butter is warmed and poured over the dry ingredients.

10.16 Low Carb Apple Crumb Muffins

Servings: 12 I Time: 45 mins I Difficulty: Easy
Nutrients per serving: Calories: 155 kcal I Fat: 12g I Carbohydrates: 9g I Protein: 5.86g I Fiber: 5.6g

Ingredients

Dry Ingredients (divided use)

- 2 cups Almond flour (190 g)
- 2 tsp Baking powder
- 1/2 cup Oat fiber (45 g)
- 1/2 cup Low Carb Brown Sugar (80 g)
- 1/2 tsp Baking soda
- 1/2 tsp Xanthan gum
- 1/2 tsp ground cardamom
- 1/4 tsp Allspice
- 1/4 tsp ground ginger
- 1/4 tsp Salt

Wet Ingredients

- 4 large Eggs
- 1 tsp Vanilla extract
- 1/2 tsp Stevia glycerite
- 2/3 cup Coconut milk (full fat)(158 ml)
- 3/4 large Granny Smith apple peeled, cored, and grated (5 oz/ 141 g)

Crumb Topping

- 1/3 cup of dry ingredients
- 1 tbsp of melted butter (ghee or coconut oil)
- 1 tbsp Granulated erythritol

Method

1. Preheat Oven to 325 °F. Line up the 12 cup muffin tin with the baking paper of the usual size.
2. Peel the Granny Smith apple.
3. Weigh 5 ounces and grate them (about 3/4 of a big apple).
4. In a medium cup, weigh all the dry ingredients and blend them to break up the lumps.
5. To use as the crumb topping, stir 1/3 cup of a mixture into a small dish.

6. Fill a large bowl with all the grated apple and wet ingredients.
7. Blend with the hand mixer.
8. Pour dry ingredients into wet ingredients and mix until they are combined.

10.17 Coconut Flour Chocolate Chip Cookies

Servings: 8 I Time: 20 mins I Difficulty: Easy
Nutrients per serving: Calories: 71 kcal I Fat: 6.44g I Carbohydrates: 2.85g I Protein: 1.31g I Fiber: 2g

Ingredients

- 2 tbsp Low carb brown sugar (or your favorite granulated sweetener)
- 2 tbsp Light Olive Oil
- 2 tbsp Almond Butter or nut/seed butter of choice
- 1/4 cup Coconut Flour
- 1/2 tsp Vanilla Extract
- 1 tbsp Lily's Sugar-Free Chocolate Chips or 85-90% dark chocolate
- 1 tbsp Flax Meal
- 1 pinch Salt

Method

1. In a medium mixing cup, prepare the flax egg by stirring 1 tbsp of flax meal and 2.5 tbsp of water together. To thicken, leave for a few minutes.
2. Using a spatula, whisk in the vanilla extract and almond butter, and sunflower oil.
3. Add low-carb brown sugar, a touch of salt, and coconut flour to taste. To shape the dough, blend well.
4. Stir in the chips or bits of chocolate. Take 1 Tbsp. of cookie dough and roll your hands into a ball. Place the ball and flatten it into a cookie shape on a baking tray (the cookies will not spread - thinner cookies result in a crisper cookie).
5. Repeat for the cookie dough that remains.
6. At 350 F/ 180 C or until crispy around the outside, bake the cookies for about 15 minutes. Don't bake over them. Enjoy when fully refrigerated.
7. Store in the refrigerator in an airtight jar. Refrigerating mitigates the erythritol-based sweetener's cooling feeling.

10.18 Keto Chocolate Chia Pudding

Servings: 2 I Time: 35 mins I Difficulty: Easy
Nutrients per serving: Calories: 336 kcal I Fat: 27.3g I Carbohydrates: 16g I Protein: 8g I Fiber: 11g

Ingredients

- 2 tbsp low carb sugar (Sukrin:1, Swerve, Lakanto, Truvia, or Besti)
- 1 tsp Vanilla Extract
- 1 tbsp Cocoa Powder (sift before measuring)
- 1 cup Coconut Milk (from a can) (or Almond Milk for fewer calories)
- 1/4 cup Chia Seeds

Method

1. To a mason jar, apply the chocolate powder and sweetener. To clear some lumps, shake well.
2. To the mason jar, apply vanilla extract and coconut milk. tIn order to mix, close the lid, and then shake.
3. Apply to the jar the chia seeds and shake again. Move the container to the fridge until the mixture is well mixed.
4. For at least 30 min, cool it.
5. Serve a chocolate chia pudding with almond yogurt and seasonal fruit in your favorite jars.

10.19 Fluffy Keto Banana Cream Pie

Servings: 8 l Time: 55 mins l Difficulty: Easy
Nutrients per serving: Calories: 526 kcal l Fat: 47g l Carbohydrates: 9.8g l Protein: 11g l Fiber: 4.3g

Ingredients

Low Carb Crust

- 1 recipe Low Carbohydrates Walnut Pie Crust

Banana Pudding (refrigerate overnight)

- 1 cup heavy cream
- 1 tbsp arrowroot powder
- 1 pinch salt
- 3 large egg yolks
- 2 large eggs
- 2 tbsp butter
- 1 tsp vanilla
- 1 tsp banana extract
- 1/2 cup low carb sugar (Swerve granulated or Lakanto)
- 1/3 cup almond milk
- 1 1/4 tsp gelatin powder
- 1/8 tsp xanthan gum

Whipped Cream (for folding into the Banana pudding)

- 2 tbsp low carb powdered sugar (or Swerve Confection or Lakanto Powdered)
- 1/8 tsp xanthan gum
- 1/2 cup heavy cream

Method

1. 1.Make the Low Carbohydrate Walnut Pie Crust according to the direction. Make it cool.
2. Ready by the stove for a strainer. To bloom, spray the gelatin over 1 Tbsp. of water.
3. In a medium saucepan, put the cream & almond milk, turn heat to medium before the milk steams, and create bubbles across the pan sides.
4. Whisk the arrowroot, sweetener, xanthan gum, and salt together in a medium dish. To mix, add the egg yolks or whole eggs and whisk.
5. Add the hot milk into the egg mixture in a thin stream while constantly whisking.

10.20 Low Carb Lemon Curd

Servings: 10 l Time: 25 mins l Difficulty: Easy
Nutrients per serving: Calories: 120 kcal l Fat: 10.7g l Carbohydrates: 2.6g l Protein: 3.74g l Fiber: 0.1g

Ingredients

- 3/4 cup (6 ounces) lemon juice, about 3-4 large lemons
- 1/4 Tsp. stevia glycerite
- 1/2 cup low carb sugar (or Swerve, or Lakanto Monkfruit)
- 4 large eggs
- 4 large egg yolks
- the zest from all of the lemons
- 6 Tbsp. salted butter
- 1 Tbsp. arrowroot powder

Method

1. Weigh and put the erythritol and the arrowroot powder in a medium bath. Stir it together.
2. To make them juicy, roll the lemons on the table, then zest the lemons, applying the zest to erythritol.
3. Separate four eggs and apply the yolks to the pot of erythritol.
4. To the bowl, add the 4 whole eggs and whisk together the eggs and erythritol.
5. Juice and weigh 3/4 cup of the lemons.
6. Strain the juice from the lemon and whisk it into the eggs.
7. Down to medium-low, switch the heat, and finish whisking.

10.21 Low Carb Lemon Lush Dessert

Servings: 15 l Time: 9 hrs 30 mins l Difficulty: Easy
Nutrients per serving: Calories: 308 kcal l Fat: 29g l Carbohydrates: 6.4g l Protein: 7g l Fiber: 1.9g

Ingredients

Lemon Curd (time: 20 minutes)
1 recipe Lemon Curd (chilled at least 4 hours)
Shortbread Crust (time: 30 minutes) (cool completely)

- 3/4 cup pecans, finely chopped
- 1/3 cup whey protein powder
- 1/3 cup of powdered sweetener (Swerve, Sukrin, or Lakanto)
- 2 cups almond flour
- 7 tbsp of salted butter (melted)

Cream Cheese Layers (time: 10 minutes)

- 1 tsp vanilla extract
- 1/4 cup heavy whipping cream (2 fl oz)
- 1/4 cup powdered sweetener (Sukrin, Swerve, or Lakanto)
- 16 oz softened cream cheese (2 packages)

Heavy whipping cream (divided use) (time: 10 minutes)

- 2 cups heavy whipping cream
- 2 tbsp powdered sweetener
- 1 tsp vanilla
- 1/8 tsp xanthan gum (optional - stabilizes the whipped cream)

Assembly (about 10 minutes)

Method

1. Before assembling the cake, prepare a lemon curd and allow it to cool fully for about 4 hours. It is possible to do this many days in advance. It is also excellent to make the shortbread crust ahead.

Pecan Shortbread Crust

1. Preheat the oven to 350 °F. Chop the pecans fairly fine and mix in a small bowl with the rest of the dry ingredients. To mix, whisk together. Melt the butter and pour the spices over it. To form a sticky, crumbly paste, combine with a fork.
2. Pour the materials into a pyrex baking dish of 13x9 inch glass and lay a waxed paper layer on the mixture. Use both fingertips, and press tightly into the bottom of a pan with a flat bottom bottle or measurement cup. Remove a waxed paper, then bake for about 15 minutes, until softly golden.

Whipped Cream

Whip the vanilla and sweeteners with the milk until it is stiff.

Cream Cheese Layer

Whip the cream cheese until nice and light with 1/4 of heavy cream and a sweetener. Adding 1/2 cup of whipped cream at a time, fold 1 1/2 cups of the whipped cream into the cream cheese. Over a shortbread crust, spread evenly.

Lemon Curd Layer

1. When loosened, whisk the lemon curd and scatter softly over the cream cheese surface. Spread the leftover whipped cream gently over the lemon curd. It is better to refrigerate for several hours or overnight.

10.22 Sugar-Free Pecan Turtle Cheesecake Bars

Servings: 16 l Time: 30 mins l Difficulty: Easy
Nutrients per serving: Calories: 439 kcal l Fat: 42g l Carbohydrates: 13g l Protein: 6g l Fiber: 8g

Ingredients

- 1 recipe Homemade Low Carbohydrates Caramel Sauce
- 1 recipe Low Carbohydrates Hot Fudge Sauce

Brown Sugar Pecan Crust

- 4 Tbsp. salted butter, (melted) (2 oz/ 57 g)
- 1/4 cup of whey protein powder (25 g)

- 1/3 cup of Sukrin Gold powdered (70 g)
- 1 cup toasted pecans, (ground) (4 oz/ 114 g)
- 1 cup of Almond Flour (4 oz / 114 g)

Vanilla Cheesecake

- 1 Tbsp. (15 g) vanilla extract
- 2 1/2 packages cream cheese, (softened) (20 oz / 567 g)
- 1/2 cup heavy cream, (whipped) (4 oz/ 118.29 ml)
- 1/2 Tsp. of Stevia Glycerite
- 2/3 cup of low carb powdered sugar (3 oz / 85 g)

Topping

- fudge sauce for drizzling
- caramel sauce for drizzling
- 1 cup toasted pecans, chopped (4 oz/ 114 g)

Method

1. Preheat the oven to 350 F and toast the pecans all.
2. Spray a 9X9 inch wide baking pan with baking spray and cover with a long enough parchment sheet such that two sides hang over it.
3. This will allow you to remove the bars for faster cutting and to serve in 1 big section.
4. 4.Grind the Sukrin Gold and add it to a medium bowl in a coffee grinder.
5. In a coffee grinder, grind the pecans and apply the sweetener to the medium dish.
6. Apply the remainder of the dry ingredients and thoroughly mix.
7. Melt and blend the butter into the dry ingredients.
8. When pressed softly in your palm, the mixture should stay together. In the microwave, heat the caramel and hot fudge sauces until soft and stir with a pour-able consistency.

10.23 Keto Sour Cream Cake

Servings: 12 I Time: 50 mins I Difficulty: Easy
Nutrients per serving: Calories: 358 kcal I Fat: 34.5g I Carbohydrates: 7g I Protein: 8.6g I Fiber: 2.5g

Ingredients

Cake:

- 3 cups almond flour (280 g)
- 1 tsp sea salt
- 3 large eggs (I always use cold)
- 2 tsp vanilla extract
- 1/2 tsp baking soda
- 1/2 cup sour cream
- 1/2 tsp stevia glycerite
- 1/4 cup salted butter, melted (4 tbsp, 2 oz)
- 2/3 cup low carb sugar

Frosting:

- 6 oz cold cream cheese
- 3/4 cup heavy cream
- 1/4 tsp stevia glycerite
- 1/4 cup salted butter (very soft) (4 tbsp, 2 oz)
- 1/3 cup low carb powdered sugar
- 1 tsp vanilla extract

Garnish:

- 12 mint sprigs
- 36 small blueberries
- 6 medium strawberries, halved

Method

1. Preheat the oven to 350 F and place the rack in the center position. Spray a 1/4-sheet tray with baking spray (small jelly roll pan).

2. With parchment paper, line the bottom and spray a paper. Whisk the almond flour to break up some lumps before weighing with a whisk.
3. Measure into a medium-large bowl all the dry ingredients. Whisk to mix thoroughly. Add all the wet ingredients to dry ingredients and combine using a hand mixer thoroughly.
4. For the best results, spread the dense batter onto the ready sheet pan and smooth uniformly with an offset spatula.
5. Bake for 20-30 minutes. When gently pressed with a finger, the cake must spring back but still sound mildly moist. Remove from the oven and perfectly cool.
6. Place a cold cream cheese with the vanilla extract, powdered sweetener, and stevia glycerite in a small-medium cup.
7. Beat until the cream cheese is fully smooth and soft with a hand mixer, around 1-2 min, scraping down each side to remove any leftover lumps.

10.24 Keto Chocolate Mug Cake

Servings: 1 I Time: 3 mins I Difficulty: Easy
Nutrients per serving: Calories: 272 kcal I Fat: 23g I Carbohydrates: 7g I Protein: 9g I Fiber: 4g

Ingredients

- 1 large egg yolk
- 1 tbsp cocoa powder
- 1 tbsp low carb sugar (Lakanto or Swerve)
- 1 tbsp mayonnaise (use sour cream in a pinch)
- 1 tsp water
- 1/4 tsp baking powder
- 2 tbsp almond flour

Method

a. Until weighing, fluff up the almond flour with a whisk and sift before measuring the cocoa powder.
b. Measure into a mug or jelly jar the dry ingredients and blend fully with a fork.
c. Add the egg yolk, mayonnaise, and water, stirring thoroughly to make sure you have all from the bottom. Leave the batter to rest for 1-2 minutes.
d. Depending on the microwave, microwave for 50 seconds.

10.25 Lemon Ricotta Cake

Servings: 9 I Time: 1 hr I Difficulty: Easy
Nutrients per serving: Calories: 212 kcal I Fat: 17g I Carbohydrates: 7g I Protein: 8g I Fiber: 3.5g

Ingredients

- 1/2 stick soft butter (2 oz/57 g)
- 1/2 cup low carb sugar (Swerve Granulated or Lakanto Classic)
- 1 1/2 tbsp fresh lemon juice
- 4 large eggs (cold) (one more egg if not using baking powder)
- 1 cup whole milk ricotta cheese (cold) (250 g)
- 1 tsp lemon zest (zest from one lemon)
- 1 tsp vanilla extract

Dry Ingredients

- 1 cup almond flour (whisk before measuring)
- 1/4 tsp salt
- 2 tsp baking powder
- 4 tbsp coconut flour (whisk before measuring)

Method

1. To 325 ºF. Preheat oven. To suit the inner bottom of an 8 x 2-inch circular pan, cut a slice of

parchment. The pan is sprayed or buttered, and the parchment is applied.

2. In a small dish, weigh the dry ingredients and whisk to remove any lumps—the cream when fully mixed with the butter, vanilla, and sweetener.

3. Add one egg and beat until fluffy and light. Stir in the ricotta cheese, lemon zest, lemon juice, and beat until well mixed.

4. Mix 1/3 of the dry ingredients into the batter by working by thirds.

5. Add the egg and blend. Repeat by starting with the last egg with the remaining ingredients. Carefully spread the batter with an offset spatula into the prepared cake tray.

6. Bake for 50 minutes or until the middle of the cake comes out clean with a toothpick inserted. Wrap every remaining cake in cling film and leave for 3 days (unless it is hot and humid) or refrigerate in the fridge.

7. Slightly warm before eating, if refrigerated.

10.26 Keto Strawberry Crepes

Servings: 4 I Time: 15 mins I Difficulty: Easy
Nutrients per serving: Calories: 316 kcal I Fat: 29g I Carbohydrates: 5g I Protein: 9g I Fiber: 0.5g

Ingredients

- 4 low carb crepes
- 4 tbsp low carb sugar (divided use)
- 3 ounces fresh strawberries, quartered and sliced
- 2 tsp Brandy, Rum, or Bourbon (optional, replace with water)
- 2 tsp water
- 1/2 cup Heavy Whipping Cream
- 1/2 tsp vanilla extract
- 1/2 cup sour cream

Method

1. In a small bowl with 1 tbsp of the sweetener, apply the brandy and water, and combine to dissolve. It does not completely dissolve. Slice the strawberries, then put them in a small dish. Apply the combination of brandy and stir. Put the bowl aside as you macerate the strawberries.

2. In a 2-3 cup mug, weigh the heavy cream, the leftover sweetener, and vanilla. Whip until very rigid.

3. In a shallow dish, apply the sour cream and whisk it to loosen. Spoon 1/4 of whipped cream onto the sour cream and mix the cream softly. Fold half of the leftover whipped cream with a large spoon or rubber spatula onto the sour cream mixture. Apply to the sour cream mixture the leftover whipped cream and fold together fully. (At this point, the filling could be refrigerated for up to a day.) (Makes around 1 1/2 cups)

4. Place half of each crepe with 1/4 of a whipped cream mixture, spreading just half of each crepe. Fold the exposed half over the filled side, then fold, like a handkerchief, corner to corner. On each tray, position one. (If sealed and refrigerated, the crepes should be filled for many hours before serving.)

5. Whisk the strawberries over each loaded crepe and spoon 1/4 of strawberries and juice on them. Serve.

10.27 Hazelnut Creme Brulee

Servings: 2 I Time: 40 mins I Difficulty: Easy
Nutrients per serving: Calories: 534 kcal I Fat: 52g I Carbohydrates: 4g I Protein: 7g

Ingredients

- 3 large egg yolks
- 2 tbsp spiced rum, brandy, or bourbon
- 2 tbsp low carb sugar (or Swerve Granular) (sugar, for non-low carbers)
- 1/4 tsp hazelnut extract
- 1 pinch salt
- 1 cup heavy cream

Optional (powdered sweetener for the top):
- 4 tsp Low carb brown sugar

Method

1. Preheat the oven to 350 °F and place the rack in the center position. Heat water until hot, not boiling, in a tea kettle. Halfway up the side of the ramekins, find a pan wide enough to accommodate 2, 6-oz ramekins and shallow enough to add water.

2. Add to a small bowl the yolks, and sweetener. With a fork, beat well to perfectly break up the yolks. Drop some giant chalazae.

3. In a small pot, pour the heavy cream and put it over medium heat. Stir with a whisk periodically before bubbles appear along the pot's edge, and the cream steams. Turn the heat off and start pouring the egg yolk into the mixture of the hot cream - very gently, in a thin stream, all the while whisking rapidly. Spiced rum (bourbon, brandy) and hazelnut extract are whisked in.

4. Divide the combination of creme brulee equally between the ramekins. Put the ramekins in the pan and fill the cooking pan with hot water halfway up the ramekin's sides (not boiling). Place the pan carefully in the oven and bake for thirty min or until the creme brulee is only centered in the very middle. (Depending on the form of the ramekin.0, it may always be just a little bit wiggly in the middle

5. In the water bath, cool the hazelnut creme brulee for 30 minutes before transferring it to a rack to cool entirely. Cover and refrigerate for about 4 hours with plastic wrap, but it's best overnight.

6. Sprinkle 1 tsp sweetener or over the tops of each creme brulee before serving. Melt the sweetener until it caramelizes, turning brown with a culinary torch. Instead, add to the top a dollop of whipped cream. Serve.

10.28 Sugar-Free Chocolate Pie

Servings: 10 I Time: 40 mins I Difficulty: Easy
Nutrients per serving: Calories: 337 kcal I Fat: 34g I Carbohydrates: 8g I Protein: 6g I Fiber: 5g

Ingredients

Flaky Pie Crust
- 5 tbsp butter
- 3 tbsp oat fiber
- 1/4 tsp salt
- 1 tsp water
- 1 large egg white
- 1 1/2 cup almond flour

Filling
- 4 ounces unsweetened baking chocolate squares, melted
- 4 large pasteurized eggs, cold
- 2 Tsp. vanilla extract
- 6 ounces (1 1/2 sticks) salted butter, very soft
- 1/2 Tsp. stevia glycerite (or more Sukrin or Swerve to taste)
- 1 1/4 cups low carb powdered sugar (or Swerve Confectioners)
- 1/4 cup heavy cream

Topping
- chocolate shavings optional - I used 2 squares of Chocolate at 86% cacao
- 3/4 cup heavy cream
- 2 tbsp low carb powdered sugar (or swerve)

Method

1. Preheat the oven to 350°F. Using baking spray to spray a pie dish. I'm using a pyrex 9-inch baking dish. (On the pie plate base, we scatter sesame seeds, so the crust should not adhere to the bottom.)
2. Measure into the food processor the oat fiber, almond flour, and salt. Cut the butter into pellets and pulse with dry ingredients until the small peas are the butter's size. Mix 1 Tsp. of water with the white egg and spill over the dry ingredients. The phase before it all comes along with the dough. For about 30 minutes to 5 days, you can refrigerate the dough.
3. For your pie plate, roll the pastry into two sheets of plastic wrap until it becomes the right size. Remove the plastic top piece and invert dough over the plate of the pie. Coax the dough softly onto the bottom and sides of a plate. Remove the plastic and bring the edge into shape. With a fork, dock the dough.
4. Bake the crust for 10-15 minutes before the golden brown starts to transform. Let it cool fully, then cover until ready to use with plastic wrap.
5. Unsweetened baking chocolate is finely diced and stored in a microwaveable dish. Heat up to 30 secs at a time before it nearly melts. The excess heat from a bowl should ensure that the remainder is dissolved.
6. In a stand mixer or a large mixing cup, place the butter and Swerve or Sukrin Melis. Apply the paddle attachment to the mixer, then beat the butter and a sweetener for around 2 minutes at medium speed. Give the bowl a scrape. Add the chocolate to the molten one and blend for 1 minute. Scrape thoroughly down the bowl. Apply 1/4 cup of heavy cream, vanilla, then glycerin stevia, and beat for 2 more minutes. Spread a filling back into a bowl and drop the paddle attachment.
7. Add the whisk attachment and switch back at medium speed on the stand mixer. Add one egg on time and let the mixer run between each addition for about 3 minutes, scraping the pan after the third and fourth additions.
8. Finish blending at high speed with a fast burst and disperse the filling into the pie's shell and refrigerate. [NOTE: refrigerate for 40 minutes if the filling splits (separates), then add 1/4 tsp of xanthan gum. Whip to release the filling for a few seconds at medium speed and then at high just a few seconds before it comes together. There could be another pinch of xanthan gum if required.]
9. With a spoon or spatula, spoon the filling onto the pie crust, then smooth it. Refrigerate, and leave open for 6 hours or overnight.
10. Whip the 3/4 cup heavy cream and finish the pie with your preferred sweetener. Additionally, by running the vegetable peeler down of a chocolate slice, chocolate curls may be added.

10.29 Sugar-free Nutella Swirl Muffins

Servings: 6 I Time: 40 mins I Difficulty: Easy
Nutrients per serving: Calories: 255 kcal I Fat: 22g I Carbohydrates: 6g I Protein: 9g I Fiber: 1g

Ingredients

Dry Ingredients
- 1/4 tsp salt
- 1 tsp baking powder
- 1 tbsp whey protein powder (We use Isopure Zero Carb)
- 1 1/2 cups Almond Flour (130 g)

Wet Ingredients
- 2 large eggs
- 1/2 cup heavy cream
- 1 1/2 tsp vanilla extract
- 1/3 cup low carb sugar

Swirl Topping
- 6 tsp Free Chocolate Hazelnut Spread (Sukrin Sugar)

Method

1. Preheat the oven to 350 F and put the rack in the center position. Strip 6 muffin wells of standard size with parchment liners. In the microwave, heat a Sukrin Chocolate Hazelnut Spread for 20-30 seconds or until a Tsp. is easy to drizzle.
2. Place the wet ingredients in the mixer. Place the dry ingredients in the mixer then. Switch down the mixer and mix. With a spatula, cut the lid and help the phase-out. Turn to medium-low and mix for 20 seconds just until the batter is smooth and well ventilated.
3. Divide the muffin batter, filling 3/4 full, among six muffin wells. Drizzle 1 Tsp. of Sukrin Chocolate Hazelnut Spread and swirl/mix with a toothpick over each muffin.
4. Bake for about 25-35 minutes or until the muffin tops are smooth to the touch and springy but still sound moist. Cool in the muffin tin for 5 minutes, then remove from a cooling rack. Refrigerate for 7-10 days in an airtight jar or stock for up to 5 days on the fridge.

10.30 Moist Chocolate Walnut Cake

Servings: 12 I Time: 55 mins I Difficulty: Easy
Nutrients per serving: Calories: 264 kcal I Fat: 23g I Carbohydrates: 10g I Protein: 8g I Fiber: 5g

Ingredients

Dry Ingredients
- 3 ounces walnuts
- 1/4 Tsp. salt
- 1/3 cup coconut flour (fluff up with whisk before measuring)
- 1/3 cup cocoa powder (sift then measure)
- 1/2 cup low carb sugar (or Swerve Granulated)
- 1 tbsp baking powder
- 1 1/4 cup almond flour (whisk before measuring)

Wet Ingredients
- 4 large eggs
- 1 Tsp. vanilla
- 1 Tsp. stevia glycerite
- 1/2 cup buttermilk (or heavy cream or full-fat coconut milk)
- 1/4 cup walnut oil (or melted butter)

Chocolate Ganache Glaze
- 1/4 cup heavy cream
- 2 oz Ghiradelli Intense Dark Chocolate (86% or any high percentage chocolate)
- 2 Tbsp. butter or coconut oil (room temperature)

Method

a. Preheat the oven to 325 °F and put the rack in the center of the oven. On the sheet of waxed paper or the parchment, trace the base of an 8 x 2 inches cake tray. Cut the circle out. Spray the cake pan with the baking spray and line the parchment circle at the pan's bottom. Weigh the walnuts and grind the sweetener until finely ground in a food processor.
b. In a medium cup, weigh the dry cake ingredients (along with ground walnuts) and vigorously stir with a large whisk to mix. Add the wet ingredients to another bowl and pound them with a hand mixer. Add the wet ingredients to the dry dish and combine until all the ingredients are thoroughly integrated.
c. To dislodge some large air bubbles, spoon the batter in the cake pan and softly tap it on a counter 2-3 times. When carefully squeezed with

your finger and insert a toothpick in the middle, bake for about 30-40 minutes or until the cake still looks moist. Do not bake in excess.

d. Take a Chocolate Walnut Cake from the oven and cover it with a clean tea towel. Let the cake perfectly cold. Then seal until ready to cover with ganache in plastic wrap. Until topping with the ganache, ensure that the cake is at room temperature.

e. Finely cut the chocolate and put it with the heavy cream and butter in a shallow microwaveable dish. Cover with waxed paper, then microwave for 30 seconds. For 1 minute, let stand, then gently whisk to mix. The ganache should be rich and shiny. Use it instantly.

f. Pour a chocolate ganache in the middle of a cake and spread it over the side with a spatula or knife, causing it to spill. Decorate, if you wish, with walnut halves (optional) or pieces of walnut while the ganache is still moist. Once the ganache has set, cut, and serve (it will still be fairly soft but not runny).

g. Hold it in the fridge or on the table. Let it arrive at room temperature for about 30 minutes before having it if refrigerated.

10.31 Blackberry Custard Pie

Servings: 10 I Time: 20 mins I Difficulty: Easy
Nutrients per serving: Calories: 357 kcal I Fat: 32g I Carbohydrates: 8g I Protein: 11g I Fiber: 3g

Ingredients

- 4 large eggs
- 3/4 cup heavy cream
- 2 large egg yolks
- 1/4 tsp xanthan gum
- 1/2 cup low carb sugar
- 1 tsp vanilla extract
- 1 tsp gelatin powder (flourished in 1 tbsp water)
- 1 recipe Low Carbohydrates Keto Graham Cracker Crust (resists soaking)
- 1 pinch salt
- 1 pinch ground nutmeg
- 1 cup buttermilk
- 1 cup blackberries (1/2 pint)

Method

1. To bloom, sprinkle gelatin with 1 Tbsp. of water. Measure the sweetener, xanthan gum, and salt in a non-reactive metal pot with a 4-6 cup size. Add the yolks and eggs and mix until thoroughly mixed. Whisk in the heavy cream and buttermilk.

2. Put the pot over medium heat until the mixture starts to thicken, whisking continuously - about 5 minutes if using Tagatesse (either a sugar) and 8 mins for Sukrin:1 or Swerve. Switch the heat medium-low and whisk for 1 minute with vigor (If whisking fails, the custard can burst). Remove from the heat and whisk for 90 seconds more. Tear the gelatin into bits and pour it into the custard and stir until it is dissolved. Include vanilla and the nutmeg, stirring until combined.

3. Only cool the mixture slowly, and pipe it onto the pre-baked pie crust. Balance the top and layer the blackberries until they are at least halfway submerged, pressing them into a custard. Refrigerate exposed before coating with cling film for several hours. Before chopping and serving, chill for at least 6 hours.

10.32 Low Carb Chocolate Chip Muffins

Servings: 6 I Time: 30 mins I Difficulty: Easy

Nutrients per serving: Calories: 270 kcal I Fat: 24g I Carbohydrates: 11g I Protein: 7g I Fiber: 7g

Ingredients

Cream Together:
- 1/2 tsp of lemon zest
- 1/2 tsp of vanilla extract
- 1/4 cup low carb sugar
- 2 oz softened unsalted butter
- 4 oz softened cream cheese

Dry Ingredients:
- 1 tsp baking powder
- 1/2 cup coconut flour
- 1/4 tsp salt
- 1/8 tsp xanthan gum

Wet Ingredients:
- 1/4 cup heavy cream
- 3 large eggs

Fold:
- 3 tbsp Lily's Sugar-free Chocolate Chips
- 4 oz strawberries, small dice

Method

1. Preheat the oven to 350 °F and place the rack in the middle. Standard muffin wells from Line 6 with paper liners. Dice some strawberries. The lemon zest. Mix the dry ingredients.

2. Cream together the whole 5 ingredients until light and smooth with a hand mixer. Again, add 1 egg and milk.

3. Apply 1/3 of the dry, well-beaten ingredients, followed by another egg. Only repeat. Make sure that a soft mousse-like appearance is preserved by fading out. The rest of the dry ingredients are added, followed by heavy cream. Half of the strawberries and half of the chocolate chips are rolled in. The batter's going to be dense.

4. Spoon the batter in a zip-lock bag and slit one of the corners with a wide hole. Squeeze the batter, placed in the middle, onto each liner. Use a muffin scoop alternately. To resist browning, brush the top of the muffins with erythritol. Arrange the remaining chocolate chips and strawberries on top.

5. In the oven center, put the muffin tin and set the oven up to 400 °F for 6 minutes. Switch the oven back to 350 °F and bake for an extra 12-18 minutes. The tops should be solid to the touch but still, look a little wet. On a wire rack, cool perfectly. Keep it softly warm in the refrigerator before eating it.

10.33 No-Bake Sugar-Free Strawberry Cheesecake Tart

Servings: 10 I Time: 35 mins I Difficulty: Easy
Nutrients per serving: Calories: 306 kcal I Fat: 28g I Carbohydrates: 5g I Protein: 10g I Fiber: 3g

Ingredients

Walnut Hemp Seeds Crust
- 2 tbsp of coconut oil (melted)
- 1/2 cup Bob's Mill Hemp Seed's Hearts
- 1 tbsp of Sukrin Fiber Gold Syrup/Vitafiber Syrup
- 1 cup walnut pieces, toasted

Cheesecake Filling
- 1 tbsp lemon juice
- 1/4 cup low carb powdered sugar
- 4 ounces cream cheese cold
- 4 ounces softened goat cheese
- 6 ounces strawberries, sliced
- zest from the lemon

- 4 ounces heavy cream, cold

Optional

- 2 tsp fresh thyme or rosemary (finely chopped)

Method

1. The oven should be preheated to 350 °F. Put on a sheet pan and then toast the walnuts for 15 minutes or until golden in color. To remove most of the loosened skin, let it cool, then rub in the tea towel.

2. In a food processor, position the hemp seeds and the walnuts and grind them until finely ground. To spread the ingredients, apply the molten coconut oil and fiber syrup (you can use honey if not low carb), then pulse. (If rolled into balls, this also produces a perfect snack.)

3. Using parchment paper to cover a tart pan. (I used a round 14x6x1 tin, but it would fit with a big circular or many small round tins.) Spread the mixture of the crust into the pan and then force it into the crust to ensure that the sides are solid. Cover tightly and place until set in the freezer and the filling is prepared or place until appropriate in the refrigerator. It thaws rapidly.

4. In a cup, add cream cheese and the sweetener, and whip until loosened with a hand mixture. Add some heavy cream, then whip until soft and light. Finally, add the cheese from the goat and whip it again. Use or cover immediately and put in the fridge until needed. Whip to loosen before expanding onto the tart crust when kept overnight in the refrigerator. (Place 1/3 of a filling in a piping bag before piping to decorate the roof. First, we place the strawberries and decorate them around.)

5. Cut the strawberries and add the filling to them. Serve instantly. If you serve later, right before eating, apply the sliced strawberries to keep them from being soggy.

10.34 Black Bottom Pie

Servings: 10 I Time: 50 mins I Difficulty: Easy
Nutrients per serving: Calories: 273 kcal I Fat: 26g I Carbohydrates: 8g I Protein: 6g I Fiber: 26g

Ingredients

- 1 recipe Low Carb Flaky Pie Crust (pre-baked)

Base Custard

- 1 tbsp gelatin
- 2 tsp cornstarch (or arrowroot powder)
- 3 large egg yolks
- 1 whole egg
- 1/2 tsp salt
- 1 1/4 cup heavy cream
- 1/4 cup water
- 1/4 tsp xanthan gum
- 2/3 cup low carb sugar
- 3/4 cup almond milk

Black Bottom Layer

- 1 cup custard
- 1 1/2 oz unsweetened baking chocolate

Chiffon Layer

- remaining custard
- 3 large egg whites
- 1/2 tsp cream of tartar
- 1 tsp vanilla
- 1 tbsp rum, bourbon, or brandy

Whipped Cream Topping

- 1/4 cup low carb powdered sugar
- 1/2 cup heavy cream

Optional

- shaved chocolate

Method

1. Separate 3 eggs into whites and yolks. Ensure the whites don't have any yolks, so they don't whip through the meringue required for the chiffon. The baking chocolate (unsweetened) is finely diced and then put in a small heat-safe bowl wide enough to hold 1 cup of custard. In a small cup, position the water and spray the gelatin over a surface to bloom.

To make the custard:

1. In a small jar, mix the 2/3 cup of sweetener, xanthan gum, cornstarch or arrowroot, and salt. Apply the egg yolks and the entire egg to the whisk. Heavy cream and almond milk are whisked in.

2. Switch the heat to low-medium. Whisk until the mixture starts to thicken, approximately 8-10 minutes, slowly but steadily, paying closer concentration to the sides and the bottom of the pot. Whisk briskly for about 2-4 more minutes as the custard begins to cook and thicken. For an extra 2 minutes, withdraw the custard from the heating and whisk.

Black Bottom Layer:

1. Drop the hot custard from one Cup and add it to the cut chocolate. Whisk once mixed with the cocoa. Let it cool, then put it into the crust of the pie. Protect and hold refrigerated.

Chiffon Layer:

1. Tear into tiny pieces the bloomed gelatin and apply it to the leftover custard. Whisk until it melts completely with the gelatin. Coat the custard with the cling film, allowing the steam to escape from a slight gap. When it has cooled, refrigerate for 2-3 hrs.

2. Place the egg albumins in a medium bowl, then sprinkle with the tartar cream until the custard's remainder has cooled. a Whisk at medium-high speed using a hand or a stand mixer until the egg albumins quadruple in volume is shiny and maintains a stiff top when the beaters are pulled straight up from the bowl. Only put aside.

3. Take the cooled custard from the fridge and use a hand or stand mixer to whisk it to loosen its texture. Include the rum and vanilla (or the flavoring of your choice) and whip again. If you like it sweeter, now is the time to change the sugar with the powdered stevia or a stevia glycerite.

4. Apply 1/3 of the meringue to custard and use a hand mixer to combine softly. Fold half the remaining meringue with the large rubber spatula into a lightened custard. Old the leftover meringue onto the custard softly but thoroughly, finishing the chiffon layer. Now spoon into a crust of the pie and smooth out to the edges. Refrigerate for several hours until exposed. Then, cover loosely and refrigerate overnight with clinging wrap.

Whipped Cream Topping:

1. Whip the sweetener with the heavy cream until it is thick. Swirl with a whisk and spoon into the pastry. Cover it with shavings of chocolate if you like. Use a vegetable peeler to shave the cocoa, as though you're peeling a carrot.

10.35 Sugar-Free Carrot Cake Cupcakes

Servings: 9 I Time: 1 hr I Difficulty: Easy
Nutrients per serving: Calories: 370 kcal I Fat: 35g I Carbohydrates: 7g I Protein: 8g I Fiber: 3g

Ingredients

Cream Together

- 1/3 cup Low carb brown sugar
- 1/2 tsp vanilla
- 4 tbsp butter, softened

Dry Ingredients

- 1/4 cup shredded coconut
- 1/4 tsp ground ginger

- 1/4 tsp salt
- 1/3 cup almond flour
- 1/3 cup coconut flour
- 2 tbsp whey protein powder (helps with texture)
- 1 tsp baking powder
- 1 tsp cinnamon

Wet Ingredients
- 2 ounces finely grated carrot (about 1 medium)
- 2 tbsp heavy cream
- 3 large eggs

Fluffy Cream Cheese Frosting
- 1 tsp vanilla
- 1/2 cup heavy cream whipped very stiffly (4 oz)
- 1/3 cup low carb powdered sugar (or Swerve Confectioners)
- 4 ounces butter softened
- 4 ounces cream cheese softened

Method

1. Preparation: Preheat the oven to 350 °F and put the rack on the oven's bottom. Wells of Line 9 cupcakes with liners. Measure in a small bowl of dry ingredients and whisk to break up some lumps. Grate the carrot finely.
2. 2. Method: In a medium cup, place the melted butter, the brown sugar substitute, and vanilla and mix until light and fluffy with a hand mixer. Add 1 egg and beat until the mixture is light, dense, and fluffy again.
3. 3. Apply 1/3 of dry ingredients and combine properly, cleaning the Cup thoroughly. Add another egg and blend until it is mixed well and light and fluffy with the batter. After the dry additions, begin mixing the dry and wet components, rubbing the bowl and leaving the texture smooth and light. At the very top, add the carrot and the heavy cream until mixed, blend. (The batter should be moist but simple to deal with. Add 1-2 more Tsp. of heavy cream if it's not, but work quickly).
4. 4. Bake: Before it thickens, get the batter into cupcake liners. Cut the batter equally between the muffin liners, then put it in the oven. To rise the flour, turn the oven to 400 °F and bake for 5 minutes. Turn the oven back to 350 F and bake for about 20 minutes or until the tops become firm but still sound moist when gently pressed with a finger. Remove and allow to cool entirely before frosting.
5. 5. Fluffy Cream Cheese Frosting: First, whip together the vanilla extract and a sweetener with the butter and cream cheese. Until it is very stiff, whip the heavy cream. 1/3 at a time, add the whipped cream into the cream cheese mixture. Frost and refrigerate the cupcakes or serve.

10.36 Strawberry Cream Cheese Crumble Bars

Servings: 16 I Time: 45 mins I Difficulty: Easy
Nutrients per serving: Calories: 284 kcal I Fat: 19g I Carbohydrates: 7g I Protein: 9g I Fiber: 3g

Ingredients

Shortbread Crust
- 1 1/4 tsp ground ginger
- 1 cup Bob's Red Mill Shredded Coconut ground
- 1/2 tsp salt
- 1/3 cup Low carb brown sugar
- 1/3 cup whey protein powder
- 2 cups almond flour
- 4 oz butter, melted

Cream Cheese
- 1 large egg
- 1/4 cup low carb powdered sugar
- 8 oz cream cheese (softened)

Crumble Topping
- Low carb brown sugar optional (to taste)
- 8 oz strawberries (small dice)
- 1/3 cup sliced almonds
- 1 cup of reserved shortbread crust mixture

Method

1. Preheat the oven to 350°F. Spray with a baking spray on a 9 x 9-inch metal pan and line with a parchment strip that occupies all or much of the pan's bottom and overhangs the two opposite sides. After frying, this will help you extract the entire dessert from the pan. Powder the coconut in the coffee grinder. Dice some strawberries.
2. Measure into a small mixing bowl all of the dry ingredients. With a whisk, blend thoroughly. The butter is melted and added to the dry ingredients. With a broad spoon or rubber spatula, stir and press a mixture until the butter is absorbed. To verify if it can stay together nicely, pinch a small amount in your palm. If not, substitute the melted butter for 1-2 more Tsp. . Drop 1 cup of the crumble topping mixture
3. In a small cup, beat the melted cream cheese with an egg and Sukrin Melis until they are thoroughly mixed.
4. Pour the remainder of the shortbread paste into the pan, spread it thinly, and cover with a sheet of waxed paper. Use a smooth glass bottom to press the crust tightly into the pan. Low the cream cheese over the crust with a spoon and spread it carefully. Accessible areas will be there. Distribute the strawberries sliced. Over the strawberries, crumble 1/2 of a reserved crust mixture and half of the almonds. And repeat. Sprinkle with extra sweetener if needed.
5. Place in the oven center and cook for 30-40 mins or until golden brown outside. Before getting it out of the grill, let it cool down.
6. Cut a strawberry cream cheese crumble with a large chef's knife into 16 circles, chopping it straight down. Put in an airtight jar in the freezer.

10.37 Low Carb Raspberry Custard

Servings: 4 I Time: 45 mins I Difficulty: Easy
Nutrients per serving: Calories: 391 kcal I Fat: 34g I Carbohydrates: 6g I Protein: 5g I Fiber: 1g

Ingredients

- 1 2/3 cups heavy cream
- 1/4 tsp stevia glycerite (or more Sukrin to taste)
- 1/3 cup low carb powdered sugar
- 1/4 tsp vanilla bean powder (or 1/2 tsp vanilla extract)
- 1 cup Brut Champagne
- 6 large egg yolks
- 2 ounces raspberries

Method

1. Simmer over medium-low heat the champagne - low heat until only 2-3 Tbsp. are remaining. Be alert that it shouldn't burn. To cool, spill into a small glass bowl.
2. Preheat the oven to 350 °F and place the rack in the center position. Heat water until hot, but not boiling, in a tea kettle. Halfway up sides of the ramekins, find a pan wide enough to accommodate 4 ramekins and shallow enough to add water.
3. In a medium dish, apply the yolks and 1 tbsp of the sweetener. Beat well to break up the yolks entirely. Remove any residual chalazia. In a small bath, mix in the heavy cream and apply the remaining sweetener and the vanilla bean powder (add later, if using extract). Place the pot over medium heat and heat until bubbles begin to boil along the edge of the pot, stirring regularly with a whisk. Turn the heat off and start

pouring the egg yolk in the hot cream mixture in a thin stream very slowly, while whisking all the while rapidly. Whisk in the champagne and stevia glycerite reduction (add the vanilla extract if you are using that instead).

4. Place each ramekin with 3 raspberries. Divide the mixture of crème Brulee equally into four ramekins. Lace the ramekins in the pan and, halfway up sides of the ramekins, fill the pan with hot water. Place the pan carefully in the oven and bake for 30 mins or until gently set at the very beginning of the crème Brulee.

5. In the water bath, cool the crème Brulee for an hour before removing it to a rack to cool fully. Cover and cool with plastic wrap for at least 4 hours (overnight is better).

6. Before eating, sprinkle 1/2 Tsp. of sweetener over the top of each crème Brulee. Use a cooking torch to heat the sweetener until it caramelizes, turning orange. Alternately, apply to the top a dollop of whipped cream. Just serve. If needed, garnish with extra raspberries. (Custards can be stored for up to 3 days in the refrigerator - no longer than that, and the raspberries start to release water).

10.38 Sugar-free Lemon Cupcakes with Cream Cheese Frosting

Servings: 6 I Time: 30 mins I Difficulty: Easy
Nutrients per serving: Calories: 375 kcal I Fat: 36g I Carbohydrates: 7g I Protein: 7g I Fiber: 3g

Ingredients

Whipped Cream Cheese Frosting

- 4 ounces cream cheese, cold
- 1/4 cup low carb powdered sugar
- 3/4 cup heavy cream (6 oz)

Sugar-free Lemon Cupcakes

- 1 tbsp lemon juice
- 1 tsp baking powder
- 1/2 cup coconut flour
- 1/2 tsp vanilla extract
- 1/3 cup low carb sugar
- 1/4 cup heavy cream
- 1/4 tsp LorAnn Lemon Oil
- 1/4 tsp salt
- 2 ounces butter, soft
- 2 ounces cream cheese, soft
- 3 large eggs (cold)
- zest from 1 lemon

Method

1. Cream Cheese Frosting: (The mixer works well, but a hand mixer also works.) To remove it, whip the cream cheese. Add and whip the powdered sweetener. When mixed, Mix, then whisk until the frosting is stiff and smooth by incorporating the heavy cream at a time. Use it immediately, or cover and then refrigerate until needed.

2. Preparation: The oven should be preheated to 350 ºF. Place the rack in the center of the oven—the lemon with zest and juice. Line a muffin pan with 6 wells and cupcake liners. Whisk the baking powder, coconut flour, and salt together in a shallow bowl to break down any lumps. Apply the heavy cream to the lemon juice.

3. Method: Beat the first 6 ingredients of the cupcakes in a medium bowl until finely ground (1-2 minutes). Add one egg and whisk until the mixture appears light and fluffy (this can split or detach, it's okay) into the butter mixture. Apply 1/3 of the dry ingredients and blend until thoroughly combined, ensuring the soft, fluffy feel is preserved. We want to have a light and fluffy - nearly mousse-like feel throughout this process.

4. Add now another egg and mix until combined fully. Apply half the remaining dry ingredients, stirring once more. Apply the last egg, followed by one of the last dry ingredients, and beat until thoroughly integrated. Beat until the batter is moist but still soft and fluffy. Finish by adding heavy cream.

5. In a plastic zip-lock bag, spoon the dense batter and snip off an edge, making around a 3/4-1 inch opening. In a muffin liner, put the snipped corner and squeeze a batter into the fat, rounded mound, filled around 3/4 of the muffin liner. To every muffin liner, repeat, adding any batter left to those who require a little extra. On your finger, knockdown if there are any peaks. Take the pan off the counter a few inches and let it drop.

6. Bake: Place a pan in the oven. For 5 minutes, switch the oven up to 400 ºF. Switch the oven back to 350 ºF and bake a lemon cupcake for a further 15-20 minutes. When gently squeezed with a finger, they are ready when they feel firm, but they still sound wet. Please remove it from the oven and cool for five minutes, then gently remove it from the pan and put it on the cooling rack to cool fully before frosting.

7. Frost: Cut the tip off a zip-loc bag of a quart size and insert a wide open-star tip. Spoon the bag with the cream cheese frosting and twist the bag over the frosting. Squeeze the frosting into a spiral, starting on the cupcake's outer edge, making it narrower in diameter when piping. Scrape a frosting off and apply it back to the bag if it's not full.

8. For 5-7 days, keep the lemon cupcakes wrapped and refrigerated.

10.39 Low Carb Blueberry Crumble Bars

Servings: 16 I Time: 50 mins I Difficulty: Easy
Nutrients per serving: Calories: 187 kcal I Fat: 60g I Carbohydrates: 7g I Protein: 13g I Fiber: 7g

Ingredients

Shortbread Crust (reserve 1 cup for topping)

- 1 cup Bob's Red Mill Shredded Coconut, powdered in a coffee grinder
- 1/2 tsp salt
- 1/3 cup low carb sugar
- 1/3 cup whey protein powder
- 2 cups almond flour
- 9 tbsp butter, melted

Blueberry Layer

- 2 cups frozen blueberries (8 oz)
- 1-2 pinches cinnamon
- 1/4 tsp xanthan gum
- 1/4 cup erythritol based sweetener
- 1 tsp cornstarch or arrowroot
- 1 tbsp water
- 1 tbsp lemon juice

Crumble Topping

- 1/3 cup sliced almonds
- 1 cup reserved shortbread crust
- more sweetener to sprinkle on top

Method

1. Blueberries: In a small pot over medium heat, put the blueberries, the lemon juice, and water to thaw. Mix the egg whites. Whisk the dry ingredients into blueberries when they have been thawed and bring them to a boil, stirring until they are thickened. Leave to cool.

2. Shortbread crust: Preheat the oven to 350 º F. Spray with a baking spray on a 9x9 inch metal pan and line with a strip of parchment that occupies all or much of the pan's bottom. And overhangs the two opposite

sides, which will allow you to extract from the pan the entire dessert. Powder the coconut in the coffee grinder.

3. Measure into a small mixing bowl all the dry ingredients. With a whisk, blend thoroughly. The butter is melted and added to the dry ingredients. With a broad spoon or rubber spatula, whisk and press the mixture until the butter is integrated. To verify if it can stay together nicely, pinch a small amount in your palm. If not, substitute the melted butter for 1-2 more Tsp. .

4. Assembly: Extract the shortbread crumb solution from 1 cup. In the prepared pan, pour the mixture's remainder, scatter it thinly and cover with a sheet of waxed paper. Use a smooth glass bottom to press the crust tightly into the pan. Over the crust, pour the blueberries. Accessible areas will be there. Crumble 1/2 of the reserved crust mixture over all the blueberries and half of the almonds. And repeat. Sprinkle with extra sweetener if needed.

5. Bake: Put in the oven center and cook for about 30-40 minutes or until golden brown outside. Before getting it out of the grill, let it cool down.

6. Cut the blueberry crumble with a wide chef's knife into 16 circles, breaking it down straight. Store in an airtight jar in the freezer.

10.40 Low Carb Chocolate Truffle

Servings: 4 I Time: 40 mins I Difficulty: Easy
Nutrients per serving: Calories: 605 kcal I Fat: 60g I Carbohydrates: 10g I Fiber: 2g

Ingredients
Low Carb Chocolate Truffle Creme Brulee

- Ghirardelli Midnight Reserve Chocolate bar 90% or 86%
- 5 large egg yolks
- 2 tbsp good Brandy
- 2 cups heavy cream (16 oz)
- 1/3 cup low carb sugar divided
- 1/2 tsp stevia glycerite

Optional Toppings

- whipped cream
- additional sweetener for sprinkling on top

Method
1. Preparation: Preheat the oven to 350 °F and put the rack in the center. Heat water until hot, not boiling, in a tea kettle. To suit the 4, 6-ounce ramekins, find a pan wide enough and shallow enough to add water halfway up the ramekins' sides. Get chocolate sliced into slivers.
2. Method: In a medium dish, add the yolks and 1 Tbsp. of the granulated sweetener. Beat well to break up the yolks entirely.
3. In a small pot, mix in the heavy cream and apply the leftover granulated sweetener and stevia glycerite. Put the pot over medium heat and heat until bubbles begin to boil along the edge of the pot, stirring regularly with a whisk. Turn the heat off and start pouring the egg yolk into a hot cream mixture - in a thin stream very slowly, while whisking all the while rapidly. To melt and mix, add the sliced chocolate and stir. Whisk the brandy up.
4. Bake: Split equally amongst 4 ramekins with the chocolate truffle cream Brulee mixture. Place the ramekins in the pan and, halfway up sides of the ramekins, fill the pan with hot water. Place the pan carefully in the oven and bake for about 30 minutes or until the creme brulee is lightly jiggly at the middle.
5. In the water bath, cool a chocolate truffle creme brulee for an hour before transferring it to a rack to cool completely. Cover and refrigerate for at least 4 hours with plastic wrap, but it's safer overnight.

6. Sprinkle over the top of each cream Brulee with 1/2 Tsp. Lakanto Monkfruit Sweetener or a Swerve Granulated until serving. Use a cooking torch to heat the sweetener until it caramelizes, turning orange. Alternately, apply to the top a dollop of whipped cream. Now serve.

10.41 Sugar-Free Coffee Creme Brulee

Servings: 4 I Time: 35 mins I Difficulty: Easy
Nutrients per serving: Calories: 510 kcal I Fat: 51g I Carbohydrates: 4.5g I Protein: 7g

Ingredients
- 6 large egg yolks
- 2 cups heavy whipping cream
- 1/4 tsp stevia glycerite
- 1/4 cup low carb sugar divided
- 1 tbsp V.S.O.P Brandy (or rum)
- 1 tbsp plus 1 tsp instant espresso

Optional Toppings
- whipped cream
- cinnamon
- additional sweetener for melting on top

Method
1. Preparation: Preheat the oven to 350 °F and put the rack in the center. Heat water until hot, not boiling, in a tea kettle. Find a pan wide enough to accommodate the 4 ramekins, and halfway up sides of the ramekins, deep enough to add water.
2. Method: In a medium dish, add the yolks and 1 Tbsp. of the granulated sweetener. Beat well to break up the yolks entirely.
3. In a small cup, pour the heavy cream and add the left granulated sweetener, stevia glycerite, and espresso. Place the pot over medium heat and heat until bubbles begin to boil along the edge of the pot, stirring regularly with a whisk. Turn the heat off and keep pouring the egg yolk into a hot cream mixture - in a thin stream very slowly, while whisking all the while rapidly. Whisk the brandy up.
4. Bake: Divide equally amongst 4 ramekins with the coffee cream brulee mixture. Place the ramekins in the pan and, halfway up sides of the ramekins, fill the pan with hot water. Place the pan carefully in the oven and then bake for about 30 minutes or until the creme brulee is slightly jiggly at the very middle - about the size of a nickel or a dime.
5. In the water bath, cool the sugar-free coffee creme brulee for an hour before shifting it to a rack to cool fully. Cover and refrigerate for at least 4 hours with plastic wrap, but it's safer overnight.
6. Sprinkle over the top of each cream Brulee with 1/2 Tsp. Lakanto Monkfruit Sweetener or a Swerve Granulated until serving. Use a cooking torch to heat the sweetener until it caramelizes, turning orange. Instead, apply a dollop of whipped cream and some cinnamon to the tip. Now serve.

10.42 Low Carb Chocolate Cheesecake With Peanut Butter Mousse

Servings: 8 I Time: 6 hrs I Difficulty: Easy
Nutrients per serving: Calories: 499 kcal I Fat: 47g I Carbohydrates: 9g I Protein: 11g I Fiber: 5g

Ingredients
- 3 ounces Lily's Original Dark Chocolate (finely chopped)
- 2 Tbsp. Cocoa powder
- 2 Eggs
- 16 ounces Cream Cheese, softened
- 1 cup Swerve Confectioners Sugar Substitute
- 1 cup Keto Peanut Butter Mousse
- ⅔ Cup Sour cream
- ½ Tbsp. Vanilla

Method

1. Preheat the oven to 350°F.
2. By oiling it with butter or a non-stick spray and lined the bottom with the piece of parchment paper, prepare a 6-inch springform sheet. Use aluminum foil to seal the exterior of the springform pan and place it in an oven bag. This bag should not cover the pan's surface, but you can fold it down based on its height so that it only meets the top lip of a springform pan.
3. Place the mixer bowl with the melted cream cheese and blend until smooth and fluffy. Apply the combination of sour cream and vanilla until well mixed.
4. Whisk the powdered sugar alternative and cocoa powder together in a shallow cup. Add with cream cheese mixture and blend until thoroughly mixed.
5. In a microwave-safe cup, put Lily's dark chocolate and microwave for 10 secs, stirring in it each time until melted and smooth. Let the cream cheese mixture cool for 1 min and then pour it in, stirring until it is completely mixed.
6. Add the eggs one at a time and blend until each egg is mixed. Only don't overmix. In the 6-inch springform bath, pour the mixture into it.
7. Bake it in a bath of water. In a wider bath, sit the springform pan (a roasting pan, deep casserole dish, or a disposable foil pan is best). Flush the pan with water before the side of a springform pan hits 1 -1.5 inches upwards.
8. Place in the oven, then bake for 45-60 minutes or until just barely jiggly in the very middle. Turn the oven off and open the door to allow the cheesecake to cool for 30 minutes. Remove it from the oven and let it cool at room temperature perfectly.
9. Remove it from a springform and wrap the parchment paper collar across it when the cheesecake is cooled. The sheet of parchment paper long and approximately two inches longer than the cake to fit around the edge of the cake. Tape together the ends such that the parchment paper remains in place.
10. Create the mousse with keto peanut butter and spread it over the cheesecake's top. It would be stopped from running off the side by the parchment paper.
11. Put in the fridge for a minimum of 4 hours to cool, preferably overnight. Until eating, take the parchment paper and enjoy it.

10.43 Low Carb Blackberry Pudding

Servings: 2 I Time: 5 mins I Difficulty: Easy
Nutrients per serving: Calories: 459.5 kcal I Fat: 44.04g I Carbohydrates: 4.91g I Protein: 9.1g I Fiber: 5.75 g

Ingredients

- 1/4 cup Coconut Flour
- 1/4 tsp. Baking Powder
- 1/4 cup Blackberries
- 5 large Egg Yolks
- 2 tbsp. Coconut Oil
- 2 tbsp. Butter
- 2 tbsp. Heavy Cream
- 2 tsp. Lemon Juice
- Zest 1 Lemon
- 2 tbsp. Erythritol
- 10 drops Liquid Stevia

Method

1. Preheat the oven to 350 °F.
2. Separate the egg yolks from the egg whites and set aside the yolks. Measure out and set aside the dry ingredients. Measure and set aside the butter and the coconut oil.
3. Beat the egg yolks until the color is pale, then add the erythritol and stevia. Beat once more before well mixed.
4. Add lemon juice, heavy cream, lemon zest, butter, and coconut oil. Beat again before completely mixed.
5. Sift dry ingredients over ingredients that are damp and blend well again.
6. Between 2 ramekins, spread the batter, then press 2 tbsp blackberries in any single ramekin. Before moving them into the batter, you want to gently smash the blackberries with the finger.
7. Bake, let cool for 20-25 minutes, and then enjoy

10.44 Low Carb Chocolate Peanut Butter Cookies

Servings: 10 I Time: 25 mins I Difficulty: Easy
Nutrients per serving: Calories: 230 kcal I Fat: 20g I Carbohydrates: 6g I Protein: 6g I Fiber: 2g

Ingredients

- 1 tsp Vanilla Extract
- 1 Egg, large
- 2 tbsps Cocoa Powder, unsweetened
- 10 Sugar-free Peanut Butter Cups
- 1 1/2 c Bob's Red Mill Fine Almond Flour
- 1/4 c Unsalted Butter, softened
- 1/4 c Sucralose granulated sweetener
- 1/4 tsp Baking Soda
- 1/4 tsp Salt

Method

1. Combine the cocoa powder, almond flour, baking soda, and salt in a shallow cup. Only put aside.
2. Cream the butter and sweetener in a blender until smooth, around 2 minutes.
3. Stir in the butter with the egg and vanilla and proceed to blend.
4. Gently add dry ingredients to a bowl before all the ingredients are thoroughly combined, then begin to blend.
5. Preheat the oven to 350 °F.
6. Scoop 2 tbsp of dough from the bowl and shape a sugar-free cup of peanut butter around it. If all of the dough is used, repeat this process.
7. Put on a lined baking sheet with cookies and then bake for bout 10-12 minutes.
8. Let the cookies on the baking sheet chill for 5 minutes, then switch them to a cooling rack for cooling completely.

10.45 Spicy Chocolate Cookie Truffles

Servings: 2 I Time: 1 hr 35 mins I Difficulty: Easy
Nutrients per serving: Calories: 152 kcal I Fat: 14g I Carbohydrates: 4g I Protein: 2g I Fiber: 2g

Ingredients

- Toothpicks optional
- 4 oz. cream cheese softened
- 3 Tbsp. cocoa
- 1/3 cup Monkfruit blend sweetener
- 1 tsp. vanilla
- 1 Tbsp. coconut flour
- 1 oz. cream cheese softened
- 1 cup almond flour
- 1 1/2 tsp. coconut oil
- 1 ½ cups sugar-free semi-sweet baking chips
- ½ cup salted butter softened
- ¼ tsp. Salt

- ¼ tsp. cayenne pepper

Method

1. Whisk in the butter and 1 ounce Of cream cheese for each other. Add and beat the sweetener before well added. Mix the vanilla in it. Apply the salt, chocolate, coconut flour, and pepper to the almond flour and blend until well mixed. On a parchment sheet or plastic wrap, put the dough and shape into a log about 2-1/2 inches in diameter. In the freezer, seal, and ice, or freeze until solid.
2. Cut the dough into 1/4 inch slices and put on a baking sheet lined with parchment. Bake for 15-20 minutes at 325. If you take them out of the oven, the cookies will be tender but will tighten up as they cool on the plate. Leave the cookies on the sheet pan to cool perfectly.
3. Add the cookies to the bowl of the food processor and pulse until crumbs are formed. Add four ounces Of cream cheese, then pulse until it forms a dough. Divide the dough into 20 mounds using a cookie scoop and put it on the parchment-lined pan you have used for your cookies. To smooth it out, roll each ball in your palm. For about twenty minutes or until stable, freeze the dough balls.
4. Merge the baking chips and the coconut oil in a mug or small bowl and microwave at intervals of 15 seconds until melted and smooth. At the top of each ball, put a toothpick (use as a stick). Dip into the melting chocolate for coating. And let excess drip off and put it back on the pan lined with parchment. For both of the balls, repeat. Until set, refrigerate. When the chocolate shell dries, carefully rotate the toothpick to clear any residual molten chocolate and drizzle with it.

10.46 Keto Rice Pudding

Servings: 4 I Time: 4 hrs 15 mins I Difficulty: Easy
Nutrients per serving: Calories: 228 kcal I Fat: 20g I Carbohydrates: 6g I Protein: 4g I Fiber: 1g

Ingredients

- Pinch salt
- 1 cup cauliflower rice, steamed (cooled and pressed dry)
- 4 large egg yolks, beaten
- 1 tsp. vanilla
- 1/2 cup unsweetened almond milk
- 1/2 tsp. ground cinnamon
- 1/3 cup Allulose Blend Sweetener
- 1/4 tsp. cardamom
- 1 can (13.5 oz) full fat coconut milk

Method

1. Combine the coconut milk, almond milk, sweetener, cardamom, salt, cinnamon, cauliflower rice, and egg yolks in a medium saucepan. Heat the mixture softly, stirring continuously over medium-low pressure. For 7-10 minutes, continue cooking, stirring continuously, until the mixture dense and reaches 170-180ºF. Don't let it simmer in the mixture. The back of a spoon should coat the mixture.

Withdraw from the sun. Add the vanilla and pour it into four serving bowls. Cover and chill until set, around 4 hours, with plastic wrap—store for up to 3 days in the fridge.

10.47 Keto Cranberry Brie Tart

Servings: 20 I Time: 27 mins I Difficulty: Easy
Nutrients per serving: Calories: 171 kcal I Fat: 14g I Carbohydrates: 5g I Protein: 7g I Fiber: 2g

Ingredients

- 1 cup coconut flour
- 2 Tbsp. Monfruit/ Erythritol Blend Sweetener
- Zest from one small navel orange
- 2 oz. cream cheese
- 2 eggs
- 18 oz. double cream brie cheese rind removed
- 1/8 Tsp. cayenne
- 1/4 Tsp. paprika
- 1/4 cup toasted chopped pecans
- 1 jalapeno finely diced
- 1 ½ Tsp. apple cider vinegar
- 1 ½ cup fresh cranberries
- ½ Tsp. salt
- ½ cup of water
- ½ cup Monkfruit/Erythritol Blend Sweetener
- ½ cup butter cold and cut into pieces
- ¼ Tsp. paprika

Method

1. Combine the coconut flour, sweetener, spices, and salt in a food processor and pulse to combine. Apply the eggs, cream cheese, and slices of cold butter and pulse until the mixture gets together and away from the bowl's edges. Place them in a plastic wrap and cool for 30 minutes.
2. Press the dough uniformly into a tart pan that has been gently sprayed. Bake for 20 minutes at 325 ºF or until it is golden. Set to cool aside.
3. In a saucepan, mix the cranberries, jalapeno, water, vinegar, sweetener, orange zest, and paprika and bring a boil over medium heat to simmer. Simmer for almost 5 minutes or before the mixture thickens, and the cranberries erupt. Remove the orange zest and chill for at least 30 minutes in the refrigerator before it cools.
4. Place the brie into a bowl of a stand mixer, with the rinds cut. Beat around 5-7 minutes or until it becomes smooth and silky with a paddle attachment at low velocity. Scrape down the sides as appropriate, every minute. Only put aside.
5. Spread uniformly over the bottom of a crust with the whipped brie. Next, the cranberry sauce is poured over the top of the brie. Sprinkle and serve with toasted pecans, then slice. Store in the fridge while covered.

10.48 Keto Molasses Cookies

Servings: 24 I Time: 18 mins I Difficulty: Easy
Nutrients per serving: Calories: 89 kcal I Fat: 8g I Carbohydrates: 3g I Protein: 2g I Fiber: 2g

Ingredients

- 2 Tbsp. coffee flour
- 1/8 tsp. black pepper
- 1/3 cup + 2 Tbsp. Monkfruit/Erythritol Blend Sweetener like Lakanto
- 1 Tsp. cinnamon
- 1 Tbsp. grass-fed gelatin powder
- 1 egg
- 1 ½ Tsp. ground ginger
- 1 ¼ cup almond flour
- ¾ Tsp. baking soda
- ½ Tsp. vanilla extract
- ½ Tsp. ground clove
- ½ cup butter
- ¼ Tsp. salt
- ¼ cup of creamy almond butter (well stirred & room temperature)

Method

1. Preheat the oven to 375°F.

2. Combine the sugar, sweetener, and almond butter and beat until well mixed. In the egg, mix. Mix well with the almond flour, baking soda, salt, coffee flour, gelatin, ginger clove, cinnamon, vanilla, and pepper. For 15-20 minutes, refrigerate the dough.

3. Scoop the dough onto a sheet pan lined with parchment and bake for about 8 minutes. Cool in the jar. Store the cookies at room temperature in a sealed jar.

10.49 Keto Lemon Loaf Cake

Servings: 12 I Time: 55 mins I Difficulty: Easy
Nutrients per serving: Calories: 173 kcal I Fat: 16g I Carbohydrates: 4g I Protein: 6g I Fiber: 2g

Ingredients

- Zest of 2 lemons
- 4 oz cream cheese softened
- 4 eggs room temperature
- 2 Tsp. baking powder
- 2 Tbsp. coconut flour
- 1/4 cup butter softened
- 1/2 Tsp. salt
- 1/2 cup Lakanto Monkfruit Sweetener or equivalent sweetener of choice
- 1 Tsp. vanilla extract
- 1 1/2 cup almond flour

Method

1. Preheat a 350 °F oven and oil a 9-5-inch loaf pan. Only put aside,

2. Combine the almond flour, baking powder, coconut flour, and salt in a medium dish.

3. Cream butter with a sweetener in the large mixing bowl until smooth & fluffy. Add the cream cheese and blend to ensure no lumps.

4. Add the eggs one at a time to the butter mixture, combining thoroughly after each addition. Include vanilla and zest.

5. For butter and eggs, add the dry ingredients to the mixture. Mix well before blended well.

6. Load the batter into a 9-5 inch oiled loaf bowl. For 40-45 minutes, bake. After 30 minutes, start testing for density.

7. Remove from the oven and leave to cool for 25 minutes, then cool fully on the rack before slicing.

10.50 Keto Chocolate Zucchini Bread

Servings: 16 I Time: 55 mins I Difficulty: Easy
Nutrients per serving: Calories: 153 kcal I Fat: 13g I Carbohydrates: 8g I Protein: 6g I Fiber: 4g

Ingredients

- 1 cup almond flour
- 1 cup grated zucchini
- 1 tsp. baking soda
- 1 tsp. vanilla extract
- 1/2 cup coconut flour
- 1/2 cup sugar-free semi-sweet chocolate chips (divided)
- 1/2 tsp salt
- 1/4 cup + 2 Tbsp. cocoa
- 1 1/2 tsp. baking powder
- 3/4 cup Lakanto Golden Monkfruit Sweetener
- 6 Tbsp. butter, ghee or coconut oil, melted
- 8 eggs

Method

1. Preheat the oven to 350°C. Oiled and 8-9" loaf pan with parchment or spray.

2. Combine the coconut flour and almond flour, and the other 5 ingredients in a small bowl and whisk well to blend. Only put aside.

3. Whip eggs until light & foamy triples in volume using the stand mixer and then whisk. This can also be accomplished with a handheld mixer, but to reduce splatter, use a big bowl.

4. Turn to the paddle attachment if a stand mixer is used. Add the eggs to the mixture of almond flour and blend properly. To the egg mixture, apply the rubbed zucchini, extract and the melted butter and whisk at a medium pace until mixed, scratching the sides at least once. Stir in the reserved chocolate chips with 1 Tbsp. Up to the end of the loaf.

5. Now spoon the batter into a prepared loaf pan uniformly and smooth the top out. Sprinkle with the remainder of 1 Tbsp. Chips uniformly around the batter's top. Bake for 45 minutes to one hour at 350°F or until a tester looks clean. "The baking time is slightly shorter if you use a 9" plate, so keep an eye on it, starting for 30 minutes

6. Cool in the skillet. Take the loaf out from the pan and slice with the parchment. Enjoy a cup of coffee. This bread can be rolled and placed in the refrigerator or frozen completely or in slices.

10.51 Double Chocolate Coconut Flour Muffins

Servings: 12 I Time: 20 mins I Difficulty: Easy
Nutrients per serving: Calories: 83 kcal I Fat: 6g I Carbohydrates: 3g I Protein: 2g I Fiber: 1g

Ingredients

- 3 Tbsp. unsweetened almond milk (or a coconut milk)
- 3 Tbsp. sugar-free chocolate chips
- 3 ½ Tbsp. coconut oil melted
- 2 Tbsp. Lakanto Monkfruit (Powdered) Sweetener
- 2 eggs
- 1½ Tbsp. cocoa
- 1/3 cup of coconut flour
- ½ tsp. Vanilla
- ½ tsp. Salt
- ½ tsp. baking powder
- ½ Tbsp. Gelatin
- ¼ tsp. baking soda

Method

1. Preheat the oven to 350 °F and spray the nonstick spray into a mini muffin pan. Only put aside.

2. In a shallow mixing cup, combine the first 7 ingredients and whisk to combine, breaking up the clumps. To mix, add the next 4 ingredients and whisk well. Stir in the crisps of cookies. Scoop batter into any muffin cup with a cookie scoop (approximately 1 tbsp. of the batter). If needed, put 2-3 extra chocolate chips on every muffin and bake for about 10-12 minutes or until baked, at 350 °F . Do not bake in abundance. Before extracting, chill in the pot for 5-10 minutes and cool fully before enjoying.

10.52 Low Carb Dairy Free Coconut Cake

Servings: 12 I Time: 45 mins I Difficulty: Easy
Nutrients per serving: Calories: 257 kcal I Fat: 23g I Carbohydrates: 7g I Protein: 7g I Fiber: 3g

Ingredients

For the Cake

- 6 eggs room temperature
- 2 cup almond flour
- 3 tsp. baking powder
- 1 Tsp. vanilla extract
- 1/2 tsp. salt

- 1/2 tsp. coconut extract
- 1/3 cup coconut oil melted
- 1/3 cup coconut cream
- 1/4 cup coconut flour
- 3/4 cup Lakanto Monkfruit Sweetener

For the Coconut Glaze

- Garnish: Whipped Coconut Cream
- 1/2 cup coconut cream
- 1/2 Tbsp. Lakanto Monkfruit Sweetener
- 1/4 tsp. coconut extract

Method

1. Preheat the oven to 350 °F and oiled a 9-inch circular inch cake pan with parchment on the sides. Only put aside.
2. Beat the 6 eggs in a medium-high to the stand mixer's high mixing bowl for 3-4 minutes. You need them to almost double volume and to be fluffy and light. Meanwhile, in a small bowl, combine the next five ingredients and mix to combine.
3. Include the eggs' dry ingredients until the eggs are fluffy and light and doubled in volume, and blend well to mixed. Now, apply the extracts, coconut milk, molten coconut oil, and mix one more time to scrap the bowl's sides and ensure that it is well blended.
4. Give the batter one last swirl to guarantee that you have the batter from the bottom of the bowl. Pour the batter into the prepared cake pan and bake for 25-30 minutes at 350 or until checked by a tester. Do not bake in excess.
5. Combine the coconut glaze ingredients in a microwave-safe mixing cup while the cake is baking. Heat at intervals of 30 seconds, swirling each time until the sweetener has fully dissolved. That can also be accomplished in a tiny saucepan over medium-low heat on the stovetop.
6. Let it rest and cool for about 5-10 minutes until the cake is finished. Then pour over the warm cake with the coconut glaze. Before turning it out, cool the cake in a pan completely. Cut and serve with a whipped coconut cream garnish.

10.53 Buttered Rum Cake

Servings: 15 I Time: 1 hr I Difficulty: Easy
Nutrients per serving: Calories: 208 kcal I Fat: 16g I Carbohydrates: 5g I Protein: 5g I Fiber: 2g

Ingredients

For the Cake:

- 8 eggs
- 7 Tbsp. butter salted
- 3/4 cup coconut flour
- 2/3 cup Lakanto Golden Monkfruit Sweetener
- 2 tsp. baking powder
- 1/2 tsp salt
- 1 tsp. vanilla extract
- 1 tsp. baking soda
- 1 cup almond flour
- ¼ cup dark rum
- ¼ cup + 2 Tbsp sour cream

For the Glaze:

- ¼ cup of Lakanto Golden Monkfruit Sweetener
- 2 tbsp water
- 3 tbsp dark rum
- 4 tbsp butter

Method

1. Preheat the oven to 350°F. Oil or spray an 8-9' loaf pan and line the bundt pan with parchment either spray

and prepare it. Melt butter in a small skillet over low-medium heat, like a 3-4 environment. Continue to cook the butter for around 7-10 minutes, stirring until the butter is nutty and browned. The caramel color can be the solids in the butter. Remove from the heat and cool off.

2. Whip eggs until light, foamy three times in volume using the stand mixer and a whisk. This can also be achieved using a handheld mixer, but to avoid splatter, use a big cup.
3. Turn to paddle attachment while using a stand mixer. Add sweetener and blend. Add almond and coconut flour, cinnamon, baking powder, and baking soda to the egg mixture and mix until mixed at low pressure, rubbing downsides for at least once. Add the butter with sour cream, vanilla and browned butter, and rum and mix until combined. Spoon the batter uniformly into the pan and smooth the top. Bake for 35-40 minutes with a bundt at 350 °F or 45 minutes to an hour. Halfway through baking and partially covered with foil to avoid browning. The baking period would be marginally shorter if you have a 9' loaf pan, so keep an eye that it starting at 30 minutes.
4. Please prepare the glaze while the cake is baking. Mix all the ingredients for a glaze in the same pan you used to brown the butter. Over medium pressure, bring the mixture to a boil and simmer for 2-3 minutes.
5. Take it out of the oven and spread the glaze uniformly over the warm cake until the cake is finished. In the dish, cool the cake. The day before it's served, this cake is better made. Switch out onto your cake stand or tray of choice. Use the parchment to remove the loaf from a pan and slice to life if you cooked it in a loaf pan. Serve and eat with a coffee cup with a dollop of delivered milk. The cake can be stored at room temperature.

10.54 Chocolate Sour Cream Cake with Cream Cheese Frosting

Servings: 12 I Time: 35 mins I Difficulty: Easy
Nutrients per serving: Calories: 226 kcal I Fat: 20g I Carbohydrates: 3g I Protein: 6.2g I Fiber: 2g

Ingredients

- 8 eggs
- 1/3 cup Pyure
- 1 tsp vanilla
- 1 ½ tsp baking powder
- ½ tsp salt
- ½ cup coconut flour
- ½ cup of butter melted
- ½ cup almond flour
- ¼ cup sour cream
- ¼ cup dutch cocoa (I use Rodelle Baking Cocoa)

Cream Cheese Frosting

- 3 Tbsp butter softened
- 3 oz Cream Cheese softened
- 1 Tbsp heavy cream
- ½ tsp vanilla (I use Rodelle Pure Vanilla Extract)
- ½ cup powdered Lakanto Sweetener

Method

1. Preheat the oven to 325°C. Spray or oil a 9-inch circular cake pan put it aside, and line the base with parchment.
2. Beat the 8 eggs in a medium-high to the stand mixer's high mixing bowl for 3-4 minutes. Double in volume and to be soft and bright. Meanwhile, in a small bowl, combine the next Six dry ingredients and mix to combine.

3. Add dry ingredients in the eggs until the eggs are fluffy and doubled in volume and blend well. Now apply the sour cream, molten butter, and vanilla, then mix one more time to make sure it is mixed properly, rubbing the bowl's downsides.

4. Give the batter one last swirl to guarantee that you have the batter from the base of the bowl. Pour the batter into the lined pan and bake for 25-30 minutes at 325 or until checked by a tester. Oh, don't overbake. Before turning it out, cool the cake in a pan completely.

5. To make the frosting: In a medium dish, combine the cream cheese and the butter and beat until smooth with the handheld blender. Apply the vanilla, milk, and sweetener and stir until smooth and all the ingredients are mixed.

6. Turn the cake out on a cake tray or platter until it's cold. Top and enjoy the frosting

10.55 Coconut Key Lime Bars

Servings: 16 I Time: 30 mins I Difficulty: Easy
Nutrients per serving: Calories: 216 kcal I Fat: 20g I Carbohydrates: 4g I Protein: 5g I Fiber: 1g

Ingredients

For the crust:
- 7 Tbsp salted butter melted
- 2 tsp lime zest
- 2 cups almond flour
- 1/3 cup Lakanto Golden Monkfruit Sweetener or your 1:1 Sweetener of Choice
- ½ cup shredded unsweetened coconut
- ¼ tsp. salt

For the filling:
- 1/3 cup + 2Tbsp Lakanto Monkfruit (Golden) Sweetener
- ¼ cup key lime juice
- 2 whole eggs
- 5 egg yolks
- 5 Tbsp. butter cut into small pieces
- 1 Tbsp. coconut oil
- 1 Tbsp. powdered gelatin
- ½ tsp. vanilla extract
- ¼ tsp. coconut extract

Method

1. To 350 °F, preheat the oven. Spray a 9 to 9 square pan with the parchment and line it. Lift the bars from the pan to remove them if you make the parchment strips, which are 9 inches wide enough to go up two on foot.

2. Combine the first 5 ingredients for the crust in a mixing bowl and blend well to combine. To achieve a crumbly texture, apply the melted butter and blend. Uniformly press this mixture onto the bottom of a lined tray. Made sure you have decent corners and margins. Bake about 10-12 minutes or until the crust begins to light golden brown at 350 °F. Take it out of the oven and set it aside.

3. Blend the main lime juice, eggs, sweetener, and yolks in a saucepan and whisk well to merge. To the pan, apply the butter and coconut oil. Turn the heat to low-medium (3-4 attitude) and start heating the mixture, stirring continuously. The butter will continue to melt as the mixture heats, stirring constantly. All the butter will melt after about 5 minutes, and the filling will then start thickening. Keep stirring, but do not boil. Remove from the heat until the filling is thickened to a loose pudding. Sprinkle the gelatin generously over the surface of the filling and stir to mix instantly. Stir the extracts in.

4. Pour the filling of lime uniformly over the top of a crust. Bake for 10-12 minutes at 350 or until set. Until cutting, cool properly. Use the overhanging parchment for lifting the bars from the pan until it is cool. To end up with 16 bars, make 4 even cuts horizontally and vertically.

10.56 Keto Lemon Pound Cake with Blueberries

Servings: 12 I Time: 30 mins I Difficulty: Easy
Nutrients per serving: Calories: 239 kcal I Fat: 21g I Carbohydrates: 7g I Protein: 8g I Fiber: 3g

Ingredients

- 1 1/4 cup almond flour
- 3/4 cup Lakanto Monkfruit Sweetener or any equivalent sweetener of choice
- 1/4 cup butter softened
- 1/2 Tsp. salt
- 1/2 cup fresh blueberries
- 4 oz cream cheese softened
- Zest of 2 lemons
- 4 eggs room temperature
- 1 Tsp. vanilla extract
- 1 Tbsp. coconut flour
- 1 Tsp. baking powder
- 2 tsp confectioners sweetener

Method

1. Preheat a 350-degree oven and oil a 9-5-inch loaf pan. Only put aside,

2. Combine the almond flour, baking powder, coconut flour, and salt in a medium dish.

3. Cream butter with sweetener in a mixing bowl until fluffy and smooth. Apply the cream cheese and blend to ensure no lumps.

4. Add the eggs one at a time to the butter mixture, combining thoroughly after each addition: Include vanilla and zest.

5. For butter and eggs, add dry ingredients to the mixture. Mix well before blended well. Fold in the blueberries, taking care not to break them down. You should toss the blueberries with 2 tsp whether you have a powdered swerve or some other sweetener, which will make the cake's bottom to sink.

6. Load the batter into a 9-5 inch oiled loaf bowl. For 40-45 minutes, bake. After 30 minutes, start testing for density.

7. Remove from the oven and leave to cool for 25 minutes, then cool fully on the rack before slicing.

10.57 Mini Orange Cranberry Cheesecake

Servings: 12 I Time: 35 mins I Difficulty: Easy
Nutrients per serving: Calories: 144 kcal I Fat: 8g I Carbohydrates: 8g I Protein: 8g I Fiber: 2g

Ingredients

For the Crust:
- Pinch salt
- 3 Tbsp salted butter melted
- 2 Tbsp Lakanto Monkfruit (Classic) Sweetener
- 1 cup almond flour
- ¼ tsp. cinnamon

For the Filling:
- 2/3 cup Lakanto Monkfruit (Classic) Sweetener
- 2 eggs
- 16 oz. packages cream cheese softened
- 1 tsp. vanilla
- ½ tsp. fresh orange zest

For the Cranberry Compote:
- 1 cup of water
- 1/2 cup Lakanto Gold Monkfruit Sweetener
- 1/8 tsp. ground clove
- 12 oz. bag fresh cranberries
- 2 Tbsp. Pyure Organic Stevia Blend
- 3-4 pieces orange peel inch wide by 4 inches long
- Pinch salt

Method
1. Put all the ingredients in the compote in a medium saucepan on medium heat. Simmer for 10-12 minutes before the cranberries burst and the sauce thickens. Remove from the heat and encourage to stay for thirty minutes. Remove the peel, drain into the serving bowl, and cool before serving time. In a zip-top bag or plastic ware, you can freeze as well. To serve, thaw in the refrigerator.
2. Preheat the oven to 350 °F and use liners to cover a muffin tray. Mix the ingredients for a crust in a medium mixing bowl and blend until combined and crumbly. Place roughly 1 Tbsp. In each muffin cup, blend the crust mixture and press it into each cup's rim. Only put aside.
3. Mix the ingredients for filling in a medium mixing bowl and blend with a hand mixer. Between the 12 muffin cups, split the filling. Bake for 15-20 minutes at 350 °F or until set. Don't bake too much. Cool at room temperature and prepare until served in the fridge.
4. Remove the cooled cheesecake wrapper and put it on the counter. Spoon the top of each cheesecake with about two Tbsp. of cranberry compote and enjoy.

10.58 Keto Double Fudge Cookies

Servings: 12 I Time: 15 mins I Difficulty: Easy
Nutrients per serving: Calories: 63 kcal I Fat: 5g I Carbohydrates: 3g I Protein: 2g I Fiber: 1g

Ingredients
- ¼ cup creamy almond butter
- ½ cup Lily's Chocolate Chips
- ½ cup Rodelle Gourmet Baking Cocoa
- ½ tsp. Baking powder
- ½ tsp. salt
- 1 Tbsp. coconut flour
- 1 tsp. Rodelle Vanilla Extract
- 1/3 cup + 1 Tbsp. Lakanto Monkfruit (Powdered) Sweetener
- 2 eggs
- 2 Tbsp. salted butter softened

Method
1. Preheat the oven to 350 °F and use parchment to cover a sheet plate. Mix the butter and the almond butter in a medium bowl until thoroughly integrated. Include the vanilla and eggs and combine until smooth.
2. The next Five ingredients are added and blend properly. Stir in the crisps of cookies. Use a cookie scoop to release flour on the lined sheet pan about 2 inches apart. Slightly flatten those cookies with wet fingertips. They won't scatter much throughout the baking process.
3. Bake for Six minutes for the fudgy texture or the less fudgy texture for 7 minutes. Don't bake too much. Let it cool on the sheet pan for 2-3 minutes, then remove to cool fully. They will set up as the cookies cool, so be careful.

10.59 Low Carb Acai Berry Bowl

Servings: 1 I Time: 5 mins I Difficulty: Easy
Nutrients per serving: Calories: 202 kcal I Fat: 13g I Carbohydrates: 18g I Protein: 2g I Fiber: 10g

Ingredients
Acai Berry Base
- 4 strawberries
- 3 tsp acai powder
- 1 tsp Pyure Organic Stevia Blend
- Pinch of Himalayan Salt
- 1/3 cup avocado
- 1/3 cup unsweetened almond milk
- 1/4 cup blueberries

Garnishes / Topping Optional
- blueberries or raspberries
- chia seeds
- low carb granola
- pecans
- shaved coconut
- sliced strawberries

Method
1. Combine all the Acai Berry base ingredients in a high-speed blender and then blend for 10 seconds or until smooth and fluffy.
2. Pour into a little mug, garnish, and enjoy your morning as desired.

10.60 Keto Fudge Ribbon Cake

Servings: 16 I Time: 1 hr I Difficulty: Easy
Nutrients per serving: Calories: 258 kcal I Fat: 23g I Carbohydrates: 8g I Protein: 7g I Fiber: 4g

Ingredients
- ½ cup avocado oil
- ½ cup coconut flour
- ½ tsp salt
- 1 ½ cup almond flour
- 1 ½ tsp baking powder
- 1 cup Lakanto Golden Monkfruit Sweetener (we use Lakanto and Highkey Allulose)
- 1 tsp vanilla
- 1 tsp. baking soda
- 1/2 cup cocoa
- 1/2 cup full-fat sour cream
- 6 eggs

Cream Cheese Frosting
- 1 tsp. vanilla
- 2 eggs
- 2 Tbsp. butter softened
- 2 Tbsp. coconut flour
- 6 Tbsp. powdered Lakanto Sweetener
- 8 oz. cream cheese softened

Method
1. Preheat the oven to 350°C. Oiled a 10 cup tray and sprinkle with cocoa thoroughly. By tapping the pan on the sink, extract any extra cocoa. Oil the inside, line the bottom layer and sides with parchment while using loaf pans, and set them aside.
2. Beat the 6 eggs in a medium-high to the high mixing bowl of a stand mixer for 2-3 minutes, until light and fluffy. In the meantime, in a tiny cup, combine the next Seven dry ingredients and combine them.
3. Add the eggs' dry ingredients until the eggs become light and fluffy and doubled in volume and blend well to mixed. Now apply oil, sour cream, and vanilla and mix one more time to scrape down the bowl's sides to ensure that it is well mixed and pour the batter into the bowl.
4. Mix the cream cheese, butter, vanilla, powdered sweetener, coconut flour, and eggs in a separate cup,

and beat until well mixed. Pour the combination of cream cheese generously on the chocolate batter.

5. For 45-50 minutes, bake at 350. Cool the cake in a pan for 10-15 minutes to cool entirely on a rack or plate before turning out. Cold top once as needed and serve. Store at room temperature up to 3 days.

10.61 Keto Pecan Toffee Crunch

Servings: 12 | Time: 12 mins | Difficulty: Easy
Nutrients per serving: Calories: 660 kcal | Fat: 60g | Carbohydrates: 7g | Protein: 13g | Fiber: 7g

Ingredients

- Pinch Himalayan or sea salt
- 4 cups pork rind pieces
- ½ tsp vanilla
- ½ cup butter
- ¼ cup finely chopped pecans
- ¼ cup + 2 Tbsp Lakanto Monkfruit (Golden) Sweetener

Method

1. Line and set aside a sheet pan with the parchment. Place bits of pork rind in a medium bowl and place them aside.
2. Combine the sweetener and butter in a tiny saucepan and melt on medium heat. Get it to a boil, continuously stirring. Switch the heat to medium-low and continue cooking for 5 minutes or so. To the butter mixture, add the pecans and finish cooking for a further 1-2 minutes or until the toasty pecans smell. Stir in the vanilla and salt and lift the butter mixture to the heat.
3. Pour half of a butter mixture on the pork rinds or spoon it over and toss to cover it. Repeat with the mixture of butter that remains. You may also put the pork rinds on the pan and let them cool to harden in the refrigerator. Store it in a sealed jar at room temperature and enjoy.

10.62 Jalapeno Mexican Fudge

Servings: 16-24 | Time: 45 mins | Difficulty: Easy
Nutrients per serving: Calories: 660 kcal | Fat: 60g | Carbohydrates: 7g | Protein: 13g | Fiber: 7g

Ingredients

- 1 jar (12oz) pickled, sliced jalapenos (drained)
- 1/2 Tsp. garlic powder
- 1/4 Tsp. onion powder
- 2 lbs Cheddar cheese (medium or mild), grated
- 2 lbs Monterrey Jack cheese, grated
- 7 oz cream or evaporated milk (Only a little over 3/4 cup)
- 7 whole eggs, beaten

Method

1. Preheat the oven to 350 ºF. Oiled a 9-to-13 pan gently.
2. Range the sliced jalapenos in a single layer around the bottom of a plate. Test the heat with jalapenos. If you want less flame, you can use less or chop them up with jalapenos.
3. Combine the shredded cheese, eggs, cream, garlic, and onion powder in a large mixing cup. Blend well.
4. Pour the mixture of cheese over the jalapenos and scatter equally. Bake for about 45-55 minutes or until bubbly and golden brown.Until carving, cool for at least 20 minutes. Cool perfectly for optimum cutting results.
5. Use 1lb of both Monterrey jack and cheddar, 3 beaten eggs, 6 tbsp of milk or cream, 1/8 tsp of powdered onion, and 1/4 tsp of garlic powder for a 9/9 pan. Similarly, cook the pan using half a packet of jalapenos. Then bake for 25-35 minutes.

10.63 Keto Banana Blueberry Muffins

Servings: 14 | Time: 30 mins | Difficulty: Easy
Nutrients per serving: Calories: 192 kcal | Fat: 16g | Carbohydrates: 6g | Protein: 6g | Fiber: 3g

Ingredients

- ¼ cup coconut flour
- ¼ cup sour cream
- ½ tsp salt
- ½ tsp. baking soda
- 1 cup diced raw zucchini
- 1 egg yolk
- 1 Tbsp. flaxseed meal
- 1 tsp. cinnamon
- 1 tsp. vanilla extract
- 2 cup almond flour
- 2 tsp. baking powder
- 2 tsp. quality banana extract, not imitation
- 3/4 cup frozen wild blueberries
- 5 eggs
- 6 Tbsp. butter melted
- 7 Tbsp. Lakanto Monkfruit (Golden) Sweetener, divided

Method

1. Preheat the oven to 350°C. Using liners or mist to cover a muffin pan.
2. In a shallow saucepan, pour 1 Tbsp. Of blueberries over medium heat. A pinch of salt and Lakanto. Bring the blend to a boil and drop the berries to a simmer, crushing them. Simmer that blueberry sauce until it thickens and the back of the spoon is coated for about 7 minutes.
3. Combine the eggs, zucchini, egg yolk, and extracts in a blender and mix for about 10 seconds before the zucchini is pureed and light and fluffy.
4. Combine the coconut flour and almond flour with the remaining sweetener, baking soda, salt, flax, and baking powder in a large bowl or the stand mixer bowl.
5. Add the egg mixture to the dry ingredients, then mix with a paddle attachment at medium pace or by hand, once mixed, scraping the sides at least once. Apply the sour cream and molten butter to the batter and stir until mixed.
6. Spoon that thickened blueberries into the batter and whisk the blueberries softly over the batter, not perfectly rubbing it in.
7. Spoon the batter uniformly into the already prepared muffin pan (approximately 3-4" full) and then bake at 350 F for 20 minutes or until baked.
8. Bake until completed or for 20 minutes. Cool for 10 minutes in the pan and switch to the cooling rack to cool fully. Enjoy it with a coffee cup. These can be wrapped up and frozen for up to 3 days. And can be at room temperature for up to 5 days in the fridge.

10.64 Low Carb Shortbread Cookies

Servings: 24 | Time: 35 mins | Difficulty: Easy
Nutrients per serving: Calories: 62.2 kcal | Fat: 5.4g | Carbohydrates: 3.2g | Protein: 0.9g | Fiber: 0.3g

Ingredients

- 5 Tbsp. Monkfruit Sweetener
- 1 Tsp. Pure Vanilla Extract
- pinch of Salt
- 1/2 cup Ghee, at room temperature, the consistency of softened butter
- 2 1/2 Tsp. Pure Almond Extract
- 1/2 cup Tapioca Starch, plus 1 Tbsp. , 73g

- 3/4 cup Almond Flour, 73g

Method

1. Preheat your oven to 350 ° F and line 2 parchment paper or silpats with baking sheets.
2. Put the monk fruit in a SMALL food processor and process until perfect, and the powdered sugar consistency is around 3-4 minutes.
3. In a large bowl, apply the monk fruit, with the ghee and all extracts. Using the electric hand mixer, run on high speed until very light yellow, around 3 minutes.
4. Apply the flour, starch, and salt and beat for another 3 minutes again, stopping as needed to scrape the edges.
5. Scoop back through the piping and pipe in 3/4-inch-high mounds on the prepared cookie sheet. These spread a lot, so leave space between them-I put 16 on one sheet of cookies. Do not down-press them.
6. Bake for about 11-13 minutes before the edges just start to turn golden brown. Put the other sheet at room temperature before the first batch of cookies is finished if you can't get all sheets in at once.
7. When baked, cool on the pan for about 10 minutes. Then turn a wire rack to cool fully.

10.65 Low Carb Corn Dog Muffins

Servings: 6 I Time: 25 mins I Difficulty: Easy
Nutrients per serving: Calories: 274 kcal I Fat: 25g I Carbohydrates: 7g I Protein: 6g I Fiber: 3g

Ingredients

- 6 Tbsp. butter, melted
- 3 large eggs
- 2 Tbsp. sugar substitute
- 2 hot dogs
- ½ Tsp. salt
- ½ cup coconut flour
- ⅓ cup heavy cream
- ¼ Tsp. baking soda

Method

1. Preheat the oven to 350°C. Using non-stick spray to spray a muffin pan.
2. To a mixing cup, add the melted butter, milk, and eggs and whisk to blend.
3. To mix, add the coconut flour, artificial sweetener, baking soda, and salt to the bowl and whisk well.
4. Cut the hot dogs into little fragments and fold them into a mixture of cornbread. Spoon the mixture uniformly between the 6 muffin wells.
5. Now Bake for about 15 minutes or until the muffin core comes out clean with a toothpick inserted into it. Until consuming, cool for 5 minutes.

10.66 Keto Buckeyes

Servings: 34 I Time: 1 hr 30 mins I Difficulty: Easy
Nutrients per serving: Calories: 164 kcal I Fat: 13g I Carbohydrates: 12g I Protein: 3g I Fiber: 2g

Ingredients

- 3½ cups confectioners swerve (if not keto, use powdered sugar)
- 3 cups lily's semisweet chocolate chips (if not keto, you can use chocolate wafers for easiest melting)
- 1⅓ cup all-natural peanut butter (for keto, use Just natural, if not making keto, use Jif)
- 1 Tsp. vanilla extract
- 1 Tbsp. coconut oil
- ½ cup salted butter softened

Method

1. In a big bowl or mixer, combine the peanut sugar, butter, vanilla, and milk for about 30 seconds.
2. In the cup, sift the swerve or powdered sugar and beat till smooth. For 30 minutes, cool the mixture in a refrigerator. Line a parchment paper baking sheet, slice out the peanut butter mixture with the medium cookie scoop and then roll it into balls.
3. Put them on a cookie sheet and chill for 20 to 30 minutes in the fridge. Melt the chocolate and coconut oil in a large glass at 30-second intervals just before extracting the balls from the fridge, swirling each of them until fully melted.
4. Spear the balls with a toothpick and dip them into the molten chocolate. Using a fork to help extract the ball from the toothpick and bring it back on the parchment pad.
5. To lightly cover the toothpick opening, use your finger or the paring knife. Set until it hardens with the chocolate.

10.67 Keto Cookie Dough Ice Cream

Servings: 15 I Time: 1 hr 5 mins I Difficulty: Easy
Nutrients per serving: Calories: 660 kcal I Fat: 60g I Carbohydrates: 7g I Protein: 13g I Fiber: 7g

Ingredients

ICE CREAM

- 2 large organic eggs
- 2 cups organic whipping cream
- 1 Tbsp vanilla extract
- 1/2 tsp fine sea salt
- 1/8 tsp almond extract (optional)
- 3/4 cup Lakanto Monk Fruit 1:1 Sweetener
- 2.5 cups organic whole milk

COOKIE DOUGH

- 2 Tbsp milk
- 2 Tbsp Lakanto maple-flavored syrup
- 2 pinches sea salt
- 1/4 cup (50g) sugar-free chocolate chips
- 1 tsp vanilla extract
- 1 cup packed (150g) almond flour

Method

1. Chill Fridge Ice Cream Canister (if directed by your ice cream machine instructions). To store ice cream in the fridge, you may want to cool the container you plan to use.
2. Beat eggs with the whisk attachment on high in the stand mixer until foamy. Reduce the pace to low and include the sweetener progressively.
3. Beat for 1 minute or before it thickens somewhat.
4. Include the ice cream, sea salt, vanilla extract, and almond extract. Mix on medium until fully mixed.
5. Pour in the ice cream canister and then pour the milk into it. If you double the formula and use a regular bucket ice cream unit, fill the full filling line with milk (no more than 5 cups of milk).
6. Or a spoon or a spatula, blend properly.
7. In compliance with its directions, run the ice cream machine. Before operating the computer, this could involve cooling the liquid well. Simply search the manuals for your particular computer brand.
8. Create cooked dough when churning the ice cream. In a medium-sized mixing bowl, combine all the ingredients except the chocolate chips. Stir well until it shapes dough. Stir in the chocolate chips and blend until blended. Form into small cookie dough balls by hands (approx 1cm in diameter). Apply a little extra almond flour if the dough is a little sticky. In the fridge, put the cookie dough balls (make sure they don't touch).

9. Stir the cold cookie dough balls softly with a long spoon or spatula until the ice cream is done churning. At this point, your ice cream should have a soft serving consistency.
10. To harden up the ice cream texture, put ice cream in a freezer in your storage vessel. Enjoy. Hold it in an airtight jar in the fridge.

10.68 Keto Buttermilk Biscuits

Servings: 6 I Time: 25 mins I Difficulty: Easy
Nutrients per serving: Calories: 660 kcal I Fat: 60g I Carbohydrates: 7g I Protein: 13g I Fiber: 7g

Ingredients

- 1/4 cup grass-fed collagen
- 1/4 cup reduced-fat buttermilk
- 1/2 tsp fine sea salt
- 2 cups packed (300g) finely ground blanched almond flour
- 2 tsp aluminum-free double-acting baking powder
- 2 Tbsp (28g) grass-fed butter
- 4 large egg whites

Method

1. Preheat the oven to 375oF and cover the parchment paper with a baking sheet.
2. In the medium-sized mixing dish, combine the dried ingredients.
3. Using a cheese grater, grind in cold butter. Toss to merge those bits that have stayed together and split them up.
4. Apply the buttermilk and the egg whites to the mixture and blend well.
5. Make biscuits simply like drop biscuits. And then scoop the batter on the parchment paper (so you can form them by hand), or if you want good biscuits and don't mind the extra work, you need to spoon a mixture into a well-oiled cup and then softly press the batter down with your fingertips into the measuring cup and flip it.
6. For 20-22 minutes, bake. This cooking time is for the biscuits with 1/3 cup of batter. If you've made the drop biscuits and smaller ones, you need to reduce the cooking time a little. When they have a good golden hue on them, the biscuits are finished.
7. Leave the pan to cool for around 5 minutes, then switch off a cooling rack to stop cooling. Due to their soft texture, such biscuits are better if you let these cool for a minimum of 10 minutes before consuming them. For around 15-20 minutes, leave them.

10.69 Keto Crockpot Candy

Servings: 24 I Time: 1 hr 3 mins I Difficulty: Easy
Nutrients per serving: Calories: 660 kcal I Fat: 60g I Carbohydrates: 7g I Protein: 13g I Fiber: 7g

Ingredients

- 2 1/2 cups (425g) Lily's Milk Chocolate Chips or Lily's Semi-Sweet Chocolate Chips
- 2 cups (280g) raw cashews
- Decorative sprinkles,

Method

1. In a small or a medium crockpot, place cashews in a layer. On top, pour the chocolate chips. You don't stir.
2. Place the top of the lid and put it on low heat. Leave 1 hour for a seat.
3. Line the parchment paper with a large baking sheet.
4. Drop the cover after 1 hour and mix well. The chocolate should be molten, still not runny, but still a little dense. Rapidly scoop out candy on the parchment that is lined baking sheets using a soup spoon. Each candy should be around.
5. Leave 5 minutes to cool, then decorate, if desired, with sprinkles.

6. Place them in the refrigerator and leave for 45 minutes to harden. Take it from the fridge and enjoy it. Up to 1 week, you can store at room temperature in an airtight container.

10.70 Keto Cinnamon Roll Holes Donut

Servings: 24 I Time: 30 mins I Difficulty: Easy
Nutrients per serving: Calories: 660 kcal I Fat: 60g I Carbohydrates: 7g I Protein: 13g I Fiber: 7g

Ingredients

DONUT HOLE DOUGH

- 1/4 cup (36g) of coconut flour
- 1 1/3 cup packed (200g) finely ground almond flour
- 1/2 tsp fine sea salt
- 2 Tbsp (28g) of Lakanto Monk Fruit (Golden) Sweetener
- 2 Tbsp (12g) grass-fed collagen
- 4 tsp aluminum-free double-acting baking powder
- 4 large eggs, beaten (about 210g)

FOR ROLLING THE DONUT HOLES

- 3 Tbsp grass-fed butter or ghee, melted but not hot
- 1 Tbsp cinnamon
- 1/3 cup Lakanto Golden Monk Fruit Sweetener

CREAM CHEESE FROSTING

- 1 tsp vanilla extract
- 1/3 cup cream cheese, softened
- 1/8 tsp sea salt
- 2 Tbsp grass-fed butter or ghee, softened
- 2 Tbsp powdered erythritol or Lakanto Golden
- Coconut milk or almond milk to thin

Method

1. Preheat the oven to 350oºF/170ºC and cover the parchment paper with a baking sheet.
2. Just make the dough. Combine the dried ingredients in a large mixing bowl and blend well. Add the eggs and blend well until they form a dough. The dough can hold well together, but it's always going to be sort of wet, not dry.
3. "Make "sugar with cinnamon. Mix the cinnamon and the 1/3 cup of Lakanto Golden in a small bowl or plate to produce the cinnamon sugar. Through a small dish, pour molten butter.
4. Shape the balls into a pastry. Scoop out rounded tbsp of dough using a tbsp measurement and roll with your hands to make balls. Roll throughout the butter to coat as you shape each ball, then roll in cinnamon sugar. Place it on a baking sheet lined with parchment and begin with the remaining dough.
5. For 15 minutes, roast them. Create the frosting before icing the donut holes. Whip the melted butter & cream cheese together for a few minutes, using a stand mixer or a hand mixer. Add erythritol, sea salt powder, vanilla, and whip for another few minutes until soft and light. To thin to the desired consistency, blend in coconut or almond milk as needed. Drizzle and serve with frosting.

10.71 Low Carb Pumpkin Spice Meriques

Servings: 55 cookies I Time: 25 mins I Difficulty: Easy
Nutrients per serving: Calories: 2 kcal I Fat: 1g I Carbohydrates: 2g I Protein: 1g I Fiber: 1g

Ingredients

- 4 large egg whites
- 2 tsp. pumpkin pie spice, no sugar added
- 1/2 tsp. cream of tartar
- 3/4 cup erythritol, powdered in a blender

Method

1. Preheat the oven to 200 °F.
2. Beat the whites of the egg until they are almost stiff.
3. Fold and finish pounding before you have stiff peaks in the erythritol and pumpkin pie spice.
4. Place on a parchment-lined baking sheet with dollops of whipped egg. Use your size judgment.
5. With the oven door partly open, bake for 2 1/2 to 3 hours. By inserting a wooden spoon between the door and the oven, this can be accomplished.

10.72 Keto Sugar-Free Lemon Meringue Pie

Servings: 8 I Time: 3 hrs 45 mins I Difficulty: Easy
Nutrients per serving: Calories: 199 kcal I Fat: 16g I Carbohydrates: 14g I Protein: 7g I Fiber: 3g

Ingredients
- 1 batch of low carb pie crust

Keto Lemon Curd
- 3/4 cup lemon juice
- 3 large eggs yolk
- 1/8 Tsp. stevia powder
- 1/3 cup powdered erythritol
- 1 Tbsp. lemon zest
- 1 Tbsp. arrowroot powder

Meringue Topping
- 3 egg whites
- 1/2 Tsp. cream of tartar

Method
1. As per directions, prepare the low carb crust. Press the dough into a tart pan or an oiled pastry—Bake for 15 minutes at 325 °F.
2. Prepare a lemon curd by putting a small pot on medium-low flame. Apply the juice of the lemon, then heat until lukewarm.
3. Whisk together the egg yolks, arrowroot powder, powdered erythritol, stevia powder, and the lemon zest in a medium sized-mixing bowl. To temper the eggs, whisk the mild hot lemon juice in the egg mixture and continue whisking until whole juice is poured.
4. Return the lemon curd to the pot on its whole back and heat on medium heat, stirring at a medium pace. (NOTE: Steady stirring is the secret to a good custard. Not as easy as scrambled eggs, but not so sluggish that things burst or boil.)
5. Continue to stir before the gravy thickens (about 3-5 minutes). Pour the lemon curd in the prepared pie crust until thickened and put uncovered for at least 2 hours in the fridge to stiffen and cool.
6. In a medium bowl with tartar cream, make your meringue top by beating egg whites until egg whites become glossy and form firm peaks.
7. To build peaks for browning, spoon meringue on top of a pie dab. Set for a few minutes under a high-heat broiler, regularly rotating to cook uniformly. Look carefully if you want to toast the meringue, but not roast it. Once it achieves the quality, you expect. Leave it to cool for another hour in the refrigerator before serving.

10.73 Keto Chocolate Fudge

Servings: 30 I Time: 40 mins I Difficulty: Easy
Nutrients per serving: Calories: 143 kcal I Fat: 12g I Carbohydrates: 14g I Protein: 2g I Fiber: 3g

Ingredients
- 4 Tbsp. butter
- 3 cups low carb chocolate chips
- 2 Tsp. xanthan gum
- 2 Tbsp. monk fruit sweetener
- 1 Tsp. vanilla extract
- 1 1/2 cups heavy whipping cream

Method
1. In a small pot, pour heavy whipping cream and bring to medium heat to boil. Reduce to simmer for about 30 minutes until boiling. To avoid the development of skin, whisk or stir regularly.
2. Apply the vanilla, butter, and sugar at room temperature to the simmering cream and then whisk until well mixed.
3. Include the xanthan gum and mix thoroughly so that no clumps are present.
4. Remove from the heat and add the chocolate chips immediately, whisking until thoroughly mixed. After several minutes of whisking, if not smooth, adjust to low heat and whisk until it is smooth.
5. In an oiled or parchment-lined 6x9 or 8x8 pan/casserole dish, pour immediately.
6. Chill uncovered for at least 4 hours in a refrigerator, overnight if feasible.
7. Cut between parchment paper sheets for gifting and serving or packaging.

10.74 Low Carb Chocolate Cake

Servings: 8 I Time: 45 mins I Difficulty: Easy
Nutrients per serving: Calories: 237 kcal I Fat: 10g I Carbohydrates: 41g I Protein: 4g I Fiber: 3g

Ingredients
- 3 tbsp butter unsalted and melted
- 2 eggs at room temperature
- 2 cups low carb vanilla frosting
- 1/4 tsp salt
- 1/4 cup powdered sweetener
- 1/4 cup brown sugar alternative
- 1/2 tsp vanilla extract
- 1/2 Tsp. baking soda
- 1/2 cup unsweetened cocoa powder
- 1/2 cup unsweetened almond milk
- 1/2 cup coconut flour
- 1 tsp apple cider vinegar
- 1 Tsp. baking powder

Method
1. Preheat the oven to 350 °F
2. Pre-oiled two pans of the 6-inch round cake.
3. Mix the almond milk and the apple cider vinegar in a shallow bowl.
4. Mix the dry ingredients in a big bowl: sweetener, almond flour, baking soda, coconut flour, salt, baking powder, and brown sugar. Build a well for the wet ingredients in the middle.
5. Add the vanilla powder, sugar, and eggs and blend to combine. Pour the combination of milk in and blend well.
6. Distribute the cake batter uniformly into your rectangular cake pans. Tap pans to disperse the cake mixture thinly around the pan on a flat surface to eliminate excess air.
7. Now Bake for 20 to 25 minutes before it comes out clean when the toothpick is inserted. Until frosting, cause your cake to completely cool.

10.75 Keto Chocolate Cheesecake Mousse

Servings: 5 I Time: 10 mins I Difficulty: Easy
Nutrients per serving: Calories: 329 kcal I Fat: 34g I Carbohydrates: 15g I Protein: 5g I Fiber: 1g

Ingredients
- 1/4 cup powdered erythritol
- 1/4 cup cocoa powder
- 1 cup heavy whipping cream

- 1 cup cream cheese

Method

1. Add all of the ingredients to a big bowl and use a hand mixer to mix the ingredients for 2 minutes. Scrape the bowl's sides off. Mix for a further 3 minutes until the stiff peaks are produced, and the mixture is dense and creamy.
2. To taste, apply additional sweeteners. In the airtight container, store your chocolate whipped cream in the refrigerator for 3 days.

10.76 Low Carb Chocolate Cauldron Cupcakes

Servings: 6 I Time: 40 mins I Difficulty: Easy
Nutrients per serving: Calories: 320 kcal I Fat: 30g I Carbohydrates: 34g I Protein: 8g I Fiber: 5g

Ingredients

Low Carb Chocolate Cupcake

- 3/4 cup almond flour
- 3 large whole eggs
- 1/4 cup unsweetened cocoa powder
- 1/2 cup grapeseed oil
- 1/2 cup erythritol
- 1 tsp. pure vanilla extract
- 1 tbsp of baking powder

Chocolate Frosting

- 1/2 cup coconut fat
- 1/4 cup erythritol
- 1/4 cup unsweetened cocoa powder

Method

1. Wash the cauldrons and, if used, dry them. Place them on a parchment-lined cookie sheet. Otherwise, line the muffin tins with the liners you've picked.
2. Preheat a 350 F microwave. Combine the cupcake items in a medium mixing dish, swirling well to mix.
3. In the cauldrons or the cupcake liners, part the batter out. Bake for 20-30 minutes, roughly. .Notice that in a convection oven. That can be done with a cake tester, which pulls out clean when poked.
4. When cupcakes are in the oven, prepare the frosting by combining the frosting products in a small-medium mixing bowl with the electric beater—store until available to use in the refrigerator.
5. Cool them fully before top with the frosting when the cupcakes are completed baked. Serving and enjoying

10.77 Keto Pound Cake

Servings: 10 I Time: 1 hr 5 mins I Difficulty: Easy
Nutrients per serving: Calories: 175 kcal I Fat: 16g I Carbohydrates: 23g I Protein: 5g I Fiber: 1g

Ingredients

- 4 eggs
- 1/4 cup cream cheese
- 1/4 cup butter
- 1/2 cup sour cream
- 1 Tsp. vanilla extract
- 1 Tsp. baking powder
- 1 Tbsp. coconut flour
- 1 cup monk fruit sweetener
- 1 cup almond flour

Method

1. Preheat the oven to 350 Fahrenheit
2. By oiling with butter and then lining with parchment paper, prepare the 9-inch flat bottom plate.
3. Whisk the almond flour, baking powder, and coconut flour together in a big dish.

4. Add butter and cream cheese in a different dish. Microwave on high for about 30 seconds, whisk and microwave for additional 30 seconds if desired before butter and the cream cheese melts together. Stir in the vanilla extract, sweetener, and sour cream. Then mix properly.
5. Pour the cream cheese butter mixture into a dry mixture. Stir once mixed properly. Apply the eggs to the batter when well mixed, one at a time.
6. Pour the batter into the dish. Bake for 55 minutes or until it comes out clean with a toothpick.
7. In a bundt pan, allow the cake to cool entirely; we've found it's best to let it cool completely for hours before it reaches room temperature (just like a cheesecake)
8. Serve with whipped cream and fresh strawberries.

10.78 Low Carb Mock Apple Pie

Servings: 8 I Time: 1 hr I Difficulty: Easy
Nutrients per serving: Calories: 190 kcal I Fat: 16g I Carbohydrates: 20g I Protein: 6g I Fiber: 5g

Ingredients

- 3 cups chopped zucchini, peeled and finely chopped
- 1/8 tsp ground allspice
- 1/2 tsp ground nutmeg
- 1/2 tsp ground cardamom
- 1/2 cup monk fruit sweetener (or another low carb granular sweetener)
- 1 tsp. pure liquid stevia
- 1 tbsp lemon juice
- 1 tbsp butter, chopped
- 1 batch low carb pie crust
- 1 1/2 tsp ground cinnamon

Method

1. Have the pie crust primed, but under-cook it (for almost 5-7 minutes).
2. Mix all the ingredients in a mixing bowl and stir well to cover the zucchini evenly with spices and sweetener.
3. For about 40 minutes or until a zucchini cooked to your taste, pour a zucchini into pie crust, wrap loosely with foil, and bake.
4. Until serving, cool perfectly.
5. Remember that this is good with low carbohydrate whipped cream

10.79 Keto Ice Cream

Servings: 4 I Time: 6 hrs 45 mins I Difficulty: Easy
Nutrients per serving: Calories: 439 kcal I Fat: 45g I Carbohydrates: 13g I Protein: 5g I Fiber: 1g

Ingredients

- 4 egg yolks, beaten
- 1 Tsp. vanilla extract
- 1/2 cup low carb syrup
- 1 3/4 cup heavy cream

Method

1. Whip the heavy cream with the hand mixer in a large bowl until it forms stiff peaks. Only put aside.
2. In a small dish, heat the low-carb syrup until it boils.
3. Meanwhile, add a big glass bowl of pounded egg yolks. Slowly drizzle the pounded egg yolks with sweet syrup until you have a pale and cream combination. Add an extract of vanilla.
4. Fold in the egg mixture with the whipped cream.
5. In a loaf tin, pour the mixture and cover it with plastic wrap. Put in the freezer and leave to set for at least 4-6 hours.

10.80 Low Carb Chocolate Fondue

Servings: 7 I Time: 1 hr 5 mins I Difficulty: Easy

Nutrients per serving: Calories: 194 kcal I Fat: 19g I Carbohydrates: 21g I Protein: 3g I Fiber: 4g

Ingredients

- 1 cup coconut milk (canned, full fat)
- 1 oz. brandy
- 1/2 cup erythritol (or another low carb granular sweetener)
- 1/4 tsp. pure liquid stevia
- 6 oz. unsweetened chocolate

Method

1. In a small and 1 quart slow cooker, combine all ingredients and mix to combine.
2. Switch the low setting slow cooker and cover with the lid.
3. Cook for approx 1 hour or until it's melted with chocolate.
4. To mix everything in the pot, stir or whisk.
5. Switch the temp to "Keep Warm" and serve with low carb fruits such as raspberries or blueberries and strawberries from the crock.
6. Don't miss the forks of fondue

10.81 Low Carb Sugar-Free Peppermint Patties

Servings: 24 I Time: 30 mins I Difficulty: Easy
Nutrients per serving: Calories: 90 kcal I Fat: 1g I Carbohydrates: 61g I Protein: 0g I Fiber: 2g

Ingredients

- 1/4 Tsp. peppermint extract
- 1/2 cup heavy cream (or dairy-free alternative)
- 6 1/2 cup powdered erythritol (like powdered swerve)
- 2 cups low carb chocolate chips

Method

1. Using parchment paper to prepare the large baking sheets.
2. Put 1 Tbsp. of milk, peppermint oil, and powdered erythritol in a large mixing bowl. Add the remaining 1 Tbsp. of cream one at a time, slowly. Continue to blend until it starts shaping a ball.
3. Pick one tbsp of the dough you have made, roll it into a small ball, and press it flat. And continue until all the patties of peppermint are made. Freeze yourself for 1 hour.
4. Add chocolate chips and microwave for 30 seconds in a microwave-safe cup, mix, and proceed until the chocolate fully melts. (1.5 minutes approx)
5. Dip the peppermint patties into molten chocolate easily with a fork, tap on the bowl edge to extract excess chocolate, and put back on parchment paper to make the placement of chocolate.
6. If you want to speed up the chocolate sets, put 5-10 minutes in the freezer.

Store in an airtight jar.

10.82 Crustless Pumpkin Pie

Servings: 9 I Time: 1 hr 8 mins I Difficulty: Easy
Nutrients per serving: Calories: 40 kcal I Fat: 1g I Carbohydrates: 23g I Protein: 2g I Fiber: 2g

Ingredients

- 2 large eggs
- 1/4 Tsp. salt
- 1/2 cup erythritol
- 1 Tsp. pure liquid stevia (optional)
- 1 Tsp. ground cinnamon
- 1 Tbsp. pumpkin spice
- 1 cup unsweetened almond milk (or heavy cream)
- 1 (15 oz) can of pure pumpkin puree

Method

1. Preheat the oven to 425°F
2. In a mixing cup, whisk together all the ingredients.
3. If you would like, spill it into an oiled 8x8 plate or pie pan.
4. Then raise the heat to 350 °F—Bake for 15 minutes. For a further 35-40 minutes, continue to bake, or until the pie is set up and cooked. The knife in the middle should come out clean.

10.83 Low Carb Chocolate Covered Bacon

Servings: 12 I Time: 25 mins I Difficulty: Easy
Nutrients per serving: Calories: 164 kcal I Fat: 16g I Carbohydrates: 6g I Protein: 2g I Fiber: 0g

Ingredients

- 1 cup low carb chocolate
- 12 wooden skewers
- 14 strips cooked bacon

Method

1. Take bacon that is freshly hot and fried. Skewer through a piece of bacon carefully. Leave the bacon to cool perfectly.
2. Create a baking sheet out of parchment paper.
3. Add the low carb chocolate and microwave for about 30 seconds, swirl and repeat until the chocolate is fully melted in the microwaveable glass cup.

10.84 Low Carb Zucchini Bread

Servings: 18 I Time: 1 hr 10 mins I Difficulty: Easy
Nutrients per serving: Calories: 155 kcal I Fat: 15g I Carbohydrates: 9g I Protein: 5g I Fiber: 2g

Ingredients

- 1/2 cup monk fruit sweetener (+ 1/4 cup for more sweetness)
- 1/4 tsp. ground nutmeg
- 1/4 tsp. salt
- 1 1/2 cups almond flour
- 1/2 cup pecan pieces
- 1/2 cup coconut oil
- 1/2 tsp. pure liquid stevia
- 1 tbsp. baking powder
- 2 tsp. ground cinnamon
- 6 large eggs
- 1 tbsp. lemon zest
- 1 cup grated zucchini

Method

1. Preheat the oven to 350 °F.
2. In a medium to big mixing cup, combine all the ingredients.
3. Line parchment paper with a regular loaf pan and pour a batter into a pan.
4. Bake for around 50-60 minutes, or until the knife inserted in the center is clean.
5. Until slicing, cool fully.

10.85 Low Carb Chocolate Bars

Servings: 9 I Time: 10 mins I Difficulty: Easy
Nutrients per serving: Calories: 169 kcal I Fat: 18g I Carbohydrates: 8g I Protein: 0g I Fiber: 1g

Ingredients

- 10 drops pure liquid stevia
- 1 tsp. pure vanilla extract
- 1/2 cup unsweetened cocoa powder
- 1/4 cup erythritol

- 3/4 cup coconut oil, melted and hot

Method

1. Using a safe microwave cup to heat the oil in the pot on the burner or in a microwave.
2. Stir the remainder of the ingredients. When the oil is heated, then whisk to remove the lumps from a cocoa powder. It will take a couple of minutes. When all is properly mixed, the mixture should be smooth and fluffy.
3. Pour chocolate into a baking dish or chocolate mold or option lined with parchment and put in a refrigerator for 2 hours or until the chocolate is completely hardened.
4. Set the dish out for about 20-30 minutes on a counter to leave the chocolate melt a little before cutting.
5. Keep in the refrigerator or freezer in an air-tight jar.

10.86 Low Carb Orange Almond Cake Bars

Servings: 28 I Time: 40 mins I Difficulty: Easy
Nutrients per serving: Calories: 84 kcal I Fat: 7g I Carbohydrates: 3g I Protein: 2g I Fiber: 1g

Ingredients

- 1 tsp. pure liquid stevia
- 4 large eggs
- 2 tsp. baking powder
- 1/2 cup unsalted butter (softened - I used a non-dairy butter)
- 1/2 cup coconut flour
- 1/2 tsp. orange extract
- 1/2 tsp. almond extract
- 1 1/4 cup fine-ground almond flour
- 1/8 tsp. salt
- 3/4 cup xylitol

TOPPING:
- 1/4 cup powdered xylitol I just powdered my own in a spice grinder)
- 1/4 tsp. almond extract
- 1/4 cup sliced almonds
- 1 tsp. orange extract
- 1 tbsp. milk (you can use unsweetened almond milk)

Method

1. Preheat the oven to 325 °F.
2. Put parchment in it without oiling the pan and set aside using a quarter-size baking sheet.
3. Whip the butter in a blender until smooth, then add the sweetener. Half the flour is added. Until this is introduced into the butter, all other ingredients continue to be added.
4. It will have the consistency of whipped cream cheese or a whipped butter when the batter is finished. Thick, still tender. Scrap the dough onto the cookie sheet and spread the dough out uniformly over a cookie sheet to around 1/2 inch thickness using a recessed spatula.
5. For 20 minutes, roast them. You can prepare the topping as it bakes. Whisk together the extracts, powdered sweetener, and about 2 tbsp in a small dish. For whatever milk you want to use.
6. Move a bar dough to the cutting board when the bars are finished baking and allow it to cool completely. Place it in the freezer for a minimum of 2 hours.
7. 11. Mix the topping ingredients, except for the almonds. leave it to stay in the almond milk for around 5-10 min to reach the sweetener to dissolve completely.
8. Scatter the icing over the bars with a spoon, and then finish with almonds. Split the dough into thin strips. Use low carb hot chocolate to serve. Keep in a freezer until fit for serving. They are more like cookies and are better eaten with a fork.

10.87 Low Carb Coconut Vanilla Ice Cream

Servings: 4 I Time: 1 hr I Difficulty: Easy
Nutrients per serving: Calories: 411 kcal I Fat: 48g I Carbohydrates: 5g I Protein: 2g I Fiber: 3g

Ingredients

- 1/8 tsp. salt
- 1/4 cup erythritol
- 1/2 cup MCT oil
- 4 large egg yolks (pasteurized eggs are safest)
- 1 (15 oz.) can full-fat coconut milk
- 2 tsp. pure vanilla extract

Method

1. In a blender, add all the ingredients, and mix for 20 seconds, or until all is well mixed.
2. Move the blend to the ice cream maker and continue with the manual for the unit.

10.88 Keto Vanilla Cupcakes

Servings: 12 I Time: 30 mins I Difficulty: Easy
Nutrients per serving: Calories: 107 kcal I Fat: 10g I Carbohydrates: 8g I Protein: 3g I Fiber: 2g

Ingredients

- 3 Tbsp. unsalted butter, melted
- 2 whole eggs
- 1/4 Tsp. salt
- 1/4 cup powdered erythritol
- 1/4 cup brown sugar alternative
- 1/2 Tsp. vanilla extract
- 1/2 Tsp. baking soda
- 1/2 cup unsweetened almond milk
- 1 Tsp. baking powder
- 1 Tsp. apple cider vinegar
- 1 1/2 cups almond flour

Method

1. Preheat the oven to 350°F. Oiled or bake with cupcake liners to prepare a muffin tin.
2. Mix the almond milk and the vinegar in a small bowl and set aside.
3. Mix the dry products, almond flour, erythritol, baking powder, salt, baking soda, and brown sugar in a big cup.
4. Create a dry ingredient core and apply the mixture of eggs, butter, almond milk/vinegar, and vanilla extract. Mix once mixed properly.
5. Spoon the flour into the lined tin for baking. 3/4 complete filling of each tin. Bake for about 20-22 minutes, or until a toothpick comes out clean.
6. Leave them to cool completely before frosting and enjoy your favorite low carb frosting.

10.89 Low Carb Chocolate Ice Cream

Servings: 4 I Time: 1 hr I Difficulty: Easy
Nutrients per serving: Calories: 323 kcal I Fat: 34g I Carbohydrates: 16g I Protein: 4g I Fiber: 3g

Ingredients

- 4 large egg yolks (pasteurized are safest)
- 2 tsp. pure vanilla extract
- 2 cups unsweetened chocolate almond milk
- 10 drops pure liquid stevia
- 1/8 tsp. sea salt
- 1/4 cup powdered monk fruit
- 1/2 cup MCT oil
- 1 tbsp. unsweetened cocoa powder

Method

1. In a blender, put all the ingredients and blend for 1 - 2 minutes.
2. Put the mixture in your ice cream maker and operate as directed by the machine.
3. Scoop and then enjoying

10.90 Keto Double Chocolate Cookie Dough

Servings: 32 I Time: 10 mins I Difficulty: Easy
Nutrients per serving: Calories: 58 kcal I Fat: 5g I Carbohydrates: 3g I Protein: 0g I Fiber: 1g

Ingredients

- 1/8 Tsp. liquid stevia
- 1/4 cup of low carb chocolate chips
- 1/2 cup softened butter
- 1/4 -1/2 cup of powdered erythritol
- 1/2 Tsp. sea salt
- 1/2 cup heavy cream or coconut milk for a dairy-free alternative
- 1/2 cup coconut flour
- 1 Tsp. vanilla extract
- 3 Tbsp. cocoa powder

Method

1. Butter, vanilla extract, stevia, salt, erythritol, and the heavy cream are creamed together in a large bowl.
2. Beat until well mixed with coconut flour and cocoa powder.
3. Fold the chocolate chips together. Eat into bite-sized bits with a spoon or scoop as they become more stable after being stored in the fridge. Store it in the freezer.

10.91 Low Carb Keto Cream Cheese Frosting

Servings: 32 I Time: 10 mins I Difficulty: Easy
Nutrients per serving: Calories: 36 kcal I Fat: 3g I Carbohydrates: 9g I Protein: 0g

Ingredients

- 8 ounces cream cheese softened
- 2 cups powdered erythritol like powdered swerve
- 1/4 cup butter softened

Method

1. Take a medium-sized mixing bowl, mix the cream cheese and butter slowly add the powdered sweetener until smooth with a hand mixer or a stand mixer.
2. Onto your favorite low carbohydrates cupcakes or cake, pipe or ice and enjoy

10.92 Low Carb Raspberry Chocolate Sponge Cake

Servings: 12 I Time: 55 mins I Difficulty: Easy
Nutrients per serving: Calories: 195 kcal I Fat: 16g I Carbohydrates: 12g I Protein: 6g I Fiber: 5g

Ingredients

- 1/8 Tsp. pure liquid stevia
- 1/4 cup coconut flour
- 1/4 cup erythritol
- 1/4 cup melted butter or butter alternative
- 1 1/2 cups almond flour
- 1/2 Tsp. xanthan gum
- 1/2 cup whole milk or dairy-free alternative
- 1/2 cup raspberries
- 1/2 cup of low carb chocolate chips
- 1 Tsp. baking powder

- 1 Tsp. pure vanilla extract
- 4 large eggs
- 4 Tbsp. lemon juice

Method

1. Preheat the oven to 350°F. Oiled with the cooking spray or oil to prepare a 9x13 pan.
2. In a big dish, combine the almond flour, erythritol, xanthan gum, coconut flour, and baking powder.
3. Build a well and apply extract, eggs, whole milk, liquid stevia, and lemon juice to the middle of dry ingredients. Mix before it is mixed properly.
4. Fold in the raspberries and chocolate chips. Into a prepared pan, pour. Bake for about 35-40 minutes, or until the toothpick is clean.

10.93 Low Carb Dairy Free Raspberry Mousse

Servings: 4 I Time: 15 mins I Difficulty: Easy
Nutrients per serving: Calories: 201 kcal I Fat: 28g I Carbohydrates: 3.5g I Protein: 0.5g I Fiber: 2.5g

Ingredients

- 2 tbsp. erythritol or the low carb sweetener of your choice to taste
- 1 (4 oz.) package fresh raspberries
- 1 (15 oz.) can full-fat coconut milk (refrigerated for 2 days)

Method

1. Set aside a pair of raspberries for garnish while you are serving this to visitors.
2. In a blender, put all ingredients and blend until they become smooth.
3. Pour into the serving cups, then top and serve with a fresh raspberry.

10.94 Keto Low Carb Pumpkin Bars

Servings: 18 I Time: 2 hrs 15 mins I Difficulty: Easy
Nutrients per serving: Calories: 171 kcal I Fat: 13g I Carbohydrates: 14g I Protein: 2g I Fiber: 5g

Ingredients

- 1 (15 oz.) can full-fat coconut milk
- 1 (15 oz.) can pumpkin puree (not pumpkin pie filling)
- 1 tbsp. coconut flour
- 1 tsp. ground cinnamon
- 1 tsp. pure liquid stevia
- 1/2 cup erythritol or another low carb sweetener
- 16 oz. food-grade cocoa butter
- 2 tsp. pumpkin pie spice, no sugar added

Method

1. Then melt the cocoa butter in a small-medium pot on low to medium heat.
2. Stir in the milk from the coconut and then a pumpkin puree. To prevent burning, stir in all the other ingredients and keep the heat on the low side. More of a custard consistency should thicken the mixture.
3. Pour it into the parchment-lined casserole dish until it reaches that consistency, then put the dish for at least two hours in the freezer.
7. Remove, cut, sprinkle with sliced pecan parts from the freezer, and enjoy.
8. Store in a fridge the rest.

10.95 Low Carb Blackberry Ice Cream

Servings: 6 I Time: 25 mins I Difficulty: Easy
Nutrients per serving: Calories: 158 kcal I Fat: 14g I Carbohydrates: 31g I Protein: 2g I Fiber: 3g

Ingredients

- 1/4 tsp. almond extract (optional)
- 1/2 tsp. ground cinnamon
- 1/2 cup erythritol
- 1 (15 oz.) can full-fat coconut milk
- 1 tsp. pure vanilla extract
- 4 large whole egg yolks, set aside in a medium bowl
- 1 (6 oz.) package fresh blackberries

Method
1. Bring coconut milk to a low boil in a medium cup.
2. Stir in the cinnamon and the vanilla, and the cinnamon will break up any clumps.
3. Take the heat-proof spoon or a small cup and gently pour about 1/4 of a cup of the hot milk into the eggs while whisking rapidly. Pour slowly and whisk immediately.
4. When you've stirred the hot milk into the shell, gently pour the egg into a simmering pot of coconut oil. The egg temperature is steadily increased by this process so that it blends into the milk without making you scrambled eggs.
5. Apply the erythritol to the pot of milk until you have the egg in it. With the potato masher or a fork, add the blackberries and crush them.
6. Remove that from the sun and cool in the refrigerator with all the batter.
7. Shift to your ice cream maker until fully cooled and continue to the manufacturer's instructions for your computer. Store in a food-safe jar in the freezer until ready to taste.

10.96 Sugar-Free Marshmallows

Servings: 16 I Time: 1 day 30 mins I Difficulty: Easy
Nutrients per serving: Calories: 4 kcal I Fat: 1g I Carbohydrates: 14g I Protein: 1g

Ingredients
- 1 1/2 cups powdered erythritol (or favorite powdered sugar substitute)
- 1 cup of warm water
- 1/4 Tsp. sea salt
- 2 Tbsp. unflavored gelatin
- 2 Tsp. vanilla extract

Method
1. In a wide dish, position 1/2 cup of the warm water. This dish should be big enough as the marshmallows in that bowl can be combined. You'll get a mess otherwise.
2. Sprinkle gelatin on the top of hot water and whisk, set aside, before adding.
3. Place the remaining half cup of water, powdered sugar replacement, and salt in a medium saucepan over medium-low heat. Whisk the components together until they are transparent. As soon as you see, bubbles start forming, extract them from the sun.
4. In your large mixing cup, add the warm mixture into it. You have the little air in a mixture and shape stiff peaks using the hand mixer or a stand mixer with the whisk attachment, then whisk for about 15-20 minutes before the color changes from light brown to white.
5. In an 8x8 baking dish, put the parchment paper. To help avoid sticking, dust with the powdered sweetener.
6. In a lined baking dish, add the marshmallow mixture and refrigerate overnight. The dough on the surface can become solid and not soft.
7. Use the parchment paper to clear it from the jar. Coat a bit of powdered sweetener with your sharp knife, carve it into the marshmallows, and make 16 squares. If the dough seems to be a little moist, you should sprinkle the marshmallows with a bit more erythritol to protect them from sticking. Store in an airtight jar.

10.97 Keto Coffee Popsicles

Servings: 4 I Time: 1 day I Difficulty: Easy
Nutrients per serving: Calories: 123 kcal I Fat: 14g I Carbohydrates: 0g I Protein: 0g I Fiber: 0g

Ingredients
- stevia to taste (or maybe low carb sweetener you prefer)
- 4 tbsp. food-grade cocoa butter
- 1 tsp. pure vanilla extract
- 1 1/4 cup brewed coffee

Method
1. Blend it all in a blender together.
2. Pour and chill overnight in Popsicle molds.

10.98 Low Carb Sugar-Free Meringue Cookies

Servings: 24 I Time: 2 hrs 40 mins I Difficulty: Easy
Nutrients per serving: Calories: 2 kcal I Fat: 0g I Carbohydrates: 10g I Protein: 0g I Fiber: 0g

Ingredients
- 3 large egg whites at room temperature
- 1 Tsp. vanilla extract
- 1/2 cup erythritol
- 3/4 cup powdered erythritol

Method
1. Preheat the oven to 200°F
2. Line the baking sheet or oiled parchment paper with a non-stick silicone pad. The silicone mat fits best, I think.
3. Add the egg whites to a medium bowl with a hand blender and beat for 1 minute at the medium-low level. Egg albumins should be frothy and white.
4. Continue to blend at medium speed, add 1 tbsp of erythritol (powdered) at a time, and continue whisking until rigid peaks shape. The batter should be thick and shiny. Stir in the vanilla extract.
5. On lined baking sheets, spoon meringue flour into mounds or spoon into the piping bag, then pipe into small mounds.
6. Bake for 2.5 -3 hours or before the meringues on the outside is dried. And a parchment paper with the intact bottoms is discarded, and the centers inside are not sticky. Switch the oven off and inside the oven, allow them to cool.

For up to 2 weeks, you can preserve it in an airtight container.

10.99 Keto Blackberry Clafoutis

Servings: 6 I Time: 50 mins I Difficulty: Easy
Nutrients per serving: Calories: 163 kcal I Fat: 13.4g I Carbohydrates: 7g I Protein: 3.7g I Fiber: 3.5g

Ingredients
- Pinch of sea salt
- 2 Tbsp. plus 1 Tsp. butter
- 2 large eggs
- 2 cups blackberries
- 2 ½ Tbsp. coconut flour
- ½ Tsp. pure vanilla extract
- ½ Tsp. baking powder
- ⅓ cup powdered erythritol
- ⅓ cup heavy cream
- ¼ cup coconut milk, almond milk, OR cashew milk

Method

1. Preheat the oven to 350 °F. Oiled up a 10" oval baking dish gently.
2. At low pressure, heat a small saucepan. Melt the butter in a pan and then heat it until it becomes golden brown, take very good care, and not let it burn.
3. Remove the container from the heating and stir in the eggs, vanilla extract, and erythritol Whiskey until the mixture becomes creamy and light in color.
4. In the coconut flour, stir gently. Then add in the milk, yogurt, salt, and baking powder of the coconut. Mix until all the ingredients are well blended.
5. Pour the mixture into the baking dish prepared and covered with blackberries—Bake in the middle for 40 minutes.
6. The core will still be somewhat wobbly but will begin to set as it cools off. You can cook it for 5 - 10 minutes longer if you like a somewhat crispier clafoutis.
7. Before eating, sprinkle with powdered erythritol, or finish with low carbohydrate vanilla ice cream or the whipped cream.

10.100 Pumpkin Spice Cupcakes With Marshmallow Frosting

Servings: 6 I Time: 40 mins I Difficulty: Easy
Nutrients per serving: Calories: 2 kcal I Fat: 60g I Carbohydrates: 7g I Protein: 13g I Fiber: 7g

Ingredients
FOR THE PUMPKIN SPICE CUPCAKES:

* 3 Tbsp. coconut flour
* 2 Tbsp. chopped walnuts
* 2 Tbsp. coconut oil, butter, or butter flavored coconut oil (melted)
* 2 large eggs, separated
* 1 Tsp. pure vanilla extract
* 1 Tsp. baking powder
* 1 ½ Tsp. Pumpkin Pie Spice
* ¾ Tsp. ground chia seeds
* ¾ cup blanched almond flour
* ½ Tsp. apple cider vinegar
* ⅓ cup plus 1 Tbsp. pumpkin puree (unsweetened)
* ¼ Tsp. of sea salt
* ¼ cup almond milk (unsweetened)
* ¼ cup golden monk fruit

FOR THE MARSHMALLOW FROSTING:

* ¼ Tsp. cream of tartar
* ¼ Tsp. of sea salt
* 1 cup powdered erythritol or monk fruit
* 1 Tsp. pure vanilla extract
* 4 large egg white, room temperature

Method
FOR THE PUMPKIN SPICE CUPCAKES:

1. Preheat the oven to 350°F.
2. Mix the almond flour, coconut flour, walnuts, ground chia, baking powder, salt, and pumpkin pie spice in a large mixing cup. Mix once well blended with all ingredients.
3. In a mixing cup, position the egg whites and use the electric mixer to beat until stiff peaks develop.
4. Beat the egg yolks for about 30 seconds in the third large mixing bowl. Add honey, vanilla extract, almond milk, apple cider vinegar, and pumpkin puree. Whisk when well mixed with all ingredients.
5. Include the dry ingredients in the egg yolk mixture and swirl to blend using a rubber spatula.
6. Fold the whipped egg albumins carefully into the mixture, but be careful not to overmix the egg whites and deflate them.
7. Divide the mixture uniformly into 6 wells of a muffin tin, silicone muffin cups, or silicone muffin pan.
8. Bake for 25 - 30 minutes until the tops are gently browned, and a toothpick can be inserted in the middle and removed without sticking to it. (Start testing at the mark of 22 minutes).

FOR THE MARSHMALLOW FROSTING:

1. Place a heatproof bowl over a saucepan filled with around 1 inch of the simmering water to set up a double boiler. Ensure the bowl shouldn't hit the water, and the pan's bottom is suspended over the waterline.
2. Place the egg albumin, sweetener, tartar cream, and salt in a bowl and whisk for 4 minutes with the electric mixer or an electric whisk.
3. Remove a bowl from the heat and begin whisking for 7 - 9 minutes until frosting becomes thick, or shift the mixture to the stand mixer. Gently add in the vanilla extract until the frosting is smooth and thick.
4. Spoon the frosting back into a pipe and pipe the marshmallow frosting for each cupcake.
5. Sprinkle a small pinch of a pumpkin pie spice with each cupcake before serving. Place the leftovers for up to 3 days in the refrigerator.

Chapter 11 – Keto-Friendly Snacks Recipes

Snacking between meals can help moderate hunger and keep you on track while following a ketogenic diet. Because the ketogenic diet is filling, you may only need one or two snacks per day, depending on your activity level. These keto snacks not only sustain fullness among meals, but they also help in weight gain if you've these too much throughout the day. It is essential to eat the appropriate number of calories based on your activity level, weight loss goal, age, and gender.

11.1 Golden Potato Croquettes

Servings: 4 I Time: 5 mins I Difficulty: Easy
Nutrients per serving: Calories: 331 kcal I Fat: 30g I Carbohydrates: 2g I Protein: 13g I Fiber: 0g

Ingredients

- 2 oz. butter
- 8 oz. (2 cups) cheddar cheese or provolone cheese, in slices

Method

1. On the large cutting board, put the cheese slices.
2. Cut the butter with the cheese slicer or us1e a knife to cut tiny bits.
3. Use butter to coat every cheese slice and roll-up. Now Serve as snacks.

11.2 Sugar-Free Keto Low Carb Granola Bars

Servings: 12 I Time: 40 mins I Difficulty: Easy
Nutrients per serving: Calories: 194 kcal I Fat: 17.4g I Carbohydrates: 8.3g I Protein: 5.5g I Fiber: 4.6g

Ingredients

- 4 Tbsp Monkfruit
- 3/4 tsp Sea salt
- 2 Tbsp Almond butter
- 1/4 cup Stevia chocolate chips (sweetened and dairy-free)
- 1 Tbsp Coconut oil
- 1 large egg
- 1 cup coconut flakes (Unsweetened and tightly packed (65g))
- 1 Cup Slivered almonds (85g)
- 1 Cup Raw almonds, Chopped (140g)

Method

1. 1.Heat your oven up to 375 ºF and line parchment paper with an 8x8 inch pan. Leave some hanging on the sides to be used later as a handle.
2. On 3 separate small baking sheets, put the sliced almonds, coconut flakes, and slivered almonds. Bake until toasted and golden colored. It takes 2-4 minutes for the coconut, about 3-5 minutes for the slivered almonds, and about 7-12 minutes for the chopped almonds. Please enable it to cool fully. Also, decrease the temperature of the oven to 350.
3. Whisk the egg and the monk fruit in a large bowl together.
4. Melt the almond butter and the coconut oil in a separate, tight, microwave-safe bowl until smooth, for about 30 seconds. Whisk in the combination of eggs when well mixed.
5. Put in all the almonds, salt, and coconut and mix until well mixed. Whisk in the chocolate chips at last.
6. Put a few muscles into it because then they stay together; you have to pack these in.
7. Cook until the top seems set, at 350 ºF for about 15 minutes. Let it cool fully in the pan to room temperature. Slice and DEVOUR when cold

11.3 Sauteed Broccolini

Servings: 4 I Time: 20 mins I Difficulty: Easy
Nutrients per serving: Calories: 40 kcal I Fat: 3.4g I Carbohydrates: 1g I Protein: 1g I Fiber: 1g

Ingredients

- 1/2 Cup Water
- 1/2 tsp Garlic, diced
- 1 Lb Broccolini
- 1 Tbsp Olive oil
- Salt

Method

1. Cut off the broccolini's stalky ends and drop some flowers.
2. Place the broccolini with the water in a vast, high-sided skillet and move to medium heat. Cover and cook until a broccolini is light green and stirring regularly, around 8-10 mins.
3. Uncover and cook for about 1-2 minutes before the water dries.
4. Push the broccolini aside and add the garlic and oil. Stir and cook together until the broccolini is brown and burnt a little.
5. Season with salt and DEVOUR to perfection.

11.4 Marinated Olives

Servings: 6 I Time: 20 mins I Difficulty: Easy
Nutrients per serving: Calories: 161 kcal I Fat: 16.31g I Carbohydrates: 4.96g I Protein: 0.28g I Fiber: 0.5g

Ingredients

- 3 tbsp olive oil

- 2 tsp chopped fresh parsley (basil or tarragon)
- 1-2 tbsp red wine vinegar (or lemon juice)
- 1/4 tsp salt
- 1/4 tsp red pepper flakes
- 1 tsp whole fennel seeds
- 1 tsp chopped fresh rosemary (or thyme)
- 1 medium garlic clove, minced
- 1 cup medium pitted green olives (6 oz)
- 1 cup medium pitted black olives (6 oz)

Method

1. In a small saucepan on medium-low heat, heat the fennel seeds until fragrant.
2. Switch the fire to medium and add the flakes of olive oil, vinegar, garlic, rosemary (or thyme), and red pepper. Heat until fragrant with the oil, around 8 minutes.
3. Pour the olives over them and stir. Add salt and parsley, swirling to mix. Serve instantly, then let marinate for an excellent taste for about 2 hours.
4. Alternately, in a mortar with the pestle, smash the fennel seeds. Garlic is then added and worked into a paste. For the next seven ingredients, stir in. For the marinade, toss the olives. For the most pleasing taste, marinate for many hours.
5. STORE: Put in an airtight jar or a film-coated bowl and can refrigerate for one week.

11.5 Keto Snickerdoodles

Servings: 8 | Time: 10 mins | Difficulty: Easy
Nutrients per serving: Calories: 57 kcal | Fat: 5.2g | Carbohydrates: 8.6g | Protein: 1.2g | Fiber: 1g

Ingredients

- 0.63 cups Almond Flour (125g)
- 2 Tbsp Coconut flour, packed (28g)
- 0.5 tsp Vanilla
- 0.5 Egg
- 0.5 tsp Cream of tartar
- 0.5 tsp Cinnamon
- 0.13 tsp Salt
- 0.25 cup + 1 Tbsp Swerve, divided
- 0.25 tsp Xantham gum (do not omit)
    - 2.5 Tbsp Unsalted Butter, softened to room temperature (70g)

Method

1. Heat the oven to 350 °F. Place parchment paper on a baking sheet.
2. Mix Cream Butter and 1/2 cup swerve until smooth with the electric hand mixer. Include the egg and vanilla, then beat until well mixed.
3. Apply all the remaining ingredients, except cinnamon and the remainder of Swerve, and stir until combined.
4. On a small pan, mix the cinnamon and swerve. Roll the dough into balls and measure 1 Tbsp, and put on the cookie sheet.
5. Slightly press the 1/3 inch thick balls and bake for 12-13 minutes before the edges start to feel set. And let pan fully cool down and DEVOUR.

11.6 Roasted Air Fryer Cauliflower

Servings: 4 | Time: 25 mins | Difficulty: Easy
Nutrients per serving: Calories: 41 kcal | Fat: 2.4g | Carbohydrates: 4.4g | Protein: 1.7g | Fiber: 2.1g

Ingredients

- 2 tsp Olive oil
- 3/4 Lb Cauliflower, cut into florets
- Sea salt

Method

1. In a wide cup, put cauliflower florets and drizzle with the oil, tossing them to cover. Then, sprinkle with salt generously.
2. Place in a single layer in the air fryer's mesh basket and cook at 400 F until golden brown and fork-tender, around 17-22 minutes.

11.7 Salt And Pepita Hard Boiled Egg Snack

Servings: 8 | Time: 35 mins | Difficulty: Easy
Nutrients per serving: Calories: 94.5 kcal | Fat: 6.7g | Carbohydrates: 0.7g | Protein: 7.7g | Fiber: 0.3g

Ingredients

- 8 large Eggs
- 1 tsp Sea Salt
- 1/4-1/2 tsp Black Pepper (depending on you, how peppery you like your eggs)
- 1/4 cup Pepitas

Method

1. Preheat to 400°F in your oven.
2. Place the eggs in the thin layer in a huge jar. Cover them and put them to a boil on high heat with 2 inches of water. Switch off the heat (but do not remove the pot from), cover and pot until they hit a rolling boil, and leave around 10-12 minutes. Pour the water and cover it with cold water, and let it stand for 10 minutes.
3. Place the pepitas over a small baking sheet while the eggs become fried and bake until softly golden brown, around 5-7 minutes.
4. Switch the toasted pepitas, pepper, and salt to the small food processor or the spice grinder and pulse until these broken down, but there are some small bits of texture.
5. By dipping into the mixture of pepitas, peel the eggs and DEVOUR

11.8 Crispy Air Fryer Brussels Sprouts

Servings: 4 | Time: 35 mins | Difficulty: Easy
Nutrients per serving: Calories: 78.2 kcal | Fat: 3.7g | Carbohydrates: 10.1g | Protein: 3.8g | Fiber: 4.3g

Ingredients

- Sea salt
- 1 Tbsp Olive oil
- 1 Lb Brussels sprouts

Method

1. Heat your fryer in the air to 350 F
2. Trim the ends of the sprouts in Brussels, cut the leaves and not look good. After trimming, you can end up with around 3/4 lb of the Brussels sprouts,
3. Place the Brussels in a bowl and toss with salt and olive oil. Remove and set aside any singular leaves for later.
4. Put the Brussels inside your air fryer's mesh basket and cook for about 12 minutes. Next, shake the basket, then cook for a further 10-12 minutes before you're done with the Brussels look. Put the singular leaves in the air fryer at this stage and cook for 2 to 3 minutes until crispy.

11.9 Sugar-Free Keto No Bake Cookies

Servings: 12 | Time: 10 mins | Difficulty: Easy
Nutrients per serving: Calories: 156.4 kcal | Fat: 14.4g | Carbohydrates: 5.7g | Protein: 3.8g | Fiber: 2.8g

Ingredients

- pinch of Salt
- 6 tbsp Almond Butter (the no-stir kind)
- 2 tbsp of Unsalted Butter (or dairy-free butter)

- 2 tbsp of Sugar-Free Chocolate Chips (or dairy-free)
- 2 1/2 tbsp Monkfruit Sweetener
- 1/2 cup Unsweetened Coconut Flakes
- 1 1/4 cups Almond Flour, (125g)

Method
1. Melt the almond butter & butter until they become smooth and creamy, around 1 minute, in a big, microwave-safe dish.
2. Whisk until it is absorbed in the monk fruit. Then stir in almond flour, the flakes of coconut, and salt.
3. To cool, put the bowl in the fridge for 15 minutes.
4. Whisk in the chocolate chips until cooled.
5. Roll into balls of 1 1/2 Tbsp and put on a cookie sheet lined with parchment paper. Slightly push out, to around 1/2 inch thick.
6. For at least an hour, cover and refrigerate.

11.10 Grilled Avocados With Feta Tahini Sauce

Servings: 6 I Time: 10 mins I Difficulty: Easy
Nutrients per serving: Calories: 199 kcal I Fat: 18.1g I Carbohydrates: 9.4g I Protein: 3.2g I Fiber: 6.2g

Ingredients
- 1 Garlic clove
- 2 tsp Fresh lemon juice
- 2 tsp Olive oil
- 3 Large Fresh Avocados
- Salt

For The Sauce:
- 1/4 cup Feta cheese, crumbled (37g)
- 1 1/2 Tbsp Tahini
- 1/2 - 1 Tbsp Reduced-sodium chicken broth (depending on how thick you like your sauce)
- 4 tsp Fresh lemon juice
- 1 tsp Honey
- Pinch of salt

Method
1. Preheat to medium-high heat on your barbecue.
2. Cut the avocados in half, and the seeds are removed. Peel a clove of garlic and take the top off. Everywhere on the cut side of avocado, rub the cut portion of the garlic.
3. In a shallow bowl, mix the olive oil and the lemon juice and spray over the avocados. Sprinkle salt on it.
4. Place the cut side down over the grill and cook for around 5-6 minutes before excellent grill marks are created.
5. Place the feta in the small microwave-safe bowl, then microwave it for about 10-15 seconds before cooking and softening, using a small food processor to mix all the sauce ingredients. To make sure it gets clean and creamy, you'll need to pause, scrape down each side, and then resume blending again—season with salt to taste.
6. Divide the sauce among the avocados, squeeze with the fresh lemon juice (not mandatory) and scoop to DEVOUR straight from the pod.

11.11 Keto Cucumber Salad

Servings: 4 I Time: 3 hrs 15 mins I Difficulty: Easy
Nutrients per serving: Calories: 49 kcal I Fat: 3.2g I Carbohydrates: 3.3g I Protein: 1.2g I Fiber: 0.7g

Ingredients
- 5 Tbsp Full-fat sour cream
- 2 tsp Fresh dill, minced
- 1 Large Cucumber, thinly sliced

- 1 1/2 Tbsp White vinegar
- 1 1/4 tsp Monkfruit Sweetener (you can use regular sugar too)
- 1/4 tsp Sea salt, or to taste
- 1/8-1/4 tsp Black pepper, to taste
- 1/4 of a Large Onion, sliced thinly

Method
1. In a big dish, blend all the ingredients until the cucumber is well combined.
2. Bring the cucumber & onions into the mixture and stir.
3. To produce flavors, cover, and refrigerate for about 3 hours.

11.12 Baked Zucchini Fritters

Servings: 16 I Time: 45 mins I Difficulty: Easy
Nutrients per serving: Calories: 222 kcal I Fat: 21.8g I Carbohydrates: 6.9g I Protein: 3.8g I Fiber: 2.8g

Ingredients
The Fritters:
- 1 cup Almond flour (100g)
- 1 Egg white
- 2 Tbsp of Olive oil, divided
- 2 tsp Coconut flour
- 2/3 cup diced Onion
- 20 Twists Real Salt Organic Garlic Pepper
- 3 Cups Grated zucchini, packed (2 large zucchinis)
- 20 Twists Organic Lemon Pepper Real Salt
- 3/4 - 1 tsp Real Salt Sea Salt
- 6 Tbsp Parsley, minced
- Olive oil spray

For The Dip:
- Real Salt Sea Salt, to taste
- 5 tsp Fresh lemon juice
- 4 Twists Real Salt Lemon Pepper
- 4 tsp Fresh dill, chopped and tightly packed
- 1/2 Cup Paleo-friendly Mayo

Method
1. Heat the oven to 400 °F. Line a parchment paper baking sheet. If you have one, use a dark-colored baking sheet as it helps crisp them
2. Place grated zucchini in the kitchen towel and apply as much moisture as possible to the loop. Put some muscle in it to keep the patties from becoming soggy. In a wide dish, add it.
3. In a wide skillet, heat 2 tsp of oil over medium heat and set aside the remainder for later. Cook the onion and add it to the zucchini until it's smooth and golden brown.
4. Add up all the Lemon pepper, parsley, salt, garlic pepper, coconut flour, and almond flour. Stir before it's blended properly. Add the white egg and cook until the zucchini is coated.
5. Drop 16 meager 1/4 cup balls on the baking sheet - or around 3 Tbsp. Push flat out (approximately 1/4 of an inch) and coat the tops with a spray of olive oil. (You would need to cook in two separate batches)
6. Bake for about 25-30 minutes, until the sides are golden brown as well as the top becomes slightly crispy. Then, change your oven to broil HIGH and broil for around 2-3 minutes until crisp. Look carefully at how they can burn quickly.
7. . Mix with all the dip ingredients and DEVOUR with fritters.

11.13 Keto Paleo Baked Chicken Nuggets In The Air Fryer

Servings: 4 I Time: 25 mins I Difficulty: Easy
Nutrients per serving: Calories: 286kcal I Fat: 11.6g I Carbohydrates: 10.3g I Protein: 29.9g I Fiber: 5g

Ingredients

- Pinch sea salt
- A cooking spray of choice
- 6 Tbsp Toasted sesame seeds
- 4 Egg whites
- 1/4 Cup Coconut flour
- 1/2 tsp ground ginger
- 1 tsp Sesame oil
- 1 Lb Free-range boneless, skinless chicken breast

For The Dip:

- 4 tsp coconut aminos (or GF soy sauce)
- 2 tsp Rice vinegar
- 2 Tbsp Natural creamy almond butter
- 1/2 tsp Monkfruit
- 1/2 tsp ground ginger
- 1 tsp Sriracha, or to taste
- 1 Tbsp Water

Method

1. Preheat the air-freezer for 10 minutes to 400 °F.
2. Cut a chicken into the nuggets (approximately 1-inch pieces), dry them, and put them in a bowl as the air fryer heats. Toss once covered with the salt and sesame oil.
3. In a wide Ziploc container, put the coconut flour and the ground ginger and shake to mix. Add a chicken and shake until the chicken is sealed.
4. Put the egg whites in a wide cup, add the chicken nuggets, and toss them until they are entirely well covered in the egg.
5. In a large Ziploc bag, put the sesame seeds. Shake the chicken off some extra egg and apply the nuggets to the bag and shake until coated well.
6. A mesh air fryer basket is generously coated with cooking oil. Put the nuggets in the basket; make sure that they are not crowded or crispy. Spray with the touch of cooking oil.
7. For 6 minutes, cook. For cooking oil, turn each nugget and spray it. Then cook an extra 5-6 minutes until the interior is no longer pink, with a crispy exterior.
8. While the nuggets are cooking, in a medium bowl, whisk together all sauce ingredients until smooth. DEVOUR nuggets and serve.

11.14 Keto Garlic Parmesan Zucchini Fries

Servings: 6 I Time: 40 mins I Difficulty: Easy
Nutrients per serving: Calories: 44 kcal I Carbohydrates: 5g I Protein: 3g I Fiber: 1g

Ingredients

- 4 zucchinis, tops, and bottoms cut off
- 1 tbsp garlic powder
- 1/4 cup parmesan cheese, fresh shredded
- 1/4 tsp salt
- 1/4 tsp pepper

Method

1. Preheat the oven to 375 °F.
2. Halve the zucchini into slices, widthwise.
3. Again, slice in two, lengthwise.
4. Slice the halves into four, making long, slender types of fry. If you have a giant zucchini, continue slicing until long, thin strips are available.

5. Pat with paper towels to rinse.
6. Toss the garlic powder, salt, parmesan, and pepper in a big bowl over the fries.
7. Place your fries on a baking sheet with parchment paper. Space out, so the fries don't hit.
8. Reduce the oven heat to 350.
9. Based on the size of the fries, bake until crunchy and brown around 20-35 minutes.
10. If browning fries are too fast, reduce the heat to 300 °F. increase the cooking time.

11.15 Keto Coleslaw

Servings: 6 I Time: 10 mins I Difficulty: Easy
Nutrients per serving: Calories: 262 kcal I Fat: 27.42g I Carbohydrates: 2.78g I Protein: 0.56g I Fiber: 1.1g

Ingredients

- 1 cup mayonnaise
- 1 tsp toasted sesame oil
- 1/4 cup sugar-free powdered sugar
- 10 oz Bag Angel Hair Coleslaw Dressing
- 3 tbsp white vinegar

Method

1. Mix the dressing. Taste to change the tastes.
2. Apply the angel hair slaw to 3/4 of a dressing and turn. Add more if required. Better if consumed within the next few hours.
3. To Make Ahead: Blend, cover, and then refrigerate dressing for up to 2 days. Only before eating, dress the cabbage.

11.16 Keto Chorizo Stuffed-Mushrooms with Cheese

Servings: 6 I Time: 40 mins I Difficulty: Easy
Nutrients per serving: Calories: 390 kcal I Fat: 33.79g I Carbohydrates: 5.47g I Protein: 17.66g I Fiber: 1.3g

Ingredients

- 8 oz cream cheese, softened (226 g)
- 2 tbsp minced cilantro
- 1/4 cup chopped green onion
- 1 lb chorizo (16 oz/ 453 g)
- 1 1/2 lb mushrooms (around 12 mushrooms) (24 oz/680g)

Method

1. Preheat the oven to 350 °F.
2. Cook and then cool the chorizo.
3. Add the melted cream cheese, cilantro, and onions into a medium dish. With a slotted spoon, scrape the chilled chorizo from the pan (leaving the oil behind) and add it to the dish's ingredients.
4. Wash the mushroom caps and pat dry with the tea towel under hot water. By bending, remove the roots. (With a melon, widen the hole if necessary).
5. Place the caps and stuff on a rimmed baking sheet with the mushrooms. To cover the crust, add plenty of water to the bottom and bake the mushrooms for about 20-30 minutes until they are browned.
6. If you want additional browning, put it under the broiler. Remove carefully to the serving dish and serve sweet.
7. With cling wrap, cover any remaining stuffed mushrooms and refrigerate. Microwave again or spray with foil and reheat for 20-30 minutes in a 350 F oven. Enjoy it within five days.

11.17 Graham Crackers With Almond Flour

Servings: 24 I Time: 27 mins I Difficulty: Easy
Nutrients per serving: Calories: 71 kcal I Fat: 6.4g I Carbohydrates: 2.6g I Fiber: 1.1g

Ingredients

- 2 1/2 Cups Almond Flour (250g)
- 1/2 cup + 2 Tbsp Monkfruit
- 2 1/2 tsp Baking powder
- 1/2 tsp Salt
- 1 Egg white
- 2 Tbsp Coconut oil, melted
- 2 tsp Molasses

Method

1. Preheat the oven to 400 °F. Use parchment paper to cover a baking sheet. Stir together the monk fruit, baking powder, almond flour, and salt in a big cup. Add white, oil, and the molasses to the egg and whisk until the sticky dough forms -it's best to blend with fingertips.
2. On the table, place a large parchment paper's piece and put the dough on the top, covering it with another parchment paper's piece. Roll out to a thickness of just under 1/4 inch.
3. Cut into 24 squares (approximately 3x3 inches) and put each square gently on the baking dish. Use a fork to softly stab the core on its own with a few holes.
4. Bake for around 6-7 minutes until the sides are only golden brown (you will need to do them in 2 lots depending on your pan's size) but do not over-bake or get too hard when cold. Let the cool pan Full.

11.18 Cauliflower Pizza Crust

Servings: 2 | Time: 30 mins | Difficulty: Easy
Nutrients per serving: Calories: 342 kcal | Fat: 0.14g | Carbohydrates: 10.16g | Protein: 32.88g | Fiber: 3.6g

Ingredients

- 2 tbsp Whey Protein Powder (optional)
- 10 oz. of frozen cauliflower rice (thawed)
- 1/3 cup Kraft Parmesan cheese (in the can)
- 1-ounce cream cheese (28 g) (cut into small pieces)
- 1 large egg white
- 1 cup low moisture shredded mozzarella cheese (4 oz/ 113 g)

Optional Seasoning

- 1/4 tsp granulated garlic
- 1/4 tsp dried basil
- 1/4 tsp dried oregano
- 1/4 tsp fennel seeds

Method

1. Preheat the oven to 425 °F. Place the rack in the middle. Line the parchment with a wide-rimmed baking sheet. Place the metal blade cutter in the food processor.
2. Squeeze as much water as you can out of an empty bag of defrosted cauliflower rice on a clean, flat, tea towel. Up with your fingertips, fluff.
3. Melt the mozzarella and cream cheese together for 1 minute in a healthy microwave dish. At 30-second intervals, stir and melt into molten. Now Scrape the cheese and add the white egg to the food processor. Process until smooth.
4. Include and process the remaining ingredients before they fit together in a ball.
5. Scrape up the cauliflower crust dough in the middle of a parchment-lined baking sheet with a rubber spatula.
6. Pat, the dough in a 10-inch disc, ensuring that it is spread uniformly.
7. Put in the oven the cauliflower pizza crust and bake for about 8-10 minutes or until one side is lightly browned. Flip over the crust and bake for 8-10 minutes. Control the crust closely so that the cheese does not burn.

8. About 3-5 minutes or just until the cheese melts, cover the pizza with your desired toppings and transfer to the oven. Serve for your salad.

11.19 Chipotle Keto Deviled Eggs with Bacon

Servings: 12 | Time: 40 mins | Difficulty: Easy
Nutrients per serving: Calories: 26 kcal | Fat: 6.47g | Carbohydrates: 0.36g | Protein: 3.6g | Fiber: 0.1g

Ingredients

- 1 1/2 tbsp melted butter
- 1 tsp chipotle powder
- 1/2 tsp salt
- 1/4 tsp granulated garlic
- 2 tsp low carb powdered sugar (Swerve, Sukrin, Lakanto, Besti)
- 2 tsp sugar-free ketchup
- 3 tbsp mayonnaise
- 4 tsp white vinegar
- 6 large hard-boiled eggs

Topping

- 2 tbsp minced cilantro
- 3 regular slices cooked bacon (crispy)
- Paprika (for sprinkling)

Method

1. Halve horizontally with the eggs. In a medium cup, scrape the yolks and place the half egg albumin on a platter or plate.
2. With a fork, mash the yolks or drive them with the pan's backside into a fine sieve. Stir in the melted butter and the mayo, blending well.
3. Apply the remainder of the ingredients to the filling and blend well to combine. Adapt the taste to your preference: lemon juice, sweetener to mellow and complement flavors, or salt to intensify flavors for more brightness. It is safest to let them stay overnight to blend the flavors. (You should cover the half egg whites at this stage and fill and refrigerate until appropriate the next day).
4. Cover the halves with the egg and dust with paprika.
5. Cut the bacon rather thinly, then drop it in a small dish. Mince up the coriander and weigh 2 tbsp. To remove some of the juice, put the cilantro in the folded paper towel, then squeeze it. It would not wilt or spill water in this manner.
6. Mix the bacon, then cilantro, and scatter over each deviled egg uniformly. Cover and refrigerate softly or eat.

11.20 Shrimp Caprese Bites

Servings: 4 | Time: 10 days | Difficulty: Easy
Nutrients per serving: Calories: 79 kcal | Fat: 6g | Carbohydrates: 1g | Protein: 6g

Ingredients

- 1 1/3 ounce mozzarella cheese
- 1 tbs olive oil
- 1 tsp freshly squeezed lemon juice
- 12 basil leaves
- 12 extra-large cocktail shrimp
- 2 cherry tomatoes (cut into 8ths)
- salt and pepper

Method

1. in a small bowl, add shrimp mozzarella and whole cherry tomatoes. Add lemon juice and a tbsp of olive

oil and season with pepper and salt to taste. To combine, toss.
2. Cut the tomatoes into eighths and the balls of mozzarella into thirds.
3. It would be best if you started assembling the skewers until the cheese and tomatoes are prepared. Insert a toothpick, right behind the tail, into the back of the shrimp. Then add a slice of tomato and mozzarella so that they stay in the shrimp's inner "c" shape. Fold up one leaf of basil and slip it on the toothpick. Finally, shift the toothpick to the other side of a shrimp.
4. For each shrimp, repeat.
5. Serve as is, or garnish with extra citrus, basil pesto, or the low carb vinaigrette instantly. Enjoy.

11.21 Low Carb Mozzarella Sticks

Servings: 4 | Time: 1 hr | Difficulty: Easy
Nutrients per serving: Calories: 94 kcal | Fat: 6g | Carbohydrates: 1g | Protein: 8g

Ingredients

- 1 egg beaten
- 1/2 tsp dried basil
- 1/4 tsp garlic powder
- 2/3 cup grated Parmesan cheese (the pasta aisle type)
- 8 sticks whole milk string cheese

Method

1. Cut those sticks of cheese in two. Then smash the egg and lb it in a tiny bowl until it's all mixed. In another cup, weigh the Parmesan cheese. For the Parmesan cheese, add the basil and the garlic powder and whisk together to mix.
2. First, dip the sliced mozzarella slice into a Parmesan mixture, then into the egg, and then into a Parmesan mixture again. On a baking sheet, put a dipped mozzarella stick on it. Repeat unless you have dipped all the bits of mozzarella. For one hour, put the baking sheets in the fridge.
3. To 400 F, preheat the oven. For 8-10 minutes, bake the icy mozzarella sticks, turning once halfway. Serve hot, if desired, with tomato sauce. Enjoy

11.22 Pan Fired Turnips Recipe with Onions and Spinach

Servings: 4 | Time: 30 mins | Difficulty: Easy
Nutrients per serving: Calories: 84 kcal | Fat: 6.25g | Carbohydrates: 6.52g | Protein: 1.06g | Fiber: 2g

Ingredients

- 2 tbsp scallions
- 1/4 tsp salt
- 1/4 tsp pepper
- 1 tbsp olive oil
- 1 tbsp butter (or more olive oil)
- 1 sprig lemon thyme (or regular)
- 1 lb turnips
- 1 cup fresh spinach loosely packed

Method

1. Peel and cut the turnips into quarters or sixths, if broad.
2. Over medium fire, position a large frying pan. Apply the olive oil to a pan when heated and swirl it to coat. When the oil shimmers, add the turnips.
3. Cook the turnips when one side is browned. Turn these over add to the pan with scallions and thyme. When the fork pierces, the thickest section slips quickly in the turnips.
4. Apply the butter and spinach to the skillet and sauté before the spinach wilts. Has the thyme sprig removed?

5. Season with pepper and salt, taste, and serve.

11.23 Bacon Wrapped Asparagus Bundles

Servings: 6 | Time: 31 mins | Difficulty: Easy
Nutrients per serving: Calories: 224 kcal | Fat: 46g | Carbohydrates: 7g | Protein: 21g | Fiber: 2g

Ingredients

- olive oil spray
- 6 slices regular cut bacon
- 1 whole lemon, quartered
- 1 tsp lemon pepper
- 1 lb asparagus, trimmed (see post)

Method

1. Preheat the oven to 400 °F. Put the rack in the center.
2. If required, wash and dry the asparagus, peel, and trim. Split into 6 bundles.
3. Wrap a slice of bacon in each package, slightly overlap the bacon, tuck the end under a bundle, and put it on a sheet tray. Using olive oil to spray and season with the lemon pepper.
4. With the asparagus, put the quartered lemon on the sheet plate.
5. Roast for eight minutes, turn over and roast for a full eight minutes. Crisp bacon under a broiler, if needed.
6. Squeeze for service with a lemon.

11.24 Zucchini Pizza Bites

Servings: 12 mini pizzas | Time: 40 mins | Difficulty: Easy
Nutrients per serving (6 mini pizzas): Calories: 92 kcal | Fat: 7.2g | Carbohydrates: 3.6g | Protein: 4.4g | Fiber: 1.3g

Ingredients

- 1/4 cup Low Carb Marinara Sauce
- 1/4 cup Pitted Black Olives
- 1/2 medium Zucchini sliced into 12 rounds
- 1 slice Mozzarella Cheese or a vegan alternative like Daiya

Method

1. To 350F, preheat the oven.
2. In 12 1/4 inch slices, dice the zucchini. Place them on a tray for baking. Coat the slice with 1 tsp (or more/less per your preference) of marinara sauce.
3. Cut an olive in half for making the spider pizzas for the body, then slice the other half into the crescents to shape the legs. On the zucchini pizzas, arrange the olive bits.
4. Assemble thin slices of the cheese and top the marinara to make mummy pizzas and put two olive slices.
5. Bake now the pizzas for about 10 minutes or unless the cheese melts. Enjoy, enjoy.

11.25 Roasted Brussels Sprouts with Walnuts and Blue Cheese

Servings: 6 | Time: 40 mins | Difficulty: Easy
Nutrients per serving: Calories: 110 kcal | Fat: 8.25g | Carbohydrates: 6.93g | Protein: 4.35g | Fiber: 3g

Ingredients

- 1/4 tsp salt
- 1/4 tsp pepper
- 1/4 cup walnut pieces
- 1/4 cup crumbled blue cheese
- 1 1/2 tbsp olive oil divided use
- 1 lb Brussels sprouts (trimmed and quartered)

Method

1. Preheat the oven to 400 °F. Shift the rack to the middle spot.

2. Trim the Brussels sprouts and quarter them and position them in a medium dish. Mix the sprouts with 1 tbsp of olive oil, salt, and pepper.
3. For 25-35 minutes, roast at 400°F, stirring half-way round. For the last 10 minutes, add the walnuts to the plate.
4. Remove them from the oven and toss with the remaining oil in the serving bowl and change the seasoning.
5. Just before serving, top with the crumbled blue cheese.

11.26 Keto Cornbread

Servings: 8 I Time: 40 mins I Difficulty: Easy
Nutrients per serving: Calories: 254 kcal I Fat: 20.4g I Carbohydrates: 5.2g I Protein: 13.7g I Fiber: 2g

Ingredients

- 3 large eggs (cold is fine)
- 2 cups almond flour (6.5 oz)
- 1/8 tsp salt
- 1/4 cup cream cheese, softened (2 oz)
- 1/2 tsp sweet corn extract
- 1 tbsp butter for the skillet
- 1 tbsp baking powder (or 1 1/2 tsp baking soda)
- 1 jalapeno
- 1 cup white cheddar cheese (or skim mozzarella) (4 oz)

Method

1. Preheat the oven to 350°F. Put the rack in the center of the oven. Now Butter an 8-inch skillet of cast iron. (You will need an 8-inches baking dish, but it can differ in cooking time. Check for over-browning). Slice the jalapeno into dense circles of 1/8 inch.
2. In a bowl of the food processor, put all ingredients for cornbread in order. Process the materials before a sticky dough emerges.
3. Scrape the dough in a prepared skillet and scatter lightly over the sides and finish with slices of jalapeno.
4. Bake for about 25-30 minutes or until gently browned at the tip. Until running a sharp and thin knife along the side and slicing to serve, remove it from the oven and cool for 10 minutes.
5. Store the leftovers in the refrigerator in an air-tight bag. Reheat in a microwave or put on a baking sheet, then reheat a 300°F (about 15 minutes).

11.27 Keto Fried Green Tomatoes

Servings: 4 I Time: 35 mins I Difficulty: Easy
Nutrients per serving: Calories: 251 kcal I Fat: 19.5g I Carbohydrates: 3.2g I Protein: 13g I Fiber: 1g

Ingredients

- 3 tbsp olive oil (for frying)
- 2 large eggs, beaten
- 1 lb green tomatoes slices, 1/2-inch thick

For dredging (optional)
- 1 tbsp whey protein powder (optional)
- 1 tbsp oat fiber (optional)

Keto Bread Crumb Coating
- 1/4 tsp pepper
- 1/4 tsp granulated garlic
- 1/4 tsp onion powder
- 1/2 cup grated Parmesan cheese (1 oz/ 29 g)
- 1/2 tsp salt
- 1 cup crushed pork rinds (1 oz/ 29 grams)
- 1 tsp dried oregano
- 1 tsp dried basil

Method

1. Place a slice on a wide sheet pan of waxed paper or parchment paper. Slice the tomatoes and let the paper towels drain on them.
2. In a small dish, whisk together protein powder and the oat fiber (dredging blend, if using). Mix the ingredients for the keto bread crumbs and put them in a shallow dish. Beat the eggs with a fork in a shallow dish.
3. With a fork, pick up the tomato slice and put it in a dredging mixture, covering both ends. Shake the waste off.
4. Within the beaten egg, put these dredged tomato slices, covering both sides. Let drain off some waste.
5. In the crumb mixture, put a wet tomato slice and cover both sides well. With crumbs, cover up the top side and press softly to ensure that they stick.
6. Shift the tomato to the lined sheet pan, and the remaining slices of tomato remain to be sprayed.
7. Over medium heat, heat a non-stick or a cast iron frying pan until clean. To coat the plate, apply 1 tbsp of oil and swirl. Add some tomato slices as the oil shimmers, then fry until browned. Switch the tomatoes, and the other hand is orange. As required, add more oil.
8. To drain and cool when frying the remaining tomatoes, add the fried tomatoes to the paper towel or a cooling rack. Serve with a dipping sauce as a side or a dessert.
9. Mix the mayo, siracha, powdered sweetener, and prepared horseradish (for a simple sauce to taste).

11.28 Baked Garlic Parmesan Chicken Wings

Servings: 4 I Time: 55 mins I Difficulty: Easy
Nutrients per serving: Calories: 512 kcal I Fat: 38.5g I Carbohydrates: 2.71g I Protein: 37.98g I Fiber: 0.75g

Ingredients

- 3 lb chicken wings, cut into pieces (about 11 whole wings)
- 1 cup grated Parmesan cheese (the good stuff - about 4 oz)
- 2 tbsp Garlic (or your favorite spice blend to taste)
- 1/2 cup mayonnaise

Method

1. Cut each wing of the chicken into three parts: the wing, the drum, and the tip. Bone broth, discard all the tips, either pop in a bag and freeze.
2. Preheat oven to 375 °F. Use foil or parchment paper to cover a wide sheet pan.
3. In a medium shallow dish, mix 2 tsp of the seasoning mixture with the Parmesan cheese.
4. Add mayonnaise to a big plastic zip bag, add bits of chicken wing, and seal. To uniformly coat each piece, maneuver the chicken wings with your hands. Instead, bring the mayo in a big bowl and cover the chicken with your mouth.
5. Stab the wing with a fork and place it on seasoned Parmesan cheese. Coat a chicken wing with your hand and fork. On the lined sheet pan, put a chicken wing. Now repeat.
6. Bake for about 40 minutes or until fully golden brown and baked through.
7. If you use foil, quickly remove these chicken wings from the pan, or the cheese will adhere to the foil.

11.29 Oven-Fried Chicken Skin Cracklings

Servings: 4 I Time: 30 mins I Difficulty: Easy
Nutrients per serving: Calories: 126 kcal I Fat: 12g I Carbohydrates: 0g I Protein: 4.5g

Ingredients

- 8 raw chicken skin pieces from thighs or breasts

- salt and pepper
- seasoning of your choice

Method

1. Remove the thighs or the chicken breasts from the chicken shell. With a knife, trim some big bits of fat off the sides. Underneath the skin, scrape away any additional fat or skin.
2. Dry the skins thoroughly on paper towels and scatter in a single layer on the parchment paper.
3. With the salt and pepper or your preferred spice, season gently. Go easy because the chicken's skin can shorten when it heats, focusing the seasoning (as much as 50 percent). In its fat, the chicken skin will fry.
4. Bake for about 20 minutes or until the mixture is brown and crisp. Remove the extra fat from the pan and drain it on paper towels. Cool thoroughly and store in the fridge in an airtight jar. For several minutes, put on a sheet pan in the oven at 350 F to re-crisp if necessary.

11.30 Braised Escarole with Onions

Servings: 4 I Time: 25 mins I Difficulty: Easy
Nutrients per serving: Calories: 124 kcal I Fat: 11g I Carbohydrates: 7g I Protein: 2g I Fiber: 4g

Ingredients

- vinegar of your choice
- Freshly ground black pepper
- Diamond Crystal kosher salt
- 3 tbsp olive oil or ghee
- 1 onion thinly sliced
- 1 large head of escarole ~2 lb
- 1 garlic clove minced

Method

1. The first thing you have to do is isolate and wash the escarole leaves properly (lots of mud and dust can be there at the base of these inner leaves). Drain and cut coarsely.
2. Heat the ghee over medium heat in a large skillet and sauté the onions until tender. Throw the garlic in and stir for about 30 seconds and then pour the escarole in it (damp greens are acceptable).
3. The greens and the onions are finely salted and cooked until the leaves are wilted and soft (about 12-15 minutes). Add salt and pepper to season, and add a dash of your preferred vinegar.

11.31 Keto Cheese Chips

Servings: 6 I Time: 18 mins I Difficulty: Easy
Nutrients per serving: Calories: 74 kcal I Fat: 4.88gl Carbohydrates: 0.61g I Protein: 6.76g

Ingredients

- Herbs, spices, spice blends
- 4 oz Parmesan Cheese

Method

1. Preheat the oven to 400 °F. Put the rack in the center position. Line the parchment paper with a large baking sheet. If you don't have a grated Parmesan, process the cheese into fine crumbles.
2. Measure the tspful of cheese and put it on a parchment-lined Panipat every mound of cheese softly (about 1 1/4 to 1 1/2 inches) in a circle with a finger. Until baking, dust with any herbs, sauces, or flavorings.
3. Cook the Parmesan crisps for 6 to 8 minutes before they begin to turn golden brown. Let it cool fully for up to 30 days before storing; put it in an airtight jar for about a week or in the fridge.

11.32 Rosemary Roasted Rutabaga

Servings: 4 I Time: 45 mins I Difficulty: Easy
Nutrients per serving: Calories: 100 kcal I Fat: 6.51g I Carbohydrates: 10g I Protein: 1.47g I Fiber: 3g

Ingredients

- 1 lb Rutabaga (peeled and cut into the 3/4-inch cubes)
- 1/8 tsp Freshly ground pepper
- 1/4 cup diced onion (1 oz)
- 1/4 tsp Salt
- 1 tbsp Chopped fresh rosemary
- 1 tbsp Olive oil
- 1 tbsp butter or ghee

Method

1. Preheat the oven to 400 °F. Put the rack in the center. Using parchment paper to cover a sheet pan.
2. Toss the onion, olive oil, pepper, rosemary, salt with the cubed rutabaga and spread it uniformly over the sheet pan. Bake about 20-30 minutes or until tender with a fork.
3. Over lower heat, heat a medium to the large frying pan. Apply the butter and swirl when heated to coat the plate. Fry a rutabaga until browned lightly.
4. To eliminate additional carbs, serve with fried, pan-seared, or roasted meat and a side salad.

11.33 Oven-Fried Parmesan Green Beans

Servings: 6 I Time: 30 mins I Difficulty: Easy
Nutrients per serving: Calories: 133 kcal I Fat: 9.88g I Carbohydrates: 6.19g I Protein: 5.3g I Fiber: 2.7g

Ingredients

Parmesan Green Beans

- 1/4 tsp salt
- 1/2 cup Parmesan cheese (Kraft in the can is fine)
- 1 lb green beans (stem end trimmed and dried with paper towels)
- 1 tsp minced garlic
- 1 large egg white (whipped until very frothy)

Sweet Mustard Dipping Sauce

- 1/4 cup mayonnaise (4 tbsp)
- 1/4 tsp dried dill, rubbed (or tarragon)
- 1/4 tsp pepper
- 1 1/2 tsp yellow mustard
- 1/2 tsp garlic salt
- 1/2 tsp smoked paprika (or regular)
- 2 tbsp sweetener of choice

Method

1. Preheat the oven to 425 °F. Put the rack in the center spot. Using parchment paper to cover a large baking dish.
2. In a shallow cup, mix these Parmesan cheese & minced garlic, and 1/4 tsp salt.
3. In a large cup, put the green beans and toss with the white egg until fully coated. Add the combination of cheese and toss to cover.
4. On the parchment-lined baking dish, scatter the green beans and sprinkle any leftover cheese on top.
5. Bake around 15-20 minutes or unless the beans become cooked and browned with the cheese.
6. Mix the ingredients for Sweet Mustard Sauce as the beans cook.

11.34 Crispy Pepperoni Chips

Servings: 1 I Time: 13 mins I Difficulty: Easy
Nutrients per serving: Calories: 150 kcal I Fat: 14g I Carbohydrates: 1g I Protein: 5g

Ingredients
- 15 Pre-sliced pepperoni slices (about one inch in diameter)

Method
Oven/Toaster Oven:
1. Preheat the oven to 400 °F. 375 F for the toaster oven and place the rack in the center. Line parchment on a sheet pan. Put the pepperoni on a parchment, spread them evenly or if you're filling the sheet pan, let them just hit.
2. Bake for 4 minutes. Be careful not to damage yourself with a paper towel—Bake for a further 4 minutes or until slightly browned with pepperoni. On a paper towel, remove and rinse.

Microwave:
1. Place the pepperoni on the paper towel on a healthy microwave plate and cook until crispy, at the interval of 20 seconds. Since microwaves differ in strength and wattage, the approximate time will rely on your microwave.

11.35 Tangy Ranch Chicken Wings

Servings: 4 | Time: 1 hr | Difficulty: Easy
Nutrients per serving: Calories: 341 kcal | Fat: 27.8g | Carbohydrates: 3g | Protein: 26g | Fiber: 2.4g

Ingredients
- Olive oil spray
- 2 tsp olive oil
- 2 tsp Baking Powder
- 2 lb Chicken wing pieces
- 2 1/2 tsp Homemade Ranch Seasoning
- 1/4 tsp Salt

Method
1. Preheat the oven to 375 °F with the middle rack in place.
2. Dry the chicken wings with paper towels and place them in a wide dish.
3. Mix 2 tsp of olive oil with the chicken wings once seasoned. Sprinkle the baking powder with 1 tsp and blend. Only repeat.
4. Place the chicken wings over a wide sheet pan and skin-side-up on a wire rack. Bake the chicken for 40 minutes, flipping it halfway through.
5. Take the chicken out of the oven and turn it upside-down again, for about 5-10 minutes just until the chicken is browned and crispy and put under the broiler.
6. Take a big bowl of chicken and gently brush it with olive oil. Over the chicken, sprinkle 1 tsp of ranch seasoning and stir to cover. Repeat with the seasoning, but add 1/4 of a tsp of salt. Just serve.

11.36 Cabbage Noodles

Servings: 4 | Time: 20 mins | Difficulty: Easy
Nutrients per serving: Calories: 82 kcal | Fat: 5.9g | Carbohydrates: 7.3g | Protein: 1.8g | Fiber: 2.7g

Ingredients
- 1/4 cup onions, sliced thinly (1 oz)
- 1 lb cabbage (cored and cut into strips)
- 2 cloves garlic, sliced
- 2 tbsp butter or oil
- salt and pepper to taste

Method
1. Cut into quarters of the cabbage. Slice the onions thinly and peel the garlic.
2. Over medium fire, heat a skillet. Apply the butter or oil when it is scorching and swirl to cover the plate. Add the cabbage, garlic, and onion and then saute until the cabbage becomes soft - about 10 minutes—salt to taste and pepper.

11.37 Oatmeal Sugar-Free Cookies

Servings: 20 | Time: 29 mins | Difficulty: Easy
Nutrients per serving: Calories: 119 kcal | Fat: 11.3g | Carbohydrates: 2.94g | Protein: 3.2g | Fiber: 1.8g

Ingredients
- 3/4 tsp cinnamon
- 1/4 tsp baking soda
- 1/4 tsp salt
- 1/3 cup Low carbohydrate brown sugar (50 g)
- 1/2 tsp of vanilla extract
- 1 1/2 cups sliced almonds (5 oz/142 g)
- 4 oz unsalted butter, softened (113 g)
- 1 cup of almond flour (95 g)
- 1 large egg, cold (room temperature)
- 2 tbsp of oat fiber (10 g)
- 2 tsp of grass-fed beef gelatin

Method
1. Preheat the oven to 350 °F. Put the rack in the center position. Line parchment on a sheet pan. In a food processor or just by hand, cut sliced almonds to imitate the size of oats. Quantify and stir together the dry ingredients to remove the lumps.
2. Sukrin Gold, vanilla extract, and Butter softened together until they become light and fluffy - around 1 1/2 minutes. Scrape the bowl down.
3. At once, add all the dry ingredients and beat until mixed. Include the egg, and beat until mixed. The cut sliced almonds fold in.
4. Scoop the dough and put on the baking sheet two inches apart using the 2 tbsp cookie scoop.
5. Bake for 8 minutes, take from the oven, and softly bang a cookie sheet on the oven or counter to flatten the cookies - about 6 times. Keep in the oven for an extra 6 minutes.
6. Take the cookies from the oven and use the spatula to slap each cookie gently. Before removing them from the cooling rack, let them cool for around 5 minutes. Until eating it, again cool these thoroughly.

11.38 Pulled Pork Stuffed Avocado Boats

Servings: 4 | Time: 15 mins | Difficulty: Easy
Nutrients per serving: Calories: 423 kcal | Fat: 34g | Carbohydrates: 9g | Protein: 23.5g | Fiber: 5g

Ingredients
- 1/4 cup BBQ sauce
- 1 1/2 cups pork or chicken (pulled)
- 2 avocados, halved and pitted

Garnish
- 1 tbsp snipped chives or green onion
- 2 tbsp BBQ sauce (sugar -free)
- 2 tbsp ranch dressing (thinned slightly)

Method
1. Halve the avocados and drain the pit. To make space for the filling, scoop out some of the avocados. (You may mash it and blend or put it on the top of pulled pork with a ranch dressing. I gave it to the children.)
2. In a microwave or the frying pan, heat the pulled pork, and mix it with 1/4 cup of BBQ sauce of your choice. Dispense equally between the halves of the avocado.
3. Drizzle each half with the remaining ranch dressing and BBQ sauce. Add chives or green onion to garnish.
4. You can eat as it is or pop put it in the microwave to warm it. Alternatively, put in a 350 F preheated oven and bake for around 20 minutes, sealed. Cover some leftovers and refrigerate them.

11.39 Sweet Bell Pepper Salad

Servings: 6 I Time: 15 mins I Difficulty: Easy
Nutrients per serving: Calories: 112 kcal I Fat: 9g I Carbohydrates: 6.4g I Protein: 2g I Fiber: 2g

Ingredients

- 2 oz feta cheese crumbled
- 2 oz. onion, sliced thinly
- 1/2 tsp garlic, minced
- 1 lb mixed bell peppers, sliced
- 1 fennel bulb, sliced thinly

Dressing

- 1 pinch pepper
- 1/2 tsp Fines Herbs (basil, tarragon, parsley, dill)
- 1/4 tsp salt
- 2 tbsp Champagne vinegar (you can also use rice wine vinegar)
- 3 tbsp extra virgin olive oil

Method

1. Cut and soak each onion in 1/4 cup of water and 2 tbsp of white vinegar for 10-15 minutes if you use heavy onions. Drain, use, again.
2. Cut the vegetables into a medium-large serving bowl and add them.
3. Mix up the dressing ingredients. Ensure that the fines herbs are rubbed on your palm or rubbed on your fingers to crack the flavor to extract it.
4. To change the seasoning, toss, and taste. Apply the cheese to the feta and toss gently. Only serve it cold.

11.40 Keto Baba Ganoush

Servings: 8 I Time: 55 mins I Difficulty: Easy
Nutrients per serving: Calories: 81 kcal I Fat: 6g I Carbohydrates: 6.3g I Protein: 2.3g I Fiber: 3.3g

Ingredients

- 1/4 cup Greek yogurt
- 1 large eggplant, sliced lengthwise (1 1/2 lb)
- 2 tsp minced garlic (1-2 cloves)
- 1/2 tsp ground cumin
- 2 tbsp tahini paste
- 2 tbsp extra virgin olive oil
- 1 tbsp lemon juice
- salt and pepper to taste

Method

1. Preheat the oven to 400°F. Please put it in the middle spot on the oven rack. Using parchment paper to cover a sheet pan.
2. Lengthwise, slice the eggplant, salt generously, and leave to rest for 15 minutes to remove the bitter juices. Quickly scrub, then pat dry. When pierced with a fork, put the eggplant having cut side down, then roast for 45 minutes or when the eggplant is fully tender. Remove and cool from the oven
3. Scoop the skin from the soft eggplant pulp and put it in a food processor. Now Pulse to split-up. Include the other ingredients and process until the dip becomes smooth and creamy in the blender.
4. Taste the seasoning and adjust. Serve right away, or cover and refrigerate for up to five days. The next day it tastes better. Serve mildly warm like room temperature.

11.41 Low Carb Keto Taco Shells

Servings: 6 I Time: 25 mins I Difficulty: Easy
Nutrients per serving: Calories: 171 kcal I Fat: 13.6g I Carbohydrates: 1g I Protein: 10.6g

Ingredients

- 9 oz pre-shredded cheddar cheese

Method

1. Put one rack in the upper third and the other rack in the lower third of the oven and preheat the oven to 375 °F. Using parchment paper to cover two wide sheet pans. (Flip the parchment over so that the cheese doesn't have a pencil or pen.)
2. Quantify 1/3 cup (1 1/2 ounce) per circle of shredded cheese and spread uniformly over the sides of the circle.
3. Bake about 5 minutes and swap the baking sheets' places. Bake for another 5-10 minutes, or until the cheese layer has small holes and the edges tend to tan.
4. Before removing onto wooden spoons or the spatulas supported by glasses to form taco shells, remove from oven and blot with the paper towel. Leave for chalupa or the tostada shells to cool flat on the pans.
5. Cool thoroughly and place for a few days in an air-tight jar. Or for up to two weeks in the refrigerator.

11.42 Low Carb Peanut Butter Balls

Servings: 20 I Time: 10 mins I Difficulty: Easy
Nutrients per serving: Calories: 104 kcal I Fat: 6g I Carbohydrates: 2g I Protein: 8g I Fiber: 1g

Ingredients

- 1 1/3 cup whey protein powder
- 1/2 tsp stevia glycerite
- 1 cup smooth peanut butter

Method

1. In a medium cup, add the ingredients and blend (knead) with the rubber spatula until thoroughly mixed.
2. Pinch-off sized sections of the dough with walnut and roll into the balls.
3. Up to 10 days in an airtight jar placed in the refrigerator.

11.43 Mexican Green Beans

Servings: 6 I Time: 25 mins I Difficulty: Easy
Nutrients per serving: Calories: 84 kcal I Fat: 7g I Carbohydrates: 6g I Protein: 1g I Fiber: 3g

Ingredients

- 1/4 cup chopped onion (1 oz)
- 1 tsp fresh oregano, minced (or 1/4 tsp of dry but fresh tastes different)
- 1/4 tsp ground cumin
- 1/2 cup Roma tomato, seeded and diced (4 oz)
- 1 lb green beans, trimmed and cut
- 1 clove garlic, minced
- 2 tbsp avocado oil or good olive oil
- 1 tbsp butter, ghee, or another tbsp of oil
- 2 tbsp water
- 1 whole bay leaf, crumbled
- 1 tsp chicken base
- salt and pepper to taste

Method

1. Wash the beans, strip them, and cut them. To separate seeds, split the tomato in half, squeeze carefully over the garbage, and then dice. Chop the onion, ginger, mince, and fresh oregano (if using).
2. Heat 1 tbsp of oil over medium heat in a large frying pan. Add the onion, tomato, garlic, and bay leaf when it is hot until the onion starts to soften. Add water, oil, oregano, green beans, and cumin, and for another tbsp to the chicken's base. Whisk to coat the beans and use a sheet of foil or a cap to cover them loosely. Cook for about 4 minutes or when the beans become cooked or according to your preference.

3. Apply butter, add garlic, pepper, or more oregano and the cumin to change the seasoning. Now serve.

11.44 Broccoli Fritters With Cheddar Cheese

Servings: 4 | Time: 18 mins | Difficulty: Easy
Nutrients per serving: Calories: 204 kcal | Fat: 16g | Carbohydrates: 5.8g | Protein: 12g | Fiber: 3g

Ingredients

- 1 cup shredded cheddar cheese
- 1 Tbsp avocado oil
- 1 tsp Cajun seasoning
- 2 large eggs, beaten
- 2 Tbsp oat fiber or almond flour, or the powdered pork rinds
- 8 oz. broccoli (cut into small pieces or chopped)

Method

1. Cut the crowns of fresh broccoli and stems into half-inch by half-inch sections. In the oven or a steamer, steam gently. If damp, remove any extra water and then dry with paper towels. (Drain well and cut into small bite-sized bits if surplus broccoli is used.)

2. With the flour of your choosing and a Cajun seasoning, toss or swirl the broccoli to coat. Mix the egg and stir. Apply the cheddar cheese and whisk until mixed thoroughly.

3. Once heated, put a cast iron or the non-stick pan on medium heat. To oil the pan, apply the oil, and swirl. Less oil is essential for a non-stick pan. The mixture is visually separated into fourths and spooned into the tray, placed in a low mound or a patty. Back into the piles, scrape some tumbled pieces.

4. In one hand, cook until the cheese starts to melt on top of the patty and the bottom becomes crusty brown around 2-3 minutes. Flip and sear until browned on the other hand.

5. Serve with an egg or a dipping sauce on top.

11.45 Low Carb Hamburger Buns

Servings: 5 | Time: 23 mins | Difficulty: Easy
Nutrients per serving: Calories: 294 kcal | Fat: 25g | Carbohydrates: 7g | Protein: 14g | Fiber: 3g

Ingredients

- 2 tbsp oat fiber (or protein powder or 1/4 c. more almond flour)
- 2 oz cream cheese
- 1 tbsp baking powder
- 1 large egg
- 1 1/4 cup almond flour
- 1 1/2 cup part-skim grated mozzarella cheese

Method

1. Place the cream cheese and mozzarella cheese in a healthy microwave bowl, then microwave for about 1 minute. Whisk and microwave for an extra 30 seconds to 1 min. Scrape the cheese along with the egg into a food processor and process until they become smooth.

2. Include the dry ingredients, then process them until they form a dough. It's pretty sticky. Let it cool for a few minutes if it's too hot to touch.

3. Preheat the oven to 400 °F. Put the rack in the center of the oven. Cover a sheet with parchment for baking. At the bottom of an oven, put a cheap metal pan.

4. Cut into 5 sections equal to each other. Lightly oil your hands and roll each piece into a ball. Place your hand on the parchment paper and softly flatten it slightly while still maintaining the domed shape.

5. At the bottom of an oven, put 6 ice cubes in a metal tray. Then the rolls are put in the oven. That will help raise and disperse the rolls.

6. Bake for about 12 minutes or until golden brown on the outside. These will be soft still, so before removing them from the baking sheet, let them cool. Store in the refrigerator after cooling. Slightly warm for pleasure.

7. Hold the burger buns in an air-tight jar in the refrigerator. They can be stored for 7-10 days and freeze well too.

11.46 Crispy Fried Eggplant Rounds With Parmesan Cheese and Marinara Sauce

Servings: 4 | Time: 30 mins | Difficulty: Easy
Nutrients per serving: Calories: 233 kcal | Fat: 17.26g | Carbohydrates: 7.15g | Protein: 11.38g | Fiber: 4g

Ingredients

- 1 cup crushed pork rinds (1 oz/ 28.35 g)
- 1 lb eggplant (cut crosswise into 1 cm - 1/2 inch rounds, 453.6 g)
- 1 tsp dried basil
- 1 tsp dried oregano
- 1/2 cup grated Parmesan cheese (1 oz/ 28.35 g)
- 1/2 tsp salt
- 1/4 tsp granulated garlic
- 1/4 tsp onion powder
- 2 tbsp olive oil
- 2 large eggs, beaten
- 1/4 tsp pepper

Method

1. Preparation: Put the eggplant in 10-12 rounds, sprinkle with salt, and leave to drain for 15 minutes in a colander. Dry full-on towels with paper. Meanwhile, in a shallow bowl (soup or cereal bowl), put the eggs wide enough to hold an eggplant round and scramble with the fork. In another small dish, blend the pork rinds, cheese, and seasoning. Get a little sheet pan packed.

2. Procedure: Use a fork to pick up around and flip this back and forth along the egg until fully coated. Grab a fork and let the egg fly away. Place in the crumb mixture, and crumbs cover the end. To the end, click the crumbs. Then use the fork to turn the round over and do this again. Raise the round eggplant and shake the excess crumbs. Lay yourself on a pan of paper. On all of the rounds, repeat the process. Depending on how large they are, you should've enough for 10-12 rounds.

3. Cook: Over medium-high cook, heat an iron skillet or non-stick pan. Alternatively, a large pancake skillet may be used, and both fit on the skillet at once. Add the oil when it is hot (you will need much less oil in a non-stick skillet). When the oil becomes hot, add 3-4 rounds to the pan and cook on either side for 3 minutes. To rinse, switch to a paper towel and then to a cooling rack. You may have to add a few more oil to the skillet as you go or adjust the heat just slightly. It'll be brown and crispy with the eggplant. Serve with hot mayo, tomato sauce, or serve as it is.

11.47 Easy Low Carb Roll

Servings: 8 | Time: 18 mins | Difficulty: Easy
Nutrients per serving: Calories: 165 kcal | Fat: 13g | Carbohydrates: 3g | Protein: 10g | Fiber: 1g

Ingredients

- 2 tbsp whey protein powder (or oat fiber or coconut flour or 1/4 cup more almond flour)
- 2 oz. cream cheese, cubed
- 1 tsp baking soda (or 1 tbsp of baking powder)
- 1 large egg

- 1 1/4 cup almond flour
- 1 1/2 cup shredded skim mozzarella cheese

Method

1. a microwave-safe dish, melt the cream cheese and mozzarella together for 1 minute at maximum strength. Stir, then heat for a further 30-45 seconds to melt. Scrape the cheese into a food processor's bowl and process until mixed completely. Add the egg and whisk until mixed.
2. The food processor adds the dry ingredients and process until thoroughly mixed (about 10-15 seconds).
3. Using oil to spray a sheet of cling film to scrape the bread dough into the middle of the cling film. It's VERY STICKY. Shape the dough softly into a disc or oval and cool it in the freezer until the oven is ready. (NOTE: the dough doesn't have to go into the freezer if it's not sticky.)
4. Preheat an oven to 400 °F. Put the rack in the center of the oven. Line a piece of parchment or Silpat with a baking sheet.
5. Remove the dough from the freezer when the oven is ready, and cut it into 8 pieces. The dough would stick to the knife-like crazy. It's all right.
6. To flatten the rim, softly oiled your hands, carefully roll the dough portion into a ball and lower it onto the prepared cookie sheet. For the remaining dough, reverse the procedure. Sprinkle with sesame, poppy, or dehydrated onion seeds, pressing very softly to bind to the dough.
7. Bake for 13-15 minutes, roughly. It will brown the dough, and it will break. Enjoy, enjoy. Hold the extra rolls in the fridge (or freezer) and warm them gently before feeding.

11.48 Asparagus with Hollandaise Sauce

Servings: 4 I Time: 15 mins I Difficulty: Easy
Nutrients per serving: Calories: 248 kcal I Fat: 26g I Carbohydrates: 3g I Protein: 4g I Fiber: 1g

Ingredients

- salt and pepper to taste
- 1 tbsp water
- 1 lb asparagus, trimmed

Hollandaise Sauce

- 1 tbsp water
- 1/2 tsp Dijon mustard
- 1-2 pinch cayenne pepper
- 1-2 pinch white pepper
- 1-2 tsp freshly squeezed lemon juice (or white vinegar)
- 2 large egg yolks
- 4 oz. salted butter

Method

1. If the asparagus' thickness is medium-large, cut 1 inch from the bottom and use a vegetable peeler to gently peel the stalks. Start from the top at around 1/3 and proceed at the bottom of every spear. Keep a spear at the bottom. If the asparagus is thin, then bend it until it snaps. Split to the same length as the remaining bows. Separate the eggs for another use, reserving the whites.
2. In a microwave-safe dish, put the asparagus and add 1 tbsp of water. Cover with the plastic wrap and cook, depending on the microwave, at high power for 1 1/2 - 2 1/2 minutes. Drain the water out to leave it hidden. Alternatively, in boiling broth, blanch the asparagus until crisply tender, rinse, and keep warm.
3. In a mixer, mix the egg yolks, 1 tbsp of water, 1 tsp of lemon juice, and mustard. Put the lid on top, then remove the piece from the center. In a medium-sized to the large frying pan, put the butter and melt the

butter over a medium flame. Turn the heat to medium-high and rotate the pan softly every couple of moments. Turn the heat off as the solids at the bottom of a pan start to turn brown. Turn the blender down and start pouring that hot butter in the blender, leaving behind the brown solids in the pan.
4. Add the white pepper and cayenne pepper after the butter has been absorbed, and mix. With more vinegar, salt, or pepper, change the seasoning. Pour on the asparagus and quickly eat.

11.49 Green Beans Almondine

Servings: 4 I Time: 15 mins I Difficulty: Easy
Nutrients per serving: Calories: 177 kcal I Fat: 16g I Carbohydrates: 9g I Protein: 3g I Fiber: 4g

Ingredients

- salt and pepper to taste
- 4 tbsp butter
- 1/4 cup flaked or slivered almonds
- 1 tbsp lemon juice
- 1 lb trimmed green beans

Optional (any, not both)

- 1 clove garlic, minced
- 1 tbsp shallots, minced

Method

1. Preparation: Wash & trim the green beans for a good appearance, cutting on the bias. Mince when using garlic or the shallots. To make squeezing simpler, roll a lemon on the table.
2. Beans: Put the green beans with 1-2 tbsp of water in the microwave-safe dish and cover with a clinging wrap. Microwave until practically crisp-tender for 2-3 minutes; the duration will depend on the microwave. Drain and stir the water. To release gas, leave it exposed.
3. Boil a pot of water and keep a big bowl of ice water standing by the Conventional method. Add the green beans while the water is boiling and cook when crisp-tender and light green. To stop frying, pour the beans and drop them directly into the ice bath. Drain them a little and dry them.
4. Over medium heat, put a large saute pan and add the almonds and butter. Cook just until the almonds have just started to brown. (Add now and mix until fragrant if using garlic cloves or shallot). Add the green beans immediately and stir in the butter to cover. All the way through, steam the beans, then squeeze lemon juice over them. To taste and serve, add salt and pepper.

11.50 Spicy Jalapeno Coleslaw

Servings: 10 I Time: 15 mins I Difficulty: Easy
Nutrients per serving: Calories: 109 kcal I Fat: 10g I Carbohydrates: 4g I Protein: 1g I Fiber: 1g

Ingredients

- ¼ cup Mayonnaise
- ¼ cup Red Bell Pepper, julienned
- ¼ cup Yellow Bell Pepper, julienned
- ½ tsp Chili powder
- 1 Jalapeno pepper, seeded and finely diced
- 1 lime, juiced
- 1 tbsp Cilantro, minced
- 1/2 cup Ranch dressing
- 2 oz. Red cabbage, finely sliced
- 8.5 oz. Coleslaw mix

Method

1. Toss the coleslaw mixture, red bell pepper, jalapeno pepper, and yellow bell pepper together in a big dish.

2. Mix the ranch dressing, lime juice, mayonnaise, chili powder, and cilantro in a shallow dish.
3. Using the slaw to spill the dressing over and toss to cover.
4. Until serving, refrigerate for about 30 minutes.

11.51 Cucumber Avocado Tomato Salad

Servings: 10 I Time: 15 mins I Difficulty: Easy
Nutrients per serving: Calories: 136 kcal I Fat: 12g I Carbohydrates: 8g I Protein: 2g I Fiber: 4g

Ingredients

- ¼ cup Olive Oil
- ¼ cup Red Wine Vinegar
- ½ Red Onion
- ½ tsp Salt, plus more to taste
- 1/4 tsp Black pepper,
- 2 Avocados
- 2 large Cucumber
- 3 tbsp Lime juice
- 4 large Tomatoes

Method

1. Cut the vegetables into bite-size pieces.
2. In a little mug, mix the olive oil, vinegar, salt, lime juice, and pepper.
3. In a wide dish, toss the cucumbers and tomatoes together and then spray the seasoning over them, turning them until all is well seasoned.
4. Add the bits of avocado and fold them carefully into the salad.
5. Immediately serve.

11.52 Easy Pickled Cauliflower

Servings: 8 I Time: 2 days 20 mins I Difficulty: Easy
Nutrients per serving: Calories: 39 kcal I Fat: 1g I Carbohydrates: 6g I Protein: 1g I Fiber: 1g

Ingredients

- 1 small Cauliflower
- 1 cup White vinegar
- 1 cup Apple cider vinegar
- 2 cups Water
- 4 cloves Garlic
- 2 Tbsp Sugar, (or sugar substitute)
- 1 tbsp Kosher salt
- 2 tbsp Mustard seed
- 2 tsp Coriander seeds
- 1/2 Red Pepper
- 1/2 orange bell pepper
- ¼ tsp Red pepper flakes
- 2 tsp Black peppercorns

Method

1. Divide a sliced cauliflower into 2 wide mouths pint mason jars and bell peppers equally.
2. In a small pot, add vinegar, water, garlic, sugar, coriander, mustard seeds, peppercorns, salt, and red pepper flakes and put to a boil on medium-high heat.
3. Remove it from heat until the mixture hits a boil and let it cool about 5 minutes before pouring it into each jar. Make sure that in each container, you have an equal distribution of spices.
4. Before screwing a lid on and sticking the jars in the fridge, let that mixture cool completely. Let it rest for 24 to 48 hours before eating.

11.53 Italian Antipasto Skewers

Servings: 12 I Time: 10 mins I Difficulty: Easy

Nutrients per serving: Calories: 224 kcal I Fat: 46g I Carbohydrates: 7g I Protein: 21g I Fiber: 2g

Ingredients

- 8 oz. Primo Taglio Mozzarella Cheese
- 5 oz. Artichoke Hearts
- 3 oz. Primo Taglio Prosciutto
- 24 leaves Fresh Basil
- 2 oz. Primo Taglio Italian Sliced Salame (Dry)
- 16 oz. Roasted Red Peppers
- 12 Olives

Method

1. Split three strips of 1/2 inch mozzarella. Cut the slices into 4 quarters each.
2. Cut 6 lengthwise artichoke hearts in half.
3. On a 5 inch skewer, arrange the ingredients. Start with a slice of salami. To form a wedge shape, fold it in half and then again in half. Push on the skewer for that.
4. thA slice of folded basil accompanies it, then a wedge of mozzarella cheese as well as the other folded basil leaf.
5. Now Cut roasted red pepper into the 1-inch wide strip 2-inch high, fold and slip onto the skewer.
6. Roll it up and cut a piece of prosciutto in two. Press it on the skewer, preceded by half of the artichoke's heart and one of the olives.

11.54 Oven Roasted Cabbage Steaks

Servings: 6 I Time: 40 mins I Difficulty: Easy
Nutrients per serving: Calories: 125 kcal I Fat: 10g I Carbohydrates: 9g I Protein: 3g I Fiber: 4g

Ingredients

- 1/4 cup Olive oil
- 1 head Cabbage
- 2 tbsp Parmesan (finely grated)
- 1 clove Garlic (finely minced)
- ½ tsp Crushed red pepper flakes
- ½ tsp Kosher Salt

Method

1. Cut cabbage into half-inch-thick slices, then put it on a baking sheet lined with foil.
2. Mix the olive oil, parmesan cheese, garlic cracked red pepper flakes, and salt together in a shallow cup.
3. Slightly covering each side, brush the mixture on the cabbage slices.
4. Bake for 15 minutes in an oven at 400ºF. Flip the slices of cabbage and finish baking for a full 15 minutes.

11.55 Keto Colcannon

Servings: 12 I Time: 15 mins I Difficulty: Easy
Nutrients per serving: Calories: 58 kcal I Fat: 4g I Carbohydrates: 5g I Protein: 2g I Fiber: 2g

Ingredients

- Salt to taste
- 6 oz. cabbage (cut into thin 1-inch long slices)
- 4 tbsp butter, divided
- 36 oz. Cauliflower, chopped

Method

1. To a simmer, put a big pot of water. Add the cauliflower and let it simmer for 10 minutes or so. You will feel that when it is soft to quickly split off with a fork, the cauliflower is finished.
2. Melt 1 tbsp of butter in the large skillet while the cauliflower is cooking. Include the cabbage and saute until softened for 5-7 minutes.
3. When the cauliflower has done frying, pour the water into a strainer and rinse it thoroughly. To eliminate water as possible, let it stay for several minutes.

4. In the empty cup, pour a cauliflower back in and add cabbage and the leftover butter. Marinate together until the consistency of mashed potato.

5. To taste, apply salt and serve.

11.56 Keto Blueberry Scones

Servings: 8 | Time: 33 mins | Difficulty: Easy
Nutrients per serving: Calories: 110 kcal | Fat: 8g | Carbohydrates: 6g | Protein: 2g | Fiber: 2g

Ingredients

- 3/4 cup Almond flour
- 1/4 cup Coconut flour
- 1/4 tsp salt
- 1/4 cup butter, unsalted, softened
- 1/4 cup Almond Milk (Unsweetened)
- 5 tbsp Granular erythritol sweetener
- 2 tsp gluten-free baking powder
- 2 tsp Vanilla extract
- 1 large Egg
- 1 cup Blueberries

Method

1. Preheat the oven to 350 °F.
2. Mix all the dry ingredients in the bowl of your blender (except the chocolate chips).
3. Include the softened butter and milk it until it is well combined and there are no bits of butter along with the dry ingredients.
4. Include the vanilla extract, almond milk, and egg and begin combining until well mixed.
5. Apply the blueberries and then roll them into the dough using a spatula.
6. Shape 2.5 oz of dough into a triangle shape with your palm. Place a cookie sheet on an unoiled one. Repeat until you consume all of the dough. Approximately 8 scones you can receive.
7. Bake for 18-23 minutes or when the sides are golden brown in the oven at 350 °F. You start to see some golden brown patches on top.
8. Takeout from the oven and leave to fully cool the scones before placing them in an airtight jar.

11.57 Cheesy Bacon Brussels Sprouts

Servings: 6 | Time: 35 mins | Difficulty: Easy
Nutrients per serving: Calories: 261 kcal | Fat: 23g | Carbohydrates: 8g | Protein: 8g | Fiber: 3g

Ingredients

- 6 slices cooked bacon, chopped
- 4 tbsp Olive oil
- 2 oz. Cheddar cheese
- 1.25 tsp salt, divided
- 1 lb Brussels sprouts
- ½ tsp Onion powder
- ½ tsp Garlic powder
- ½ cup Heavy cream
- ¼ tsp Salt

Method

1. Preheat the oven to 375° F.
2. Over medium heat, heat a large size oven-safe skillet.
3. Add the olive oil and the sprouts from Brussels. Sprinkle with 1 tsp of salt and simmer until the sprouts appear to soften and brown in patches, for about 10 minutes.
4. Mix the heavy cream, garlic powder, onion powder, and the remaining ¼ tsp of salt as the brussels sprouts become cooked.

5. Remove them from the sun until the Brussels sprouts are prepared and pour a heavy cream mixture on them.
6. Sprinkle the Brussels sprouts with cheddar cheese and bacon over them.
7. Place the skillet in an oven until the cheese is fully melted and bake for 10 minutes.

11.58 Keto Chocolate Chip Scones

Servings: 8 | Time: 30 mins | Difficulty: Easy
Nutrients per serving: Calories: 156 kcal | Fat: 20g | Carbohydrates: 5g | Protein: 2g | Fiber: 2g

Ingredients

- 4.5 oz. Lily's Dark Chocolate Chips
- 3/4 cup Almond flour
- 1/4 cup Coconut flour
- 1/4 tsp salt
- 1/4 cup butter, unsalted, softened
- 1/4 cup Unsweetened Almond Milk
- 5 tbsp Granular erythritol sweetener
- 2 tsp gluten-free baking powder
- 2 tsp Vanilla extract
- 1 large Egg

Method

1. Preheat the oven to 350 °F.
2. Mix all of the dry ingredients in the bowl of your blender (except for the chocolate chips).
3. Apply the softened butter and milk it until it is well combined, and there are no bits of butter along with the dry ingredients.
4. Apply the vanilla extract, almond milk, and egg and begin combining until well mixed.
5. Include the chocolate chips and then roll them into the dough using a spatula.
6. Shape 2.5 oz of dough into a triangle shape with your palm. Place a cookie sheet on an unoiled one. Repeat until you consume all of the dough. Approximately 8 scones you can receive.
7. Bake for 17-21 minutes or until the sides are golden brown in the 350 °F ovens, and you have to see golden brown patches on top. Remove from the oven and leave to fully cool the scones before placing them in an airtight jar.

11.59 Classic Cheese Ball Recipe

Servings: 10 | Time: 10 mins | Difficulty: Easy
Nutrients per serving: Calories: 238 kcal | Fat: 22g | Carbohydrates: 3g | Protein: 8g | Fiber: 1g

Ingredients

- 8 oz. Cream Cheese, softened
- 8 oz. Cheddar Cheese shredded
- 2 tsp Worcestershire sauce
- 1 tsp Lemon juice
- 1 tsp Green onion, finely chopped
- 1 cup Pecans, roughly chopped
- ¼ tsp Salt

Method

1. 1.In the bowl of the stand mixer, put the cream cheese, green onion, cheddar cheese, Worcestershire sauce, salt, lemon juice, and blend until all the ingredients are thoroughly mixed.
2. Scrape the bowl with the mixture and shape it into a ball.
3. Use the chopped pecans to roll the ball until it is completely enclosed.
4. Cover the ball of cheese in plastic wrap and put for 1 hour in the refrigerator to cool.

5.   Serve with crackers and vegetables.

11.60 Air Fryer Chicken Wings

Servings: 4 I Time: 40 mins I Difficulty: Easy
Nutrients per serving: Calories: 375 kcal I Fat: 31g I Carbohydrates: 1g I Protein: 23g I Fiber: 1g

Ingredients

- 1 tsp Pepper
- 1/2 cup Frank's Red Hot Sauce
- 1/4 cup butter, melted
- 2 lb Chicken wings (cut into drumettes and flat)
- 2 tsp salt

Method

1.   Pat's chicken drumettes and the wings dry with a paper towel and put them on the baking sheet or a cutting board.
2.   Sprinkle salt and pepper on the chicken.
3.   Put the chicken in an air-fryer basket and cook for 25 minutes at 380 °F. Cut the basket halfway through and use tongs to dip the chicken around and shift it around so that bottom reaches the top.
4.   Turn the heat to 400 °F after 25 minutes and continue cooking for 5 minutes or when the skin is crispy.
5.   Take the chicken from the basket and put it in a wide bowl with the fryer.
6.   Over the chicken wings, add the sauce and throw them until well seasoned.
7.   Immediately serve.

11.61 Inst. Pot Turnip Greens & Collard Greens

Servings: 6 I Time: 20 mins I Difficulty: Easy
Nutrients per serving: Calories: 256 kcal I Fat: 23g I Carbohydrates: 8g I Protein: 3g I Fiber: 3g

Ingredients

- 20 oz. Turnip greens or collard greens (stem removed and roughly chopped)
- 1 cup Chicken broth
- ½ cup Onion, diced
- 2 tbsp Vinegar
- Salt and pepper to taste
- 6 oz. Salt pork (diced into about 1/4-inch pieces)

Method

1.   Set the Inst. Pot to saute, add pork or bacon salt and onions, and cook until the pork is crisp and the onions become softened.
2.   Pour the chicken broth into a pot and deglaze the pan's bottle to ensure the browned bits get up. To stop the saute feature, click cancel.
3.   In the greens, add some vinegar and the package so that the pot is around 2/3 of the way finished.
4.   Lock the lid and turn the valve to the SEALING position. For 10 minutes, set to high Intensity.
5.   When the timer goes off, adjust the valve to Ventilation and let all the air out by rapidly opening it.
6.   To blend it, remove the lid, swirl the pot's contents, and apply salt and black pepper.

11.62 Keto Avocado Coleslaw

Servings: 8 I Time: 10 mins I Difficulty: Easy
Nutrients per serving: Calories: 123 kcal I Fat: 10g I Carbohydrates: 8g I Protein: 2g I Fiber: 4g

Ingredients

- 1/2 cup Sour Cream
- 1/2 tsp salt
- 16 oz. Coleslaw mix (or shredded cabbage)
- 2 Avocado
- 3-4 tbsp Lime Juice (more to taste)

Method

1.   Stir mixture into coleslaw.
2.   Mash avocado with sour cream, lime juice, and salt.
3.   Keep refrigerated until you are ready to serve.

11.63 Buffalo Chicken Jalapeño Poppers

Servings: 8 I Time: 50 mins I Difficulty: Easy
Nutrients per serving: Calories: 408 kcal I Fat: 33g I Carbohydrates: 4g I Protein: 21g

Ingredients

Buffalo Chicken Dip

- 8 oz. Cream Cheese, softened
- 3 tbsp Ranch Dressing
- 2 Chicken Breasts (approximately 12 oz.)
- 1/2 cup Frank's Red Hot sauce
- 1/2 cup Cheddar Cheese, (shredded)

Buffalo Chicken Jalapeño Poppers (Make Almost 30 Poppers)

- 16-20 Jalapeños, halved
- 16-20 Strips Bacon
- Buffalo Chicken Dip,

Method

Buffalo Chicken Dip

1.   Boil the water.
2.   For 15 minutes, or when cooked through, put the chicken breasts in the boiling water.
3.   Remove the chicken breasts and insert them directly in the mixing bowl of the stand mixer. (You should use the fork to shred a chicken by hand if you do not have a stand mixer.)
4.   Turn the mixer to medium for about 1-2 minutes or until the chicken is entirely shredded using a dough hook. To make sure all the chicken becomes shredded, stir once or twice.
5.   Transfer the chicken to the softened cream cheese and mix it thoroughly.
6.   Apply the hot sauce and thoroughly mix.
7.   Include the ranch and shredded cheese and mix thoroughly.

Buffalo Chicken Jalapeño Poppers

1.   Preheat the oven to 400° F.
2.   Cook bacon partly, making it partly crisp but still flexible enough to coil around the poppers.
3.   With a heaping tbsp of buffalo chicken sauce, stuff the jalapeno halves with it.
4.   Wrap a slice of bacon for each jalapeño popper.
5.   On a baking sheet, place the stuffed poppers.
6.   Bake until the jalapeños are softened, and the bacon is crispy in the oven. 20 minutes roughly.

11.64 Low Carb Big Mac Bites

Servings: 16 I Time: 35 mins I Difficulty: Easy
Nutrients per serving: Calories: 182 kcal I Fat: 12g I Carbohydrates: 1g I Protein: 10g

Ingredients

- ¼ cup Onion, finely diced
- 1 tsp salt
- 1.5 lb Ground beef
- 16 slices Dill Pickle
- 4 slices American Cheese
- Lettuce

SECRET SAUCE

- 1 tsp Garlic powder
- 1 tsp Onion powder

- 1 tsp Paprika
- 1 tsp White wine vinegar
- 1/2 cup Mayonnaise
- 2 tbsp yellow mustard
- 4 tbsp Dill pickle relish

Method
1. Preheat the oven to 400°F.
2. Mix the onions, ground beef, and salt in a large dish. Mix when mixed thoroughly.
3. Roll the beef into balls of 1.5 oz.. To make the mini burger patty, press every one slightly down to flatten it and put it on the lined baking sheet.
4. Now Bake for 15 minutes or until fully baked at 400 °F.
5. When cooking burgers, add all the secret sauce components to a bowl and mix to blend.
6. Switch off the oven when the burgers baking finished and remove them—Pat off the extra oil.
7. Cut four squares of each cheese slice and put a square on each mini-patty. Place the cheese back in the oven and let it melt.
8. Place a few lettuces (squares) and a pickle slice on top of each meatball, and drive a skewer through it. Serve or have the special sauce.

11.65 Ranch Baked Pork Chops

Servings: 4 I Time: 35 mins I Difficulty: Easy
Nutrients per serving: Calories: 252 kcal I Fat: 9g I Carbohydrates: 7g I Protein: 32g

Ingredients
- 4 Pork Chops, 1 inch thick
- 2 tsp Dried Parsley
- 2 tsp Garlic Powder
- 2 tsp Paprika
- 1 tsp Dried Dill Weed
- 1 tsp Dried Minced Onions
- 1 tsp Sea Salt
- ½ tsp Dried Chives
- ½ tsp Onion Powder
- 1/2 tsp Ground Black Pepper
- 1/4 cup Dry Buttermilk Powder

Method
1. Preheat the oven to 400°F.
2. To make the ranch seasoning, add all the dry ingredients in the bowl and blend thoroughly.
3. In the ranch seasoning, dip each pork chop, turning it over when it is thoroughly coated. Before lying on a baking sheet, shake off the residue.
4. In the oven, put the pork chops and bake for 15 to 25 minutes. When it touches an internal temperature of 145 °F, the pork chop is cooked.
5. Until eating, let the pork chops rest for about 5 minutes.

11.66 Low Carb Nachos

Servings: 8 I Time: 35 mins I Difficulty: Easy
Nutrients per serving: Calories: 227 kcal I Fat: 14g I Carbohydrates: 6g I Protein: 18g I Fiber: 1g

Ingredients
- Toppings such as avocado, sour cream, tomatoes,
- 8 oz Cheddar Cheese (shredded)
- 20 Mini Sweet Peppers (halved and seeded)
- 2 tbsp Chili Powder
- 1/2 tsp salt
- 1 tbsp Cumin
- 1 lb Ground Beef, chicken, steak, or pork, cooked

- 1 Jalapeno, sliced

Method
1. Cook your favorite meat in a skillet, adding cumin, chili powder, and salt. On a sheet plate, put the mini sweet pepper halves.
2. Sprinkle the cooked meat over the mini peppers and hold it in peppers to spill into the pan. Cover the mini peppers with jalapeno slices and shredded cheese.
3. Put in a BROIL-set oven for about 5-6 minutes or when the cheese is completely melted.
4. Apply some low carb toppings you need for the nacho.

11.67 Air Fryer Low Carb Mozzarella Sticks

Servings: 6 I Time: 20 mins I Difficulty: Easy
Nutrients per serving: Calories: 267 kcal I Fat: 20g I Carbohydrates: 4g I Protein: 18g I Fiber: 1g

Ingredients
- 1 tsp Italian seasoning
- 1/2 cup Almond flour
- 1/2 cup Parmesan cheese (the powdered form)
- 1/2 tsp Garlic Salt
- 12 Mozzarella sticks, string cheese (cut in half)
- 2 large eggs, beaten

Method
1. Mix the almond flour, Italian seasoning, parmesan cheese, and garlic salt in a dish. Whisk the eggs together in a separate dish.
2. Coat the mozzarella stick halves in your egg one at a time and then toss throughout the coating combination. Please place them in a suitable jar.
3. Place parchment paper among the mozzarella sticks layers if you need to make more than 1 sheet. Freeze for 30 minutes the sticks of mozzarella
4. Remove it from the freezer and placed it in the Philips AirFryer.
5. Adjust to 400 °F for 5 minutes and cook.
6. Open the air fryer and then let for 1 min before moving to a plate of low carbohydrate mozzarella sticks.

11.68 Crab Cakes With Roasted Red Pepper Sauce

Servings: 8 I Time: 40 mins I Difficulty: Easy
Nutrients per serving: Calories: 65 kcal I Fat: 4g I Carbohydrates: 4g I Protein: 6g

Ingredients
- 2 tsp Old Bay seasoning
- 2 tsp dijon mustard
- 2 Tbsp parsley, chopped
- 2 Tbsp coconut oil
- 1.5 Tbsp coconut flour
- 1 Tbsp fresh lemon juice
- 1 egg, beaten
- 1 cup lump crab meat

Method
1. 1.Pick the crab carefully to ensure the absence of shells or the cartilage in meat and add it to a small bowl. Mix the lemon juice, egg, and dijon mustard in another small cup, blending until smooth.
2. Mix the parsley, old bay, and coconut flour in a third dish, stirring thoroughly. Add the mixture of eggs to the crab softly, folding when mixed. Then apply to the crab mixture the dry ingredients and gently blend in. Try not to cut up the crab bits or shred them too far.

3. Heat the coconut oil in a nonstick saute pan over medium heat. Create 8 small cakes and carefully put them in the hot oil. Cook on either side for around 2-3 minutes, or until golden brown. Move to a plate lined with paper towels from the dish.
4. Sprinkle with kosher salt and serve with the Roasted Red Pepper Sauce and half squeeze a fresh lemon over it.

11.69 Low Carb Taco Bites

Servings: 30 I Time: 1 hr I Difficulty: Easy
Nutrients per serving: Calories: 73 kcal I Fat: 5g I Carbohydrates: 1g I Protein: 4g

Ingredients

- Pico de Gallo for garnish
- 8 tsp Sour Cream for garnish
- 2 tbsp Cumin
- 2 tbsp Chili Powder
- 2 cup Packaged Shredded Cheddar Cheese
- 1 tsp salt + more to taste
- 1 lb Ground Beef

Method

1. Preheat the oven to 350 °F. Place 1 tbsp pile of cheese 2 inches apart on the baking sheet lined with a silicone or mat parchment paper
2. Place the baking sheet in an oven and bake until the edges of cheese become brown, or for 5-7 minutes.
3. Let that cheese cool for 1 min, then pick it up and press it down into a mini muffin tin cup to shape a cup.
4. Let the cheese fully cool, and then cut it.
5. As you begin to bake the cheese and make your cups, over medium-high heat heating, put the ground beef in the skillet until it is fully cooked.
6. Drain the beef from the fat and then add 1/4 c of water and the spices.
7. Stir once mixed, then add some more salt to taste and boil for 5 minutes.
8. For cheese cups, substitute meat and finish each with 1/4 tsp of sour cream. If you like, you can also include fresh pico de gallo as well.

11.70 Bacon Cheese Balls

Servings: 24 I Time: 10 mins I Difficulty: Easy
Nutrients per serving: Calories: 89 kcal I Fat: 8g I Carbohydrates: 1g I Protein: 2g

Ingredients

- 10 slices bacon (finely chopped)
- 4 oz. Cheddar cheese (shredded)
- 4 oz. Salted Almonds (chopped)
- 8 oz. Cream cheese

Method

1. In a dish, mix the first 3 ingredients.
2. Roll the cheese mixture in 1-inch balls and roll and widen the ends slightly to gently mold them in an oval shape.
3. Roll out the sliced almonds with the mini cubes.

11.71 Shrimp Cocktail Deviled Eggs

Servings: 12 I Time: 30 mins I Difficulty: Easy
Nutrients per serving: Calories: 142 kcal I Fat: 11g I Carbohydrates: 1g I Protein: 8g

Ingredients

- 1 1/2 tsp Horseradish
- 1/2 cup Mayonnaise
- 12 eggs, hard-boiled & peeled
- 24 Shrimp, steamed
- 3 tbsp Ketchup
- Paprika for garnish
- Salt to taste

Method

1. Put the eggs in half and place the yolks in a different bowl to remove them.
2. Apply the yolks to the horseradish, mayonnaise, ketchup, and salt and mix until creamy.
3. In a piping bag, put the yolk mixture and pipe in the egg halves.
4. Place a shrimp over each shell. Garnish with Paprika.

11.72 Shrimp Pil Pil

Servings: 8 I Time: 10 mins I Difficulty: Easy
Nutrients per serving: Calories: 275 kcal I Fat: 25g I Carbohydrates: 2g I Protein: 14g I Fiber: 2g

Ingredients

- 1 lb Shrimp, large (around 30 shrimp)
- 5 tbsp Butter
- 4 tbsp Tabasco
- 1 tbsp Spanish paprika
- 1 tsp Salt
- 2/3 c Olive oil

Method

1. Mix in the olive oil, sugar, Tabasco, paprika, and salt.
2. Place each ramekin with 3-4 shrimp and many slices of garlic.
3. Until the shrimp is partially covered, add the sauce in.
4. Put the ramekins on the baking sheet and broil them for 4-5 minutes in the oven or until the shrimp's oil bubbles and the shrimp become pink.
5. Remove from the oven and serve when hot.

11.73 Easy Guacamole

Servings: 12 I Time: 40 mins I Difficulty: Easy
Nutrients per serving: Calories: 178 kcal I Fat: 15g I Carbohydrates: 14g I Protein: 3g I Fiber: 8g

Ingredients

- 1 Roma or vine tomato
- 1/4 cup chopped fresh cilantro
- 1/4 cup chopped red onion
- 1-2 jalapeño or serrano chilis
- 2 ripe avocados
- 2-3 limes
- sea salt

Method

1. Peel and pit the avocado and cut the onion thinly, and add it to a dish. Mush up the entire avocado with a fork.
2. Drop the seeds and the liquid, wash and slice the tomato into half, then dice just the flesh and return it to the cup.
3. Wash and spin fresh cilantro dry and cut when you have around 1/4 cup of cilantro chopped and return it to the dish.
4. Season with lime juice and sea salt, stir it together well, and serve
5. Add freshly chopped chili to the hot guacamole, too.

11.74 Keto Parmesan Roasted Broccoli

Servings: 5 I Time: 30 mins I Difficulty: Easy
Nutrients per serving: Calories: 157 kcal I Fat: 13.8g I Carbohydrates: 4.5g I Protein: 5.5g I Fiber: 2.2g

Ingredients

- 3 Tbsp. salted butter, melted

- 2 Tbsp. avocado oil
- 1/3 cup grated Parmesan cheese
- 1/2 tsp. salt
- 1/2 tsp. garlic powder
- 1 lb fresh broccoli florets
- 1 1/2 tsp. lemon pepper

Method
1. Line and set aside a sheet pan with the parchment. Preheat the oven to 400°F.
2. Place the florets of the broccoli in a wide dish. Mix the melted butter, avocado oil, garlic powder, lemon pepper, and salt in a separate bowl and mix.
3. Drizzle over the broccoli with the butter mixture and toss to mix. Sprinkle the broccoli with parmesan and flip to cover it.
4. On the ready sheet pan, put the broccoli into a single layer. Bake for about 20-25 minutes or until it is soft and golden brown.

11.75 Spicy Sautéed Mushrooms with Anchovy

Servings: 4 | Time: 20 mins | Difficulty: Easy
Nutrients per serving: Calories: 111 kcal | Fat: 8g | Carbohydrates: 9g | Protein: 3g | Fiber: 3g

Ingredients
- Juice from 1 lemon optional
- 3 garlic cloves minced
- 2 tbsp butter or ghee
- 2 medium anchovy fillets
- 1 lb mixed mushrooms
- ¼ tsp red pepper flakes

Method
1. Heat butter over medium-high heat in a large skillet. Apply the pepper flakes, anchovies, and garlic, as the butter melts and the foam subsides and cooked, splitting the anchovy fillets with a wooden spoon before the mixture is fragrant (approx 1 minute).
2. Include the mushrooms and cook for about 12 minutes, stirring regularly, until the mushrooms' liquid disappears and the mushrooms are finely browned. Season to taste with salt, squeeze one lemon juice (if used), and serve immediately.

11.76 Keto Cheese Crackers

Servings: 11 | Time: 30 mins | Difficulty: Easy
Nutrients per serving: Calories: 183 kcal | Fat: 17g | Carbohydrates: 4g | Protein: 6g | Fiber: 2g

Ingredients
- 5 Tbsp. butter salted & softened
- 4 oz. Pepper Jack cheese shredded
- 2 Tbsp. coconut flour
- 1 oz cream cheese softened
- 1 cup almond flour
- ¼ tsp. Salt
- ¼ tsp. Onion powder
- ¼ tsp. Garlic powder
- ¼ tsp. cumin
- ¼ cup finely chopped pecans

Method
1. Cream together the butter and cream cheese in the tank of the stand mixer. Apply the melted cheese and blend until mixed properly. Add the 6 ingredients, then continue blending. Stir the chopped pecans together.
2. Layer dough in plastic wrap and shape around 2 ½ inches thick into a roll. Tightly cover-up and cool or freeze until solid.
3. Cut the chilled dough into ¼' thick slices and put on a sheet pan lined with parchment. Bake for 20-25 minutes at 300 °F or until softly golden brown. Before withdrawing, cool crackers entirely in pots.

11.77 Cheesy Squash Bites

Servings: 28 | Time: 30 mins | Difficulty: Easy
Nutrients per serving: Calories: 76 kcal | Fat: 6g | Carbohydrates: 2g | Protein: 3g | Fiber: 1g

Ingredients
- 4 Tbsp. butter melted
- 3 Tbsp. coconut flour
- 3 eggs
- 2 Tbsp. sour cream
- 2 cloves garlic finely minced
- 2 ½ tsp. baking powder
- 1/2 tsp. Monkfruit or Erythritol Blend Sweetener
- 1 tsp. salt
- 1 Tbsp. chopped parsley
- 1 Tbsp. butter
- 1 cup almond flour
- 1 ½ cup shredded squash
- ½ tsp. Pepper
- ½ cup Colby or Medium Cheddar cheese
- ¼ tsp. Fiesta Brand-Zesty Italian Delight/Italian Seasoning
- ¼ cup shredded Parmesan
- ¼ cup diced onion

Method
1. Spray and set aside a mini muffin tin or fill a mini muffin tin with liners. Spray well and put aside if you are using the silicone mini muffin tray.
2. Melt one tbsp of butter in a shallow pan. Garnish with cabbage, rubbed squash, ginger, and 1/2 tsp. Add salt and sauté for 5-7 minutes, just until the onion is shiny. Put aside to cool. There should not be any liquid in the container.
3. Mix the flour and the next 6 ingredients in a large bowl and mix well to combine. Mix the eggs one at a time. Apply a mixture of melted butter, squash, and sour cream and mix well. Stir the cheese in.
4. Drop the entire tbsp or put the dough in a ready mini muffin pan using a cookie scoop.
5. For 20 minutes, bake at 350 F or until the tops are only golden brown. Cool for 5 minutes in a pan, then remove from the pan and cool thoroughly on a rack. They can be eaten warm and also store at room temperature.

11.78 Roasted Cauliflower Keto Hummus with Red Peppers

Servings: 10 | Time: 45 mins | Difficulty: Easy
Nutrients per serving: Calories: 137 kcal | Fat: 12g | Carbohydrates: 5g | Protein: 3g | Fiber: 2g

Ingredients
For the Roasted Cauliflower
- 3-4 Tbsp. olive (or avocado oil)
- 1 large head cauliflower (cut into florets)
- ½ tsp. Garlic powder
- ½ tsp. cumin
- 1 tsp. salt

To Finish the Hummus:
- 2-5 Tbsp. water

- 2 Tbsp. olive or avocado oil
- 2 Tbsp. fresh lemon juice
- 1-2 cloves garlic
- 1/2 tsp. Cumin
- ¾ tsp. Salt
- ¼ tsp. Pepper
- ¼ cup roasted red pepper
- ¼ cup + 2 Tbsp. tahini

Method

1. Preheat the oven to 400°C. Toss the cauliflower florets with olive oil, garlic powder, salt, and cumin in a large cup. Load it onto a sheet pan lined with parchment. Be sure to hit the pan with all the florets for full caramelization. For 30-35 minutes, roast the cauliflower or until the florets become brown and very tender. 5-10 minutes to cool.
2. Mix the roasted cauliflower, tahini, lemon juice, and the next 6 ingredients in a food processor or the high-speed blender. Puré the mixture until it is smooth. Add a tbsp of water at a time if the hummus is too dense to achieve the target consistency. Serve with keto crackers or vegetables.

11.79 Keto Spinach Balls

Servings: 16 I Time: 30 mins I Difficulty: Easy
Nutrients per serving: Calories: 96 kcal I Fat: 8g I Carbohydrates: 1g I Protein: 5g I Fiber: 1g

Ingredients

- 1/3 cup red onion finely minced
- 1/3 cup parmesan cheese (finely shredded)
- 1 Tbsp. butter
- 3 cloves garlic (finely minced)
- 1 cup pork rind crumbs
- 1 tsp. kosher salt
- ¼ tsp. poultry seasoning
- 10 oz. frozen spinach (squeezed dried & thawed)
- ½ cup fontina cheese (finely shredded)
- ¼ tsp. Black pepper
- 1 Tbsp. heavy cream
- 5 Tbsp. butter salted melted
- 3 eggs

Method

1. Preheat the oven to 350°F. Line up and set aside a large sheet pan.
2. Melt the butter in a small skillet on medium heat. Include the onion then sauté until soft and translucent for 5-7 minutes or when solid. Add garlic and simmer for an additional minute. Remove from the sun and place to cool aside.
3. Mix the dried spinach, cooled onion, pork rind crumbs, garlic, and the next eight ingredients in a medium mixing dish. Mix well and let the mixture sit for 5-10 minutes in the fridge.
4. Divide the mixture into 16 portions using a small scoop, and use your hands to shape each part into a ball. Place balls about an inch apart on the lined cookie sheet and bake for about 15-20 minutes or until they are golden. Take from a sheet pan and put to cool on paper towels. Serve at room temperature or hotter.

11.80 Cajun Pork Rinds

Servings: 14 I Time: 1 hr 13 mins I Difficulty: Easy
Nutrients per serving: Calories: 51 kcal I Fat: 5g I Carbohydrates: 1g I Protein: 1g I Fiber: 1g

Ingredients

- 6 Tbsp. melted butter
- 2 Tbsp. Worcestershire Sauce gluten-free
- 2 3.25 oz bags of plain pork rinds
- 1/8 tsp. cayenne pepper
- 1/2 tsp. paprika
- 1/2 tsp. onion powder
- 1/2 tsp. garlic powder
- 1 1/4 tsp. Fiesta Brand-Cajun All Seasoning

Method

1. Preheat to 250 F in the oven. Line up and set aside a large sheet pan lined with parchment.
2. Through a large dish, pour the pork rinds. In a small cup, mix the next 7 ingredients and blend well to mix. Drizzle over the pork rinds with half the butter mixture and toss to cover. Repeat with the mixture of butter that remains. Cover the coasted pork rinds over the pan of prepared sheets and bake for 80 minutes at 250 F, stirring after every 20 minutes.
3. Take the pork rinds from the oven and pass them to paper towels to make cool. When cold, place at room temperature in an air-tight bag.

11.81 Jalapeno Stuffed Hamburger Steak Bites

Servings: 8 I Time: 25 mins I Difficulty: Easy
Nutrients per serving: Calories: 262 kcal I Fat: 23g I Carbohydrates: 2g I Protein: 10g I Fiber: 1g

Ingredients

For an Avocado Ranch:

- 2 tsp. of Worcestershire sauce
- 1/3 cup of avocado
- 1 tsp. of creole mustard
- 1 clove garlic
- 1 ½ tsp. Hot sauce
- ½ tsp. salt
- ½ Tbsp. parsley (Dried)
- ½ cup unsweetened almond milk
- ½ cup mayonnaise
- ¼ tsp. Onion powder
- ½ tsp. of Italian seasoning

For Steak Bites:

- 2 tsp. Worcestershire Sauce
- 1 tsp. salt
- 1 lb ground beef 80/20
- 1 fresh jalapeno (seeded, deveined and finely diced)
- ½ tsp. Garlic powder
- ½ tsp. Fiesta Brand Fajita Seasoning (Salt-Free)
- ¼ tsp. black pepper
- ¼ cup purple onion (finely diced)

Method

Avocado Ranch preparation:

1. In the blender, first mix the mayo and then the next 8 ingredients and mix until smooth and blended. Whisk in the dried herbs and pour into a cup, cover, and cool before ready to eat.

Steak Bites preparation:

1. Cut off the ground beef in the medium mixing bowl, and then add the next seven ingredients. Mix softly, blending all the meat with the seasoning and vegetables. The meat mixture or even the steak bites would be dense. You wouldn't want to over mix or execute more. Divide the mixture into 8 pieces equally, roll each potion softly into a ball, and then flatten it to around 1/4 inch thick. For all 8 parts, repeat.

2. Over medium-high heat, preheat the heavy skillet. Add up the 4 patties and cook for around 3 minutes/side or achieve the ideal point.
3. Serve hot with the Ranch Avocado

11.82 Roasted Cauliflower with Chili Lime & Browned Better

Servings: 4 I Time: 40 mins I Difficulty: Easy
Nutrients per serving: Calories: 207 kcal I Fat: 18g I Carbohydrates: 9g I Protein: 3g I Fiber: 3g

Ingredients

- 6 Tbsp. butter melted
- 1/2 Tbsp. kosher salt
- 1/2 fresh lime
- 1 tsp. chili powder
- 1 head fresh cauliflower, dried
- 1 dash -1/8 tsp cayenne pepper
- ½ Tbsp. Granulated garlic
- ¼ tsp. cumin
- ¼ tsp paprika

Method

1. Preheat the oven to 425 ºF and set aside a sheet pan with the lined-parchment.
2. Place the florets of the cauliflower in a wide cup. In a small bowl and wick, mix melted butter and the other 6 ingredients to combine. Toss the butter and spices with the florets until they are fully covered.
3. Disperse the florets on the ready sheet pan and bake for 25 to 30 minutes at 425 ºF or until the florets become golden brown; whisk during the baking period. Remove from the oven and strain the florets with fresh lime. Now immediately serve.

11.83 Keto Chili Cheese Bites

Servings: 36 bites I Time: 15 mins I Difficulty: Easy
Nutrients per serving: Calories: 81 kcal I Fat: 6g I Carbohydrates: 0g I Protein: 3g I Fiber: 0g

Ingredients

- 8 oz. cream cheese, softened
- 6 pieces crispy cooked bacon (chopped finely)
- 4 cups Colby jack cheese (shredded)
- 1/4 tsp. salt
- 1/2 tsp. paprika
- 1 tsp. Worcestershire sauce
- 1 tsp. hot sauce
- 1 tsp. granulated garlic
- 1 scallion or green onion (thinly sliced)
- 1 1/2 tsp. chili powder (divided)

Method

1. Mix melted cream cheese, onion, garlic, paprika, shredded cheese, 1 tsp in a large mixing cup. Chili powder, sauce from Worcestershire, sweet sauce, and salt. To blend, balance well. In a stand or portable mixer, you can mix this as well.
2. Mix finely chopped bacon and half tsp of the chili powder in a pie plate or other flat dishes. Roll the mixture of cheese into 1″ cubes. Then roll each ball in the crumbs of bacon, pressing them into the cheese mixture gently. To smooth them out, roll each cheese ball in your palms. Refrigerate then for 1 hour.

11.84 Creamy Mashed Turnips

Servings: 6 I Time: 30 mins I Difficulty: Easy
Nutrients per serving: Calories: 128 kcal I Fat: 46g I Carbohydrates: 7g I Protein: 21g I Fiber: 2g

Ingredients

- salt & pepper to taste
- Chopped Green Onion or Chive for Garnish
- 5 medium turnips of baseball-sized (peeled & diced)
- 3 tbsp butter
- 2 tsp kosher salt
- 2 tbsp heavy cream
- 2 oz cream cheese
- 1/4 tsp Lakanto Monkfruit Sweetener

Method

1. Add the turnips to the big pot of cold water (approximately 6 cups) and add 2 tsp of salt and sweetener to the water, if necessary. Boil and then reduce to the simmer and cook for around 20 minutes until smooth and tender.
2. Drain the turnips well, and return to the pot. Let it hang for a minute or 2 to evaporate some of the excess moisture.
3. Include the cream cheese, sugar, cream, and mash until you achieve the perfect consistency. To taste, season with salt and pepper. Use an immersion blender if you like a smoother consistency.

11.85 GG's Oil & Vinegar Coleslaw

Servings: 4-6 I Time: 20 mins I Difficulty: Easy
Nutrients per serving: Calories: 224 kcal I Fat: 46g I Carbohydrates: 7g I Protein: 21g I Fiber: 2g

Ingredients

- 4 T red wine vinegar
- 3 T finely diced purple onion
- 3 cups cabbage (shredded)
- 2 2.5 oz cans - sliced black olives (drained)
- 1/3 cup light olive oil or avocado oil
- 1 cup diced English cucumber
- 1 cup diced celery
- 1 cup diced bell pepper
- 1 4oz jar diced pimentos (drained)
- 1 ½ tsp salt
- ½ tsp onion powder
- ½ tsp dry mustard
- ¼ tsp Pyure (or 1 tsp of your preferred sweetener)
- ¼ tsp pepper
- ¼ tsp granulated garlic

Method

1. In a wide dish, mix the first 7 ingredients.
2. Whisk together the vinegar, seasonings, and the sweetener of choice in a medium dish. Slowly stir the oil into the seasonings and vinegar.
3. Pour dressing over the vegetables with oil and vinegar and toss to coat.
4. Cool at least an hour before serving. The longer it remains, the cooler it gets. Store it in the freezer.

11.86 Spicy Salmon Cucumber Bites

Servings: 4 I Time: 20 mins I Difficulty: Easy
Nutrients per serving: Calories: 112 kcal I Fat: 11g I Carbohydrates: 4g I Protein: 1g I Fiber: 1g

Ingredients

- Ground black pepper
- Diamond Crystal kosher salt
- 4 cherry tomatoes quartered
- 1 tbsp shallots minced
- 1 tbsp chives chopped
- 1 English cucumber (peeled and cut into ¾-inch thick slices)

- 1 bunch chive sprigs garnish
- ½ lb cooked salmon
- ¼ tsp Tabasco sauce
- ¼ tsp smoked paprika
- ¼ cup Paleo mayonnaise

Method
1. In a shallow dish, mix the smoked paprika, mayo, and Tabasco and blend thoroughly. If you like spicy stuff, taste the seasoning and add further Tabasco.
2. Grab the cooked flake and salmon into large bite-sized pieces.
3. Put the salmon, chives, salt, diced shallots, and pepper in a dish and mix the spicy mayonnaise gently.
4. Grab the cucumber slices, then scoop out the middle of each cucumber slice using a melon baller or tsp. Do not dig too hard, or it will turn into open-ended tubes for your cups, and the salmon filling may fall right through.
5. Divide a salmon mixture in each cup and apply a cherry tomato slice and a few chive tops.

11.87 Crispy Mushroom Chips

Servings: 2 I Time: 1 hr I Difficulty: Easy
Nutrients per serving: Calories: 171 kcal I Fat: 15g I Carbohydrates: 9g I Protein: 5g I Fiber: 3g

Ingredients
- Kosher salt
- Freshly ground pepper
- 2 tbsp avocado oil or melted ghee
- 10 oz. 300 grams of king oyster mushrooms

Method
1. Preheat the oven to 300 °F (or 275 °F on convection baking) and use parchment paper to line several rimmed baking sheets. You'll either need to use several trays or bake in many batches for this recipe.
2. Split the mushrooms lengthwise in half, and then cut them into 1/8-inch slices using a mandolin slicer.
3. On the parchment-lined baking sheets, assemble the slices into a single layer. Make sure you have super-dry mushrooms and leave some room between the slices.
4. Brush all sides of the mushroom slices with avocado oil or melted ghee, and season with pepper and salt to taste.
5. Bake until the chips become golden brown and crispy, or for 45 minutes to an hour. If they are out of the microwave, these chips will not begin to crisp, so do not take them out if they are already sort of fluffy.

11.88 Chili Lime Chicken Wings

Servings: 10 I Time: 1 hr 45 mins I Difficulty: Easy
Nutrients per serving: Calories: 588 kcal I Fat: 25g I Carbohydrates: 5g I Protein: 27g I Fiber: 1g

Ingredients
- Zest from 2 limes
- Freshly ground pepper
- 6 lb chicken wings and drumsticks
- 4 limes cut into wedges
- 3 garlic cloves peeled
- 2 tbsp Paleo-friendly fish sauce Red Boat.
- 2 tbsp coconut aminos
- 2 jalapeno peppers or 1 serrano pepper
- 1-2 tbsp melted fat of choice
- ½ medium onion roughly chopped
- ½ cup cilantro tightly packed
- ¼ cup lime juice

Method
1. In a blender, mix the onion, peppers, cilantro, ground pepper, garlic, lime zest & juice, fish sauce, coconut aminos, and process until the bright green purée appears.
2. In a wide bowl, put the chicken wings and add the marinade. In your palms, blend well.
3. Marinate the chicken for about 30 minutes and up to 12 hours in the refrigerator. For more than 12 hours, the wings should not marinate because the acid can make the beef mushy.
4. Remove the wings from the fridge 30 minutes before you expect to roast them.
5. These chicken wings can be baked either in the oven or on your backyard barbecue if you can stand the cold weather outside.
6. Arrange a rack in the oven center, and on convection roast, preheat it to 400 ° F (or 425 ° F on the standard-setting). Cover with foil on a rimmed baking sheet and put a wire rack on top. Then set the wings for 30 minutes or when the wings become golden brown on the oiled wire rack and roast them.
7. If you are grilling chicken wings, then first use the long-handled tongs with the wad of paper towels dipped in molten fat to oil the cooking griddle. Then cook the wings on medium-hot coals for around 15 minutes, rotating once, until the fat is made and the skin becomes crisp and golden, or with the gas grill burners that set to medium.
8. Serve with wedges of lime, and let the frenzied feeding begin.

11.89 Crispy Prosciutto Chips

Servings: 12 I Time: 20 mins I Difficulty: Easy
Nutrients per serving: Calories: 355 kcal I Fat: 34g I Carbohydrates: 1g I Protein: 11g

Ingredients
- 3 oz. of very thinly sliced Prosciutto di Parma

Method
1. Having the rack in the center, preheat the oven to 350°F.
2. With a piece of parchment paper, line the rimmed baking sheet, and put the prosciutto on top in a single layer. Don't overcrowd the pigs; otherwise, it won't be appropriately crisp.
3. Place the tray in the oven until the oven is ready. Bake for about 10-15 minutes or until crunchy (based on the slices of prosciutto). To make sure they don't burn, watch those chips like a hawk.
4. To cool, move the chips onto a wire rack. (As they cool, they get crunchier).

11.90 Brussels Sprouts Chips

Servings: 2 I Time: 15 mins I Difficulty: Easy
Nutrients per serving: Calories: 169 kcal I Fat: 15g I Carbohydrates: 8g I Protein: 3g I Fiber: 3g

Ingredients
- Lemon zest optional
- Kosher salt to taste
- 2 tbsp melted ghee olive oil or avocado oil
- 2 cups Brussels sprout leaves

Method
1. Preheat the oven to 350 °F.
2. In a wide cup, mix the leaves, salt, and ghee (or avocado oil).
3. Line two large parchment baking trays. Divide the leaves uniformly on each tray into a single sheet.
4. Bake each tray for about 8-10 minutes or crispy and brown across the edges.

5. Microplane over the chips with some lemon zest (optional), then chow immediately.

11.91 Green Pork and Shiitake Sliders

Servings: 6 | Time: 35 mins | Difficulty: Easy
Nutrients per serving: Calories: 346 kcal | Fat: 27g | Carbohydrates: 8g | Protein: 18g | Fiber: 4g

Ingredients

- 6 reconstituted shiitake mushrooms (dried & finely chopped)
- 2 large eggs lightly beaten
- 1/8 cup coconut flour up to 1/4 cup
- 1/4 cup full-fat coconut milk
- 1/2 cup yellow onion (finely chopped)
- 1/2 cup fresh cilantro leaves
- 1/2 cup celery small-diced (around 2 medium stalks)
- 1 tbsp Red Boat fish sauce
- 1 tbsp coconut oil (or fat of choice)
- 1 tbsp coconut aminos
- 1 lb ground pork
- 1 lb frozen chopped spinach
- 1.5 tsp freshly ground black pepper
- 1 tsp Diamond Crystal kosher salt

Method

1. In a secure microwave dish, pour the frozen spinach and cover it with a lid. To defrost it, microwave the bowl on top for about 4 minutes.
2. In a colander, put the defrosted spinach and press all the liquid out.
3. In a large cast-iron skillet, heat 1 tbsp coconut oil over medium heat.
4. Toss along with salt & pepper to taste in the onions (chopped) and mushrooms. Sauté the ingredients unless they've evaporated the liquid and softened the onions.
5. Use a hand blender, blitz the coconut milk, cilantro, and celery.
6. Replace the spinach, puree, mushrooms, onions, eggs, coconut flour (1/8 cup), coconut aminos, fish sauce, pepper, and salt, and put the ground pork in a big dish.
7. Mix all the ingredients gently
8. Shape into the tiny patties of the meat mixture (2 inches in diameter).
9. Heat 2 tsp of coconut oil on medium heat in a cast-iron skillet (the oil should make a thin layer). Fry the sliders on both sides for 3 minutes.

11.92 Broiled Herb-Stuffed Sardines

Servings: 3 | Time: 25 mins | Difficulty: Easy
Nutrients per serving: Calories: 415 kcal | Fat: 36g | Carbohydrates: 5g | Protein: 20g | Fiber: 2g

Ingredients

- 1 large lemon
- 1/2 cup Italian parsley (chopped)
- 2 tbsp oil
- 3 tbsp butter or ghee
- 4 green onion stalks (chopped)
- 6 large fresh sardines 2 lb
- Diamond Crystal kosher salt
- Freshly ground black pepper

Method

1. Preheat the broiler to a high degree and put the top rack four inches from the heating unit.
2. Take the kitchen knife out of it and gut the fish. Cut out a shallow path around the fish's belly and take the innards out. Rinse the fish, then pat it dry.
3. In the food processor, put along the butter or ghee, green onions, salt, parsley, and pepper. Pulse until you have formed a uniform paste.
4. Spoon each sardine cavity with 1 tbsp of filling.
5. Brush the fish's skin with the molten bacon fat and sprinkle on top with salt and pepper.
6. Place the ready-made sardines on top of the foil-lined baking sheet on a wire rack and place them in the oven.
7. Broil for about 5 minutes, tossing at the halfway point with the cod.
8. Spritz the new lemon juice with it.

11.93 Oven-Roasted Tomatoes

Servings: 2 | Time: 55 mins | Difficulty: Easy
Nutrients per serving: Calories: 185 kcal | Fat: 15g | Carbohydrates: 13g | Protein: 3g | Fiber: 4g

Ingredients

- 1 tbsp Sunny Paris seasoning (or your preferred dried herb blend)
- 10 plum tomatoes (Choose a tomato type with more flesh & fewer seeds).
- 2 tbsp extra virgin olive oil (or your favorite fat)
- Diamond Crystal kosher salt
- Freshly ground black pepper

Method

1. Preheat the 400 F toaster oven and sweep up the tomatoes.
2. Slice the tomatoes in half lengthwise and scatter them on a single sheet on the foil-lined baking tray, in a cut-side-up position.
3. Sprinkle the seasoning mixture of dried spices, salt, and pepper on tomatoes and the virgin olive oil (extra).
4. Pop the tray in an oven and roast these tomatoes for about 45 minutes, turning the tray several times to cook uniformly. Tomatoes are finished when the sides are a little brown, shrunk a little, and soft and chewy.

11.94 Simple Crab Salad

Servings: 4 | Time: 10 mins | Difficulty: Easy
Nutrients per serving: Calories: 146 kcal | Fat: 6g | Carbohydrates: 1g | Protein: 21g | Fiber: 1g

Ingredients

- 1 lb cooked lump crab meat
- 1 tbsp lemon juice
- 2 scallions thinly sliced
- 2 tbsp chopped Italian parsley
- 2 tbsp paleo mayonnaise
- Diamond Crystal kosher salt
- Freshly ground black pepper

Method

1. Assemble and cut your herbs with your ingredients. Crack open the 'o crab can' and squeeze the excess liquid out.
2. In a medium-sized dish, pour the crab and blend in the scallions, salt, parsley, and pepper.
3. Next, in a separate bowl, put the mayonnaise and lemon juice together. When mixed, apply the combination of mayonnaise to the crab dish. Taste it to see if more mayo, salt, lemon juice, or pepper is required.
4. Serve it with avocado or guacamole over the greens. Or, if you're looking to put a short appetizer together, mix the crab salad with several finely diced red bell pepper, then spoon it into some spears of endive.

11.95 Green Sliders

Servings: 6 | Time: 50 mins | Difficulty: Easy
Nutrients per serving: Calories: 354 kcal | Fat: 27g | Carbohydrates: 10g | Protein: 20g | Fiber: 5g

Ingredients

- 1 medium garlic clove (minced)
- 1 lb frozen spinach (chopped)
- 1 lb ground beef
- 1 tbsp unsalted butter (or coconut oil)
- 1 tsp Diamond Crystal kosher salt
- 1.5 tsp freshly ground black pepper
- 1/2 cup celery (small-dice)
- 1/2 cup Italian parsley leaves loosely packed
- 1/2 cup medium yellow onion (chopped)
- 1/2 lb cremini mushrooms (finely chopped)
- 1/4 cup coconut cream (or coconut milk)
- 1/4 cup coconut flour
- 1/4 tsp freshly grated nutmeg
- 2 large eggs beaten
- 2 tbsp coconut oil for frying
- Fleur de sel

Method

1. Pour the spinach box into a microwaveable bowl and then microwave it on high to defrost it for about 4 minutes. (Without an oven, you should even let it defrost overnight).
2. In a colander, put the defrosted spinach and press all the liquid out.
3. In the large cast-iron skillet, heat the butter or the coconut oil on medium heat and toss in chopped onions & mushrooms with salt & pepper.
4. Sauté the vegetables until they have evaporated the liquid and softened the onions. In a wide dish, add the ground beef. Just put aside.
5. Put in a dish of coconut milk, celery and parsley and mix with a hand blender.
6. Pour it on the ground beef until a puree is developed, and then include the chopped spinach, garlic, measured salt & pepper, coconut flour, fresh nutmeg, beaten eggs, and a mixture of cooked mushrooms.
7. Mix all the ingredients gently and shape little patties with the meat mixture (about 2 inches in diameter). There are about 30 patties you can have.
8. In a cast-iron skillet, heat 2 tbsp of coconut oil on medium heat and cook the sliders in 3 batches. Cook the sliders on either side for 3 minutes.
9. Place the patties on the plate until they're finished cooking. Dig in for a heated sauce of marinara

11.96 Roasted Portobello Mushrooms

Servings: 4 | Time: 35 mins | Difficulty: Easy
Nutrients per serving: Calories: 51 kcal | Fat: 4g | Carbohydrates: 3g | Protein: 2g | Fiber: 1g

Ingredients

- Sunny Paris seasoning (or your preferred salt-free herb blend)
- Minced fresh herbs optional
- Melted ghee melted coconut oil (or your preferred fat)
- Lemon or lime juice (or your preferred vinegar)
- Kosher salt
- Freshly ground pepper
- 4 large Portobello mushrooms (clean with a paper towel or damp cloth)

Method

1. Preheat oven to 400 ºF. Put an aluminum foil on the middle rack or a parchment-lined baking dish.
2. Grab and cut the stems from the mushrooms, scrape the gills with a spoon, and turn down the gill-side caps.
3. On top of each mushroom, cut a shallow 'X,' brush the entire cap (top & bottom) with molten fat, and season with salt and pepper on both sides.
4. Before sticking these on a hot baking tray in an oven, sprinkle a few Sunny Paris seasoning (or your preferred salt-free herb blend) over the caps, gill-side up.
5. For 10 minutes, roast the shrooms and then flip them to cook for an extra 10 minutes (total 20 minutes). If the cooking caps are used as buns, you are done.
6. Cut them up and then squeeze some lemon juice and the minced fresh herbs if you are eating the shrooms as a side dish.

11.97 Cauliflower and Carrot Puree

Servings: 6 | Time: 40 mins | Difficulty: Easy
Nutrients per serving: Calories: 138 kcal | Fat: 11g | Carbohydrates: 9g | Protein: 2g | Fiber: 3g

Ingredients

- Splash of heavy cream optional
- Freshly ground black pepper
- Diamond Crystal kosher salt
- 4 tbsp ghee (or fat of choice)
- 3 large carrots (cut into small chunks)
- 2 garlic cloves (minced)
- 1 large cauliflower cut up into florets
- ½ medium onion coarsely (chopped)
- ¼ cup of water
- ¼ cup organic chicken broth

Method

1. Chop up your vegetables and, over medium heat, melt 3 tbsp of ghee in a big stockpot.
2. Within the bubbling fat, put the veggies, broth, and water. Cover the pot as the liquid begins to boil, turn the heat down to the minimum, and let it steam until softened (25-30 minutes). Make sure don't dry your pot.
3. Add another tbsp of ghee, the splashes of heavy cream, salt, and pepper, and mix until creamy, using an immersion mixer.

11.98 Sausage and Spinach Stuffed Portobello Mushrooms

Servings: 5 | Time: 1 hr 5 mins | Difficulty: Easy
Nutrients per serving: Calories: 425 kcal | Fat: 35g | Carbohydrates: 11g | Protein: 20g | Fiber: 4g

Ingredients

- Sunny Paris seasoning
- Freshly ground black pepper
- Diamond Crystal kosher salt
- avocado oil (or cooking fat of choice)
- 5 medium portobello mushrooms
- 2 tbsp ghee (or fat of choice)
- 1½ cups marinara sauce
- 1 tbsp coconut flour
- 1 lb uncooked sausage (removed from its casing)
- 1 large egg lightly beaten
- ½ small onion minced
- ½ lb frozen spinach (defrosted & squeezed dried)

Method

1. Keep the rack in the middle of the oven, preheat an oven to 400° F, and put the foil-lined baking sheet over the rack.
2. Gather your shrooms, wipe the tops with a moist cloth, and take a spoon from the stems and gills. Place them in the shallow baking dish until washed.

3. Using a sharp paring knife, cut a shallow "X" on the top of each shroom and brush an avocado oil in the shrooms, and salt and pepper season the tops & bottoms.
4. Place the mushrooms in the oven, position the gill side up, and then bake for 10 minutes on a pre-heated baking sheet. Flip each mushroom and cook them down on the gill side for an extra 10 minutes. Take the tray from the oven and leave to cool at room temperature for the mushrooms.
5. To broil, raise the oven temperature.
6. You should start preparing the stuffing when the mushrooms are cooking. Heat the ghee over medium heat in a large skillet and sauté the diced onion (with salt & pepper) until tender and translucent.
7. Apply to the pan the bacon and a few dashes of a Sunny Paris seasoning. Cook the meat until the meat is not pink anymore.
8. Remove a meat mixture and leave it to cool at room temperature in a medium cup.
9. Add the egg, coconut flour, spinach, salt, and pepper until the sausage is cooled and blended. Shift now this cooled roasted mushrooms to another foil-lined baking sheet (lots of mushroom liquid would be on the initial baking sheet), layer the stuffing on each shell, and press down to make it more compact.
10. For around 5 minutes, put the tray under a broiler (center rack), rotating halfway during the cooking process.
11. When the mushrooms are full, the stuffing should be uniformly browned (not burned).
12. Add marinara sauce to the stuffed mushrooms and serve instantly.

11.99 Roasted Portobello Mushroom Packets with Garlic, Shallots, and Balsamic Vinegar

Servings: 5 | Time: 40 mins | Difficulty: Easy
Nutrients per serving: Calories: 141 kcal | Fat: 12g | Carbohydrates: 7g | Protein: 2g | Fiber: 2g

Ingredients
- 1 tbsp Balsamic vinegar
- 10-15 garlic cloves peeled
- 2 medium shallots (coarsely chopped)
- 3 tbsp ghee or fat of choice
- 5 large Portobello mushrooms tops (wiped clean, stems & gills removed)
- Diamond Crystal kosher salt
- extra virgin olive oil
- Freshly ground black pepper

Method

1. Preheat an oven to 400°F and cut the shallots coarsely, and trim the garlic ends. In a food processor, throw the shallots to finely mince them (or mince by hand).
2. In a 3:1 fat to vinegar ratio, apply fat and vinegar to the minced alliums. By using an acceptable salt and fresh ground black pepper sprinkling, season this vinaigrette mixture.
3. Place each of the Portobello mushrooms, stem side up, on a sheet of heavy-duty aluminum foil. Each shroom is lightly coated with some extra virgin olive oil and salt and pepper. Put into each mushroom a dollop of vinaigrette, spreading unless the cap is filled.
4. Seal every mushroom packet tightly and put it on a baking tray. In the microwave, stick the tray and roast for about 25 minutes.
5. Take the mushrooms from the packages and slice them up.

11.100 Collard Greens

Servings: 4 | Time: 30 mins | Difficulty: Easy
Nutrients per serving: Calories: 138 kcal | Fat: 9g | Carbohydrates: 14g | Protein: 12g | Fiber: 9g

Ingredients
- Freshly squeezed lemon juice (or balsamic vinegar)
- Freshly cracked black pepper
- 3 cloves of garlic minced
- 2 lb assertive greens (such as collards, kale, mustard, or turnip greens; coarsely chopped and stemmed)
- 1½ tsp Diamond Crystal brand kosher salt
- 1 tbsp olive oil
- 1 cup diced ham (or bacon optional)
- ¼ cup chicken broth

Method
1. In a deep kettle, boil 2 quarts of water. Include the greens and salt and whisk until wilted. Cover it and cook until just tender (approx 7 minutes) for the greens.
2. In a colander, rinse the collard greens. To cool the pot, clean it with cold water and refill it with cold water and a few ice cubes. To pause the cooking process, pour the greens into the ice water.
3. Shift the greens back to a colander and put a small handful to squeeze out much water as possible into a potato ricer. Repeat unless all the greens are no soggier any more. In a locked jar in the freezer, you can store these greens for up to 4 days.
4. Now you're set for the greens to sauté. If you need your greens to be sliced smaller, do it now.
5. Over medium heat, heat a big skillet. When the pan is warmed, stir in the olive oil.
6. Then throw in some bacon or ham and add your fried collard greens. Top with ¼ cup of chicken broth and cover for 2 minutes. When required, taste and change with salt & pepper, and squeeze a lemon juice or vinegar.

Conclusion

There should be about 75% fat, 10-30 percent protein and no more than 5 percent or 20 to 50 g of carbohydrate per day in a balanced ketogenic diet. Focus on low-carb, high-fat foods such as low-carb vegetables, meats, dairy, and eggs, as well as sugar-free drinks. Make sure that highly processed products and LDL fats (Bad/unhealthy Fats) are limited. Now, it has been easier to look up a wide diversity of fascinating and nutritious keto meal recipes online because of the success of the ketogenic diet. You will set up for success by using this guide to get started on the keto diet and make switching to a high-fat, low-carb diet an easy thing.

Ketosis is a normal metabolic condition which can be accomplished by adopting a diet. It has a number of health advantages, including:

- Reduced seizures in epileptic children.

- Lower blood sugar levels.

- Weight loss.

It can be very hard, however, to adopt a strict diet to trigger ketosis, and there could be some harmful side effects. Moreover, not all experts believe that the only way to lose weight is via a keto diet.

If you'd like to lose weight quickly, even in your fifties, the keto diet is one of the easiest ways to do it. For women in their fifties, it is suitable since it tackles many of the difficulties that follow menopause.

The low carb diet is not only a diet for weight loss, it is a hygienic diet, and while it can be difficult for the first 1-2 weeks, it's a treat after that. There's no hunger, no cravings, and you're going to have more energy than ever.

That is because one of the most common diets around is keto. And note, a century earlier, it was developed, and that indicates it does work!

Printed in Great Britain
by Amazon